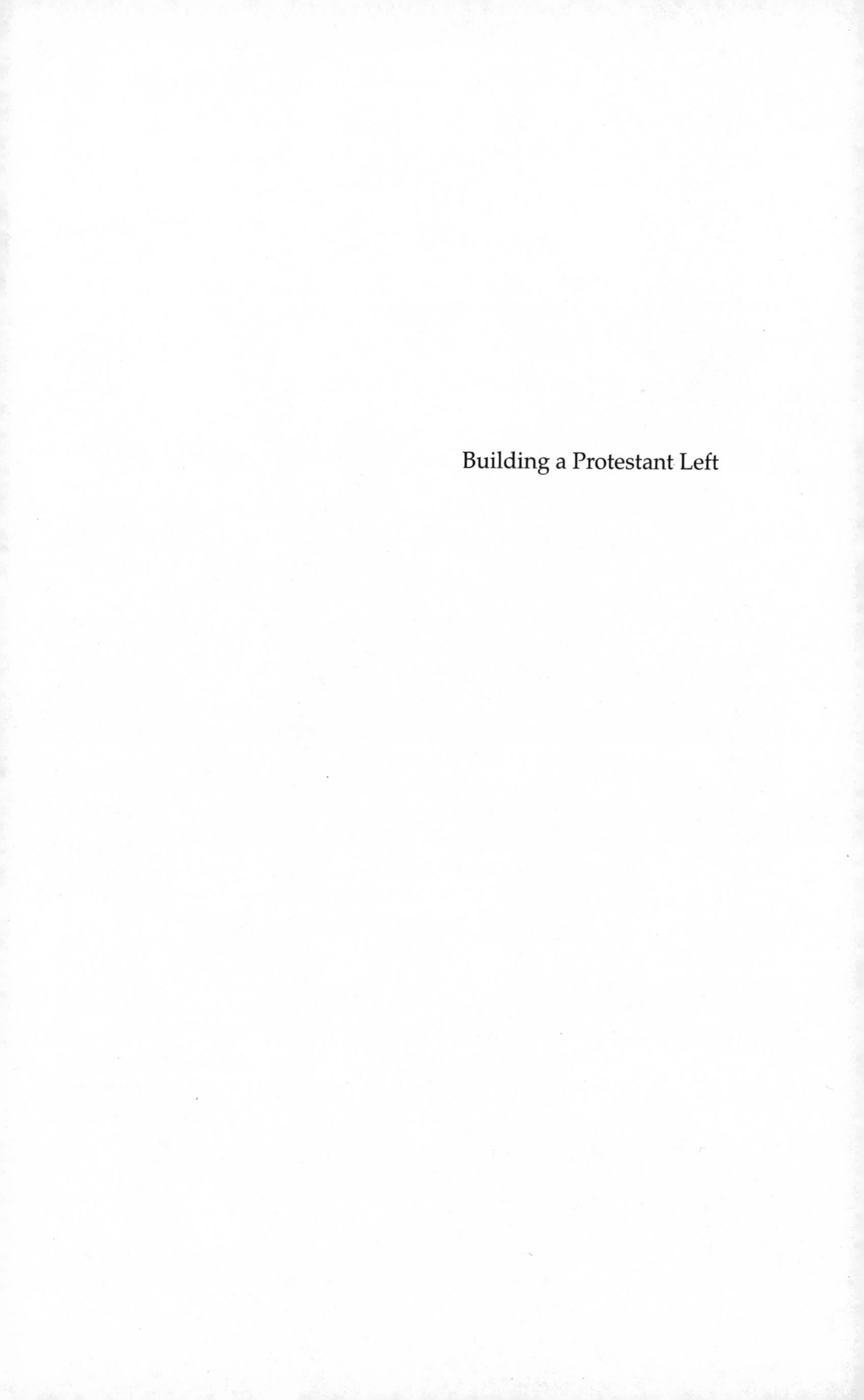

Building a Protestant Left

Mark Hulsether

Building a Protestant Left

Christianity and Crisis Magazine, 1941–1993

The University of Tennessee Press / Knoxville

First Edition.

The paper in this book meets the minimum requirements of the American National Standard for Permanence of Paper for Printed Library Materials. ♾ The binding materials have been chosen for strength and durability.

♻ Printed on recycled paper.

Library of Congress Cataloging-in-Publication Data

Hulsether, Mark.
Building a Protestant left : Christianity and crisis magazine, 1941–1993 /
Mark Hulsether. — 1st ed.
p. cm.
ISBN 1-57233-022-8 (cl.: alk. paper)
1. Christianity and crisis. 2. Christianity and politics—United States—History—20th century. 3. Liberalism (Religion)—Protestant churches—History—20th century. 4. Liberalism (Religion)—United States—History—20th century.
5. New Left—United States—History—20th century.
I. Title.
BR1.C64173 H85 1998
261.8'0882044—ddc21 98-19738

Contents

Preface

This is a study of changing ideas about religion and society in a small but influential journal of liberal Protestantism called *Christianity and Crisis,* or *C&C.* It uses *C&C* as a case study to tell a larger story about trends in postwar Protestant social thought and political activism, from the rise of Reinhold Niebuhr's Christian realist positions of the 1940s, through Protestant participation in the complex social movements of the 1950s and 1960s, to the emergence of various liberation theologies—black, feminist, Latin American, and others—that used *C&C* as a central arena of debate during the 1970s and 1980s. It places these changes in the context of postwar cultural and social history, relating *C&C*'s theological and ethical positions to broader social and political issues that the journal treated in detail.

When an earlier version of this book was published as a dissertation in 1992, I dedicated it to my parents and my children saying, "I hope this work will be a bridge between old and new generations of spiritually sensitive and socially engaged thinking." I was thinking about a bridge between two kinds of divides. The first was a generational divide within liberal Protestantism. My parents and many of my teachers came of age at roughly the same time as *Christianity and Crisis;* my children, like most people under age twenty-one today, have no personal memories before Ronald Reagan's presidency. The second was the chasm that often exists between the study of religion in the twentieth-century United States, on one side, and broader studies of social movements and cultural history, on the other.

My goal of bridging these gaps remains. However, since 1992 a lot has changed. On the personal front, I moved halfway across the country from a school with a left-liberal ethos in a community where activist mainline

Protestants were a strong presence, to a school where the majority of my students are conservative evangelicals who have difficulty even imagining a form of Christianity that is left of center and focused on political activism. On the national Protestant scene, *C&C* went out of existence, unable to imagine how to survive in a situation of rising costs and shrinking financial support. In national politics, the Republicans swept the 1994 elections, pushing President Bill Clinton far to the right and symbolizing a sort of vacuum of left-liberal hopes. Globally, the logic of capitalism moved forward, with pockets of creativity and resistance inside it to be sure, but still transforming the world into a place of heartless competition and ecological disaster, where decisions about everyday life are determined not by what is needed but by what will produce the most profit for the rich.

Even more has changed since I first began thinking about these issues in the mid-1980s, and the cumulative weight of this change has shifted how I see the purposes of this book. When I started my research, I was a partisan in the battles between moderates and radicals that raged in and around *C&C*. On my more conciliatory days, my studies were an attempt to understand how my teachers saw the world, so that I could take what was good and move beyond their limitations. But I still thought that people like John Bennett (*C&C*'s leading voice from 1955 to 1970) were essentially passé. On my angrier days I was mainly looking for dirt on my enemies, and these enemies quoted *C&C*'s founder, Reinhold Niebuhr.

I no longer see the *C&C* of the 1950s and 1960s as either passé or the enemy. Instead, I have become a partisan of unity between moderate liberals and radicals of various stripes, despite all their real and significant differences, against the greater enemy of neoconservatism. I would like to believe that this change has come about not solely because the dangers of the right have grown in proportion to those of old-time Protestant liberals, but because I have really learned something about the positive virtues of the moderates by studying the past. As I searched for the beginnings of the radical tradition in *C&C* within which I placed myself, I discovered that they reached back into the mid-1950s. They emerged then because even in *C&C*'s most conservative period, between 1947 and 1957, radical voices were alive as a minority current within its debates, and this current reached back into critiques by the left wing of the social gospel in the first half of the century. In any case, *C&C*'s cold war positions were not conservative compared with the main currents of U.S. culture during the same period but only compared with *C&C*'s later positions and with 1950s radicals such as C. Wright Mills and W. E. B. Du Bois. Thus John Bennett appears in this book as an exemplary pragmatic activist, much as Martin Luther King Jr. has been presented by Cornel West.[1] In sum, I still study the recent past to help people from my generation to understand their parents and teachers. But it is less to criticize and more to heal.

My greatest fear, as I send this long-developing book out into the world, is that I have tried to bridge so many gaps that I am left standing not with feet planted solidly on both sides but in midair over a chasm. Probably I remain grounded enough in feminist, multiculturalist, and other radical critiques to rub salt in old grievances of moderates and neoconservatives; yet it remains to be seen how my kind words for John Bennett's pragmatism will play on the left, where it remains safest to pen attacks from standpoints of ever greater sociopolitical marginalization and ever more uncompromising poststructuralist suspicion. In addition, I am sufficiently interested in religion to rouse the suspicions of prospective allies in cultural studies, yet committed deeply enough to the project of cultural studies to rouse suspicions among some scholars in religion. But there is little I can do about this now; it is too late to worry about it.

I cling to a modest hope that the bridges will hold, at least for limited traffic, because of the community that has nurtured the project so far. I have been extremely privileged to learn from excellent teachers in several schools. My deepest thanks go to Letty Russell and Cornel West, with whom I worked at Yale University, and to my key advisers in the American Studies Program at the University of Minnesota, George Lipsitz, Roland Delattre, and above all David W. Noble, who is the single greatest influence. Thanks also to Riv-Ellen Prell, Sara Evans, Nancy Roberts, and Elaine and Lary May at Minnesota; David Montgomery, Sydney Ahlstrom, Bruce Mullin, and other teachers at Yale. At Luther Seminary Paul Sponheim, Steve Charleston, and especially Paul Sonnack gave guidance and friendship as I wrote a thesis that formed some of the infrastructure of this work. I learned much from responses by Richard Fox, Richard Flacks, Mel Piehl, Louis Weeks, and Preston Williams to conference papers based on this research.

Many people connected with *Christianity and Crisis* provided interviews; a complete list appears in the appendix. I thank each and every one and would like to express special thanks to Richard Butler, James Cone, Wayne Cowan, Leon Howell, Robert Hoyt, Rosemary Ruether, Roger Shinn, Peggy Steinfels, and James Washington. Above all, I would like to give recognition to Beverly Harrison, Vivian Lindermayer, and the late John Bennett for their extremely helpful insights and cooperation.

Many friends and colleagues inside and outside the academy formed a community that shaped my thinking about the issues I discuss—although we certainly do not agree about every issue—and they supported me in various ways during the long years of writing and revision. Along with

Anne McKee, who is by far the most important influence, and others whom I no doubt have overlooked, I would like to acknowledge Elizabeth Bounds, Rachel Buff, Laura Castor, Derek Curtis, Dan Deffenbaugh, Virgil Foote, Chuck Foster, Larry Golemon, Rosalind Hackett, Marlene Helgemo, Ron Hopson, Sue and Sara Hulsether, George Hutchinson, Janet Jakobsen, Serene Jones, Frieda Knobloch, Dick Lundy, Mary Ann Lundy, Laurie Maffly-Kipp, Doug McAdam, Russell McCutcheon, José Antonio Machado, Joyce Mercer, Lyle and Jeanne Meyer, Kenny Mostern, Joy and Davie Napier, Tom and Julia Tipton Rendon, Charles Reynolds, and Elizabeth Shaw. My children—Lucia, Mark, and Doug—deserve special recognition for their good questions, and for putting up with the many weekends and evenings when this book kept me away from them.

Drew Kadel of Union Theological Seminary in New York went beyond the call of duty in helping me work through a mass of uncataloged *C&C* archives, housed in a nearly inaccessible part of Burke Library. Various support staff at the University of Tennessee were indispensable, especially Joan Riedl. Thanks also to Joyce Harrison and Stan Ivester at the University of Tennessee Press, and to Elaine Otto, freelance copyeditor.

Last but not least, my work was supported financially by a Professional Development Award for Faculty Research from the University of Tennessee, a summer research grant and a dissertation fellowship from the Louisville Institute, several travel grants from the University of Minnesota American Studies Program, and, most importantly, by the hard work of Anne McKee.

Since Anne is in first place as emotional, intellectual, and financial supporter for this project, the book is dedicated to her.

Introduction: Who Cares about *Christianity and Crisis*?

"Among the many journals of opinion published in the United States is one of comparatively short years and small circulation, having a title that suggests a parochial concern relevant only to the very devout."[1] So began an article on the December 1, 1966, financial page of the *Rockland Record*, a newspaper serving an upscale suburb of New York City. One might ask why this newspaper should care if, as its article discussed, a small Protestant journal withdrew $25,000 from New York's First National City Bank to protest its investments in South Africa.[2] Come to think of it, why should I have spent several years writing a book on this journal? Why should you bother to read about it?

The *Record* provided some clues. "With most periodicals the measure of influence is how many readers," it said. "With '*C&C*,' as it is called in church circles, the measure of its readers is who they are." Quoting *Time* magazine, the *Record* judged that *C&C*'s influence "is well out of proportion to its size," with readers like former Secretary of State John Foster Dulles, theologian Paul Tillich, liberal pundit Walter Lippmann, and civil rights leader Martin Luther King Jr.[3] Despite its small size, *C&C* readers held strategic positions in establishment Protestantism and the secular liberal intelligentsia. *C&C* enjoyed the prestige of its founder, Reinhold Niebuhr, "the most formative contemporary influence on American liberalism," and his long-time colleague and coeditor, John Coleman Bennett of Union Theological Seminary in New York.[4] *C&C*'s influence was strongest among liberal Protestant academics, clergy, and bureaucrats. Its subscribers included the leaders of mainline seminaries, religious social action agencies, and ecumenical organizations. Historian Martin Marty is convincing when he says *C&C* had "public influence greater than the denominational magazines with hundreds of thousands of subscribers"—not because one bureaucrat is worth ten thousand laity, but because *C&C* was at the forefront of evolving conversations.[5]

C&C also gained attention from secular elites. Consider how it boosted the career of Ernest Lefever, who was nominated by Ronald Reagan to be assistant secretary of state for human rights. Lefever's big break came in 1954 when he wrote a *C&C* article pressing the World Council of Churches (WCC) to be realistic about the dangers of communism. According to Lefever, "[My article] was read by Justice Frankfurter who asked Dean Acheson, 'Who is this who writes with such clarity and dynamism?' Acheson did not know but asked Paul Nitze to find out. . . . [Nitze approached] Dean Rusk, then president of the Rockefeller Foundation and arranged a one-year grant for me to work with him."[6] This story brings together a Supreme Court justice, two secretaries of state who served during the Korean and Vietnam Wars, the head of the State Department policy planning staff who wrote the most important policy directive of the cold war [NSC-68], and a foundation that channeled hundreds of millions of dollars of Standard Oil profits into Protestant institutions—all looking to *C&C* to recruit a future member of the Washington establishment.

Stories about *C&C*'s links to power are easy to multiply. Many prominent intellectuals with religious connections, from Cornel West on the left to Michael Novak on the right, built their early reputations largely through writing in *C&C*. Senator Eugene McCarthy helped *C&C* with fund-raising; Nitze and famed anthropologist Margaret Mead served on its editorial board; Israeli prime minister Menachem Begin wrote to complain about its coverage; Frankfurter's spouse personally complained to Niebuhr about a change in *C&C*'s logo. Niebuhr appeared on the cover of *Time*'s twenty-fifth anniversary issue, served on the State Department policy planning staff, was a leading organizer of Americans for Democratic Action, and has been called "perhaps the most influential thinker" in the United States during the cold war era.[7]

All this meant that *C&C*'s trickle-down importance was considerable. A *C&C* article about *Playboy* was reprinted in *Redbook* and dozens of anthologies.[8] In 1946 Niebuhr published an article in two versions, one for *C&C*'s seven thousand readers and one for *Life* magazine's four million.[9] The *New York Times* often reported on *C&C* editorials, with a large ripple effect when others picked up the stories. When *C&C* attacked Billy Graham for preaching in the Nixon White House, this was discussed in the *Spartanburg (S.C.) Herald, Dowagiac (Mich.) News, Attleboro (Mass.) Sun, Galveston (Tex.) News, Manitowoc (Wis.) Herald-Times,* and *Mesa (Ariz.) Tribune.*[10] Of course, such evidence does not prove any direct correspondence between

C&C and an average churchgoer's ideas or even between *C&C* and the sermons of mainline ministers. However, it does suggest some broad correlation between trends inside *C&C* and among a wider Protestant constituency.

Thus the *Rockland Record*'s financial editor had valid reasons to care about *C&C*'s choice of bank. And this in turn helps explain why the *Record* concluded with a warning shot across *C&C*'s bow. It used an argument that hit *C&C* where it hurt. *C&C* prided itself on actions for justice that remained within the bounds of the pragmatically attainable; its watchword was responsible realism as opposed to idealistic utopianism. But the *Record* pointed out that the return on South African investments was 19 percent compared with an average of 11 percent elsewhere in the world. Therefore, the *Record* instructed, *C&C*'s "impact on the realities of business with South Africa remains to be seen."[11]

In retrospect, the *Record*'s skeptical comment stands out in bold relief and has an ominous ring. In 1966 *C&C* radiated confidence about its alliance with Great Society liberalism, and its morale was high. Vice-President Hubert Humphrey had just spoken at its twenty-fifth anniversary banquet, and *C&C* was even operating without a deficit from year to year, making the decade an anomaly within its history. But *C&C* was about to enter a prolonged period in which elite newspapers were far less interested in reprinting its articles and recruiting its writers. Clouds were already gathering in 1966, when *C&C*'s anniversary banquet featured not only Humphrey but also an antiwar speech from the podium, antiwar pickets at the door, and feminist theologian Anne McGrew Bennett (John Bennett's spouse) seated at the head table with a large white dove pinned to her black dress. In time the storm hit and the rain took its toll, and by 1993 *C&C* had died of demoralization and shrinking institutional resources. The great Protestant voice of bold and realistic social action could not discover a realistic way to survive in the chilly new world order of the 1990s.

C&C's protest against First National City Bank was only the tip of an iceberg. It was just one blip amid *C&C*'s total concerns in 1966, a year in which *C&C* threw itself into anti-Vietnam protests, came to terms with black power, and debated whether God was dead. Moreover, 1966 was just one moment in a five-decade transformation that is the subject of this book: the transformation of liberal Protestant social thought in the postwar United States, and especially the emergence of liberation theologies during the 1960s and 1970s. As more and more of this iceberg came into view, the warning shots from *C&C*'s right became more insistent. *Newsweek* had praised Bennett's "astute commentary" on a range of issues, but as *C&C* steered left, FBI chief J. Edgar Hoover placed his activities under surveillance.[12] *New York Times* coverage began to drop off.[13] Centrist commentators became less respectful, as when *C&C*'s widening interests and sharper critical voice led Marty to conclude that almost the opposite had occurred—that *C&C* had become "a more focused and less critical advocate of radical causes."[14] Attacking from the world of neoconservative foundations, Richard John Neuhaus called *C&C* the "little magazine that trashes the Reinhold Niebuhr legacy that it claims." No longer did *Commentary* editor Norman Podhoretz say, as he did in a message to *C&C*'s twenty-fifth anniversary celebration, that *C&C* "has, from my point of view, been the most valuable journal to issue forth from American Protestantism. . . . May it endure millennia."[15]

Therefore, with three decades of hindsight, a skeptic might extend the line of criticism introduced by the *Rockland Record* when it said that *C&C*'s impact remained to be seen. Just as the *Record* doubted that *C&C*'s moral logic plus $25,000 of capital could outweigh an 8 percent gap in profits on a multibillion-dollar investment portfolio, so also the legacy of *C&C*'s general left turn remains to be seen in a society where left-of-center politics have produced markedly lower returns than neoconservatism for the past two or three decades. If there were ever any doubts that such arguments held some force, *C&C*'s 1993 death dispelled them with an exclamation point.

I believe that such a skeptical dismissal would be misleading in two ways. First, *C&C*'s history was by no means a steady downhill slide after the 1960s. Despite the clouds and the rain—or perhaps even because of them—*C&C* remained one of the premier forums of Protestant debate on public issues, especially in the late 1970s (when its circulation peaked) and early 1980s. Although it lost conservatives like Ernest Lefever and Michael Novak, it gained leading left intellectuals like Cornel West and Rosemary Ruether. According to Gayraud Wilmore, in the 1960s and 1970s "it was difficult to find someone who was really making waves on the Christian social justice front who did not read *C&C*." Its "public was always small, but savvy, secular in the best sense, relatively free of the most doddering pieties and conservatism of the mainline, and yet influential enough to effect strategic changes in certain sectors."[16] Indeed, an important factor in *C&C*'s death alongside dried-up resources and discouragement was the fact that many of the new approaches pioneered in its pages had become common wisdom in the mainline Protestant academy by the 1980s, so that *C&C*'s niche was less unique.

Such an upbeat spin on *C&C*'s problems—that it worked itself out of a job by pouring its life into mainline Protestantism at large—might not reassure our hypothetical skeptic, since it risks putting a better face on *C&C* by shifting its problems onto a larger canvas. It is well known that liberal Protestantism has become significantly weaker since the 1960s and that its major problem has been a failure to sustain the interest of upcoming generations.[17] Some people may ask whether *C&C*, which was often "ahead" of the mainline's curve on social issues, was also ahead in a process of institutional decay. I would suggest turning this question around and accenting the positive. How was *C&C* able to survive for as long as it did, as an arm of an institution that seems determined to alienate so many of its primary constituents, especially among those who were born after 1950 and have left-liberal values? If loyalty to mainline Protestantism is decaying, its failure to support journals like *C&C* is surely one important reason.

A second reason not to overstress *C&C*'s decline is implicit in the *Record*'s own skeptical argument. When it asked whether *C&C*'s call for divestment from South Africa would be persuasive, it presupposed that the answer would vary for different people, depending on what I call their cultural standpoints. By this I mean their mix of material interests (are they investors or workers?), social locations (are they young women in African townships or middle-aged men in U.S. suburbs?), their ethnic, religious, political, and sexual identities—and, not least important, their capacities for compassion and solidarity. Different cultural standpoints generate different priorities, kinds of facts that count as relevant, and yardsticks for success. They lead people to experience significantly different realities. This is a critical issue for a journal that always evaluated its moral claims in relation to "the real social context."

Now, it is possible to go overboard with this contextualist line of thought. Differences grounded in distinct cultural standpoints are not absolute; for example, a rich banker and a poor community activist might assess the same evidence and agree that, in the long run, apartheid will lead to a revolution that lowers profits. Nor should we think about differences in rigid and single-minded ways. Most people embrace many standpoints at the same time, in layers of identity that can overlap and gain cumulative weight, but seldom fall into sweeping binaries such as the homeless Haitian lesbian versus the rich male Anglo-American heterosexual. When does identity politics promote group empowerment and social justice, and when does it help elites divide and conquer? When does the radical self-perception of postmodernists unmask false universals, and when does it function as an esoteric form of depoliticized pluralism? There are no easy answers to these questions.

Nevertheless, we underestimate differences in cultural standpoint only at the risk of blindness. Standpoints are often decisive for setting priorities and interpreting complex sets of facts—and this remains true whether one bemoans or celebrates this situation when writing theoretical articles. In the *Rockland* case, *C&C* was more persuasive for people with a passionate desire to overturn apartheid than for those concerned only with the short-term bottom line. Similarly, people will assess *C&C*'s overall transformation in differing ways, even if they agree on abstract principles such as "oppression is bad" or documented facts such as "*C&C* had greater institutional resources in 1966 than 1993." For people concerned about a bottom line of influence in the mainstream culture, *C&C*'s death provides limited inspiration. And who does not care about this bottom line at some level? On the other hand, no one cares *only* about the bottom line, excluding all other considerations. We can only answer the question about *C&C*'s long-term success through discovering what groups find its approaches (as reflected in the larger Protestant left) to be persuasive in the years to come.

The cumulative weight of my argument, throughout this book, explains why I believe that *C&C*'s transformation from the 1940s to the 1970s was constructive, on balance and despite various qualifications. But I will defer speaking about this directly until my conclusion, after I have earned a greater right to do so. Until then, I will use an analytical voice which clarifies *C&C*'s clash of standpoints in a way that I hope will be persuasive and illuminating, even for skeptics who may not share my assessment of whether *C&C*'s approaches constitute success. Are *C&C*'s criteria for success—which, on balance, are also my own—shared by enough people to carry forward *C&C*'s legacy in the years to come? In the *Record*'s words, this "remains to be seen."

One thing is certain. *C&C*'s changes across time are fascinating. Consider how its 1966 decision to divest from South Africa fits within its long-term trajectory. Thirteen years earlier, a *C&C* board member had written a glowing endorsement of South African government plans for its bantustans, the notorious tribal "nations" imposed by the white minority government to keep the black majority divided, impoverished, and dependent. He foresaw a rosy future for bantustans through pro-western economic development. Such bullish positions on development were still surviving well into the 1960s, as when *C&C* stated that "we have a clear obligation to take the Cold War to Africa" and that "the net impact of European colonialism in every area has been good" because without it there would be widespread "cruelty, cannibalism, slavery, and torture, all sanctioned by superstition and abetted by self-serving witch doctors."[18] At the same time, also leading up to *C&C*'s divestment decision, a growing stream of articles had begun to support the movement for black majority rule led by Nelson Mandela and to argue that capitalist development would reproduce paternalism and dependency. In later years, *C&C* would publish African liberation theologians like Desmond Tutu, defend the WCC's funding of revolutionary groups in southern Africa, and compare abuses by U.S. police (the kind later symbolized by the beating of Rodney King) to precedents in Nazi Germany and South Africa.[19] In 1976 *C&C* exhorted investors to "name things by their names"—to state loudly and clearly that "the high mortality rate of babies in South Africa [is] a condition of the high rate of return on the stock there; for the return would be lower if people were allowed to live under human conditions."[20]

C&C's overall transformation was as striking as these shifting positions on Africa. At *C&C*'s birth in 1941, the crisis in its title referred to the rise of Nazism and the opposition of many liberal clergy to the United States' entry in World War II. To attack their pacifist arguments, *C&C* used an approach called Christian realism that blended liberal social activism with a stress on two themes: God's transcendent judgment on sinful human pride plus the resulting need for a defensive stance toward all types of Progressivism. After the war, *C&C*'s concrete deployment of these concepts took the standpoint of liberal elites. When *C&C* criticized sinful pride and power, it did so from within the larger social formation of cold war liberalism. Its personnel, perspective, and institutional matrix were almost exclusively white male, and its editor later recalled its original readers as "the sort of people Republicans call moderates."[21] *C&C*'s major sociopolitical concerns were anticommunism, New Deal type economic reform, and pro-western international development. Thus *C&C* writers could advocate a policy of "imperialistic realism," justify scenarios for nuclear war "in retaliation with all possible restraint," caution that desegregating the army was "going too far" strategically, and attack the Kinsey Report for documenting the "disintegration of the family" as well as "sexual perversions" that should no more be welcomed than statistics about murder.[22] One of *C&C*'s very few articles before 1970 that was written by a woman or that criticized discrimination against women stated that "heterosexuality is the most 'given' of all natural distinctions . . . and belongs to what theologians call the 'order of creation.'" It also argued that most women should stay out of the paid labor force at least until their children enter school. In general, *C&C* perceived, as Niebuhr stated on the eve of the 1960s, that "in the modern day domestic problems have been tolerably solved."[23]

Over time *C&C* came to listen to new voices and deploy two of its core themes—God's will for justice and the need for self-critical social action—from different cultural standpoints. Its writers became frustrated with the links between its inherited positions and status quo power structures. They embraced liberation theology, an umbrella category for various forms of radical Christianity that stressed possibilities for radical change from the standpoint of oppressed communities—black, feminist, Latin American, and many others. This polarized the journal internally, at the same time as similar dynamics polarized its secular allies in the New Deal coalition. By the 1970s *C&C* was overtly anti-imperialist, had feminists and black nationalists on its editorial board, and advocated democratic socialism. It gave qualified support to black militant James Forman when he interrupted worship at Riverside Church to read a manifesto demanding $500 million in reparations ("15 dollars per nigger" by his calculation) from white churches and synagogues to fund a revolutionary black power movement.[24] *C&C* published leaders of a group called WITCH who celebrated that "over against the prevailing sense of reality [defined by patriarchal sex roles] androgyny is anarchy." A contributing editor judged that the doctrine of Christ's sacrificial atonement (as opposed to a feminist understanding of Jesus that accents passion for justice) "represents the sadomasochism of Christian teaching at its most transparent."[25]

We must not overstate these contrasts. Within *C&C*'s dialectical approach, it always criticized abuses of power and promoted the strongest forms of left-liberal activism it perceived realistic and self-critical. *C&C* never spoke in single voice, either about bantustans or black power. It had oppositional subcurrents in its earlier years, and its liberation discourse blended with a substantial amount of standard-brand liberalism in later years. Moreover, a leading Niebuhr scholar rightly insists that many liberationist critics of Christian realism presuppose the same underlying arguments used by the liberal realists: "To see what Christian realism is, we need to attend not only to the work of those who chose the label for themselves, but also to those who have used its methods to move beyond the limitations of its first practitioners."[26] Still, there were striking changes in the pragmatic uses of *C&C*'s moral reasoning, its concrete alliances, and its place within structures of power.

The central goal of this book is to analyze this transformation. Our task is complex because three kinds of change unfolded at the same time: straightforward extensions of *C&C*'s original ideas in relation to emergent issues, radical breaks from received ideas, and shifts in *C&C*'s constituencies and sociopolitical allies. These three changes happened in varying proportions, on timetables that varied from issue to issue: for example, every four years, like clockwork, *C&C* supported the Democratic presidential candidate as a lesser evil, whereas feminist shifts appeared relatively late and proposed major changes.[27] I will use two underlying ideas to clarify patterns in this complex transformation. First, I present it as a paradigm shift, from the realism associated with Niebuhr toward the paradigms associated with liberation theologies. In other words, *C&C*'s transformation comes into helpful focus if we assume that anomalies build up within a given pattern of thought until the stress is intolerable and there is a shift toward a new pattern. A new paradigm is not necessarily a brand-new set of ideas; it may simply be a new hierarchy of concern that reshuffles ideas within an ongoing community of discourse. The key is how it reorients a general way of seeing in response to new evidence and experience.[28]

Second, I relate *C&C*'s paradigm shift to broader sociopolitical issues, framing my story using theories of cultural hegemony. Some basic definitions may be useful.[29] By hegemony I mean a pattern of "normal reality" that is taken for granted as common sense in a society but that works in the interest of some people (the hegemonic groups) more than others. For example, if both men and women accept a common sense notion that a woman's place is in the home, this works in male interests and is an example of male hegemony. If everyone in a classroom assumes that the teacher can normally assign work to students, but students cannot assign work to each other, such common sense behavior reflects the hegemony of the teacher. These examples suggest that hegemonic relations are not necessarily good or bad, but someone is sure to point out that I am a male teacher whose judgment on this matter is suspect. This is precisely the point; underdogs in hegemonic relationships need to think carefully about these relationships. If they decide that they want to change systems that are stacked against them, they must develop a persuasive sense of alternative possibilities (counterhegemonic ones). An oppositional consciousness cannot create change by itself, but it is a precondition for taking further steps and is one factor of power in its own right.

It is crucial to recognize that there is no monolithic structure called "*the* hegemony": life is too multilayered for one rigid definition to hold. (One could be a female teacher, a male student, and so on.) Nor is there any such thing as "total hegemony," since underdogs in any part of a system never completely accept elite definitions of normal reality, and the system is always shifting and being renegotiated, not through totalizing abstractions but through everyday forms of power and persuasion. Thus the question for theories of cultural hegemony, simply put, is how hegemonic coalitions come together and how they come apart—and how the paradigms that define particular communities (such as the realist paradigm defining *C&C*'s consistency during the cold war) relate to these shifting coalitions.[30]

Returning to our larger analysis with these definitions in mind, the key point is that *C&C*'s liberal Protestant tradition is complex enough to be used for hegemonic or oppositional goals. (Cultural theory speaks of the multivocal and contested nature of all culture, as well as its articulation and disarticulation with larger social forces.) Through tracing *C&C*'s changing positions, I will argue that *C&C* spoke for a multivocal tradition of liberal Protestantism that was ongoing throughout the century, and that *C&C*'s

transformation between the 1940s and the 1970s was a paradigm shift from a primarily hegemonic articulation of this tradition to a largely oppositional form—one that sought to distance Protestants from problems with cold war liberalism and articulate it with more radical strategies and coalitions.

C&C's transformation is fascinating on its own terms, and some readers may want to skip ahead to chapter 1 and simply follow the story through its particular drama. However, *C&C* is also a fruitful case study for wider discussions in two broad scholarly camps: a cluster of Protestant ethicists, theologians, and social thinkers, on one side, and a broader group of scholars in cultural studies, American studies, and postwar cultural history, on the other. Before turning to my main narrative, I will present my case for interchange across the divides that separate these two groups, and I will underline some of the connections embedded in my chronological narrative. Imagine the study of *C&C* as a set of concentric circles. At the center is *C&C*'s particular story. The inside circles represent *C&C*'s place within a larger map of postwar U.S. Christianity. The widest levels of interest represent how it fits into broader discussions in cultural studies and postwar cultural history. Let us start on the outside and work our way in.

Bill Graham and Billy Graham: Why C&C Is Not Just for Scholars of Religion

The study of *C&C* fits within a broad context of interpreting the nature, limitations, and legacy of the so-called cold war liberal consensus. Many scholars identify a trend in postwar U.S. culture from a relatively strong liberal hegemony in the cold war era to a partial collapse of liberal dominance in the 1960s and the growth of cultural alternatives, including counterhegemonic movements.[31] At a minimum, the study of *C&C* tests how these larger trends worked themselves out in one key case within Protestantism. However, this study has implications that reach beyond documenting one more group within standard patterns of explanation; therefore, it may have broader effects on how we conceptualize this change.

The title of this section comes from David Farber's *The Sixties: From Memory to History,* a collection currently staking a claim as cutting-edge scholarship on postwar U.S. cultural politics. Farber frames his book by arguing that the decade was not only a time when left-liberal movements flowered. It was also a seedbed for the rise of conservatives who have dominated U.S. national politics from Nixon's election to the present. He notes that they succeeded by creating a backlash against radicalism, largely through the institutions and ideologies of the new religious right. This is a crucial argument, but unfortunately the analysis of religion is hardly more than a gesture in his book. With the exception of a section on Martin Luther King Jr. and a few sentences on the religious antiwar group called Clergy and Laymen Concerned about Vietnam, or CALCAV, none of the key players in Christian religious-political debates appear in the book. We hear about funk singer James Brown, *Cosmopolitan* editor Helen Gurley Brown, folk singer Jackson Browne, black power activist H. Rap Brown, and politician Jerry Brown—but not *C&C*'s Robert McAfee Brown or Harold O. J. Brown, a social theorist associated with the evangelical magazine *Christianity Today*, even though both played key roles in debates about civil rights, Vietnam protest, and women's rights. We learn about Bill Graham, the music promoter who helped launch the Grateful Dead—but not Billy Graham, the evangelist who preached at the White House and invited Richard Nixon to speak at his nationally televised revival, immediately after the Kent State killings. My point is not to trivialize James Brown and Bill Graham. I do insist that a book that begins and ends by portraying the 1960s as a seedbed for the new religious right should not spend three hundred intervening pages neglecting religion.[32]

C&C is a promising place to explore how postwar religion and broader social movements fit together. As I have suggested, it was a leading space for conversation about religion and politics for the ecumenical left as well as a select group of secular intellectuals who chose to join the discussion. Many *C&C* contributors commanded respect far beyond religious circles: Hannah Arendt, Peter Berger, Noam Chomsky, Vine Deloria Jr., Michael Eric Dyson, John Kenneth Galbraith, Michael Harrington, bell hooks, June Jordan, George Kennan, Martin Luther King Jr., Robert Lekachman, Margaret Mead, A. J. Muste, Rigoberta Menchú, Hans Morgenthau, Lewis Mumford, Arnold Toynbee, Cornel West. One of my goals is to persuade more of my colleagues who do not specialize in religious issues to enter this discussion.

Sometimes making this case is an uphill battle, despite the fact that cultural studies scholars like to cite Benedict Anderson's argument that nationalisms and religions are two key forms of imagined community.[33] Both are powerful cultural constructs; they are multivocal and contestable, "imaginary" but no less real in their effects for identity formation and the exercise of sociopolitical power. If nationalisms are like religions, as Anderson suggests, isn't it relevant to explore what *religions* are like? We might answer no if we consider nationalisms as successor movements to religions, ones that have largely supplanted religions in some pockets of our world. Yet religions remain alive and well on every continent. They coexist with nations and often function as bulwarks for them. They seem more likely to bury theories of secularization than vice-versa.[34] Does cultural studies have anything to say about the imagined communities commonly designated religious? I do not suggest *substituting* a focus on religions for attention to factors such as race, class, gender, and nation. But I do suggest *integrating* religious identities as variables in the mix of analysis: for example, analyzing both gender and religious differences within nations, both race and religious identities cutting across national boundaries, both race and religious differences within classes, and so on. No one attempting a broad account of the contemporary world can ignore nationalism—not even the poststructuralists who are most determined to dissolve the fixity of national boundaries, accent the oppressive dimensions of nationalism, and write complex accounts of structures like race that cut across nations. However, almost *anyone* in cultural studies can choose to ignore religions without being challenged to think twice about it. One need not claim that religions are the sole variables in contemporary cultures, or the most important ones, to be troubled by this situation.

When it comes to sparking interest in what *C&C* brings to discussions in the wider academy, I sometimes feel that *C&C* has three strikes against it. First, there is a relative lack of interest in twentieth-century religion of any kind. Second, when postwar religion *is* addressed, the tendency is to make simplistic critiques, often focused on fundamentalists, that are tone deaf to the internal complexities of religions. Third, there is a widespread suspicion of classic forms of cold war liberal consensus-building, including Niebuhr's version, among postmodern theorists and cultural pluralists of various stripes. Three strikes and liberal Protestants are out—or at least pushed to the margins of dominant intellectual maps.

It is easy to turn back the first two objections. Anyone can see that academic apathy about contemporary religion stands in striking contrast to the continuing importance of religious belief and practice in the wider society. For example, more than half of the people attend church, synagogue, or mosque; 80 percent expect to appear before God on judgment day; and 85 percent accept the Bible as divinely inspired.[35] Centrist politicians and popular musicians often speak about God. When Pat Robertson writes a book in which he claims that George Bush was complicit in a Satanic conspiracy to institute "an occult-inspired world socialist dictatorship," this cannot be ignored, because he commands a large television audience and is a major force in the Republican Party.[36] Of course, religion is not the sole key to U.S. culture. Less than half the people who claim that they want to live by the Ten Commandments can name four of them, and Robertson no longer speaks in tongues on television because "it comes on as cornball or zany."[37] Nevertheless, developments in the religious arena have been highly significant for the broader society, not least in the case of Niebuhrians and another group that loomed large at *C&C:* the coalition led by Martin Luther King Jr.

In this context, studying *C&C* contributes to the ongoing remapping of postwar cultural history, especially on the political left. It is now common for feminists to point out that standard histories of the 1960s are biased toward male leaders of national New Left organizations.[38] My example from Farber suggests that the same histories tilt toward *secular* actors. *C&C* people played key roles in the civil rights and antiwar movements, roles that are increasingly well documented but poorly integrated into standard histories. For example, the major seedbed of the New Left at the University of Texas was the campus YMCA, inspired conceptually by the social gospel and existentialist theology—in other words, some of their key leaders read *C&C.*[39]

Stuart Hall argues a similar point in more abstract terms, designed to speak to his colleagues in cultural studies. He says that despite valid reasons for leftists and feminists to be suspicious of religions, such that "it would be idiotic to think that you could easily detach religion from its historical embeddedness and simply put it in another place," nevertheless, "Religion has no necessary political connotations. . . . Its meaning—political and ideological—comes precisely from its position within a formation. . . . To struggle around religion in [a particular] country, you need to know the ideological terrain, the lay of the land. . . . [Sometimes] no political movement in the society can become popular without negotiating the religious terrain. Social movements have to transform it, buy into it, inflect it, develop it, clarify it—but they must engage with it."[40]

Unfortunately, when secular leftists do turn their attention to religion, the second problem I have mentioned arises. Often they display such suspicion and lack of nuance that one wishes they had *continued to ignore* the issues. Consider the case of Samuel Ruiz, the bishop of San Cristóbal de las Casas, Mexico, who has long advocated indigenous rights and Latin American liberation theology. He was a major player in the historical process that produced the Zapatista army of Chiapas in 1994 and a key broker in negotiations between the Mexican government and the Zapatistas. Thus he appeared in the *Nation,* a secular left journal, where we are told that he "began a hunger strike—which he prefers to call a religious fast."[41] Perhaps we should marvel that the *Nation* printed something sympathetic toward a bishop. Nevertheless, this quotation signals deeper problems. By the same logic, shall we say that Martin Luther King Jr. "gave motivational pep talks to his church—which he preferred to call sermons and prayers"? Do musicians like Chuck D of Public Enemy "give topical political commentary—which they prefer to call rap music"? The *Nation*'s sentence implies a subtle disrespect for Ruiz's beliefs as well as a general attitude that disables critical analysis. We must analyze Chuck D's rhythms and rhymes, as well as the complex social forms through which they are received by his listeners, if we hope to understand their impact.[42] Likewise, we must seriously interrogate the semiotics of Ruiz's act—which includes exploring the meanings of Christian theology and ritual within larger social formations—to understand his ability to galvanize support. Ruiz's institutional and discursive position as a bishop gives him specific resources and limitations. It enables certain forms of praxis and closes off others. Religion was a factor in the effectiveness of his strike/fast at every level—from the local context, to the Mexican nation, to his impact on U.S. elites who influence Mexican policy, to the support he attracted from international human rights networks. It was not the *only* important factor, and we must not romanticize liberation theologies, whether Ruiz's or more grassroots variations. Still, no one can understand the lay of the land in Chiapas if they split off Ruiz's fast from his strike and proceed to ignore it.[43]

Thus I conclude that the first two pitches used to discount the value of a case like *C&C* are not really strikes but big slow floaters to smash out of the ballpark. The third pitch—the objection, "Haven't we heard enough about cold war liberals?"—is a hanging curve ball. But it *is* a curve ball, and we must recognize that there is some truth to it. Niebuhr's realism fits within so-called consensus history and the myth and symbol school of American studies, two approaches that have long been under attack as overgeneralized and ahistorical.[44] Perhaps we *have* heard too much about these liberals—at least too much that is uncritical of their limitations, as well as too much that is misinformed and dogmatic in its hostility. But precisely because of the ongoing influence of liberal approaches, we need studies that clarify both their strengths and limitations, study the process through which their assumptions began to break down, and rethink them in light of collapse of the New Deal coalition, the end of the cold war, and the rise of the new religious right. *C&C* is an excellent case study for approaching these issues. Above all, it sheds light on the current impasse of the left and current debates about morally grounded struggles for hegemony in the public sphere. Critical analysis of *C&C*'s history—both its successes and failures—engages one directly with some of the most pressing current issues for left-wing intellectuals today, caught as we are in a complex web of commitments that do not always work together.

After a generation of scholarship on cultural difference and conflict, many scholars perceive a problem of fragmentation in U.S. culture. We might debate whether diversity and conflict have actually increased since the 1960s; I think recent changes are relatively small compared with ongoing structural differences. In any case, it is clear that since the 1960s it has become harder for elites to ignore the perceptions of people further from the centers of power—African Americans, Latinos, women of many backgrounds, and so on—who insist that from their standpoint, traditional History appears as "a compilation of the depositions made by assassins with respect to their victims and themselves."[45] Perceptions have changed in analogous ways within philosophy and social theory, which have seen a marked suspicion toward "master narratives" and "totalizing" moral agendas—especially in explicitly theological forms.

In this context, the radical positions of the later *C&C* stand in dialogue with well-funded conservatives and centrist liberals who lament the loss of a cultural center. For our purposes, the most relevant dialogue partners are not conservatives like Allan Bloom, author of *The Closing of the American Mind,* but liberals like historian Arthur Schlesinger Jr.—a friend of Niebuhr—who stated in 1990 that a "cult of ethnicity" had gone too far: "We used to say *e pluribus unum.* Now we glorify *pluribus* and belittle *unum.* The melting pot yields to the Tower of Babel."[46] This lament, which is echoed by scholars in religious studies such as Robert Bellah and William Dean, interests me because it overlaps with discussions on the academic left about multiculturalism and poststructuralism.[47] Broad social movements involving complex alliances are needed to transform oppressive power structures, and such movements are difficult to create when their prospective participants have radically diverse ideas about what forms of suffering and oppression, linked to what power structures, should be in focus. This challenge is acute today. I say this, presupposing rather than lamenting the turn to multicultural approaches. I also presuppose insights of the best postmodern scholarship, which complicates overly simple conceptions of power structures and suffering—including the idea of liberal consensus progressively overcoming "extremism" and "backwardness" as well as Marxian accounts of one capitalist power structure creating one basic form of economic suffering. The challenge of coalition-building cannot be addressed simply by reasserting one of these approaches. If older approaches fail to account for differences based on race, gender, sexuality, and so on, the obvious response is to rethink these approaches rather than to discount the differences.

Unfortunately, diverse definitions of oppression and difference, linked to equally diverse postmodernist analyses of how power works, can result in methodological gridlock when each "different" group seeks priority in the academy and broader coalition-building. An influential article by Audre Lorde accented the importance of cultural difference by quoting Adrienne Rich's line, "The master's tools will never dismantle the master's house." But Hazel Carby replied: "Theories of difference and diversity in practice leave us fragmented and divided but equal in an inability to conceive of radical social change. . . . We are not supposed to use revolutionary theories of history, the 'master narratives,' because they are the master's tools. It is my contention that the master appropriated those tools along with the labor of those he exploited and it is high time that they be reclaimed."[48] In this context, academics must walk a tightrope between respecting complex differences and stressing how various forms of oppression interlock. Often this shifts the priority from accenting diversity to seeking spaces for dialogue. The key task becomes exploring possibilities for struggle in the current situation—proximate teleologies with no assurance of success or advance blueprint for coalescence.

This is the context in which the pitcher delivers the third pitch . . . and by this time in the ball game some of the players have heard enough from liberals like Schlesinger. Yet a formal perception of Babel can be shared across the political spectrum: by conservatives like Bloom, liberals like Schlesinger, and radicals like Carby. Conservatives approach this issue from above in an effort to revitalize a status quo consensus perceived to be slipping away, while radicals advocate coalitions from below to undermine and transform a status quo perceived as all too strong. For an analysis centered on cultural hegemony, the crux question is to what degree, and in what contexts, liberal calls for greater attention to cultural centers function to revitalize an old exclusionary dominant culture, and to what degree they are open to counterhegemonic meanings.

Consider how a study of *C&C* relates to the many recent calls for strengthening the public sphere in general and (at least among *C&C*'s old constituents) public religions in particular. An essential point implicit in the breakdown of liberal consensus approaches is the coexistence of many publics, overlapping in complex ways, holding varying amounts of power, and sometimes standing in conflict. With so many kinds of public on the table, and in light of the growing body of scholarship showing the historical connections between national public spheres, patriarchal metaphors, and racial exclusions, it is tempting to throw up our hands and say that the national public simply does not—or should not—exist.[49] On the other hand, as Bruce Robbins points out, this response is uncomfortably close to what Walter Lippmann argued in the 1920s: that society has become so complex that the masses cannot be adequately informed to participate in decisions about social policy, and have no viable choice except to delegate authority to technocratic elites or trust the invisible hand of the free market. Thus Robbins says, "If there is some reluctance to see the public melt conclusively into the air, the cause may not be vestigial piety so much as the fear that we cannot do without it." He calls for building publics that can defend collective democratic interests against elite interests. At the same time, he insists on abandoning unitary conceptions of the public and recasting them in pro-feminist and multiculturalist forms: it becomes "a matter of local investigations into particular collectivities and practical politics."[50] One of the best versions of this approach is Nancy Fraser's concept of counter-publics committed to social transformation. They form a creative middle ground between unitary concepts of the public, on one side, and various approaches that abandon public work toward sociopolitical change, on the other.[51]

C&C's left turn is easy to interpret in these terms. As a study in the rise of *counter*-publics, *C&C* shows how pluralist and radical critiques unfolded—why they seemed essential and why current debates cannot be resolved by reasserting older approaches. *C&C* exposes the limits of neoconservative proposals for consensus and presses liberals like Schlesinger and Bellah to clarify their mixed signals about social transformation. As a case study in counter-*publics*, *C&C* provides a relatively coherent community of discourse that—however imperfectly—developed a morally grounded approach to radical politics, sustained a dialogue among white liberals and a variety of radical groups, and practiced the type of publicly engaged cultural criticism that Cornel West has called prophetic pragmatism.[52]

C&C did not fully theorize these issues, much less "solve" them. Yet one might suspect from reading critics who lament the rise of atomized individualism and poststructuralist theories, as well as the fragmentation caused by the "micropolitics of identity" and "special interest groups" in religion, that *C&C*'s approach was barely even conceivable. *C&C* created a forum which, despite numerous imperfections, managed to bridge several divides: between generations within the liberal Protestant tradition, among several contentious communities committed to liberation theologies, and between religious discourses and broader public issues. It managed to sustain this broad approach for nearly three decades, from its left turn in the 1960s until 1993. Anyone who assumes the need for coalition-building in the public sphere might well reflect on its successes and failures.

C&C and the Internal Politics of Protestantism

I began with an effort to persuade my secularized academic colleagues to engage with *C&C*, because I take it for granted that specialists in Protestant social thought will be interested. For readers in the know, it is enough to recall the names of *C&C* writers. Over the years *C&C* published an international who's who of religious thinkers including Karl Barth, Dietrich Bonhoeffer, James Cone, Gustavo Gutierrez, Hans Kung, Jurgen Moltmann, H. Richard Niebuhr, Rosemary Ruether, and Paul Tillich. That's a short list. The honor roll includes Rubem Alves, Robert Bellah, Daniel Berrigan, Elizabeth Bettenhausen, Allan Boesak, Leonardo Boff, José Míguez Bonino, Emil Brunner, Dom Helder Camara, Will Campbell, Carol Christ, Chung Hyung-Kyung, John Cobb, William Sloane Coffin—and so on throughout the entire alphabet. More important than their names were the issues they discussed. *C&C*'s story is entwined with three topics of current interest in the study of U.S religion: the simultaneous upsurge of fundamentalism and stagnation of liberalism in postwar Protestantism, the explosion of multiculturalist approaches to U.S. religion, and controversies about Niebuhr's legacy in light of critiques launched by liberation theologies.

The relative power of mainline Protestantism has declined sharply since the 1950s, and scholars are debating the merits of several religious-political alternatives that have arisen. These range from resurgent fundamentalism on the right, through various forms of neoconservatism, moderate evangelicalism, religious communitarianism, and unrepentant liberalism struggling for the middle ground, to liberation theologies on the left. *C&C*'s leftward shift exemplifies one major trend within this larger map of religious-political contestation.[53] When liberal Protestants abandoned their inherited roles of baptizing U.S. nationalism, capitalism, and "family values," people like Billy Graham and Pat Robertson were waiting to fill the vacuum they left. This was a major context for a widely heralded scholarly discovery in the 1970s that conservative evangelicals were reviving. In fact, their numerical growth had been steady for decades, but this had largely been ignored in mainstream discourse. The cumulative effect of evangelical growth was not trivial, nor was the trend of liberal youth abandoning mainline churches that they considered bland and vaguely repressive. Still, the most important change around 1970 was not demographic: it was a massive shift of money, elite resources, and morale into the conservative camp. In this context, *C&C*'s former constituency polarized between neoconservative versions of Niebuhrian theology like Michael Novak's and left-liberal versions like Cornel West's.

This struggle for control of mainline Christianity continues today, and it is not fully clear whether the leftward shift exemplified by *C&C* was *imprudent* from the standpoint of mainline Protestant success.[54] I maintain that this remains to be seen, depending on the definition of success and what new allies the mainline attracts in the long run. Neoconservative journals clearly have had greater success in attracting institutional backing, compared with *C&C*, which folded largely for lack of comparable resources.[55] However, since the major explanation of mainline membership losses since the 1960s is the defection of youth, a shift to the left would appear to be a plausible strategy for maximizing mainline demographic strength. Although some of this might be debated, one thing is clear. Analyzing *C&C* can reveal a great deal about the central issue of who within Protestantism, in what sociopolitical contexts, attracts which powerful allies.

C&C is especially useful for relating this spectrum of Protestant debate to the explosion of pluralist and multicultural scholarship, which among historians of U.S. religion often marches under the banner of "outsider" religious traditions.[56] Scholars interested in these issues have tended to emphasize autonomous alternative subcultures and have given relatively low attention to the *relationships* between insiders and outsiders. (The major exception to this rule is the discourse about public religion, where a leading tendency is to approach cultural pluralism as a problem to overcome.) Mutual relationships among elites and subcultures are at the heart of this book, since I will focus on some extremely well connected insiders as they came to terms with the critiques of outsiders from Roman Catholicism, the women's movement, African American religion, and the third world. Through studying *C&C*, we can explore the impact that the rising consciousness of pluralism and conflict made on the work of establishment writers, as well as the shifting power relationships that unfolded as *C&C* began to place outsider concerns at the center of its agenda.

In ongoing debates about the future of U.S. religion, scholars across a wide spectrum appeal for authority to Niebuhr, who is widely considered "the unrivaled political ethics teacher to several generations of pastors . . . [and] the political gatekeeper to North American Christendom."[57] Neoconservatives often use the Niebuhrian gate to keep liberation theologies and their radical agendas outside of acceptable religious discourse, while liberationists attempt to kick this gate open or frame their arguments so that they can squeeze through it. This is not an abstract speculation akin to monks debating how many angels fit on the head of a pin. On the contrary, it is a major way that the concrete sociopolitical priorities of U.S. Christians are negotiated.

Debating the question "What would Niebuhr say?" is not the most helpful process that might be imagined for evaluating current issues. At best it is indirect, and at worst it presupposes Niebuhr's ideas as the standard when this should be critically evaluated, while it deflects attention from the differences between current situations and ones he addressed.[58] However, as long as proposals about the future of U.S. religion keep appealing to Niebuhr, it is almost impossible to avoid considering what he would say. Such appeals are not found only in academic journals. For example, during the Persian Gulf War, a syndicated newspaper columnist cited Niebuhr as an authority who supposedly demonstrated that the peace movement "sees no values worth fighting for," "strips life of true moral concerns," and "accepts a view of man that denies the possibility of human evil." Peaceniks were appeasing Saddam Hussein, just as Britain had appeased Hitler at Munich.[59]

For anyone who is drawn into these debates about Niebuhr's legacy, however eagerly or reluctantly, *C&C*'s history is very important. Of those who collaborated with Niebuhr during his lifetime and carried his analysis into the post-Vietnam era, such *C&C* leaders as Bennett have the strongest claims to authority. Bennett was a central architect of Christian realism; Niebuhr stated in 1970 that he had "consulted with Dr. Bennett in all difficult academic and journalistic problems" since 1928 and had in every case "achieved an essential accord."[60] During the 1970s and 1980s, one of the best ways to learn what Niebuhr would say was to read what Bennett *did* say in *C&C.* It is also fascinating in this connection to analyze how *C&C* polarized in the 1960s. Among leading neoconservative Niebuhrians, Richard John Neuhaus and Peter Berger both wrote for *C&C,* and Michael Novak was a contributing editor from 1968 to 1976.[61] Neuhaus sees his well-funded journal, *First Things,* playing a role in current debates somewhat similar to *C&C*'s role during the 1940s.

Although the connection with Niebuhr creates interest in this book, it also raises a question about what is new, since so much research related to *C&C*'s career has already been published. Niebuhr has been studied *ad nauseum,* especially from theological perspectives, and there are several excellent theological texts on the clash between Niebuhrian and liberation theologies.[62] The systematic study of *C&C* contributes to this literature, because as Bennett has said, "To understand Niebuhr's thought we must move back and forth between his books, which provide the theological frame for his thought, and his articles and editorials, which show his response to contemporary events. . . . The dialectical structure of his thought as a whole often leaves us with a delicate balance between opposite positions . . . [and] it is only in the light of his concrete decisions for action that we can be sure where his emphasis finally lies."[63]

Nevertheless, this is not the ten thousandth book on Niebuhr, nor the thousandth on liberation theologies, but the first book on *Christianity and Crisis.* To gain a quick sense of why it fills a distinctive niche amid the scholarly literature, consider how it relates to four recent texts: Christian Smith's *Emergence of Liberation Theology,* James Cone's *Martin and Malcolm and*

America, Richard Fox's *Reinhold Niebuhr: A Biography*, and Robert Wuthnow's *Restructuring of American Religion*.[64] It is in dialogue with each of these texts, yet in each case it provides a fresh angle of vision.

Like Fox's biography, this book places Niebuhr and his circle of colleagues in the context of cultural and sociopolitical history. However, Fox keeps a tight focus on Niebuhr, so that his study winds down (along with Niebuhr's health) in the late 1960s, just when debates about left-right polarization and the rise of liberation theologies became especially interesting in Niebuhr's community. For example, Fox hardly addresses the debate between feminist theologies and male Niebuhrians because it was barely under way before the 1970s. In contrast, I focus on a much larger group of people and trace a continuous institutional and personal bridge between classic Niebuhrian positions and liberation theologies. I am centrally concerned with radicalization and polarization within Niebuhr's community in and around Union Seminary, not only during the final decades of his life but also continuing beyond his death in 1971.

The breadth of my argument falls midway between Fox's tightly focused study and Robert Wuthnow's wide-ranging survey of white Christianity since World War II, *The Restructuring of American Religion*. Because *C&C* had such broad interests, studying it amounts to something like a survey of postwar Protestant religious politics, albeit from a distinctive perspective. Like Wuthnow, I accent liberal-conservative realignment, which split *C&C* wide open during the 1960s. Like him, I map the rise of evangelicalism and the easing of strife between Catholics and Protestants. (*C&C* began by attacking Roman Catholicism as a form of totalitarianism comparable to communism, and ended with liberal Catholics in its inner circle.)[65] Unlike Wuthnow I do not attempt to tell a comprehensive story from a stance "above" the left and right; rather, I describe how the various dialogues appeared from within left-liberal circles. Also, whereas Wuthnow is a sociologist who relies on quantitative surveys, I stress narrative and cultural interpretation. As a source, *C&C* cannot offer the advantages of Wuthnow's "hard" survey data, but it has the compensating strength of providing "thicker" interpretation of cultural meanings. For whatever *C&C*'s case may be worth, it also qualifies Wuthnow's interpretation of certain issues; I will argue that *C&C*'s changes are hard to explain through his theories about the new class.

Both Fox and Wuthnow devote limited effort to placing their protagonists within race, class, and gender hierarchies in postwar America and to charting relationships between so-called insiders and outsiders. Fox sticks so closely to Niebuhr's life that the effect is to minimize dialogues between Niebuhr and his more radical critics, despite Fox's sympathies with some of these critics. Wuthnow interprets the left turn of *C&C*-type liberals mainly in categories that are blind to gender and race, and presents their activism as part of a fragmented civil religion, a problem that he hopes national consensus-building can overcome.

My work is more attentive to the limits of liberalism stressed by feminist and pluralist scholarship and to positive aspects of the rising religious-political left. My analysis of *C&C*'s gender dynamics overlaps strongly with books on the rise of feminist spiritualities such as Judith Plaskow and Carol Christ's *Womanspirit Rising*, a classic reader with several articles that appeared in *C&C*.[66] However, in this introduction I will discuss two studies that treat a somewhat earlier period: Cone's *Martin and Malcolm and America* and Smith's *Emergence of Liberation Theology*.

Cone, Smith, and I all highlight the historical process through which liberation theologies emerged. This reflects a growing trend in scholarship on these movements, to put less stress on methods of normative theology and more stress on bridging the discourses of secular historians and cultural critics, on one side, and religious studies scholars, on the other. Like *The Emergence of Liberation Theology*, this book explores how liberation theologies became influential in the Americas, using methods that are primarily historical and informed by social theory. But whereas Smith's subjects are Roman Catholics from Latin America, mine are U.S. Protestants. *C&C*'s surging interest in Latin American liberation theology is just one strand in my argument, and I approach it in the context of U.S. cultural history. Also, in partial contrast to Smith's sociological methods, I place more stress on the cultural-historical analysis of a representative case study.

In *Martin and Malcolm*, Cone also uses a historical case-study approach, and he addresses the same broad question as this book: how did radical theologies emerge in the postwar United States? Much like Cone explores the roots of recent black religious thought by analyzing King and Malcolm X in their cultural-political contexts, my book analyzes the emergence of a wider Protestant radicalism by placing *C&C* in its context. Cone's sources allow him to study this process from the underside, far more than is possible using *C&C*, which was monopolized by white male liberals until the late 1960s. However, *C&C* provides certain advantages over Cone's sources for analyzing developing *relationships* among various currents of radical religion—feminist, black, womanist, Latin American, mujerista, queer, ecological, and so on—all in conversation among themselves and with white liberal theologies. The challenge of sorting out these complex relationships is near the top of scholarly agendas in religious studies today.

One of the patterns within this multifaceted conversation—the tension between liberals and various liberationists—brings us back full circle to the question in Fox's book about Niebuhr's legacy for the present.

If one were to imagine these four books as points on a circle, my book would fit somewhere in the center, engaged in a dialogue with each one. I hope that my analysis can mediate among their emphases in a useful way, and to a limited extent even integrate their various strengths within a single case study, at the same time as I tell the distinctive story of *C&C*'s transformation.

Further Thoughts on Generational Bridge-Building

In my preface, I expressed the hope that my book could build bridges between generations of liberal Protestant social thought. This bridge cannot succeed, and I will be left suspended in midair over a chasm, unless I can gain trust on both sides of generational battle lines, among two sets of people who are scarred by Oedipal conflicts: old-time New Deal liberals and a cohort of various New Left, feminist, and multiculturalist radicals. Many of their battles have been fought over questions about continuity and change in *C&C*'s tradition: how radical a repudiation of liberal approaches is needed to address the most pressing issues on the current scene? Several *C&C* old-timers, notably John Bennett and Roger Shinn, tried to impress on me a greater sense of *C&C*'s continuities over time, compared with the stress I placed on generational discontinuity in the early stages of my research.[67] I considered their advice carefully, and I believe that I have incorporated a good deal of their wisdom. In part, I see this book as a corrective to liberationist texts from the past three decades that are overly harsh toward Niebuhr and Bennett's generation and simplistic about the internal dialectic within Christian realism. As I have discussed this book with people from my own generation, I have often been amazed at the limits of their knowledge and/or memory of history before the 1970s. I can sympathize with the lack of personal memory because I was only nine years old in 1966, but it still comes as a shock to consider that many entering graduate students were not even born before the publication of classic texts by *C&C*'s "new young radicals" such as Rosemary Ruether and James Cone. I hope that by telling *C&C*'s story, presupposed by an older generation and little known by upcoming generations, this book can build bridges. I especially hope it will revalorize John Bennett's role in opening Protestant social thought to broader perspectives. Through studying *C&C*, I gained a tremendous respect for his role in guiding it through its critical years, and in many ways he emerges as the hero of the book.

Nevertheless, my argument does steer into generational controversy. I remain unconvinced that liberal continuity should be my dominant theme, and I argue in the vein of liberation theologies about the limitations of cold war Niebuhrianism. At times I document a selective memory among Niebuhrian old-timers. They have a tendency, fueled by justifiable outrage at neoconservative appropriations of Niebuhr, to exaggerate *C&C*'s prophetic bite in its early years. Some of the evidence I present may make them squirm. For example, whereas liberal Niebuhrians commonly claim that *C&C* was a forceful critic of cold war culture during the 1940s and a vigorous advocate of civil rights in the 1950s, I demonstrate that in most cases its criticism was quite cautious and circumscribed, although an element of critique was usually present as a secondary theme.

Reading these cautious articles which *C&C* old-timers recall as bold and biting, I sometimes ask myself if *C&C*'s bite was analogous to a certain type of hostile book review. I mean the sort of tactful evaluation that says, "I like point A, and point B is solid, and I certainly agree that point C is crucial. However, let me say this about point D"—where the zinger about point D calls everything else into question and would be considered the main point of the review by people who had ears to hear. Sometimes I wonder whether, due to my youth or some other limitation, I lack the ears to hear the zingers that old-timers recall, and I only hear how *C&C* shared in a cold war mentality on points A, B, and C.

Let us recall, however, that there is another kind of book review, in which agreement on A, B, and C means 99 percent support on all the essential points, and the "zinger" at point D corrects a spelling error. It is not always easy to assess the zing in *C&C*'s point D zingers, which criticized U.S. policies in its early years. No doubt readers responded in different ways, and—more importantly—*C&C*'s audience changed over the years. In its early years, *C&C* writers liked to speak to establishment insiders as establishment insiders, or at least as experts who were trying to imagine how issues appeared from insider points of view. Often *C&C* adopted elite standpoints explicitly, as when its writers analyzed options for U.S. foreign policy, using the word *we* interchangeably for the nation as a whole, government policy planners, the U.S. army, and themselves. Other times they may have implicitly fueled aspirations toward elite standpoints through their rhetoric of objective policy planning and universal ethical judgment. Insiders did listen, as when Paul Nitze recruited Ernest Lefever and when Arthur Schlesinger Jr. (then a special assistant to President Kennedy) wrote to complain about *C&C* coverage of Latin America.[68] However, in later years, *C&C* increasingly adopted a peasant's eye view of U.S. bomber planes, a prisoner's eye view of confrontations such as the

Attica prison revolt, and grassroots views of various minority and low-income political movements. As it integrated the standpoints of people further from the centers of power—both directly and by trying to imagine how issues looked from their points of view—*C&C* stressed the drawbacks of its earlier links to status quo power structures, as well as the difficulties of attaining a "God's-eye" perspective on theological questions.

Feminist ethicist Sharon Welch interprets this change as a move away from an ethic of control that presupposes a standpoint of top-down power—an ethic which can easily turn into "an ideology of cultured despair" if the people who are actually in control pay no attention to advice from ethicists.[69] To minimize this problem, Welch calls for an ethic of risk grounded in "communities of solidarity and resistance." As *C&C* radicals moved in this direction, they did not necessarily abandon core insights of Christian realism such as the need to deflate arrogant pride and meet oppressive power with countervailing power. On the contrary, they frequently used the central realist principle—that God stands in judgment on sinful human pride—to criticize aspects of pride specified as economic exploitation, militarism, racism, sexual violence, neoconservative arrogance, and so forth. In any case, whether they recast realist critiques of pride within a liberation paradigm, or pushed further along lines suggested by Welch, they assumed accountability to a different community of readers.

Liberal Niebuhrians like Ronald Stone argue eloquently that radicals like Welch should give Niebuhr greater credit: "To Niebuhr, the U.S. was an empire in a struggle. Critics often seem to find fault with Niebuhr as if he were responsible either for the empire or the struggle. . . . [His views] are rooted in reality as well as perspective. A sympathetic reading . . . finds him urging a cautious policy of statecraft, the upbuilding of the developing world, a nuclear partnership, a decrease in American reliance on military power, and so on—the most constructive policies that he saw as real possibilities within the inevitable boundaries of nationalism, empire, and Cold War."[70]

These points are well taken. Yet at the same time they illustrate a problem: the limitations of Niebuhr's postwar perspectives, in which the main realities were those perceived by government elites and their advisers—experts who spoke for "all of us Americans" (black and white, male and female), focused on geopolitical struggles with communism, and took empire for granted as an "inevitable boundary." Thus *C&C* churned out countless variations on the goal of defending against totalitarianism and resisting naive idealism. It assumed that neither feminism nor racial justice was a high priority.[71]

All this leads to an irony that has been argued elegantly by William McGuire King: it is quite possible that the prophetic voice of mainline

Protestants had a relatively minor impact, in terms of making a practical difference in outcomes, when they were considered the most influential. This is true because the price of influence was prior agreement with elites on a whole string of points A, B, C, D, E, F, and G.[72] Conversely, Protestants might have had a greater independent impact when *Time* ignored them and the State Department no longer tried to recruit them. Obviously, one can press this line of thought only so far. Sometimes influence means influence, weakness means weakness, and marginality is well deserved. Nevertheless, these considerations complicate the problem of judging the zing of a given zinger. They return us to the problem of how to respond if a skeptic complains that the impact of *C&C*'s left-wing activism remains to be seen. Once again, the crucial question concerns cultural standpoints and the criteria for success that emerge from them.

When I first began to study *C&C*, I vowed to avoid arguments like the one that is emerging here, in the style of rhetoric that continually says, "On the one hand X is true . . . but on the other hand we must not forget Y."[73] I fear, however, that this refrain from *C&C* has come into my book by extension, despite my best efforts. *C&C* continually expounded on "dialectical" or "paradoxical" situations: *X, but at the same time Y.* Often *C&C* leaned these two "hands" against each other without explicitly endorsing either one, but the reader was supposed to conclude that one of these hands held the preferred solution. My shorthand term for the dominant hand representing *C&C*'s lesser evil is "the X hand," and I will speak about the hand with the job of adding secondary nuance or qualification as "the Y hand." This is the hand where conflicting arguments are duly acknowledged but weighed as lacking.

Can the idea of X and Y hands promote peace between the generations? At least it clarifies my dual claim, first, that *C&C* changed from a realist to a liberationist paradigm, but second, that this was an organic change within a continuous tradition. I will argue that even during *C&C*'s most conservative period, its Y hand kept alive oppositional sensibilities that were by no means trivial and that sometimes grew to become the X hand.

Consider *C&C*'s blend of continuity and change on the issue of democratic socialism. Most of *C&C*'s leaders had been socialists during the 1930s. Niebuhr was famous for attacking the New Deal from the left, and he had even run for office on a socialist ticket. At *C&C*'s birth, he and his *C&C* colleagues were midstream in a process of converting to New Deal capitalism—but they were by no means all the way there. In 1949 Paul Tillich (a *C&C* contributor) captured their spirit when he commented in the *Christian Century* on the rise of global conflict between the United States and Soviet blocs: "The expectation that we had cherished after the First

World War that a *kairos* 'a fulfillment of time' was at hand has been twice shaken [by Nazism and the cold war]. . . . I do not doubt that the basic conceptions of religious socialism are valid. . . . I am *not* sure that the adoption of religious-socialist principles is a possibility in any foreseeable future. Instead of a creative *kairos,* I see a vacuum which can be made creative only if it is accepted and endured and . . . transformed into a deepening 'sacred void' of waiting."[74]

Thus the matter rested for many years. Respectable Protestants had two choices: scaling back their goals to fit the political-economic realism of the cold war, or embracing the vacuum of socialist hopes provided by Tillich's existentialist theology. *C&C* was rooted in the first of these options and increasingly shifted toward the second during the 1950s. But however deep Tillich's void of waiting may have been in 1949, the wait for socialist principles had clearly ended in *C&C* by its 1976 anniversary banquet. There *C&C*'s editors reaffirmed their fidelity to a Niebuhrian perspective—defined as a commitment to social action linked with an awareness of the realities of power and the imperfection of all social orders. They alluded to *C&C*'s inaugural issue, which had berated pacifists "who choose to exist like parasites" on democracy while Nazi tyrants threatened to destroy it. But returning to Niebuhr's 1941 image, *C&C*'s editors argued in 1976 that the United States was "'parasitically' dependent upon the third world to maintain our standard of living and power. . . . We are now confronted once again by the class structure of our own nation, by the realities of unequal distribution of power—and by the resulting serious undermining of the foundations of and rationale for democracy."[75]

Tillich's 1949 statement that "the basic conceptions of religious socialism remain valid" was the sort of critique that *C&C* often proposed on its Y hand during the cold war era, but overrode on its X hand with arguments about the pragmatic superiority of the New Deal and the totalitarian dangers of communism. Many people at *C&C* never abandoned this position. Yet Tillich's 1949 position can be interpreted as a sort of move underground or pragmatic retreat within a tradition of socialist critique that flowered on *C&C*'s pages both before and after the cold war. This illustrates a common pattern in *C&C*'s history, relevant for a wider range of issues.

Thus it turns out, despite all my stress on shifting standpoints and generational conflict, that my underlying analysis presupposes continuity at *C&C*. More precisely, my core argument is about the multivocality of one broad tradition and about ongoing internal battles over the preferred ways to align that tradition with larger social forces. In this sense, John Bennett has posthumously won me over to his position about stability at *C&C,* just as he so often converted others during *C&C*'s history.

Nevertheless, it is not always clear which level of analysis—the strong paradigm shift against the background of a continuous tradition, or the strong continuity of tradition with shifting articulations—is the proper point to stress in particular conversations. When I am in dialogue with liberal Christian realists such as Stone, I insist on the strong substantive shifts in *C&C*'s basic intellectual paradigms and communities of accountability. But when I am in dialogue with academic radicals of my own generation, I often find myself stressing continuities and pointing out how much *C&C* old-timers like John Bennett resemble contemporaries like Stuart Hall, Beverly Harrison, and Cornel West within a larger scheme of things. I will leave it for each reader, then, to assess whether *C&C*'s transformation represents continuity or change, growing wisdom or decline, on the issues most dear to their own hearts.

The bottom line is that a *C&C* exchange from the early 1970s remains remarkably fresh. At the height of *C&C*'s acrimony about its unraveling liberal consensus, Richard Shaull, a leading proponent of Latin American radicalism, asked whether radicals of various stripes pointed to real problems that liberals could not solve. If so, then liberal objections to radical innovations were "out of context," and it was necessary to acknowledge a "new historical situation in which the struggle for social justice and human well-being must be defined in new terms." Bennett responded that the issue was "the viability of the American political system as an instrument of radical change"—not in the abstract but as compared with other methods that were actually available. Bennett was pessimistic about working through the system—and even *more* pessimistic about working outside it. He maintained that radicals could create "urgency within the political process" and that *C&C* could be a forum for "communication between those who are near enough to the center to influence policy and those who are quite far out in their radicalism."[76]

This is a white male Protestant variation on the exchange between Lorde and Carby, in which Carby contended that, despite the problems of dismantling the master's house with the master's tools, we should stress that "the Master appropriated these tools along with the labor of those he exploited, and it is high time that they be reclaimed." In *C&C*, Rosemary Ruether captured a related tension as the struggle "to bridge the gap between a liberalism too easily co-opted and a radicalism too easily turned into impotent tantrums."[77] From the 1970s until *C&C*'s death, neither radicals nor moderates in *C&C*'s spectrum of debate could ignore each other. They were forced to live in the tension between their positions.

I fear that I am getting ahead of my story. If this debate is to be resolved, inside Protestantism or in wider circles, this can only happen within the force fields of history that made the arguments develop as they did—which includes the wider resonances that memories carry for participants on all sides. In my conclusion, I will reflect on the state of this debate as we approach the end of the century. Meanwhile, let us explore how *C&C*'s history unfolded.

1

The Social Gospel and C&C's Prehistory

C&C was created for the specific purpose of attacking another journal, the *Christian Century,* on a specific political issue, its opposition to U.S. involvement in World War II. However, this dispute was only the tip of an iceberg. At stake were profound differences over the role of the United States on the global stage, the prospects for social justice inside the United States, and the basic purposes of Christianity. The rise of *C&C* involved discrediting the political and religious assumptions that undergirded the *Century*'s position, which was known as the social gospel, and substituting its own Christian realist positions. This was not an attack from outside the *Century*'s broad constituency but a rebellion from the inside. *C&C*'s leaders emerged from the same traditions as the *Century,* which was "the central arena of Protestant debate in America."[1]

In 1939 Reinhold Niebuhr published a *Century* article called "Ten Years That Shook My World" as part of a famous series called "How My Mind Has Changed in the Last Decade." In this symposium a cross-section of Protestant leaders addressed two major issues: a "new theological outlook" that was challenging "the foundations of liberal theology" and the fact that World War II was breaking out, with the *Century*'s constituency sharply divided about how to respond.[2] Niebuhr began by stating that "about midway in my ministry, which extends roughly from the peace of Versailles to the peace of Munich . . . I underwent a fairly complete conversion of thought which involved rejection of almost all the liberal theological ideals and ideas with which I ventured forth in 1915." Niebuhr then launched a merciless assault on liberal theology. He said it was naively optimistic and engaged in illusion. It was like tilting at windmills and preaching "simple little moral homilies" that were irrelevant to "the brutal facts of life." According to Niebuhr, his conclusions about theology had come "not so much through study as through the pressure of world events."[3] Reality had revealed the social gospel as bankrupt, Niebuhr said, and forced him to a more profound Christianity.

The *Century*'s editor, Charles Clayton Morrison, shared Niebuhr's sense of crisis but rejected his conclusions. Like several other contributors to the symposium, Morrison denied many of Niebuhr's charges against the social gospel. He did not believe that he now had to accept or reject a complete conversion from all aspects of liberalism. However, tension was building between people who shared Niebuhr's sweeping disdain for liberalism and people like Morrison who proposed fairly minor adjustments within an ongoing social gospel paradigm. In 1939 these debates remained within the *Century*, and their outcome was unclear. By 1941 the strains would become an open rift, and Niebuhr and his allies would break away to form *Christianity and Crisis* as a base to press their attacks.

C&C's story begins by clarifying the positions its leaders had recently shared but were coming to repudiate. Exactly what did Niebuhr mean when he spoke of "liberal theological ideals" which he had embraced in 1915 but now found worthless? What specific experiences created a crisis between the Treaty of Versailles, which ended World War I, and the Munich Conference, which appeased Hitler in 1938? This chapter introduces the social gospel, discusses how Niebuhr came to reject it, and describes the *Century*'s response to his criticisms which formed the immediate backdrop for *C&C*'s birth.[4]

The Social Gospel

The network of Protestant social activists and religious thinkers known as the social gospel was a multifaceted movement, one that appears to shift in shape depending on the definitions that scholars use in their efforts to identify its center and describe its boundaries. In this section I will try to capture some of its complexity by approaching it from three directions: as part of a larger Progressive movement, as an expression of Anglo-American middle-class values, and as a politicized form of liberal theology. Before turning to this task I will make a more general point, one which became important for *C&C*'s later career. In each of its three faces, the social gospel was influenced—not as a sole explanation but alongside other factors—by a long-standing tradition that understands the United States as distinctively virtuous, entrusted with a special mission and destiny in the world. This may represent a stumbling block for some members of my postmodern, post-Vietnam, post-Madonna generation, who have been taught to roll their eyes and wait for the ironic joke when this tradition is mentioned.[5] Precisely for this reason, it is worthwhile to reflect on this tradition, since many people in the past (and more than a few in recent years) have taken it very seriously.

Although this tradition often takes secular forms, as in the idea of American democracy versus foreign tyranny or American progress versus third world backwardness, one of the richest historical vocabularies to articulate this sense of mission and identity has been Christian theology. People sometimes speak of an "America under God" struggling against adversaries described as Godless, idolatrous, or immoral. Scholars have shown how millennial expectations, in combination with "the Protestant ethic," have led key sectors of the populace to understand their identity as that of a redeemer nation. Historians have discovered variations on this theme in the Puritans' attempt to build a city on a hill at Massachusetts Bay, the civil millennialism of the Revolutionary era, the evangelical revivals and reform movements of the nineteenth century, and the televised prayers of Pat Robertson.[6] Scholars in American studies have shown how these religious ideas can blend with other notions of national identity and work their way deeply into the popular culture, for example, in best-sellers such as *Uncle Tom's Cabin* or speeches by Ronald Reagan.[7] At times, participants in this tradition have believed quite literally that they were building the Kingdom of God on earth. At other times, they have rejected overt theology but substituted rhetoric with unmistakable religious overtones. For example, the committee that designed the Great Seal of the United States rejected the suggestions of Benjamin Franklin and Thomas Jefferson, both of whom proposed the image of the Exodus; instead, they settled on the slogans *Annuit Coeptis* (God smiles on our undertaking) and *Novus Ordo Saeclorum* (a new order of the ages). Related ideas remained very much alive in the early twentieth century. David Noble reports, "When I attempted to analyze the controlling assumptions of the *New Republic* magazine, which had been founded in 1914 explicitly as the voice for [Progressivism], I found that the editors of this journal expected something very much like the millennium to appear between 1914 and 1917."[8]

Scholars call this the tradition of the American jeremiad. Named after the biblical prophet Jeremiah, who warned that Jerusalem would fall unless its people repented, the jeremiad is a form of logic and rhetoric which proclaims that the United States has been chosen for a special role in history, then laments that the people are falling short of their mission. According to Sacvan Bercovitch, what makes this style of thinking an *American* jeremiad is its third step. It is not merely a two-step lament about backsliding from an ideal vision to a current fallen condition. On the contrary, it presents the backsliding as a mere obstacle along the way, which can be transformed into success in carrying the mission forward in the future.[9] Consider the Puritans' goal of building a city on a hill, a vision often cited by U.S. politicians. Puritan theocrats executed witches, Pequots, and Quakers. Does this call into question their status as founders of American liberty? Ah, no, says the true believer. Those were temporary problems which the Puritan tradition overcame; its rebellion against the Anglican state church and its love for learning developed into tolerance and religious freedom in the long run, so that it still represents the best available model. Or consider the so-called American dream of democracy. The rich males who wrote "all men are created equal" also wrote slavery into the Constitution. Did this discredit the United States as a system of liberty and justice for all? Ah, no, can't you see that female abolitionists could also appeal to the Bible and that even the Black Panthers quoted the Declaration of Independence?

The American jeremiad is very much out of favor in the U.S. academy today. This is true, first, because many of the classic arguments for the unique promise of the United States were based on a perceived contrast between a virtuous New World in North America and a corrupt Old World in Europe. Scholars are now more prone to interpret the U.S. and European worlds as two similar variations within the same broad modern world—the one defined by the rise of capitalist nation-states led by the middle classes of Europe and North America. All modern capitalist nations saw themselves undergoing analogous experiences of progress from a feudal "old world" to a modern one. This implies that U.S. history was not a righteous alternative to a European pattern, so that, for example, Europe practiced imperialism and the United States did not. Rather, U.S. history was part of the imperial expansion of a transatlantic capitalism.[10] Second, scholars of the American jeremiad have too often assumed that a Euro-American middle-class jeremiad defined the identities of U.S. citizens as a whole. Everyone agrees that this tradition was a preferred interpretation of U.S. identity for middle-class males who held disproportionate power and that these elites frequently attempted to "uplift" outsider groups through assimilation into their purportedly more virtuous civilization. In addition, non-elites sometimes used versions of the American jeremiad for their own purposes, as for example in the speeches of Martin Luther King Jr. However, this does not yet prove that elite traditions defined the culture of immigrants, blacks, women of all races and classes, and others outside the dominant groups. Their degree of cultural autonomy and their specific responses to elite influences must be studied on a case-by-case basis.

Despite these major qualifications by present-day scholars, the main point for present purposes is that Euro-American leaders during the Progressive era—including almost everyone who wrote for the *Century*—inherited this tradition of U.S. destiny and were seeking to carry it into the twentieth century. As our story opens, the tradition was changing. In the nineteenth century, some of its more influential proponents had feared that the true promise of America would be derailed by the rise of industrial cities, with their aristocratic elites and historic entanglements with Europe. The hope of America, so these earlier theorists had reasoned, was based on small towns and yeoman farmers who lived free of the oppressions symbolized by parasitic bankers, railroad barons, and dark satanic mills. By the twentieth century, a new generation had come to believe that the transition to an urban and industrial society was inevitable. Thus, the vision of American virtue and destiny enters our story, not as the hope of living on the land as a self-reliant producer but as a vision of building democracy inside the modern industrial city.[11]

At the level of culture, this was the general goal of Progressives, both secular and religious. They linked this symbolism to a variety of concrete commitments—everything from unionism, democratic socialism, and progressive state regulation for the collective good, through wishful thinking about harmonious class cooperation, to various kinds of moral reform to clean up the lingering evils of the city. The *Century*, as the leading voice of Progressivism among Protestants, published articles by or about leading reformers such as Jane Addams, Herbert Croly, Vida Scudder, and Washington Gladden, plus a stream of reports on the eight-hour day, prison reform, and so on. "The World Is Getting Better" and "Social Survey" were regular features that "reported on as many developments of (or impediments to) the social-gospel movement as [they] could identify."[12] The *Century* supported civil liberties, attacked laissez-faire economics, and supported the right to strike. It chided the American Federation of Labor for being too conservative to bring industrial democracy; its preferred approach to labor issues was in some ways more radical (indeed often socialist) yet weaker in practical application (since it appealed to uncoerced cooperation between labor and capital).

Early in the twentieth century, many Progressives framed their hopes in global terms. They envisioned industrial democracy triumphing over plutocratic capitalism and feudal backwardness in Europe, the United States, and throughout the world. Progressive nations such as the United States would bring civilization, along with military conquest and trade, to places like Cuba and China. This way of thinking could support a policy that proved fateful for the United States in the twentieth century: the extension of conquest and economic expansion from a continental to intercontinental scale, and the entrance into World War I, the war which was expected to end all wars and institute world democracy.[13]

Of course, the actual experience of World War I was markedly different, and this led to a shift within Progressive thinking that would be crucial for *C&C*. In the aftermath of the war, the idea of a civilizing mission for Euro-American armies appeared to many people as unpersuasive—indeed, as repulsive and dangerous. When Niebuhr spoke of the peace of Versailles as the beginning of his disillusionment, he signaled his agreement with this perception; he had embraced pacifism during a 1923 trip to Europe, when he was appalled by the French treatment of Germans after the war.[14] In a similar vein, leading Progressive intellectuals such as the historian Charles Beard abandoned hopes for the democratizing mission of the United States on a global stage. This did not mean that Beard and Niebuhr gave up all hope for progress; rather, it meant that they moved toward an antimilitaristic vision of progress. Beard fell back on promoting a unique tradition of struggle for democracy inside the United States—a classic variation on the American jeremiad which understood the United States as a special case set apart from the rest of the world—while simultaneously warning that democratic values might be overwhelmed by capitalist leaders. Their internationalist entanglements threatened to draw the United States into another imperialist war, Beard argued, and this threatened to destroy democracy at home—but there was still hope for progress inside the United States if these pitfalls could be avoided. This was Beard's argument in best-selling works of history that he and his spouse, Mary Beard, produced in the 1930s.[15] It was also the underlying political logic of the *Century*'s opposition to U.S. entry in World War II. As we will see, during the 1930s Niebuhr moved from a similar logic to a sharply opposed one.

Before we turn to Niebuhr's shift, let us note a second general point about the social gospel: its middle-class Anglo-Protestant standpoint on the goals and priorities of social reform. Beard's worldview, in which the major axis of struggle pitted economic and political democracy against corporate capitalism in general and the military-industrial complex in particular, overlaps with arguments that recently have been advanced by left-wing intellectuals like Noam Chomsky and William Appleman Williams.[16] But Beard's worldview differs from present-day activists in one crucial respect. For Beard, as for many other theorists of the American jeremiad from his generation, Anglo-Protestant males were the main carriers of the national democratic tradition.[17] Upholding democracy in the face of capitalism and militarism was linked in Beard's mind to upholding Anglo-Protestant purity and virtue against the perceived corruption of Roman

Catholic and Jewish immigrant communities. Many aspects of Progressive reform, from educational reform through social work to anti-immigrant repression, were conceived and justified in light of such thinking. Secular Progressives and clergy alike frequently supported efforts to "uplift" and discipline immigrant groups through assimilation and social control.

Often the specifically religious dimensions of this quest were played out through Protestant missions. Missionary societies attempted to convert non-Christians, and often Roman Catholics, to their theological positions and moral codes. Of course, mission workers drew on a far broader range of motives and precedents than Progressivism alone, and their priorities covered a wide spectrum—from a focus on fundamentalist theology and personal morality to a stress on liberal theology and social reform.[18] However, at the liberal end of this spectrum, missions blended with the larger social gospel movement, and both overlapped with Progressive reform in general. For example, the settlement house movement was closely related to the churches. Student Christian missionary movements sometimes became quite radical. In these cases, the general Progressive response to the challenge of the new industrial order—democratizing it from within—took the specific form of missionizing it. The *Century*'s title reflects this approach. Before 1900 it had been known as the *Christian Oracle,* but its editor renamed it, reasoning that "this new century must be made a *Christian* century."[19]

Consider how the *Century* approached women and non-Anglo men. It had a column on Modern Womanhood that advocated women's suffrage and discussed female workforce participation. As evidenced by this column and the presence of Addams and Scudder among social gospel leaders, there was a reasonably strong alliance between male social gospelers and moderate middle-class feminists.[20] Yet there is no doubt that the *Century*'s constituency was male dominated and heavily weighted toward middle-class Anglo-Protestants. Organized labor and African Americans were objects of concern but rarely actors in the coalition. The *Century*'s articles on labor issues were read by the leaders of churches filled with management and their middle-class peers; in this context even the *Century*'s support for the right to strike was controversial.[21] On issues of antiracism, one scholar claims that the *Century* was among the most supportive journals in the country (presumably he means mainstream white journals), but it endorsed "separate but equal" schools in Gary, Indiana; another scholar describes its racial ideology as "Anglo-Saxonism."[22] Jews and Catholics were seen largely as threats.

The crusade for Prohibition was the greatest symbolic focus of Progressive efforts, and the *Century*'s commitment to this cause sometimes reached the point of obsession. In the 1928 presidential race it endorsed the dry Protestant candidate, Herbert Hoover, rather than the wet Catholic, Al Smith, even though it agreed with Smith on more issues. In 1932, in the depths of the Great Depression, the *Century* again favored the Republicans over Franklin Roosevelt, largely because of this issue. As late as 1936, when the *Century* finally endorsed Roosevelt, this provoked a storm of protest from readers because of its perceived apostasy on this issue. Out of a huge volume of letters to the editor, only one supported its decision.[23]

Prohibition is a good example of the complex motives of social gospelers. From the perspective of many feminists, Prohibition was a crusade against the abuse and neglect of women and children, somewhat like recent campaigns against domestic violence and "deadbeat dads." Most social gospelers understood it as one plank in a larger Progressive platform. Niebuhr supported it, although not as a high priority, and for many the alcohol industry symbolized the evils of a whole corrupt (male-dominated) capitalist system. However, it is well known that an anti-immigrant and anti-Catholic animus linked to a vision of middle-class decorum was a major impulse in Prohibitionism.[24] Just as issues blended in complex ways within Prohibitionism, the same was true for other issues in the Progressive repertoire. Pacifist anticapitalism was combined with Anglo-American suspicion of cultural pluralism in Progressive thinking. The whole combination, both the good and the bad as judged by recent liberal criteria, resonated with Progressive visions of special national virtue.

So far I have presented the social gospel as the overtly religious part of a wider Progressive movement reflecting middle-class values. Approaching from a different direction, the social gospel was also the overtly Progressive part of a wider liberal approach to religion. Recall how nineteenth-century interpreters of American democracy adapted to the rising industrial system. They reasoned that if urbanization was inevitable, Progressives must do more than valorize yeoman farmers who resisted evil cities; rather, Americans would have to democratize the city. Similarly, nineteenth-century interpreters of Protestant theology were also forced to respond to changes, notably the rise of historical criticism, cultural pluralism, and modern science. If these challenges were inevitable, liberals reasoned, religious thinkers would have to develop a modern form of Christianity. However, when liberal theologians proposed innovations to address this challenge, this led to controversies about the proper method of theology—that is, about what sources people could use for authority when their goal was explaining God's will for the city or the truth status of Trinitarian doctrine in an age of science.

The challenges were formidable. Most earlier Protestants had accepted orthodox Christian doctrines and assumed that they could defend these doctrines through direct appeals to the Bible. But now science seemed to contradict orthodox teachings, most famously in the clash between Darwin's theory of evolution and inherited teachings about creation. The method of higher criticism analyzed the Bible as a set of historical and literary texts. It made direct appeals to the Bible difficult by presenting it as a text written by humans, one which had changed over time and was often self-contradictory even in its canonical version, to say nothing of its many textual variations. In general, many believed that rational and scientific thinking made "dogmatic" and "magical" ideas inappropriate for a modern age.

Liberal Protestants responded to these challenges by steering a middle course between fundamentalists who resisted and denied the challenges of science and historical criticism, on one hand, and secularists who simply abandoned religious belief and commitment, on another.[25] Making the home of Christian theology within modern thought, they began to rethink Christianity within that horizon. They presupposed the historical methods and scientific assumptions of the day, then reconceptualized theology in terms consistent with them. For example, rather than questioning historical evidence in the name of the Bible, they tried to learn as much about the Bible as they could using historical methods. They drew a contrast between the deeper abiding truths of Christianity and the external forms which had sought to express these truths at different times. Commonly this entailed discounting orthodox teachings and rituals—especially those that liberals associated primarily with Judaism or Roman Catholicism—and presenting them as external forms that masked and distorted deeper truths. Liberals granted that some prescientific language, such as Bible stories about miracles, may have expressed truths in ways appropriate for prescientific eras. However, liberals reasoned that modern Christians must express the deeper truths of faith in a modern way, somewhat like a world traveler might translate the same story into different languages in different places. Morrison, the *Century*'s editor, is a good example of the liberal method for identifying true religion. He had been an urban minister in Chicago and a student of John Dewey at the University of Chicago before he bought the *Century* in 1908. He had chosen the philosophy department over the divinity school because "I had a theory that the problems of theology originated in philosophy, and I wanted to get to the bottom of things."[26]

Liberal theologians used such logic to defend several characteristic themes. They appealed to the immanent presence of God in the processes of nature and history, as opposed to divine transcendence over history. They based their theological claims on rational thought about common human experiences, rather than leaps of faith and special revelations. They stressed the human aspects of Jesus' life as moral teacher, rather than his traditional image as God and savior. They centered their spirituality on human virtue; this extended a move already begun by revivalists, away from strict Calvinist teachings about predestination and human depravity and toward a stress on human moral decisions and a reformed life. All these themes were linked to the idea of millennial progress: God was immanent in the progress of history, Jesus taught a moral life of progress toward the Kingdom of God, and so on.[27]

It is best to reserve the term *social gospel* for the activist wing of liberal Protestantism, even though a wide range of liberal Protestant leaders used at least mild social gospel rhetoric. This allows for distinctions between committed social gospelers and other liberal clergy who were less interested in politics, more individualistic and complacent about business, and quicker to provide biblical justifications for social Darwinism—traits that described many Protestants, to the dismay of serious social gospelers. Not all liberal clergy shared all the activist views expressed in the *Century.* Even Harry Emerson Fosdick, a leading minister in the moderate social gospel camp, led a congregation so thoroughly dominated by John D. Rockefeller Jr. that one critic suggested taking the cross off its building and replacing it with a sign reading "SOCONY": Standard Oil Church of New York.[28] Closer to the ideal type of a social gospel activist was Walter Rauschenbusch, a German-American Baptist who became a minister in the Hell's Kitchen area of New York City. There he became convinced that the economic system was moving toward "a new feudalism, dominated by robber barons and served by a new class of industrial peasants." His Christian Sociology has been described as "a hermeneutic of social history that allowed [him] to see the power of God's Kingdom being actualized through the democratization of the economic system."[29] For Rauschenbusch, theology focused on overcoming social sin through building up the Kingdom of God. Although he is sometimes accused unfairly of blindness to human evils and the ambiguities of power, there is no doubt that he accented the possibilities of positive change. And although he did not reduce building the Kingdom of God to Progressive reform in any simple way, there is no doubt that he correlated them.

Summing up this section, let us recall how Niebuhr disparaged "liberal theological idealism" in his "How My Mind Has Changed" article and take an inventory of some key components of this idealism. The social gospel was a territory where several things overlapped: Progressive thinking about U.S. destiny, the Protestant missionary impulse (including its Anglo-Protestant standpoint), the new theological liberalism, and a commitment to religious-political activism. All the people who founded *C&C* were nurtured within this general territory. But as Niebuhr's scathing comments dramatize, they were also breaking away from it. Let us look more closely at why they were dissatisfied and what alternatives they had in mind.

From the Social Gospel to Christian Realism

The transition from the social gospel to Christian realism involved complex developments in theological method, biblical interpretation, cultural history, and politics. We can clarify some of its key dynamics using the concept of paradigm shifts that I discussed in the introduction: the idea that anomalous evidence builds up within a group's worldview until the stress is intolerable and there is a shift toward a new pattern of thought.[30] It is nearly impossible to persuade a true believer in the paradigm of the American jeremiad that any other approach might be more helpful—that judging by the evidence, perhaps the nation may *not* have a special virtue and promise—since the believer can always respond by saying, "Yes, look how far we have fallen from our true identity and how hard we must work to fulfill our destiny in the future!" It is equally hard to refute a social gospel paradigm of struggle toward the Kingdom of God in America. This is why Niebuhr accused liberals of believing that "appeals to love, justice, good will, and brotherhood are bound to be efficacious in the end; if they have not been so to date, we must have more appeals to love, justice, good will, and brotherhood."[31] Still, even for a true believer in the social gospel, the evidence challenging the vision during the years from Versailles to Munich was formidable. Progressives with extravagant hopes for Anglo-Protestant democracy had to face an array of unexpected anomalies: the experience of World War I, the failure of Prohibition and the increasingly obvious realities of cultural pluralism, the power of corporate capitalism over its would-be reformers during the 1920s and 1930s, and the rise of fascism. In this context many social gospelers found it necessary to rethink their positions. They moved toward a new paradigm, Christian realism.

I have already mentioned the first shock, the disillusionment caused by World War I. As we have seen, the war by itself convinced many Progressives to give up their faith, but most social gospel leaders responded by reconceiving wars (even wars for democracy) as a form of backsliding on the road to progress and by making pacifism and international cooperation central to their visions for the future. Niebuhr shared in this movement, and John Bennett was a committed pacifist when he entered Union Seminary in 1926. It is difficult to overstate the centrality of antiwar themes to the social gospel during these years.

A second shock to Protestant expectations was the inability to enforce Prohibition, with all that this failure symbolized about the rising pluralism of twentieth-century cities. Protestant leaders had grown up in a world where they assumed their cultural hegemony—for example, Protestant clergy dominated higher education. But now they faced a second disestablishment at the hands of pluralistic cities, anticlerical intellectuals, and secular popular culture. Progressive Anglo-Protestants found it harder to ignore or suppress cultural changes from a new youth culture, feminism, the so-called lost generation in U.S. literature, and the growing urban subcultures of African Americans and European immigrants. Although these issues were not unique to the 1920s, they struck white Protestants with special force during these years. For some, these challenges led to discouragement and / or the embrace of greater pluralism. In many cases it led Protestants to redouble their efforts to maintain their influence through Prohibition, film censorship, and other Progressive reform movements.[32]

In this context, the fortunes of the social gospel were mixed. Some scholars describe the 1920s as an American religious depression because of a relative numerical decline and loss of confidence by mainline Protestants. One standard book on Protestant social action between the world wars, *Decline and Revival of the Social Gospel,* presents a decline in the 1920s.[33] These were years when, for example, Bruce Barton's book describing Jesus as the greatest businessman who ever lived was a national best-seller and an ambitious Interchurch World Movement funded by John D. Rockefeller Jr. ended in a highly publicized collapse (which coincided with the organization's advocacy of collective bargaining during a major steel strike).[34] On the other hand, another standard book on Protestant social thought documents a continuous commitment to Progressive reform.[35] On balance, the debacle of World War I and the growing pluralist challenge to Anglo-Protestant leadership led to stress within the social gospel vision, as well as numerous defections from it. However, true believers interpreted these challenges as the latest forms of declension from a still-intact promise of the American jeremiad. This spurred the leading social gospelers to work harder for progress.

A third challenge was harder to assimilate, and it became Niebuhr and Bennett's main focus during the 1920s and early 1930s. This was the frustration of hopes for industrial democracy—both because of the general power of corporate capitalism and the shock of the Great Depression. After World War I, President Harding had called for a return to normalcy, and of course his normal world did not include a millennial victory over parasitic capitalism. Corporations held preponderant domestic power, crippling the forces associated with industrial democracy. Social gospel appeals to harmonious labor-management cooperation and peaceful evolutionary progress toward socialism came to appear illusory and irrelevant. It was in responding to this situation that Niebuhr made his first distinctive contributions to the social gospel movement.

Until the early 1930s Niebuhr's positions fell generally within the social gospel camp, although he advanced them with unusual energy and ambition. He grew up in a rural German-American community rather than the genteel world of Anglo-Protestant elites; this background produced a creative dissonance in his thinking about cultural pluralism and probably helped him move toward new ideas. Still, he was educated at Yale Divinity School as a liberal theologian. During World War I he held a job overseeing military chaplains, producing Wilsonian war propaganda, and campaigning against his denomination's German ethnicity in the name of Americanism. Then, as we have seen, he converted to pacifism shortly after the war.[36] Niebuhr seemed motivated by the gap between his ideals and actual social experiences to work even harder. He became a pastor in Detroit, a star on a national campus lecture circuit, and an activist involved with many journals and organizations, including the pacifist journal *World Tomorrow* and the Fellowship of Reconciliation. Beginning in 1922 he wrote dozens of articles for the *Century* every year, and in 1925 he turned down the job as its associate editor. After 1928, he taught at Union Theological Seminary and continued an astounding schedule of writing and activism.

Like many other U.S. intellectuals, Niebuhr moved left during the 1930s. During the Great Depression it was easy to radicalize a tradition that opposed the virtuous goals of the people to the corruptions of capitalist interests. The revival in the book on *Decline and Revival of the Social Gospel* refers to religious aspects of this trend.[37] Niebuhr became extremely hostile toward corporate capitalism and outspoken in his socialism. In the mid-1930s, students of Niebuhr and his colleague Harry Ward even flew the flag of the Soviet Union from the Union Seminary flagpole, infuriating president Henry Sloane Coffin. The students (who called Coffin a "fascist despot") were eventually expelled; this in turn caused the *Century* to fret that Union Seminary might "degenerate into another training camp for priests."[38]

Niebuhr's distinctive role in the social gospel network was not in calling for a more just economic system—many others were equally active on this front—but in making the most influential criticisms of prevailing liberal models for cooperative, peaceful, and evolutionary change. In his 1932 book, *Moral Man and Immoral Society,* he dropped a bombshell on his social gospel comrades by turning to an explicit model of violent class conflict and group self-interest. Both this book and his 1935 *Reflections on the End of an Era* stressed that moral ideals alone could not solve problems of class oppression, which were rooted in deep-seated human sinfulness. A realist, as opposed to a sentimental utopian idealist, had to admit that political force, possibly including armed struggle, would be necessary if change were to come.[39]

Niebuhr was arguing that progress toward a more just society might still be possible, but only through class struggle. Could this be the route toward the Kingdom of God? For liberal social gospelers committed to peaceful cooperation, this idea was no better than denying progress entirely and cutting out the heart of Christianity. One former friend of Niebuhr stated, "Jesus' serene trust in human nature, his stern acclaim of the moral law . . . his sunny optimism, his radiant passion would all have seemed a little ridiculous to Niebuhr. [He] would not have opposed the Man of Galilee, but he certainly would have despised him. And with what relief he would have turned to the 'cynical and realistic' Pilate as the man of the hour"![40]

Niebuhr was outraged by this review, but he agreed that his new Christian socialist vision denied the social gospel version of progress, which he now described as pathetic. He drastically lowered his expectations for progress, undermining the idea that a Kingdom of God in America was possible. In scathing attacks like his "How My Mind Has Changed" article he explained how realism about human selfishness and power politics had forced him to these conclusions. The upshot was complex. Christians should participate in class struggle but understand that they were not progressing toward any ideal society. For the rest of his life, Niebuhr assumed this basic logic: deep-seated human sinfulness chastened unrealistic utopian hopes, but Christians should continue to engage in social action for truly realistic objectives. As we will see, his mid-1930s version of this logic, in which progressive socialist commitments blended with attacks on progressivism, proved to be an unstable halfway house on the road to later forms of Christian realism.

The fourth and decisive challenge to the social gospel paradigm was the rise of Nazism. If paradigmatic shifts are like earthquakes, we might say that challenges to Anglo-Protestant cultural dominance were a constant source of stress, and World War I and class conflict created major fault lines, but that it was Hitler, above all, who shook the foundations and rearranged the landscape. In the context of rising fascist power, it seemed extremely inappropriate to correlate sociopolitical change with the fulfillment of God's will in human history. Could the rise of Hitler represent progress toward the Kingdom of God? Optimism about human moral capacities seemed totally inappropriate. Didn't it make more sense to emphasize human tendencies toward sin and evil? Moreover, the social gospel commitment to peaceful international cooperation appeared as a reprehensible form of moral perfectionism. However well intentioned, wouldn't it do more harm than the forthright choice of a lesser evil? The greater evil was fascism; a less-than-pacifist military defense of a less-than-socialist democracy was necessary to combat it.

Thus by the late 1930s Niebuhr shifted the particular aspect of human sinfulness that was the focus of his polemic. In his earlier realist writing, the number one sin had been class oppression; he had argued that an awareness of human sinfulness implied that class struggles were a fact of life and that fighting on one side of these struggles was a high-priority course of action. As Hitler's power grew, Niebuhr focused on sin expressed in Nazi violence and tyranny. Just as he had earlier accused liberals of blindness to the realities of class conflict because of their idealist hopes for class harmony, he now claimed that their naive illusions about international cooperation blinded them to the realities of fascism.

Changing the number one sin targeted for prophetic denunciation—from U.S. plutocrats to foreign fascists—led to a rhetorical move from offense to defense. Niebuhr's socialism had assumed forward progress toward a better society. Now Niebuhr began a steady shift toward defending an imperfect status quo against a greater external evil. Less and less he argued that democratic socialism could overcome the evils of capitalism. More and more he upheld an imperfect but realistic New Deal democracy *together* with capitalism against international totalitarians and the naive idealists who closed their eyes to their threat. Niebuhr drew two morals from Munich. Politically, he concluded that when nations abuse power they cannot be stopped by idealistic pronouncements but must be stopped by force, and better sooner than later. Theologically, he interpreted the biblical prophetic tradition more as a defensive weapon unmasking the abuse of power, and less as a vision calling humans toward a better society.

In sum, when Niebuhr shifted toward antifascism, he laid down the basic foundations of Christian realism that would dominate mainline Protestant social thought for the next quarter century. This paradigm stressed, above all, the transcendence of God, especially as a critical judgment on human pretensions. Second, it highlighted human sin, conceptualized as self-centered pride; sin implied limited possibilities for utopian progress, and the constant tendency for the leaders of political movements to abuse power. Third, realist rhetoric took a primarily defensive stance, constantly on the lookout for Munich analogies and geared to using countervailing power against leaders whose sin caused them to abuse power. Fourth, realists continued to promote energetic liberal social action for the positive goals deemed realistic, provided that such action was self-critical enough to avoid utopian illusions and the corruptions of power.

With only two more small changes, the Niebuhrians arrived at their classic postwar positions. First, they came to generalize their arguments against fascism into arguments against all forms of totalitarianism; soon they would deploy these arguments mainly to advocate defense against communism through the global exercise of U.S. military power. Second, they completed their shift away from socialism; soon they would deploy their arguments for social action to support cold war liberalism of the Harry Truman type, conceptualized as interest group politics within a pluralist democracy.

Know Your Enemy: Progressivism "Bandaged but Unbowed"

But I am getting ahead of my story. At *C&C*'s inception in 1941, the Niebuhrians saw their immediate task as converting social gospelers at the *Century* to realism about fascism. To understand why this took center stage, it is essential to grasp that the four shocks to social gospel expectations which I have just described—the discrediting of wars for democracy in World War I, the collapse of Prohibition and gradual decline of Anglo-Protestant cultural dominance, the weakness of industrial democracy in the face of capitalist power, and the rise of Nazism—are not a description of an obstacle course that all liberal Protestants marched through in lockstep under Niebuhr's orders. Rather, they are an ideal model, a useful abstraction, to clarify major patterns in a wider discussion. The lived world of everyday decision making and moral discernment was considerably messier. At each stage in my model, in the face of each challenge to the social gospel paradigm, there were some social gospelers who turned away from their former vision and others who tried to sustain their worldview—perhaps in a modified form. That is, if they did press forward toward some aspect of the social gospel vision, such as the hope of economic justice, they could make adjustments to their religious ideas without simply opting for or against "complete . . . rejection of almost all the liberal theological ideals," as Niebuhr put it in 1939. They could take more than one position toward any of the issues I have underlined—without even mentioning other developments outside my model—and they could do so with various motives ranging among complacency, opportunism, blindness to important aspects of their situations, nostalgia for past Anglo dominance, resistance to future Anglo dominance, tragic failure of imagination, and principled pragmatism. In the resulting free-for-all, neither the Niebuhrians nor the social gospelers had a monopoly on wisdom and virtue.

I have not attempted to sort out all the variations. Nor have I attempted to prove what I will state as my informed opinion: that Niebuhrian-influenced historiography has tended to paint the Niebuhrians in the best possible light and their social gospel opponents in the worst.[41] I have simply focused on one point that was crucial for *C&C:* that the *Century* put up a spectacular resistance to abandoning the pacifist plank in the social gospel platform at the fourth stage I have described. In terms of my earthquake analogy, the *Century* was trying to hold on to its inherited landscape as the ground shifted, and its motives were informed by all the baggage that the social gospel carried, as discussed in the first section of this chapter. The *Century*'s resistance included a mix of good intentions, blindness, sensitivity, and arrogance, and it was argued with intense passion. The Niebuhrians' equally passionate disagreement with the *Century*—also with mixed motives, although they got the better of the argument—was the reason they created *Christianity and Crisis.*

Before discussing their confrontation over the war, we must pause to disentangle the *Century*'s arguments about militarism from its arguments about method in theological ethics. These issues were related—indeed, Niebuhr fused them in his 1939 attack on "liberal theological ideals"—but they were distinct in important ways. Recall what is at stake in debates about theological method: it establishes what evidence will count for supporting claims such as "God is on our side in this war" or "feminist theology is heresy." On the issue of method it is instructive to place Niebuhr in dialogue, not merely with theological liberals at the *Century* but also with Karl Barth, the most influential theological challenger to liberalism in Europe.[42] If we do so we discover, to put it bluntly, that Niebuhr was basically a liberal.[43] The term *neoorthodoxy* is often used to describe both Barth's theology and the Niebuhrian paradigm I have described. As general positions they have much in common: stress on divine transcendence and judgment, sympathy for socialism and resistance to fascism, and hostility toward middle-class "culture Christianity." But there is a major distinction between their theological approaches. Far more radically than Niebuhr, Barth rejected theological liberalism's basic method of elaborating the insights of Christianity within the terms set by the contemporary intellectual context. Barth appealed to biblical revelation and used it to criticize the whole project of liberal theology. Against theologies based on experience and reason, he insisted on revelation and faith, and his transcendent God was "Wholly Other." On each of these issues, Niebuhr's shift was relatively moderate, and that of his key *C&C* colleague John Bennett was even more limited. Bennett and Niebuhr both sought a middle ground between classic forms of theological liberalism and Barthian theology, which they considered anti-intellectual and dogmatic: a halfway house to fundamentalism.[44] Each appealed to common human experience as a major source for his religious claims—as when Niebuhr said that the doctrine of original sin was empirically verifiable—even though their perception of this experience was influenced, sometimes decisively, by an understanding of Christian revelation rooted outside modern liberalism, in the prophetic writings of the Bible and the theologies of St. Paul and Augustine.

Consider Bennett's contribution to the "How My Mind Has Changed" debate. While Niebuhr hurled rhetorical bombs at his social gospel enemies, Bennett tried to imagine a compromise. "We shall not come nearer to the truth about God if we cut loose our idea of God from the highest human moral standards," Bennett said. Thus he qualified the tendency of neoorthodoxy to stress human finitude and sinfulness, as contrasted with God's transcendent otherness. "We should not yield to those who write volumes to exalt the absolute supremacy of Jesus Christ and at the same time suggest that his teachings are relatively unimportant." Thus he defended the idea of Jesus as a human moral teacher and rejected the Barthian theology in which Jesus' role as savior displaces him as a human role model. Turning from theology to world affairs, Bennett continued to defend a qualified liberalism: "We should not allow dogmatic pessimism to take the place of the discredited dogmatic optimism about the possibilities of human progress."[45]

Thus far he stood firm for liberal theology. However, his disavowal of dogmatic optimism was just one of many signs that his liberalism was under stress. Like Niebuhr, Bennett was becoming disillusioned with socialism and pessimistic about the international situation. He was "torn between the conviction that a general war would not save the world from fascism but spread the seeds of fascism, and the strong suspicion, which goes against my habits of thought, that the democratic nations must arm in order to make possible the balance of power without which . . . [the only possibility is] withdrawal before the threat of force." The watchword for Christian teaching was moral realism. Still, this was "realism and not cynicism, or even pessimism." Bennett's title summed it up: he was "A Changed Liberal—But Still a Liberal."[46]

Other participants in *Century*'s "How My Mind Has Changed" series were also suspicious of neoorthodox emphases on divine revelation and transcendence, as opposed to liberal appeals to reason, human moral capacities, and divine immanence. Robert Calhoun of Yale captured their sentiments. He referred to a discussion group in which he participated with Niebuhr, and in many ways their theological dispute was quite narrow. Calhoun granted much of the neoorthodox argument about transcendence and revelation. No longer could he rest content, he said, with the liberal attempt to fit biblical texts and creeds into "illustrations of familiar logical formulas." On the contrary, "I have been driven to admit that theology cannot get on without special revelations. . . . It must start from such revelations, above all those which center about Jesus Christ, and the faith which they evoke. This amounts to a Copernican change in my orientation."[47] Nevertheless, Calhoun remained "no fit material for a good Barthian, nor for any kind of theologian except some obstinate form of liberal." Theology based on special revelations seemed "likely to slip into the very subjectivism it deplores." It needed to be tested by scripture, historical study, and current human experience. Calhoun believed that all members of his theological group, including Niebuhr, would agree at least in principle.[48]

This latter argument was convincing, and in this respect Niebuhr's polemical outburst about rejecting *all* his liberal ideas was misleading. However, in 1939, Niebuhr's polemics were driven by his passionate focus on what Calhoun called a Copernican revolution and on its implications for the U.S. role in international politics. Like Barth, Niebuhr turned away from an appeal to human reason and moral capacity as ground for optimism about human history, toward a focus on human sinfulness before the judgment of God. He found it crucial to stress the themes of revelation and human limits. This is why Niebuhr is considered a great figure of neoorthodox theology in the United States, despite his essentially liberal theological method, and why his liberalism was not the same *kind* as the social gospel's.

These subtle theological nuances among Barth, Niebuhr, Bennett, and Calhoun—how much to stress the Copernican shift—functioned in the 1939 *Century* as signals in an intense political debate. Was it necessary to redraw the battle lines of the social gospel—the lines which pitted pacifism, democracy, and true Christians against capitalism, militarism, and imperialism? Calhoun was uncompromising on the political issue, despite highlighting his common ground with Niebuhr in theological method. Although he agreed with Niebuhr that the Munich agreement was a scandal, he insisted that "however bad the alternative, a general war is almost certain to be worse." (Thus he accepted Niebuhr's insistence on lesser evil reasoning, but tried to trump it.) He concluded, "I am still a pacifist then, set against war—most of all against expeditionary war in defense of democracy, peace, freedom, religion, or anything else high and noble." In short, Calhoun remained "A Liberal Bandaged but Unbowed."[49]

Calhoun's phrase is an apt description of the *Century*'s political position in the late 1930s. For two decades the only issue rivaling Prohibition in its hierarchy of concern had been antimilitarism, and this issue had grown during the 1930s as Prohibition faded. The *Century* agreed with broader Progressive opinion that war was futile and that staying out of war was necessary for the survival of democracy. Its position is commonly labeled "isolationist," which makes sense if the point is to highlight the *Century*'s desire for peace and distaste for Euro-American imperialism. The label also makes sense to convey the idea that *Century* was *relatively* reluctant to confront the challenge of European fascism, compared with both the communists who sought U.S. intervention in the Spanish Civil War and Niebuhrians who sought stronger policies against the Nazis. (In no sense was the *Century* sympathetic to either Franco or Hitler; the issue for them was whether war would be a greater or lesser evil, especially in light of the nexus between capitalism and militarism inside the United States.) Some scholars also use the isolationist label as shorthand to describe an attitude that is really more like overenthusiastic internationalism: the *Century*'s naiveté about the prospects for global cooperation and international law. For example, in the 1920s Morrison was deeply committed to a campaign to outlaw war. Reporting from the 1928 conference that produced the Pact of Paris, he informed *Century* readers, "*Today international war was banished from civilization*" [his emphasis] and the treaty was "water-tight, bullet-proof . . . [with] not a single loophole in it."[50]

However, it is misleading to use the isolationist label to conflate the *Century* with a type of "America First" isolationism linked to right-wing domestic policies, such as the positions of the *Chicago Tribune* in the 1930s and Pat Buchanan in recent years.[51] Whatever we say about the rank and file of mainline Protestant laity, the *Century* was left of center on most political issues and clear in its support for many forms of internationalism. It consistently supported initiatives toward international law and movements for unity and cooperation between rival Christian groups, both domestically and internationally. It had long-standing interests in international missionary work, especially in China. This led to some ambivalence and confusion when its missionary commitments came into conflict with its rejection of imperialism. Faced with this tension, the *Century* liked to remind missionaries of their true calling, which it interpreted as opposing conquest and exploitation, gaining converts, and promoting peaceful cooperation.[52]

The *Century*'s concentration on politics may surprise those who assume that religious journals focus on another realm. The issue of February 8, 1939, provides a good example. Along with Bennett's "How My Mind Has Changed" article, it featured an article called "Apply the Gandhi Method to Japan!" Its book reviews were about Japanese politics. Five of its short opening editorials discussed war and peace, three addressed New Deal politics, and one touched on international ecumenism. A longer editorial reported that a fundamentalist had denounced Niebuhr and three other Protestant leaders as communists before a congressional committee. The *Century* rejected this charge, quoting the accused favorably as Christian socialists and presenting this as the antithesis of Marxist-Leninist ideology.[53] Another major editorial discussed Roosevelt's plan to fortify Guam and send arms to France and England. It argued that the public did not support Roosevelt and that democratic control should be asserted: "To understand the meaning of this Guam proposal the American citizen who does his own thinking has only to turn it around hypothetically. What . . . would be the effect on the American public if Japan [built] 'a major advanced fleet base' [near] our Pacific coast? . . . A great base at Guam means one thing—decision by the U.S. to maintain a permanent empire in the Philippines and to play a leading part in that struggle for the control of Asia which will fill the next century."[54]

Most of the letters to the editor in this typical issue discussed an earlier *Century* attack on Roosevelt for asserting that European fascism was a threat to U.S. religion. "There comes a time in the affairs of men," Roosevelt had said, "when they must prepare to defend not their homes alone, but the tenets of faith and humanity on which their churches, their governments, and their very civilization are founded. The defense of religion, of democracy, and of good faith among nations is all the same fight." The *Century* had called this speech an "Invitation to a Holy War"—"the most misleading and dangerous appeal made to the American people by a chief executive in the history of the republic." The idea of an attack on the Western Hemisphere was "fantastic"; it was a mere attempt at "destroying the sober, calm judgment" of the citizens and drumming up emotional hysteria. The actual reason for military expenditures, said the *Century,* was a desire by corporate elites for economic pump-priming, and the result would be dragging the nation into a European war. Since no one would believe Roosevelt if he proposed war taxes to make the world safe for democracy, he had in desperation retreated to the slogans of a religious crusade. His ideas "should be utterly and instantly rejected" by the churches. Seven of the ten letters in our sample issue agreed with this editorial, although two were rather fatalistic about the coming of war. Three defended Roosevelt.[55]

Throughout 1939, while Niebuhr churned out essays like his "How My Mind Has Changed" article, the *Century* countered with editorials such as "Our Frontier Is on the Potomac." "Well Said, Mr. President" approved the policy of staying neutral as war broke out. "Keep the Arms Embargo!" appeared the following week.[56] By the second half of 1941 the *Century* asked, "Who Rules America?" Was it Roosevelt or the Congress and the people? Morrison concluded indignantly that the "peace policy has been abandoned. . . . Nothing remains but the final plunge into full participation in the slaughter."[57]

Despite this growing sense of helplessness, the *Century* steadfastly opposed internationalist military commitments. "Is Neutrality Immoral?" asked Morrison in an explicit response to Niebuhr. Touching lightly on the immediate crisis in Europe, he warned that Niebuhr's arguments would not merely be useful "as an apologetic for *this* war" but that, if one assumed Niebuhr's definitions of responsibility, the United States could be "responsible for participation in any war waged anywhere in the world."[58] When *Time/Life* publisher Henry Luce wrote his famous manifesto calling on the United States to shape the world order by creating an "American Century," Morrison published a response called "A War for Imperialism." It said that Luce's essay had provoked a general outcry among the people but had nevertheless been officially acknowledged as government policy. The complicated business of international cooperation and negotiation had been rejected, and

> the American citizen, with his boundless belief in his own capacities, is asked to prepare to fight a war so that he and his kind can take over the control of the world. The world is in a mess; now let the omnicompetent Anglo-Saxon step in to straighten it out! . . . Here is a simple picture anyone can understand—the business of running the world taken out of the untrustworthy or inefficient hands of all other nations and entrusted to the sole care of the freedom-loving, justice-serving, God-fearing, English-speaking white peoples of Britain and America! . . . Behind this simple picture there waits the prospect of the most ambitious imperialism ever projected, an imperialism which will gradually but inevitably bring to focus against itself the jealousies and hatreds of all the other nations and races on earth.[59]

The *Century* did not perceive itself attacking the Niebuhrians with naive moral idealism. On the contrary, it labeled the internationalists as "romanticists" and contrasted Niebuhr's "fanatical cult" with a *really* realist position, based in an objective analysis of the world situation and "what effects are likely to flow from America's belligerent participation." In the end, "the realist [i.e., as defined by the *Century*] sees a different course for the country"—a nonimperialist course, where the United States is "strong in her military preparedness" and in "the justice and vigor of her own democratic institutions."[60] To follow this agenda would shorten the war and make the United States better able to help with postwar reconstruction.

The last-quoted article appeared in the issue dated December 10, 1941, after Japan had attacked Pearl Harbor and the United States had declared war. The following week the *Century* grudgingly gave up the fight. "We, too, must accept the war," it said. Yet citizens should see the war as "an almost unrelieved tragedy, a tragedy which need never have happened." In the words of the *Century*'s title, it was "An Unnecessary Necessity" that could only be accepted with deep grief, dismay, and shock. Two weeks later, a majority of letters to the editor were angry about Morrison's compromise.[61] By this time, however, the exchange between *Century* writers and readers could no longer be described as "*the* central arena for Protestant debate in America." Earlier in the year, the *Century* had gained a major competitor; *Christianity and Crisis* had been created.

2

The Emergence of *Christianity and Crisis*

C&C's first issue was dated February 10, 1941. It began by defining "The Crisis"—the "ultimate crisis of the whole civilization of which we are a part." This civilization was "differentiat[ed] . . . from all others" by its commitment to freedom, democracy, and Protestantism. It was centered on the North Atlantic, but its influence "spread to the ends of the earth." The crisis was stark: "the most powerful state in Europe has sworn to destroy" this civilization. Hitler had overrun most of Europe. Now "Britain alone stands guard against the westward march of tyranny." The urgent moral task was to stop "exist[ing] like parasites" on the liberties of a democratic culture that tyrants were threatening to destroy, and to "put the full resources of America at the disposal of the soldiers of freedom."[1]

The parasites in question were the social gospelers who opposed U.S. entry in World War II. The reasons for their opposition were complex: their bandaged but unbowed vision of Christian pacifism, their reluctance to come to terms with Nazi power, and their political analysis, which centered on a clash between democracy and the military-industrial complex. Recall the *Century*'s warning that there was more at stake in the war preparations than stopping Hitler: the "God-fearing, English-speaking white people" were preparing to take control of the world through the "most ambitious imperialism ever projected."

Niebuhr perceived such objections as unrealistic, naive, dangerous, and callous toward the victims of fascism. It was like fretting about the redesign of one's garden "at the very moment when [one's] house faces the imminent peril of destruction from a tornado."[2] He granted that imperialism at its worst was raw exploitation by the powerful. Even at its best it was corrupted by human selfishness, like all human activities.

However, "The sin of imperialism . . . may well be a less dangerous form of selfishness than an irresponsible attitude toward the task of organizing the human community. . . . No world organization will be possible without a willingness on the part of Britain and the United States to assume 'imperial' tasks in the best sense of the word."[3]

By the late 1940s Niebuhr's view dominated mainline Protestantism. Talk of U.S. imperialism gave way to calls for responsibility: the need to defend western civilization from totalitarians on the left and the right as well as from naive left-wing idealists who might become their dupes. Western democracy was seen to merit defense, despite its admitted imperfections, because it respected civil liberties and provided relative political and economic justice. It was also understood to be closer to God's will because it had a more realistic appreciation of human sinfulness and it guaranteed religious freedom. Niebuhr became a celebrity and an adviser to government elites, the "official Establishment theologian."[4] *C&C* became his major channel of communication with Protestant opinion leaders. As we have seen, it also served as a bridge between Protestants and secular leaders, from the financial editor of the *Rockland Record* to the vice-president of the United States.

Throughout the 1940s and 1950s, *C&C* worked from the logical foundations that it had built during the debate about Hitler: God's prophets critiqued sinful pride without abandoning self-critical social action. However, its concrete deployment of these concepts did not carry forward the democratic socialist radicalism of the 1930s, except as a distinctly subordinated "Y hand" within *C&C*'s dialectic. No longer did Niebuhr's students fly the Soviet flag over Union Seminary. More and more, they deployed their realist logic from the standpoint of liberal elites. *C&C* made consistent attempts to critique pride and power, but from within the larger social formation of cold war liberalism. Its major sociopolitical concerns were anticommunism, New Deal type economic reform, and pro-western international development. This chapter discusses these core components of *C&C*'s basic cold war vision, beginning with the original crisis that gave *C&C* its name.

The Original Crisis of World War II

Niebuhr founded *C&C* with backing from key leaders of Union Seminary and its ecumenical Protestant network, as I discuss more fully in a separate chapter on *C&C*'s institutional history. They began on a small scale with an eight-page newsletter aimed at a specific constituency: not Niebuhr's hard-core devotees who read his socialist journal *Radical Religion* (renamed *Christianity and Society* in 1940); not academics who read him in *Foreign*

Affairs and *Theology Today,* and not his secular audience in such journals as the *Nation* and the *New Republic,* both of which followed a trajectory somewhat like *C&C*'s from Progressivism to support for World War II.[5] *C&C* aimed for the same broad liberal Protestant readership as the *Century.* Its basic mission was to convert as many *Century* readers as possible and neutralize the rest. *C&C* was produced on a shoestring budget at Union Seminary and had eight thousand subscribers at the end of the war—less than the *Century* or the *Nation* but more than the *Partisan Review.*[6]

Aesthetically *C&C* was spartan in the extreme. Only by the most functional standards would anyone judge its layout attractive or its articles consistent in stylistic excellence. *C&C*'s founders were, in fact, single-mindedly focused on *C&C*'s function—to respond, as its opening article said, to "the ultimate crisis of the whole civilization of which we are a part." Such an attitude meant that *C&C* often achieved a raw passionate eloquence that was quite compelling and well matched to its bare-bones production standards. Fox's comment about Niebuhr's writing in *Radical Religion* also applies to *C&C:* "He would never bother with matters of style. . . . Words were vehicles for conveying ideas and sparking action, they were not aesthetic objects. Likewise clothes were for keeping warm and food was fuel to be rapidly taken in at the pit stop. . . . He was capable of poetic expression. . . . But calculated attention to form struck him as self-indulgent, diversionary. The point was to convince and mobilize, not beautify."[7]

In *C&C*'s first years, the war was the great issue, and combating the *Century* was the overriding concern. Niebuhr saw his shifts away from pacifism toward U.S. internationalism as reluctant, realistic, and purely defensive; Morrison perceived him as an imperialist rushing into an unnecessary war that would have disastrous consequences. This difference set the terms of debate. Of course, there is no reason to doubt Niebuhr's sincere belief in the need for the defense of western civilization.[8] But neither is there any doubt about the expansive definition of the borders he wanted to defend.

Over and over, *C&C* hammered out variations on its opening manifesto: the crisis of civilization, the need to rally to its defense, and the parasites who failed to grasp these elementary points. One study of Niebuhr comments that *C&C* was at first "wholly devoted to representation of the Allied cause" and that "in the ten months between its first issue . . . [and] Pearl Harbor, there is no development of views to be traced."[9] Almost every issue had a section called "World Church: News and Notes" with short articles on the war, giving special attention to the fate of Protestants under fascist regimes. *C&C* writers developed the fine points of ethical reasoning about self-defense. Until Pearl Harbor they took every opportunity to assault the *Century*'s positions, and afterward they monitored the *Century*'s grudging support for the war, denouncing all signs of weakening resolution.[10] In 1943 *C&C* featured a series of articles by prominent government and business leaders promoting "Six Pillars of Peace," a report of the Federal Council of Churches (FCC) Commission on a Just and Durable Peace.[11] (This committee included Bennett and Niebuhr and was chaired by John Foster Dulles, who later became Eisenhower's secretary of state; one scholar calls this "the only example I know of parlaying church committee work into a cabinet post.")[12] *C&C* provided a running commentary on war-related issues. It quoted St. Paul to admonish antiwar students not to oppose the draft simply to save their own skins, argued that if George Washington were alive he would try to "end international anarchy and establish world organization," suggested that Nazi prisoners of war in the United States should be "educated" (but not "indoctrinated" in violation of the Geneva convention), and called for progressive tax codes to finance the war.[13]

C&C took pains to deny a central charge from the Morrison camp: that its support for the war was a replay of World War I, when preachers confused U.S. military policy with a crusade for Christianity. *C&C* replied that, on the contrary, it had learned humility from that earlier mistake. It had gained an appreciation for God's transcendent judgment on all sides of the conflict, without thereby becoming blind to the relative virtues of democracy compared with fascism.[14] *C&C*'s opening manifesto hotly denied that it proposed a holy war, as the *Century* charged. It simply sought an "alternative between fanaticism and inaction," which was military action "undertaken with a proper sense of contrition."[15] *C&C* liked to denounce the *Century* for clinging to a discredited jeremiad that sought the Kingdom of God in America. This enabled *C&C* to understand itself as *less* prone to identify God's will and the nation compared with the *Century*, even when *C&C* backed national policy and the *Century* opposed it. However, by hammering on the idea that God stood in judgment on all human kingdoms, *C&C* provoked a question. Should Protestants pray for an Allied victory? Would this not imply that God was taking sides in the war? A minor controversy ensued when Niebuhr supported such prayers.[16] A Presbyterian compromise formula captured *C&C*'s spirit: We do not "identify our purposes nor those of any people with the holy will. . . . But we are of good conscience that our cause is in line with His righteousness."[17]

C&C offered some criticisms of U.S. wartime policies, usually aligning itself with positions within the mainstream of government debate: support for civil liberties, relatively nonpunitive plans for postwar reconstruction, and support for Zionism. *C&C* was relatively hopeful about cooperation with the Soviet Union, which was a U.S. ally in the war.[18] Often

C&C delimited its criticisms with the caution that experts had to make the final decisions based on their superior access to information. On balance, *C&C* presented the U.S. and British governments as exemplary. When Roosevelt died in 1945, Niebuhr described his career as a "providential emergence" and a "symbol to the world of our nation's growing maturity." FDR's "sagacity" and realism about centralized power had led the nation from a childish and "almost psychopathic" desire for peace. Later, when Winston Churchill retired as British prime minister, Niebuhr mentioned in passing that he was a "romantic imperialist," yet called him "the very embodiment of all that is best in both the democratic tradition and the Anglo-Saxon version of that tradition."[19]

Commentators impressed with *C&C*'s critical distance from U.S. policy sometimes point to its criticism of the "conventional" Allied terror bombings of cities such as Dresden. But an article sometimes cited as evidence, "Is the Bombing Necessary?" answered its own question with a qualified but clear yes. Half of this article's words and most of its passion were devoted to attacking an article by Vera Brittain against the obliteration bombing of German cities. *C&C* called her article unconvincing for anyone except pacifists who believed that "victory over Nazism is not a prerequisite of a tolerable world order." Such idealists were "unable to understand the tragic necessities of history"; they forgot that prolonging the war "would bring additional misery and death to millions." Turning to its own position, *C&C* rejected obliteration bombing as a means to shorten the war unless all alternative means were tried first, especially offering the Germans economic incentives for postwar reconstruction. It voiced doubts that the indiscriminate bombing of homes could be justified, but unambiguously supported "precision" bombing of "the industrial and transportation centers of the enemy," and stated that only experts could make final decisions about targeting. On balance, even though *C&C* clearly desired to minimize the bombing of civilian targets, its major suggestion was to approach the bombing in a more theologically profound and humane way: to understand it as necessary but tragic.[20]

C&C often projected itself into the role of military chaplain. Using a special $2,000 grant, it sent free subscriptions to all U.S. chaplains, and it defended chaplains against criticisms from pacifists. Sometimes it published articles by military personnel. It developed positions on such issues as Catholic soldiers' observance of the Sabbath and how chaplains could improve the sexual ethics of the troops. It endorsed the army's program of political education, which used pamphlets which the "American Historical Association has prepared, in collaboration with the Education Branch of the Morale Services Division."[21]

C&C's easy assumption of military perspectives was built on the personal experiences of its writers. Henry Sloane Coffin, who as president of Union Seminary was the major institutional backer of *C&C*, was a close friend of the secretary of war. Roger Shinn, then a Union student and later a major *C&C* editor, became a prisoner of war. Union thought he had died and held a memorial service for him. The Union faculty also organized itself into civil defense teams, in case of an enemy attack on New York. Paul Tillich was to staff the "gas squad and decontamination center" at Union, whereas Niebuhr's projected role was "guard in charge of shelters and security."[22] Among Niebuhr's many official roles during the war, this was probably the least important. He became a high-level adviser to the Roosevelt administration, toured bases in England to report on troop morale, advised the War Department on the situation in Germany, and wrote articles that were used as government propaganda. After the war he served on many ecumenical commissions linked to the U.S. government and/or the United Nations, and he even served at the highest level of the State Department, on the policy planning team chaired by George Kennan.[23]

By the end of the war, *C&C* was more likely to project itself into the role of international policy planner than chaplain.[24] From the beginning, *C&C* consistently discussed the postwar international order. Consider *C&C*'s opening manifesto, which defined "The Crisis," attacked pacifist "parasites," and argued that raising skeptical questions about postwar planning was like planning a new garden while a tornado approaches your house. Despite the tornado, this article went on to argue that responsibility did, indeed, demand preliminary plans for addressing a remarkable range of problems in the international garden, including European reconstruction, disarmament, economic reorganization on a global scale, "the future of small, weak, or less-developed nations," and "a world political order and the abridgment of national sovereignty." None could be solved without "some measure of [U.S.] responsibility for world order."[25]

Or recall the article in which Niebuhr called on the United States to assume "'imperial' tasks in the best sense of the word." Sounding less like a homeowner facing a tornado than a banker contemplating an investment, Niebuhr appealed to a biblical text about servants who are given talents by their Master and use them to gain more: "In the Lord's parable it is the servant who hid his talent in the ground who is condemned. The other servants seemed to have profited from usurious interest rates. But censure falls upon the irresponsible servant alone."[26]

C&C's forthright advocacy of imperialism was not a minor theme during these years. A lengthy piece called "Plans for World Reorganization" developed an argument for "imperialistic realism." Another article on "Anglo-American Destiny and Responsibility" stated that "the world cannot be organized by Anglo-Saxon hegemony" because this was not pragmatically possible. Prophetic insight from the churches was needed to combat complacency, since "without a religious sense of the meaning of destiny, such a position as Britain and America now hold is inevitably corrupted by pride and lust for power." Nevertheless, "Only those who have no sense of the profundities of history would deny that various nations and classes, various social groups and races, are at various times placed in such a position that a special measure of the divine mission in history falls upon them. In that sense God has chosen us in this fateful period. . . . It so happens that the combined power of the British Empire and the United States is at present greater than any other power. It is also true that the political ideals that are woven into the texture of their history are less incompatible with international justice than any other previous power of history."[27]

By the final years of the war, *C&C* was established as a successful competitor to the *Century* and its Progressive paradigm of theology and politics. Ironically, at the same moment that *C&C* helped discredit a jeremiad of millennial hopes for Anglo-American destiny in the *Century*'s liberal Progressive version, it helped revive the same tradition in a postwar liberal form. As *C&C*'s immediate concerns about mobilizing for war became a dead issue, its preoccupations steadily changed. Armed with confidence that U.S. policy was "in line with [God's] righteousness" even though not "identified with the holy will," *C&C* turned to its perceived responsibility: helping plan and police what Morrison had called "the most ambitious imperialism ever projected."

The Ethics of Atomic War

In his first public announcement of the atomic bomb, President Truman said, "We thank God that it has come to us, instead of our enemies, and we pray that He may guide us to use it in His ways and for His purposes." *Life*'s first statement after Hiroshima blended themes of danger and promise, concluding with a broadly Niebuhrian moral: "Our sole safeguard against barbarism is the kind of morality which compels the individual conscience. . . . No limits are set to our Promethean ingenuity, provided we remember that we are not Jove."[28]

What did *C&C* add to this high-level theologizing about the dream of ultimate power and the dangers of nuclear extinction? On the whole it dovetailed with mainstream establishment opinion. After Hiroshima, *C&C* called on readers to "accept [the bomb] as we accept the mysteries of radio." The bomb could be used for good or bad, and *C&C* challenged Christians to "accept the fact that the world is one and order the institutions of society accordingly." Niebuhr had no doubt about the justice of the nuclear attack. "We were indeed the executors of God's judgment," he stated. Still, "victory leaves a strange disquiet and lack of satisfaction" and the bomb causes "uneasiness of conscience." Niebuhr seemed touchy about charges that the U.S. exhibited racism in its choice of target; he was quick to point out that "certain types of incendiary bombs were perfected too late to be used against Germany." He warned the United States to avoid imperial arrogance and racism during its military occupation of Japan. Only in this context, as a diatribe against unnamed liberals with overly sweeping ideas about democratizing postwar Japan, did Niebuhr's editorial on the bomb unleash the critical side of his rhetoric: sarcastically he spoke of liberal plans to "destroy nations in order to make 'democracies' out of them."[29]

Debates about the bomb were a key transition between *C&C*'s original crisis, World War II, and its classic concerns about the crisis of the cold war. As already noted, *C&C* had begun to discuss the bombing of civilians in places like Dresden well before the attack on Hiroshima. One locus of this debate was a 1944 Federal Council of Churches commission chaired by Robert Calhoun, whom we have already met as the *Century*'s "Liberal Bandaged but Unbowed." The Calhoun commission agreed to denounce "the massacre of civilian populations," but was split on major nuances. A minority condemned Allied policies unambiguously, but the majority (those aligned with *C&C*) supported "all needful measures" necessary to defeat the Axis powers—and some members "explicitly endorsed the obliteration bombing of cities."[30] In 1946, a second Calhoun commission convened, this time narrowing its attention to atomic bombings. Again *C&C* paid close attention, since the commission included Bennett, Niebuhr, and others from *C&C* circles. Again the committee reached consensus on some fairly critical rhetoric. It called the Hiroshima bombings "morally indefensible" and repented because "we have sinned grievously against the law of God and people of Japan."[31] Yet, Edward Long wrote, the report also produced "a barrage of arguments trying to apologize for our use of the atomic bomb in such a way as to deny any need for contrition." Many of the key nuances dividing the committee were buried in a footnote. Some members were straight pacifists. Others condemned all obliteration bombings. Those allied most closely with *C&C* condemned the Hiroshima bombing only because of its particular circumstances, holding that "the use of atomic weapons under some circumstances [may be] right" because "the only effective restraint upon would-be aggressors might be fear of reprisals."[32]

Thus the Niebuhrians and *Century*-type liberals struggled to control FCC policy pronouncements. Seeking added leverage in this debate, *C&C* appealed to a British religious statement on atomic war, which argued that Christians must accept atomic technology and use it responsibly. Its variation on the jeremiad form was especially interesting. Since secular progress had been discredited, it argued, there was a need to draw on the "inexhaustible resources of [Protestant] faith to restore men's confidence" in the possibility of bringing power under social control and building an effective world community. The world needed a "counterpart of the secular myth of progress, rendered more profound by the insight of the gospel."[33]

Finally, in 1950, the FCC came up with a resolution on nuclear war that satisfied *C&C*. After four years of intensifying cold war, the FCC convened a third commission, which removed many members of the two Calhoun commissions, replacing them with leading supporters of government policy, such as *C&C* writer Arthur Compton. This committee was chaired by Angus Dun, a member of *C&C*'s board of sponsors; once again it included both Niebuhr and Bennett. *C&C* devoted a full issue to the Dun Commission report, which included little or no expression of guilt or call to repentance, and argued that responsible Christians could not make judgments in advance about the future use of atomic bombs. To rule out nuclear war "would leave the non-communist world with totally inadequate defense," the commission stated. "We believe it could be justifiable for our government to use [atomic bombs] in retaliation with all possible restraint."[34]

The two dissenting members of the Dun Commission received half a page in *C&C*'s following issue. Georgia Harkness commented that "us[ing] atomic weapons 'in retaliation with all possible restraint' seems a contradiction in terms." She also complained about unfair attacks on straw versions of pacifist arguments. Calhoun observed that, for the Niebuhrians, "Christian conscience in wartime seems to have chiefly the effect (certainly important but scarcely decisive) of making Christians do reluctantly what military necessity requires."[35]

This was one of the rare occasions when articulate voices opposed to *C&C*'s dominant positions received space. When they did, it was often with editorial comments framing their contributions as an opportunity to know your enemy. During the war, *C&C* almost never opened its pages to pacifists. In my random sample, only two of sixty pieces had a clear peace focus, and both were short letters of protest.[36] Coverage of the peace movement was from the outside looking in. Niebuhr considered nonviolence a respectable calling for Christian minorities who are "frankly irresponsible in the social struggle as the best ascetics of Christian history were."[37] The only catch was that such pacifists must admit that their witness was irrelevant to real world debates about government policy. In these terms, *C&C* upheld the right of conscientious objection to the military draft, even as it called on Christians not to exercise this right.[38]

Coverage of peace issues picked up slightly after the war. Leading pacifist A. J. Muste occasionally published telling criticisms on atomic issues. Few from *C&C*'s inner circle engaged him seriously, but Bennett was an exception. In 1954, Muste launched devastating objections to the argument that a war which might destroy the human species could be justified as a lesser evil. He also raised questions about the practical value of deterrence. Did it not increase, rather than decrease, the danger of war by heightening fear? How exactly could it be used, for example in Asia, without backfiring for the self-interest of the United States?[39] Significantly, Bennett replied that Muste had raised many criticisms that "are entirely sound," some of which "represent real questions in my own mind about my own position." Still, Bennett reaffirmed *C&C*'s X hand position that "it would be intolerable to have the free world menaced by a Communist world with weapons which it could not match." According to Bennett, Muste insisted on a choice between red and dead. Bennett was prepared to agree that red was preferable if it came to this choice—but he still hoped "to prevent both war and universal Communism." Deterrence was the best hope of buying time to find an alternative.[40]

In later years *C&C* liked to recall its reservations about the bomb as having been large. This is certainly true compared with conservative Protestants. Evangelist Billy Graham launched his career largely through a revival that began only three days after the United States learned that the Soviets had exploded an atomic bomb. Graham told his congregation that the Soviets were aiming a bomb at them and that the world might end unless they repented. This was the context in which publisher William Randolph Hearst gave his famous directive to his media empire, "Puff Graham." In addition, Graham's father-in-law, L. Nelson Bell, was among leading conservative Protestants who called for a nuclear attack on Russia in the name of Christianity.[41]

On the other hand, *C&C*'s criticisms were weaker than many of its liberal colleagues and journalistic counterparts—and not only compared with the *Century* (which published several pages of letters against the bomb) or people who were committed to peace activism. *C&C*'s tortured attempts to justify scenarios for an atomic holocaust contrasted with other voices, even from among *C&C*'s intellectual allies. For example, Niebuhr's friend Lewis Mumford contended in *Saturday Review,* "Madmen govern our affairs in the name of order and security. . . . [T]hey have been carrying through a series of acts which will lead eventually to the destruction of mankind, under the solemn conviction that they are normal responsible people." In a nationally broadcast sermon, Harry Emerson Fosdick (a *C&C* sponsor) denied that "mass murder of whole metropolitan populations is right if it is effective."[42]

"The power to blow all things to dust / Was kept for people God could trust," quipped Edgar Guest, reducing the theology of nuclear war to its bare bones. *C&C* probably assumed that this poem was not directed at sophisticates like themselves, since they spoke continually about tragic choices and the dangers of complacency. Still, Paul Boyer's summary judgment is persuasive. Even in their most critical 1946 report, the one which the Dun Commission overturned, Protestant leaders "condemned the concept of total war, the deliberate terror bombing of civilians, and the destruction of Hiroshima and Nagasaki. But [they] grant[ed] moral legitimacy to the retaliatory use of atomic weapons under certain conditions—precisely the theory that would provide the ethical foundation of the nation's nuclear policies for the next generation."[43]

The Central Vision of Cold War Liberalism

Of course, *C&C* did not justify U.S. nuclear policy in a vacuum. It assumed the existence of a unified communist movement on the verge of world takeover. It conceived this as a threat to democracy—a political vision blending liberal political rights, freedom of religion, and a global free market system. In this context, *C&C*'s justification of the bomb was just one variation on its first great geostrategic theme, defense against communism, which coexisted with two other themes: cautions about excessive reliance on military solutions and the promotion of international economic development.

Having supported atomic war, *C&C* had no trouble justifying other U.S. military initiatives that could be presented as defensive. Consider how it covered a major escalation of the early cold war, the Truman Doctrine of 1947. This was the U.S. decision to replace Britain as the dominant colonial policeman in the Middle East, beginning by intervening in a Greek civil war, where it took the side of fascist elites against a communist-led coalition which had recently led the resistance to Nazism. *C&C* said that U.S. interest in Middle Eastern oil could by itself justify the new policy, but *C&C* stressed, "A firm stand . . . [is] the most effective way to stop the expansionist drive of the Soviet Union. No convincing case can be made for a hands-off policy. . . . Moscow is either committed to an aggressive course, or is too inept or desperate to be allowed to play with the destiny of Europe."[44]

When Truman and his advisers prepared a speech to announce this new policy, they scrapped their first draft, commenting that it sounded "like an investment prospectus" when they needed a speech that would "scare the hell out of the American people." Economics and fear converged again in 1950 as the United States opted (in the famous NSC-68 document drafted by Paul Nitze) for a full-scale military remobilization linked to an escalation of the cold war. Throughout this period U.S. policymakers wished to prevent another economic collapse like the Great Depression, and they were committed to using government fiscal policies and economic expenditures (or Keynesian policies, after economist John Maynard Keynes) to keep the economy humming. The path of least resistance was to keep it humming in a way which minimized forms of state intervention that cut into corporate profits and which maximized chances for the United States to take advantage of its global economic dominance on a "level playing field" of free trade. For these purposes, military Keynesianism—concentrating government pump-priming and social investment on a military buildup—was a path that had worked during the war and that could minimize conservative resistance to expanding the pro-labor policies of the New Deal. As 1950 approached, this path also appeared more politically viable than renewing and expanding the Marshall Plan (and parallel initiatives in Japan) for global pump-priming. Secretary of State Dean Acheson famously recalled that "Korea came along and saved us." Coming at the same time as Mao's triumph in the Chinese Civil War and the Soviet Union's new atomic bomb, a war in Asia provided ample evidence for scaring the hell out of taxpayers.[45]

Fear was very much in evidence as the United States entered the Korean War: *C&C* speculated that "history may record that the Third World War began on June 25, 1950—if historians continue to inhabit the earth." In light of this prediction, it is remarkable that *C&C* showed neither remorse nor any doubt that U.S. policy was inevitable. It spoke of putting teeth into NATO, placed all the blame on the Soviets, and virtually ignored the internal dynamics of the Korean civil war. When the United States attempted (briefly and unhappily) to roll back the frontiers of communism by invading North Korea, *C&C* approved and even speculated that "adequate protection of Formosa may require comparable action against Communist China."[46]

On issue after issue, *C&C*'s judgment on international issues flowed within the main currents of liberal anticommunist opinion.[47] Almost half of its articles focused on international issues, and the majority supported cold war liberal policies.[48] What made *C&C* distinctive, compared with other liberal journals of opinion, was its greater stress on religion. Its political analyses appeared within a matrix of writing focused more narrowly on theology and religious issues. A third of its articles focused on concerns unique to mainline Protestantism, and a great majority touched on religious issues, at least in passing.[49] *C&C* published small but steady streams of theological essays,[50] reviews of major works in theology and ethics,[51] devotional pieces that were often reprinted sermons,[52] and miscellaneous articles on psychology and religion, religious education, and liturgy.[53] Many were informed by the involvement of *C&C* personnel in the ecumenical movement, especially around 1954 when the WCC met in Evanston and much of the preparation was done around Union Seminary. *C&C* often reported ecumenical news, and its articles were an organic part of larger discussions in the WCC.[54]

Relating theology to cold war policies, Niebuhr spoke of a "strong affinity at one point between democracy and Christianity: the toleration which democracy requires is difficult to maintain without Christian humility; and the challenges to pretensions of every kind which are furnished in the give and take of democratic life" provide "strong external supports for the Christian grace of humility."[55] Other articles said that "the perennial choice with which man is confronted—God or an idol—reduces itself, under contemporary conditions, to the stark alternative; *God or Stalin.*" Communism had an "erroneous conception of human nature"—the "utopian illusion that the abolition of a social institution will redeem man of sin."[56] This same theological error was present in a muted form among Progressives who supported politicians like Henry Wallace.

Secular opinion leaders picked up a vulgarized variation of these ideas about sin. In 1948 Niebuhr appeared on the cover of *Time*'s twenty-fifth anniversary issue. *Time* and *Life* regularly featured him, as when *Time* gave his *Nature and Destiny of Man* a glowing review under the title "Sin Rediscovered." In 1946 *Life* published "The Fight for Germany" with the subtitle "A distinguished theologian declares America must prevent the conquest of Germany and Western Europe by the unscrupulous Soviet tyranny."[57]

C&C's first major theme, military defense, was constantly shadowed by its second—a stream of arguments cautioning policymakers not to overemphasize military confrontation as a result of arrogant pride, unnecessary fear and hatred, or a crusade mentality. This constant sniping on *C&C*'s "Y hand" often called to mind Calhoun's complaint about the Dun Commission: that *C&C* merely exhorted readers to do what military logic required, only more reluctantly. *C&C*'s editorial on the Truman Doctrine is a good example. *C&C* would have preferred to see the United States intervene through the UN rather than unilaterally. When Truman spoke about "our date with destiny," *C&C* pointed out that this might remind people of Manifest Destiny. *C&C* also acknowledged some evidence of Soviet weakness, thus raising questions about their aggressive expansion-ism claimed by Truman. *C&C* refused to endorse a "war for preservation of an economic system," and even compared U.S. allies in Greece with the notorious Spanish fascist, Francisco Franco. (As *C&C* gingerly put it, support for U.S. policy in Greece risked "putting the prewar Spanish situation in reverse.") Rather than refute these arguments, *C&C* briefly acknowledged them on its Y hand and overrode them with anticommunism on its X hand. It summed up the overall arguments, pro and con, with the idea that U.S. policy was tragic and must be undertaken self-critically.[58]

C&C's strongest reservations about the cold war mentality were voiced during the relatively fluid period before 1948, when moderate positions were live options for policymakers. *C&C* speculated about cooperation with the Soviets, as when Bennett argued that the differences between Nazism and communism "make possible future reconciliation with Russia."[59] The key test case for cooperation was Germany, which was the perennial hot spot of the European cold war and a country that especially interested Niebuhr because of his German-American background. During the war *C&C* often spoke against punitive postwar policies, and for a brief period after the war, it was attracted by the vision of a neutralist Germany.[60] Although Niebuhr was moving toward a harder anti-Soviet line in 1946, some *C&C* articles at this time were almost as critical of the West as of the East. An East German theologian suggested that his country's attitude toward the United States and USSR should be like the biblical Kingdom of Israel between Egypt and Babylon. He seemed undecided which was the lesser evil: peaceful coexistence with atheistic communists, or an alliance with anticommunist western Christians. The United States was like the flesh pots of Egypt, with their temptations of capitalist individualism; Russia was like Babylon in the book of Jeremiah, an "arrogant blasphemer" who nevertheless might be used by God as an "instrument of wrath" against the sins of Israel / Germany. Perhaps, in the best case scenario, pressure from "Babylon" could move the Germans to a prophetic middle ground between east and west, overcoming the problems of an "outworn bourgeois spirit."[61]

By 1950 *C&C* had moved to the position that Nazism and Communism were parallel forms of totalitarianism. Thus it abandoned its wartime idea that western democracy and communism were like a thesis (liberty) and an antithesis (economic equality) that could reach a creative synthesis. As Paul Merkley says, "It became less and less a case of thesis and antithesis, and more and more a case of Gog and Magog."[62] Richard Fox compares Niebuhr to "a debater summoned suddenly to argue an opposite viewpoint": "[Niebuhr] declared that once upon a time there were 'more creative elements in Communism than in Nazism. . . . But the actual tyranny which has emerged and the fanatical fury [generated] are, unfortunately, not distinguishable from the practices derived from the purer paganism and cynicism.' The 'absence of a race theory' in communism had always been its prime virtue for Niebuhr; now he managed to assert that lack of such a doctrine 'gives this new tyranny an advantage over the old one in bringing nations under its subjection.'"[63]

Many of the strongest critiques of the cold war that *C&C* published appeared in the context of a debate between pro-NATO and neutralist tendencies in the World Council of Churches (WCC). It must be said, however, that *C&C*'s major goal was to hold up the neutralist writers for criticism rather than to commend them. *C&C* often attacked Karl Barth both on theological grounds (as discussed in chapter 1) and because of his unwillingness to take sides in the cold war.[64] Niebuhr said that Barthians were "obliquely pro-Communist"; in the face of Nazism they had "discovered that the church may be an ark in which to survive a flood. Today . . . they have decided to turn the ark into a home on Mount Ararat and live in it perpetually."[65] Yet *C&C* printed Barth's powerful reply to those (like *C&C*) who questioned his neutralist stance. When his critics asked him to equate the 1951 Soviet policy with the 1938 Nazi threat, Barth responded, "There is no evidence for, and much evidence against, the idea that [the Soviet Union] wants war." The task of the hour was working for peace and economic justice; failing this, Europe would soak up socialism "as a sponge draws in water." "A war which is not forced on one, a war which is any other category but the *ultima ratio* of the political order, war as such is murder. . . . Every premature acceptance of war, all words, deeds and thoughts which assume that it is already present, help to produce it. For this reason it is important that there be people in all nations who refuse to participate in a holy crusade against Russia and communism, however much they may be criticized for their stand."[66]

Variants of such reasoning appeared often enough to show that *C&C* took it seriously and considered it a temptation for its readers. Its most sustained dialogue was with Josef Hromadka, a Czech theologian who cooperated with his government. Although *C&C* leaders were suspicious of Hromadka, they knew him through the WCC and respected his judgment enough to consider it carefully.[67] In 1951 they gave him space (albeit with a strong disclaimer) for a blistering attack on the WCC. How could a legitimate world organization of Christians support the United States in the Korean War (as a recent WCC meeting had done) without addressing the "economic expansion of the Western world . . . [as a] breeding place of military aggression," without calling for Soviet and Chinese participation in Korean peace negotiations, and without condemning "the bloody suppression of the colonial peoples in Viet Nam"? Hromadka denounced the "disquieting self-assurance" of people in *C&C*'s circles who believed "that they are free of any self-imposed prejudice and that only 'the other side' might be a victim of propaganda pressure, a police supervision, and of a systematic indoctrination." Such people were "suffocating . . . [in an] atmosphere of self-complacency and self-righteousness . . . and do not know about it."[68]

C&C's critique of U.S. military logic was stronger when discussing Asia, compared with Europe. To some extent *C&C* merely *sounded* more critical, without seriously questioning actual U.S. policies, because its editorials stood with U.S. liberals against the Republican China lobby. In any case, *C&C* regretted the legacy of imperialism and cautioned against military interventions in Asia. It paid the most attention to China, largely because of the influence of China missionaries in *C&C*'s circles.[69] Throughout the 1950s, *C&C* stressed that right-wing plans to roll back communism in Asia were bankrupt; it decried "hysterical journals" that hammered on the Democrats for their supposed "loss of China."[70]

Bennett's 1950 article, "The Problem of Asiatic Communism," set forth reasoning used in many subsequent editorials. Reflecting on a recent speaking tour in Asia, Bennett identified the key issue as poverty and said that "social revolution is overdue." For many Asians, "Communism is the only movement that has a program that *seems* drastic enough to be relevant to the economic needs." On his trip, listeners had not rallied to abstract rhetoric about freedom. They did not perceive the hand of the Soviets everywhere, and had resisted Bennett's contention that the theological implications of communist ideas would lead inevitably to totalitarianism. Worst of all, Marxist propaganda had convinced them that western nations were the *real* imperialists. In light of this situation, said Bennett, U.S. military pressures had limited value and might make things worse. Asia needed programs modeled on the New Deal, informed by Christian understandings of human nature rather than communist total systems. Only this approach had a realistic chance of addressing the central economic issues and stopping "the serious threat of indirect aggression" through the spread of communist ideas.[71]

C&C's consensus on minimizing military strategies in Asia blended two distinct lines of thought, closely entwined in this period but destined to polarize in the decade after 1956. One was Bennett's logic of relative trust and respect for third world nationalists, linked to a relatively strong critique of imperialism. The other was the idea that U.S. military interventions were unrealistic in countries that did not have "viable" cultures for democracy. Later *C&C* would adapt this second idea for sharp attacks on U.S. Vietnam policy, but in the 1950s it was a more gentle reminder that U.S. intervention in certain countries could not advance U.S. self-interest—perhaps because too many people there supported left-wing social movements, or local elites were too corrupt, or the economy was too far removed from industrial capitalism.

Often *C&C* unpacked this idea of viable civilization with racist and paternalistic presuppositions. Typical arguments judged that "millions of Africans are not yet ready for modern political leadership of any kind"; that "new nations" emerging from colonialism were like young children and sprouting flowers that may not be capable of democracy, and that Latin American Catholicism was "unable to develop that type of individual who is fitted for life in a democratic society." The problem in Latin America was that "justification by faith creates responsible individuals who are the ideal citizens of a democracy, while the Catholic sacramental-sacerdotal system fails precisely at this point." Therefore, without help from Anglo-American Protestants, the Latin American Catholic "will always continue to be a minor" who is "incapable of practicing liberty."[72] Statements like these were common well into the 1960s. Niebuhr wrote that "democracy was not viable in unreconstructed feudal economies" like those in Latin America, where the leaders "obviously do not have the resources for correcting their own faults." Also, in Africa the United States had been a "tutor in civilization to these primitive cultures," but they show a "fever of resentment." Ernest Lefever even claimed that "the net impact of European colonialism in every area has been good." Without it, "cruelty, cannibalism, slavery and torture, all sanctioned by superstition and abetted by self-serving witch doctors, would be widespread."[73]

C&C assumed that imperialism was mainly a European problem. According to Niebuhr, "Western imperialism was morally ambiguous rather than purely evil," and he found it "irrelevant" when Dutch Protestants repented of imperialism after they "lost Indonesia," because the Dutch had "made solid contributions, advertently or inadvertently, to the budding Indonesian nation." He stated that "America . . . was not involved in overt imperialism."[74] He found it ironic when communist propaganda called the United States imperialist, given that "we were never imperial in the classical sense of the word" and "the one portion of our 'empire,' namely, the Philippines, was given its independence without a struggle." The only problem Niebuhr concedes is too much stress on military solutions in U.S. Asian policy, which "has given the colored part of the world this wrong picture of the realities."[75] Thus on the bottom line, despite *C&C*'s many significant caveats about the details of U.S. policy and a great deal of talk about disengaging U.S. missionaries and diplomats from the taint of western imperialism, *C&C*'s overall tension with U.S. policy was limited.

It should already be clear that *C&C*'s second geopolitical theme—these significant but circumscribed questions about excessive reliance on military crusades that we have been discussing—shaded into its third theme: full-scale advocacy for nonmilitary forms of U.S. global influence, which offered the hope of containing communism in a positive way. *C&C* unambiguously supported economic development based on integration into the world capitalist market, in both Europe and the former colonies. This does not mean that *C&C* favored the type of free market proposals championed by Henry Luce in the cold war era and Milton Friedman in later years. *C&C* saw these approaches fostering economic injustice and excessive individualism, whereas *C&C* favored limited government mechanisms for redistributing wealth within each country. However, any proposal that *C&C* judged incipiently communist was out of bounds, as were autarkic policies in Latin America and elsewhere.

The official 1948 mission statement of *C&C*'s board of sponsors judged that the "present foreign policy . . . is essentially correct." The United States was like a wise doctor responsible for economic and political health of an impoverished world through the Marshall Plan.[76] *C&C* often proposed extending the Marshall Plan to Asia, carrying it out behind a military shield of containment from India to Japan. Failing this, *C&C* promoted a U.S. development program called Point Four and a related WCC initiative. "If only the people of America could catch a vision of the enormous possibilities of this enterprise, and take fire!" preached one editorial, perhaps "again this country might be animated by a sense of mission, captured by a high purpose, a purpose broader and more constructive than that of the containment of Russian Communism by military might alone."[77]

The logic of development pervaded *C&C*'s entire worldview. A piece on postwar European reconstruction advocated a "spiritual economy of abundance" along with material aid. "Like international trade, spiritual fellowship has to travel both ways—else it speedily ceases to move at all."[78] The general mind-set reached across *C&C*'s political spectrum—we will explore disagreements about appropriate *kinds* of development in later chapters—and continued well into the 1960s. A 1961 article called Africa a new front of the cold war, where "our guiding principle must be to maintain access to all of Africa."[79] The economic dimensions of this access were explicit in an article by Roy Blough, a former member of Truman's Council of Economic Advisers. After a detailed discussion of "international economic integration," Blough concluded that the "basic requirement is that each country be willing to give up possible gains in specific clashes of interest in order to reap for itself, and assume for others, the larger advantages of a peaceful, stable, prosperous, developing world. Responsibility in this as in other matters is correlative with strength. The lead must be taken by the powerful and prosperous."[80]

No doubt, this was useful advice in some contexts and had significant positive effects. Nevertheless, *C&C* had a tendency to use development as a panacea for problems that were more deeply rooted, as when *C&C* repeatedly attempted to finesse the Israeli-Palestinian conflict through an economic development project modeled on the Tennessee Valley Authority, perhaps on the Jordan or Euphrates River, which would persuade the Palestinians to give up their claims.[81] *C&C* touched lightly on the drawbacks of capitalist development for people who were disadvantaged by it. *C&C*'s most flagrantly uncritical support for development appeared in a 1953 article on South Africa. Based on a short visit, Henry Pitney Van Dusen was confident that the "wave of the future bears the cause not of Nationalism but of moderation." Speaking about the government technocrats who oversaw economic development in bantustans, he said, "I seldom have met a more competent or enlightened group of highly trained and informed social scientists." They had "detailed evidence of the well nigh limitless economic potential of the 'reserved areas.'" And they were committed to the "total advance of the population, not merely economic progress but economic, educational, social, cultural and spiritual factors in their organic unity."[82] Niebuhr and Bennett may have disagreed with parts of Van Dusen's article and published it because he was their boss, as president of Union Seminary. But they did not clearly dissociate themselves with the position when it appeared, as they often did with other articles to which they objected.

One is frequently unsure, when reading *C&C*'s calls for developmentalist solutions to third world social conflicts, whether to interpret its arguments as prophetic critiques of the dangers and blindnesses of existing military policies or as something more like cheerleading for U.S. capitalists committed to an American Century. In one sense it does not matter. In another sense, however, the point is crucial. *C&C*'s rhetoric justifying U.S. economic expansion was at its most powerful, because most prone to self-deception and least vulnerable to critique, when the economic jeremiad (progress through global capitalist development) was implicit within overtly antiprogressive critiques (suspicion of military pride and socialist utopianism) designed to deflate alternative positions. It was relatively easy for *C&C* to second-guess U.S. elites when they moved toward a military crusade mentality, because *C&C*'s central arguments stressed that all political regimes (whether the

United States or its enemies) were prone to the sin of pride. Yet when the United States projected economic power and sought to create an ever-expanding market based on each group pursuing its self-interest—when it promoted a level playing field in which the United States was the dominant economic force because its rivals had been largely leveled to rubble after the war—*C&C* could present this as an example of *criticizing* pride and militaristic pretension. *C&C* managed to perceive the dominant strategies of corporate capitalism being undertaken with a defensive posture, in the name of a "humble acceptance of the fallen nature of humanity."[83]

Domestic Liberalism and McCarthyism

For many years *C&C* paid more attention to international issues than domestic ones. This was an outgrowth of *C&C*'s original concerns and reflected its belief that the great unresolved crises of the era were foreign and military, whereas "in the modern day, domestic problems have been tolerably solved."[84] However, after the war *C&C* broadened its focus, with a quarter of its articles focusing on domestic politics.[85]

By the early 1950s, *C&C* had come to question the wisdom of virtually any social movement that sought economic changes more radical than the New Deal. *C&C* moved from its inherited socialism to this position through a gradual process centered on the 1940s. Bennett still cautiously endorsed socialism in a 1948 book that undergirded many *C&C* editorials. He said that it was "essential for Christians to emphasize the moral limitations of capitalism," which was an ideology of business elites. Christians should "avoid altogether the tendency to give religious sanction to capitalism."[86] However, Bennett also endorsed the free market as a technique for organizing society, and he spoke of a "gradual revolution in the American system" since 1932 which had resulted in "the control by the community through government of the powerful economic institutions upon which the welfare of the people depend." He worried that "unless [the] people are very vigilant and resourceful, a socialist society may degenerate into a totalitarian society."[87] His doubts about socialism increased in subsequent years. By 1956 he could say that Niebuhrian theology "was never really consistent with democratic socialism which had too optimistic an attitude toward the problem of incentive and toward the tendency to unite economic and political power." Still, even at this low ebb of *C&C*'s socialism, Bennett seemed pleased to report that Niebuhr had in his younger days opposed capitalism for more than thirty years and that Niebuhr had "often expressed his belief that capitalist institutions were the most putrid aspect of a decaying civilization and the oligarchs of the business world the chief examples of social stupidity."[88]

Niebuhr converted more quickly and emphatically than Bennett. By the late 1940s he typically struck phrases like this: "The uneasy conscience of sensitive spirits about the injustices which arose from disproportions of power in a liberal society have been overcome by the fact that the alternative organization of society, when carried through consistently, leads to a monopoly of power; and a monopoly of power leads to all the evils which the Russian tyranny exhibits."[89] According to Niebuhr, any system of thought which focused on historical progress rather than "transhistorical interests of the Christian faith" led to attempts to "establish a heaven upon earth." Unfortunately, "This heaven on earth turned out in the case of orthodox Marxism to be a communist hell." Liberal utopianism produced results that were "less dangerous but equally pathetic."[90]

Niebuhr spoke more boldly for socialism in places besides *C&C*. In a 1976 address to a later generation of *C&C* readers, Bennett attempted to put the best face on Niebuhr's (and his own) past. He jokingly recalled that "*C&C*'s constituency was not like you here tonight; it was a very respectable constituency. Most of the people in it were the kind of people the Republicans call moderates." Bennett maintained that, when Niebuhr wrote for *C&C*, "he very carefully avoided subjects that would be outside the consensus of this group. At the time Niebuhr was also editing another journal called *Radical Religion* and in that journal he said everything he wanted to say. . . . Niebuhr's socialism came out very strongly in it."[91]

Bennett's chronology was off, since *Radical Religion* (the journal of the Fellowship of Socialist Christians) changed its name to *Christianity and Society* (the journal of the Frontier Fellowship) before *C&C* was born. His larger point does stand, but only with a significant qualification. *Christianity and Society* was in decline. "With Niebuhr's attention focused elsewhere, it gradually shrank to a shadow of its former self. . . . Socialist critique was not explicitly denied but circumscribed, exiled to [its] little-read pages."[92] Niebuhr also stopped writing for the *Nation*. His main secular outlet became the *New Leader*, which Fox calls "the most simplistically anticommunist journal on the liberal side of the political spectrum."[93]

C&C offered vague support to the noncommunist labor movement, but its passions were elsewhere. It spoke about labor with an us-them rhetoric, with *C&C* as the sympathetic but paternally chastising "us." A comment on the 1959 steel strike caught the spirit: "A plague on both your houses . . . but a little more on management's house."[94] Liston Pope, the *C&C* insider best informed about labor, argued that "fresh indications of social vision have been rather lacking in labor circles in the last decade. . . . [Labor] must on occasion be itself restrained from using [its new] power to subvert the common good." This was part of a near-despairing lament by Pope about the decline of socialist and agrarian radicalism after the war. Communists had destroyed left-wing forces from within, and third parties were a dead end. In short, Pope saw a "vacuum on the left" and thought that "the New Deal is dead." Searching for the way forward, Pope turned away from labor and called for more voluntary organizations, including church-based ones.[95]

Electoral politics sparked somewhat more interest. One of *C&C*'s founders, Francis P. Miller, repeatedly ran for senator of Virginia and expounded in *C&C* about the difficulties of being a moral person and effective politician at the same time.[96] Robert McAfee Brown, who was soon to become a professor at Union and a *C&C* insider, discussed his volunteer work for Senator Eugene McCarthy's 1952 campaign, in which Brown learned firsthand about the red-baiting tactics of Republicans.[97] *C&C* covered each presidential campaign with forums that argued the merits of each candidate, as well as follow-up editorials giving advice to the incumbents. Anyone could see that *C&C* preferred liberal Democrats such as Adlai Stevenson, but members of its board of sponsors wrote to support moderate Republicans such as Dwight Eisenhower. Given Niebuhr's love for polemics, *C&C*'s overall editorial voice was surprisingly bipartisan and decorous.

C&C's greatest passions on the domestic front were aroused by the anticommunist blacklists and purges known as McCarthyism. To a greater extent than *C&C* old-timers like to recall, *C&C* was caught up in the general movement of repression. This went beyond its efforts to destroy the academic reputations of its Progressive opponents through scholarly debate and infighting—behavior that seems to be par for the course in every academic generation. *C&C* also supported more heavy-handed forms of discipline such as academic blacklists and loyalty oaths. Robert Fitch reported on a case at the University of California. Striking a disdainful pose toward the "stupidity" of the controversy, Fitch stated that communists were "disqualified" to teach. It was necessary to protect academic freedom, but "impossible to believe that a bona fide member of the Communist party has not . . . committed himself to the subversion of both liberty and truth." Even if such people were sincere, they were sheep running with wolves. Thus they had no right to complain if they were shot during a hunt.[98]

C&C kept its bearings in the atmosphere of anticommunist hysteria far better than many of its contemporaries. This was a period when the John Birch Society deduced that President Eisenhower was a communist, and a politician stated, "If someone insists that there is discrimination against Negroes in this country or that there is inequality of wealth, there is every reason to believe that person is a Communist."[99] Serious anticommunists were more prone to perceive *C&C* as communist than to greet it as an ally, and *C&C* writers took real risks when they criticized McCarthyism as idolatrous and hypocritical. Although *C&C* agreed that loyalty was needed, the X hand of many articles cautioned against hysteria. "What is wrong is not the searching out of teachers and administrators who are hostile to our way of life," said a typical article, "but rather the dragnet method of going after them."[100] Bennett advocated amnesty for anyone who had been involved with the Communist Party before 1948. He complained that a red-hunter who specialized in attacking the religious left, J. B. Matthews, lumped together communists with anyone who signed any petition of any leftist organization at any time for any reason—including people that Bennett knew personally as anticommunist pacifists. Bennett described how a group on Matthews's blacklist asked him to sign a petition: "I see a few names on the letter-head which make me suspicious but I fully agree with the statement and most of the names inspire confidence. I do not know whether this committee is a Communist front or not but I have learned to be cautious and so I do not sign. Is this wise caution or is this cowardice? Is this chiefly an indication that I am in my own way a victim of McCarthyism?"[101]

Bennett's final question is compelling, provided we keep a sense of proportion about Bennett's "own way" of being a victim—and that of Niebuhr, whose early career made him a target of government security investigations. Around the same time that Bennett wrote this article, *C&C* supported the death penalty for Ethel and Julius Rosenberg after they were convicted of spying in one of the most controversial trials of the cold war.[102] Ten days after their execution, a public relations branch of the State Department aired a radio broadcast—"Ideological Special no. 256"—based on a Niebuhr article called "Why Is Communism So Evil?" This piece, which *C&C* later used in a promotion, stated that communism was "an organized evil which spreads terror and cruelty throughout the world and confronts us everywhere with faceless men who are immune to every form of moral suasion."[103]

C&C was indeed in its own way a victim of McCarthyism—but the main way was self-censorship. It deflected more acute consequences by allying itself with liberal anticommunists.

C&C and the American Jeremiad

How shall we summarize *C&C*'s cold war vision? Compared with positions within *C&C*'s tradition that came before and after, this is a story of complacency. Bennett later described it as a "too bland acceptance of national trends of the 1940s and 1950s."[104] However, interpreting *C&C* solely in these terms is potentially misleading on two counts. First, although *C&C* worked within the framework of cold war liberalism, it often took positions to the left of actual policy. This placed *C&C* even further left of the mainline Protestant laity to whom it hoped its views would trickle down, who voted Republican at higher rates than either Catholics or fundamentalists. Often *C&C* endorsed positions that it explicitly described as lesser evils within a political climate it deplored. Within the dialectical style of argument that *C&C* favored—with its omnipresent rhetoric of "on the one hand X, on the other hand Y"—*C&C* maintained some limited rhetoric of anticolonialism, anticapitalist economic struggle, and racial justice. Critical stances on the Y hand were subordinate to the anticommunism and technocratic liberalism of the X hand. Yet *C&C*'s ability to sustain a tradition of oppositional prophetic Protestantism, even in a circumscribed form, was not trivial. This would become clearer in later years, as the "realistic" political space for critique increased.

There is a second sense in which *C&C* battled complacency. Even when *C&C* identified with dominant trends, it felt a strong subjective sense of crisis for the nation. Niebuhr's fifteenth anniversary article in 1956 said that *C&C* was "engaged in a desperate struggle with a despotism on the edge of an abyss of atomic destruction." On the tenth anniversary he said that *C&C*'s original crisis was deeper than he had expected: "We confront the necessity of developing an armed camp with all of our economic and man-power resources partially, and possibly totally, mobilized."[105]

The mobilization Niebuhr had in mind was ideological and spiritual as well as political and military. True, he avoided bald statements about God's will for America that might provide aid and comfort to conservatives as well as fall prey to his own antiprogressive arguments. His best defense of liberal America was a good offense. Still, his perception of crisis implied God's transcendent judgment on evil and the urgent need for responsible Christian action. An explicit goal of *C&C* was to mobilize the moral strengths of its religious constituency.[106]

A 1950 article by Charles Malik on "The Crisis of Faith" revealed the underlying assumptions. In classic jeremiad style, his article opened by asking, "When the Son of Man cometh, shall He find faith on this earth?" A long section lamented a decline caused by materialism and insensitivity to transcendent values: "Real creative faith . . . has to an alarming extent departed from the earth," said Malik. "The stout men of faith of the past, meeting the typical modern man . . . [will] turn away their faces in disgust." Moreover, communists were attacking the entire western intellectual tradition including "reason, order, . . . human dignity, history, God, love, and the higher things."

What was to be done? Two givens were the resolute containment of communism and a renewed commitment to the Marshall Plan and New Deal. But these were the easy tasks compared with the underlying problem of faith. "Civilizations have perished not so much because they have been materially weak," argued Malik, "as because they lost their soul and ceased to have a fighting faith in themselves as bearers of light and being to the entire world." The West needed spiritual values stronger than communism. But there was hope: God "will surely have compassion on us and come to the rescue of his inheritance." The only thing required was hearkening to *C&C*'s jeremiad: listening to God's judgment, repenting, and devoting the nation to the divine will.[107]

Although this perception of world crisis and national mission was not complacent, neither did it represent much opposition to the main lines of establishment policy. In fact, it echoed classic traditions of the American jeremiad. It was in line with John Foster Dulles, who said, "It was the religion of the West that made the colonial system of the West profoundly different from the empires of the past."[108] *C&C* also echoed the famous "Mr. X" article by diplomat George Kennan (a classic document of containment theory), which argued that U.S. citizens "should experience a certain gratitude to a Providence which, by providing the American people with this implacable challenge, has made their entire security as a nation dependent upon their pulling themselves together and accepting the responsibilities of moral and political leadership that history plainly intended them to bear."[109]

3

White Male Protestants on Blacks, Women, and Catholics

Christianity and Crisis wrote almost exclusively from a white male Protestant standpoint as it elaborated on its worldview. This is not a problem—everyone writes from *some* standpoint—if it does not perpetuate unjust power relationships between white male Protestants and various others. However, *C&C*'s standpoint was frequently linked to limitations in its domestic social vision during the decade after World War II—problems of limited imagination and lukewarm support for changes in unjust power hierarchies. Here again, there were X and Y hands. *C&C* supported mild reforms related to civil rights and women's issues, and made a striking shift toward openness to Roman Catholicism. On all these fronts, *C&C* assumed slow and steady progress toward a more pluralistic society. It kept alive a significant commitment to social criticism. At the same time, it was relatively complacent about the status quo and assumed that white male Protestant experience was the norm. In retrospect, *C&C*'s limited concern with race and gender justice and its hostility toward Catholics loom large.

Visions of Gradual Progress toward Racial Integration

As I grew up, when I was taught about Protestants and civil rights, I gained two images. The first was of southern whites who resisted change. I am thinking, for example, about people who assumed the inferiority of African American culture and the need to move slowly in view of state's rights—the sort of people who criticized President Truman's decision to integrate the army as going too far, too fast. Alongside this image was a vision of African American churches and northern liberal clergy as allies in famous civil rights struggles such as the Montgomery bus boycott. I envisioned mainline clergy reading speeches of Martin Luther King Jr. to their parishioners to firm up support for civil rights legislation or helping convict the consciences of the segregationists and fence-sitters. Such images are supported by heroic narratives such as James Findlay's important *Church People in the Struggle*—narratives that are sometimes linked to a lament for what was lost with the rise of black nationalism and multiculturalism in the 1960s and 1970s.

The history of *C&C* before 1960 does not always fit this image. Parts of it do. However, the negative images of white racism that I just mentioned are taken not from southern fundamentalists but from *C&C* articles. After the 1954 *Brown v. Board of Education* decision that outlawed segregated schools, Niebuhr argued that force "must not be used to enforce the Court's decision." He asked *C&C* readers to step into the shoes of white southern parents who feared corruption by a backward race: According to Niebuhr, such whites had some valid grounds for fear because "the race is backward." Don't worry, Niebuhr continued. This was a temporary result of substandard educational opportunity. It would be overcome through slow, steady progress if both sides were patient.[1] Findlay is well aware of the limited antiracist commitments of mainline leaders before 1960. He notes that the National Council of Churches (NCC) refused to pass a resolution condemning the murder of Emmett Till, a young black from Chicago who was killed during a visit to Mississippi for flirting with a white woman, and he adds damning evidence from later years such as NCC cooperation with FBI surveillance of civil rights organizations.[2] But Findlay does not dwell on these problems; rather, he focuses on a "kairos" moment of activism in the 1960s. In this book, we must linger somewhat longer on these problems, more as James Cone does in *Martin and Malcolm and America*, and consider how they may have shaped the attitudes of *C&C*'s black allies who moved toward more radical positions.[3]

It is somewhat surprising that *C&C*'s early commitment to civil rights was so limited, given that two of its major themes were the need to resist racist tyrannies by force and the superiority of liberal democracies because they respected pluralism. The Niebuhrians developed these critiques largely to attack Nazism, but carried them forward as standard rhetoric after the war. Unfortunately, *C&C* did not think much about the implications of this approach for U.S. racism until the 1960s. It was so busy making connections between Hitler and Stalin that it paid scant attention to analogies between Hitler and U.S. racists.

This means, first of all, that race was a low priority. Out of 158 articles in my cross section from 1945 through 1956, only 5 had domestic race issues as a major theme. Seven more addressed race as a secondary theme, often because they attacked racism in foreign countries or used rhetoric with striking racial connotations. (For example, *C&C* posed a stark alternative between the rule of international law or "the continued chaos of jungle ethics.")[4] *C&C* completely ignored Latinos and Native Americans, and its attention to Asian Americans was only the smallest afterthought of the war. Its editorial boards, sponsors, and staff were all white with the exception of contributing editor J. Oscar Lee, who was also the sole African American staff person at the NCC in the early 1950s. I can identify only one article by an African American in *C&C*'s index from 1952 to 1956.[5]

This article, by Benjamin Mays of Morehouse College, embraced theories of integration and universal humanity so enthusiastically that he could speak as follows: "No sane man has ever denied the fact that the Gospel of Christ is super-racial, super-cultural, super-national, and super-class. Christ died for all mankind." (So much for contextual theologies and postmodern theories of racial difference!) Mays's article was a lengthy compendium of arguments against scientific and religious justifications for segregation, ending with a call to enforce the Supreme Court's school desegregation decision from earlier in the year.[6]

In theory *C&C* was fully committed to integration, and in practice it was willing to use its standard arguments about resistance to tyranny in a way that justified some use of force by federal and state governments to overturn segregation. What is striking in retrospect, however, is how often *C&C* failed to endorse even mild activism by African Americans and wrote almost exclusively from the standpoint of government policymakers and white southern clergy. *C&C* stressed slow and restrained change that could maintain relative consensus in the community, by which it primarily meant the *white* community. Attention to *C&C*'s logical allies in the African American Protestant churches was virtually lacking, especially before 1954. It is interesting to contrast this failure to approach domestic racism from the standpoint of minorities with its somewhat more frequent efforts to take the standpoint of Asians and Africans toward Euro-American imperialism.

C&C's most ambitious statement on race published before the 1960s, which took up an entire issue in 1955, was by Frank Graham, a former North Carolina senator then working at the UN. It approached school desegregation in a cold war framework, opening and closing with passionate statements about integration's "strategic moral power in the worldwide struggle between democratic freedom and totalitarian tyranny." Resentment of racism by colored people worldwide impeded the "high morale of a common front." In this context the school desegregation decision was "louder than the explosion of the hydrogen bomb," and the United States faced the challenge of refuting communists who predicted that the new policy was just so much rhetoric that would never be put into practice. *C&C*'s article was addressed to whites; it was filled with details about specific policy options such as integration phased in over twelve years, one grade at a time. It rejected "immediate complete integration in all communities" as pragmatically unwise, because this would result in stalling tactics explicitly aimed at noncompliance, which might slow long-term progress. There might even be open defiance of the law, which would be a disaster for anticommunist propaganda.[7]

This is a good example of how international considerations helped to focus the attention of white elites on domestic racism and to shift the balance of power on racial struggles so that grassroots movements gained leverage in the postwar period. When a traveler was refused a haircut in Cincinnati because his skin was too dark, or when a black student at a Baltimore bus station asked for a drink of water and was told, "The place for you, my man, is the spittoon outside," this was par for the course, part of the "realities" of the United States. But when the traveler was a Ceylonese diplomat, and the student was Kwame Nkrumah, who later became the president of Ghana, such events became headaches for the State Department. In 1961, when the Dallas Hilton refused a room to another black visitor—the ambassador from Ghana—Vice-President Lyndon Johnson phoned the hotel manager and explained the situation as follows: "These people have twenty odd votes in the United Nations. . . . It is going to be explosive internationally. We are outnumbered 17 to 1, black to white in this world. . . . If this gets out that [Dallas] has refused him, we will have Freedom Riders all over the town. . . . [Moreover,] you can't afford to hurt [the ambassador's] feelings . . . [because] it would take a lot of white people to fill up a hotel in Ghana. . . . If word gets out that Hilton Hotels are segregated, Hilton Hotels all over the world are in trouble."[8]

Niebuhr commonly argued that moving too slowly to enforce the Brown decision would "reduce the majesty of the law," yet moving too fast risked white resistance. He spoke of the "knotty problem" of conflict between law and "the customs and prejudices of the community" and regretted that the (white) churches were being "sub-moral" as the conflict unfolded. As we have seen, he advised against using force to implement the decision and said that whites had legitimate fears of corruption by a backward race.[9]

During the 1957 desegregation crisis in Little Rock, Arkansas, when local authorities resisted so intensely that President Eisenhower sent in the army to enforce the law, Niebuhr wrote almost exclusively from the standpoint of "responsible leaders"; black agents were almost invisible in *C&C*'s text. He argued that Eisenhower and Governor Orval Faubus were bungling the pragmatic tactics of integration. Niebuhr placed most of the blame on Faubus, the irresponsible one playing with matches around "inflammable material." But he said that Eisenhower should have known that he would "harden hearts of the racists" by sending the troops—who remained in the Little Rock high school protecting black students for a whole year—and should not have allowed the controversy to escalate until the army was needed. Niebuhr pointed to Louisville as a model city which proved that integration could work if "every official from governor to school superintendent proceeded with caution and a sense of responsibility."[10]

Before 1954 *C&C* typically took weaker antiracist stands than this lukewarm support for federal activism in Little Rock. During debates about desegregating the army in 1948, one *C&C* article stated that "sweeping and indiscriminate application of a policy of non-segregation throughout the armed services" was "going too far" strategically. Another article favored integrating the military by executive order, but criticized efforts by activist A. Phillip Randolph to organize a nonviolent protest to demand this change. This could not succeed, *C&C* judged, partly because African Americans lacked "the great spiritual and emotional discipline required."[11] In 1952 *C&C* cautioned that legal challenges to segregation in South Carolina by the National Association for the Advancement of Colored People (NAACP) might, in practice, result in driving "a further wedge of resentment" between the races; a better strategy was to "consolidate the beachheads already won before advancing into the hedgerows."[12] *C&C*'s writer identified less with the "impatient" NAACP than with committees for interracial dialogue which had limited influence—not the most logical agents for *C&C*'s realist strategy of meeting injustice with countervailing power.

It was an innovation when, after 1956, *C&C* occasionally brought up the subject of "the church and race," then went on to treat African American churches as active subjects. Before 1956, its writers' minds almost always jumped to the white Protestant churches.[13] In light of the stress on Rosa Parks and the Montgomery bus boycott in the popular memory, it is interesting that *C&C* gave the boycott limited attention—mainly brief notices in its small-print News and Notes section. One notice from four months into the boycott spoke of Protestant elites from the North sending letters of support; the only person from Montgomery mentioned by name was an A.M.E. Zion pastor, Solomon Seay.[14] More typical coverage was an article describing five representative types of southern clergy, all apparently white. They ranged from "Rev. Hard Core Resistance," a fundamentalist committed to segregation, through "Mr. Power," who wants "reconciliation" and whose motto is "Be firm, but don't stick your neck out," to the two models recommended by *C&C:* "Mr. Strategy," who supported integration but was waiting for a more opportune moment to play his cards, and "Mr. Action," who was actually participating in civil rights organizing despite ostracism from friends and threats of violence.[15]

It is fascinating to observe how racial conflict made *C&C* jump out of the ruts in its typical reasoning about pacifism. When discussing racism—and *only* when discussing this issue—pacifism was seen as good. A 1957 editorial praised nonviolent protest because of its "sober," "calm," "patient," and "pacific" approach. *C&C* commented that "it is almost too much to ask of human nature" to "play this role in the tense drama of suffering and redemption."[16] By mentioning human nature, *C&C* arrived at a sort of switch point where nine times out of ten its standard realist argument would click in—the need to build countervailing coercive power against sin and the bankruptcy of perfectionist utopianism. During these same years, Malcolm X was working only a few blocks from Union Seminary, where he was drawing conclusions that overlapped significantly with such reasoning—the need for black self-determination and the limitations of nonviolent liberal protest.[17] But whenever *C&C* writers began to enter the well-worn rut of antipacifist argument that might have led in Malcolm's direction, they stopped in their tracks. Insofar as *C&C* used realist arguments to discuss race, it almost always did so from the standpoint of government elites, with solicitude for people who hedged their support for the NAACP, on the grounds that it exhibited not only "the will to equality but [also] the will to power."[18]

We should not conclude from this litany of relative timidity about reform that *C&C perceived itself* resisting challenges to institutional racism. On the contrary, *C&C* felt that it was part of a steady movement toward equality, and it went so far as to debate whether clergy should risk their jobs for the cause. In no way did *C&C* perceive itself as unsympathetic to change, but rather as *more* sympathetic than most of its readers, and merely concerned to manage a timetable of progress with the best pragmatic results. Typical was a 1950 article by Liston Pope that celebrated Jackie Robinson's 1947 integration of major league baseball, the desegregation of the military, various court rulings, and economic gains for some blacks. Pope concluded that "a revolution in racial patterns is sweeping American society."[19] As federal activism increased, so did *C&C*'s confidence on this point.

Even *C&C*'s most cautious articles assumed that inevitable changes were unfolding. The article that cautioned against advancing into the hedgerows concluded with an Exodus image: the (white) church was called into a "strange territory" that might be "a land flowing with milk and honey or a wilderness infested with brigands." Unfortunately, the church "which should be ready to lead her children, seems to have lost sight of the cloud and the fire."[20] Of course, *C&C* assumed that its mission was to provide this vision. As we will see, *C&C*'s contributions to antiracist struggle in the 1960s were by no means trivial, but *C&C* would also have to face an identity crisis as increasing numbers of blacks questioned its qualifications as leader.

Good Wives and Priestesses: Treatments of Gender and Sexuality

C&C's most important positions on gender during the decade after World War II were not self-conscious but implicit in its virtually all-male personnel and its masculinist rhetoric about both God and everyday life. For the most part, *C&C* writers paid no attention to the rights of women or the construction of gender and sexuality; they simply presupposed prevailing cultural patterns. Only two issues received minimal concern: women's ordination and trends in sexual behavior analyzed by the Kinsey Reports. In both cases *C&C* was lukewarm toward women's equality and hostile toward gay/lesbian concerns, although it was slightly more sympathetic than the liberal Protestant churches at large.

At this time *C&C* published almost no female writers. Between 1952 and 1956, indexes show a cumulative total of seven articles by women. Three were written by Ursula Niebuhr, who was married to Reinhold Niebuhr. My sample of 158 articles between 1945 and 1956 includes only 4 articles by women, none of which addressed gender overtly, plus 4 more pieces by men that did touch self-consciously on gender issues.[21]

Of course, this does not mean that *C&C* failed to engage implicitly with the construction of gender before the 1960s, when it began to write about this self-consciously. Gender relations are present and important whether males notice them or not. Women's historians have shown that history often appears in a different light if the conditions of women's lives are in focus than if other issues take center stage. Triumphant moments of cultural revitalization for males may have mixed results from female perspectives. The United States in the cold war era is a good example. This was a period of resurgent self-confidence for male liberals but reverses for movements seeking women's equality. Although the overall trend of female workforce participation has been upward for a century, and although women gained new access to desirable industrial jobs during the mobilization for World War II, many of these gains stalled or reversed after the war. Women were pushed out of better-paying jobs back toward the so-called pink-collar ghetto of secretarial and service work. In the cult of female domesticity, they were groomed by education and culture to work without pay in the home, and they were discouraged from pursuing professions.[22] Elisabeth Schüssler Fiorenza, now a world-famous Harvard biblical scholar, recalls that "just as in the 1950s I could not imagine typing this article on a word processor, so could I not conceive of a woman as a theological scholar." Even in the mid-1960s, after Fiorenza had earned two graduate degrees with honors and published a book, she could not obtain a doctoral fellowship; her adviser told her "he did not want to waste the opportunity on a student who as a woman had no future in the academy."[23]

Part of the way that such double standards came to be understood as normal was through the rhetoric of cultural leaders. In 1945 *C&C* used these words to celebrate the founding of the United Nations: "Men are the children of God. Men constitute God's one great family. . . . They must recognize that fact and embody it as well as they can in the world structure. . . .God's great human family is one and His purpose is inexorable." For anyone whose perceptions of the world were shaped by these images, God and the emergent UN leadership were linked through an image of a father caring for—and implicitly disciplining—his family. All the other people in this family (including females described as "men") are imagined as children, and since the father has inexorable power, the realities of this gendered world are presented as nonnegotiable. In fact, the article went on to say that to fight against them was to "defy ultimate reality."[24]

Or let us return to *C&C*'s editorial on the Truman Doctrine and note how much of its imagery is open to a phallic interpretation. *C&C* called the new policy a "vigorous thrust of American power into the arena of international affairs. [It] does not fall into the conventional pattern of political penetration by means of economic policy . . . [which would fulfill] the economic needs of Greece and Turkey. . . . All is out in the open. . . . The President has thrown soft diplomacy to the winds and called a spade a spade."[25]

C&C's board probably did not intend a phallic reading of its editorial, yet such a reading gains plausibility from the explicit way that other cold war intellectuals used sexual imagery. *The Vital Center* by Niebuhr's friend Arthur Schlesinger Jr. was an influential manifesto of cold war liberalism, contrasting the "virility" of liberals to the "political sterility" of its opponents on the left and right. Schlesinger described communism as "something secret, sweaty and furtive like nothing so much . . . as homosexuals in a boys' school." *C&C*'s review did not mention this image, but did endorse Schlesinger's vision of a liberal state "reunit[ing] individual and community in fruitful union." It said that Schlesinger's book "express[ed] in its fundamental faith what would seem to be a normal expression of Christianity."[26]

The most immediate way that sexist and homophobic double standards are enforced is not through gendered rhetoric, however important it may be, but through overt discrimination by structures of economic power. For the most part *C&C* was silent about this issue, but it did condemn the worst aspects of job discrimination in mainline churches. These denominations have undergone long processes in which women first gained equal rights as laity, later access to professional jobs as Christian educators, the right to be ordained as regular clergy, and finally a struggle (still ongoing) for equal access to the best jobs. The timetable and specific details have varied in each tradition, but many mainline denominations began accepting female clergy in the third quarter of the century, with the United Methodists moving relatively early in 1956 and the Episcopalians relatively late in 1976.[27]

Although *C&C* personnel were not on the cutting edge of this process, they were somewhat closer than many of their peers. In 1949 Niebuhr criticized Episcopalians for refusing to seat elected female delegates at their convention; he complained that churches generally lagged behind civil society on equal rights for women because of a traditional "enmity between the priest and the woman." Some feminist historians stress the disadvantages for women caused by the rise of industrial labor markets and the bourgeois family.[28] However, Niebuhr argued that liberal modernity was solving women's problems and that churches would soon catch up. His basic principle, cited from St. Paul, stated that in Christ "there is—neither male nor female." Not all *C&C* readers agreed. A letter to the editor defended the Episcopalians because their church had a women's auxiliary just like the Masons and the Lions' Club. "It is not a case of being exclusive, but being practical," he said. "Consider the business transacted, and you will understand."[29]

Even *C&C*'s boldest articles on women's ordination—which were their *only* major articles on women's rights before the 1960s—partly embraced this letter's "separate but equal" logic. An article by Ursula Niebuhr agreed with her spouse that there should be no male or female within the Christian community. She used this idea to support women's ordination, offering many examples of "sub-Christian" discrimination, which she compared to apologies for slavery. In contrast to the antimilitarism of many contemporary feminisms, she pushed the logic of women's equal rights to the extreme of celebrating "Mrs. Rosenberg"—Anna M. Rosenberg—as the "best 'man'" for assistant secretary of defense. However, alongside Niebuhr's dominant logic of gender equality, she also spoke of sexual difference as irreducible and positive. This part of her argument overlaps with much feminist theory, both in accenting the construction of gender and in complaining that many forms of Christianity have had a repressive attitude toward sexuality and no positive view of sex difference. However, unlike most such theories, Niebuhr used the idea of gender differences largely to defend the nuclear family against feminist extremists. She said that most women should stay out of the paid labor force at least until their children enter school and that heterosexuality was part of the God-ordained "order of creation." A committee that she chaired on women and the church concluded that women deserved full rights, but that because of their responsibilities as wives and mothers, their roles should be suited to "their own distinctive gifts."[30]

What exactly *were* these distinctive gifts? *C&C* unpacked their meaning in a fascinating article by Cyril Richardson, a Union Seminary professor. He used arguments compatible with feminism to support women's ordination, attack gender hierarchies, and advocate feminine metaphors for the theological categories of Holy Spirit and Church. He also emphatically denied that "a woman is just another kind of male" and stated, "This misleading notion encourages all the evils of the 'feminine protest.' We do not want women *priests.* What we need is *priestesses* whose functions and authority are appropriate to their nature." These functions, based on the natural role of motherhood, were to work with "the feminine aspects of the Word"—identified as sacraments and pastoral care. Richardson used a medical analogy to dig himself steadily into a hole from a feminist perspective: an ambitious woman either "becomes a doctor and loses much of her femininity" or becomes an administrator, in which case she loses "her peculiar talent as the healing mother of the patient, implying . . . a type of healing of which the doctor by nature is incapable." In short, the distinctive gifts of male and female clergy were modeled by male doctors and female nurses. *C&C* reported that the Prussian Union Church had used similar reasoning in a 1952 decision to ordain women. Women "will have the same rights as their male colleagues," they decreed. Yet women "normally will be restricted to positions for which they are particularly fitted, such as leadership of women's, youth, and children's work, Sunday schools, Bible reading groups, and pastoral care to women in prisons and hospitals."[31]

In their own everyday practice, *C&C* people roughly matched this Prussian example of separate but equal complementarity. I have noted the lack of female writers; in addition, during *C&C*'s first twenty years it had only one woman on its masthead—Rhoda McCulloch, a founding member of the editorial board and contributing editor from 1948 to 1951.[32] The only major female role in producing *C&C* was secretarial, and even that was largely male during the 1950s.

C&C leaders who were seminary professors—most of the key figures—had a few female students. *C&C*'s home base, Union Seminary, can serve as a fairly representative case study, although *C&C* board members were drawn from several schools, including some with a weaker female presence.[33] Before World War II, a third of Union's students were women; many were enrolled in the Christian education track or the music program. The figure dropped to about 20 percent after the war and remained there as late as 1972. President Henry Sloane Coffin was "not particularly keen on women as theological students" because he thought "the presence of young women was 'hazardous.'" When he saw a female student smoking Reinhold Niebuhr's pipe, he proposed a rule that no women could smoke, which was voted down only after a five-hour filibuster by Union's two female faculty.[34] In the 1950s there was an increase in married students, even though the school discouraged marriage before graduation and required students planning otherwise to meet with the president for a lecture that highlighted their responsibilities as parents. Married students received no additional financial aid.[35]

The majority of *C&C* personnel were married. Some of their spouses were known as strong women, including Anne McGrew Bennett, who later published a book of feminist theology.[36] Others were career women, including the prominent church leader Mildred McAfee Horton, spouse of *C&C* sponsor Douglas Horton. Ursula Niebuhr taught at Barnard College, although she curtailed her career to take primary responsibility for child care (since Reinhold was often traveling) and to care for Reinhold after he suffered a stroke in 1952.[37] However, most *C&C* leaders embraced conventional middle-class gender roles. Roger Shinn has spoken of "all the assumptions that all of us had about the male being the main professional in the family and so on."[38]

C&C underlying beliefs about gender rose quickly to the surface if they were challenged, as they were when the Kinsey Reports on sexual behavior appeared in 1948 and 1953, reporting unexpectedly high rates of homosexuality and the sensational findings that a quarter of middle-aged women had committed adultery and half had engaged in premarital sex. *C&C* agreed with *Life* that these reports were an "assault on the family as a basic unit of society, a negation of moral law, and a celebration of licentiousness."[39] Niebuhr spoke about the "disintegration of the family" and widespread "sexual perversion," which "approach[ed] the license which characterized Roman civilization in the period of its decay." He argued that Kinsey's method reduced sexuality to mere biological urges, and he was outraged that people interpreted its empirical findings as moral justifications for a "crude hedonism." It made no sense, argued Niebuhr, that perverts "would have their consciences eased if they only knew how much more widespread these perversions are, than they had supposed." By this logic, "would murderers have an easier conscience if they were told that the rate of this crime had increased markedly in recent times?" The report was not merely amoral; it even ignored scientific evidence for the need to control sexual drives, such as what Niebuhr claimed was the "universality of the prohibition of adultery" in all human cultures. "Women have a particular stake in this issue," continued Niebuhr, "for the male is usually the aggressor in sexual intimacy and the woman 'gives herself.'" Without a strong framework of values, "the unscrupulous male may use every wile and stratagem to secure sexual satisfaction from the female without offering her the love and respect which would make the experience tolerable to her as a person."[40]

Niebuhr conceded that Christianity was sometimes too sexually repressed, although he thought this was mainly a Catholic problem. In any case, he refused to condone premarital sex simply on the grounds that there was a biological drive for sexual expression between puberty and the end of schooling (which he took as the time when most people would get married). He pronounced petting to be an acceptable outlet for this drive, but drew the line at intercourse. Niebuhr thought that young people were "solving this problem creatively" by marrying while still in school. This gave the advantage of early childbearing and helped solve the "problem of frigidity." He welcomed Kinsey's finding that "the devout are in every case . . . least given to promiscuity and masturbation."[41]

Responding to this article, a professor of counseling encouraged Niebuhr to tone down his rhetoric about hedonism and ignorance. Would it not be better simply to speak about trade-offs in Kinsey's method, as well as to underline the dangers of Protestant legalism and asceticism? Did Kinsey really document the decay of the family? The evidence was mixed: there was a trend toward greater female sexual satisfaction, less prostitution, more mutuality. "The crucial point is that the patterns of women's sex life are approaching those of men more than before, thus also producing some change in men's patterns as a consequence."[42]

In sum, by 1955 *C&C* had advocated several positions that later became common feminist themes. It had called for women's ordination, advanced biblical warrants for gender equality and feminine images of the divine, and valorized female difference. *C&C* writers were no more hostile to women's equality, and in some ways friendlier, than most of their colleagues in other parts of mainstream U.S. culture.

Nevertheless, as we have seen, these female-friendly precedents on *C&C*'s Y hand were an extremely low priority, voiced primarily by males, and loaded down with antifeminist qualifications. In the cold war era *C&C* generally moved in harmony with conservative trends on gender issues in the dominant society. Perhaps this was best symbolized when the Rockefeller Foundation cut its funding for Kinsey's research in 1954 and at the same time granted Union Seminary half a million dollars "to aid in the development of vital religious leadership."[43] Beverly Harrison, who later became one of *C&C*'s leading feminists, comments that whatever one might say about a submerged undercurrent of protofeminist ideas and practice in *C&C*'s circles, she was raised and educated in these circles. "So far as I was aware growing up, no such reality as feminism had ever existed . . . it was an unspeakable impoverishment of my life to grow up and live so long without any knowledge of [earlier feminist] critique and struggle."[44]

"I Regret That You Do Not Detest the Pope": C&C before Vatican II

From its original polemics against Nazism, *C&C* inherited not only a rhetoric of democracy versus racism but also the claim that democracies were superior because they respected religious freedom. Yet in its early years *C&C* found no contradiction in publishing a stream of articles extremely hostile to Roman Catholicism.[45] In fact, it attacked Catholics *in the name of religious freedom,* perceiving Catholicism as a third great totalitarian threat alongside communism and Nazism. Extending historic Protestant suspicions that rising Catholic power could undermine home-grown American virtue—recall the discussion of Charles Beard and Prohibition in chapter 1—*C&C* leaders entered the 1950s perceiving Catholicism as a threat to democracy.

At its most defensible, *C&C*'s anti-Catholicism simply opposed the political activities of Catholic leaders, such as Cardinal Francis Spellman, who were allied with McCarthyism.[46] Unfortunately, *C&C* tended to generalize such views to all Catholics; it had such trust in the monolithic unity of Catholicism and its top-down ideological control by people like Spellman that it could write, "Catholics will take a lot of kicking around as long as the Pope is left in his place, but touch him and they'll fight to the last man."[47] In any case, insofar as we can abstract away from such overgeneralization (and the assumptions behind it), one strand within *C&C*'s anti-Catholicism was not much different from its opposition to the secular political right.

A second strand in *C&C*'s thinking is understandable if we posit a broad continuum between proper self-confidence and respect for one's own religious beliefs, at one pole, and improper arrogance about universalizing those beliefs and imposing them on nonbelievers, at the other. Some aspects of *C&C*'s anti-Catholic polemic can be understood as efforts to defend the integrity of Protestant faith against Catholic leaders (again, assumed to be monolithic) who refused to accept Protestant religious commitments as valid or to work with Protestant clergy as equals. For example, *C&C* often asked why Protestant ministers should cooperate with Catholic priests who demanded that in every Protestant-Catholic marriage the couple must marry in "the one true faith" of Rome.[48] One of the few times that *C&C* supported its theological nemesis, Karl Barth, was in his exchange of letters with Cardinal Jean Daniélou, a prominent Jesuit. Barth had scandalized Daniélou when he expressed satisfaction (rather than a pious lament about Christian disunity) when no cardinal attended a major World Council of Churches assembly. For Daniélou, who fervently hoped to reunite Protestants and Catholics, Barth's attitude was an example of willful divisiveness. But Barth replied that Catholics only wanted unity on their own terms. People like Daniélou excluded themselves from sitting at an ecumenical table, thought Barth, because they assumed that they already had all the answers. Protestants were also clear about their God-given mission and goals. Under the circumstances it was better for the two groups to remain separate.[49]

Barth also offered a textbook case of how self-respect can shade into intolerance when he said to Daniélou, "I regret that you do not detest the Pope." Most Christians consider their faith claims as in some sense true *for everyone*—at least within situated contexts—even if they do not claim a universal need to embrace specific Christian doctrines.[50] Whenever two groups' insights about religious truth come into conflict, it is always possible for one group to charge the other with intolerance. Obviously, Catholics could interpret Barth's comment about the pope as the mirror image of alleged Catholic intolerance and insensitivity.

Few *C&C* writers advocated detesting the pope, but in the decade after the war, defensible strands in *C&C*'s anti-Catholicism did typically come blended with intolerant rhetoric. *C&C* cofounder Henry Sloane Coffin saw a "kinship at point after point between the methods of totalitarian Moscow and those of equally totalitarian Rome."[51] A 1947 article said that Protestants would "betray their lord the Christ" by cooperating with priests and bishops. Catholicism was "ecclesiastical totalitarianism." It was "the most tough and wily and intransigent hierarchy on earth," and Catholic laity succumbed to its ruthless power-hunger much like German citizens did to Hitler. Since the Catholic partner triumphed in every interfaith marriage, "one begins to wonder . . . how Protestant tolerance and birth-control can ever stand up against Catholic intolerance and fecundity." Liberals refused to face up to Catholic power, just as they had earlier failed to stand up to Nazis. They needed another dose of realism.[52]

One rallying point for Protestants who held such views was Paul Blanshard's *American Freedom and Catholic Power,* an alarmist exposé of Catholic plans to replace U.S. democracy with a "Catholic America."[53] *C&C* distanced itself from Blanshard's contention that religion should not be taught in the public schools. Well into the 1960s, *C&C* upheld the importance of religious education, both Catholic and Protestant.[54] But Coffin wrote a glowing *C&C* review of Blanshard's book, praising his "precise documentation" and "patent aim to be fair." Coffin stated that "the gratitude of all freedom-cherishing Americans goes to him." After an important book rebutted Blanshard's distortions, *C&C* published a rather embarrassed review conceding major problems with his method. Most telling was Blanshard's conflation of abstract principles in theological documents with the actual practices of U.S. Catholic leaders. (Replying to similar Protestant attacks in the 1920s, Catholic presidential candidate Al Smith had exclaimed, "Will somebody please tell me what in hell an encyclical is?") Yet the main goal of *C&C*'s revised assessment of Blanshard was to call for future exposés that were better conceived.[55]

Another flashpoint of anti-Catholicism was the U.S. government's 1951 decision to open diplomatic relations with the Vatican. This provoked widespread outrage in Protestant circles, and *C&C* writers divided into two camps: passionate and alarmist opponents versus cool and moderate ones. One of the alarmists stated that creeping Catholic power could supplant the nation's Reformation heritage, and the United States could end up like Poland, Spain, and Latin America—totalitarian. A somewhat calmer editorial by Henry Pitney Van Dusen described diplomatic recognition as "a long step" toward "abandonment of the American principle of Church-State relations." Speaking for *C&C*'s least intolerant wing, Bennett called the new embassy "inconsistent with the spirit of American institutions," but the main point of his editorial was to minimize objections from alarmists.[56]

Throughout the 1950s, Bennett and Niebuhr steadily guided *C&C* toward more tolerant, realistic, and self-critical positions. Gradually *C&C* abandoned the idea of a monolithic Catholic subculture and began to distinguish reactionaries like Spellman from possible *C&C* allies. As early as 1952, Niebuhr began to shift gears, directing attention to Catholic laity and pointing out that the main political struggles in the United States "would appear to be between Jews and Catholics who are left of the Center and Protestants who are right of it" because of their lamentable individualism.[57] Robert McAfee Brown's "Confessions of a Political Neophyte" speaks about his surprise at making common cause with Catholics and Jews against a candidate who, like Brown, was a Presbyterian. Niebuhr spoke well of the Catholic bishops' capacity, because of the top-down organizational structure of their church, to impose pro–civil rights priests on southern laity in places where Protestants would have simply fired the minister.[58] Bennett wrote about the range of Catholic views on McCarthyism, praising the liberal Catholic journals *Commonweal* and *America*.[59] He surveyed divisions within Catholicism and highlighted signs of internal change.[60]

To a large degree *C&C*'s willingness to make peace with Catholics hinged on Catholic teaching about religious freedom. *C&C* wanted Catholics to repudiate the official teachings that so worried Blanshard—the ones that declared it desirable to unite the government and church in a Catholic America. However, Catholic Archbishop Robert Lucey argued in *C&C* that the forms of church-state cooperation that Catholics actually had in mind were no different from what Protestants already did. He pointed to the role of the Anglican Church in British politics, as well as the many links between Protestant religion and public institutions in the United States. Lucey held onto the theory of a Catholic America only in case of a far-fetched scenario of an overwhelming majority of citizens converting to Catholicism. Until that happened, he claimed that his commitment to religious tolerance was at least as firm as the Protestants'.[61]

C&C duly noted these assurances but remained suspicious. Niebuhr introduced the archbishop's article as a document that revealed how "official Catholic doctrine stands in contradiction to our constitutional expressions of church and state."[62] *C&C* did not shift unambiguously to an open posture until it could welcome the growing influence of the position associated with John Courtney Murray, who argued that the traditional Catholic teaching on church and state was historically conditioned and now inappropriate; Catholics should endorse the separation of church and state as a positive good.[63]

By the late 1950s, as Murray's ideas gained momentum, *C&C* published a major series of articles by liberal Catholics, including Gustave Weigel and Daniel Callahan. Despite sniping from *C&C*'s old guard (including Van Dusen), *C&C*'s top leaders moved decisively toward an alliance with liberal Catholics.[64] It was cemented in the early 1960s during Vatican II, the famous Vatican Council during which the Catholic Church officially made peace with modernity by endorsing Murray's theories on religious freedom, shifting away from the Latin Mass, reconceiving the role of the laity, and so on. *C&C* followed the council's progress closely, taking the standpoint of its victorious liberal wing. *C&C* insider Robert McAfee Brown was among a select group of official Protestant observers at Vatican II.[65]

During John Kennedy's 1960 presidential campaign, prominent evangelical leaders including Billy Graham and Norman Vincent Peale formed a lobbying group called the Citizens' Committee for Religious Freedom to support Kennedy's opponent, Richard Nixon. They claimed that Kennedy would put his allegiance to the pope before the U.S. Constitution. By this time *C&C* was so unimpressed with such thinking that it attacked this so-called Peale group for its "blind prejudice" and ran an editorial criticizing Kennedy for his assurances of patriotism. It said that Kennedy *should* put his faith above loyalty to the Constitution—and so should any orthodox Protestant.[66] As the debate about Kennedy's religion heated up, *C&C* countered the evangelicals by publishing the first major Protestant statement that minimized religious concerns about his candidacy. Niebuhr refused to make this a joint statement of the whole editorial board, which would have increased its weight in places like the *New York Times*. This was not because he disagreed with it but because he favored Hubert Humphrey's candidacy over Kennedy's.[67]

Will Herberg, author of the book *Protestant Catholic Jew*, provided much of the infrastructure of *C&C*'s changing thought about Roman Catholicism.[68] In a 1953 *C&C* article, Herberg exhorted U.S. religions to stop fighting each other and make common cause against secularism and communism. "Blanshardism," he said, "constitute[s] a much more serious threat to our democracy than any of the horrendous Romanist plots that Paul Blanshard has been so fond of conjuring up."[69] In 1962, Herberg gave a sociological account of the changes, placing them firmly in the past tense. "There was a time," he argued, "when Protestants met Catholics nowhere in the important areas of community life: not in the civic organizations, nor in the service clubs, not in the medical societies, nor in the bar associations." Protestants formerly treated Catholics as hired laborers who were "marginal to the society"; there were few separate Protestant associations because "the ordinary community organizations were Protestant organizations." Over time, as Roman Catholics became part of the mainstream, an older generation of Protestants had become defensive, sometimes even "paranoid," about its loss of status. Fortunately, the current generation presupposed religious pluralism.[70]

By 1960, *C&C*'s anti-Catholic tradition had been largely abandoned, and most of what survived had been transmuted into polemics on behalf of *C&C*'s liberal Catholic allies against their conservative Catholic opponents. One article even proposed that Protestants should recognize the pope as their "spiritual leader."[71] *C&C* now correlated U.S. democracy, not with a Protestant America defined against the enemy of Catholicism, but with a triple alliance of liberal Protestants, Catholics, and Jews, defined against secularism, communism, and all the other enemies of pluralism, including the conservative wings of the three major faiths.[72]

Drawing together all three sections of this chapter, we have seen that *C&C*'s willingness to consider the standpoints of racial minorities, women, and Roman Catholics was limited during the decade after 1945. However, *C&C* was able to reevaluate its stance toward Catholics, as well as to advocate limited reforms on civil rights and women's ordination. In the following decade, *C&C* made changes on a range of issues that were equally striking as its 1950s shift on Catholicism. To this story I now turn.

4

Evolving Liberalism and Emerging Polarization

In light of *C&C*'s original crisis—its battle with religious pacifism—one of the most striking moments in its history was a brief editorial that appeared with no fanfare in 1958. It marked the twenty-fifth anniversary of the *Catholic Worker,* a pacifist journal founded by Dorothy Day. Bennett said that Day's group was "very small and far removed from most of our readers"; it "exists but there are few existing things that are more improbable."[1] Even more improbably, given *C&C*'s inherited suspicion of Catholics and pacifists, Bennett spoke warmly about the *Catholic Worker.* He even applauded Day for her civil disobedience against air raid drills, which at the time were major public spectacles that functioned as rituals of the cold war. (In these drills, everyday life stopped and people rehearsed what they would do if a nuclear attack had just been launched.) According to Bennett, Day's protest was "wrong on one level," since the government needed the drills. Yet, "on a deeper level, as human beings, [Day and her friends] were protesting against the madness and inhumanity of the whole nuclear race and that is good."[2]

From such tentative beginnings, *C&C*'s second thoughts about its inherited positions steadily increased. By 1966 they had ripened. In that year Bennett edited the preparatory documents for a WCC consultation on social ethics, in the context of rising third world criticism of "the responsible society." This was the WCC's shorthand term for the same basic vision shared by *C&C* during the cold war era: anticommunism, liberal democracy, capitalist development, and so on. Bennett wrote that the ideal of the responsible society reflected the needs of western democracies but "does not fit the context . . . of nations which must first go through a period of revolution in which socially transforming justice has priority." He compared his second thoughts about the responsible society to his rethinking of social gospel pacifism during the 1930s. In both cases, "the political choices may seem intolerable according to all the 'principles' learned in church in the past," but shifts were necessary in light of new situations.[3]

These two articles by Bennett make suggestive bookends for the decade from the mid-1950s to the mid-1960s, underlining *C&C*'s steady move toward bolder, more activist forms of liberalism. Since *C&C* moved in harmony with the rise of Kennedy-style liberalism, we would exaggerate if we described its general mood as critical of the dominant culture. Yet *C&C* moved distinctly to the left, gaining an unambiguous commitment to civil rights activism, a bolder advocacy of economic reform, a sharper critique of the arms race, and a greater willingness to approach third world issues outside a cold war framework, though still within the framework of pro-western development. *C&C* also explored innovations in theology and culture, giving attention to existentialist novels, contextual ethics, the sexual revolution, and death of God theology. As space increased for left-liberal positions in "respectable" mainstream discourse, *C&C* consistently moved into that space. On some issues *C&C* no doubt helped, in its modest way, to push out the boundaries of respectability.

These changes did not happen without resistance. Because *C&C* had always tried to side with underdogs against tyranny and to be self-critical, it naturally considered the views of blacks and third world colleagues as events forced these people into its field of vision. Moreover, as the McCarthyite idea of the United States as an underdog versus communism lost momentum in the larger culture, some *C&C* writers began to raise questions about the cold war mind-set, building on the Y hand resonances of peacemaking and anticolonialism in *C&C*'s tradition. However, every time one writer backed away from classic realist positions, another usually stepped forward in reaction, determined to pass on the cold war vision intact. From the late 1950s forward, *C&C* insiders frequently aired their disagreements about neocolonialism and the arms race, as well as the cultural issues discussed in chapter 5.

In retrospect we know that these trends would intensify: *C&C* would become increasingly frustrated with the status quo, advocate radical change, and identify with black militants and third world radicals who saw themselves as separate from liberal elites and opposed to them. Already by the mid-1960s, *C&C* was publishing editorials with such titles as "It Is Difficult to Be an American." It regretted that "there is no indication that anyone in political power really takes the Gospel very seriously" and called its readers to identify more strongly with the poor—even if this implied that churches could not "preserve undiminished" their "channel to the power structure of the nation through [their] influential members."[4] Such fault lines continued to deepen until consensus shattered.

C&C did not enjoy our advantages of hindsight as it entered the decade after 1955. Polarization remained in the future, and *C&C* saw itself as part of an ongoing New Deal coalition. Its main goal was not to critique the limits of liberal policies—although it tried to support the boldest currents in "respectable" policy debates—but rather to overcome resistance to its liberal vision from its perceived enemies: southern racists, backward nations, and others whose propensities to sin prevented an optimum response to poverty, injustice, and the specter of communism. *C&C* insiders maintained relative harmony, with their conservative and liberal wings receiving equal space and everyone trying to be decorous. *C&C*'s typical response to internal dissent was to publish a joint editorial with a range of comments spinning out divergent nuances, or, if this proved impossible, then a balanced symposium respectfully outlining disagreements. Most of its articles from "far right" to "far left" endorsed existing policies of U.S. elites. Thus, during *C&C*'s 1957 controversy about European versus Arab control of the Suez Canal, *C&C*'s most daring "pro-third world" position supported (on the surface) nothing more radical than President Eisenhower's foreign policy. *C&C*'s strongest "pro-peace" position in a 1961 debate about nuclear weapons repudiated pacifism and explicitly (albeit grudgingly) endorsed Kennedy's policies.[5]

On the whole, this was a period of confidence and growth for *C&C*—a time that its old-timers remember as a golden age. After a moment of crisis in the early 1950s when *C&C* nearly folded, its circulation quadrupled from 1954 to 1965 and its number of pages per issue doubled.[6] Bennett became Niebuhr's co-chair and *C&C*'s most important leader, while a steadily expanding editorial board shared the decision making from its base at Union Seminary. *C&C*'s changes represented an organic unfolding of earlier positions, with new tendrils of growth exploring in a left-liberal direction. Disagreements seemed manageable, and morale was high.

The High Tide of Civil Rights Activism

As we have seen, *C&C* entered the decade between 1955 and 1965 eager to advise government officials about the pragmatics of desegregation. However, black writers were extremely rare, and *C&C* assumed a clear distinction between us and them, with African Americans involved in civil rights organizations typically among the "them." A 1958 symposium called "The Southern Church and the Race Question" completely ignored black churches and focused on white Protestant clergy.[7]

By the early 1960s, the gap between *C&C* and the civil rights movement was greatly reduced. In fact, *C&C* had largely adopted the standpoint of the movement. The "us" language functioned less to keep "them" outside the picture than to search for the most helpful roles "we" (*C&C*'s white readers) could play in relation to "them"—and to imagine the issues, as far as possible, from "their" point of view. *C&C* board member John Maguire wrote "When Moderation Demands Taking Sides" to describe how he became a freedom rider, part of an interracial movement organized by the Congress for Racial Equality (CORE) to flout southern laws against integrated buses. Freedom riders often suffered harassment and violence from racist mobs, and their actions were profound learning experiences for *C&C*'s white liberals. In a superb memoir, John Raines later described his civil rights activities as his second education; he marveled at the ways that solidarity from black strangers had saved his life when he went south, and explained how this permanently transformed his life's priorities.[8]

The heart of *C&C*'s worldview in the early 1960s was a commitment to civil rights. *C&C* covered almost every civil rights issue that gained national attention, from celebrated southern campaigns such as Mississippi Freedom Summer to northern efforts against housing discrimination, as well as special concerns of Protestants such as the integration of church colleges.[9] Invariably *C&C* sympathized with civil rights activists. Unlike in earlier years when foreign policy was its top priority, between 1960 and 1965 one-third of its articles focused on race or domestic issues such as urban planning that had major racial implications, while less than one-quarter addressed international issues. Later in the decade, only Vietnam gained more attention.[10]

When Martin Luther King Jr. was arrested for civil disobedience in 1963, *C&C* published excerpts from his famous "Letter from Birmingham Jail." This was a fascinating moment in *C&C*'s history, since King's letter was a response to mainline clergy who attacked him using arguments that sounded like Niebuhr's mid-1950s *C&C* editorials—the type that cautioned against goals that were pragmatically too ambitious. By this time *C&C* preferred to forget this part of the past; in a 1961 special issue on race, Roger Shinn's lead editorial stated that a middle ground between the segregationist white citizens' councils and the NAACP was "always a hypocritical stance"—with no mention that *C&C* had sometimes promoted this stance.[11] It is instructive to observe how *C&C* edited King's letter. Although its introduction noted that King was responding to critics, *C&C* edited out most of King's reply to the charge of irresponsibility, including his famous comment (devastating for people like Niebuhr who liked to speak about the "majesty of the law") that Hitler had risen to power through the established legal channels. *C&C* tended to downplay the pacifist aspects of King's approach. Instead, it accented his rhetoric of cultural lag between a liberal norm and a backward South, where King's daughter was prohibited from going to "Funtown" and blacks moved at a "horse and buggy pace toward the gaining of a cup of coffee," while Asia moved "with jet-like speed toward the goal of political independence."[12]

The problem, in *C&C*'s view, was helping blacks speed their progress into the liberal mainstream. This underlying logic informed *C&C*'s whole approach to race. In the 1961 special issue, one writer argued that if African Americans could make a "brisk climb up the economic ladder" and pass literacy tests for voting, then voting rights legislation would lead to general empowerment. This was a common *C&C* position; in 1957 Niebuhr agreed with King's "irrefutable logic" that if blacks gained voting rights, "all other injustice would be eliminated in time" without violence.[13] An article on northern housing discrimination stressed that the problem was ensuring each family's equal right to buy what it could afford, rather than redistributing income. It was a mistake to "confuse problems of racial segregation with problems of socioeconomic segregation. Mixing neighborhoods by race does not mean mixing them by social class too. Persons of similar cultural and economic status have more in common regardless of race."[14]

C&C's advocacy of civil rights included a growing emphasis on telling concrete stories "from the bottom up," as opposed to analyzing elite policy options. For example, a seminary professor described how he was drawn into debates about police brutality when he was appointed to a civilian review board. While trying to be even-handed in respecting police points of view, he clearly sympathized with black complaints and provided *C&C* readers with several vivid examples of police violence. Stephen Rose filed a lengthy report from Birmingham during the week of the notorious terror bombings of black churches that killed four children. Writing from a standpoint within the moderate civil rights movement, Rose gave voice to a wide range of ordinary people, including some with quite militant views. He reported with disgust that on the morning of the terrorist attack, fifty feet from an area blockaded by a police line, worshipers at a white Presbyterian church said nothing about the murders. They merely had a moment of silence to pray for peace in Birmingham and a vacuous sermon about Mother's Day.[15]

As I will discuss below, in the mid-1960s *C&C* faced an identity crisis as race riots exploded in northern cities and many African American activists accented the shortcomings of the civil rights movement and white liberalism. Early in the 1960s *C&C* began to notice that frustration was building. It almost goes without saying that before this time *C&C* did not publish, and indeed barely seemed aware of, articulate black nationalist voices. By black nationalism I mean the broad tradition that accents a distinct cultural identity for people of African descent and the need for an autonomous base of power to press this community's interests. Often it is premised on historical memories of white untrustworthiness and doubts about the possibility of integrating into a truly race-blind society, as opposed to simply being co-opted and brainwashed by a white hegemonic norm. As James Cone argues, a paradigmatic integrationist such as the early Martin King would assume that America is a dream and that in time, with enough hard work, blacks will see the dream come true for them. In contrast, a paradigmatic nationalist like Malcolm X would respond that this dream itself is a form of false consciousness. That is, the ideology of equal opportunity and success through hard work obscures the reality of everyday experience, which is a nightmare—an ongoing structural problem of institutionalized racism at the heart of U.S. history, which can only be transformed, if at all, through building countervailing power from within the black community.[16]

The broad nationalist tradition is internally complex. It can take anti-Christian and separatist forms, as it did for Malcolm X and his colleagues in the Nation of Islam, or root itself in Christian churches. Its strategies can run the gamut from armed struggle to building a distinctive black power base through the same kinds of interest-group politics that were used by the Irish, Jews, and other ethnic groups. But for *C&C* the variations on these positions hardly mattered before the late 1960s. A 1958 editorial condemned Adam Clayton Powell Jr., pastor of Abyssinian Baptist Church in Harlem and longtime congressional representative, for what *C&C* called his "racist demagoguery" and "racism in reverse." His offense was a speech sponsored by the NAACP to mark the four-year anniversary of the Brown decision on school desegregation. Noting that this decision had still not been enforced in much of the nation, Powell had stated that this was "a white man's country of dedicated hypocrisy" that showed "organized and frequently legalized contempt of the law." For *C&C* this observation was "inflammatory." It was a "virtual incitement to violence."[17]

As for the Nation of Islam, in 1961 one of *C&C*'s boldest white leaders called the doctrine of "Muhammed X" [*sic*] "hair-raising" because it was an "exact counterpoint to the White Supremacy lie."[18] He also stated that James Baldwin's relatively sympathetic presentation of the Nation of Islam in *The Fire Next Time* was "the most gripping evidence yet of how dangerously close to the brink of serious paranoia so many Negroes stand."[19]

One of *C&C*'s major steps toward engaging with black nationalist critiques, as well as exploring the limits of liberal integrationism, was a 1964 controversy about James Baldwin's play, *Blues for Mister Charlie*. The play was based loosely on the case of Emmett Till, a young black who was murdered by white vigilantes in Mississippi, and it addressed the psychosexual dimensions of North American racism, a topic largely taboo for liberals at *C&C* who stressed that the races were the same under the skin and could integrate harmoniously through educational and legal changes. Baldwin portrayed a breakdown of moderation as the father of the Till character (a Protestant minister) picked up a gun and a white liberal character was forced to choose sides. *C&C's* Tom Driver said the play had caused an uproar for a good reason: it broke with more reassuring plays such as Lorainne Hansberry's *A Raisin in the Sun,* which taught northern whites that they had nothing to fear from blacks. In contrast, Baldwin taught that "there is plenty to fear" because blacks were not as whites wanted them to be, racism was not limited to the South, and technocratic reform would not be enough. According to Driver, the "sober citizens of the North . . . will have to learn that some (we don't know how much) violence is unavoidable. . . . Violence itself is far from the worst of evils, even in a peaceable democracy. The repression of violence by a force that perpetuates injustice is worse."[20]

This was by no means a consensus position for *C&C*. Bennett granted that Baldwin's diagnosis of deep racial conflict might be all too realistic. (He pointed out that if whites wished to condemn racial violence, then white violence against blacks was the biggest problem, not vice-versa.) Still, Bennett stressed that it was wrong and self-defeating to let "predictions of violence shade into a defense of strategies of violence."[21] Charles Lawrence expanded on the issues at stake; he accused Baldwin of racist stereotyping and insisted that black attitudes "resemble those of whites of similar occupations, income and educational attainment, except where questions of racial discrimination are concerned."

Tom Driver responded that this was a large exception. It was true, Driver conceded, that "if we abstract the Negro and the white from their cultural and historical communities, I suppose the only differences left . . . are not significant. But people do not exist abstracted like that." Lawrence disagreed: he insisted that blacks wanted to be included as consumerists in a color-blind society, that Baldwin confused the mythology of black sexual prowess with violence in unhealthy ways, and that nonviolent strategies remained valid. Driver replied that *Blues for Mr. Charlie* had not asked liberals to take up arms. It simply asked them to avoid compromise with racism, and this included facing up to the complexity and gravity of the problem: "Sooner or later one has to choose sides."[22]

Since this exchange appeared at the height of *C&C's* enthusiasm for civil rights, some readers may have considered it a side issue. For the moment, *C&C's* typical way to acknowledge the black militancy was to suggest heading it off with more ambitious civil rights activism. Thus

C&C's leading expert on race, Robert Spike, spoke of a "Muslim threat" that made King look moderate; he hoped it would make anti-integrationists wake up.[23] *C&C* became a strong promoter of the NCC's new Commission on Religion and Race. This commission, masterfully described in Findlay's *Church People in the Struggle,* was directed by Spike and enthusiastically backed by NCC head Eugene Carson Blake, who was an important *C&C* writer. Among other projects, the commission launched an ambitious campaign to mobilize support for the Civil Rights Act of 1964 and Voting Rights Act of 1965. This campaign was especially effective in midwestern states that had many Protestant voters and congressional fence-sitters.[24] *C&C* was deeply invested in the project. For example, during a conservative filibuster against the 1964 bill, *C&C* ran an editorial refuting the conservative arguments, point by point, and offering detailed advice about lobbying Congress.[25]

At this moment, *C&C* was fully integrated into the infrastructure of the civil rights movement. Unlike in his 1950s editorials, Niebuhr showed strong sympathy for nonviolent activists and spent little effort putting on brakes; a typical use of *C&C*'s gradualist reasoning by 1963 was a rationale for compromise between stronger and weaker versions of the civil rights bill. Niebuhr said that white supremacists were "increasingly desperate." He even dared to hope that he was seeing the "ultimate, or at least penultimate, chapter in the long history of overcoming the American dilemma."[26]

Christianity and Camelot: The Politics of Domestic Liberal Reform

As the 1960 election approached, *C&C* was looking for a change. Sarcastically, Robert McAfee Brown joked that the only biblical warrant for conservative civil religion was "This . . . nation . . . under . . . God" (Esther 9:17; Isaiah 1:4; Genesis 1:7; and 2 Kings 1:2) and that the warrant for Christian capitalism was an obscure parable of Jesus that concludes, "Make friends for yourself by means of unrighteous mammon."[27] *C&C* clearly despised the Republican candidate, Richard Nixon. This feeling was longstanding. One of the least convincing attempts at impartial bipartisanship that *C&C* ever published ran in 1952, purporting to criticize the "political self-righteousness" of both major parties, but devoting most of its attention to a visceral attack on Nixon for red-baiting and accepting illegal corporate contributions. Bennett's editorial on Nixon's 1960 presidential nomination also stretched bipartisan decorum to the breaking point. He regretted that Nixon, rather than Nelson Rockefeller, was the Republican candidate, and he reviewed Nixon's career with obvious distaste. He gamely tried to present both strengths and weaknesses, but commented that "anyone who tries to be fair to Nixon and who has the past in view labors under serious difficulties."[28]

In a revealing 1959 editorial, political scientist Kenneth Thompson dropped his usual voice—the objective geostrategic pundit—and delivered an impassioned jeremiad on the decline of U.S. culture. The decade of the 1940s had "some of our finest hours," judged Thompson, but the 1950s had been "bereft of great ideas." The people were to blame because "the popular mood asked this much and no more," and the leaders pandered to their sloth. A famous scandal of a rigged TV quiz show was an apt symbol of the corruption. Thompson called citizens to recover a sense of purpose.[29]

At the end of Thompson's article, one could almost hear him intone John F. Kennedy's famous words, "Ask not what your country can do for you, but what you can do for your country." And indeed, at this time *C&C* became very excited by Kennedy's blend of technocratic liberalism and cold war machismo. True, *C&C* insiders privately discussed—although tactfully did not mention in print—their concerns about Kennedy's "moral character," that is, his sexual promiscuity.[30] Largely for this reason, Niebuhr supported Hubert Humphrey's candidacy. Still, *C&C* was elated when Kennedy won the election. Although *C&C* had always followed Washington politics, such coverage exploded during the Kennedy and Johnson presidencies, with *C&C* often publishing articles with such titles as "One Year of the New Frontier" and "President Kennedy and the 87th Congress: A Preview."[31]

The background assumptions informing *C&C*'s approach were nicely stated in Adlai Stevenson's 1960 article, "The Survival of the Free Society," which was later chosen to conclude a "best of *C&C*" retrospective. Stevenson, who had been the Democratic presidential nominee in 1956, wrote that a recent steel strike was the "end of an era" because "the public interest" could not tolerate similar future disruptions in a climate of cold war competition. The U.S. needed to work harder to remain ahead of the Soviets, in light of their new Sputnik satellite and the powerful missile (adaptable for bombs) which had launched it. Stevenson advocated mandatory federal mediation to prevent future strikes and force collective bargaining. He attacked "irresponsible private power" and called for higher government spending on "defense, economic aid, education, and basic research." In his introduction, Bennett tried his best to put a peaceful spin on this proposal, stressing that Stevenson's "emphasis is a positive one not tied primarily to defense."[32]

C&C had never given up on mildly class-conscious New Deal economics, and as the pressures of McCarthyism receded, *C&C* began to speak up for such policies more often.[33] Discussing a proposed labor law in 1959, it reminded readers that "labor was the one [power bloc] whose real interests were closest to the public interest," especially when labor was led by people like Walter Ruether of the United Auto Workers.[34] However, *C&C* stayed fairly aloof from the labor movement, explaining that racketeers such as Jimmy Hoffa of the Teamsters Union showed the need for stronger laws to "check the power of unions" and "provide for sufficient safeguards against self-seeking human nature." It described the Newspaper and Mail Deliverers' Union, which forced a strike in 1959, as a "Frankenstein monster . . . peopled by assorted thugs, racketeers, and experts at the shakedown."[35]

C&C typically offered pragmatic support to existing liberal initiatives while calling for bolder experiments. It cast a wide net: advocating national health insurance, hyping Edward Murrow's documentary on hunger called *Harvest of Shame,* discussing a "Crisis in the International Monetary System," and expounding on "The Moral Meaning of Transportation" (a call for improved public transportation).[36] Overlapping with this coverage, *C&C* also carried on a thriving discourse about "the City" and the prospects for its renewal.[37] Stephen Rose proposed liquidating 90 percent of the budgets of church bureaucrats and using the savings to consolidate local congregations into interdenominational grassroots ministries. He envisioned ministries with less "chaplaincy" functions and more of a focus on social action and community building. In response to criticism, Rose denied that his proposal was radical—it was a moderate middle ground between a stagnant status quo and the trend of youth abandoning churches altogether.[38]

In 1964 *C&C* dropped all pretense of political neutrality, officially endorsed Lyndon Johnson for president, and charged his Republican opponent, Barry Goldwater, with "an immoral nationalism, an immoral nuclear recklessness, an immoral racism, . . . an immoral economic individualism," and a general extremism that placed him outside the bounds of national religious consensus.[39] This was only one of many widely publicized statements with unusually strong passion—one editorial even speculated that the Goldwater right might embrace paramilitary tactics after its defeat.[40] Of course, we now know that the trajectory of the right was quite different. Ronald Reagan rose to power (starting with the California governorship in 1966) not through a extremist coup d'état but rather through a feel-good style of conservatism, winning the hearts and minds of a big part of the religious mainstream. But during the 1960s, *C&C* could not seriously consider that U.S. culture had right-wing capitalists like Reagan at its center, within what Michael Rogin calls a dominant countersubversive tradition. With rare exceptions, *C&C* was bullish on the type of "vital center" associated with Arthur Schlesinger Jr. and Richard Hofstadter, which was quick to dismiss people like Reagan as self-marginalizing extremists who came into view only during occasional crises, as external threats to a healthy liberal mainstream.[41]

One partial exception to this rule was an article by Niebuhr that presented Republicans as examples of a dominant culture based on individualism. Another piece by Rose cautioned liberals to be less contemptuous of Goldwater; they would be better off trying to understand the frustrations of sincere people tempted by him and proposing better solutions.[42] In retrospect, it is easy to see that if *C&C* had placed more stress on these trains of thought, accenting aspects of the right that represented widely shared aspects of the dominant culture, the right would have appeared no less dangerous, compared with paramilitary schemers. However, the right would have been harder to dismiss—as well as easier to refute when it presented itself as a group of outsiders, out of sync with U.S. dominant culture.

C&C's attack on Goldwater had repercussions. Least troublesome, but interesting, was a letter from Goldwater in which he complained that *C&C* had "aligned me with the anti-Christ for purely political reasons." Goldwater concluded piously (or blasphemously), "Forgive them, Father; they know not what they do." It was easy for *C&C* to shrug off this sort of objection—in fact, too easy, because Goldwater also posed a good question: exactly where was the evidence of the national religious consensus that *C&C* had claimed to represent?[43] Harder for *C&C* to dismiss was an attack from Paul Ramsey, a prominent member of the guild of Protestant ethicists, who argued that God was above political partisanship.[44] Most alarmingly, the federal government revoked *C&C*'s tax-exempt status over the incident—an ironic development since *C&C*'s endorsement of Johnson was certainly not its most important political commitment during these years. The tax ruling was eventually overturned with the understanding that *C&C* would make no more direct endorsements in editorials, although it could express political opinions in articles.[45] Thus the stage was set for one of the most bizarre episodes in *C&C*'s history. A sympathetic article on the Catonsville protest of radical priest Daniel Berrigan, during which he burned draft records with homemade napalm to protest the Vietnam War, was printed right next to an article from *C&C*'s 1968 presidential forum, which boosted Ronald Reagan for president! One wonders whether a single *C&C* reader took this endorsement seriously, yet *C&C*'s forum was scrupulously balanced.[46]

This spectrum of opinion from Reagan to Berrigan serves as a useful reminder that *C&C* was not always unified behind the Democratic Party's standard-bearer. By 1965 *C&C* was raising pointed questions about the corporate bias in Great Society programs and their failure to redistribute wealth and power to low-income communities. One article argued that the Job Corps created no new jobs and failed to redistribute income. At best it subsidized employers through a redundant vocational education system; at worst it was nothing but an "aging vat" to train people for jobs that would never exist. Wouldn't it be simpler, *C&C*'s writers asked sarcastically, to "give the money directly to the private employer, eliminating all the bureaucratic overhead?"[47] Linked to such skepticism was *C&C*'s rising interest in community organization, which overlapped with its writing on black power. *C&C* moved naturally from lobbying for top-down reforms to supporting the bottom-up demands of such groups as the National Welfare Rights Organization (NWRO), which organized welfare recipients to demand improved benefits. *C&C* reported NWRO figures that a family of four required $4,500 a year to stay out of poverty, but New York paid only $3,400 and Mississippi $408. It endorsed a NWRO campaign to disrupt New York welfare agencies, a strategy which led the state to increase services substantially.[48]

Despite scattered radical explorations, *C&C*'s dominant voice remained bullish about the prospects for Great Society liberalism through the mid-1960s. As late as 1969, one writer remained optimistic enough to claim that even though Brooklyn had its problems, "If one saw this borough . . . as a social system whose input is one-half million raw human stuff every ten years and whose output is one-half million who now fit the dimension of being suburban, he would have to say that the most dramatic things happening today are transpiring in these great urban places. He who does not see this as a good is standing in the middle of history, and it is passing him by."[49] Residents of some Brooklyn neighborhoods may have agreed that a trend of upward mobility was passing them by—but not necessarily in the sense intended by this article. In later years, their voices were destined to have greater weight in *C&C*'s pages.

Second Thoughts about Developmentalism

Most of *C&C*'s writing on international development remained within established patterns in this period. Much of it remained paternalistic, as when Niebuhr bemoaned the tragic "Congo problem" caused when "the Belgians set untutored tribesmen adrift" or when Lefever said that "the net impact of European colonialism in every area has been good."[50] And most of *C&C*'s arguments were familiar, aside from their application to new situations. Consider the blend of anticommunist and pro-development arguments in a 1960 article by Kenneth Thompson about the Cuban revolution. In the past, said Thompson, U.S. elites had claimed an exclusive sphere of interest in the Western Hemisphere because we "could not afford to allow imperialism in Latin America to go unanswered." Although gunboat diplomacy had been morally ambiguous, it had "expressed the realities of the American position." Now, in the face of Castro's success, "we" (North and South American elites) faced both a military threat, if Cuba made an alliance with the Soviets, and an economic threat if the Cubans successfully rebelled against "alleged American injustices." In the latter case, "the symbolic effect elsewhere would be far-reaching and tragic." There was a pressing need for development aid, since "Latin America can no longer be taken for granted."[51]

Not all of *C&C*'s positions were mere extensions of past trends. In the decade after 1955, *C&C* theorized about international development in more explicit and complex ways, and there were variations among the *kinds* of development that *C&C* recommended. Some *C&C* writers—more from *C&C*'s periphery in the world ecumenical movement than *C&C*'s inner circle—began to publish more radical critiques that would blossom in the late 1960s.

One of *C&C*'s most revealing articles on this subject was by Vassar professor Elisha Greifer. He began by observing that radical ideas were gaining influence in many third world nations that faced intense poverty and injustice. He asked, "How, then, are we to think about the revolutionary temper which is so distasteful to our own?" According to Greifer, "any college student" could "refute Marxist ideas." Citing Louis Hartz's influential interpretation of U.S. history, *The Liberal Tradition in America,* Greifer argued that the United States had never provided conditions in which radicalism could become attractive. All Americans were basically liberal individualists. Slavery was the one "grand exception" to this rule. However, Greifer argued that this exception "ought to be explained away." He attempted to do so using Stanley Elkins's *Slavery,* a book which argued that African culture had been totally destroyed in the American South and replaced by a "Sambo" personality. According to Greifer, contemporary African Africans had either been absorbed into the mainstream and had become liberals like everyone else, or else they were so marginal that they were "not part of the society at all."[52]

Shifting gears from a theory of U.S. exceptionalism to the vision of universal progress that so often accompanied it, Greifer went on to suggest that Hartz's liberals could interpret the strange revolutionary temper through Walt Whitman Rostow's *Stages of Economic Growth.* All nations modernized through economic stages similar to the rise of corporate capitalism in Britain and North America, but unscrupulous radicals could exploit social turmoil and nostalgia during a "danger point" caused by the transition from traditional backwardness to modernity. Following political scientist Seymour Martin Lipset, Greifer suggested that modernizing leaders should maintain resources for social stability by pursuing a responsible evolutionary road, rather than overturning traditional patterns too quickly. The question was how to apply these insights in particular. For example, should Castro be overthrown? [53]

Armed with these theories, *C&C* had the resources to support authoritarian allies of U.S. elites against revolutionary movements like Castro's, on the grounds that at least modernizing authoritarians, while distasteful and not to be supported complacently, might be lesser evils who could keep developing nations on track toward a possible democratic future. Reading such *C&C* arguments, it was sometimes easy to forget that they presupposed a universal "track"—in bad communist and good democratic variations—that every society was on. Greifer clearly stated that "sooner or later all 'traditional' agrarian economies develop." They passed through Rostow's four stages—preconditions for take-off, take-off, drive to maturity, and high mass consumption—and northern investment (both government aid and private speculation) could jump-start their take-offs and move them more quickly toward maturity.[54] But Greifer's clarity was atypical. *C&C*'s implicit progressivism was often masked by a barrage of overtly antiprogressive arguments that stressed the limits of U.S. power to promote its political ideals throughout the world. Such arguments extended *C&C*'s familiar argument that democracy was not viable in some parts of the third world and that it was a fantasy—at best sentimental and at worst dangerous—to try to impose it on a universal pattern. Thus *C&C* could understand its support for modernizing elites in the third world, not as an example of imperialism and liberal idealism, but as an alternative to them. (Later, in the Reagan era, conservatives would justify U.S. support for authoritarian leaders such as Philippine dictator Ferdinand Marcos with a retooled version of this same theory, sometimes invoking Niebuhr's authority.)[55]

C&C's search for optimum government techniques to manage a process of modernization could be—and in this period usually was—turned against revolutionaries such as Castro, either for moving too quickly or for starting down the wrong (pro-communist) road to industrial development. But the same logic of managing development could also be turned around and deployed against U.S. policies, especially if *C&C* inquired about the practical limits of U.S. power. Thus even as Greifer aimed his big intellectual guns at Castro, he also asked whether Castro's successors would be more legitimate if the United States overthrew Castro. Perhaps if democracy was not viable in Cuba, Castro could be the best lesser evil. And even though Niebuhr said that some third world dictators "may be bastards but are at least our bastards," echoing Franklin D. Roosevelt's oft-quoted comment about the notorious Dominican dictator Rafael Trujillo, *C&C* did not necessarily agree with the government's application of this logic.[56] At some point "our bastards" could be seen, not as wisely restraining others who were too impatient for change, but as themselves moving too slowly or ineptly. U.S. policy of propping them up could be criticized for its own universalist pretensions, rather than lauded for restraining the universalist idealism of their enemies.

Where did this crossover point fall? In the Dominican and Cuban cases *C&C* waffled, showing somewhat greater sympathy for the left than U.S. policymakers, but doing so more in the spirit of friendly advice than sharp opposition to their positions. Bennett caught the dominant flavor when he called Fidel Castro a "distasteful nuisance" but not an "intolerable danger."[57]

The leading edge of *C&C*'s leftward exploration was its dialogue with Christians from Asia, Africa, Europe, and Latin America organized in the international ecumenical movement. The WCC began the period with ideas similar to Greifer's.[58] But through its network, *C&C* learned about the gap between lived experience and the rhetoric of democratic responsibility in the former colonies. Many emerging WCC leaders understood that such thinking, although sometimes helpful, could be used to justify the repression of popular movements and to justify economic policies with mixed practical results for the majority of people. Ecumenical conferences and publications introduced *C&C* to perspectives unavailable in the mainstream press, creating a productive cognitive dissonance when missionaries and trusted international colleagues began to talk like "communists." The following exchange illustrates dynamics that were played out in various ways.

A religion professor from Wake Forest University, McLeod Bryan, toured Africa. Upon his return, he wrote that Africa's "supreme test" was whether "African nationalism can keep open the frontiers that the outside forces of colonialism and Christianity cut through the jungle of closed, suspicious tribal communities." Could Africa's "toddling democracies" achieve a nationalism that was "restrained and internally corrected by a transcendent Christian value system?" Or would radical pan-African leaders such as Ghana's Kwame Nkrumah produce a "selfish black nationalism that destroys itself" in indiscriminate "anti-white hatred" and tribal warfare? Bryan was sad to report that many Africans were guilty of "making of independence an absolute final good." They appealed to Christian universalism to support pan-Africanism, replaying the errors of the social gospel, even to the extreme of using Methodist missionary hymns about "the golden age" [i.e., the millennium] as political campaign slogans. Luckily, some African Christians understood that "realistic democracy can impose the necessary restraints" on one-party political systems. Bryan was thrilled to report that in Nigeria he read "a line upon line, precept upon precept argument that some Nigerian had studied under Reinhold Niebuhr!" At least a few Africans had learned that "absolute satisfaction of political ideals" and "absolute equality" were not practical possibilities.[59]

In reply, an anonymous African asked, "Do Mr. Bryan and Niebuhr's students the world over really believe that one needs to be a Christian and opposed to the so-called Social Gospel in order to realize that . . . absolute satisfaction of political ideals is an impossibility? Since I do not know what he means by absolute equality I cannot say whether it is a practical possibility. . . . [However,] any pagan with any amount of experience in interpersonal and inter-group living, let alone a politician, should be able to realize that life is a series of compromises." The letter then inquired whether the Wake Forest faculty practiced what Bryan preached about racism. If so, they too "would soon be labeled as followers of the Social Gospel school of theology, and thereby lose the respectability that comes with maintaining the sane and realistic balance between sanity and madness. African nationalists cannot afford to stand aside and make wise judgments on both sides of the struggle."[60]

At the opposite extreme on *C&C*'s spectrum from Lefever's apology for colonialism was 'Bola Ige, a Nigerian lawyer known to *C&C* through the Student Christian Federation. Ige published one of *C&C*'s most militant early statements on Africa (or any other subject). He spoke from a pan-African socialist stance hostile to the black bourgeoisie and argued that the anticolonialist struggle should be "waged by us Africans alone" because economic development aid would reproduce paternalism and dependency.[61] By the mid-1960s, some of *C&C*'s core writers were moving toward this position. This was in the background when Bennett edited the preparatory documents for the 1966 WCC conference mentioned at the beginning of this chapter, the one in which he defended 1960s third world revolutionaries on an analogy with *C&C*'s 1930s rebellion against the *Century*.

C&C's report on this conference was written by Wayne Cowan, who was rising through *C&C*'s ranks from secretary in 1954 to editor after 1968. He underlined the confrontation between third world voices and North Americans, leaving the impression that he had expected to side with delegates from the South but had been surprised by the vehemence of their critique. According to Cowan, many U.S. delegates were offended by the radical rhetoric, and others came home changed. One thought that Americans were "almost masochistic in responding to the criticism with silence." But Indian intellectual M. M. Thomas (a *C&C* contributing editor) said the silence was typical: "They think we're second-class citizens; they don't even reply to our criticisms."[62]

More typical than such sharp confrontations around 1960 was the argument of Paul Devanandan, a scholar from India who taught at Union Seminary as Luce Visiting Professor. Devanandan inquired whether accepting western aid would subvert his country's national political independence, "economic self-sufficiency," and cultural cohesion. He answered that western values could go hand in hand with overcoming the caste system and that development aid could advance "cultural and social objectives" including national economic planning for socialism.[63] By this time, articles like Devanandan's, which drew clear distinctions between various uses of development aid from informed third world standpoints, represented *C&C*'s developmentalist thinking at its most nuanced. Such writing increasingly supplanted more racist variations allied to U.S. government standpoints such as Lefever's. Radicals such as Ige who doubted whether there was a realistic pro-western, social democratic "third force" for the former colonies remained a minority, although one that was gaining momentum.

The Suez Crisis and the Turn from East-West to North-South Thinking

When *C&C* began to approach economic development from third world standpoints, this was not necessarily incompatible with a cold war mind-set; recall *C&C*'s long tradition of promoting development as the most viable alternative to communism. Still, the change did have some tendency to call a cold war mind-set into question. *C&C* gradually came to analyze Asian, African, and Latin American issues more on their own terms and less through an approach that has been compared to wearing "East-West glasses" with "2-D lenses"—glasses that let their wearer "see U.S. vital interests and a Soviet menace anywhere" but unfortunately also make the wearer "lose some of the detail."[64] Although East-West considerations remained important, *C&C* began to consider them just one factor alongside local issues such as land reform and national self-determination. These latter issues often seemed more important within a North-South paradigm that focused on overcoming the legacies of colonialism, including alliances between local elites and neocolonial powers such as the United States.

C&C's first major controversy between writers who maintained an East-West paradigm and those who were turning to a North-South paradigm was the Suez Crisis of 1956. Bennett later recalled this as a turning point in *C&C*'s history.[65] In the crisis, Egyptian leader Gamal Abdel Nasser seized the Suez Canal in the name of pan-Arab nationalism. A British-French-Israeli military force then invaded Egypt to reclaim the canal. The

United States, forced to choose between angering one important ally or another, sided with the Arabs and condemned the invasion. In this context *C&C's* editors spoke of their "surprising disagreements."[66] Unable to reach consensus, they published a position paper by Thompson with several critiques. This ignited a controversy that lasted several months, with no clear winner except a meticulous search for balance.

For Thompson, the crisis represented the decline of the western alliance just at the moment when it desperately needed unity against the Soviets, who intervened in Hungary at the same time. He complained of a "legalistic-moralistic" approach in which "peace, anti-colonialism, and the UN [were] invested with absolute ethical value." This was a "comfortable substitute for discriminate moral and political judgments," said Thompson. It formed "the new creed of a crusading, conservative political and religious movement." While such moralists talked abstractly about colonialism, European weakness in the Middle East "has created a vacuum into which Soviet influence has flowed"—a real world result far worse than colonialism. "Historians may record that with [U.S. Suez policy] we lost the 'Cold War' and paved the way to a third world war."[67] Niebuhr seconded Thompson, decrying "fatuous idealism" and stating that, although he generally opposed colonialism, he could not do so when Egypt "develops imperialistic ambitions of its own, seeks to dominate the Islamic world and gets its hand on the life-line of European economy." UN condemnations of the European intervention were irrelevant, judged Niebuhr, because "the UN without a strong Anglo-American core of power becomes a rudderless ship."[68]

At *C&C's* anticolonialist pole, a reader from India attacked the realists' "occidental centrism."[69] Bennett charged that Thompson "sees the present crisis too exclusively in the context of the 'Cold War.'" Shrugging off the charge of abstract moralism and conservatism, Bennett proposed to talk about a specific "attack on Egypt as a reversion to the worst kind of colonialism." He pointed out that Thompson refused to "see the problem even a little from the point of view of Egypt and the other Arab nations." Perhaps Thompson was the *really* unrealistic theorist blinded by his presuppositions. Would U.S. support for the British and French actually advance U.S. power interests? Would it not backfire, even as an anticommunist tactic, by alienating most of the world? Could it actually defend oil pipelines? Shouldn't Eisenhower be commended for respecting "the emerging Afro-Asian bloc which is, to be sure, dominated by undiscriminating anti-colonial resentments but represents half of the world's people and has become a third force with which we and the Communists must reckon"?[70] Accused of ignoring a threat to vital interests, Bennett replied that if there were such interests, it was doubtful that the United States could defend them without Arab cooperation. "This kind of proposal shows the danger of thinking of Arabs as though they were like the American Indians and could be managed or pushed around by us."[71]

Since Israel participated in the Suez Crisis by invading the Sinai Peninsula, *C&C*'s debate blended with its long-standing dispute about Zionism. From its earliest days, *C&C* insiders had agreed to disagree about the Israel-Palestine conflict. Niebuhr was the leading pro-Israeli voice, reinforced by his personal friendships with Jewish intellectuals in the United States. Until his death in 1954, Henry Sloane Coffin was *C&C*'s leading anti-Zionist, reinforced by his abiding Progressive assumptions about U.S. Jews and his personal friendships with missionaries who had concrete relationships with Arab Christians.

Some of *C&C*'s arguments supporting Palestinian rights lost credibility because they were mixed, especially in *C&C*'s early years, with Anglo-Protestant condescension and hostility toward domestic Jews. In 1949 Coffin had lamented that Jews were bringing justifiable oppression upon themselves by retreating from the logic of universal humanity assumed by "thoughtful" Jews. In other words, they were turning toward Zionism from the anti-Zionist liberalism that had been embraced by many Jews (including the mainstream of Reform Judaism) before the 1930s but by relatively few thereafter.[72] According to Coffin, "benighted" and "partially Americanized" Jews were falling prey to "fanatical Jewish nationalism." They would gain "the suspicion of being hyphenates" and set back the good cause of defeating anti-Semitism.[73]

In a move highly unusual for *C&C* at the time, Niebuhr printed a barrage of letters to the editor that attempted to instruct Coffin on the arrogance of his position and the ways that times had changed.[74] Not only did Niebuhr repudiate the idea that Jews were "ready to be melted down in our famed melting pot." He was so far removed from Coffin's attitude that he called on Christians to "remove Jews from the scope of Christian missionary activity." He explicitly denied that Christian revelation was superior to Judaism; indeed, he seemed to prefer Judaism to orthodox Christianity when he spoke of the Nicene Creed as a "Hellenistic corruption of Hebraic faith" and the Gospel of John as "frankly anti-Semitic."[75]

In any case, Zionists remained suspicious that Protestants who overtly shared Coffin's defense of Palestinian rights covertly shared his domestic attitudes toward Jews. These suspicions would later explode, but during the Suez Crisis they were muted, and *C&C*'s disagreement about Israel was running within long-established channels that remained similar from the creation of Israel in 1948 to the Six-Day War of 1967.

C&C was divided between unambiguous Zionism and a compromise position sympathetic to Palestinian rights. *C&C* Zionists accented Jewish suffering, treated Palestinians as external threats to Israel, and defended the dispossession of Palestinians in various ways: as the just spoils of a war initiated by Arabs, as an unavoidable tragedy, and as an opportunity for Arabs to learn the skills of technological development from Israel's advanced civilization. In 1949 one writer described moral questions about the Jewish takeover of Palestinian farms and homes as an "obviously hostile" position mainly interested in "punishing Jews." He painted a rosy picture of democratic guarantees and social harmony within Israel. Unfortunately, in the context of war (which he blamed on Arabs rather than the Israeli takeover) Palestinians were a fifth column. Israel was "most charitable" in letting a few refugees return; however, it was in the Palestinians' "best interests" to move to Iraq.[76]

C&C's pro-Palestinians were far more willing to grant the justice of Israeli claims than *C&C* Zionists were to grant Palestinian claims. For them, Israel's existence and its boundaries after the 1947–49 war were givens that should not be renegotiated. However, they accented Palestinian suffering, disapproved of Israeli expansion, raised questions about U.S. aid to Israel, and called for the return of Palestinian property inside Israel. A missionary in Egypt presented one of *C&C*'s strongest pro-Arab arguments. He said there were good reasons for the "deeply ingrained [Arab] suspicion of all forms of Western imperialism" and serious concerns about religious freedom and minority rights within Israel, as well as Israel's long-term goals for expansion. There was a need for a "complete change of attitude on the part of the Jews toward the Arabs."[77]

YMCA executive Eugene Barnett revealed the key to *C&C*'s uneasy truce when he segued from telling concrete stories about Palestinian suffering to discussing policy alternatives in a geostrategic voice. Barnett explained that large-scale Palestinian resettlement within Israel was not realistic; he called for western development aid for resettlement elsewhere in the Arab world. Despite the impasse over who would control Palestine, Barnett hoped that "statesmanship and creative human engineering could forge a new and more inclusive unity in that part of the world, bent on the united conquest of backwardness and all its woes."[78]

Such visions of progress became *C&C*'s standard formula: support for the state of Israel coupled with increased western developmental aid for Arabs, to be used to resettle most Palestinians elsewhere.[79] Whereas Barnett's spin on this argument underlined Palestinian grievances and asked for Israeli compromises, other spins tilted toward Israel. One writer agreed that all sides should "work together to rid the Middle East of its feudal character and foster the growth of democratic institutions," but complained that Barnett was unfair to Jews, since Israel was a "pilot light in the darkness of the backward, depressed Arab world."[80] Neither of these spins seemed concerned that U.S. support for Israel was concrete and tangible, but the benefits to Palestinians from development aid and Israel's pilot light were at best uneven and largely hypothetical.

The Suez Crisis revived this simmering disagreement because Israel took part in the invasion and the conflict pitted pro-western forces against Arab nationalism. Bennett described the Suez Canal and the Israeli state as twin symbols of colonialism, while Thompson saw Israel (as a pro-western democracy) battling Nasser (as Soviet proxy). Both sides were relieved when the UN brokered Israel's withdrawal from the Sinai Peninsula. Both saw increased development aid as the way forward.

These controversies about the Middle East were important for *C&C*'s long-term transformation because they showed that not all conflicts translate well into cold war morality plays or developmentalist jeremiads. One of *C&C*'s best articles on the Middle East between 1948 and 1956 made a virtue out of its inability to forge one coherent and objective narrative, calling the Middle East a kaleidoscope of experiences that only partly fit western assumptions.[81] Even Niebuhr and Thompson, who were almost never at a loss for words, seemed unsure how to respond when the United States sent troops into Lebanon in 1958. Niebuhr pontificated in various directions at the same time: If U.S. intervention was correct now, this proved that inaction had been a mistake during the Suez Crisis. On the other hand, the current policy of sending troops to Lebanon was a disaster. Niebuhr was glad to see Eisenhower doing something in the face of a Munich analogy with Nasser playing Hitler—but he was unsure what good U.S. policy would do, since it was an act of desperation that squandered U.S. moral prestige and there was not really any communist threat in Lebanon. Thompson was better informed, more confident, and pleased to report that the United States had learned from the Suez Crisis that "the status quo is vital to the West." Still, as he analyzed the complex issues at play in Lebanon, his overall cold war argument, like Niebuhr's, approached paralysis. He concluded vaguely that "neither a policy of massive intervention nor one of non-intervention is feasible."[82]

Such testing of cold war paradigms in light of specific conflicts was not limited to the Middle East. On the contrary, it was generalized. Herbert Butterfield wrote forceful articles moving toward a new outlook. In contrast to Thompson, he called for a "radical revision" of U.S. and British approaches. Both nations had been "tripped into being on the wrong side of . . . the primary issue in international affairs" and had been "put in retreat by the problem of resentful people who are under some form of subjection."[83] Defending the status quo was morally indefensible and unrealistic—indeed, it would benefit the Soviets. Butterfield explicitly denied that analogies with the Munich Crisis and the cold war were appropriate for understanding the Suez Crisis, the Algerian revolution, and the crisis in Lebanon. Rather than "merely seek to hold the fort, to dam the flood," said Butterfield, the West should put its weight behind alternatives to the neocolonial status quo that were equally committed as Communists to the material improvement of popular majorities and more committed to democratic freedom.[84] For the moment, *C&C* largely channeled such hopes into support for programs like Kennedy's Alliance for Progress. Still, Butterfield's challenge to the cold war paradigm was clear.

Rethinking the Ethics of Nuclear War

According to a Bennett article in 1959, there was a "Great Conflict of Opinion" about the cold war in *C&C*'s circles. One side was suspicious of the Soviets and refused to negotiate with them because they felt this implied moral parity. The opposing side supported peaceful coexistence, the superpower summits of the late 1950s, and reductions in cold war tensions.[85] More and more, *C&C* began to tilt toward the conciliatory side of this debate, which was associated with Senator William Fulbright in national politics. Many articles explored the prospects for cooling the arms race in the wake of changes in the Soviet Union after Stalin's death. Early in 1958 Bennett proposed what he called a trial balloon: to adopt a live-and-let-live attitude toward communism. Perhaps the United States could coexist with "irreversible" communist systems in Russia and China, while remaining opposed to their expansion and hoping that their systems would mellow. Bennett supported the movement against nuclear testing and chaired a National Council of Churches (NCC) committee that supported U.S. diplomatic recognition of Communist China, provoking an intense debate with the evangelical magazine *Christianity Today.*[86]

By now it should come as no surprise that *C&C* hawks tried to shoot down the doves' trial balloon; they remained suspicious of communism in all its works and all its ways. Both hawks and doves claimed that their opponents were ideologues and they were objective moderates. Whereas the doves saw themselves as cautious mediators between unreconstructed *C&C* cold warriors and overenthusiastic pacifists, the hawks positioned themselves midway between right-wingers and *C&C* doves who had already taken their idealism to dangerous extremes. After Stalin's death in 1953 and Nikita Khrushchev's famous 1956 speech denouncing his crimes, Niebuhr weighed in on the side of the hawks. He argued that de-Stalinization did not make communism any more palatable but merely more dangerous. It was evidence of the "superior tactical skills of the new Soviet overlords."[87] Another editorial asked, "Is There a New Russia since Stalin?" and its short answer was no! De-Stalinization was an illusion, since the party remained in command. Some factions wanted real reform, others did not, and because the Soviet Union was a closed society it was like "parapsychology" to investigate, but the reforms were probably a "warmish day on the brink of a Russian winter."[88] When a superpower summit was derailed after U-2 spy planes were shot down over Russia, Kenneth Thompson gloated in an editorial that basically said, "I told you so": Eisenhower had bungled in numerous ways that he could have avoided by listening to Thompson's advice all along. Especially foolish was the idea that people could work for peace on the basis of mutual interest, rather than engaging in constant struggle to balance power against power.[89]

Niebuhr made shifting and often ambiguous attempts to synthesize themes from both poles of the Great Controversy. After the Soviets launched the Sputnik satellite in 1957 with their new intercontinental missiles, Niebuhr warmly reviewed a book by Henry Kissinger (later Richard Nixon's national security adviser), who argued that the strategic calculus had changed. It was time to reject the Republicans' all-or-nothing strategy of massive nuclear retaliation, in favor of building up conventional forces to fight "limited wars." Around 1960 Niebuhr's editorials on the cold war presented Kennedy's "posture of firmness and calmness" as exemplary. "The obvious fact of our destiny" was a need for patient and restrained, yet firm and resolute, struggle over many years.[90] Although Niebuhr's concessions to doves were limited, they were clear. He began to put more stress on his long-standing argument for nuclear restraint; since there was a "nuclear stalemate," the two superpowers needed to "establish some minimal community of coexistence." He began to speak of "phenomenal changes [in the Soviet Union] which may increase the power and prestige of the adversary but which also offer new hope for relaxing the Cold War."[91]

Until the early 1960s none of these explorations—even those that were most optimistic about peace—seriously questioned *C&C*'s basic argument about deterrence. Ever since the 1930s Niebuhr had argued that realism required using countervailing power against tyranny, whether capitalist, Nazi, or communist. Bennett had argued that nuclear pacifism would "play into the hands of any nations that are unscrupulous enough to use the threat of atomic attacks as blackmail" and judged that "Christians . . . cannot put their communities in the position of being forced to yield to overwhelming power if there is any way of avoiding this."[92]

In 1961 Bennett wrote a major *C&C* article questioning whether this logic justified nuclear threats against communists. He emphasized changes within the Soviet Union and divisions among various communist governments. In addition, he denied that nuclear war could ever be considered a lesser evil, given the destruction it would unleash. On these grounds he rejected the first use of nuclear weapons and questioned whether nuclear retaliation, the central idea of deterrence, could ever be justified. The immediate context for this argument was a U.S.-Soviet confrontation that led to the building of the Berlin Wall. How could a nuclear holocaust possibly be a lesser evil than negotiating a compromise over Berlin?[93] Bennett was cautious in policy recommendations, praising "the combination of firmness and flexibility emphasized by President Kennedy." But his rhetoric pushed further: he called for a shift in emphasis "from the fear of being destroyed to the awareness of the moral meaning of being destroyers." Rather than assuming a defensive posture against a faceless communism, he asked, "When will we cease threatening the use of ultimate violence every time there is a crisis involving Russia?"[94]

In a symposium by *C&C*'s inner circle, Niebuhr and famed political scientist Hans Morgenthau backed Bennett's proposal. Tillich also gave qualified support, saying that "atomic armament is justified" but disapproving first use and stressing that war would "annihilate what it is supposed to defend."[95] Paul Ramsey offered "support" that was probably less appreciated, since he disavowed nuclear retaliation but waxed enthusiastic about other kinds of military power: "Better Red than to perform the deed that obliterates people wholesale, even in retaliation against their government. Better Dead than to yield to nuclear blackmail and cease to be a nation with its just purposes armed with limited and just weapons intended to be used for military and political objectives."[96]

C&C's conservative wing attacked full force. Kenneth Thompson decried a "revival of past illusions" and said it was "sophism" to claim that nuclear war was "morally more offensive than killing one man."[97] Carl Mayer of the New School for Social Research bitterly lamented that Christian realism had come to an end, with *C&C* regressing to the level of the prewar *Century*. If *C&C*'s editors were truly realistic, said Mayer, they should be smart enough to know that the United States would use nuclear weapons whether Christian ethicists liked it or not. Moreover, these weapons could be used for good. The "utopian illusions" of *C&C*'s emerging positions were in no way helpful. In fact, by undermining deterrence they made nuclear war more likely.[98]

In response to these attacks, Niebuhr backpedaled. He said that Mayer was right to stress "peace by grace of the balance of terror," although Niebuhr still thought there was room for disagreement on the value of working for peace.[99] Bennett hedged his position in a similar way during a bizarre exchange of views, which started when *C&C* heard that Kennedy had hesitated on moral grounds before bringing the earth to the brink of a nuclear holocaust during the Cuban Missile Crisis. *C&C* found this "very reassuring" because it supposedly revealed Kennedy's moderation and responsibility. Subsequently, Zbigniew Brzezinski (who later became national security adviser to Jimmy Carter) criticized Kennedy's alleged scruples, and attacked the press for talking about them, on the grounds that war in Berlin had become more likely, now that more people suspected that Kennedy had been bluffing. Bennett responded that Brzezinski had posed "a real dilemma."[100]

Bennett did not back down, however, in his confrontation with Thompson and Mayer, which was the main event in *C&C*'s internal controversy. He denied their accusation of perfectionist legalism, and he spoke of the judgment of God on all positions, including Mayer's. Bennett denied that Christian realism could support any and all forms of amoral power politics. The heart of the issue was whether there were limits to the evils that could be baptized in the name of realism. Bennett insisted that nuclear war went beyond any such limits.[101]

This controversy ended inconclusively, with Niebuhr sitting on the fence and the other protagonists maintaining an uneasy coalition because they all supported Kennedy. But in the process, the contours of *C&C*'s debate had shifted markedly toward peace making. Roger Shinn, a *C&C* moderate, spoke for most of the board when he wrote about "Changing Tides of History" that undermined inherited cold war reasoning. By 1964 Bennett could speak of "Cold War slogans long since out of date."[102]

Drawing this chapter to a close, let us recall *C&C*'s editorial about Dorothy Day and her civil disobedience against air raid drills, which Bennett described as "wrong on one level" yet "on a deeper level . . . good." I believe that this reveals a great deal about Bennett's writing between 1955 and 1965, which was in the forefront of *C&C*'s process of rethinking the cold war. By extension, it illumines wider meanings of *C&C*'s omnipresent "X but on the other hand Y" rhetoric during these years. More than any other *C&C* insider, Bennett was fair-minded in presenting multiple sides of contested issues, but this goal was not unique to him. On the contrary, it was part of the general mind-set of cold war realism. It reflected *C&C*'s assumptions that its cultural standpoint could approach neutrality and that all human options are fallen, so that all sides had mixed motives. It also had affinities with the Niebuhrian fondness for talking about everything under the rubric of paradox, from indecisiveness and muddled thinking to insoluble political conundrums and profound spiritual mysteries.

In later years this "X but also Y" rhetoric came to appear to *C&C*'s left wing as excessively cautious, because it balanced and qualified every statement in ways that appeared repressed and lacking in commitment. A later generation judged that realist rhetoric tended to act as a brake on constructive change, because realists continually brought up counterarguments and second-guessed the motives of activists. In some ways, this is a fitting criticism of *C&C*'s dominant voice between 1955 and 1965. After all, Bennett was not the only one who used this rhetoric; so did the most conservative voices in the debates I have described. Moreover, Bennett was not himself at the *Catholic Worker* protest; he called it "far removed from most of our readers" and "wrong on one level." However, in this case where Dorothy Day was on the Y hand, Bennett was obviously tempted to join her in overt opposition to status quo military policies. Whatever we say in retrospect about his inhibitions, it is worth noting the costs of being arrested for peace in 1958 compared with the late 1960s, when Bennett actually did participate in illegal antiwar protests. Simply by defending Day, Bennett risked a limited but real loss of prestige in his professional circles, as well as attacks from McCarthyites who remained powerful throughout the 1950s. By repressing his own voice and insisting that all sides be heard, Bennett reduced the risk and created space on the Y hand for voices that might not otherwise have been heard in *C&C* at all. From this point of view, *C&C*'s objective voice and the "X but Y" balancing functioned less like a brake or distancing mechanism, and more like a wedge to open a door nearly shut by hegemonic forces. Indeed, the door remained open a crack because realists had kept a toehold outside it—on the Y foot—as the forces symbolized by McCarthy attempted to close it.

The days when *C&C* became an unambiguous ally of Day (and other activists such as Baldwin) remained in the future. No doubt, many people at *C&C* read the *Catholic Worker* editorial in light of *C&C*'s standard qualifier—we can humor the pacifists as long as they concede their irrelevance to the real world. Still, Bennett and his allies leaned on their wedge in their cautious and steady way.

5

Sex, Movies, and the Death of God: Changing Approaches to Culture and Theology

Starting with its inherited Christian realist paradigm and working from within it, *C&C* shifted between the mid-1950s and mid-1960s toward more contextual approaches to theology, ethics, and culture. This shift toward contextualism was broadly correlated with *C&C*'s leftward explorations and its greater attention to nonwhite perspectives. It also correlated, in a more complicated and qualified way, with greater openness to analyzing gender and sexuality. Thus a rough operational definition of "the context" in *C&C*'s contextual theology and "the situation" in its situation ethics was *C&C*'s turn to bolder liberalism, greater pluralism, and more talk about sex.

It is crucial not to oversimplify this correlation. Contextualism is a big tent, covering many approaches. It makes a difference, for example, whether one writes contextual theology from the context of North American female Protestant solidarity workers in postrevolutionary Nicaragua or from the context of "modern man." Similarly, one can adopt the basic approach of situation ethics—de-emphasizing abstract rules of behavior and accenting a search for behaviors appropriate to particular situations—and come up with a wide range of conclusions. Under the rubric of contextual ethics, *C&C* discussed everything from the suggestion that *Playboy* magazine had matured and was "now a literary-type magazine," to a debate about *Blues for Mr. Charlie*, which asked whether a violent insurrection could be justified in the context of inner-city racism, to the claim that one should enact love (*agape*) in every situation and that "on a vast scale of 'agapeic calculus' President Truman made his decision about the A-bombs on Hiroshima."[1] Clearly *C&C* did not always conceptualize contexts from the standpoint of underdogs in power hierarchies! Nor did *C&C* writers who sympathized with the underdogs necessarily turn toward contextualist methods to argue their points; sometimes they simply used radicalized versions of the same old realist methods.

It is important to note that *C&C*'s writing about the arts and theology was more haphazard and sporadic than its writing on politics. Its political discourse was not only more sustained. It also represented for *C&C*'s largely clerical constituency one of the more sophisticated discussions of the issues that they knew. In contrast, *C&C*'s contribution to specialized theological debates and cultural analysis was more like the tip of an iceberg, presupposing a broader literature.[2] The point is not that *C&C*'s constituents were more knowledgeable about politics than they were about theology—on the contrary, they were more likely to read and publish in specialized theological journals than to read widely in the social sciences. The point, rather, is that the submerged part of this iceberg concealed multiple complexities which *C&C* writers presupposed but did not always address directly in *C&C*'s pages.

Bearing in mind these complexities, it remains possible to document a general trend. *C&C* made a contextual shift on theological and cultural issues that was broadly correlated with its leftward political shift. Over the entire period discussed in the next few chapters, from the mid-1950s until the mid-1970s, *C&C*'s contextual theology became increasingly linked to pluralistic understandings of context, to radical analyses of structural conflicts, and to levels of experience such as gender, embodiment, and local community. Its operational definitions of context shifted from issues like modernity to issues like the church in Nicaragua. This chapter treats the first part of this period, the mid-1950s to the mid-1960s. In these years *C&C* usually articulated context from middle-class male perspectives, presupposing technocratic optimism and accenting relationships between liberal individuals and a generalized secularity. *C&C*'s discussions unfolded in three overlapping patterns: the analysis of novels and film, debates about method in Christian ethics (especially its application to sexuality), and a trend toward secular and pluralistic approaches to theology. Viewed in a longer perspective, these explorations formed a halfway house between *C&C*'s classic realist positions and its later full-blooded liberation theologies.

From Zion to Bohemia: Religion, Literature, and the Arts

Beginning in the mid-1950s, peaking in the late 1950s, and continuing sporadically in the 1960s, *C&C* greatly increased its attention to the arts and culture.[3] A 1956 editorial note announced *C&C*'s "plan to scan a wider horizon" and give attention "to other areas of life in which the 'crisis' was manifest." By this crisis *C&C* understood an ongoing divine judgment on human culture, and it argued that the arts offered promising ways to articulate this judgment. Largely to signal this shifting focus, *C&C* introduced a new layout and logo with a lighter feel and allegedly more sophisticated art. Citing Paul Tillich, *C&C* editor Amos Wilder called for a bridge between "Zion and Bohemia" and encouraged readers to "move out into a general cultural encounter" involving not just high art but also the mass media, all the way down to the comic strip. They should appreciate art with "integrity, reality, [and] wholeness of vision"—wherever it could be found—and avoid shallowness, sentimentality, escapism, and sensational violence.[4]

To interpret the relationship between this cultural turn and the long-term shifts in *C&C*'s standpoints, it is useful to recall the Tillich article that I cited in the introduction—the one in which he reaffirmed his confidence in the "basic conceptions of religious socialism" but saw a vacuum of hope for putting these concepts into practice, which could "be made creative only if it is accepted and endured and . . . transformed into a deepening 'sacred void' of waiting."[5] When people like Tillich faced the collapse of their Progressive hopes, they could move in at least two directions. One was *C&C*'s dominant strategy: keeping overt political activism alive in a chastened key and revitalizing aspects of the Progressive mind-set to support international development and the cold war. However, another response became attractive to *C&C* in the mid-1950s, when *C&C* was most demoralized by McCarthyism. This was to accent a void of overt political hopes but keep an oppositional sensibility alive in the realms of imagination and individual moral decision. This path led toward existentialism and a concern with literature.[6] *C&C* insiders who followed this path—notably Robert McAfee Brown, Harvey Cox, and Tom Driver—also tended to be *C&C*'s pioneers in contextual ethics and its leading partisans of cultural pluralism. This suggests that *C&C*'s cultural turn of the 1950s could function to carry forward a prophetic tradition of political hopes and cultural criticism that began before this period and continued after it.

This argument remains somewhat speculative—an interpretive hypothesis rather than a conclusive thesis—because *C&C*'s coverage of the arts was too sporadic to carry a heavy interpretive weight and because not every literary text addressed by *C&C* can be understood as oppositional.[7] Many parts of the postwar literary scene that interested *C&C* were politically complacent and uncritical of consumer culture. Moreover, even if we zero in on writings that best support the idea of keeping a counter-hegemonic imagination alive within a void of more practical hopes, and leave the rest aside, we still cannot assume that either *C&C* or the artists it discussed were self-consciously trying to produce texts that functioned as tactical moves toward a radical politicized goal. In fact, *C&C*'s key motive for turning toward culture, given the hypothesis I am proposing, was precisely the difficulty of producing believable accounts of any such overt goal—these were precisely the types of visions that realists saw tainted by idealism and prone to slide into totalitarianism. In other words, I am speaking about latent meanings and long-term functions that *C&C*'s writers and original readers may not have perceived.

Despite these caveats, the idea of opposition driven underground or diverted to a cultural terrain works as an analytical tool to interpret a good deal of *C&C*'s turn toward culture in the 1950s and 1960s. Consider, for example, the seething hostility to capitalism in Arthur Miller's play *The Death of a Salesman,* the commentary on race relations in Ralph Ellison's novel *Invisible Man,* or the cultural criticism of Beat poets like Jack Kerouac.[8] On this reading, *C&C*'s interest in literature allowed its writers to explore cultural criticism—however circumscribed or ambiguous in its opposition—that would be ruled out of bounds by the criterion of short-term pragmatic realism.

For *C&C,* the classic locus of this discussion was the existentialist novelist Albert Camus. Robert McAfee Brown described Camus as an exemplary critic because he was committed to authentic ethical action and he kept Christians honest by attacking "cheap" forms of uncritical hope, much as Niebuhr had done. Others praised Camus for his honest look at human mortality, his stress on the duty of relieving suffering, and his corrective to realists who tended to "overlook the evil and the summons to witness that lie near at hand" because they were too much oriented to ruthless calculations about future goals.[9]

This discussion was set within *C&C*'s larger approach to literature, well summarized by critic Nathan Scott of the University of Chicago. He began by claiming that the "literary intelligence is recognized as having dealt more creatively with the human problem in our period than either the philosophical intelligence or the social scientific intelligence." Novels were a "kind of modern scripture," said Scott. The best authors such as Camus, Franz Kafka, and William Faulkner "strike us as having lived nearest the center of modern experience," especially because of the way they articulate "dread, despondency, anguish, and alienation."[10] Christians could approach them sympathetically through the theology of God's incarnation in human life.

However, continued Scott, a Christian critic could not rest at this stage of analysis, because much modern literature lacked "a deep restoration of confidence in the stoutness and reliability and essential healthiness of the things of the earth." Although Scott cautioned against criticism that was merely "judicial and rejective," he insisted that theology must do more than simply give "adulatory enshrinement" to great literature. It must enter into dialogue with it, bringing a positive Christian contribution. For example, *C&C* judged that Faulkner did a fine job of expressing the theme of incarnation into a sinful world, but he needed a more positive vision of grace. *C&C* described *JB,* a Broadway version of the book of Job, as shallow and lacking in transcendent grounds for hope.[11]

For related reasons, a simmering dispute between Niebuhr and Tillich boiled over when Tillich said in a television interview that Pablo Picasso's painting *Guernica* was the most "Protestant of modern works of art." Niebuhr complained that Tillich's comment about Picasso was preposterous, no better than a segment of an NCC television show called *Look Up and Live,* which had billed itself as "theology of dance" but in practice merely featured a ballerina dancing *Swan Lake,* with a narrator who described ballet as a tradition that had been handed down from generation to generation, just like Christianity. Niebuhr insisted that Christians must do more than echo social critiques by secular artists; they should propose a cure for the "tragedy of contemporary history." If Tillich's comment was the best that theologians could say about art, Niebuhr judged, then "we had better keep silent." In a lucid and icy response, Tillich agreed that Picasso did not exhibit a complete Christian theology—the TV producer had edited his comment about *Guernica.* But what was the point of stifling what was helpful in Picasso or in other artists who could better meet Niebuhr's objections? Keeping silent, Tillich retorted, was exactly the wrong response.[12]

Arts and literature were important to *C&C,* not only for promoting ethical action and reinforcing theological themes, but for opening up windows to concrete experience that were closed in *C&C*'s abstract theology and geostrategic punditry. During the 1950s, Mary Ann Lundy, later a top ecumenical bureaucrat and *C&C* board member, was one of Union Seminary's few female students. She recalls Union's literature courses, especially by Brown, as one of the few academic spaces where everyday life could be discussed. In the absence of self-consciously feminist arguments (such as those she embraced after the 1963 publication of Betty Friedan's *Feminine Mystique*), she gravitated toward these courses.[13]

If art was one of *C&C*'s main windows on concrete experience, what was in view outside this window? We know from Nathan Scott that it involved dread and despondency, but in what forms and from whose standpoint? Occasionally *C&C* touched on overtly countercultural and non-elite standpoints. For example, Robert Spike wrote about the Beats with qualified sympathy, speaking of "real affinities between this American type existentialism and the Christian faith."[14] *C&C* paid little attention to be-bop or rock and roll (the leading art forms rooted in the multiracial urban working class), but the contexts in which these styles came up were interesting. In a piece promoting inner-city ministries, Kilmer Myers spoke of the need to understand the "be-bop lifestyle." He said that street priests should "go native in all things save in faith and morals." George Todd of East Harlem Protestant Parish, an urban ministry related to Union Seminary, insisted that "the Body of Christ, his church, must know, accept, and share in the life of young people who drink . . . , have out-of-wedlock sex experience, dance the 'fish' and the 'grind,' carry guns and knives, are truant or have quit school, and who do not hold jobs."[15] Both articles were by white liberals rooted outside inner-city neighborhoods, but Myers told concrete stories from the street that gave his article more of a bottom-up perspective than most *C&C* fare, and Todd clearly questioned the class-bound decorum of white Protestant culture.

More typically, *C&C*'s writers were highbrow. They argued, for example, that Shakespeare presupposed a societywide concept of moral order which the United States could use as a model, that clergy should read Robert Spiller's *Literary History of the United States* (a leading postwar authority on the U.S. literary canon), that Abraham Lincoln's moral vision was "keen[er] than anyone since the inspired writers of the Bible," and that the trends in Protestant church music had been going steadily downhill since Bach.[16] In a 1959 eulogy, *C&C*'s writing about John Foster Dulles moved beyond politics into the realm of cultural capital. It described how Dulles had broken his mother's heart when he decided not to enter the clergy, but later fulfilled her wish by becoming a "Minister of State—a Minister of Christ in his sacred calling." Dulles confirmed the wisdom of Plato when he said that "statesmen should be philosophers."[17] The 1966 "best of *C&C*" collection included two film reviews, but only of highbrow Italian films like *La Dolce Vita* and *The Gospel According to St. Matthew.*[18]

Along with highbrow tastes came condescension toward popular culture. I have already mentioned how *C&C* used TV quiz shows as a metaphor for a decade without greatness. *C&C* was also appalled by the philistinism of NCC leaders who, one writer charged, alienated all true artists by sponsoring religious broadcaster Norman Vincent Peale. Worse yet, they refused to condemn the artistic styles used on the covers of Protestant church bulletins.[19] Frequently *C&C* reviewers heaped contempt on Hollywood, although there were exceptions such as a glowing review of Stanley Kubrick's satirical antiwar film, *Dr. Strangelove.* More typically,

C&C called Cecil DeMille's biblical epic *The Ten Commandments* a "spectacle lacking either religious or dramatic significance"—a "monstrosity" based on culture-religion.[20]

Even hip urban ministers like George Todd were not suggesting that the children of *C&C* readers should dance the fish and the grind; in fact, his article can easily be read as defining *C&C*'s culture in contrast to the inner city. When another inner-city minister wrote a poem about a God who "hangs out on street corners . . . smells . . . is pregnant without husband . . . is a bum . . . whose name is spick, black nigger," *C&C* drew the line. Brown agreed that all people were formed in God's image and that God was incarnate in the city—but even so, equating God and the city was idolatry.[21]

If the arts helped *C&C* to think more concretely about experience in general, they played a special role in breaking *C&C*'s silence about one particular aspect of experience: sexuality. During this period *C&C*'s masculine rhetoric continued unabated. It published almost nothing that explicitly advocated gender equality except one lonely editorial on equal pay for comparable work, in which associate editor Frances Smith forcefully criticized the finding that women only earned sixty-one cents for every dollar earned by men.[22] However, there was a thriving debate about the representation of sex in novels and the mass media.

In "*Playboy*'s Doctrine of Male"—reprinted in *Redbook* and dozens of other places—Harvey Cox agreed with *Playboy* that moralism about sex and the rejection of all sexual representation was inappropriate and counterproductive. But Cox argued that *Playboy* was "basically anti-sexual" because it kept women at arm's length as objectified images for consumption. *Playboy* "departmentalized" sex and presupposed "a repressed fear of involvement with women." Cox celebrated the "mysterium tremendum of the sexual" and called it "the basic form of all human relationship." *Playboy* had a "deep-set fear of sex" in this authentic form, which involved risk and self-exposure rather than objectification and control. Alluding to a famous slogan associated with Tillich, Cox claimed that *Playboy* represented a "lack of 'the courage to be.'"[23]

In light of later debates in *C&C* about goddess spirituality, it is fascinating to learn that Cox also identified a "re-emergence of pre-Christian fertility cults" in the contemporary United States. He found them in an unlikely cultural archetype that he called "The Girl," symbolized by Miss America. Like the Virgin Mary, The Girl had many manifestations. But whereas Cox respected some of Mary's virtues and her famous biblical speeches attacking the rich, he saw The Girl as "a kind of anti-Madonna" and in the end as an idol, even though she "functions in many ways as a goddess." Cox argued that Protestant hostility to Marian devotions and biblical attacks on fertility cults were both well founded. In a phrase that was picked up in a half-page *Time* magazine report on his piece, he lamented that Protestants only railed against Mariology, while failing to notice the "vampire-like cult of The Girl."[24]

Cox did not focus on women's agency in struggles for change, and he presupposed a root self-image in which a male prophet of a male God attacked sins associated with the body. Nevertheless, for *C&C* such articles were a step toward problematizing, rather than presupposing, received gender relations. This, along with their relatively open and nonpunitive stance toward sexuality, provoked a counterattack from *C&C* conservatives like Robert Fitch and Paul Ramsey. Fitch wrote that he was no Puritan "bluenose"—but "a Protestantism that has lost the sectarian impulse to stand in judgment on the civilization of the day has lost its Protestantism." He excoriated the idea of using appeals to sincerity and honesty to provide a "halo" for "any dish of obscenity served up on the stage, any collection of trash spread out in a novel." Consider how he summarized the themes of the film *Cat on a Hot Tin Roof*: "Man is a beast . . . the only honest man is the unabashed egotist . . . [and] the human comedy is an outrageous medley of lechery, alcoholism, homosexuality, blasphemy, greed, brutality, hatred, and obscenity."[25] Echoing the same complaint more concisely, another writer said that the theme of the film *Baby Doll* was that "hav[ing] sex, preferably adulterous, is the means of grace and the hope of salvation, and if you don't get it you are damned!"[26]

Tom Driver replied, speaking for *C&C*'s emergent cultural cutting edge, that if Fitch and his allies wanted to criticize the modern world, novels and films could do this using realism and irony just as well as Fitch could do it through moralizing. In any case Driver pointed out that Fitch endorsed classic literature full of sex and violence such as Shakespeare's *Romeo and Juliet*.[27]

Situation Ethics and Sexual Mores

C&C's debate about the media in general, and media representations of sex in particular, became entwined with more abstract debates among academic ethicists about the proper weights of general rules as opposed to analyses of specific situations. Rule-based approaches roughly correlated with Niebuhrian rhetorics that stressed a need for transcendent judgments to restrain sin and selfishness. Contextual approaches tended to have somewhat more confidence in human wisdom and capacity for virtue.

Fitch and Ramsey were *C&C's* most vehement anticontextualists not just when attacking *Cat on a Hot Tin Roof* but across a range of issues. Fitch lumped together Darwin's evolutionary theory, Einstein's relativity theory, contextual ethicists, and cultural anthropologists like Ruth Benedict who confused people by showing "diverse and contradictory patterns of culture." *All* assisted what he called "a creeper-crawler approach of relativism in ethics." Contextualists trusted people to make wise judgments about what was good in the absence of fixed ethical principles. But Fitch asked, "Would you [trust] Big Daddy in the *Hot Cat?*"[28]

Although the dispute between contextual and rule-based ethics defined *C&C's* central axis of ethical debate at this time, this way of drawing the lines conceals important inner complexities that we must take a moment to unpack.[29] Consider the diverse array of theological colleagues whom Fitch placed in a broad contextualist camp, accusing them of betraying principles to justify immoral permissiveness. They included theological liberals who appealed to the "sacredness of personality" so much that they were silent about principles to restrain evil, Lutherans who spoke so much about grace and forgiveness that they forgot about law, sophisticates like Niebuhr and Tillich who undermined the principles of bourgeois culture, and Barthians who spoke so much about God transcending every particular human culture that they "obliterat[ed] all principle before the holiness of God."[30] Within this motley group, analysts from the most theologically liberal to the most neoorthodox—if they were left-liberal in politics and attentive to contexts—could find common ground against more conservative colleagues with a similarly diverse range of theological methods.

Similarly, there were strange bedfellows on the other side of the divide between contextual and rule-based methods in ethics. Cultural conservatives like Fitch and Ramsey called for ethical principles. But so did Bennett, their opponent on most political issues, who advocated "middle axioms" to mediate between overly abstract principles on one hand and attempts to make decisions in concrete situations without any moral guidelines on the other. So did the NCC's Eugene Carson Blake, an energetic activist who took his stand on the "ecumenical consensus" of prophetic Christianity and saw situation ethics as indistinguishable from "secularistic relativism."[31]

Further complicating this debate, almost all *C&C* writers rejected the most famous contextual argument, Joseph Fletcher's *Situation Ethics,* which set up one and only one transcendent principle of love (*agape*) and proposed that moral agents decide on a case-by-case basis how best to enact it in particular contexts. This was the book I mentioned earlier, which proposed that the United States had debated whether to drop a nuclear bomb, using "a vast scale of 'agapeic calculus.'" Shinn dismissed Fletcher's book as nothing but "utilitarian hedonistic calculus," and a *C&C* writer trivialized a famous book called *Honest to God* (which agreed with Fletcher on ethics) by calling for a sequel called *Who in Hell?*[32] However, Shinn took pains to distinguish Fletcher from Paul Lehmann, a more liberal Union Seminary theologian, who in practice was almost as contextual as Fletcher but in a more grandiose Barthian vein: for Lehmann the task of ethics was to discern in each new situation "what God is doing in the world to make and to keep human life human."[33]

One question, more than any other, made sense of *C&C*'s actual disagreements, uniting contextualists like Lehmann and rule-based ethicists like Bennett against their more conservative opponents like the rule-based Fitch and contextualists who were apolitical. Which ethical methods, in the hands of which ethicists, were responding positively to *C&C*'s explorations toward new experiences and standpoints, and which proposed to judge and reject these trends? This question remained helpful, whether the innovators introduced new standpoints directly, presupposed them as part of their operational understanding of "what God is doing to make life more human," or approached them under the heading of a middle axiom such as organizing the disempowered for social justice. However, since various kinds of contextualists were the loudest voices among the new approaches, sometimes the term *contextualism* became a shorthand label for this whole group. Thus we circle back to the central battle line between contextualism and rule-based approaches.

C&C board member Alexander Miller stepped forward to refute Fitch's claim that all contextualists were on a slippery slope toward moral anarchy. He argued that Reformation theology rejected all forms of natural law—including Bennett's middle axiom approach, which "lack[ed] theoretical cogency," although it did provide a working basis for action. All products of human reason, including human ethical systems, were corrupted by sin and relativized by God's transcendence, said Miller. He cited *C&C* board member Joseph Sittler, who suggested an ethics modeled on Jesus' teaching, which moved by "occasional lightning flashes and gull-like swoops into concrete situations." The problem with Fitch, said Miller, was that he wanted to "cage the gull." Miller argued that ethical guidelines were social products rather than ahistorical metaphysical principles. Therefore, his central ethical question was "what community generates our basic commitments" and defines "basic loyalties." Miller refused to seek a "content" of ethics, although he observed that patterns of action (understood as habits rather than laws) often emerged. Rather than systematizing content, Miller suggested "pragmatic calculation of the maximum human good." Ethicists should approach decisions with a combination of "faith and facts," trusting people to choose the good through their "innate impulse of justice and compassion."[34]

For Fitch and Ramsey, it was ridiculous to think that gull-like swoops were an adequate basis for ethics—and, as already noted, they harbored doubts about Big Daddy's innate impulses. They pressed Miller to admit that his appeal to justice and compassion was already a principle—however vague and fuzzy—and to clarify what he meant when he spoke of basic loyalties.[35] Since these criticisms had a good deal of force, Miller's best defense was a good offense—he challenged Fitch and Ramsey to suggest a "'law' that is not another yoke of bondage." He stood ready to deconstruct it with his Reformation theology and the complexity of relevant facts.[36]

The sexual revolution provided a good deal of the subtext in these abstract debates about situations and contexts. In 1963 *C&C* analyzed a document by British Quakers which argued that decisions about engaging in sex should be judged, not by the presence or lack of wedding vows, but by whether the sexual acts would "express and encourage the responsible behavior of the whole person" or, on the negative side, "whether they involve exploitation." On these grounds the Quakers defended premarital sex, homosexuality, and "triangular heterosexual relations" in some contexts, placing the moral agency in the hands of the people involved. Driver's review, "On Taking Sex Seriously" (later selected for the twenty-fifth anniversary "best of *C&C*" collection) is a good example of *C&C*'s contextualism as a halfway house between Niebuhrian realism and feminism. Driver seemed torn between the logic of celebrating embodied sexuality and the logic of judging sinful license; he compromised by arguing that Christians should "put sex in its place" not by directly refuting the Quaker argument and making overt moral condemnations but by refusing to take sex too seriously—by laughing at it. Driver used a dualistic logic of spiritual transcendence versus sex as an impersonal force. He said it was a mistake to integrate sexuality with a higher spiritual side of human personality. As he put it, "Sex is not essentially human, it is not inseparable from the human in us." However, in its place sex was natural and positive. Thus Driver's half-critique of the Quakers represented more, not less, openness compared with *C&C*'s inherited approach.[37]

Shortly after this article appeared, *C&C* opted for a new stand on sex outside marriage. Harvey Cox proposed to reject across-the-board rules about premarital sex, presupposing a logic similar to the Quaker document. (He kept silent about homosexuality, which had troubled Driver the most.)[38] Cox said that the issue was not "to bed or not to bed." Rather, he asked, "How can I best nourish the maturity of those with whom I share the torments and transports of human existence?" Cox pointed to various hypocrisies in prevailing practice: advertisers used sex incessantly to sell things, yet youth were expected to remain chaste for years; a female college student had told him she had necked to orgasm every weekend for the past two years, but was still a "virgin." Young people would justly ignore church teaching if it was too legalistic and hostile to the positive expression of sexuality.[39]

Cox's article was delayed for six months by an intense debate among *C&C* editorial board members. Shinn attacked Cox's position as "theologically invertebrate" for abandoning specific moral guidelines and falling into an "ethic of self-fulfillment, curiously hitched to the gospel." Niebuhr said that Cox failed to recognize that young women engaged in sex "as a pledge of love" while young men did so "most likely motivated by pure lust." He cautioned against substituting "a thoughtless antinomianism for the old hypocrisy and prudery."[40] When they finally published the piece, *C&C* editors hedged their endorsement and braced for a firestorm of controversy—but were greeted with a yawn. The result, as Cowan later recalled, was "deafening silence; not one word of praise or blame" from readers. Conservatives like Ramsey were outraged by these developments, but they represented *C&C*'s past. Cox represented its future.[41]

These debates about sexual ethics formed some small part of *C&C*'s long-term shift toward feminism, because their attention to male-female interactions and their stress on consulting particular human agents in particular contexts provided a marginal increase in the legitimate space for women's experience to be considered and, more important, an opening wedge for consideration of overtly feminist standpoints. Feminist ethics later took over and radicalized Miller's contextualist argument that ethics are social products rather than transcendent principles and that the key ethical question is what communities generate basic moral commitments.

I would not overstress this line of thought, even for *C&C*'s more innovative voices on sexuality. Articles focused overtly on gender remained highly limited until the 1970s. Even if we consider *C&C*'s most liberal and partially "feminized" writing on gender issues, and approach it through the most positive feminist interpretations of the sexual revolution, *C&C*'s discourse was still, in the end, a debate among males who could be interpreted as proving their virility in a new context and justifying their fascination with magazines like *Playboy*. Almost everything I have discussed was prefeminist, if a minimal definition of feminism includes focused analysis of gender systems from the perspective of the underdog, with a focus on female agency and a view toward transforming the structures of injustice. To whatever degree this discourse was open to feminist uses, they mainly came into the pages of *C&C* later.

Meanwhile, male self-definition in contrast to behaviors understood as feminine remained central for *C&C* writers at every point on the spectrum from Fitch to Cox. *C&C* tended to blend macho poses with endorsements of Kennedy's perceived revitalization of culture after "a decade without greatness." Shinn said that it seemed "prissy" to use Niebuhrian arguments about the moral ambiguity of all positions, if this meant evading a clear option for Martin Luther King against southern racists like Bull Connor.[42] Virtuous social action in the inner city was masculinized, and complacent suburban culture religion was feminized. Brown trivialized suburban Christianity using an image of women preening in Easter hats, and Lehmann cited a poem in which the women of "St. Status Episcopal" prepared the Eucharist using "a tempting cheez-dip with the Body and lovely crystal-punch-cups for the Blood." Compare this with the virile faith Lehmann recommended: "the bearer in the long stream of history . . . of the cutting edge of prophecy." This faith was present whenever "usurpation of power in the common life of men, over their minds or over their institutions, has raised its head and where a halt must be called."[43]

Secular Theology and Religious Pluralism

As *C&C* reevaluated theology in this period, its major preoccupation was not sex but secularity and pluralism. True, sexuality was enough of a theme in battles over contextual ethics to ensure that whenever *C&C* appealed to new contexts, some readers might suspect that greater openness to changing gender roles was associated with the appeal. But sexual politics was a low priority compared with civil rights and a host of other issues.[44] The leading way *C&C* talked theologically about new experiences and contexts during this period was through the vaguer and purportedly more universal category of secularity.[45]

C&C's debate about situation ethics—did new situations take methodological priority over traditional ethical principles?—can be understood as a particular case within broader and more abstract patterns of theological debate. Did modern secular experience make it necessary to reconsider inherited theistic language or recast ethical arguments based on God's transcendence? Should theologians substitute an approach that paid more attention to science and human autonomy? Should they place more emphasis on divine immanence and incarnation?

C&C's new standpoints in ethics and theology tended to reverse or at least reprioritize themes within neoorthodoxy. Its writers moved from a dominant note of transcendent judgment on the cultural given, in which "the situation" was approached on an analogy with bourgeois complacency or Nazi oppression, to a positive acceptance of "the situation" as a given that included possibilities for positive transformation. As they embraced positive aspects of the situation, they used images such as participation in the biblical Exodus, building God's kingdom, or maturing toward individual fulfillment in a "world come of age." In this sense—which is not the only important sense—contextualists emphasized the linear and Progressive aspects of liberal Protestant traditions, compared with the unreconstructed realists' tendency to stress what they called "vertical" parts of the paradigm such as human mortality and God's perennial judgment on sin.[46] In the vertical logic, sin and grace were often used to explain the inevitability of choosing lesser evils, as well as to justify the agents who chose them. For the contextualists, sin tended to be less of a given, and grace was understood to undermine received structures of law (such as rules about sex in the situation ethics debate) and empower Christians to transform sinful social structures (such as Jim Crow segregation in the theology of Martin Luther King Jr.). Although these themes had always been present in Christian realism, *C&C*'s dominant accents changed markedly in this period.

Often *C&C* argued explicitly that the inherited rhetorics and priorities of neoorthodox theology were inadequate for addressing new political challenges. South African novelist Alan Paton replied to critics who perceived him as extremist simply because he had decided "to choose justice and not injustice and not to seek some middle ground between them." "The greatest danger to Christianity is [not communism but] pseudo-Christianity . . . [which] always prefers what it considers realism to love. . . . It says, 'you know, Paton, you are really talking a lot of bloody nonsense. . . . You don't understand human nature. You are trying to achieve the impossible.'. . . I think that ultimately if one wants to be a good man one must live by the law of love no matter what the cost of it may be. . . . If that is not the meaning of faith, then I don't know what is."[47]

Henry Pitney Van Dusen expressed related frustrations, recommending that realists should pay more attention to Jesus' advice, "Let what you say be simply 'yes' or 'no.'" Some paradoxes were profound, Van Dusen said, but too much neoorthodoxy logic fit the dictionary definition of paradox: "palpably incorrect, contradictory, absurd." It was fine to speak about complexity, but the crucial question was "how much 'yes' and how much 'no'; at what point between a categorical 'yes' and an unqualified 'no' does truth lie?" Too much equivocation led to saying, "Lord, Lord," but not doing the commandments.[48]

C&C began to rehabilitate the theology of the Kingdom of God, which had been under a cloud of suspicion ever since the Niebuhrians routed the social gospelers in the 1940s. Bennett granted that social gospelers had sometimes misused this image, but he insisted that Jesus' prayer, "Thy will be done on earth as it is in heaven" remained a basic Christian theme. Part of the truth, underplayed by neoorthodoxy, was the possibility that God's will could be imperfectly but partially expressed in history. This theme (known in technical terms as realized eschatology) should be revived, Bennett argued, and not focused too narrowly on sacraments and institutional churches.[49]

In his theological best-seller, *Honest to God,* Anglican bishop John Robinson attacked the language of transcendence and called for an honest admission that traditional orthodoxy was becoming irrelevant and should be rephrased in terms accessible to secular culture. Lehmann, Bennett, and sociologist Robert Bellah all reviewed *Honest to God* favorably, although it struck Bennett as a "delayed reaction to sermons preached by Paul Tillich in the Union Seminary chapel twenty years ago." Bellah (in his first *C&C* article) argued that the book should go even further toward eliminating a rhetoric of a transcendent God "out there"; he suggested that a social science approach to symbolic aspects of human experience was more appropriate than the remaining vestiges of theological language. However, Bennett objected that *Honest to God* "tends to identify God with the totality of being and so to threaten the transcendence and freedom of God." Without transcendence, "God may be only another name for The System." Surprisingly, Bennett had come around to arguing that his colleagues should read more Karl Barth![50]

Barth found more favor at *C&C* by the 1960s, partly because he was then emphasizing incarnational theology more than in his earlier texts, and partly because *C&C* was belatedly coming to appreciate his cold war neutralism and tendency to describe the United States with images like the fleshpots of Egypt. Bennett said that Barth's later theology of grace "closely resembles a Christian universalism," and he expressed surprise that Barth showed a new "capacity to be fair to those with whom he disagrees, especially when they are dead."[51]

C&C devoted a special issue to another theological best-seller, *The Secular City* by its own Harvey Cox. The responses—both pro and con—revealed *C&C*'s growing internal conflict over theology. Lehmann's review, "Chalcedon in Technopolis," welcomed Cox's translation of traditional theology into the language of urban modernity. For example, Cox said that "just as . . . the deity of Jesus [may be seen] as his readiness to accept and execute God's purpose for him, so the secular city signifies that point where man takes responsibility for directing the tumultuous tendencies of his time."[52] Lehmann said that Cox's book had been a revelation: "Anonymity, mobility, bureaucracy, and organization—which I had hitherto regarded as the principal foci of dehumanization in modern society—I have now come to see as the principal foci at which the purpose and activity of God and the responsibility and activity of man for the humanization of man intersect."[53]

David Little, on the other hand, said that "one gains the impression that he has heard this song before." Little clearly did not like the song either time. He said that Cox's "unprincipled contextualism" presupposed unacknowledged norms by default. Point by point, he compared *The Secular City* with Walter Rauschenbusch's *Theology for the Social Gospel* and complained bitterly that Cox failed to acknowledge the link. According to Little, "Rauschenbusch was considered unsophisticated and a shallow activist." "Theologians were appalled . . . [and] very nearly apoplectic" about his positions. "But Cox uses almost the identical language and people find him exciting."[54]

Cox replied that there was a simple reason why he had not cited Rauschenbusch—he had not drawn on him while writing his book—and so what if they had things in common? In any case, Cox said, Little failed to understand that Cox presupposed a critique of the social gospel much like Barth's and Niebuhr's. His intent was to heighten the "Protestant principle" of transcendent critique of all human projects. This desacralized the profane world just as secularization did, spurring Christians to social action.[55]

Indeed, from the perspective of theologian William Hamilton, *The Secular City* was nothing but "pop Barth." As Hamilton perceived the theological scene in 1965, there was a passé establishment (including Cox) which continued in the "ecumenical, Barthian, neo-Reformation tradition." There was a hermeneutical approach associated with Rudolph Bultmann; it used an existentialist approach in which individuals were called to authentic faith through hearing a demythologized gospel message. There were new kinds of "natural, metaphysical or philosophical" approaches such as phenomenology and process theology. Finally, there were the secular theologies, or death of God approaches, which Hamilton recommended. He challenged theologians to face up realistically to the "loss" of God and said, "I do not see how preaching, worship, prayer . . . can be taken seriously by the radical theologian." In a similar vein Gabriel Vahanian argued that science had taken over; God was "neither necessary or unnecessary, he is irrelevant. He is dead."[56]

Some of what death of God theologians denied on one hand with sensational formulations of this sort—which were debated none too insightfully in *Time*—was reaffirmed on another hand (at least by key members of their diverse group) when they presented Jesus as a model for faith. They had in mind a highly incarnational Jesus who was uncompromisingly human, rather than the Jesus in standard doctrines of Christology. Even so, *C&C*'s inner circle showed minimal interest in death of God theology. They considered it respectfully, much as they appreciated the moral but atheistic novels of Camus. But like Niebuhr contemplating *Guernica*, in the end they wanted to correct and supplement it—which they attempted to do as part of the media's feeding frenzy surrounding the movement.[57]

In *C&C*'s definitive statement on death of God theology, Langdon Gilkey defined secularity as "the 'modern mind' minus its elements of 'ultimacy' and linear purposiveness." For such raw secularity, modernity was a condition "in which no ultimate order or meaning appears." This understanding was "expressed both by positivism and by secular existentialism, especially in the latter's literary forms." Gilkey expressed some sympathy for attacks on neoorthodoxy from such a secular standpoint. As he put it, neoorthodoxy "accept[ed] the whole modern understanding of the spatio-temporal process, now de-sacralized of all ultimacy. Out of this came an uneasy dualism, with a naturalistically interpreted world and a biblically understood God giving meaning and coherence thereto. . . . The present crisis in theology illustrates the increasing difficulty of this strange marriage of heaven and earth."[58] (In a similar vein, historian Sydney Ahlstrom later described neoorthodoxy as a "thin sheet of dogmatic asphalt over the problems created by modern critical thought.")[59]

For Gilkey, however, "the effort to interpret Christian theology without God is a failure." It would not work to adopt the death of God approach and speak only about a human Jesus, nor to follow Bultmann's approach, which was to say as little as possible about God except as outmoded myth, and instead focus on the power of demythologized preaching, or what Bultmann called *kerygma.* (As Gilkey put it, for Bultmann, "God was shoved farther and farther back into the never-never land of sheer kerygmatic proclamation.") Both of these approaches evaded the core issue: whether there was any *real* God connected either to Bultmann's biblical word-event that ostensibly *proclaimed* God, or to Jesus, who undoubtedly saw himself doing God's will, even assuming the least Christological interpretation of his life. Gilkey assumed that "the secular denial of all categories of ultimacy makes theology impossible." But he continued: "I also think it reflects a false analysis of man's secular experience. . . . A more valid analysis, probably of a phenomenological sort, of those realms of ordinary experience that we call secular will reveal dimensions for which only language about God is sufficient."[60]

C&C basically presupposed this solution to "the strange marriage of heaven and earth." But the more that emergent theological debates shifted toward the terrains suggested by Gilkey—abstract language analysis and phenomenology—the less closely *C&C* followed. Arguing in a vein similar to Gilkey but with a much different tone, Niebuhr dismissed death of God theology as futile; he said that life would always have realms of value, and this was what theological language was talking about. Niebuhr even claimed that Marx and Freud were preferable to death of God theologians because at least they provided alternative systems of meaning; he quipped that a leading book on death of God theology had been dedicated to Tillich, but "it may well be that Tillich is dead."[61] Shinn spoke for many at *C&C* when he later commented that "to the extent that Christian ethicists were involved in moral crusades against social evils, *they knew* what they meant and did not take much time out for subtle theorizing about their language."[62] Instead, they moved toward various forms of liberation theology.

Not all of *C&C*'s theological dialogue with "modern secular experience" was channeled through debates about scientific rationality and historical critical thought; equally important was the experience of secularity as cultural pluralism. We have seen that by the early 1960s, *C&C* had moved more or less gracefully toward an alliance of liberal Protestants, Catholics, and Jews against more conservative religious positions. A key milestone was Vatican II, which met near the height of *C&C*'s interest in secular theologies. *C&C* spent much energy analyzing the theology of Vatican II and its ramifications for Protestant-Catholic relations.[63] Many of the divisions in *C&C*'s treatment of Vatican II mirrored intra-Protestant disputes about how much to trust and welcome modernity. When Pope John XXIII issued *Pacem in Terris* in 1963, Bennett welcomed its call for cooperation with Protestants, its moderate views on the cold war, and its generally open stance toward the modern world based on liberal principles such as the dignity of the person. Niebuhr, on the other hand, complained that *Pacem in Terris* had naive utopian ideas about the cold war. Also, it tried to fuse Catholic natural law traditions with a bad kind of modern liberalism, so that "the Church absorb[ed] some of the voluntarism of the social contract theory" and attempted to create universalistic communities unrooted in organic traditions. *Pacem in Terris* was "thoroughly modern" and "breath[ed] a Pelagian, rather than an Augustinian spirit." At least, Niebuhr conceded, its defense of religious freedom might "leaven the lump of Latin Catholicism."[64]

As *C&C* came to terms with religious pluralism, a question arose about the future of Protestant elites who were heirs to the assumption that their views articulated a moral consensus for the society. For example, what of Fitch, who believed that a Protestantism without the "impulse to stand in judgment on the civilization of the day has lost its Protestantism," or Niebuhr, who stated in 1959 that within "the whole spectrum of Christian doctrine" in all of history, "seventeenth-century Calvinism would come off best" because of its "devotion to the creation of a just political order" linked to a defense of civil liberties. Niebuhr saw little reason to rethink the Calvinist tradition in light of religious pluralism. He celebrated its "theory of religious toleration" and argued that even when Calvinists had not fully enacted the theory they had splintered into so many denominations that toleration resulted anyway "by the providence of God."[65] But what if articulate non-Calvinists—let us say, social historians who sympathized with victims of seventeenth-century Puritans such as accused witches, Pequot Indians, and executed Quaker missionaries—were less impressed with the Calvinist record on religious pluralism?

Consider a good news/bad news report on Christian theology from two death of God theologians. Bearing the bad news, Rabbi Richard Rubenstein argued that Christian theism was one important cause of the Holocaust. William Hamilton agreed but looked for the silver lining—perhaps the death of God would improve Christian-Jewish relations.[66] This was obviously not Niebuhr's idea of how Calvinism and religious pluralism fit together! Niebuhr presumably welcomed the response to Rubenstein from Rabbi Arthur Hertzberg, who argued that theism did not ordinarily cause evils such as the Holocaust but helped to restrain them. Nevertheless, Hertzberg's response to Hamilton provided limited comfort. Hertzberg reminded *C&C* readers that earlier innovations in Protestant theology had been mixed blessings for Jews. Martin Luther had assumed that the Reformation had solved all of Christianity's problems, so there was no longer any valid reason for Jews to resist conversion. Nineteenth-century liberal theologians had argued that Jews should convert to an upgraded, universal form of Christianity, unless they wanted to become a backwater in history. Was Hamilton's new and improved, less anti-Semitic secular theology a further example in this tradition? Had he thrown off orthodox doctrine, only to retain a cultural religion—in this case a cultural Christianity that could easily turn into cultural imperialism?[67] Consider the problem for Niebuhr. If even a liberal like Hertzberg thought that Hamilton's death of God theology was too aggressive in its Christian "sectarianism," what would less friendly critics think about Niebuhr's Puritans?

In recent years there has been much discussion of "the naked public square." This is Richard John Neuhaus's term for a national discourse in which Christian leaders can no longer assume that their views articulate a moral consensus for the society. (Let us not pause to debate how far this assumption has ever been valid, and how much has actually changed for non-Protestants; the point at hand is the internal crisis of elite Christian identity when they perceived a square that appeared to them newly naked.) In its 1962 symposium on "Protestantism in a Post-Protestant America," *C&C* aired several issues that later became prominent in debates about the naked public square.[68] In this symposium, the idea of a square naked because of rising pluralism and the idea of a square naked because of secularism were interwoven. This raises the question of how much God's death at the hands of secularity was linked to the death of a credible Anglo-Protestant self-perception of cultural dominance.

I have argued that *C&C*'s appeals to secular context were broadly correlated with its turn to a more pluralistic range of standpoints. In *C&C*'s symposium these links were explicit. Will Herberg focused on Protestants losing their establishment role in a pluralistic culture; Lehmann addressed the challenge to Protestantism from secular thought. But each speaker addressed both issues: Herberg called for Protestant vigilance against secularist "culture religion," while Lehmann warned about rising Catholic power. Robert McAfee Brown's introduction wove their articles together and provided *C&C*'s editorial response. He said that the United States was now "post-Protestant" and possibly even "post-Christian." Could Protestants accept this gracefully and make "witness as the leaven since we can no longer make that witness as the leader?" This would mean "accepting the role of tenants in a land we thought we owned." Protestants should gladly embrace the minority role of a "church set against the world."[69]

Many themes from this chapter came together in an all-star symposium that *C&C* organized for its twenty-fifth anniversary in 1966, on the general subject of philosophical interpretations of "the crisis." Exactly what *C&C* meant by "crisis" was never clear, but the symposium gathered scholars attentive to pluralism in a variety of contexts, and it included a strong concern for the arts. Theologians were not major presenters; their role was listening to secular colleagues analyze their context, rather than proclaiming God's judgment on that context.

This symposium was so diverse that it is hard to summarize, but this very fact underlined the theme of a breakdown in common values across the society, coupled with doubts about common purposes. Foreign policy specialist Richard Goodwin and civil rights activist Bayard Rustin kept alive *C&C*'s standard call to liberal political action. But experts on culture—philosophers, artists, and scientists—spoke forcefully about various kinds of crises, including the political crisis that was on everyone's mind: the breakdown of consensus about U.S. intervention in Vietnam.[70] Harvard physicist Gerald Holton spoke of the "relativity of values or, more correctly, the coexistence at different levels, of a variety of sometimes contradictory values." He explicitly denied that there was any single religious truth, and said that aggressive religious advocacy of common values functioned to support the U.S. war machine. Theater critic Herbert Blau spoke of "entropy running wild" as evidenced in the bleak vision of contemporary literature. He commented on a recent trip to Vietnam by Hubert Humphrey, who in the keynote speech of the anniversary celebration invoked Niebuhr to justify his actions. Blau said, "It was very hard for me to believe . . . that [Humphrey] was going off to Saigon to teach that good clean Vietnamese kid Marshall Ky, who had previously praised Hitler, something about the American way of life and midwestern agricultural methods."[71]

These quotations underline a point that I have been arguing throughout this chapter—that *C&C*'s cultural debates and political stances must be understood together, and that in many cases cultural analysts were *C&C*'s boldest voices pushing for new approaches. What was true of critics like Blau and Holton was also true of contextualists in *C&C*'s inner circle.

The anniversary symposium also suggests that by the mid-1960s *C&C* was pushing the limits of generalized understandings, both of context in theological ethics and cultural experience in the arts. Increasingly *C&C* asked pointed questions about specific groups of people who were locked in conflict within particular contexts. Although these questions grew naturally out of *C&C*'s contextual turn, they stretched *C&C*'s consensus to the breaking point.

6

The Shattering of Consensus over Black Power and Vietnam

"It is no longer the case that those of us who read and write for *C&C* argue within a mutually recognized set of theological, ethical, and political premises. Those very premises are now in question."[1] With these matter-of-fact words, *C&C* opened its 1969 volume, in an editorial by James Kuhn that looked back on the previous year. Kuhn argued that Great Society liberalism remained valid and *C&C* should stay the course. But the center was not holding.

This editorial appeared as the flames were settling down from one of the most heated debates in *C&C*'s history. The larger fire in question—the tension between classic realists and their critics—had been smoldering for years, and throughout the 1960s the fuel of various disputes kept it well stoked. However, during 1968 *C&C* writers heaped on unusually large amounts of fuel, and the flames were fanned by social crises such as the assassination of Martin Luther King Jr. and the Chicago police assault on antiwar protesters at the Democratic National Convention.

Late in 1968, *C&C*'s fire flared to a peak of intensity after Harvey Cox editorialized that "Enough Is Enough!"—readers should not support Democratic candidate Hubert Humphrey for president. They should boycott the election, since the "race is already lost no matter who wins."[2] Pouring on extra gasoline, Will Campbell and James Holloway added, "Four years ago we were told that a vote for Goldwater was a vote for some sort of manifestation of anti-Christ. . . . So Christians from bishops to the omnipresent concerned laymen spent themselves electing in the name of Christ crucified and resurrected . . . Lyndon Baines Johnson." According to Campbell, Christians should stand for "the sign of Jonah [an allusion to Jesus] and not the sign of the swastika or donkey or elephant." They should drop out of politics and "weep for those who stayed in."[3] Pete Young added that the question was simple: "Are you on the side of the folks, or the system? If the former, you will find more important things to do than elect McCarthy delegates to the meat grinder in Chicago. If the latter, to hell and be damned with you."[4]

C&C's unreconstructed liberals had no intention of stopping their search for lesser evils, and they did not appreciate such comments from anyone—especially not from Cox, whose writings on sex, theology, and the New Left made him a magnet for controversy. They vehemently protested that Humphrey was better than Nixon—a point that Cox had already granted, although not without adding that both candidates "personify discredited responses to the major issues." *C&C's* "stay the course" faction pronounced "a pox on Mr. Cox."[5]

Cox's editorial appeared when passions were already running high from another controversy. This one pitted *C&C* moderates and radicals together against emergent neoconservatives like Ramsey, whose contempt for *C&C's* dominant line steadily escalated. In 1967 Ramsey had provoked another flare-up when he published *Who Speaks for the Churches?* This book excoriated Protestant leaders for taking "prophetic" positions more radical than their rank-and-file constituents, and insisted that they should keep silent unless they could speak from consensus.[6] The tone of this debate was bitter. Since Ramsey conceded that his principle had limits—he thought that German clergy should have condemned Auschwitz even lacking a consensus of German laity—Bennett asked why he could not condemn burning Vietnamese civilians with napalm, even though many U.S. Protestants might support this. Ramsey retorted that Bennett should condemn "throat-slitting and disembowelment" by the Vietcong (which, of course, Bennett was not endorsing, simply because his priority was to stop war crimes by his own government). Moreover, continued Ramsey, Bennett should pay attention to the geopolitical instability caused by the "immoral insurgency" of the Vietnamese, as well as the "destruction being wrought in our domestic political life" by the peace movement.[7]

Ill will carried over from this exchange into the "Enough Is Enough" controversy. But whereas Ramsey's attack on Bennett seemed to presuppose that Bennett was betraying an expected responsibility, Ramsey's attack on Cox was sarcastic and resigned—the discussion was between camps of mutual disrespect. Mocking left-wing rhetoric, Ramsey called for "Political Repentance Now!" and he spoke of "a luminous, almost mystical moment of apprehension" when he grasped the truth: liberals were totally insincere and their actual goal was to destroy the New Deal, elect Richard Nixon, and alienate voters from the Democrats. Only then did liberal behavior, which he called "acts of politicus interruptus," make any sense.[8]

Reactions to this outburst were revealing. Trying to cool down the rhetoric, one writer suggested that "*C&C* neither advocates nor supports 'revolutionary violence.' It is only that some of us recognize as a main job of liberals now not criticism of the vagaries of those who demand change but a struggle against those who resist change." To say the least, *C&C*'s right wing was unwilling to extend leftists the benefit of doubt in this way. Ernest Lefever claimed that "romantic idealists are dupes of revolutionaries," and he spoke of a "totalitarianism of the left" that was comparable to the "prelude to Hitler's Germany." He called for a "return to the political realism and honesty that characterized *C&C* during its first two decades."[9] Meanwhile, a writer from *C&C*'s left wing challenged Ramsey to apply his argument to Jesus. Since Ramsey was quick to attack people who were trying to follow Jesus' teachings in the modern world, would he also call Jesus a "self-appointed Messiah" who was completely irresponsible? Judged by Ramsey's criteria for responsible ethics, did not Jesus appear to be "unbearably naive, totally unaware of the consequences of his teaching" about love and justice? Perhaps "the better explanation is that [Jesus] was insincere, even malicious. . . . He certainly knew that the result would be the exact opposite of what he said he wanted."[10]

Sometimes when two lovers break up, their hardest task is articulating their disagreements and deciding whether to keep working on their relationship, especially while both have a stake in maintaining it. At some point—often after disagreements have ripened for a long time—something clicks to articulate the conflicts unmistakably. The controversy over Cox's "Enough Is Enough" editorial provided that kind of click for *C&C*. Cox said, "Mr. Lefever has demonstrated to me more cogently than any New Leftist ever could that the liberal consensus is indeed finished."[11] Cox placed himself closer to the New Left demonstrators than to Chicago mayor Richard Daley and closer to Guatemalan guerrillas than to the Green Berets. His comment, and the whole surrounding controversy, dramatized *C&C*'s impasse—and Kuhn's editorial, which opens this chapter, was responding to it explicitly.

After 1968 everyone at *C&C* perceived polarization on the continuum between its left and right wings. Unrepentant cold warriors like Lefever abandoned *C&C* in disgust. But *C&C*'s core constituency shifted left. People like Bennett from its former liberal vanguard became its centrists, and *C&C* picked up new allies on the left—radicalizing voices like Cox as well as new constituencies, especially feminists. *C&C*'s continuum of debate was reconfigured. This was a process that included breakdown and rebuilding, both of which were ongoing throughout 1960s and 1970s. However, the note to accent in the late 1960s—and the focus of this chapter—was the shattering of *C&C*'s inherited consensus.

The Breakdown of Civil Rights and the Debate about Black Power

As Martin Luther King Jr. prepared for his 1968 Poor People's Campaign, C. Eric Lincoln's editorial looked back on events of the previous three years: urban uprisings, associated police violence, and the rise of militant black nationalism. Black moderates had "abandon[ed] non-violence one by one," said Lincoln, "because we exploited their non-violence with cynicism and deceit." Now King proposed one last effort to "redeem non-violence." "He is asking for bread. Will you give him a stone? . . . If he fails, his present portfolio will be exhausted."[12]

Lincoln sensed failure; he saw whites denying the roots of racial strife and merely seeking out conservative blacks who would blame the problems on "Negro Crime." Lincoln's opening sentence set the tone: "Futility is what I feel. Sadness and futility. America is rocketing to perdition, and nobody seems to give a damn." He continued: "Perhaps America has the intent to destroy what frightens her. This is what frightens me. Perhaps it should frighten you. It is the promise of blood implied in the frantic stockpiling of Stoner guns, machine guns, sawed-off shot guns, gas masks and immobilizing chemicals by police departments across the country. . . . It is the organization of vigilantes. . . . This is madness. I know it can't happen here. But there is a worrisome uneasiness that . . . it is happening. After all, there are precedents—in Germany and South Africa. And in America."[13] Within a few weeks King had been murdered, riots had erupted, and the Poor People's Movement had collapsed. *C&C*'s next issue had a blank front page, except for a small italicized note: "We have run out of words, and we are running short of hope."[14]

As we have seen, *C&C*'s hope had been overflowing in the early 1960s as *C&C* lobbied for civil rights laws and wrote that it might be witnessing the "ultimate, or at least penultimate, chapter in the long history of overcoming the 'American dilemma.'"[15] During the late 1960s, however, *C&C*'s integrationist vision suffered a series of shocks. As unfolding events called its vision into question, three strands entwined in *C&C*'s response. First, many writers attempted to maintain their hopes for progress toward color-blind harmony in the face of new challenges; this was linked to a basic confidence in the dream of American democracy, at least as an ideal to keep striving for. The second strand was a turn toward black nationalist standpoints that accented pride in a distinct black identity and sought black self-determination. This vision perceived America more as a nightmare than a dream for blacks; it assumed that the U.S. psyche and social structure were racist to the core, although it sometimes tried to build power selectively through the system. *C&C* eventually developed updated variations on both these strands, and they came to dominate its coverage of race. However, visions of integration became markedly less credible after 1965, and *C&C* was never completely comfortable with black nationalism. Therefore, a third strand in *C&C* response—confusion and demoralization—took center stage in this period. *C&C* never fully recovered from it.

We have seen that before the mid-1960s, *C&C* knew of critiques raised by Malcolm X and other black nationalists, but kept them at arm's length, mainly using them to spur civil rights activism. After Malcolm X was assassinated in 1965, Roger Shinn wrote some positive words about him. Shinn highlighted the end of X's life, when he had moved toward a more open form of black nationalism which Shinn interpreted as simply calling for "a better deal where [blacks] lived," as opposed to Elijah Muhammad's far-fetched visions of a new black state. Yet Shinn saw the Nation of Islam's organizational achievements as "amazingly small" and its appeal as a "fantastic foolery" based on an "outlet for pent-up aggressions." Some might say—Shinn said *he* would not say it—that Malcolm's death was a case of chickens coming home to roost.[16]

No one at *C&C* could minimize the challenge of black militancy after a triple whammy of crises that began with the Watts riot of 1965. After Watts, Shinn typified *C&C*'s received positions by maintaining an "outside looking in" standpoint toward the black community. He spoke of "the appalling cries of 'burn, baby, burn'" that "left people so mystified that each man could only resort to his most treasured clichés as a defense against the fury." Although he described the riot as "a mass cry for attention to deep corporate wrongs," he saw "no alternative to putting it down by force."[17] However, some *C&C* writers began to explore how the issues looked from the other side of the barricades. A lawyer from the NCC Commission on Religion and Race reported that the people of Watts suffered from rampant police violence and were cynical about empty white promises. *C&C* quoted a young black male who told whites to forget about solving inner-city problems and leave him alone. For him, whites were the enemy.[18]

A second shock, the controversy sparked by the Moynihan report on *The Negro Family*, produced intellectual conflict that was nearly as intense as the Watts riot. This report, written by Daniel Patrick Moynihan as a rationale for Lyndon Johnson's policies toward African Americans, identified the key problem as a dysfunctional family structure in which women were too dominant and men too irresponsible. The report assumed that African American culture had essentially been destroyed during slavery and replaced by a culture of poverty. Therefore, if blacks wanted a viable culture, reasoned Moynihan, they needed to integrate into the dominant society and become more like liberals. Moynihan had good intentions of helping blacks make this transition, rather than blaming them for their problems. His policy proposals addressed significant structural issues. Unfortunately, one of his background assumptions was that whites could define the major problem of African American communities as a deficient culture, deflecting the blame away from institutional racism. Many blacks perceived this as contemptuous and paternalistic—especially since people on Moynihan's right used the report as ammunition for punitive policies that simply blamed the victims and exhorted them to pull themselves up by their own bootstraps.

C&C divided over its response to the Moynihan report. Robert Spike and Benjamin Payton (who replaced Spike as head of the NCC Commission on Religion and Race) said that Moynihan exaggerated problems in the black community, screened out positive evidence that did not fit his theory, neglected structural problems of the city as a whole, and advocated programs that had been discredited among the black masses.[19] But others at *C&C* were more positive. After one writer described a White House conference linked to the Moynihan report as "rigged" and "drugged" by Lyndon Johnson, others responded that, on the contrary, the conference had been "hard-nosed and visionary." The acrimony became so intense that Niebuhr resigned and withdrew from *C&C*'s masthead in anger at *C&C*'s criticism of Johnson's policies, as well as embarrassment when Moynihan complained directly to him.[20] Niebuhr soon returned because some people saw his resignation as support for the Vietnam War, but this did nothing to resolve *C&C*'s underlying dissension about race.

This was the context in which *C&C* first began to explore the internal complexities of black power. *C&C* gave far more support to pluralist forms of black power that were like traditional ethnic politics than it did to radical versions of black cultural and political separatism.[21] James Breeden wrote that there was some truth in the claim by NAACP leader Roy Wilkins that "black power means black death" because in its most militant forms it would simply provoke a right-wing backlash—and that this sad truth would remain no matter how much Wilkins was vilified by militants as an Uncle Tom or valorized by hypocritical whites at the *New York Times*. Turning to his positive vision, Breeden appealed to the authority of black leaders from Frederick Douglass through W. E. B. Du Bois to Martin Luther King Jr., claiming that each had presupposed pride in black culture and worked for black empowerment; he added that Du Bois had rejected black self-assertion if it was merely "the feeling of revolt or revenge."[22] In 1967, after an African American, Carl Stokes, was elected mayor of Cleveland, C. Eric Lincoln stressed in *C&C* that Stokes had won through broad-based appeals to all citizens. This was a case of black power achieved through the simple logic (compatible with civil rights approaches) of electing the best person for the job.[23]

C&C embraced moderate versions of black power like Stokes's at a moment when they represented only the tip of an iceberg of nationalist bitterness. Beyond *C&C*'s pages, in the freedom movement at large, leading voices were turning in the late 1960s toward positions that were far less optimistic about working within established channels. They echoed Malcolm X's judgment that the 1963 March on Washington, at which King gave his famous "I Have a Dream" speech, had been a "Farce on Washington" orchestrated by whites to channel black rage in degrading and innocuous ways. Assata Shakur later evoked the period's mood of rising militancy when she spoke of "the so-called responsible [black] leaders, the ones who are 'responsible' to our oppressors." She commented: "I have heard 'liberals' express every conceivable opinion on every conceivable subject. . . . As long as some white middle-class people can live high on the hog, take vacations in Europe, send their children to private schools, and reap the benefits of their white skin privileges, then they are 'liberals.' But when times get hard and money gets tight, they pull off that liberal mask and you think you're talking to Adolf Hitler."[24]

Such criticisms set the stage for the third and most decisive shock to *C&C*'s integrationist vision: calls from black leaders to exclude whites from the freedom movement. They argued that whites were a strategic impediment because they weakened morale from within, attempted to control movement agendas, and generally short-circuited black self-determination and pride. For many at *C&C*, it was a severe blow to be vilified by a movement so central to their identity, for which some had even risked their lives.

C&C responded to these shocks in various ways. One was to backpedal. Veteran activist Howard Moody, a white minister and *C&C* board member, defended black power against white attacks. "Power of, by, and for blacks" should be uncontroversial, he said, and this implied less stress on nonviolent integration and more stress on black pride. "Only extreme paranoia could interpret this as black racism."[25] Still, *C&C* resisted a worldview that pitted all blacks against all whites; it clung doggedly to distinctions between whites who were more or less promising allies for blacks, as well as between black activists and a co-opted "black bourgeoisie." A Nation of Islam member told *C&C* writer Malcolm Boyd, "I consider you more black than many blacks," and Boyd presented this as a model approach: judging people by their humanness. Above all, *C&C* groped for constructive things to do as an ally. Moody staked out *C&C*'s preferred self-understanding. White liberals should "become an advocate before the white power structure," working in their own backyards to pay "empty promissory notes" that revealed white hypocrisy.[26]

This role as bridge to the power structure was easier when the proposals being advocated had a reasonable chance of being implemented. But as the civil rights coalition polarized and *C&C*'s black allies radicalized—and especially after Richard Nixon won the presidency in 1968 on a "Law and Order" platform—this bridging role became harder to sustain. Let us consider a few cases of ascending difficulty faced by *C&C* between 1964 and 1971.

As we have seen, it was second nature for *C&C* to shift from technocratic models toward visions of greater community control. In 1964 *C&C* steered left in a controversy about Saul Alinsky, a community organizer who was interested only indirectly, if at all, in interracial harmony or technocratic solutions. Alinsky targeted a problem, identified an enemy, and mobilized community resources against the enemy—and he organized black communities against white power structures.[27] The *Century* found him "sub-Christian," largely because his approach seemed to imply backsliding from King's vision of racial harmony toward amoral divisiveness. But Bennett said that as far as he was concerned, Alinsky's principle of meeting oppressive power with countervailing power had been old hat ever since Niebuhr wrote *Moral Man and Immoral Society* in the 1930s. We have noted how seldom *C&C* applied this Niebuhrian moral to race before the 1960s, but for Bennett in 1965, building black power was elementary Christian realism. It was hypocritical for whites to condemn blacks for using power tactics, at the same time that white power structures presupposed violence against blacks.[28]

So far so good for *C&C* as an ally of black nationalists. But as its allies radicalized, the prospects for successful advocacy became harder. Payton stressed that the black power movement sought equality as "social reality and not just a legal theory" and that this opened an "ideological chasm" between the races.[29] Spike reported a crevasse in the movement, with the New Left and "militant Negroes" on one side and Great Society liberals ("we") on the other. Although Spike spoke about "we liberals," he also claimed to identify with militants who recognized that the masses would not respond to Great Society slogans. Even Alinsky-style community organizations and projects such as the Mississippi Freedom Democratic Party (which sought black representation in southern politics) were too limited, said Spike.[30]

If whites should not pay off their empty promissory notes toward these goals, then toward what? *C&C* advocated for an ecumenical project in

Mississippi called the Delta Ministry, defending it against an NCC investigation that charged it with financial corruption, separatism, and fomenting conflict rather than reconciliation. The last of these charges was galling, since efforts by the ministry to reach out to whites had been rebuffed, but future *C&C* editor Leon Howell put it in historical perspective, commenting, "Niebuhr faced [a similar] charge in his support of labor against the automobile industry years ago." Howell added that a Delta Ministry leader had told him that Martin Luther King Jr. and black power militant Stokely Carmichael (now Kwame Ture) were "both correct, but Carmichael was more realistic."[31] In this way, Howell maintained *C&C*'s role as advocate. But the conflict with Delta Ministry's backers at the NCC was troubling, and *C&C*'s room to maneuver was dwindling due to the expulsion of whites from black organizations. Even more alarming was Spike's murder under suspicious circumstances shortly after he radicalized on the racial front, even though no one ever proved a connection between these two events.[32]

Moving further onto a limb, in 1968 John Fry cleared space for advocacy by defining his job at a downtown Chicago church as ministering to a politicized gang called the Blackstone Rangers; this eventually led him before a Senate investigatory committee. Few *C&C* readers followed this model. I know of none who enacted a proposal by Harvey Cox after the Chicago police murdered Black Panther leader Fred Hampton in 1969, attacking him with massive firepower while he slept at home with his pregnant companion. Cox compared the Chicago police to Hitler's Gestapo and suggested that white volunteers might volunteer to sleep in Black Panther houses to deter police assaults. He evoked Martin Niemoller's famous comment that the Nazis had come for communists first, then Jews, then unionists, then Catholics—but Niemoller did not speak up for any of these groups because he did not belong to them. Finally, when the Nazis came for dissident Protestants like him, there was no one left to speak up.[33]

Whites did not necessarily reject Cox's advice because they lacked commitment—after all, many civil rights workers had faced clear dangers of beatings and snipers, and some *C&C* readers later faced similar risks in Nicaragua. Of course, it is true that many whites did "tune in, turn on, and cop out," as black musician Gil Scott-Heron charged in his famous pun on the countercultural slogan, "tune in, turn on, and *drop* out."[34] But consider the problem of finding a context to support the level of commitment that Cox suggested. For northern whites in the early 1960s, a brief stay in jail for civil rights protest often involved limited risks while conferring significant prestige. But what about an indictment for conspiracy with the Black Panthers in 1970, after King was dead and Nixon was in power? Moreover, let us suppose that Cox had volunteered. In what context could he and the Panthers have built trust and common vision? Let us further suppose that they created this context. Would it imply burning every bridge to the mainstream churches? Quite likely the answer would have been yes. A mild Presbyterian resolution had recently been attacked simply for supporting nonviolent civil disobedience; Senator Sam Ervin, a "loyal Presbyterian," had compared this to condoning rape and murder. Imagine the difficulties when the Presbyterians (endorsed by *C&C*) contributed $10,000 to the legal defense fund of Angela Davis, a self-described communist who supported militant black power![35]

I have dramatized *C&C*'s dilemmas with a far-fetched image of respectable liberals volunteering as human shields for Black Panthers, but it is crucial not to overdramatize these dilemmas. After all, *C&C* could play more plausible advocacy roles even in relation to the most radical groups. Rebutting police lies about Fred Hampton's murder, however limited, was not trivial. *C&C* helped popularize black power and worked for fairness in the celebrated political trials of Angela Davis and Benjamin Chavis.[36] *C&C* published "Inside Attica," a major article about the Attica prison strike and ensuing massacre. It was an interview with a member of the inmate negotiating team, and with its eloquence, specificity, and controlled rage, it was a superb resource for understanding the revolt from the prisoners' perspective and refuting government versions of the story.[37]

Although such advocacy roles were more modest than sleeping in Black Panther houses, they were more than enough to polarize *C&C* readers. One letter writer claimed that government abuses at Attica were not systematic and that *C&C* should have underlined problems in the prison yard. He implied that the government had negotiated in good faith—precisely what *C&C*'s evidence called into question—and that the prisoners' demands were too stubborn. Another reader called it "hogwash" to defend Fred Hampton because he was armed; *C&C* should only support "justified protest." (This provoked a reply entitled "Yes, Virginia, There Is Police Harassment," which pointed out that police had been killing blacks for years.)[38]

More than any other issue, the Black Manifesto controversy dramatized the collapse of the civil rights coalition and the difficulties of *C&C*'s advocacy role. This drama unfolded in two acts. In the first, black activist James Forman interrupted worship at the Riverside Church, a center of establishment Protestantism that was only one block from *C&C*'s office. (This is the same congregation we met earlier, when a critic dubbed it SOCONY, or "Standard Oil Church of New York.") After a fiery anti-imperialist preamble, Forman said, "We are therefore demanding of the white Christian churches and Jewish synagogues, which are part and parcel of the system of capitalism, that they begin to pay reparations to black people in this country. We are demanding $500 million. . . . This total comes to 15 dollars per nigger. . . . [This] is not a large sum of money and we know that the churches and synagogues have a tremendous wealth, and its membership, white America, has profited from and still exploits black people."[39]

Forman's demand caused an uproar within the mainline churches. It also created a specific problem for *C&C,* because Bennett was president of Union Seminary and students occupied his office to demand that Union kick into the reparations fund. Under Bennett's leadership, Union's board donated $100,000, shifted $500,000 in investments into Harlem, and pledged to raise $1 million more. But this was not a happy decision. It provoked resignations from Union's board and failed to satisfy the militants because little money went to Forman's group. Rather, Union's reparations (like most other contributions from church groups) funded "safe" projects such as minority scholarships at Union and black caucuses within white denominations.[40]

Meanwhile, in the second act of the drama, Union's governing body, which had been newly reorganized to share power with students and staff, voted $400,000 of Union's endowment to post bail for a group of Black Panthers who were then on trial. Union's board responded by overthrowing the new governance system and vetoing this decision. These two acts, along with Union's new affirmative action policy, caused extreme internal dissent at the seminary and the withdrawal of corporate support. This was not an everyday sort of crisis but the near-collapse of Union as an institution. Union's faculty was cut in half between 1970 and 1974.[41]

C&C reacted cautiously to these exhilarating events at the school it relied on for personnel and subsidies. On one hand, it supported the Black Manifesto and attacked the strings attached to funding as "Colonial Brokerage." It compared reparations to paying outstanding debts on an estate before dividing the inheritance, and it defended Forman's program, which centered on large-scale community organizing efforts and included economic development organizations, strike funds, communications media, and a school—in short, as Gayraud Wilmore summarizes, a complete "apparatus for institutionalizing black power."[42] But another article attacked the Manifesto as a "candidly Socialist and racist" proposal by "self-appointed" leaders. "If someone were to propose a Free State of Harlem" with an elected government, said this article, it might make sense to transfer wealth to it from the state of New York. But the Black Manifesto was too indistinct.[43]

Around 1970, *C&C* still clung to its role as bridge and advocate, but only by the barest thread. Rose noted that radicals saw Union's decision about bail for the Panthers as a betrayal, while liberals perceived it as an attempt to avoid "institution-destroying polarization." He tried to imagine a creative polarization that could lead to an alliance between radicals and liberals. At a *C&C* anniversary banquet in 1971, Bennett said that *C&C* provided a "platform to those who push the white man hardest, for we see that white racism is a deeper cultural sickness than we realized in the early sixties." He specifically mentioned Forman.[44]

This role as platform and funding resource for radicals was not trivial. Nonetheless, it seemed slightly unsatisfying, and the rhetoric sounded hollow, given three problems: *C&C*'s limited ability to imagine a movement with a clear role for white liberals and black nationalists, its lack of a black constituency whose day-to-day concerns could be addressed, and the increasing costs of advocacy. In this context, there was some tendency for *C&C* to disengage from race issues. We must not overstress this point, because in some ways *C&C*'s commitment was steady. In time it rebounded from demoralization and moved toward alternative approaches such as black theology, womanist theology, and various grassroots organizing projects. *C&C* remained among the top religious journals addressing racial justice, and increased its nonwhite readership from 2 percent to nearly 10 percent by 1990.[45] Yet *C&C* never regained the level of engagement with race that it sustained in the early 1960s. Race moved from the center of its agenda and the vanguard of its evolving radical discourse, to a distinct third place behind Latin American radicalism and feminism. *C&C*'s dominant mood at the end of the decade was unmistakable. As Lincoln put it in 1968, "Futility is what I feel. Sadness and futility."

The Vietnam War: Niebuhrian Hawks, Niebuhrian Doves, and Radical Anti-Niebuhrians

C&C's process of rethinking the cold war came to a head over U.S. intervention in Vietnam. As *C&C*'s leaders questioned cold war approaches to the war and attacked U.S. policies, unrepentant cold warriors at *C&C*'s hawkish pole were outraged. Meanwhile, moderate doves from *C&C*'s "right-center" and more radical voices on its "far left" (who were not very radical compared with the New Left) split on major issues. Vietnam was *C&C*'s highest priority between 1965 and 1970, accounting for 20 percent of its articles.

The favorite story used by *C&C* old-timers to dramatize their history was provoked by Vietnam. *C&C*'s twenty-fifth anniversary fell in February 1966, just when the United States drastically escalated the war. This turned almost all *C&C* insiders against the war, including some who had earlier been noncommittal. Niebuhr's old friend from Americans for Democratic Action, Vice-President Hubert Humphrey, was scheduled to speak at the anniversary banquet—and this turned out to be his first public speech after a high-profile trip to Asia promoting U.S. policy. Behind the scenes, *C&C* debated whether to withdraw the invitation, then decided against it. Humphrey shuttled in from Asia and visited Niebuhr at home, since he was too sick to attend. (Niebuhr later reported incredulously that Humphrey had told him that the notorious Vietnamese leader Marshall Ky was "a patriot, an anti-communist, and now we're going to make him a Democrat.") Antiwar protesters from Union picketed outside the banquet. Inside, Bennett and Hans Morgenthau preceded Humphrey with antiwar speeches. Humphrey then gave a "Tribute to Reinhold Niebuhr," which Niebuhr later vilified for "claiming my anti-Nazi stance of the thirties for the present war." Anne Bennett, seated near Humphrey at the head table, "removed her black shawl to reveal a large white dove" pinned to her dress.[46]

This confrontation would soon seem tame compared with other *C&C* antiwar activities. However, *C&C* could not embrace more radical protest until it came to terms with its past. We have seen that *C&C* entered the 1960s with an X hand that used anticommunist and pro-development arguments to support the basic outlines of U.S. foreign policy and, frequently, to support third world dictators whom it deemed the best "viable" leaders for their countries. At the same time, *C&C*'s Y hand stressed that such U.S. clients were lesser *evils* and cautioned against overly ambitious attempts to impose U.S. will through military action. Moreover, by the late 1950s, *C&C* was giving increased respect to anticolonial standpoints and rethinking the cold war.

C&C had never been completely sure how to respond to what the Vietnamese call their thirty years' war—their anticolonial struggle, which was already under way in 1941.[47] During World War II, Ho Chi Minh led a successful war for national independence, complete with a victory speech quoting the Declaration of Independence. The United States responded by funding the French to reconquer Vietnam and integrate it into the periphery of Japanese capitalism. After a decade of struggle, the Vietnamese defeated the U.S./French forces, and in the 1954 Geneva Accords they accepted a temporary North-South partition based on the promise of elections to unify the country. Everyone knew that Ho Chi Minh would win the elections, so a series of South Vietnamese governments postponed them indefinitely. These governments were largely created by the United States; as one Asian ecumenical leader put it, "To say that the government of South Vietnam approves of the U.S. policy is to say precisely nothing."[48] These regimes also proved extremely unpopular and corrupt, so that by the early 1960s the government of Ngo Dinh Diem was losing a civil war against a revived National Liberation Front (the Vietcong) rooted in the south and allied with Ho's government in North Vietnam.[49]

Before Diem's regime collapsed, *C&C* generally went along with U.S. policy, reasoning that "if we withdraw, the Communists will overrun the whole of southeast Asia." *C&C* criticized French colonialism, yet supported what it called "obviously necessary military action against the hostile threat of Ho Chi Minh."[50] Niebuhr blandly rewrote the Geneva Accords as partitioning Vietnam indefinitely "between a Communist and a 'democratic' section." He said that "there ought to be an island of isolation for women like . . . the sister of President Diem," but that Diem himself was "our bastard."[51] On the other hand, ever since Mao had defeated Chiang Kai-shek, *C&C* had stressed the futility of trying to defeat Asian nationalism with the U.S. military alone.

Thus *C&C* could interpret Vietnam through various political analogies. The default option was a Munich analogy, with China in the role of Hitler; this led to the conclusion that communism must be resisted at all costs. However, *C&C* vacillated between this and a Korean War analogy. No matter how much it hated Ho Chi Minh, it saw no sense in risking a stalemate like the Korean War, when the United States had invaded North Korea to roll back communism, only to be turned back (as a U.S. commander put it) by a "glut of Chinamen." Such a war would not be viable; resistance to communism had to focus on nonmilitary initiatives. Blending a little from both approaches, *C&C* thought arms might supplement nonmilitary policies on a NATO analogy—the United States could try to hold a military line behind which an Asian Marshall Plan could work. But it remained unclear whether this plan was viable.[52]

Given this background, *C&C* faced a crossroads as doubts increased about "our bastard" Diem's ability to win the Vietnamese civil war. What if *C&C*'s vision of a "free and stable [South] Vietnam . . . at peace with its neighbors" was not realistically attainable? If not, was a "semi-free, semi-stable, somewhat imperiled Vietnam worth the costly effort and risk of conflict with Communist powers?"[53] For *C&C*'s hawks the answer was obvious. Kenneth Thompson said that the West must "tam[e] the latest aggressor . . . threatening peace in the world, Red China," in order to "preserve [an] international order in which [democracy] can grow." Van Dusen added that "one must search" to find anyone who disagreed with the domino theory; he charged religious doves with "inexcusable wishful thinking."[54]

At first *C&C*'s centrists were unsure. In 1965 Niebuhr called Vietnam "an insoluble problem" and seesawed between pro- and antigovernment arguments. Stressing *C&C*'s omnipresent concerns about viability, he said that "we cannot construct a democratic government for this 'client nation' because the peasants are too ignorant to understand the issues"—they saw Ho Chi Minh as a patriotic hero rather than a tyrant. Moreover, "only a highly advanced European culture . . . [can] sustain democratic autonomy." Yet the inexorable logic of deterrence remained: "We cannot afford strategically to deliver the whole of Southeast Asia to the Communist empire." Niebuhr's only positive suggestion was to "explain [the problem's] insolubility with candor."[55]

By 1966, Niebuhr was tilting distinctly toward the antiwar side of this seesaw.[56] By this time, Bennett had been producing a steady stream of editorials against the war for two years. A month after Niebuhr's insoluble problem editorial, Bennett asked far sharper questions. Why not negotiate seriously with North Vietnam? Who is being killed? Do hawks really believe that "all that it takes to win is more resolute use of force?" This idea was "terribly wrong" because "the Vietcong represents an indigenous revolution in South Vietnam." In general, U.S. policy "rests [its] whole structure . . . on a swamp."[57]

Bennett addressed *C&C*'s leading hawk, Ramsey, who complained that "Reinhold Niebuhr signs petitions . . . as if Reinhold Niebuhr had never existed." How could "a journal founded . . . to support the war against Hitler and combat pacifism" now criticize U.S. policy and "make common cause with today's pacifists?" Bennett replied that *C&C* still believed in checking power with power; it wanted negotiations rather than immediate withdrawal. Yet the Munich analogy was flawed—first, because peaceful coexistence with Hitler had been impossible, but it was now possible with some forms of communism; and second, because the "viability" argument, as Bennett now deployed it, unambiguously critiqued U.S. policy. The threat of Asian communism was not primarily military—rather, it was based on "exploit[ing] revolutionary situations" which U.S. intervention would intensify. Bennett said, "We need to be realistic about what . . . a predominantly white country can do to counteract Communism in Asia," especially when the people involved "need stable governments and revolutionary change." Hawks ignored factors that "could cause military success to lead to political and moral defeats." Bennett insisted that *C&C* was more realistic than its realist opponents.[58]

In 1966, *C&C*'s whole board (except Kenneth Thompson, who by this time was conspicuously out of step) signed a widely publicized editorial against the war. It called for "de-escalation, disengagement, multi-lateral diplomatic efforts and economic reconstruction," and insisted that any drawbacks of this plan were lesser evils.[59] There was less consensus on this statement than met the eye. When board members presented their individual spins, Searle Bates added so many qualifications that he effectively repudiated it. Shinn proposed a "sober factual" approach: "Dig in for a while, keep casualties at a minimum instead of escalating the war, and wait for the other side to negotiate." Meanwhile, Brown called for a peace candidate in the 1968 elections, and Driver accused the government of complete cynicism.[60]

Far more than his colleagues, Driver spoke about the positive self-organization of the National Liberation Front, rather than a faceless communism emanating from North Vietnam or China. Vincent Harding also presented the history of the conflict as a popular civil war, tilting toward the standpoint of the South Vietnamese opposition.[61] This focus on Vietnamese points of view was rare, but *C&C* did begin to integrate the Vietnamese through what we might call a dual-track approach—one which stressed a pragmatic convergence of interest between the Vietnamese and U.S. people. The joint editorial said that the war was "destructive to the people whom we claim to be helping . . . and to our best interests." The dominant calculus was responsible U.S. self-interest, but the Vietnamese gained some status in the debate through passages like this: "The burning of villages, the killing . . . of civilians . . . the use of napalm and chemical destruction of crops inflict . . . suffering that makes incredible the official promises of pacification and remote benefits. . . . Such tactics alienate and harm the very people we purport to save." Note that such a dual-track approach only works as long as U.S. self-interest and morality run smoothly together. What if a corrupt third world regime—say, that of the Emir of Kuwait—could win a "viable" war against an opponent identified by U.S. elites as a threat to their self-interest? *C&C* was still open to supporting this. Its joint editorial treated the domino theory as a serious concern and endorsed "efforts to strengthen viable governments that afford alternatives to Communism."[62]

In this context, straightforward moral criticism of the human costs of U.S. policy were like a breath of fresh air in a stuffy room. One of *C&C*'s earliest critiques in this vein was by a self-described conservative, Peter Berger. He rejected the dual-track approach because he thought U.S. policy *was* viable—that is, victory was plausible. Moreover, he placed himself above knee-jerk liberals: "If all that one could reproach the U.S. Government with is that it is imperial, that it uses military force and that it tells lies, one's own moral economy would remain fairly undisturbed." Still, Berger was "morally outraged by American actions in Vietnam," such as torturing prisoners, making war against the whole population, and "dropping napalm on children." Berger was proud to be a realist. But even if such behavior was strategically prudent, it went beyond limits—it was crime. U.S.

citizens were viewed worldwide "with the same pastoral solicitude with which people used to approach 'good Germans'" after World War II.[63]

After 1966, *C&C* steadily increased its reliance on such straightforward arguments and turned toward unambiguous peace activism. Bennett said, "It Is Difficult to Be an American," because his government refused to consider compromise to stop the killing, while it committed "atrocities . . . that surpass in inhumanity all of the atrocities we charge against our adversaries."[64] We might pause to reflect that this statement, although cautious by the standards of the antiwar movement, was intended (as Nixon's famous phrase put it) to "play in Peoria." It received respectful coverage in the Protestant press, the *New York Times* and *Village Voice*.[65] It also received this response from the *Danville (VA) Register*: "The peaceniks of Dr. Bennett's ilk see only one side . . . if [he] finds it so difficult to be an American, why does he not try being something else? It should be easy, quite easy, for someone at such odds with the cause and course of his country."[66]

After a history of identifying with U.S. officials—indeed, working as government officials in some cases—*C&C* came to assume that official news reports about the war were lies. It reported how a military officer who handled the Vietnam press corps had told reporter Morley Safer, after Safer questioned U.S. propaganda, that he expected reporters to be "handmaidens of government" and that he could "deal with you [i.e., Safer] through your editors and publishers back in the States." The same officer stated, "If you think any American official is going to tell you the truth, then you're stupid."[67]

Antiwar activities became *C&C*'s top priority. Bennett was a key organizer of Martin Luther King Jr.'s famous Riverside Church speech against the war.[68] Most important, Bennett, Brown, and many others in *C&C*'s orbit were among the central organizers of CALCAV, or Clergy and Laymen Concerned about Vietnam (later renamed Clergy and Laity Concerned).[69] Although groups like the Catholic Worker and the American Friends Service Committee had long opposed the war, CALCAV was the first major nonpacifist (as they said, "responsible") religious antiwar organization. Some scholars place it among the nation's most effective peace groups because of its social location and pragmatic sophistication.[70] CALCAV often ran advertisements in *C&C* for such projects as Vietnam Sunday—a day to pray for peace and teach about Vietnam during Christian worship—and mobilizations in Washington where antiwar clergy heard speeches and lobbied Congress. *C&C* in turn reported on CALCAV and its process of radicalization. By the time of its second Washington Mobilization in 1968, CALCAV had given up on selling its program to the administration. Instead of going to Capitol Hill with petitions, the group marched in Arlington Cemetery to pray for the dead.[71]

Although *C&C* did not stop petitioning Congress and promoting moderate outreach to local churches until the bitter end, it also began to embrace more flamboyant methods.[72] It defended draft resistance, citing St. Peter, who was jailed for the principle "We must obey God rather than men."[73] CALCAV sent a chaplain to U.S. draft resisters exiled in Sweden. Anne Bennett traveled to Vietnam with a group that documented South Vietnamese torture of prisoners in its notorious "tiger cages." John Bennett (then president of Union Seminary) went to jail for a protest at the White House—in the year after the president of Union's board of directors resigned to become Nixon's undersecretary of state.[74] The radical Catholic priest Daniel Berrigan appeared in the first—and only—centerfold poster in *C&C*'s history. His brother Phillip wrote from prison after their famous Catonsville protest, at which they destroyed draft records with homemade napalm—the protest for which Daniel wrote his famous poem: "Apologies, good friends, for this fracture of good order, the burning of paper instead of children."[75]

By 1967 Niebuhr had tilted decisively against the war. He supported CALCAV within the limits of his health, and when a group of seminarians burned their draft cards, he called them "heroic." In 1966 he had retired from the *C&C* masthead; thus he had not signed its joint antiwar editorial, which appeared in *C&C*'s first issue with Bennett as sole chair. *C&C*'s hawks who saw themselves as the true Niebuhrians were gratified, since they assumed that this signaled Niebuhr's disagreement with *C&C*'s emerging line. But he quickly returned as a "special contributing editor" and called the war a mistake. In 1967 he said it was an "error [to] regard the issue as the containment of communism, when we are in fact dealing with the nationalism of a small nation in Asia." In a 1969 interview, he sidestepped questions that were framed as openings to attack the utopianism of radicals, and responded that nonradicals also had illusions—a case in point being Richard Nixon. However, Niebuhr was never among *C&C*'s most radical voices. In the same interview he confessed that "a mystery of life to me is how the devil we should have been submerged in . . . this quagmire." He never fully moved beyond approaching Vietnam from a U.S. elite standpoint as an unfortunate mistake within a more-or-less intact vision.[76]

This approach was under severe attack by the late 1960s. An internal position paper by staff member Robert Harsh granted the value of promoting policies with a real chance of adoption, but he maintained that liberals were hemmed in places where all their options were intolerable: "'responsible' dissent means criminal cooperation [and] playing the game of options only means choosing how you or someone else will die." Harsh recalled *C&C*'s founding editorial, which had defined The Crisis and rallied

Protestants to defend western civilization. Did it not seem strange that Germany had been expelled from this civilization? "What if . . . Nazism is in some respects a horrible consequence of Western civilization and not a wholly alien tyranny imposed from without? What if Viet Nam is not just a mistaken choice among several Asian policy options, but is rather a fairly clear indication of the 'realism' which has always informed our foreign policy?"[77]

Thus Harsh no longer used realist moral logic to defend a nationalist, capitalist form of democracy, against murderous expansionist states such as Nazi Germany. Rather, he saw two *kinds* of murderous expansionist states (one self-described as realistic) against . . . what? *C&C*'s answers varied and interlocked: First, these states were against people who simply wanted to get off the killing train. This was the Berrigans' answer. Second, they were against direct victims of U.S. power who resisted it on its various frontiers—Vietnamese, Native Americans, black activists, feminists, and other groups in many places. This was the answer of liberation theologies. Third, they were against anyone still convinced by the original realist arguments against tyrannical power and the arrogance of expansion. But since realist arguments had come to justify postwar imperialism, realism was deployed, in the most radical way, against itself. This last possibility is extremely useful for conceptualizing how *C&C* could arrive at radical positions (on Vietnam and other issues) through a logical process within its former cold war paradigm.

These three answers—in their convergences and differences—help clarify debates about liberalism versus radicalism that became acute in the years around 1970 and have echoed through scholarship since then. Many people, within *C&C* and beyond it, attacked Niebuhrian realism as establishment ideology. George Williamson's 1972 article, "The Pentagon Papers and the Desecration of Pragmatica," was a major *C&C* statement of this theme, attacking Niebuhr directly.[78] But others defended Niebuhr. In light of the third answer—realism against realism—it is possible to see how both sides were correct. Realist logic was at the heart of elite U.S. policy in Vietnam, and realism could undermine it radically. Both Beverly Harrison and Bennett defended Niebuhr from overly sweeping attacks by Williamson. Bennett said, "I have no desire to preserve that word [*realism*] to refer to the sum of theological wisdom . . . [yet] you lose perspective if you fail to see that the logic of realism as understood in theology should be used against the assumptions, structures, and policies Williamson condemns."[79]

Bennett and Harrison could say such things with some credibility on the left. Harrison was emerging as the leading feminist scholar at Union, and she later used a "feminist realism" to inform an important moral defense of abortion rights.[80] A leader in the draft resistance movement lauded

Bennett at *C&C*'s thirtieth anniversary banquet. In the course of a lucid radical analysis of Vietnam, he said he respected few people from the older generation—especially not university presidents who were generally "the chauvinist, racist imperialists that the radicals say they are." Bennett, on the other hand, was a model for youth because of his activism and "ability to work through the political naiveté of Cold War Christian realism."[81]

It must be said, however, that the practice of blurring distinctions between realist and radical criticism gives rise to justifiable suspicion on the left. Although politely ignored by "respectable" discourse, Noam Chomsky makes devastating attacks on the sort of liberal Vietnam criticism that accents how "we" (all of us Americans, rich and poor together) miscalculated "our" interests in this war, but our motives were good and we should go ahead—preferably with a more enlightened self-interest next time.[82] Some academic arguments in this vein downplay differences between liberal and radical critiques with a primary result, less of legitimating radical critique, and more of neutralizing it by absorbing it into establishment realism. The classic example is Robert Tucker's 1971 book, *The Radical Left and American Foreign Policy,* which demonstrated the blurry boundaries between realists and the best revisionists such as William Appleman Williams—but essentially did so to isolate and dismiss other anti-imperialist critiques (or at least straw versions of them) and move forward with business as usual. By the 1980s, for Tucker, business as usual included economic arguments for U.S. military control of oil in the Persian Gulf.[83]

The basic dispute between the realists and the anti-imperialists has been recycled in complicated debates between "postrevisionists," world systems theorists, and a growing cast of other interpretations.[84] *C&C*'s relation to these debates is doubly complex because *C&C* sided with radicals when discussing events from Vietnam through the Persian Gulf War, without ever recanting its realist analysis of the early cold war, which is the classic locus of disagreement in the scholarly debate. This is not the right place to sort out all these issues. For present purposes, the central issue in this tangled discourse is *C&C*'s dispute about radical uses of realist insights—for example, the gap between Harrison and Williamson's evaluation of Niebuhrian themes. It returns us to the central issue of *C&C*'s standpoint. Let us assume that fair-minded analysts on all sides can recognize the blurry boundaries between the best realist and radical positions. Let us further grant that, despite many complexities, everyone can agree at some level that there has been an identifiable structure of international power (whether "national security" or "corporatism" provides the best language for it) and a real set of elite policies interacting with it (whether a given policy may be driven ideologically, bureaucratically, racially, defensively, imperialistically, or through soft-headed "American innocence"). Given a hierarchy of power and specific U.S. policies, with whom was *C&C* siding? With whom was it making alliances? From whose point of view was it evaluating what was at stake? These questions provide no escape from evaluating particular disputes in political theory or day-to-day policy formation. Nonetheless, they are crucial questions to orient more specific inquiries and test their pragmatic value.[85]

The main point is that almost everyone at C&C—both its centrists like Bennett and its radicals like Harsh—broke with an elite standpoint on U.S. policy. They stopped talking about "our" interest and began to ask who, in particular, would profit and die from specific policies, and to think about these policies from the perspective of the victims—among which they increasingly included themselves. C&C's debate was no longer between pro-war and antiwar variations of Niebuhrian realism. Rather, it was between moderate antiwar activists who maintained aspects of realism and critics who self-consciously broke with it on the left. What they learned in Vietnam was deeply entwined with what they learned from the black freedom movement. They soon began to explore what these lessons meant for a wide range of other issues.

7

Flashpoints of Conflict: Third World Radicalism, the Religious Right, and the Student Left

Of course *C&C* followed many issues in the late 1960s besides race relations and Vietnam, the poles around which its debates revolved.[1] This chapter treats four of the most important: the Israel-Palestine conflict, Latin American radicalism, the rise of neoconservatism and the New Christian Right, and the counter-culture. Each of these issues in its own way contributed to *C&C*'s polarization.

"I Must Conclude That You Are a Cheat and a Liar": Conflict over the Middle East

One of *C&C*'s most heated controversies occurred when it began to tilt toward moderate pro-Palestinian positions and away from mainstream Zionism. Until after the Six-Day War of 1967, *C&C*'s running dispute about the Israel-Palestine conflict continued in the same patterns established at the founding of Israel in 1948 and the Suez Crisis of 1956. *C&C*'s Zionist tendency remained strongly entrenched. Even though Israel's powerful military easily won the Six-Day War, Niebuhr's commentary was called "David and Goliath." He said, "David, of course, is little Israel, numbering less than 2.5 million souls" against an alliance of Egypt, Syria, and Jordan that blockaded its outlet to the Red Sea and shelled it from the Golan Heights. "David" struck with "astounding victories" because "a nation that knows that it is in danger of strangulation will use its fists." Thompson approached the war with a cold war calculus so strong that he nearly ignored Arabs and Israelis: "The Russians seem bent on maintaining the foothold they gained in 1956 . . . and persist in heightening instability there." Niebuhr added, "The Mediterranean is becoming a Russian lake."[2]

C&C's moderate pro-Palestinian position also held steady, as Bennett called Israel to return Arab territories occupied in 1967—the West Bank, Golan Heights, Gaza, and Sinai—and rejected an accusation by Rabbi Balfour Brickner (his colleague in antiwar and civil rights work) that *C&C* was biased against Jews. Bennett said that "we should not go back" to debate "whether there was originally an injustice" at the formation of Israel, and that he presupposed Israel's right of self-defense; this remained *C&C*'s position until its death. But Bennett was adamant in his call for Israeli reconciliation with Arab refugees. Rejecting Brickner's argument, which used Hebrew Scriptures to defend Zionist land claims, Bennett said, "Theological premises . . . [do not] override issues of justice as between Israel and her neighbors. . . . Nothing that was true in an earlier century in regard to relations of Israel to Jerusalem can sanctify the right of conquest in the twentieth century."[3]

The attempt to mediate between these positions remained *C&C*'s center of gravity. Alan Geyer proposed a compromise on refugee resettlement and trotted out *C&C*'s familiar theory of forging solutions through development schemes like a "Jordan Valley Authority." After a 1969 Middle Eastern trip, Roger Shinn sympathetically reported both Jewish and Palestinian perspectives and argued that "there must be answers" which both sides would prefer to war. "People of different faiths can live together in peace. Lebanon shows that."[4]

In retrospect, this comment echoes with heartbreaking irony, since we know how the historic truces in Lebanese politics dissolved into bitter hostility.[5] The uneasy peace in *C&C*'s Middle East analysis did not fare much better. By 1970, *C&C*'s overall tilt had shifted toward a moderate pro-Palestinian position—and Zionists were outraged. The balance was already beginning to tip in 1967. The tone of Geyer's piece, which played the crucial mediating role between Zionist and pro-Palestinian articles, was more unsettled than analogous pieces in earlier years; it also used stronger language when discussing Palestinian points of view, as when Geyer wrote, "Israel's portrait of Nasser as the new Hitler is all too readily countered with Arab charges that Israeli militarism is pursuing a policy of *lebensraum* and 'genocide.'"[6] The turning point in *C&C*'s coverage, however, did not come until after a 1969 Middle East trip by a group of religious journalists, including Cowan, who by this time was *C&C*'s editor, and Bob Hoyt, who would later join him on *C&C*'s staff.

Cowan said that it was a "mind expander" to meet people on both sides of the conflict. After speaking with Palestinian refugees, he was appalled to hear Israeli Prime Minister Golda Meir "fervently plead for help in overcoming Soviet reluctance to let Jews come to Israel—and coldly insist there could be no Palestinian nation because there were no Palestinians." Cowan later recalled, "It was not easy to write about my new realization of complexity: Two people, with just but conflicting claims, not one good cause but two. I knew many of my Jewish friends would . . . feel betrayed." But he did write an article that underlined Palestinian grievances and asked the United States to address them more seriously. He said that even airline hijackings by the Palestine Liberation Organization (PLO), although "not to be condoned," were "the only way the Palestinians have been able to draw attention to their plight." Cowan argued that "one man's piracy is another man's guerrilla warfare"—and that this was true not only of the PLO but also of Israeli leader Menachem Begin (who had been a terrorist during the war to establish Israel) and of Errol Flynn movies about English explorers raiding Spanish galleons.[7]

One year later the American Friends Service Committee (AFSC) published a document called "Search for Peace in the Middle East." After it was attacked by the B'nai Brith and American Jewish Congress, *C&C* devoted two issues to debating its arguments. In an outraged tone, A. Roy Eckardt accused the AFSC of bias, hypocrisy, and "below-conscious anti-Semitism."[8] The idea that both Israelis and Palestinians had legitimate moral claims infuriated him—granting the two sides moral parity was anti-Semitic. Other writers balanced Eckardt with defenses that were far more cogent and evenhanded, though tilting toward Arab perspectives. They agreed that Christians must not forget Jewish fears of another Holocaust—and by the same logic they should also respect Arab grievances.[9] Two Jews joined this discussion. For Steven Swartzchild, defining all opposition to Israeli policy as anti-Semitic was like defining all Vietnam protesters as anti-American. On the other hand, Arthur Hertzberg said that the AFSC was "morally unforgivable." He questioned whether Israeli concessions suggested by the AFSC would work, given that Israel had already tried to negotiate when it withdrew from conquered territory after the Suez War. (How this withdrawal helped Palestinians was unclear.) Hertzberg said that the AFSC's goal was "moral pressure on Israel." But then why didn't Christians, if they really sought peace, "write a document addressed primarily to Arabs to suggest that Israel is a necessity and even a moral good?"[10] (Of course, from a Palestinian perspective, this sort of pressure on Palestinians had been a basic premise of western policy since the 1940s, backed by both ethical writings and military force.)

Israel Shahak, a survivor of the Bergen-Belsen concentration camp during World War II and chairman of an Israeli human rights group, replied to Hertzberg. He denounced the Israeli annexation of East Jerusalem as immoral and unjust. He also said, "I here declare emphatically, as a Jew (living in Jerusalem for the last eighteen years) that I trust many Arabs more than I trust Arthur Hertzberg." Why had Hertzberg dismissed evidence such as Israelis desecrating Arab cemeteries and repressing Arab dissent? Perhaps during his visit to Jerusalem he "was so busy in protesting the injustice done to Soviet Jews that he did not see the abominations against Arabs committed under his very nose."[11]

For *C&C* Zionists, this comment was the last straw. Franklin Littell perceived Zionist voices at *C&C* being swallowed up by an outrageously pro-Arab bias, and he described Niebuhr as a "revered teacher" who had written more for German Jews than "any other man or group of men." According to Littell, "It is a bitter shame and scandal that *C&C* should have descended to the level that it has, and that . . . [it] is now the predictable exponent of a position which on this issue . . . is indistinguishable from *Deutsches Christentum*"—that is, the Nazi Christianity sponsored by Hitler. Shahak was a "renegade Jew," a propagandist comparable to the Nazi Joseph Goebbels, and a communist whose claim to be a human rights activist was a lie. *C&C* stood by its information about Shahak's identity and repeatedly asked critics to address Shahak's specific charges, even if they believed that he was a communist. No such replies were forthcoming, but behind the scenes, Littell and Cowan exchanged extremely bitter letters and Littell attacked *C&C* in the newsletter of his group, *Christians Concerned for Israel*.[12] The controversy spilled over into the national press when Dean Francis Sayre of the Washington Cathedral quoted Shahak in a Palm Sunday sermon.[13]

In an open letter to Littell, which *C&C* chose not to publish, Shahak denied that he was a communist or even had Marxian sympathies, commenting that "this information about me is very easy to ascertain" in Israel. Thus, "I must conclude that you are a cheat and a liar." Since Littell had implied that Shahak supported terrorism, he stated that he

> always opposed any acts of terror by any individual or organization whatever . . . [including] terrorist acts committed by the Palestinian organizations. *But* I always made equally clear that I include . . . terrorist acts committed by order of the Israeli government—my government. I condemned . . . the use of napalm to burn Arab children alive—as was done by my government in Jordanian towns (A-Salt and Irbid) in June 1968. . . . I condemn even more the action of Golda Meir, who only a few months ago gave publicly her approval to those nauseating terrorists. . . . It is remarkable that you who dared to bring an accusation of alliance with terrorism against me are so silent about those acts.[14]

The climax of this drama came when Ursula Niebuhr, who accepted Littell's information about Shahak and dismissed all contrary evidence as communist disinformation, told *C&C* to remove Reinhold's name from its masthead, where he had been listed as founding editor since 1969. For several years before his death, she said, Reinhold had been troubled by some of *C&C*'s changes, and now "it is impossible . . . to have Reinhold's name still on the paper when it consistently publishes articles with anti-Israel animus." In response, Cowan reprinted a 1949 editorial note to remind readers, in Reinhold's own words, that *C&C* had always published critiques of Zionism. In a letter to Ursula, Bennett echoed this point, stressed the wide spectrum of opinion in *C&C*'s recent articles, and stated that Reinhold was "so much a part of [*C&C*'s] history that it seems strange and ungrateful not to record this fact in some way." In May 1972 *C&C* complied with Ursula's request.[15]

In *C&C*'s later years, despite occasional twists in its coverage of Middle Eastern issues, *C&C* continued on the basic trajectory laid down by 1972. The rough parity between Israeli and Palestinian claims that so enraged Littell was maintained, and within this framework *C&C* still sought a balanced approach and advocated a two-state solution. Thus when the United Nations passed a resolution identifying Zionism as a form of racism, Bennett said, "I share the general indignation and distress," since Zionism was "a form of nationalism designed to protect the Jewish people" from racism (not unlike black nationalism) and its exclusivism "is not directed against any race." But he also criticized Zionist policies toward Palestinians, which he said exacerbated hostility from the third world and helped to account for the vote.[16] Later *C&C* periodically endorsed compromises that would expand Palestinian rights, and it reported sympathetically on the Palestinian intifada, an upsurge of protest in the late 1980s.[17] *C&C* did not understand its positions as anti-Israel but, rather, as support for the compromises necessary to build long-term solutions. Thus one writer quoted an ex-member of Israel's general staff who spoke of "blindly chauvinistic and narrow-minded support [by U.S. liberals] for the most intransigent and suicidal tendencies within Israel."[18] Rosemary Ruether, one of *C&C*'s strongest advocates for Palestinian points of view, was also its most insistent critic of Christian anti-Semitism. She attacked it as a foundational dualism in western thought, with roots at the heart of Christian theology. In fact, it was "the left hand of Christology." Anti-Judaism was implied by exclusive Christian truth claims about Jesus as the Messiah, which assumed that Jewish beliefs about the Messiah were wrong. She argued that Christians should rethink their theology and accent the less exclusivist, more pluralistic dimensions of their traditions.[19]

From 1973, when the Organization of Petroleum Exporting Countries (OPEC) sharply increased oil prices, to the Persian Gulf War of 1991, *C&C* periodically debated the wisdom and morality of projecting U.S. power to "protect" Middle Eastern oil fields. In a mid-1970s exchange, Shinn and economist Robert Lekachman agreed that military intervention might be inevitable in certain scenarios, although they disagreed about how much domestic change should be undertaken to minimize this possibility. (Lekachman called for a nationalized U.S. oil industry, which led Shinn to query whether such a company would be as corrupt as the New York Transit Authority.)[20] However, *C&C* had a long tradition of skepticism about the logic of military intervention. Recall how Bennett asked during the Suez Crisis how raw force could successfully defend an oil pipeline in a foreign desert. One writer extended this tradition from a corporate standpoint, denying that OPEC had caused any crisis that justified war; why not stop rattling swords and just buy oil from the Arabs? Noam Chomsky pressed harder, asking why no one had proposed scenarios for invading Canada, Venezuela, and other non-Arab countries that produced oil. For that matter, why shouldn't Kuwait invade Texas to "protect" its oil, since Texas might not want to sell oil on Kuwait's terms and since Kuwait had a better record of using oil profits for humanitarian aid than Texas did? Chomsky's point was that such double standards could only be explained by racism and imperial arrogance, which had questionable morality as well as dangerous long-term implications for U.S. self-interest.[21] His questions echoed through *C&C*'s coverage until its death. By the time of the Gulf War, *C&C*'s skepticism about military motives and solutions, as well as its sympathy for the Iraqi victims, seemed unambiguous.[22]

From Developmentalism to Dependency Theory

As *C&C* embraced radical analyses of the Vietnam War, its larger thinking about foreign relations moved in similar directions. Increasingly it embraced nationalist movements with anti-imperialist agendas in Latin America, the Philippines, and southern Africa; it moved fastest and furthest to the left wherever it had radical colleagues in ecumenical networks.[23] Much of this analysis moved within a larger critique of free-market developmentalism. In 1969 a *C&C* moderate said of Henry Luce's 1941 call for an American Century: "We can, looking backward, see that we shared much of [Luce's] optimism about the U.S. spreading her productive skill and culture over the world. We had great confidence in the ability of U.S. democracy to right wrong at home and abroad; we believed that the U.S. as a world power could provide the answer to European colonialism. Today we are a little wiser."[24]

C&C increasingly abandoned the core premises of developmentalism: that Latin America, Asia, and Africa were following the same path to modern capitalism as Western Europe and the United States, and that by concentrating on their "comparative advantage"—whatever the world market decreed that their capitalists could sell at the highest profit—they could "progress" faster on the universal path from "underdevelopment" to "modernization." On the contrary, in the emerging paradigm of dependency theory, northern industrial powers and the former colonies in their southern periphery had evolved together within the same world capitalist system. Northern wealth and southern poverty both resulted in significant part—although not exclusively—from the exploitation of the South. Thus the South could not simply follow in the North's footsteps.

C&C came to insist that it was ideological mystification to use the theory of supply and demand—a closed theoretical system in which, by definition, whatever is sold is "worth" whatever is paid for it—to posit equal relationships of international trade in which strategies of comparative advantage could be freely chosen in a free market. On the contrary, market choices in every nation were continually shaped by political policies such as tax incentives, labor laws, corporate welfare, and government investment in road building and arms production. International economics involved *unequal* relationships of dependency, in which the stronger parties took advantage of the weaker through various means, from pillage and slavery in the colonial era to neocolonial arrangements like the politics of international debt in the present.[25]

For example, the theory of comparative advantage in producing raw materials consigned such countries as Cuba and the Dominican Republic to sell sugar on unpredictable and historically worsening terms to far more powerful industrial economies. Comparative advantage in the price of third world labor—that is, in human terms, starvation wages and appalling working conditions—was made possible by the repression of working-class movements by elites armed and funded by the North. Countries and movements that tried to opt out of the world system, or to reform their economies in ways deemed too radical, were attacked as communist. Sometimes the combined power of northern nations and their elite southern allies destroyed these movements through direct repression; sometimes they merely crippled them through various means (embargoes, economic sabotage, and so on) as a lesson for the benefit of other people who might be observing the radical experiments. This was to ensure that the so-called domino theory would not prove true in a backward way: not by a series of external communist conquests akin to falling dominos, but by a demonstration effect as various countries tried to copy a good thing.

A dependency analysis did not settle the question of how third world nations who inherited this history could best maximize their current economic health. Should they try to withdraw from the international market or use various political means to negotiate better terms within it?[26] In addition, the dependency analysis was potentially misleading if it assumed that the lines between strong and weak parties in a dependent relationship were the same as national border lines, as opposed to the distinctions between international classes of elites and workers—so that, for example, Mexican agribusiness executives with children at Harvard could posture as oppressed while checkout clerks in U.S. supermarkets felt guilty as oppressors. Even so, the central facts of inequality and empire remained, partly organized along national lines. (Few malnourished U.S. workers produced consumer goods that they could not afford, for sale to affluent Latin Americans; many malnourished Latin Americans grew food that they could not afford to eat, for sale to affluent U.S. consumers.) Radical analyses, typically informed by neo-Marxian theories, overthrew the modernization paradigm in many parts of the South. Radicals embraced an urgent rhetoric of structural change; often they used the vehicle of third world nationalism.

In the long run, the revolutionary nationalists who made the greatest impact in *C&C* were Latin Americans. Their influence grew through a gradual process, beginning in the early 1960s and complete by the mid-1970s. Reports from Latin America were a key part of *C&C*'s changing approach to the WCC's responsible society. For example, *C&C* board member Richard Shaull, a former missionary in Brazil, reported in 1963 that "a revolutionary mood has spread across the continent." He denied that development programs such as Kennedy's Alliance for Progress were forging a liberal center between a feudal right and an "international communist" left. On the contrary, development coexisted comfortably with a "semi-feudal order of privilege." Revolutionary workers, peasants, and youth were demanding larger structural changes, including land reform and income redistribution. Shaull said that *C&C*'s optimism about the liberal center "may no longer be justified"—the center was increasingly weak and unwilling to undertake significant reform. Instead, the best realistic option was to build broad center-left coalitions committed to national development. He argued that Marxian social analysis should have an important role in these coalitions, distinguishing between Marxism as a "general ideological inspiration" that provided tools for social analysis, and Marxism as an international conspiracy or an "all-embracing world view of dialectical materialism." In Latin America, "North Americans talk of freedom to people for whom that word connotes the freedom of a privileged few to exploit the masses; we speak of democracy to people for whom it suggests the continuation of the intolerable status quo. . . . We urge reforms . . . [with] little recognition of how they can come about." Shaull concluded that "the decline of the Center and the new role of Marxism . . . demand new categories of thought and a redefinition of responsibility" in which North Americans unambiguously took sides in a class struggle. This position apparently ruffled feathers at the White House: *C&C*'s archives contain a letter from Cowan to Arthur Schlesinger Jr., then a special assistant to the president. In response to criticism, Cowan underlined Shaull's distinction between forms of Marxism promoting "indigenous social change" and those "serving the interests of Chinese and Russian policy."[27]

In the early 1960s this was a minority position at *C&C*. Even Bennett suspected that Shaull was too pessimistic about the Latin American's vital center.[28] However, by the late 1960s, Shaull's perceptions (reinforced by *C&C*'s world ecumenical network) were becoming *C&C*'s common wisdom.[29] In 1967 Shaull argued that the status quo was bankrupt. He briefly entertained the idea that "the only way to move ahead" was through guerrilla warfare of the type made famous in secular leftist circles by Che Guevara and in church circles by the Colombian priest Camilo Torres, who died as a guerrilla and was widely revered as a martyr. But Shaull changed his mind about this vanguard approach and began to argue that a democratic transition to socialism might be possible. If so, it would require large-scale "conscientization"—a process of education for class consciousness, stressing the active agency of poor people for change—along the lines proposed by the Brazilian educator Paulo Freire.[30] At the political-economic level his vision reverted, once again, to national center-left coalitions for economic restructuring. But at the cultural and theological levels, churches could play an important role, especially if they reorganized in *comunidades ecclesiales de base* (CEBs)—grassroots groups organized within larger parishes for friendship and worship, using Freire's approach to social analysis and theological reflection.[31] *C&C* argued that if North American missionaries were to be helpful in this process, they needed Freire's education at least as much as the Latin Americans did. In a 1969 interview, the radical Mexican educator Ivan Illich described missionaries as "court chaplains" to the bureaucrats who administered U.S. development aid and "cultural propagandists for the status quo." With the best of intentions, they wanted to "colonize South America with North American Christianity." Illich organized a school for missionaries to "diminish the damage."[32]

Within this emergent framework—which provoked the predictable sniping from *C&C*'s lingering cold warriors—*C&C* followed developments in many parts of Latin America. In Chile the 1970 election of Salvador

Allende as president on a socialist platform first seemed to vindicate *C&C*'s vision of peaceful change, then seemed to discredit it as unrealistic when Allende's movement was crushed by U.S. and Chilean elites who instituted a bloody pro-capitalist dictatorship in 1973. *C&C* gave the greatest attention to Brazil, which was not only the country where liberation theology gained its strongest early foothold but also Shaull's former base as a missionary and the home of Rubem Alves, a liberation theologian who taught as a visiting professor at Union Seminary. In 1970 an important *C&C* article by William Wipfler documented large-scale torture by Brazil's military government.[33]

C&C writers were outraged and bitterly dismayed when the United States participated in Latin American repression. Many had personal friends who faced torture and murder, and sometimes they had personal knowledge that the official U.S. explanations were cover-ups and lies.[34] This was the political background for *C&C*'s later discussions of Latin American liberation theology, Central American revolutions, and the sanctuary movement. It drew *C&C* people into a process that asked them to take sides in increasingly intense conflicts, as when an NCC legal specialist coached pastors on how to respond if the FBI investigated one of their parishioners for revolutionary activities, or when the radical Nicaraguan priest Miguel D'Escoto made this comment about a conservative church leader: "I do not see how we have the same faith; we do not believe in the same Christ."[35]

Changing Relationships with Evangelicals and Neoconservatives

Although D'Escoto was speaking about a Catholic, Alfonso Lopez Trujillo of the Latin American Bishops Conference (CELAM), many *C&C* writers also found the Christ of North American fundamentalists such as Jerry Falwell to be different from the one they believed in. *C&C* provides an interesting angle of vision for exploring realignments in a larger U.S. religious landscape, especially in light of the simultaneous stagnation of mainline Protestantism, and growth among various evangelicals. (I will use *evangelical* as an umbrella term for fundamentalists, Pentecostals, neo-evangelicals, and others who stress personal conversion to Christ and Bible-centered authority.) For *C&C* after the 1960s, the key developments within this shifting landscape were its growing estrangement from the evangelical right, its budding alliance with the evangelical left, and its deteriorating relations with neoconservatives in the mainline denominations.

Despite the widespread perception that evangelical Protestants are rebels against something called "the world" or "mainstream U.S. culture"—a perception that harmonizes both with evangelical self-assessments and hostile analyses presenting them as a marginal and extremist fringe—the fact remains that most evangelicals have been comfortably accommodated to the dominant cultural trends of U.S. nationalism, white male power, and free market capitalism throughout the postwar period. At least in these important senses, they have been a steady part of the hegemonic coalition that *C&C* supported in its early years but increasingly came to criticize. Still, during the years of *C&C*'s transformation, there were two key changes among evangelicals.

First, they became increasingly central to the Protestant establishment. Indeed, by the 1980s some people were calling liberal denominations the "old-line" or even "sideline," replaced at the center by evangelicals. Between 1965 and 1985, evangelicals grew steadily—the fastest growing Pentecostal groups grew 30 percent per decade—while the mainline lost members at a striking rate: 28 percent for Presbyterians, 17 percent for Methodists, and so on.[36] Contrary to conventional wisdom, these losses had little to do with masses of laity flocking away from liberalism and voting with their feet for more conservative answers. More people who actually switched denominations moved from right to left, rather than from left to right, and the differences in growth resulted mainly from evangelicals retaining a higher percentage of youth than liberals.[37] (Evangelical youth moved toward more liberal enclaves within evangelicalism; mainline youth defected to secular culture—often a move left from churches.) Also contrary to common wisdom, these statistics represented little change in long-term demographic trends. True, the cumulative impact of evangelical growth was important, and the negative numbers did have a way of focusing the attention of mainline leaders. But the mainline's status as a numerical minority was long-standing—it was true both in the 1950s and in the 1970s—and the trend toward its declining market share had been under way since at least 1800, with the 1950s as a partial exception to the rule. The gap between conservative gains and liberal losses during the 1970s actually may have been *smaller* than in earlier decades.[38] What changed most drastically in the 1970s were a rising trend of youth alienation from the mainline and a growing perception of evangelical power (and related issues of morale) linked to evangelical leaders' ability to attract powerful allies.

It is fascinating to speculate on how *C&C*'s radical turn relates to this shift. Was a vacuum created in the elite tradition of justifying status quo policies as the will of God, when liberal Protestant leaders abandoned their inherited roles of baptizing U.S. nationalism, capitalism, and "family values"? Did people like Billy Graham and Pat Robertson gain morale and visibility, in part because elite allies turned to them to fill this vacuum?

Niebuhr had been known as the official establishment theologian, but by the mid-1960s if the *New York Times* sought a Protestant leader to bless status quo policies they had to look beyond *C&C* and its allies at the NCC. This was the context in which massive evangelical growth was discovered in the 1970s, whereas similar growth had earlier been ignored. It was also discovered that establishment Protestant leaders like those at *C&C* only spoke for a minority of the population. In addition, diagnosticians commonly discovered that the mainline churches had become dangerously liberal, indicating a need for a shift to the right.[39] This happened at the same moment that mainline youth defected in a generally left-liberal direction; one study found that only 6 percent of Presbyterians confirmed in the 1960s converted to fundamentalism, while half drifted into an apathetic or hostile stance, and the most liberal people were most likely to be alienated.[40]

Whatever impact the Niebuhrians' left turn had on the fortunes of evangelicals and liberals—of course, it was just one factor among others—and however much the rising power of evangelicals can be illuminated by asking which Protestants attract allies in broader hegemonic coalitions, one point is clear. Evangelicals could no longer be interpreted as either marginal or alienated from the establishment after the early 1970s. Politicized evangelicals such as Jerry Falwell and Pat Robertson led a key battalion in a victorious conservative army, however much they complained that Nixon or Reagan did not enact their complete agenda. Some scholars claimed around 1990 that the religious right had peaked and was now declining, as when *C&C* entitled an article "Good-bye to Pat Robertson" and predicted that the religious right was "unlikely either to grow much more . . . or fade away."[41] But such arguments are best interpreted as highlighting how evangelicals' political cup remained one-third empty, even though it was two-thirds full. As Marty has commented, by 1980 evangelicalism "claim[ed] the loyalty of all three major presidential candidates, along with entertainers and entrepreneurs, athletes and beauty queens. Obviously such a subculture can hardly be described as marginal."[42]

A second change in evangelicalism was its internal polarization between conservatives and liberals, a change somewhat like the radical versus neoconservative realignment inside *C&C*.[43] A clear majority of evangelicals remained conservative, bitterly divided among themselves on doctrinal issues and between relative moderates like Billy Graham and the rising militants of the New Right. However, a growing minority of evangelicals were liberals like Ronald Sider of Evangelicals for Social Action. There was also a thriving group of evangelical radicals such as the countercultural community that began publishing *Sojourners* magazine in 1971, with an original title of the *Post-American*. A good deal of evangelicalism's much-noted ability to retain youth (a pillar of the diagnosis which holds that institutional prudence dictates a right turn by the mainline) has in fact been linked to the growth of evangelical moderates and radicals.[44]

We have seen that *C&C* came into existence imagining liberal Protestants as good guys versus a whole gang of bad guys—Catholics, evangelicals, secularists, and sometimes Jews—but later joined an ecumenical coalition of liberal Catholics, Protestants, and Jews versus conservatives of all faiths. Throughout this process, *C&C* assumed that most evangelicals remained in the enemy camp. In the 1950s *C&C* debated about evangelicals when Billy Graham solicited help from mainline churches for a revival in New York City.[45] Niebuhr, who perceived Graham as intellectually unsophisticated and reactionary on race relations, said that he dreaded Graham's visit. This provoked an angry response from Henry Pitney Van Dusen (then president of Union Seminary), who advocated openness to evangelicals as a "third force" in Protestantism.[46] Similar arguments were recycled two months later when J. Howard Pew endowed *Christianity Today* magazine as an evangelical alternative to the *Century*.[47] These passionate exchanges did not represent sustained attention to evangelicals, who subsequently dropped out of *C&C*'s vision until around 1970, except during sporadic episodes such as the evangelical mobilization against Kennedy during the 1960 election. (At this time Bennett received national press coverage when he said that the anti-Kennedy lobbyists, who were convened by Billy Graham and included Norman Vincent Peale, were barely removed from a "Protestant underworld.")[48] Such episodes brought to the surface *C&C*'s underlying assumption that the liberal denominations were the establishment and that evangelicals did not deserve to join it.

Around 1970 *C&C* redrew its map of the religious landscape. Most evangelicals continued as *C&C* bad guys, but their rising power made them appear more dangerous. *C&C* obviously opposed the Texan Pentecostal who said that the Vietnam War "is but a narrow theater of a broader war between the free world and the communist world. The first thing that any believer should understand about the war which is now raging is that it is a holy war . . . in which the God of the universe is on one side, and against the other side. The issue in this war is nationalism. . . . The Bible is explicit that God is the author of nationalism."[49] Graham's rhetoric was more measured, but his sympathies were equally clear. When he kicked off a series of worship services in Nixon's White House, Niebuhr wrote a piece called "The King's Chapel and the King's Court," which was widely cited by the national press and subsequent scholarship. He compared the scene to the biblical confrontation between Amaziah, a court priest for the monarchy, and Amos, a prophet known for bluntly condemning oppression.

Of course, Graham played the role of Amaziah and Niebuhr played Amos. In the Bible, Amaziah had been a "high priest in the cult of complacency and self-sufficiency." Niebuhr stated that "those who accept invitations to preach in the White House should reflect on this."[50]

Writing in this vein appeared regularly until the end of *C&C*'s career. Sometimes *C&C* was bemused, as when one of the few female Southern Baptist ministers wrote that her male colleagues could preach hard-hitting sermons on political issues without raising eyebrows, but whenever she preached a sermon that challenged her parishioners, they assumed she was feeling sick and brought her casseroles. Sometimes *C&C* was bitter. As conservatives took over the Southern Baptist Convention in the 1980s, Will Campbell highlighted historic Baptist struggles for local autonomy. He recounted an episode when Anabaptist martyrs were executed with their tongues screwed to the roofs of their mouths so that they could not witness to the crowd; bitterly, he compared this to the emerging situation in which conservative Baptists silenced their own people.[51]

Meanwhile, just as *C&C* had earlier made peace with like-minded Catholics, it now explored an alliance with the evangelical left. Since the worship styles and biblical interpretations of most black churches were quite evangelical compared with mainline Protestants, *C&C*'s interest in the civil rights movement was part of this story. At the same time, the shifts on the white side of the color line were equally striking. In 1972 the *Post-American* (that is, the original *Sojourners*) offered free sample issues in *C&C*, and one year later *C&C* hyped the Chicago Declaration of Evangelical Social Concern, a document which rallied liberals in evangelical churches against the evangelical establishment. The author of an early book on the evangelical left wrote in *C&C* about "Evangelicals: Ecumenical Allies."[52]

Campbell and Cox searched for evangelical allies more diligently than most *C&C* writers. According to Campbell, "The alleged redneck is a crucial factor in the social problem of race / poverty / war. I am trying to say that he too has been manipulated, used and abused, and that what makes a man like George Wallace [the conservative populist politician] so dangerous is that about 90 percent of what he says is true, factually and historically accurate."[53] Campbell's intention was not to support Wallace but to stress that rank-and-file "redneck" anger against the establishment—partly expressed through fundamentalism—was a possible resource for future resistance on the left. He argued that white working-class southerners should be part of the coalition that *C&C* envisioned, at least on class issues, and that northern liberals should be less contemptuous toward southern whites. By the 1980s Cox had picked up a similar argument. In his sequel to *The Secular City*, called *Religion in the Secular City*, he turned his earlier pro-secular argument inside out, presenting Jerry Falwell's anti-modernism and Latin American liberation theology as parallel forms of "postmodern theology," in the sense that both made religious-political critiques of secular modernity. Ultimately, Cox judged Falwell a bad kind of "postmodernist" and the Latin Americans a good kind, but he said, "We need a liberation theology that will draw on the folk piety of Baptists, Methodists, and the rest." If not Falwell himself, perhaps some of his followers or their children might enact this.[54]

At best Cox's rednecks had a tentative—primarily hypothetical—place in *C&C's* new mental map of coalition partners. Even the alliance with *Sojourners* was rocky after the initial optimism; it was never as strong as *C&C's* alliance with the Catholic left. Major obstacles included disputes about interpreting the Bible, *C&C's* openness toward gays and lesbians, and *Sojourners'* opposition to abortion. Whereas *C&C* had several Catholics among its key writers, role models, and staff over the years (notably Ruether, Berrigan, and Hoyt), it had few people who identified primarily as evangelicals. Still, many *C&C* writers also appeared in *Sojourners.* If not through full harmony and day-to-day working relationships, then at least through a rough overlap in priorities, *C&C* embraced most evangelical leftists as allies on the majority of issues. Virtually no *C&C* subscribers read *Christianity Today* in 1967 or 1990. But by 1990, two-thirds as many *C&C* readers (14 percent) listed *Sojourners* or its kindred publication, *The Other Side,* as one of their two favorite magazines, as those (22 percent) who listed the *Century.*[55]

While *C&C* made peace with the embattled left wing of evangelicalism, its relations deteriorated with members of the old Protestant establishment who were becoming neoconservatives. I have used the analogy of a break-up between lovers. Something clicks . . . but disentangling two lives and negotiating the terms of separation may take years. *C&C's* conservatives fell away on varying timetables. Paul Ramsey disappeared after 1968. Kenneth Thompson hung on slightly longer; his last article, with its familiar omniscient voice full of geopolitics and lessons of history, appeared in 1971 as a "perspective" sandwiched between Cox's review of the countercultural film *Trash* and letters from readers.[56] Michael Novak was next in the line of critics who moved beyond *C&C's* rightward horizon, lamenting that *C&C* had betrayed a conservative version of Niebuhrian faith. Novak provided a twist on the usual pattern of starting on *C&C's* right and standing still as times changed. He began on *C&C's* left wing, and during the 1970s he claimed to attack *C&C* from within the left.

In 1968 Novak agreed with Cox that "Enough Is Enough"—that there was no significant difference between Humphrey and Nixon. In 1969 he penned a scathing attack on the academic establishment, complaining that it groomed students for conformity and used transparent double standards, as when it became alarmed about armed blacks but not about police brutality. At this time, Novak was barely civil to moderates who "believe that 'reason' and 'democratic procedures' operate in universities." Radicals should only try to dialogue with moderates, he judged, if each side could use its own chosen idiom.[57]

Novak was not the only budding neoconservative who wrote for *C&C* during the 1960s. We have seen how Peter Berger was one of *C&C*'s first writers to present a straightforward moral critique of U.S. Vietnam policy.[58] Two years later, Berger switched from upholding Vietnamese standpoints against U.S. war crimes to taking a police standpoint against young black males. He rallied to Richard Nixon's call for law and order, claiming that "the worry about a loitering young black"—that is, the assumption that black males are likely to be dangerous criminals—"is fully justified empirically, and anyone who denounces this statement as racist is obfuscating the issue." He also stated that most blacks actually supported calls for law and order; they aspired to an image which Berger had seen on a postage stamp: a "solicitous, apparently unarmed, policeman, holding the hand of a little boy."[59]

In an even more striking—even shocking—shift, by 1970 Novak had come to take the standpoint of construction workers who assaulted hippies and student protesters. His article did include a few points that were useful for a left-liberal analysis: he accented class resentments that helped account for the attacks, and he pressed leftists to stress economic grievances of workers. Yet the bulk of his article virtually celebrated the attacks, stopping just short of full identification by assuming the voice of an impartial reporter. Novak was especially impressed with the workers' banner, "MEN with a capital M," and spoke of their "apocalyptic rage that will make student riots seem like sorority teas." Liberals were for taking blacks to lunch, but Novak was for taking cops. A liberal pundit had said of the police at the Chicago Democratic convention, "They are beating our children." Novak responded, "Our children were also doing the beating."[60]

Less and less, Novak perceived *C&C* trying to build an oppositional alliance against a hegemonic coalition centered on corporate and military elites and their government allies. More and more his views converged with theories about a "new class." Within this worldview "class"—and consequently the true nature of radicals who mistakenly think they oppose an elite class—has little to do with neo-Marxian analyses of who controls structures of political-economic power. Rather, the real elite is centered on government bureaucrats and a knowledge class that controls the manipulation of ideas in a postindustrial economy. This analysis grew out of efforts to describe what kind of domination was practiced by elites in the old Soviet Union. Clearly these elites represented some sort of class, but it was not the old capitalist class and not the working class. It was something new. After theorists adapted and refined this approach to fit the United States, they were able to make some valuable distinctions among different sectors of the middle class. Unfortunately, in the debates most important for *C&C*, the most influential new class theorists focused selectively on *liberals*, rather than conservatives, within the knowledge class—conveniently ignoring people like Ronald Reagan's press team or corporate advertising firms. Thus new class theory deflected attention from analysis of race and gender—not to mention "old class" conflicts, the ones between the rich and the poor, between those who control the wealth and those who depend on them for a livelihood. A *C&C* reviewer hit the nail on the head in 1989 when he called new class analysis "a half-truth whose time has come."[61]

Novak was already arguing in the early 1970s that a "technological-social planning elite" was forming an unholy alliance with blacks (who had real but not unique grievances) and feminists (who were self-indulgent individualists) against white working-class majorities who were "family oriented." Democrats and radicals should be allying with the latter group, which Nixon called the silent majority and the press later called Reagan Democrats. In practice the liberal elites were betraying these people, according to Novak. He urged leftists to stop using vague rhetoric about peace and justice—which Niebuhr's anti-utopianism discredited—and to start building coalitions on specific issues of concern to white ethnic neighborhoods. Although other *C&C* writers explored related ideas and tried to integrate them within a left-wing multiculturalist vision, few shared Novak's "Programmatic Suggestions for a New Ethnic Politics," which included an end to busing for school integration, pro-family rhetoric versus "government child-care bureaucracy," and "confronting the pain of alienated labor" in only the vaguest way, tinged with nostalgia.[62] Novak steadily drifted to the right, where he soon completed his own map of U.S. society: it was a culture war between hypocritical liberal elites and opportunistic minorities allied on one side, against a silent majority no longer in a vacuum, betrayed, but rather led by powerful Republicans and allied with conservative elites like Novak and his sponsors at the American Enterprise Institute.

Although this was Novak's long-term trajectory, in the early 1970s he was still on *C&C*'s editorial board, and he considered himself a left-wing Democrat. He worked for George McGovern's presidential campaign in

1972, writing in *C&C* with a rhetoric somewhat like Black Power's, except that he argued that "every group is a minority." McGovern, too, was part of a minority because his father "experienced prejudice" as a Methodist fundamentalist in South Dakota. Novak was not McGovern's firmest ally, since he also praised Nixon (supposedly writing as a devil's advocate) for his "courage" in ordering the "lightning thrust" of the invasion of Cambodia. Unlike the Democrats, Nixon was "intelligent and persuasive" about the war.[63]

Finally, in 1975, when Novak submitted a piece called "The Richest Left in the World," *C&C*'s staff had heard enough. After consulting several contributing editors, they dropped him from the masthead. He fought the action, insisting in a flurry of correspondence that he did not "consider *C&C* more 'to the left' than myself" and that in loyalty to Niebuhr he wanted to "persevere until the magazine returns to sounder judgment." Roger Shinn and Robert McAfee Brown supported reinstating him, but they were overruled. He left with parting shots about *C&C*'s "radical chic and utopian thinking" and its "orthodoxy on women's issues," which he compared to the Vatican.[64] Thus, long after the click described above, no more neoconservatives remained in *C&C*'s inner circle.[65]

"Nothing Goes Right When Your Underwear's Tight": C&C and the Student Left

Insofar as "the sixties" are defined narrowly by New Left movements such as Students for a Democratic Society (SDS) or the counterculture, *C&C* remained on the margins of the sixties. Perhaps this is evidence that *C&C* was too square to deserve a place in standard narratives about the decade, or perhaps it suggests that these narratives should be framed more broadly, with more religion on the map. In any case, *C&C* was never "of" radical student movements in a way comparable to the civil rights coalition or moderate antiwar protest. Even the radicals on *C&C*'s spectrum of opinion about Vietnam were moderates compared with leading student antiwar activists. Consider this revealing story by Andrew Young, a civil rights activist and Democratic politician. He attended a planning meeting for the spring 1968 antiwar Mobilization, which was dominated by New Leftists, to tell them that King wanted to speak against the war. According to Young, "only one person there seemed even rational," so King turned to CALCAV to organize his famous Riverside Church speech against the war.[66]

C&C did publish a small stream of articles such as Shinn's acknowledgment of "Ferment on the Campus" in 1965 and an account of "The Battle of People's Park"—a 1969 confrontation at Berkeley during which

Governor Reagan put the campus under martial law—which addressed the motives of both sides in an "objective" voice but tilted toward the activists. Also, by the end of the decade *C&C* was advocating reforms in theological education; as noted above, Bennett oversaw major reforms at Union. These included shifting significant power toward students, many of whom had connections with the Columbia University student movement.[67]

Cowan noted that many of *C&C*'s younger constituents were upset that *C&C* spent so much energy dialoguing with Ramsey but had not "treated Students for a Democratic Society, the Black Panthers, and other elements of the New Left with sufficient seriousness." In the same article, however, Cowan maintained a strong us-them distinction between *C&C* and the New Left, stating that, "of course, confrontation politics is counter-productive." Writers from *C&C*'s older generation were eager to elaborate on why "they" must remain distinct from "us." One writer decried the New Left's "excess of 'prophetic zeal'" and fanatical tendency to "regard our present system as beyond redemption."[68] (Perhaps he was thinking about SDS leader Tom Hayden's statement that he was coming to the 1968 Chicago convention "to vomit on the 'politics of joy'"—Humphrey's campaign slogan—and to denounce the government as "an outlaw institution under the control of criminals.")[69] Hayden did not write for *C&C;* a more typical argument in its pages was the suggestion by historian Henry May that New Leftists in general, and Harvey Cox in particular, should reread Niebuhr's *Irony of American History.* In a private letter, Niebuhr echoed Henry Sloane Coffin's response after Niebuhr's students raised the hammer and sickle over Union Seminary in the 1930s. Niebuhr said, "These kids are all going crazy. I have an old man's peeve against the younger generation."[70]

Still, when *C&C* moderates saw the police attack Columbia University students in 1968, they were appalled. Kuhn compared the Columbia student movement to historic struggles by unions like the CIO during the 1930s; they were battling to transform the "authoritarian or monarchical structure of many universities." Bennett said, "There has been much talk about police brutality, but middle-class students and professors have seldom experienced it or seen it at first-hand on a large scale. . . . [Police] backed many [students and faculty] against fences and clubbed them while they drove others through the gate with their horses. These things had to be seen to be believed." Similarly, most *C&C* writers were outraged by the Chicago police assault on protesters at the 1968 Democratic Convention—except Ramsey, who complained about the students' "massive breakdown of good manners."[71]

Prior to 1968, *C&C*'s attention to the counterculture was sporadic at best. Whereas it knew how to respond to the New Left's political arguments, even when it disagreed with them, its early reports on hippies and the cultural aspects of the amorphous student movement call to mind Bob Dylan's famous phrase, "You know something is happening, but you don't know what it is, do you, Mr. Jones?"[72] Articles ranged from rather tame advocacy, such as a report on a church-related suburban youth center called "The House" that showed mild countercultural influences before the established churches closed it down, to extreme outside looking in analyses such as an article on youth interest in eastern religious mysticism by a prominent scholar of comparative religion, Huston Smith, who judged "psychedelic theophanies" a failure because profound experiences required greater discipline.[73]

By 1970 *C&C* began to pay more attention to the counterculture. The same internal position paper by Robert Harsh cited above—the one that compared U.S. Vietnam policy to Nazism—went on to argue that a liberal pragmatic mind-set made *C&C* "lose touch with the emotional realities of American life." Harsh said, "I usually get a tight feeling from reading *C&C*, a feeling that a certain discipline has been imposed on writers which limits their remarks to a narrow range of language and opinion. . . . 'Look at all these things that are wrong,' we keep telling our readers. 'Well,' say the readers, 'nothing goes right when your underwear's tight.'"[74]

Harsh suggested a new definition of responsibility and a "new politics" that was "willing to politicize all of life"—one that is "chaotic, playful, violent, and seemingly out of control." Along with this came a "theology of play" that sought to revalorize emotions and unlock creativities stifled by realism. One article approvingly quoted Cox: "Play is not about fun. . . . [It] is ludic consciousness. . . . It provides the link between our new theologies of 'religion' and theologies of liberation."[75] By 1970 many *C&C* articles reflected these themes. All of them rebelled against "politics as usual," but their political dimensions could be more or less emphatic. Sometimes counterculturalism shaded into activism of the Daniel Berrigan type and / or arguments about utopian consciousness in liberation theologies, as I will discuss below. Other times the political implications were individualized and indirect. "In Praise of Intimacy" sought experiences of refuge from a technological society. Reviewing pop-rock plays about Jesus, *C&C* said Bach would have liked *Godspell;* it also endorsed *Jesus Christ Superstar*'s presentation of Jesus and Mary Magdalene as lovers, as well as its interpretation of Judas as a typically unreliable pragmatist.[76]

C&C raised questions about the counterculture from both centrist and radical perspectives. One writer reported with disgust that a church conference had "aimed at blowing the mind of the conference rather than informing it," as when one small group presented its report in verse: "The fatal flaw of the white American / broods / over this conference / the fear of freedom / the fear of being out of control."[77] Another writer, using the literary pseudonym "Gammer Gurton," criticized theologians of play, including Sam Keen of men's movement fame. She echoed Gil Scott-Heron's complaint that hippies had "tuned in, turned on, and copped out." However, for Gurton the accent was on their tendency to valorize sexist role models such as Lord Krishna and Zorba the Greek, while failing to notice that "while their winsome, free and unproductive children were playing, someone was working." Gurton wanted to know, "Who's the cook?"[78]

Cox was *C&C*'s leading countercultural voice, from his 1969 *Feast of Fools,* an essay on festivity and fantasy, through his 1973 *Seduction of the Spirit,* which argued for the "reassertion of the small-scale, the spontaneous, the particular," to his 1977 *Turning East,* which described his personal exploration of non-Christian religions, from Zen Buddhism through the Hare Krishnas to peyote rituals of Mexican Indians.[79] The subtitle of *Turning East* was *The Promise and Peril of the New Orientalism,* and Cox argued that for most people in the United States, the perils of such explorations outweighed their promise. He challenged Christians to explore neglected mystical, ritual, and communitarian dimensions of their own traditions. Despite these disclaimers, it will come as no surprise that other *C&C* writers were suspicious. Even Driver, who shared many of Cox's concerns, said that *Seduction of the Spirit* "displays a certain anti-intellectual quality" and was sometimes "half-baked." In a supposedly friendly "personal letter," Martin Marty said that *Turning East* risked "what sociologists used to call 'slumming'" in its chapters about trying to learn from nonwestern traditions. Marty said, "You properly locate Orientalism as an upper middle-class luxury. . . . [It] says nothing to or for most blacks, or poor or oppressed. I am with you when you accuse its pop forms of narcissism and 'gluttony-of-experience.' Be prepared for critics who will accuse you . . . of sharing in all these shortcomings."[80]

When the *New York Times* mistakenly identified Marty as the author of *Turning East,* Robert McAfee Brown had a field day in his satirical column called "St. Hereticus." He said that a *Times* investigative reporter had been researching people with "a propensity for compulsive religious writing." (Both Cox and Marty, as well as Brown himself, cranked out books and articles by the dozen.) This reporter supposedly discovered that Marty "had a lacuna of thirty unaccounted-for minutes each day" during which he wrote under the suspicious pseudonym "*H*arvey Cox of *H*arvard College." "'Cox' was the alter-ego by means of which Marty kept his fantasy life in touch with reality. . . . Marty was the establishment spokesperson, 'Cox' the renegade social activist; Marty was the historian, 'Cox' the contemporary. . . .

[Marty] appeared in public places sporting a false beard and hairpiece, giving trendy talks and collecting 'Cox's' honoraria, after which he would double back to the University of Chicago to sit in on oral examinations about obscure eighteenth-century historians."[81]

This humorous approach to conflicts over the counterculture was more in keeping with *C&C*'s debates in the late 1970s than with *C&C*'s first bitter battles in the 1960s. Recall how during the 1968 election Will Campbell exhorted Christians to "drop out of politics and weep for those who stay in." He went on to insist that anything short of repudiating liberal politics was "political Messianism, Baalism." Appealing to the sweeping antitechnological critique of French theorist Jacques Ellul, Campbell said, "The truth is, nothing happened in Chicago . . . so let the Christian act as if nothing happened." As we have seen, Pete Young's attitude toward the liberal establishment—"to hell and be damned" with it—was even harsher. He embraced "the political task of building a new America," which he described as "a sort of Luddite rebellion in which machines of control will serve as the principal targets." Quoting novelist Norman Mailer, Young summed up his views: "There is a shit storm coming."[82]

All the issues discussed in the last two chapters were in the background or looming on the horizon—the collapse of the civil rights movement, conflict over Vietnam and the Middle East, religious polarization, and various attacks on establishment liberalism—when Harvey Cox wrote his "Enough Is Enough" editorial. For good measure, Cox followed it with another editorial called "The End of an Era," which stated that everyone agreed: liberalism had failed. "With the coming of Nixon, the New Deal is over. *Requiescat in Pace*."[83] But, of course, everyone did *not* agree; this was precisely the attitude that dismayed James Kuhn in the editorial I cited at the beginning of chapter 6, in which he exhorted liberals to stay the course. To say the least, Kuhn did not appreciate hearing his vision described as dead. He urged the left not to parrot right-wing rhetoric about the failures of liberalism, and he insisted that federal initiative remained the best hope for addressing major issues. Yet Kuhn's liberal vision presupposed a working New Deal coalition. Like it or not, that coalition was falling apart, inside and outside *C&C*. The result for liberals was an "underlying numbness." "What one senses at every level is an increasing air of futility."[84]

In time, *C&C* recovered from this shock and pressed forward with new energy. But after the 1960s neither radicals nor moderates in its new spectrum of debate could ignore the other. This was the context for the exchange I mentioned at the end of my introduction, in which two comments cut to the heart of *C&C*'s debates. Speaking for *C&C*'s emerging left, Shaull asked whether various radicals had identified real problems that liberals could not address. If so, pragmatic objections to radical strategies might be "out of context," and it was necessary to acknowledge a "new historical situation in which the struggle for social justice and human well-being must be defined in new terms."[85]

We may recall, however, how Bennett responded. He insisted that the issue was whether the U.S. system could be an "instrument of radical change"—not in the abstract but as compared with the actual alternatives that were available. Bennett was pessimistic about working through the system, but even *more* pessimistic about working outside it. He hoped that radicals could create "urgency within the political process" and that *C&C* could promote "communication between those who are near enough to the center to influence policy and those who are quite far out in their radicalism." Rosemary Ruether, emerging as a leading *C&C* theorist, expressed the tension as a struggle "to bridge the gap between a liberalism too easily co-opted and a radicalism too easily turned into impotent tantrums."[86] Her comments provided no easy answers to the problems that troubled *C&C*, but they defined *C&C*'s problematic as it entered its last two decades.

8

Picking Up the Pieces, Integrating Feminist Approaches

By the early 1970s, *C&C* had finished debating whether to take an oppositional stance toward the status quo, and its spectrum of debate had been reconfigured. Its new task was to pick up the pieces after the shattering of its former consensus and to organize them in new patterns, in relation to social concerns it had already assumed and to several new ones, especially feminism, gay/lesbian rights, and various liberation theologies. It is risky to speak about these developments in general terms, because they involved explorations in diverse directions rather than a search for any one unified vision. However, many of these explorations were loosely linked through a shift toward approaching issues "from below"—from the perspective of people at the bottom of power hierarchies—and within specific local contexts and communities.

An underlying key to this shift was revealed in 1972 when a reader complained that *C&C*'s coverage of the Attica prison strike and torture in Brazil were "simply articles" that provided "no connection between what you describe and what can be done by you and me." This was a strange argument if it implied (as it apparently did) a contrast with *C&C*'s past. Surely there had been no great connection between *C&C*'s geopolitical arguments of the 1950s and what could be done by most readers. No matter how little leverage *C&C* readers had on Governor Rockefeller's National Guard at Attica, it was greater than their leverage on, say, the Soviets' decision to invade Hungary in 1956, and no less than their leverage on Governor Faubus's National Guard at Little Rock. Why would *C&C*'s editors showcase this letter and comment that its "words cut deeply"?[1]

One clue can be found in Tom Driver's ironic comment about changes in Protestant theology since midcentury: "Our teachers, then, were warriors and heroes. They slew dragons. Their ivory towers were arsenals. We know (or fancied) that they made a difference in history. After all, the integrity of Western culture and 'the tradition' were at stake. . . . Down went the Nazis, down went the complacency of the bourgeoisie, down went the word of man. We cheered."[2]

By the 1970s a more typical example of *C&C*'s perspective on "the integrity of Western culture" was that of Dom Helder Camara, a Brazilian bishop who helped pioneer Latin American liberation theology. Invited to Harvard to receive an honorary doctorate of law, Camara asked, "What kind of law?" He listed a few possibilities and described how each was used against poor people. Then he turned to the "Four Freedoms" that Roosevelt had proclaimed as the western heritage to defend in World War II: freedom of speech and religion, freedom from want and fear. These "fundamental freedoms—portrayed so brilliantly on paper—soar like mockery, like jeers for the absolute majority of humanity," Camara said. For the sake of honesty, "Why not close . . . the schools of law and open schools of war?"[3]

C&C also perceived abstract assurances of justice as jeers at people inside the United States—and not only at poor people and racial minorities easily bracketed as the Others of a white middle class. For example, *C&C* began to examine the actual concentration of wealth in the United States, which is more comparable to Brazil's than to the vision of dispersed power in liberal ideology. And Mary Lou Suhor, editor of the Episcopal journal *The Witness* during the 1980s, reminisced about winning an academic contest in New Orleans: "The first prize was a full, tuition-paid scholarship to the Catholic University I later attended. *That* was the first prize if the winner was a 'boy.' But if the winner turned out to be a 'girl,' *the first prize was $40.*"[4] She later paid to attend this school but was not allowed to major in journalism.

Obviously, such stories posed a sharp challenge to *C&C*'s earlier defense of U.S. foreign policy and its belief that "domestic problems have been tolerably solved." What about the charge that they gave "no connection . . . [to] what can be done by you and me"? Why would this charge "cut deeply" for *C&C* editors? This question brings us to the heart of *C&C*'s changing orientation. Riding on the shoulders of dragon-slaying theologians, *C&C* readers previously had been able to identify with decisive elites managing and solving problems. But if, after reading "Inside Attica," they still identified with Nelson Rockefeller, then, true enough, *C&C*'s article failed to focus on what they should do (although certain implications were obvious); rather, it exposed them as passive supporters of a massacre. If they took the article's preferred perspective, they were challenged to consider "what could be done" from the standpoint of young black males caught in a racist legal system. Similarly, if they still resisted feminism and promoted capitalist development for Brazil after reading Suhor and Camara, they stood accused of slamming doors in Suhor's face and mocking the poor. In contrast, if they had gone through the same change as *C&C*, they were challenged to consider "what could be done" within bottom-up and small-scale contexts such as Camara's parish and Suhor's college.

For readers who made such shifts in perspective, *C&C*'s writing by the 1970s became, on balance, more helpful in identifying "what could be done." However, for those who did *not* make the shift, *C&C*'s critiques of white liberalism often undercut their received self-images and led them into a sort of vacuum, where they found it plausible to complain that there was no connection to what they could do—not only when *C&C* flirted with despair about the prospects for change or suggested far-fetched alliances like sleeping in Black Panther houses but also when it published articles that advocated moderate and pragmatic tactics supporting non-elite agendas. Some of the people who started out perceiving such a vacuum moved on to nostalgia for a golden era of vital center liberalism and ended up producing versions of Driver's jeremiad that, unfortunately, lacked his irony.

C&C's main story after its polarization of the late 1960s was that it did make this shift toward a smaller-scale, more bottom-up perspective. More precisely, it became a hub for communication among a diverse group of people, sometimes in conflict but loosely linked, who were making such shifts. Suhor said, "The women's movement did for me what the black movement did for blacks. It raised my consciousness and allowed me to see what scars I was carrying," as well as "to hear 'with black ears' what [blacks] were saying." After Driver painted his picture of dragon-slaying theologians, he contrasted it with a current situation in which "we have all been driven to find our theological identities not in the Other but in refractions of our experience. . . . The divine Wholly Other died. The Other as enemy also died, or dissolved."[5] Although Helder Camara was less prepared to dissolve his focus on elite enemies of the Brazilian masses, the emotional center of his speech was a call for small-scale communities rooted in hope. His biblical model was not Joshua's army or David's monarchy but the faith of Abraham and Sarah, who received a promise of future blessing that seemed highly improbable and required risk.

None of this means that *C&C*'s liberal-radical tension ended or that it lost a basic continuity with its past. True, *C&C*'s new debate was more decentered and its spectrum of debate was reconfigured. In addition, there were institutional changes that I discuss more fully in chapter 11: *C&C* partially cut loose from Union Seminary in the wake of Union's institutional crisis of the 1970s. It became less dominated by white males (for example, the combined nonwhite and female readership increased from 20 to 50 percent between 1967 and 1990), and more power flowed to the staff at the expense of the editorial board, which had become dysfunctional during the polarization of the late 1960s. Yet within this new framework *C&C* maintained considerable continuity. Its prestige was still based primarily on a central board of writers (renamed contributing editors in 1972) largely employed in Protestant seminaries. A moderate oppositional tendency continued to stress hope for pragmatic changes within received systems; for them, a call for more attention to "what we can do" suggested cautious liberal optimism rather than radical despair. Meanwhile, a decentered radical tendency accented the limitations of the moderates' vision and searched for alternatives; for them, the issue was despair about pragmatism versus optimism about radicalism. At worst these two tendencies merely threw mud on each other, but at best their tension was creative. Everyone agreed that problems were radical in the sense of requiring basic changes in status quo power structures and cultural patterns.

Exploring Feminist Analyses

When women in the student left presented their first explicit feminist critiques, the men who held power in the movement made notoriously revealing responses. For example, after a Women's Liberation Workshop at an SDS convention presented a major statement, the *New Left Notes* printed it next to a cartoon of a stereotypical young woman wearing a polka-dot miniskirt and matching panties, holding a sign stating, "We Want Our Rights and We Want Them Now." Such responses came to symbolize male resistance to feminism and the need for an autonomous women's movement.[6]

Judging solely by the cover of *C&C*'s first special issue on the women's movement, in 1970, *C&C* risked following a similar path. The cover photo showed a smiling white woman in a long dress, with lacy gloves, white parasol, and large formal hat that shadowed her eyes—bearing a sign that read "Equality Now." She seemed slightly out of touch with poor black people, antiwar protesters, and the gritty style of art that signified relevance for *C&C* at the time, even if she was interpreted as a latter-day suffragette using irony to promote a feminist cause. Fortunately, in this case appearances were somewhat deceiving. Despite the ambiguous cover, the issue featured a long article written from the standpoint of the women's movement, published without nonfeminist "balance."[7] The overall result foreshadowed *C&C*'s long-term trajectory. Although *C&C* always had writers who did not fully embrace feminism (so that religious feminists, like their secular counterparts, also needed to create autonomous spaces), after the mid-1970s *C&C* integrated feminist concerns as a high priority. Compared with its leading competitors in the world of Protestant journalism, such as the *Century* and *Sojourners*, it was by far the most consistent advocate of women's equality and empowerment.

During *C&C*'s radicalization in the late 1960s, it had continued to neglect gender and exclude female writers for the most part. Its habit of speaking about humans as men and the divine as Father had continued. So had its tendency to feminize positions it opposed; for example, Arthur Moore said that when U.S. government claimed it was trying to leave Vietnam, this reminded him of a woman in *Don Juan:* "A little still she strove, and much repented / And whispering 'I will ne'er consent'—consented." Bennett later recalled that he had doubted the reality of female oppression as late as 1970.[8]

On the other hand, *C&C* had substantial raw materials to draw upon when it finally turned its attention to gender. It routinely supported underdogs in hierarchies of power, had some precedent of questioning sexual codes linked to the traditional family, and had long been on record—if not as a high priority—in favor of women's ordination and against treating women as sex objects. It was not hard to rearticulate such positions in unambiguously feminist ways. For example, in 1971 Harvey Cox returned to the subject of sex in popular culture and recycled his earlier arguments—but his theme was no longer *Playboy*'s lack of the "courage to be" or the "vampire-like cult of The Girl" that required prophetic critique. Rather, he said that "the Follies girl . . . personifies the female equivalent of Stepin Fetchit," a notoriously racist stereotype from minstrel shows.[9]

It is easy to explain in general terms why it was around 1970 that Cox's writing gained a feminist edge, Bennett noticed women's oppression for the first time, and *C&C* began to publish women consistently. The revived second wave of feminism, inside and outside the churches, forced the issue to the forefront. Above all, *C&C* had to face the issues because women were being ordained in mainline denominations on a large-scale basis for the first time, and student populations at seminaries such as Union were transformed. No longer were they overwhelmingly male, with women usually pursuing Christian education degrees. Now the male/female ratios approached a rough parity, with women pursuing the same careers as men.[10]

However, grasping this point is only the beginning of analysis, because there was no single women's movement. From the beginning, feminists prominently debated their tendencies and divisions, and *C&C* was one space in which different groups battled for primacy. Amid their push and pull of argument, *C&C* evolved a position with a center of gravity in moderate socialist feminism, giving priority attention to interlocking structures of gender and socioeconomic power. *C&C* also supported liberal feminism, focusing on women's inclusion in status quo structures on the same terms as men (for example, organizing for women's ordination and related changes such as gender-inclusive language), and multicultural feminism, exploring the differences among white women and women of color. More radical forms of cultural feminism, goddess spirituality, and New Left socialist feminism were dialogue partners at times, but they lay on the periphery of *C&C*'s consciousness.[11]

These distinctions are clearer in retrospect than they were in the early 1970s, when *C&C*'s discourse on gender circled through a variety of loosely linked (sometimes incompatible) positions united by a common movement sensibility. Various components of disputed arguments were introduced under a common movement banner, in a spirit of fluid experimentation with feminist thinking that continued until the end of *C&C*'s career. Three examples from the early 1970s clarify the point.

The feature article in the special issue inaugurating *C&C*'s coverage—the one with the parasol woman on the cover—underlined the impact of feminist consciousness-raising, a common form of the early movement in which women met in small groups to compare experiences. With impressive eloquence, Kathy Mulherin and Jennifer Gardner described how their group had rethought the problems of career women, the politics of sex (if you fake orgasm, are you a whore?), males' failure to share housework, and the challenge of maintaining self-esteem in a system that devalued them. In terms of the contentious debates within feminist theory at the time, they supported the so-called pro-woman line toward heterosexual marriage. That is, they cautioned against dismissing married women as traitors who collaborated with the patriarchy, and suggested trusting them as potential allies who were making the compromises they needed to survive. Mulherin and Gardner were conscious that most feminists were relatively affluent whites, and their article does not fit the stereotype of white feminists imposing a universal women's nature on women of color. They said they understood why many black women had primary commitments to African American movements, and they expressed the hope that nonwhites would assume leadership within feminism.[12]

Not all of *C&C*'s feminists gave comparable attention to differences among women within larger social systems. Penelope Washbourn's "Religious Dimensions of Sexuality" stressed how women's bodies united them in a common experience of difference. Washbourn described in breathless prose how feminism helped her discover her connection to animal nature in the primal experience of giving birth, as well as her orientation toward emotional openness and the special fear of being penetrated that came with having a vagina. She argued that "the meaning of life and death, the question of a transcendent dimension, the experience of grace become most real on the visceral level, and most particularly so in the experience of my female sexuality."[13] Since Washbourn wrote in the first person, it was not clear whether she intended to posit a universal essence of women's nature defined by sexuality. However, she did not address other dimensions of women's experience, discuss differences among women on the issues she did raise, or say much about the down side of approaching women primarily through their bodies (notably the world-historical tendency of men to justify women's oppression in this way). Thus she left the impression that celebrating embodiment was a central pillar of feminism.

Where Washbourn presupposed biologically defined "feminine" experiences and revalorized them, Emily Culpepper and Linda Barufaldi started from a biology that was emphatically *not* destiny, and stressed how the social construction of gender squeezed people into artificial sex roles that devalued women. They advocated androgyny, describing it not as a "monotonous world of unisex, which would reduce everyone to one mold" but an approach that "multiplies and celebrates difference." Adopting a radical rhetoric, they wrote as leaders of a group called WITCH (Women's Inspirational Theology Conspiracy from Harvard, not to be confused with the more famous WITCH group called Women's International Conspiracy from Hell). "Over against the prevailing sense of reality [defined by patriarchy] androgyny is anarchy," they said. "The very consciousness that constitutes Being is changing."[14]

Cox's "Eight Theses on Female Liberation" showed that such diverse experimentation with feminist ideas had begun to influence *C&C*'s leading writers by 1971. After an abstract preamble about God supporting underdogs, Cox argued that sexism was "certainly the oldest and maybe the most basic and persistent form of seignorialty."[15] Women needed to create their own organizations, because working for socialism alongside men was not sufficient. Cox accented the complicity of the nuclear family with a gender-segregated job market, as well as the family's role in socializing people as sexist. He said that the main task for men was getting out of the way of women, although he believed that men also had a stake in the movement, since gender justice could improve their lives.

Although this was easily the strongest feminist statement to date from *C&C*'s inner circle, it did not go far enough for Carol Christ, a rising feminist scholar. She criticized Cox for taking too much personal credit for his arguments and failing to acknowledge the women's movement. In a similar vein, Anne Bennett wrote a scathing letter in which she assumed the worst about Cox's intentions. She felt that his language trivialized women (as when he lamented women's "replaceable coolie role" in the labor market) and assumed an "objective" voice that was biased toward males. Men should "move over so that women may take their rightful places . . . even on editorial boards of 'Christian journals of opinion.'"[16]

Anne Bennett was the author of a book on feminist theology, a mentor to young religious feminists, and a power behind the scenes in *C&C* circles.[17] Her feminist turn was important for *C&C*'s larger one, and at *C&C*'s 1971 anniversary banquet, which honored John Bennett upon his retirement from Union, Brown used humor to acknowledge her influence. He read a series of joke telegrams, all starting with the words "DEAR JOHN, APPRECIATE YOUR PROFOUND CONTRIBUTION TO MODERN THEOLOGICAL UNDERSTANDING." Each ending was different. Billy Graham supposedly tacked on the qualifier "EXCEPT FOR YOUR OPTIMISM REGARDING MAN." New Leftist Herbert Marcuse added, "EXCEPT FOR YOUR PESSIMISM REGARDING MAN." The culmination of this joke was the message from Anne Bennett: "EXCEPT FOR YOUR SILENCE REGARDING WOMAN."[18]

It was Rosemary Radford Ruether, however, who led *C&C* toward its socialist feminist center of gravity. In 1972 she and anthropologist Margaret Mead became the first two women on *C&C*'s board of editors in more than thirty years.[19] At first Ruether was identified largely with race issues, since she began her teaching career at historically black Howard University and wrote on such topics as the lessons whites could learn from blacks about effective protest. As noted above, she placed herself in the center of *C&C*'s spectrum of debate, calling herself a "Radical-Liberal."[20] The heart of her approach was a critique of dualistic and hierarchical thinking in western history, from the dualism between good and evil in Jewish and Christian apocalyptic, through the gnostic dualism of soul and body, to the Cartesian dualism of subject and object. Ruether showed how the positive sides of these dualistic oppositions were associated with the dominant groups in social hierarchies and how the devalued sides were identified with oppressed groups. She used this framework to analyze racism, anti-Semitism, human relations with the ecosystem, and class oppression as well as gender issues.[21] In addition to her writing on liberation theologies (discussed in chapter 9), Ruether kept *C&C* readers in touch with many other feminist concerns, such as debates about witchcraft, Roman Catholic teachings on gender, and efforts to equalize opportunities for women by shortening the work week and improving community-based child care.[22]

Like second wave feminism at large, *C&C* feminists had an internal tension between two paradigms for approaching sexuality. Insofar as the problem of sexism is identified as male objectification and control of women's bodies, the corresponding feminist attitude toward most sexual expression is suspicion. The sexual revolution and most sexual representation in the media appears, primarily, to represent easier and more dehumanized access by men to women's bodies. The core images for sexuality are rape, abuse, and objectifying pornography. But insofar as the main problem of sexism is the containment, channeling, and repression of sexuality by the "traditional" (i.e., modern bourgeois) family and its associated codes of sexual propriety, then liberation from sexual repression and overly rigid sexual mores can become a key part of feminist agendas. The core image is the erotic as the engine of liberation.[23]

These two logics are not mutually exclusive, and most *C&C* feminists blended some of each. Still, early explorations by *C&C*'s leading feminists were closer to the latter (pro-erotic) paradigm than to the former (anti-porn) logic. *C&C*'s inherited fascination with sex in the mass media, and its earlier discussions about sex outside marriage, transmuted in the 1970s into feminist critiques of sexual repression and its connection to the nuclear family. Cox's "Theses on Female Liberation" made this explicit. Related perceptions led Driver to revise the dualistic logic he had used in his 1964 article on sexual ethics. Recall how he set up a contrast between spiritual transcendence and an impersonal sexual force that was "not inseparable from the human in us." By 1977 Driver had reduced this dualism to the vanishing point and was calling on theologians to "baptize orgasm with explicit recognition of its form and teleological power." In "Toward a More Flexible Monogamy," Raymond Lawrence added that "extramarital sex may be openly and contractually integrated into a marriage with creative and positive results."[24] These articles by Driver and Lawrence were not fully feminist in the sense of highlighting women's empowerment in relation to men. However, Ruether did highlight this issue in a piece that began by restating the same argument Cox had used in his article on *Playboy*: objectification of women was a form of alienation from healthy relationships. She went on to accent how this reinforced larger social hierarchies, and she encouraged women to reclaim their sexuality from depersonalization and repression. The nuclear family could not solve this problem, Ruether judged, because it "forced women into a state of dependency" that undermined marriage as "friendship of equals." It was built on a "psychology whose sole basis is sexual friendship conceived of as a totalitarian form of exclusive private possession."[25]

The pro-erotic wing of *C&C*'s feminism continued throughout the rest of *C&C*'s career, often linked to a discourse about the positive role of passion and embodiment. Its momentum led *C&C* to reconsider Jesus' sexuality, since, as Driver argued, "Christianity has never entertained the image of a Christ who shared the sexual experience of most of the human race; hence that experience is rendered suspect, to say the least." Both Ruether and Driver cited William Phipps's book *Was Jesus Married?* This book rejected ascetic views of Jesus who, after all, scandalized his enemies by eating and drinking with sinners. Following Phipps, Driver speculated that Jesus had not been celibate; assuming that he was a typical Jewish boy of his times, he probably married in his teens. Ruether went on to argue that Jesus "appears to be neither married nor celibate"; he was more like a hippie than a respectable bourgeois husband. He had a special companion in Mary Magdalene (who, in the famous story of Jesus' post-Resurrection appearance, seemed accustomed to embracing and kissing him) as well as a "beloved disciple" who "laid his head on his breast" (John 13:23–25). Ruether admitted that these stories *proved* nothing about Jesus' sexual activity, and in fact she stressed that friendship, not sex, was Jesus' model for interpersonal relationships. But she insisted that Jesus, as a role model, did not support sexual repression or the patriarchal family.[26]

By no means did everyone at *C&C* root their feminist criticism on the sexual liberation side of the so-called sex war in feminist theory, much less embrace radical sexual experimentation. Even Ruether pulled her punches, leaving open the question of how to act on her critiques of the monogamous nuclear family, because she was also dissatisfied with the de-personalized sex of the student movement. Union Seminary ethicist Beverly Harrison recalls Anne Bennett as "prudish" on sexuality and resistant to lesbianism despite her passionate feminism and openness to other forms of radicalism. Harrison describes a late 1960s episode when John and Anne Bennett were distraught about what might happen at a Union chapel service on "Celebrating Human Sexuality." Relieved that the service turned out to be tame and tasteful, John Bennett commented matter-of-factly that his spouse would also have approved—if she had not skipped the service to picket with the Black Panthers![27]

The wing of *C&C*'s feminism that accented suspicion of male sexuality also remained strong until the end, often speaking against pornography, rape, and battering.[28] One article highlighted sexual exploitation by clergy and endorsed a code of ethics that "names as abusive and rules out all romantic relationships between clergy and parishioners, even those which are apparently mutually consenting and non-adulterous . . . because of the inherent power imbalance in such relationships and the violation of professional boundaries." It assumed that any sexual activities which included a serious power imbalance constituted abuse, and this included a large number of sex acts since, as *C&C* contributing editor Susan Thistlethwaite put it in a related article, "inequalities of power between men and women are so pervasive as to be nearly invisible."[29]

This approach to sexual ethics is a good example of how *C&C*'s two orientations to sexuality sometimes stood in tension. At one level, the basic principle was straightforward. Powerful forces in U.S. culture converged to eroticize hierarchical domination rather than mutuality, and sexual abuse occurred on an alarmingly large scale; thus it was commonsensical to teach the principle that people with power and authority should not make sexual advances to people in relation to whom they exercise power. The greater the imbalance of power between the advancer and the "advancee" (whether based on age, institutional authority, professional trust, internalized sexism, or brute coercion), the greater the problem.

At the same time, the underlying logic informing many such proposals—that sexuality as we know it should be approached with a deep suspicion that it is based on an abusive power play—coexisted uneasily with the logic of celebrating embodiment and female empowerment in other strands of *C&C* feminism. One letter pointed out that *C&C*'s approach to clergy sex had a fairly low estimate of female power and capacity for autonomous choice in the realm of the erotic. Also, it led to a concrete problem: where would clergy, of whatever sex or sexual orientation, find partners?[30] A later comment by feminist theorist Jane Gallop is relevant to *C&C*. She said that universities have trouble enforcing codes designed to stop sexual abuse because "the definition of sexual harassment is being expanded to include many things people don't really think are bad." "When sexual harassment sounds just like sex, then what you get is a situation where everybody officially says it's bad, but everybody does it, which is what we have in a society that thinks sex is bad. Societies that have very strong strictures against sex are not made up of people who don't have sex, they're made up of a kind of vast discrepancy between official discourse and practice."[31] Although *C&C* writers did not fully air their thoughts on this issue before the journal folded, disagreements were simmering just below the surface. Many *C&C* pastors and teachers (and not solely its male heterosexuals) were in consensual relationships with former parishioners and students, and many of these relationships had complex power dynamics. (Who is the predator and who is the prey in a sexual liaison between, say, a female minister and male parishioner, or between a young male assistant pastor and a wealthy female parishioner on the parish personnel committee?)

After the early 1970s, issues related to women's ordination were woven through many of *C&C*'s discussions of gender. Ordination policy became an especially heated battleground in the Episcopal Church, the last bastion of an all-male priesthood in mainline Protestantism. Old-time *C&C* stalwart Kilmer Myers—the same person we earlier met exhorting be-bop priests to "go native in all things save in faith and morals"—now wrote as an Episcopal bishop opposed to women's ordination. He reasoned that priests represented God, and God in turn represented "initiative" ("in itself, a male rather than a female attribute") and "the generative function" ("plainly a masculine kind of imagery"). The "prototype for the ministry of women" was the Virgin Mary.[32] Over the objections of people like Myers, in 1974 several women were ordained as priests, including Carter Heyward, who soon became a major force at *C&C*. Their ordination was not authorized by the proper bureaucratic channels, but *C&C* defended it as authorized by the Holy Spirit.[33] The debate was bitter, leading a psychologist to reflect in *C&C* on the need to overcome deep psychic blocks of fear and rage connected to the issue. He reported that a conservative priest receiving communion from Heyward had grabbed the chalice, "tightly held her hand, viciously scratched it, drawing blood, and said: 'I hope you burn in hell.'"[34]

By this time most *C&C* people had managed to heal or repress any lingering neuroses of this kind, and they considered it old hat to argue that women should be ordained. Although *C&C* kept its readers up to date about ongoing battles on this front, more vital discussions took the change for granted and asked whether it implied rethinking worship and ministry, how it impacted seminary curriculums, and whether feminist theorist Mary Daly might even be correct when she suggested (outside *C&C*'s pages) that a woman seeking gender equality in the church was "comparable to a black person's demanding equality in the Ku Klux Klan."[35] These discussions led directly into feminist theologies, as discussed below.

The Debate over Abortion Rights

Both *C&C*'s feminist turn and the continuing distance of some *C&C* people from feminism are easy to see in its abortion debate. From *C&C*'s earliest days it often took positions more liberal than Catholicism on issues of reproduction. But before the late 1960s *C&C* paid scant attention to abortion. Its hesitancy to defend it, if not its outright opposition, was assumed. Thus when Norway passed a liberalized abortion bill in 1961, *C&C*'s commentator, Franklin Littell, worried that cultural attitudes toward abortion were moving beyond the churches' control. He warned that the bill would be a stride toward "moral anarchy" unless "lay theologians" emerged within the medical profession. Similarly, a 1960 article on ecumenical debates about contraception—pitting tolerant Protestants against rigid Catholics—

commented offhandedly that Protestants supported contraception only in marriage and considered abortion immoral "except to save the life or health of the mother."

Incidentally, this same article presented the rhythm method, especially if improved through research, as the way forward for Catholic family planning.[36] In 1965 *C&C* extended this line of thought and linked it to abortion when John Leo, then an editor at *Commonweal,* wrote in *C&C* about a papal commission that was deadlocked over allowing the use of birth control pills. Leo mentioned a possible compromise: interpreting the pill as a form of the rhythm method that drastically slowed down menstrual rhythms and "plac[ed] the egg in a state of temporary repose." Unfortunately, scientists were still debating the details of how the pill worked. What if the pope endorsed it, only to find out later that it caused "instantaneous abortions" of zygotes?[37]

C&C's first round of sustained debate about abortion took place in 1967, after *Commonweal* stated that "abortion is equivalent to murder." This position was more conservative than any point on the *C&C* spectrum of debate. *C&C*'s center of gravity was articulated by Ronald Green's "Abortion and Promise-Keeping." Green placed himself midway between *Commonweal* and the idea that fetuses were mere tissue with no moral claims. He argued that when women engaged in sex, they implicitly promised to care for a possible fetus, but this promise, despite its strong moral force in most situations, was not the *only* relevant issue and could be overridden by such considerations as the mother's health. The law should not be rigid, and the decision should be in the hands of the women.[38]

Ramsey took his typical place on *C&C*'s right wing; he endorsed Green's logic of women's promise making, but denied that it could support liberalized abortion laws. Meanwhile, at the opposite pole of *C&C*'s debate was the sole female participant, Ruth Sprague; she advocated a "right to be wanted" that overrode Green's promise theory, and she underlined Green's neglect of *male* promise making during sex. Like Green, but with a more concrete focus on specific dilemmas, she insisted that "a decision to abort or not to abort has to be made situationally."[39] Between these poles, Bennett accepted Green's logic but, unlike Ramsey, used it for a clear defense of abortion rights. Addressing *Commonweal* directly, he suggested approaching the moral claims of the fetus "in relation to the concrete circumstances in the lives of actual persons" and argued that only a "harsh and unconvincing form of legalism" would fail to allow for other considerations. A year later he called *Humanae Vitae,* a papal encyclical prohibiting both abortion and contraception, "a disaster for the Roman Catholic church." Through each round of *C&C*'s battle over abortion, Bennett tried to build consensus for a liberal abortion law. He argued that everyone, whatever their personal views, should be able to agree that the choice of abortion should not be in the hands of the state.[40]

When this debate was revived for a second round in 1973, at the time of the *Roe v. Wade* decision, which decriminalized abortion, *C&C*'s spectrum had begun to shift toward female standpoints. Daniel Callahan argued a position somewhat like Green's, but whereas Green had been at the center of *C&C*'s 1967 spectrum, Callahan was now *C&C*'s most conservative voice (except for stray comments from Michael Novak, who was then moving rapidly beyond *C&C*'s rightward horizon). Although Callahan argued that the right to choose overrode sweeping pro-life positions, he also spoke against "Orwellian" tactics by pro-choicers, which he saw distorting the debate: for example, he rejected language that presented fetuses as mere "globs of tissue," opposed situations in which women were pressured into abortions, and insisted (against Sprague's "right to be wanted" argument) that some unplanned pregnancies produced happy children. Ethicists should give proper respect to the fetus as a potential life even as they supported the legal right to choice.[41]

At *C&C*'s pro-choice pole, Howard Moody expressed no such ambiguities. He spoke of the "conceptus" rather than "children" and compared people who gave fetuses the status of human beings to "animists" who believed that rocks have life. Moody said that pro-lifers "deify the conceptus" and that when they forced women to bear unwanted children it was like "legalized rape." Despite some problems in Moody's overall logic (after dismissing questions about when life begins, he later presupposed that fetuses were human lives and mounted a "better dead than unwanted" argument), his contributions were valuable because they approached abortion as an issue of particular women's lives. His strength was his vivid use of examples (stressing cases of failed contraception) from an abortion referral service he helped organize at his Greenwich Village church, which was one of the foremost religious alliances with women's health organizers in the years before *Roe v. Wade*.[42]

During this round of debate, anthropologist Margaret Mead used cross-cultural examples to destabilize arguments considered self-evident by pro-lifers. She described cultures in which children were not considered human until age two and times when all bodies were the property of the king. She also suggested that the logic of pro-life arguments might imply the need to end the Vietnam War or organize for the rights of the unconceived.[43]

C&C's abortion debate reached a height of both clarity and acrimony during its third round in 1977, which was provoked when conservatives lobbied to cut off Medicaid funding for abortions and pass a human life amendment to the Constitution. Dozens of prominent ethicists, including many who wrote for *C&C*, released a "Call to Concern," which *C&C* printed as an advertisement. This document placed abortion in the "realm of often tragic actions where circumstances can render it a less destructive procedure" than realistic alternatives. The Call characterized the prolifers as absolutist and extreme because of their "total preoccupation with the status of the unborn." This blinded them to other major issues, including "the quality of the entire life-cycle, the health and well-being of the mother, the question of emotional and economic resources," as well as the right to choose. Approached in a wider framework, the Call maintained, "abortion may in some cases be the most loving act possible."

The Call further argued that political lobbying by antiabortionists was unwise because, even though everyone had a right to ask for laws consistent with their beliefs, rigid laws would be counterproductive and unenforceable, somewhat like Prohibition. Moreover, such lobbying was a "threat to religious liberty and freedom of conscience" because it sought to "compel the conscience of those who believe abortion to be in harmony with their religious convictions." It would "violate the deeply held religious convictions [of many people] about when human personhood begins [and] the relative rights of a woman and a fetus."[44]

Two vehement dissents shattered the brief impression that this was becoming *C&C*'s settled approach. The inside attack was by Robert Hoyt, a Catholic journalist who had recently joined *C&C*'s staff and who would serve as editor between 1982 and 1985. Hoyt accepted the central arguments of the Call, which rejected sweeping antiabortion laws. But, he claimed, "Abortion is a Yes or No question; those who would sanction it are quite as 'absolutist' as those who would not." In reality two, not one, "coercive social policies" were being proposed: pro-lifers sought to ban abortion, whereas pro-choicers sought to "establish abortion officially . . . as a morally neutral procedure like an appendectomy."[45] Given such an idea of equivalency, such terms as *absolutist* for antiabortionists were nothing but "a pejorative denigrating noise"—and by extension, Hoyt could not distinguish between the level of absolutism involved in calling on the state to ban all abortions and arguing that abortion is sometimes a tragic lesser evil and the state is not in the best position to judge when this happens. Hoyt thought each side had too many single-minded crusaders. Although he knew signers of the "Call" who sincerely believed that abortion was tragic, their actions were helping make abortion "morally neutral, emotionless, [and] casual." "One hears women who speak of their abortions as inconveniences like dental appointments." Thus Hoyt upheld the pro-lifers' right to organize; he shared the "outrage legitimately felt by citizens who are repelled by abortion."

Because Hoyt sought a compromise that supported abortion rights, he was far more conciliatory than the Notre Dame priest, James Burtchaell, whose paid rebuttal described the Call's attack on Catholic antiabortion lobbying as "simple bigotry." Burtchaell ridiculed the idea that complex dilemmas rendered some abortions less destructive than the alternatives. Zeroing in on fetuses, which he defined as human lives from the moment of conception, he asked, "What is more destructive than death?" *Homicide* was a neutral term for abortion, he stated, and aside from a few "justifiable homicides" to save the mother's life, abortion was murder. Burtchaell claimed hard evidence that only 5 percent of abortions were chosen for the reasons cited in the Call—health, economic resources, and so on—and that "the enormous majority are abortions of expediency."[46] In a follow-up article, he compared abortion to Hitler's Final Solution, the My Lai massacre, and "giv[ing] . . . dum-dum bullets to the Mafia." He claimed he was "*in no way* insensitive to the plight of mothers who are frightened thirteen-year-olds, or supporting six children on welfare, or having to drop out of college." He simply returned to "the *point* . . . the chief and only point at issue: To abort is to destroy one's son or daughter."[47]

In response to these attacks, *C&C*'s abortion rights advocates mainly restated past positions. But the exchange produced new clarity about the importance of feminist logic in their arguments, as well as the impasse over the question of when human personhood began. Both sides perceived this impasse. Bennett asked why pro-life Catholics could not approach abortion as they did contraception: maintain their teaching and church discipline if they wished, but stop lobbying for criminalization. Hoyt said the answer was obvious: no one thought contraception was murder. Bennett was "beg[ging] the question" because he assumed that abortion could be "a question of private morality"—exactly what the official Catholic position denied. Bennett was asking antiabortionists "to conform *their* politics to *his* ethics," and he was ruling their concerns out of bounds.[48]

On the other side, Harrison argued that, when Burtchaell narrowed his focus to fetuses and assumed his theological position on when human life begins, Burtchaell "ruled out the moral standing of those who do not agree that abortion, per se, is homicide." She insisted that the "life process is a continuum" and that Burtchaell could not appeal to science to determine "when, in a continuous biological process, we are wisest to predicate a fetus's standing as a person, morally and under law."[49] (Mead's cross-cultural examples clarify this point, as do examples from U.S. culture. All can agree that a fetus is alive without settling the question of whether a miscarriage should have a funeral, whether women who miscarry should be investigated for manslaughter, or, more fancifully, whether a fetus would count as a passenger in an expressway car pool lane after gaining full legal rights.) Vivian and Eric Lindermayer agreed: "Whether abortion is homicide is . . . ultimately a metaphysical question." Pro-lifers wanted to "enforce *legally* a highly disputed moral position" and they could not defend this as social policy simply by "reiterating their controverted convictions." Yet, continued the Lindermayers, this was what Hoyt's argument amounted to: that antiabortionists "'define' abortion . . . as homicide, and that their political program is justified given the convictions they hold." It was antiabortionists who begged the question: "The justification of their position is clear—*for them*."[50]

Harrison and the Lindermayers stressed feminist logic as they defended the importance of multiple moral factors. They rejected Burtchaell's "objective" statistics that 95 percent of abortions were for expediency—of course, his finding hinged on definitions of *expediency*—and they linked his perception to sexist stereotypes of selfish and capricious women. They insisted that within the total moral calculus surrounding abortion decisions—which included concern for the developing human life both before and after birth—female well-being and collective power were major issues of concern, which were not to be trivialized. Life was not only a continuum. More pointedly, it was a continuum that "begins not only 'in' but as part of a woman's body." Thus banning abortion involved the (predominantly male) judges and legislators of the state controlling women's bodies. In general, a human life amendment "would have the profoundest negative consequences on . . . the life history of every female child born into this society."[51]

By the mid-1970s, *C&C*'s abortion debate was clearly weighted toward Bennett and Harrison's positions. For a time the debate continued. In fact, while Hoyt and Peggy Steinfels (both now at *Commonweal*) held two of *C&C*'s three top staff positions in the early 1980s, the overall balance shifted in a somewhat more conservative direction. The editors promoted a compromise formula: the continued legal right to choose, more stress on abortion as a moral evil, and stronger policies to make it illegal except as a last resort. *C&C* even invited the head of the National Right to Life Committee (plus Paul Ramsey for old times' sake) to comment on this position in a symposium.[52] However, Hoyt and Steinfels had both left *C&C*'s staff by 1985, and thereafter *C&C* supported abortion rights unambiguously. Vivian Lindermayer wrote in 1986, "*C&C* holds an editorial position favoring women's right to choose. We do not intend to keep rearguing the position. What we do intend is to create a forum for prochoice feminists to reflect not on why but on *how* women should decide about abortion."[53]

"The Scandal of Peculiarity": C&C's Critique of Heterosexism

C&C's support for feminism and gay / lesbian rights moved largely in tandem against a similar perceived enemy: the cultural supremacy of straight males. Not all *C&C* feminists supported gay / lesbian rights, not all *C&C* gays were feminists, and *C&C*'s support for gay / lesbian rights lagged slightly behind its support for feminism. But on the whole *C&C*'s antisexist and anti*hetero*sexist discourse overlapped, and in lesbian feminism it merged.

Until the 1970s, *C&C* hardly ever addressed gay / lesbian issues overtly. Homophobia often lurked below the surface, as when *C&C* celebrated Arthur Schlesinger's *The Vital Center* without commenting on its comparison between communism and homosexuals in a boys' school. And gay / lesbian sexuality made even *C&C*'s libertines uncomfortable. Recall the Quaker document that kicked off *C&C*'s debates about premarital sex in 1963. It defended responsible gay / lesbian relationships in the same terms as heterosexual ones, and Tom Driver's review generally supported its approach. Yet when Driver qualified his endorsement and called for humor to "put sex in its place," he was largely thinking about gays. Driver was untroubled by unmarried straight couples having sex; but he spoke as follows:

> [Gay partnership] can be a serious and responsible relation. But the matter cannot be left there. . . . Homosexuality is odd. All sex is odd, but homosex is odder than most. And funnier. The homosexual doesn't know what he's missing. Bigger joke: for emotional reasons, he can't know. The guy is trapped. . . . Are we to take this trap as fate (bad), or destiny (potentially good), or as a devil of a predicament from which there might be a way out? The minute we opt for fate and / or destiny we play acolyte to the bogus rituals that surround homosexuality. There is a whole literature and psychology built on this, and it's just plain cockeyed.[54]

Because Driver did not reject gay / lesbian relationships categorically, this position was *C&C*'s most positive (or least negative) stance on the issue before the 1970s. It was rivaled only by a few statements criticizing the harassment and criminalization of gay men. In one example, a pastor lamented that police harassment had caused one of his gay parishioners to commit suicide. Typically, this minister gave a mixed message; he implied that homosexuality was like a disease, since he asked whether those who harassed gays would also harass the mentally ill. It is fascinating to note that a second example supported Ronald Reagan on a gay rights issue. On one of the rare occasions in which *C&C* ever agreed with Reagan about anything, Howard Moody cautioned liberals not to attack him for appointing gays to high posts in the California state government, even though Reagan's hypocritical rhetoric about "traditional values" made this tempting.[55] Beyond such articles, *C&C*'s only explicit writing on homosexuality came when its defecting neoconservatives attacked liberal "permissiveness." Richard John Neuhaus mentioned an argument supporting gay rights in a book entitled *The Lord Won't Mind;* he stated that this "might serve as the theme of much recent writing on Christian ethics." For Neuhaus, to defend gay / lesbian rights was to extend contextual ethics to the point of absurdity.[56]

In the early 1970s, *C&C* began to write about gay / lesbian movements in roughly the same terms as black power and feminism. In an early article, James McGraw took a standpoint within the gay pride movement. He denounced the *New York Times* for suggesting that gays would prefer to be straight, adopted the word *faggot* as a defiant point of pride somewhat like black nationalists used *nigger,* and generally insisted that the problem was not the sickness of gays but the homophobia and oppression by straights. McGraw's boldest argument was implicit in his title, "The Scandal of Peculiarity." Readers with a minimal knowledge of academic theology could immediately recognize his pun on "the scandal of *particularity*"—a shorthand term for the problem of conceptualizing how Jesus could have a special relationship with God (in orthodox Christian doctrine, equal status in the Trinity) given his human incarnation in general and his execution as a criminal in particular. In other words, McGraw implied that theologians who could see God revealed through Jesus' embodied human life should also be able to see God's will and blessing expressed through (responsible) gay lifestyles—and implicitly McGraw compared the oppression of gays and lesbians to the suffering of Christ. Although McGraw did not develop this last point explicitly, his general drift was unmistakable. He compared Troy Perry's founding of the Metropolitan Community Church, a predominantly gay and lesbian denomination, to James Varick's founding of the African Methodist Episcopal Church Zion. In both cases, people left established denominations because of discrimination, and they "took Jesus with them, as he always feels more at home with the rejected."[57]

After McGraw broke *C&C*'s silence, articles in a more scholarly voice defended gay / lesbian relationships against received ethical teaching. Norman Pittenger argued that natural law ethics (which often attacks homosexuality as unnatural) in fact should support gay / lesbian rights: "For homosexuals it is entirely natural to love and to act homosexually." Pittenger's moral criterion for gays was the same as for straights: sex should avoid "cruelty, injustice to others, 'thingifying' persons-in-the-making, selfish gratification."[58] A widely reprinted article by James Nelson provided a broad compendium of biblical and theological defenses. Nelson argued, for example, that the actual sin in the leading biblical proof-text used to condemn homosexuality, the story of Sodom and Gomorrah, was inhospitality to strangers and homosexual *rape.* (If it were about heterosexual rape, would anyone conclude that all straight people should be condemned?) Nelson also argued that biblical writers had no conception either that some people had fixed and unchosen same-sex orientations or that both females and males contributed genetic material to procreation. Consider the implications: whereas conservatives assumed that the Bible was rejecting homosexuality in a sweeping way, the biblical writers may have seen themselves as condemning willful acts of *promiscuity* by people who were basically straight. They may have understood the condemnation of gays as just one part of a condemnation of *all* forms of nonprocreative male sexual activity—including masturbation—because this was viewed as the murder of fully developed human seeds, much as some contemporary pro-lifers view abortion. The assumption that all gay sex was promiscuous dissolved, as did the assumption that masturbation was akin to murder, if the best contemporary understandings were presupposed.

There should be no obstacle to adopting revised biblical interpretations, continued Nelson, because the "Protestant principle" of reforming received traditions in light of "God's invitation to human wholeness" had led Christians to revise many other aspects of biblical teaching in light of changing thought: for example, they had not maintained biblical understandings of astronomy such as the theory that the sun moved around the earth, nor biblical teachings justifying slavery and polygamy, nor biblical prohibitions against eating shellfish. (Virginia Ramey Mollenkott later added that the first church council that explicitly banned homosexuality, in 1179, also imposed sanctions against moneylenders, heretics, and Jews.) Similar changes were needed now in relation to sexuality. This was an issue of justice for gays and lesbians, but it was also in the self-interest of the society at large, since homophobia (and its connection to male sexism) caused unhealthy repressions in straight people.[59]

There was a submerged tension in Nelson's article between the changeable social and cultural constructedness of sexuality, always being reformed by the Protestant principle, and the appeal to fixed gay/lesbian orientations which must be accepted as natural and unchangeable. A key early article by Carter Heyward addressed this tension explicitly. Heyward highlighted the constructedness of the "boxes" in which people play out sex and gender roles, including the categories "gay" and "straight." Yet, she insisted, "These categories—boxes—are real. We live in them."[60] She went on to argue that it was appropriate for her, at this time and place, to identify as a lesbian feminist. The most important box to deconstruct was "the single box labeled 'heterosexual,'" which defined male and female roles in sexist ways and presupposed hierarchies of exploitation. A key problem with this straight box was that it often short-circuited the creative power of passion and its associated drive for mutuality, which refused to flow in the channels it proposed. Feminism in general, and lesbian feminism in particular, was for Heyward the most creative current box in which to situate herself because of the way it criticized such dominant social patterns and highlighted the positive role of mutuality and passion.

Of course, in the churches at large such positions were extremely embattled. For the rest of its existence, *C&C* reported on the progress of gay and lesbian ordination rights, as well as conservative counterattacks such as the case of a Methodist minister named Rose Mary Denman who was hounded out of the church when she came out as a lesbian.[61] One of *C&C*'s best articles on this subject was by the prominent theologian John Cobb. He deflated conservative pretensions to be upholding biblical values with their rule (written to exclude homosexuals) that all clergy must embrace "fidelity in marriage and celibacy in singleness." Cobb pointed out: "The Bible reflects and sanctions several ways of dealing with sexuality, ranging from the multiple wives and concubines of the patriarchs and kings of Israel to the lifelong chastity that seems to have been favored by Jesus and Paul. But I do not know where the exact pattern now being proposed [including tolerance for divorce, which was explicitly condemned by Jesus] is reflected or supported." Cobb then asked a few pragmatic questions: Did the churches really want to be on record as condemning practices of premarital sexuality that were presupposed by large numbers of its members, especially its engaged couples? If not, had they considered the implications of imposing a double standard of sexual conduct for ministers? How much did their rule reflect a lingering background assumption that "sexuality is inherently evil" except for procreation? Did they really want an official policy, for either homosexuals or unmarried straight people, that could "make no distinction between long-term faithful relationships and utter promiscuity?"[62]

Occasionally voices of backlash appeared in *C&C*'s pages. A Methodist bureaucrat received space to restate the party line in response to Cobb. A Yale Divinity student wrote to attack Nelson. He argued that the biblical idea of purity excluded homosexuality and that the Bible stressed marriage—defining it "in exclusively heterosexual terms" such that "only heterosexual relationships are natural." Biblical teaching was clear-cut, and Scripture should be the judge of Nelson, not vice-versa.[63] In addition, letters to the editor characterized homosexuality as lust and suggested that *C&C* should "hate the sin but love the sinner." A southern ecumenical leader described gay/lesbian sexuality as a "perversion of the flow of nature." If so, Nelson's reasoning was backwards: to affirm homosexuality was actually a *refusal* to "accept and affirm one's own sexuality." During thirty years of pastoral counseling this minister had "experienced most homosexuality as a conflict in identity, such as a male not being willing to affirm or accept maleness. If one fails to accept one's sex given by nature, then all the other identities are up for grabs such as ethnic group, race, regionality [*sic*], etc. . . . As for ordaining homosexuals (or lesbians) we are (in primitive terms) making a person potent. To put the blessing of the church on an impotent person does not bestow potency."[64]

C&C did not present these hostile responses as an equally legitimate pole of a balanced debate. In 1977, a special issue on Homosexuality and the Church opened by answering a new subscriber who, having read Nelson, asked whether *C&C* had published articles on the other side of the issue. One might debate the proportions of honesty and evasion in the editors' reply: "No, there is no previous issue of *C&C* arguing the other side of the question." In any case, their rationale was forthright: they said they realized that "many readers will disagree . . . and some will object strongly." Still they planned to be advocates for gay-lesbian concerns. "The real theological problem . . . [is not] reconciling acceptance of homosexuality with the scriptural passages that appear to condemn it, but rather how to reconcile condemnation of homosexuals with the criteria of morality that are truly central to the Christian message."[65]

By the late 1970s gay/lesbian issues were among *C&C*'s top priorities, so that the pseudonymous Presbyterian minister "Calvin Gay" could begin a 1978 article attacking homophobia in his denomination with the disclaimer, "This article covers ground already somewhat familiar to *C&C* readers."[66] *C&C* continued to give strong attention to gay and lesbian issues, with AIDS becoming a major concern.[67] At times its writers tried to shame the mainstream into rethinking its homophobia, as when Louie Crew described how one local church had treated him; his article was entitled "At St. Luke's Parish, the Peace of Christ Is Not for Gays." At other times, *C&C* became one of the few safe spaces in Protestant journalism to express simple outrage at the mainstream, as in a piece on "The Last Committee on Sexuality (Ever)," which denounced and withdrew from the whole "dialogue" process in which straight Christians debated whether gays and lesbians are sick.[68] Sometimes *C&C* blended both moods, as when Crew wrote about a friend who was dying of AIDS. His friend could find no sense of peace because he believed that God hated him. Crew said, "I am an atheist to the God he feared. I believe that kind of a God is a fraud [but] if that God turns out to be real, let the sucker burn me." In the end, his friend saw angels at the foot of his bed. It signaled that at least God, if not God's reputed followers in the churches, had a message of grace for gays and lesbians.[69]

9

Toward New Contexts and Standpoints for Theology

As *C&C* turned left in the late 1960s, it rarely asked if there were unique black, feminist, or third world approaches to the great themes and metaphors of religious language. To be sure, abstract principles like "God wills justice" could be *applied* to various concerns. But consider how *C&C* had assumed that God was above race, relativizing any differences caused by skin color, and that whites could take a neutral position in racial conflicts. In a similar way *C&C* assumed that God transcended differences of gender, class, and nationality, and that white North American males could speak about the universal content of theology and objective approaches to its contexts.

Feminist, black, and Latin American theologians insisted that *C&C*'s received theology was written from the context and standpoint of white North American males. They rethought the methods and priorities of theology from the standpoints of feminism, black nationalism, and Latin American radicalism. In the famous words of Gustavo Gutiérrez, theology was "critical reflection on praxis," and praxis implied concrete struggles for justice within situations of conflict.[1]

In a sense this was nothing new. *C&C* had long talked about contextualism, and even in the 1950s its pragmatic methods—if not its neoorthodox metaphors—had analyzed current situations and interpreted theology in relation to them.[2] What was different in liberation theologies was their stress on structural conflicts *within* "the context" and their commitment to rethink theology from one side of these conflicts, rather than assuming a stance from above. Even these latter themes had been present earlier in a muted way. Where the context had been global, conflict had been explicit in the cold war and semiexplicit in the clash between forward-looking development and backward-looking feudalism. Where the context had been national, conflict had been explicit in class struggles of the 1930s and semiexplicit in the civil rights movement. Even where the context had been an all-pervasive modernity, *C&C* embraced it in a way that others did not—and this could translate into conflict with fundamentalists. However, *C&C* had stressed that God did *not* take sides in these struggles but, rather, judged the tendencies to sin on all sides. If *C&C* ever came out and admitted that it thought God was "on the side of liberals"—and it went to great lengths to *avoid* saying this—this was because *C&C* believed that liberals had a more objective and universal approach, one less corrupted by particular egotisms and ideologies. Even highly contextual theologies like Cox's *Secular City* agreed on this point.

C&C's general radicalization set the stage for shifts in theology. This was easy to see in a 1968 symposium on "Christian Realism: Retrospect and Prospect" by seven members of *C&C*'s inner circle. Bennett opened their discussion by proposing that realism could be "kept up to date" with only four changes: revised thinking about nuclear war, attention to changes in the eastern bloc, realism about the limits of U.S. power, and support for "revolutionary change in the third world." He maintained that the result would be similar to Richard Shaull's theology of revolution, an early form of Latin American liberation theology. But Bennett's colleagues insisted that the cumulative effect of these changes was far-reaching. Shaull appealed to Thomas Kuhn's theories about paradigm change in science, and called for a new theological paradigm centered on "the continuing effects of redemption" in human history. Cox added that realism "function[ed] as middle-class ideology"; it was used to imply "that all causes are more-or-less equally suspect because . . . they will fall into the sin of pride." Driver agreed, claiming that realist arguments were so fused with western liberalism that "we defend one while supposing we defend the other. But it is all too defensive." Bennett responded, "I agree with you wholly. It is time to shift gears entirely on this—not with any romantic revolutionary attitude but with the recognition of an open future." Driver then insisted that Bennett's gear-shifting amounted to a basic change in theological paradigm, from limitations caused by sin to creative hopes for change. Bennett resisted this line of thought only in relation to the arms race, where he believed that the critique of pride remained essential. His main response to Driver was, "I agree. . . . It is much better to start with Christian possibilities."[3]

This was a completely white, male, and Protestant panel, no matter how much it responded to black and third world voices (not to women so far). Its "possibilities" could be understood as an extension of *The Secular*

City (published three years earlier) or Martin Luther King Jr.'s theology, at least as well as a white Protestant version of James Cone's *Black Theology and Black Power* (which appeared one year later) or documents on liberation theology endorsed in the same year by the Latin American Bishops at Medellín. But optimism about the *Secular City* was crumbling, and *C&C*'s symposium contained the outlines of its new approach.

Only one thing remained to make it unambiguous liberation theology. Its "Christian possibilities" had to be approached explicitly from the perspective of oppressed groups—and not merely defined intellectually, since liberationists stressed the need to formulate theory in explicit relation, even subordination, to practical actions for change. *C&C*'s liberals had to reimagine themselves, less as the central actors in the drama of liberation—although they remained part of the oppressed in relation to corporate elites and military planners—and more as strategic allies of people who suffered from the interlocking oppressions based on race, class, empire, sexuality, and gender.

From this point of view it was understandable for *C&C* to maintain some distance from liberation theologies. In fact, the distance was unavoidable, given that *C&C*'s readers were overwhelmingly white, male, and North American in the early 1970s. Even in 1990 they remained 90 percent white and 60 percent male. *C&C* was not a central arena for *elaborating* liberation theologies in the same strong sense that it had been for Christian realism, although it sometimes played this role for Christian feminism. Its main role—not a trivial one—was as a forum for debating the white North American *reception* of liberation theologies.

Liberation theologies challenged *C&C*'s inherited emphases on divine transcendence over all political positions and its generalized understandings of the context for theology. Their focus on conflicts within the context was unambiguous, and their mix of analytical tools for defining the context tilted away from philosophy toward social science and cultural criticism. For them, the will of God unambiguously supported oppressed groups against their oppressors. In the leading metaphors of theology, no longer did God and "his" prophets stand in judgment over all sides, with Christ offering grace for everyone—with secondary themes added when necessary, as when *C&C* said during World War II that it had a "good conscience that our cause is in line with His righteousness," since a theological stance justifying Hitler was obviously inappropriate.[4] The new paradigm centered on God struggling alongside people who suffered from oppression—since it was obviously inappropriate for theology to remain neutral between the rich and the starving, between fascist Salvadoran torturers and the nuns they raped. Liberationists approached Jesus as a human in the midst of struggle, as *part* of the oppressed. Calls for humility, objectivity, and theological self-criticism by the hungry and the raped were demoted to a lower priority—although not for that reason completely abandoned—and Carol Christ judged that "Niebuhrian cynicism" supported "a half-engaged, half-detached liberal conscience." According to Christ, "armed with this theology the liberal is justified in her/his failure to become fully committed to any of the liberation movements."[5] The point of departure for liberation theologies was *presupposing* such a commitment.

Feminist Theology

Women were mentioned only once during *C&C*'s 1968 symposium on Christian realism, in a lament about "rosy-cheeked coeds talking about guerrilla warfare."[6] But by 1974 *C&C* published a whole issue on feminist theology, with a lead article that spoke of the "familiar terms of the women's movement." It said: "Theology has reflected male experience of the world—and of God. . . . No area of life has gone untouched in past theologizing and none must be left unexplored as women theologize. . . . We move to God-talk through reflection on the reality of our own lives, thereby acknowledging that all theology is done in a context. Women's experience has not been in the traditional 'theological circle' [that is, the process of relating inherited traditions to current issues] and so a new context is introduced."[7]

Feminist theology insisted that the central theme of Niebuhrian theology—a transcendent God judging human pride—was neither objective nor gender-neutral. It was a male reflection on male experience and had to be reexamined in relation to women. The point was not that the critique of pride was irrelevant to women but that such a critique was better directed at powerful men. For women, the more pressing problem was how sexist socialization undermined self-esteem, taught deference to men, and overstressed self-sacrifice, even to the point of blurring the lines between feminine virtue and masochism in extreme cases. Thus feminist theologians revalorized female experience, embodiment, and agency.[8] This was related to *C&C*'s long-term trend toward stressing incarnation and human possibilities, but here incarnation was into female bodies and the possibilities were feminist.

C&C's feminist theologies were as diverse as its general analyses of gender, which we began to discuss in chapter 8. Controversies about sexuality, race, and theological method divided feminist theologians in complex ways. However, one continuum more than any other structured the debate, especially during the 1970s. Writers at one pole sought to revise and partly redeem Christian traditions from within; they were frequently socialist or liberal feminists. Writers at the other pole saw Christianity as oppressive to the core and worthy only of radical repudiation; they were often cultural feminists.[9]

The reformists plugged women into *C&C*'s long-standing theme of God siding with underdogs; they continued to cite Ursula Niebuhr's old proof-text, "in Christ there is no Jew or Greek, slave or free, male or female." They used the theology of transcendence to argue that God was beyond gender and, more pointedly, that it was idolatrous to use exclusively male images for the depth and fullness of God, so that a more inclusive range of images was required by orthodoxy. James Nelson's Protestant principle could be used not only to throw off the dead weight of Christian homophobia but also to overthrow Christian patriarchalism that used outmoded assumptions to defend gender inequality as part of the order of creation.[10]

Christian feminists often focused on biblical texts that shaped the self-image of oppressed groups in the interests of their oppressors. Other liberationists shared this concern, but it loomed larger for feminists because of the subtle ways that gender roles are contested in households and bedrooms. Also, the Bible has a larger supply of positive male role models than female ones. Out of 1,425 people in the Bible who have names, only 111 are women, and many of them are negative role models, such as Eve and Jezebel. Of course, this imbalance is related to the fact that the Bible was written by men, then edited, translated, and interpreted by men in a long succession of male-dominated societies. Historian Elaine Pagels says that trying to reconstruct women's lives in biblical times, solely using evidence from the Bible, is like trying to "re-create the thinking of Karl Marx on the basis of a handful of anti-communist tracts from the 1950s."[11]

Biblical scholar Phyllis Trible claimed that the encounter between "the Hebrew Scriptures and the Women's Liberation Movement . . . need not be hostile." She did not deny that much of the Bible was sexist, but she believed that she could "depatriarchalize" many texts that seemed unpromising at first glance. For example, she maintained that the antifeminist reputation of the Adam and Eve story had been read into the text by men and could be eliminated through careful interpretation. *Before* the creation of Eve from Adam's rib, Trible argued, Adam was "basically androgynous," a mere "generic term for humankind." As for the punishment, which gave men a mandate to "rule over women" and relegated women to painful childbearing, these curses came *after* the fall into sin—along with other consequences of sin which are not considered normative behavior, such as Cain's being cursed to wander the earth after murdering Abel.

Between Eve's creation and the fall, continued Trible, Eve and Adam had an exemplary mutual relationship. If anything, Eve was dominant; she ate the forbidden fruit because she was "more intelligent . . . more aggressive . . . and the one with greater sensibilities." Adam was "passive, brutish, and inept," and "his one act [was] belly-oriented." Trible further argued that the assertive, openly sexual female in *Song of Songs* showed that, even after the fall, the Bible could endorse sexual mutuality.[12]

C&C's moderates pressed such women-friendly Bible readings as far as they could. Often they stressed Jesus' iconoclasm against received gender roles, a stance that placed him within the most pro-woman currents of his culture. Some of the most powerful arguments were by Elisabeth Schüssler Fiorenza, who presented Mary Magdalene as a leader among Jesus' disciples, with a liberationist agenda and a stature as great as that of St. Peter. Unlike Trible, who uncovered a feminist Eve in the canonical text, Fiorenza argued that evidence about Magdalene had been suppressed and distorted by the men who gave the Bible its final form (somewhat like the evidence about Marx in anticommunist tracts). Magdalene's reputation had to be reconstructed by reading between the lines and tapping other historical evidence.[13]

We have seen how the sexual liberation camp among *C&C*'s feminists recast Jesus' sex life. There were also theological proposals by *C&C*'s feminists in the camp which associated sex more with being abused than with unleashing repressed passion. Sometimes they promoted inclusive metaphors of God, reasoning that to envision God as a father—or worse, as a feudal overlord—conveyed precisely the wrong idea to women whose own fathers were abusive. Taking a different tack on this same problem, Diane Tennis argued that, because real fathers were unreliable, a positive image of divine Fatherhood was all the more necessary to address women's sense of loss. Some early Christians had said, "Jesus is Lord," not to reinforce authoritarianism in their communities but to assert that "*Jesus* [not Caesar] is *my* Lord." Similarly, women could say that God, rather than fallible human males, was *their* father.[14]

As *C&C*'s moderate feminists thus tried to carve out space for a depatriarchalized Christianity, they were hampered by working in a free fire zone between anti-Christian feminists and Christian antifeminists, who penned attacks that fed on each other. *C&C* quoted a minister who said, "The women's movement rejects the Bible concept of God, Christ, the church and the home. It is now known that . . . a believer could not be a part of this movement."[15] Such arguments confirmed the suspicions of women who saw Christian commitment as a betrayal of women's self-respect—as well as the growing tide of liberal women (and men) who simply decided that it was not worth their trouble to struggle against the sexist men who dominated their churches.

The most vehement attacks on Christianity came from feminists who revived and reinvented a feminist spirituality focused on ancient Goddess religions.[16] They rolled their eyes when *C&C* quoted Mary, the Mother of Christ, saying that God "has scattered the proud, . . . filled the hungry with good things, and sent the rich empty away" (Luke 1: 51–53). For Mary Daly, the leading post-Christian cultural feminist, Mary was not a positive model but a degraded caricature of a powerful Goddess who had symbolized female procreative power. The Bible had reduced her to a "handmaid of the Lord" (Luke 1:38) or, in Daly's paraphrase, a "Total Rape Victim" of an all-male Trinity.[17] Daly's criticism did not appear in *C&C*, and few *C&C* writers embraced her style of radical feminism, especially after she repudiated Christianity entirely in the mid-1970s. In a typical treatment, Carter Heyward saw a creative tension between Daly's uncompromising go-it-alone style and Rosemary Ruether's efforts to forge links between feminism and broader issues of the left. Heyward was drawn to Daly's verve and passion, but in the end her basic sympathies remained with Ruether.[18]

For her part, Ruether engaged in a long-running dispute with Carol Christ, a proponent of feminist spirituality.[19] In *C&C* this controversy was one-sided, with Ruether hammering on the point that ancient pagan societies were not egalitarian utopias. The worship of Isis or Diana coexisted with male-dominated societies based on class oppression and slavery, and the lines between oppressors and oppressed followed power rather than ideas about the gender of the divine. Polytheists with power persecuted Christians and Jews, while Jewish monotheists without power did not persecute anyone. Although Ruether took flak from other Christian feminists for taking Goddess spirituality too seriously, she rejected cultural feminist innovations such as gynecentrism (female dominance as opposed to the multiplicity of gods and goddesses in ancient paganism) and the romanticization of the nurturing female (which she saw as a retread on the Victorian cult of "true womanhood").[20]

Still, some of *C&C*'s writing approached Daly's post-Christian positions. The first women's theology issue included a semiliturgical play from a conference at Grailville, a center for religious feminism. This play presupposed a sweeping male/female polarity. There was a "feminine principle at work in history" symbolized by "Mary-Isis called also Athena, Venus, Diana . . . Minerva, Hera," and there was a corresponding masculine principle symbolized by biblical texts showcasing Yahweh's violent intolerance. Yahweh especially hated "other gods"—and other *goddesses* such as Astarte (or Asherah), the female consort of the better-known male god, Ba'al. The play revalorized Jezebel, a worshipper of Astarte, in her struggle with Yahweh's prophet Elijah. Yahweh emerged as the villain when he said, through Elijah, "The dogs shall eat the flesh of Jezebel, and the corpse of Jezebel shall be as dung in the face of the field."[21] According to this play, harmony across the male-female divide could never happen until men gave up their traits symbolized by Yahweh and subordinated them to the female principle.

The Grailville feminists accented the worst about the Bible just where Trible accented the best, and by attacking the prophetic tradition they struck a nerve. It was one thing for *C&C* to debate whether teachings about homosexuality in Leviticus could be abandoned along with laws against eating shrimp. If someone maintained that the Bible was antigay, *C&C* found this troubling—but not because it had ever cared about Leviticus. *C&C* leaders *had* emphatically cared, at the heart of their identities, about prophets like Elijah. They had applied the prophetic model to every issue; recall how Cox took a prophet's role when attacking Miss America as a latter-day manifestation of Isis. Now an emerging group of feminists suggested that the prophets were on the cutting edge of a world-historical movement to stamp out female-centered nature religions.

Clearly there is a wide spectrum between a liberationist Virgin Mary and a male God whose prophets feed women to dogs. Throughout its last two decades, *C&C* explored this middle territory. What were the limitations of Christianity for feminists, and what was salvageable? *C&C* endorsed theologian Sallie McFague when she suggested Mother, Lover, and Friend as metaphors for God. But *C&C*'s reviewer, Catherine Keller, went beyond McFague in suggesting Native American images for the divine such as bear and serpent. In general, she called for a greater sense of rupture with patriarchal traditions. *C&C* newcomer Keller cited an old-timer from *C&C* circles, Nelle Morton, who had come to believe that patriarchal images must be shattered and reconstructed from the roots, not just overlain with a thin layer of inclusive images.[22]

Some feminists influential at *C&C* questioned almost *any* concept of a transcendent God. When attacking Christian positions that presupposed a dualism between a positive realm of disembodied spirit and the devalued realms of embodiment and the natural world, they posed their arguments so sharply that they risked crossing a line defining—for most people—the outer limits of Christianity. Carter Heyward stepped right up to this line when she spoke of "Jesus, who may or may not be, for us, The Christ, Savior, or Lord." Indeed, she seemed to imply that devotion to Jesus was ordinarily oppressive when she wrote that "many are recognizing the role of christian teachings in general, and of christology in particular, in justifying and perpetuating abuse. . . . The doctrine of atonement probably represents the sadomasochism of christian teaching at its most transparent."[23] Despite the provocative rhetoric, there was less heresy here than met the eye, since Heyward recast the meaning of Christ, taking the stress off the (male) human being Jesus and his acceptance of suffering. Her feminist christology rejected the passive embrace of sacrifice that often reinforces traditional female socialization, and underlined the empowering passion for justice that unlocked the "christic" energy in relationships of mutuality and struggle. Since most liberation theologies stress that such a passion was modeled by Jesus, it was not difficult for Heyward to backpedal on another front when she said, "We cannot dismiss Jesus as oppressive and corrupt for everyone. . . . If 'Jesus' has been largely positive, as he has been for many within the African American religious tradition, the character of his ongoing presence can indeed redeem African Americans."[24]

To understand the full resonance of this latter comment, made in 1989, we must back up and review a long-simmering controversy. From the beginning, *C&C*'s feminists had debated how their work related to other liberation theologies—especially by blacks and Latin Americans—that accented prophetic role models such as Jesus. As usual, Mary Daly was the most skeptical, charging (again, outside *C&C*) that James Cone's prophetic black God was "as revengeful and sexist as his White prototype . . . [and] at least as oppressive as the old."[25]

In 1974 Ruether wrote a *C&C* essay called "Crisis in Sex and Race: Black Theology versus Feminist Theology," which became a benchmark for subsequent discussions of race, gender, and theology. She spoke of an undeclared war between the two camps. Two of her key points were that feminists should not repeat the history of racism in the women's movement, and they should not be so patronizing toward the majority of women, as when single career women denigrated motherhood.[26] A group of Union Seminary women, including Heyward, responded that "misogyny is the most basic mode of oppression." One group member called Ruether's defense of motherhood a "product of brainwashing from a male-dominated church," and another said that motherhood for blacks might be one thing, but for whites it "perpetuat[ed] white male oppression with the presentation of a white son to inherit white male status." Overall, Ruether had "come close to dealing with the issues of feminism," but she had not discussed feminism as "an alternative culture in its own right."[27]

In reply, Ruether threw down the gauntlet: "It is evident that whenever a group of women regard sexism as the 'only' or 'most fundamental' form of oppression in an exclusivist way, they must be white and upper class. . . . Their exclusivism and separatism become a form of race and bourgeois false consciousness. I regard the three alienations of race, sex, and class as inter-structured." Moreover, continued Ruether, the Union group was uninformed about ancient religions in which "the goddess as autonomous mother is the foundation of political as well as cosmic power." In fact, "if women want to know why men are afraid of them and even hate them, they must shake off the assumption that motherhood is primarily the point of their weakness and rediscover what the symbol meant when men struggled to suppress it." When male theologians spoke of God as ground of being, they were really unwittingly saying "mother."[28]

Ruether's "Black Theology versus Feminist Theology" article was nearly as critical of black theologian James Cone as it was of the Union feminists, given the inattention to gender in Cone's first books and his tendency to link black power with black manhood. Ruether called on her colleagues to resist the divide-and-conquer strategies that pitted blacks and feminists against each other, and to pay more attention to a constituency neglected by both sides: black women. In 1974, Ruether's final point was little more than a gesture of intention toward future work, but it placed *C&C* on the path that it would in fact follow. By the 1980s, womanist, mujerista, and other theologies from women of color were major *C&C* concerns. Black women's literature, such as Alice Walker's *The Color Purple,* became key sources for *C&C*'s theological reflection. *C&C* published many leading black female scholars—for example, June Jordan, bell hooks, Pauli Murray, and Emilie Townes—and gave increasing attention to women of color from other cultures such as Ada María Isasi-Díaz, Kwok Pui-lan, and Rigoberta Menchú.[29] *C&C*'s leading womanist, Union Seminary's Delores Williams, often addressed concerns of black women; she used the image of Hagar's daughters for black women in the United States, and the image of a discordant jazz symphony for dialogues between womanists and other groups. A striking measure of *C&C*'s change was its fiftieth anniversary celebration in 1991, where Delores Williams (not Hubert Humphrey) gave the keynote speech.[30]

Whereas in 1961 *C&C* did not publish a single article written by a woman, by 1985 *C&C* could claim that "almost half were by women." Although this was a generous estimate—since the actual number was less than a third—the change remained striking. (It placed *C&C* no further from parity than leading secular left journals; for example, only 20 percent of *Nation* articles were by women.)[31] As feminist theologies became *C&C*'s top theological discourse, Ruether could look back and discern three stages of the movement. The first had exposed the sexism of inherited traditions:

for example, when *C&C* asked how men would feel if they were asked to sing hymns about "the Sisterhood of Woman" and pray "that all men as well as women will come to experience true sisterhood." In the second stage, feminists recovered alternative traditions, as when they revalorized Mary Magdalene. During these stages they had learned how often feminist critiques had been developed in the past, only to be repressed and forgotten, so that feminists were continually reinventing the wheel. The next task, said Ruether, was to move from the margins and "lay claim to the center" through constructive theological work, and to build institutional bases strong enough that contemporary feminism would not go down the memory hole, like so much work in the past. According to Ruether, divinity schools "belong to women as much as to men. We have a right to contend for their ownership and definition, and we will do so. The library budget needs to be used to buy feminist books; the curriculum to teach feminist courses. . . . Feminism is not a special interest group or a passing fad. . . . Feminist theology, along with other forms of liberation theology . . . is redefining the agenda and constituency of theology itself."[32]

Black Theology

For early black and Latin American theologies, the key questions of feminist theology—how to understand Christianity in the context of struggle for gender justice and whether to repudiate prophetic Christianity—were not at issue. The movements presupposed male agency, used analytical categories that were blind to gender, and kept the prophetic tradition from Moses through Jesus as their unquestioned center of vision. Black theology rethought Christianity in the context of black nationalism and African American traditions. *C&C* became engaged with it as an outgrowth of its passion for civil rights, and its engagement remained limited because of its standoffishness toward black power.

Before 1970 *C&C* assumed that Martin Luther King Jr.'s theology moved within the general approach that *C&C* took for granted: the fatherhood of God and brotherhood of men, liberal theology, and progress toward color-blind social harmony. *C&C* rarely spoke about King as a theologian, but when it did, it downplayed things that made King distinct, such as his interest in Gandhi and his conviction that blacks had a special calling to redeem the soul of America. *C&C* stressed King's Niebuhrian aspect: his pragmatic efforts to build power inside the political system.[33]

Indeed, *C&C* was suspicious of the black church roots that were a key to King's approach. True, *C&C* no longer discussed "The Church and Race" by talking solely about southern white clergy. But entering the 1960s,

C&C still saw black churches as otherworldly enclaves dominated by complacent ministers. In 1965 a piece called "The Separated Darker Brethren" by Charles Lawrence agreed with two leading scholars of the black church, E. Franklin Frazier and Joseph Washington, who underlined the centrality of churches to black communities, but judged them anti-intellectual enclaves with corrupt leaders. (King was an anomaly for this paradigm, but *C&C* could set him aside as a special case, educated in elite white schools.) At this time, Washington was arguing that black churches were not fully Christian but merely a syncretic folk religion.[34] Lawrence's *C&C* article softened this attack, maintaining that black churches had a "deep understanding of the Gospel" beneath their corruption. Still, *C&C* writers often lamented that Sunday was the most segregated day of the week. They approached black churches somewhat like "separate but equal" schools; that is, they perceived the solution as integrating the white churches.[35]

For *C&C*, King's mobilization of African American churches as a power base for civil rights represented a halfway house to a more positive approach. Black theologians increasingly presented African American congregations as places to sustain the autonomy of black culture and organize for black power. To be sure, black theology did not endorse everything about black churches—in some ways it intensified Frazier's critique of black clergy, accusing them of betraying nationalist (and / or proto-nationalist) traditions formed in slavery.[36] Still, black theologians reconsidered Washington's folk religion. The black churches' syncretic influences from African traditions and their distance from white Christianity were recast as strengths. *C&C* began to pay significant attention to black churches: for example, by collaborating with the militant National Conference of Black Churchmen (NCBC) to produce a double issue on the topic.[37] *C&C* never became a journal "of" African American Christianity, following its internal debates with anything like the passion it devoted to white liberalism. Still, activist black churches became a significant part of its mental map of allies. As *C&C*'s nonwhite readership increased from 2 to 10 percent between 1967 and 1990, the new 8 percent undoubtedly included much of the minority leadership in mainline denominations.

Unlike King, Cone could not be tucked into a remote cranny of *C&C*'s theological reflection, because he repudiated the liberal civil rights paradigm and worked in the framework of black nationalism, as defined above, stressing an autonomous black community against whites and the need to build power (not ruling out violence) to overturn institutional racism. Moreover, Cone's books were among the few Christian bridges to black radicalism—and among them, the most elaborated in terms of (white) academic theology. Thus they were on everyone's reading list at *C&C*.[38]

Cone's June 1970 article, "Christian Theology and the Afro-American Revolution," used Barthian theological arguments somewhat like Paul Lehmann's. Recall how during *C&C*'s debate about contextual theology, Lehmann sought to discern "what God is doing in the world to make and to keep human life human." Cone embraced a black nationalist analysis of U.S. society and argued that God was on the side of the oppressed. The heart of Christianity (read: "what God is doing to make life more human") was liberation, and the locus of Christianity in North America was black power. To be Christian at this time and place, Cone argued, was to work for black power and promote black pride. Theology should draw on sources from the African American tradition such as Nat Turner, Malcolm X, and the Black Panthers. For example, Cone wrote that "Jesus is Black. If we assume that the Risen Lord is truly present with us, as defined by his past history and witnessed by Scripture and tradition, what then does his presence mean in the social context of white racism? . . . Christ must be Black in order to remain faithful to the divine promise to bear the suffering of the poor."[39]

Cone held out only a thread of hope that white people might become black and thus part of valid Christianity. Not until the penultimate page of his first book, *Black Theology and Black Power,* did he qualify a stream of more militant rhetoric and state that blackness was not a matter of skin color; rather, "It means that your heart, your soul, your mind, and your body are where the dispossessed are. . . . Being reconciled to God does not mean that one's skin is physically black."[40] Even this comment seemed directed as much toward blacks who "were not black enough" as it was toward possible white allies. Pressed by critics, including the African American theologian J. Deotis Roberts, about the biblical theme of reconciliation, Cone held out another small thread.[41] Indeed, said Cone, the Bible did speak of reconciliation—but it involved radical repentance, and its cost was death.[42]

Cone's central arguments posed little problem for *C&C* if they were approached in the light of earlier debates about Saul Alinsky's community-organizing methods. But Cone raised red flags when read through *C&C*'s self-image as a bridge between blacks and the establishment, or in light of *C&C*'s dogged insistence that *the* overriding distinction for analyzing race did not run between all whites and all blacks—that there were at least a few trustworthy whites and a few blacks who were apolitical or conservative. The tensions escalated after the Black Manifesto controversy, which collapsed most of the Protestant bridges that were still standing by this time. As *C&C* debated whether to blame the collapse on black militancy or a white "colonial mentality," Cone took his stand with the militants. He and the Latin American liberationists Hugo Assman and

Paulo Freire announced that their stance toward white theologians would be "incommunication" rather than communication until they saw more evidence of solidarity.[43]

Bennett criticized Cone in his 1976 book, *The Radical Imperative*, and spin-off articles in *C&C*. In general, this book promoted liberation theologies and stressed connections between them and Bennett's past positions, especially from the 1930s. However, Bennett commented that for Cone, "blackness covers all forms of suffering from oppression. I suspect that blackness does not very clearly include the suffering of women." Bennett also said that all theology was properly strategic but that Cone was *too* strategic. Perhaps Bennett might have said "not strategic enough," since one of his points was that blacks needed coalitions with whites, and some whites were more promising partners than others. In any case Bennett saw "an element of unreality" in Cone's presentation of race as monolithic, and he thought Cone pandered to the "passionate self-righteousness" of revolutionaries.[44]

Bennett was not Cone's only critic in *C&C*. Julius Lester, a former black nationalist militant who later converted to mystical Judaism, harshly attacked Cone for downplaying African American traditions of religious transcendence. According to Lester, these traditions provided the strength of black religion: collective identity, dignity, and a way to make suffering meaningful and potentially redemptive. Black theology was abandoning this strength. In fact, black nationalism "is all black theology is." People like Cone were "uncertain about their identities—as blacks, and particularly as Christians." The result was a "cry to despair masked as the bark of militance," expressed in books written for white theologians and out of touch with black people. Cone was "trying to catch an airplane as it is taxiing down the runway."[45]

Lester made a few valid points. Cone's first books were in fact addressed mainly to white theologians. After all, Cone had studied in the Garrett-Northwestern Ph.D. program where in six years he was not assigned a single book written by an African American, and he taught at predominantly white Union Seminary. Moreover, there were notable gaps between Cone's normative black church and actually existing black churches; even King's civil rights activism had been too radical for the largest organization of black Baptists. Ruether echoed both of these points less polemically in the article mentioned above, "Crisis in Sex and Race: Black Theology versus Feminist Theology." Along with her argument about sexism, she said Cone was too limited to the concerns of "black caucus theology"—that is, African American leaders in predominantly white denominations—and not deeply rooted in the historic black churches. Outside *C&C*'s pages, other African American leaders including Cone's brother Cecil agreed.[46]

Nevertheless, Lester was overly harsh and unnuanced. An earlier Cone article, "Theological Reflections on Reconciliation," had been a model for writing theology from the context of black Christianity. As in his 1972 book, *Spirituals and the Blues,* Cone said more about African American religious experience than about European theology. He wrote concretely about the church in Fordyce, Arkansas, where he was raised. Responding to Lester, he refused to apologize for his focus on overcoming unnecessary suffering through social transformation, as opposed to redeeming suffering through religious transcendence. But he pointed out that he presupposed *both* a transcendent God *and* the idea that God was on the side of the oppressed.[47] Later, his commitment to a normative Christian logic was clear when he criticized a religious studies approach to black religion. Charles Long and a group of African scholars proposed to substitute a social scientific and comparative approach for a Christian theology with Jesus as its norm, but Cone responded, "With whom do we replace him?"[48] Whatever one might say about other liberationists, to dismiss Cone on the grounds that he does not stress a theology of transcendence is seriously misleading. In important ways he is *more,* not less, Barthian than liberal critics such as Bennett.

Although Cone's major *C&C* articles appeared in the early 1970s, he remained a contributing editor until 1985 and a strong influence to the end. His interests steadily diversified. Both he and his collaborator, Gayraud Wilmore, wrote extensively on black churches. And from his base in black nationalism he carried on a wide conversation with socialist, feminist, and third world theologies, adopting the idea of interstructured oppressions. His 1991 book, *Martin and Malcolm and America,* drew on cultural history as much as systematic theology; it advocated a middle ground between Malcolm X's mature black nationalism (after his break with the Nation of Islam) and the democratic socialist approach of the later King.[49] Other *C&C* voices who addressed race and theology diversified in similar ways. As already noted, womanist theology evolved into a major concern. And as I discuss in the next chapter, *C&C*'s leading African American voice in the early 1980s, Cornel West, did not call himself a black theologian but, rather, a prophetic pragmatist with interests in African American critical thought.

Latin American Liberation Theology

While Cone approached Christianity in the context of black nationalism, Latin American liberation theologians approached it in the context of dependency theory and Latin American class struggle. Their goal was to forge alliances between progressive sectors of the Catholic church and the center-left national coalitions that we saw Richard Shaull advocating in chapter 7. This implied breaking the church's historic alliance with landed elites and its identification of Christendom with the political status quo. It also implied rejecting the more liberal New Christendom approach, which was roughly the Latin American Catholic version of the WCC's "responsible society." New Christendom assumed a "distinction of spheres." God and the church transcended mundane politics but provided general moral principles; meanwhile, in the temporal sphere, individual Christians joined Catholic Action movements and Christian Democratic parties.

New Christendom broke down at the level of practical politics because Christians began to join more radical movements than the theory endorsed, beginning in Brazil in the 1950s and peaking with the integration of the Christian left within the Sandinista revolutionary coalition in Nicaragua during the 1970s. Meanwhile, at the level of elite church policy, liberationists convinced a majority of Latin American bishops at Medellín in 1968 to affirm a strong rhetorical option for the poor, although conservative bishops (and eventually Pope John Paul II) later mobilized against this idea, putting the radicals very much on the defensive by the 1980s.

New Christendom also broke down theologically as liberationists insisted that such themes as salvation and the Kingdom of God should not refer to a realm of reality distinct from day-to-day human life. Rather, there was one *unified* sacred / profane history. Although experience could be analyzed at different levels through different languages—from "scientific" Marxian analysis to metaphors of theology—salvation / liberation would come, if at all, in and through this history. Liberationists relentlessly attacked all forms of "pie in the sky" theology that could be used to legitimize poverty and fatalism. They rejected all arguments that called on churches to remain aloof from politics in the name of the distinction of planes, although they also maintained a secondary rhetoric of God transcending any particular political movement. Thus Gutiérrez said, "The growth of the Kingdom is a process that occurs historically in liberation. . . . This is not an identification [i.e., between God's Kingdom and historical events]. Without liberating historical events, there would be no growth of the Kingdom. But the process of liberation will not have conquered the very roots of oppression and the exploitation of man by man without the Kingdom of God, which is above all a gift."[50]

As the Latin Americans developed their theme of unitary history, they complained that first world theologians put too much stress on God transcending politics. They even criticized Jürgen Moltmann, whose "theology of hope" was the leading European theology that accented the human possibilities mentioned in *C&C*'s symposium on Christian realism. Moltmann transmuted critiques from "above" history into critiques from "ahead of" current history. In his theology, God critiqued the present from the standpoint of the future; he used symbols from eschatology, or the theory concerning the end of the world. According to the Latin Americans, Moltmann's God of the future was too far beyond the present; Moltmann failed to stress God's presence in current struggles, and this was an example of typical first world complacency. This led Moltmann to respond in a widely debated open letter to José Míguez Bonino in *C&C*. Moltmann maintained that the Latin Americans' ideas about the future were so similar to his own that if he was guilty of bourgeois abstraction, then so were they. He denied that he stood aloof from struggles for justice in his country. On the contrary, said Moltmann, no one could make a revolution with theory alone; visions of social change that were not attuned to the people would function like train engines tearing loose from their cars. Europeans had no choice but to advocate forms of socialism that had unambiguous commitments to democracy. He suggested, however, that the Latin Americans needed better grounding in their *own* history. They should pay more attention to popular Christianity and be less preoccupied with European debates about that Eurocentric theorist, Karl Marx.[51]

Within his framework of a unified history moving toward the Kingdom of God, Gutiérrez stressed the importance of utopia, understood as a level midway between politics and Christian faith, or between socioeconomic liberation and the deepest levels of spiritual liberation. This middle ground was the seedbed for the imagination needed to inform political practice; it was the place of "historical projection" and "annunciation" that could create new forms of solidarity.[52] Utopia was also the key term in *C&C*'s debate about Latin American theology. This debate pulled in two directions, corresponding to two levels of meaning in *C&C*'s discourse on utopia.

In the first sense, utopia was the opposite of discredited pragmatic gradualism. It was a vision reaching beyond current historical possibilities. In this sense it meant rebelling against current realities and proposing something counterfactual. For example, if a pragmatist lobbied Congress to end the war, a utopian might try (as a famous group of antiwar protesters did in 1967) to levitate the Pentagon.[53] Such thinking is natural when the pragmatic options are all intolerable, and one must imagine something new. Rubem Alves, a Brazilian liberation theologian, wrote that U.S. liberals had formerly assumed that they could identify and change their enemies. Now "the ghost of tragedy has begun to haunt this country." "We behave as if democracy were here (knowing that it is not), as if the Congress had power (knowing that it does not), as if magic rituals were political acts. We enter the world of fiction. The fact that we still use democratic tactics in a nondemocratic society is an indication that we live in a theoretical gap. We sense that power has now moved to different hands and functions through new mechanisms. But we do not know this new thing. Politics then has to become magic."[54]

In this context Alves turned to the concept of utopia, which in *C&C* at this time was linked to the theology of play. During the same years that Cox saw "an end of an era" and a need for play as "ludic consciousness," he asked how to maintain hope after Martin Luther King's assassination. Hope was not optimism, he said, nor was it based on mere probability that could be discovered empirically. It required a "different basic orientation" of faith. King had said that "we have cosmic allies." Cox asked, "Do we? The question is not answered speculatively but by living as though we do."[55] It was no longer possible to talk about "human possibilities" as if it were a matter of polling Congress to see if the votes were there for a Great Society program. Rather, utopian hope—and faith in God—involved the ability to think in a new way.

Against thinking that was utopian in this sense, Christian realists wanted to be, well, more realistic. After Gutiérrez's *Theology of Liberation* was translated in 1973, this complaint surfaced in a famous *C&C* symposium. It began when Thomas Sanders accused Gutiérrez of uncritical thought, or what Niebuhr had called "soft utopianism." Sanders thought that theologians who appealed to possibilities should be able to provide plausible empirical evidence of their grounds for hope. He claimed that the Latin Americans failed at this point because their analysis was oversimplified and moralistic. According to Sanders, there was no evidence of a general "revolutionary ferment" in Latin America; instead, technocratic decision makers had to juggle complex power struggles in national contexts. The root problem was theological: liberation theology neglected limits imposed by "the biblical view of human nature" and the "moral ambiguity that characterizes all forms of social existence."[56]

Alves responded angrily, making a sophisticated case that different paradigms delimit the realities that people are able to perceive. In Sanders's realist paradigm, Alves insisted, "the limits of the future are determined by the structure of the present." "As one takes a certain social order for granted, a rather large number of possibilities become impossibilities. Peace is a utopian dream in a society structured in terms of functions. The categories 'impossibility' and 'utopian' are not absolute but relative to the systems they want to transcend." Thus Alves claimed that Sanders's attempt to interpret Latin Americans' political possibilities for them was a patronizing "part of cultural imperialism." Its ethics "operat[ed] according to the logic of the system which totally ignores morality."[57]

For a time it seemed as if every single *C&C* writer felt compelled to comment on this exchange.[58] Bennett granted some of Sanders's points about moral ambiguities, but he pointed out that liberationists were already capable of noticing them without help from a condescending North American onlooker. He stressed that a revolutionary standpoint and commitment were needed "prior to the consideration of particular revolutionary policies."[59] Sanders subsequently granted these points, but went on to rephrase his question: was there a way to translate between normative utopian rhetoric and a more customary language of short-term policy and power? Moltmann later made a similar distinction between the *necessity* of revolution (assumed by everyone at *C&C*) and its *possibility.*[60]

Political scientist Alexander Wilde partly supported Sanders, although he found him excessively technocratic. For Wilde, "the problem is not that the forces of change are unrealistic (though they may be) but that there are so *few* of them" in Latin America at large. Wilde joked, "Today Chile, tomorrow . . . Paraguay?" Given the grinding injustices of Latin America, "the forces of change need all the help they can get." Wilde said, "I end in the same place as the Liberationists, though with a much less optimistic appraisal of the reality they wish to transform." His point soon gained force, as Allende's socialist government in Chile was crushed and a wave of U.S.-backed fascist governments came to power in Latin America. Ironically, this setback for the revolutionary hopes of the 1960s undermined Wilde's further contention that churches were "marginal to the most important processes in politics."[61] In some places churches became quite important under repression, because they were the strongest popular institutions still intact after the destruction of unions, political parties, independent presses, and so on. Dissent became channeled through the popular church.[62]

To get to the heart of the Sanders versus Alves debate, it is crucial to grasp that Alves assumed *C&C*'s second sense of the word *utopia.* Recall how the first sense suggested something counterfactual, like levitating the Pentagon. In the second sense, aspects of utopia that Gutiérrez called "denunciation" were linked to a progressive vision of a future that was not yet realized but was taken to be an *actual possibility.* Liberationists spoke of it as a "historical project." King's "I Have a Dream" speech was utopian in this second sense: it contradicted current realities and painted a rosier picture than would probably ever happen, but King's listeners thought that something approximating it was coming or at least might happen if they kept hope alive. The Latin Americans' hope for a society that redistributed wealth and combated dependency (correlated with biblical images of God's Kingdom) was utopian in this sense. This was *not* because they thought a "perfect" society could ever happen, despite claims to the contrary by a whole generation of conservatives who have been unable or unwilling to grasp this basic point. Rather, it was because they thought a better society (in Niebuhr's terms a less evil one) *was* happening, and—this is crucial—that its mix of success and failure would depend, in part, on how many people kept hope alive.[63]

As we have seen, the attraction to this second kind of utopia ran deep in *C&C*'s tradition. This in turn helps explain *C&C*'s surge of interest in Latin America, as when Robert McAfee Brown said that Gutiérrez's *Theology of Liberation* might be the most important book of the decade.[64] In Latin American liberation theology, *C&C* found a radical movement that integrated utopian thinking and included people they knew. (They knew hardly any Vietnamese, especially not as theological colleagues.) Most important, it seemed to *show hope of practical success*—at least for a time, in some key places like Brazil and Nicaragua. *C&C* progressives, reaching a dead end after King's murder and feeling uncomfortable with the Black Manifesto, shifted their interest to Medellín and Managua. There they switched sides in the class struggle, from backing anticommunist development to joining popular movements for the redistribution of wealth and the transformation of global economic relationships.

As theologian Frederick Herzog watched this process unfold, he asked whether something would be lost in the translation as Latin American theology was appropriated by North Americans. After all, north of the border the most common historical equation read as follows: liberal progressivism plus power equals Manifest Destiny. Herzog asked whether stressing a unified sacralized history would be helpful in the United States; he feared that it might not turn out much better than earlier forms of the American jeremiad. According to Herzog, U.S. theologians should highlight race and give methodological priority less to standard contextualist methods and more to listening to a transcendent / prophetic critique from the Bible. Herzog saw himself supporting revolutionary change. However, Hugo Assman charged that he was speaking about "God's action in history without going through history."[65]

We must evaluate Herzog's skepticism on a case-by-case basis because his critique of progressivism applies to some North Americans more than others. Harriet Tubman used Exodus metaphors in her work on the Underground Railroad without becoming an apologist for Manifest Destiny. Moreover, as Herzog himself stressed, his argument gave U.S. critics small warrant for charging Latin Americans with triumphalism. Even the most successful revolutionary coalitions of the 1970s in Chile and Nicaragua were never in a position of strength, and they suffered severe harassment. Thus it was offensive when, in another popular distortion of liberation theology, conservatives in the United States accused people like the Salvadoran Jesuit Jon Sobrino of progressive hubris when his order was under a death threat from a U.S.-backed death squad, his friends (from peasants to archbishops) were being slaughtered, and he wrote about facing martyrdom.[66]

The upshot of *C&C*'s enthusiasm for Latin American theology was ambiguous. Was *C&C* valorizing uncritical visionaries or latching onto realistic agents of forward progress? How relevant was the Latin American model for North America? In any case, during the 1970s *C&C*'s discourse on Latin America was its strongest attempt to keep alive an oppositional form of progressivism. As Beverly Harrison summarized, Latin American theology was the "most serious, sustained and theologically informed challenge to the Western, dominant Christian paradigm."[67] Because this challenge came at a formative moment, *C&C* leaders including Harrison, Ruether, and West later carried forward many of its central concerns, along with their commitments as feminists and black intellectuals.

C&C's engagement with Latin American liberation theology in the narrow sense—as a school of academic theology—began to fade in the late 1980s in the face of a triple whammy of changes: a systematic Vatican counterattack on the leaders of the movement, reduced hope for imminent revolutionary change in Latin American societies, and the discovery that conservative evangelicals, especially Pentecostals, were in many places thriving more than liberationist base communities.[68] Still, *C&C* remained deeply interested in Latin America until the end. It followed Central American politics closely, and leaders like the murdered Salvadoran archbishop Oscar Romero became key role models.[69] *C&C* promoted the sanctuary movement, a network of U.S. Christians who smuggled refugees from Central America into their communities, offering them sanctuary in their churches. Such religiously ritualized civil disobedience personalized and extended the transnational religious-political community that was being created in opposition to U.S. policy. In some places it was the backbone of organizing against Reagan's Central America policy, and it was enough of a brake on Reagan's plans that his administration ordered extensive illegal surveillance and infiltration of churches. *C&C* closely followed the conspiracy trials and countersuits, which involved friends and colleagues of *C&C* insiders.[70] In 1982, 15 percent of *C&C*'s articles and fully half of its editorials were about Latin America; one irate subscriber even suggested renaming the journal "Christianity and Central America."[71]

Complex Dialogues within a New Theological Paradigm

Imagine a circle with four points on its circumference representing white liberal theology, black theology, Latin American liberation theology, and feminist theology. As I have shown, *C&C* engaged in specialized debates around each of these points. But its overall theological discourse was a multileveled dialogue among everyone in this whole circle—including people at "midway points" such as womanist theology and other nodal points such as ecological theology and gay/lesbian theologies—and between this circle as a whole and the larger society. Although these debates were too complex to map here, it is useful to note some common patterns.

One pattern was a critical response to liberationists from established white male theologians. I have mentioned several examples, from friendly exchanges like Moltmann's letter to Míguez Bonino, through ambiguous comments like Driver's image of dragon-slaying theologians, to disdainful dismissals like Ramsey's. A common complaint from Niebuhrians was that liberationists lacked self-criticism, since they denied the possibility of objectivity and gave higher priority to promoting movements for change than criticizing them. This was part of Bennett's complaint against Cone, as well as Sanders's against Alves. However, the indictment could be framed in far harsher terms.

The Hartford Appeal was a 1975 statement by former *C&C* allies moving toward neoconservatism. Its argument was somewhat like Paul Ramsey's earlier attack on contextual ethics, in that it stressed the need to stand in judgment on sinful human contexts rather than build contextual ethics on a base of sin. The Appeal used this logic to accuse liberation theologies of accommodating to "the world." For the key voices behind the Appeal, this world was perceived through theories about the "new class." As we have seen, this means that they posited a world dominated by liberal bureaucrats and liberal intellectual workers rather than corporate executives and generals, that they celebrated a democratic capitalism that was upheld by these executives and generals against totalizing liberals, and that they had a blind spot when it came to noticing *conservative capitalist* members of the "class" of bureaucrats and intellectuals. Viewing through this "new class" lens, neoconservatives were able to perceive a journalist like Morley Safer as a representative of the "dominant class" in his confrontation with the military officer in Saigon who, let us recall, told Safer that he was a "handmaiden of the government," that Safer would be disciplined through his employers if he failed to cooperate, and that "if you think any American official is going to tell you the truth, then you're stupid."[72] Similarly, the Hartford Appeal claimed that liberation theologies were in fact accommodated to dominant social and intellectual trends, even though liberationists understood themselves as attempting to build oppositional coalitions among oppressed groups and their allies. Richard John Neuhaus was a key promoter of the Appeal, and several old-time *C&C* writers including Nathan Scott and Peter Berger signed it.

In a *C&C* symposium on the Appeal, liberal pastor William Sloane Coffin said he had signed it because he agreed that churches should refuse to let "the world" set their moral agenda. But Coffin perceived a world quite different than Neuhaus's, and he was among a minority that turned the Appeal's logic against U.S. nationalism. Speaking for the majority, Neuhaus maintained that liberation theologians, Norman Vincent Peale (author of the religious self-help book, *The Power of Positive Thinking*), and Billy James Hargis of the Christian Anti-Communist Crusade were comparable. Why? Because none of them stressed divine transcendence over politics. Asked how many blacks and women had been involved in a conference that could perceive the world through this lens, Neuhaus replied that there had been a few, but "unabashedly and without apology, our primary concern was to get people who could deal with these questions [i.e., the theology of transcendence] regardless of sex or race and if that be elitism, let it be elitism."[73]

Like estranged lovers who had not entirely forgotten the old days, participants in *C&C*'s symposium maintained minimal civility. After Cox attacked the Appeal for retreating from the best recent work of the churches, assuming that "God Almighty has a special fondness for America," and promoting a heretical "God-world dualism," Neuhaus responded that he and Cox "really are good friends" and that the Appeal's goal was simply "regaining of American Christian confidence" for social activism—essentially a return to the liberal consensus that Ramsey had seen slipping away in 1967. Still, one participant joked that the signers and opponents might someday wind up on opposite sides of a barricade "with weapons in our hands."[74]

Another variation on establishment hostility toward liberation theologies was harder for liberationists to confront than overt attacks like the Hartford Appeal. This was the perception that not only self-critical theology but theology as a whole was disappearing. Since the new paradigm implied different ideas about what constituted important theological problems and helpful arguments to address them, liberation theologies were not always seen by other theologians as real (or adequate) theologies at all. A generation trained to judge "serious" theological ethics by its dialogue with the history of philosophy and doctrine might perceive ethics informed by neo-Marxian sociology and feminist cultural theory as trivial. Often white males treated black and feminist theologies as nonevents.

In a 1975 symposium on "Whatever Happened to Theology?" Gordon Kaufman stated that "the once proud queen of the sciences, having lost a sense of her own meaning and integrity, had become a common prostitute" legitimating "almost any partisan position found in the culture."[75] Kaufman, near the liberal pole of the theological establishment, disparaged neoorthodoxy and called for a revival of foundational theology. Meanwhile, Van Harvey, whose method was closer to neoorthodoxy, lamented the "faddism" and "pervasive loss of vocation" among younger theologians. Citing Peter Berger's version of new class theory, he argued that theology was being swallowed up by the secular academy. Unlike the Hartford Appeal, which drew conservative conclusions from similar perceptions, Harvey described theological accommodation to the academy as "bourgeois entrapment" linked to a militaristic economy, and he urged theologians to "break out of the horizon of the bourgeois world and bring a transcendent word of judgment on and renewal to the conditions that create the 'life-worlds' of Western men and women."[76] In principle, most liberationists agreed, just as Coffin agreed with the Hartford Appeal in the abstract. However, liberationists put more stress on grounding prophetic critiques in concrete contexts of oppression—and, of course, they denied that this (necessarily) represented faddism.

Although we have noted how Latin American radicals cast Frederick Herzog as a wishy-washy gringo who wanted "to speak of God in history without going through history," Herzog did not play this role in relation to Kaufman. Herzog suggested that a better name for *C&C*'s symposium on "Whatever Happened to Theology?" would be "What's Happening to the White Male Theologian?" As in the story of the emperor's new clothes, said Herzog, "the white male theologian stands exposed. . . . The modern mind [he] has been apologizing to turns out to be a monstrous misfit," and the liberal "turns out to be his own worst enemy." Herzog suggested that, in biblical terms, "the ax is already laid to the roots," and liberals needed to repent. Along with historical criticism of the Bible, they needed "ideology criticism" of the "history of power in Protestant systematic theology," with special attention to Protestant support for Manifest Destiny. Herzog quoted the great liberal theologian Friedrich Schleiermacher, who wrote in 1830 that Christians no longer needed miracles because of "the great advantage in power and civilization that Christian peoples possess over the non-Christian, almost without exception." Herzog pointed out that, just one year later, "Nat Turner was tried and put to death by Christian people in Jerusalem, Va. . . . Who has ears to hear, let him hear!"[77]

A second pattern within *C&C*'s multileveled dialogue was sorting out the cultural differences and interstructured oppressions among various branches of liberation theology. Here again, I have already mentioned debates between Trible and Daly, Daly and Ruether, Ruether and Cone, and so on. It would be easy to multiply examples, such as the efforts by Czech theologian Jan Lochman to make peace between pacifists, who opposed all war, and liberationists who were retooling just war theories as "just revolution" theories.[78] Mexican feminist Sylvia Marcos illustrated the sort of comparative reflection that became second nature for *C&C:*

> It is not the same to live in a squatter settlement or cardboard house as it is to have five houses scattered throughout the world. Economic differences . . . create an abyss of difference. It was difficult for me to listen to the grievances of middle-class feminists after I had shared the anguishes of poor rural women . . . [who] were literally shivering with cold and never had enough to eat. . . . [Nevertheless] the concerns of those comparatively well-to-do feminists were not individual or relevant only to their class. I was also hearing Doña Maria, an urban poor woman, complaining of unending housework, the weight of children on her back, and a husband who came home from work and considered his job finished, with everything else her duty only. On the one hand, the economic differences are striking. On the other, the similarities . . . that cut across class lines are also striking.[79]

Many of *C&C*'s dialogues across various camps of liberation theology touched on a broad tension inside the liberationist discourse. On one side was the continuing appeal of progressive prophetic metaphors (if framed in oppositional ways over against specified Pharaohs). On the other side was suspicion about the limitations of a prophetic sensibility, because of its effects on groups that were Others for male prophets during the history of the West, and because of its tendency to screen out a wider range of experiences such as those celebrated by counterculturalists or the Grailville feminists. In 1989 an influential article by the Osage writer Robert Allen Warrior argued that *C&C* had taken the wrong side in its omnipresent rhetoric about the Exodus and the Promised Land. For Warrior, the biblical conquest of Canaan involved genocide—at least as portrayed in the canonical text—and native peoples were its victims. Exodus would not work as the central metaphor for Native American Christian spirituality.[80]

The Lakota writer Vine Deloria made a similar point in a 1975 interview, but in broader strokes. According to Deloria, "the very essence of Western European identity involves the assumption that time proceeds in a linear fashion; further, it assumes that at a particular point in the unraveling of this sequence, the people of Western Europe became the guardian of mankind."[81] This explained why western thought centers on biblical metaphors like Exodus and secular ones like the progress of civilization, as opposed to the idea of recurring generations and cycles of nature. And it helped explain behaviors which Deloria described as literally insane, such as assuming that the Vietnam War could be a natural unfolding of the history of North America. Deloria was able to perceive and critique this limitation of western paradigms because he spoke from an alternative community, a sense of cyclical time, and a strong sense of relationality with the natural environment.

In her influential 1971 article, "Mother Earth and the Megamachine," Ruether struck a balance between positive and negative stances toward prophetic Christianity. She began with her standard argument about dualisms in western thought. Israelite prophets had broken away from a religion that was attuned to cycles of nature, embracing a more historical and linear approach. At first this was neither good nor bad, but eventually it had degenerated into an antihistorical apocalypticism and blended with Neoplatonic dualisms between mind and body, male and female. The Enlightenment had continued this theme through its practice of considering dominant groups (men, whites, technocrats, etc.) as rational subjects and the victims of hierarchies (women, blacks, the natural world, etc.) as their objects. Thus western assumptions of objectivity and gender-neutral rationality were deeply suspect.

To a point, Ruether argued, Enlightenment logic was helpful for addressing these problems. It could transform received traditions about women by extending the logic of human equality to give women an equal chance at rationality and initiative. Moreover, third world versions of progressivism were addressing crucial issues. But neither of these logics went far enough, Ruether judged, and first world liberal theologies were barely helpful at all, insofar as they portrayed a gospel freedom "to depart endlessly from natural and historical foundations into the contentless desert of pure possibility." Such theologies were "happy to baptize modern technology as the expression of the freedom to transcend and dominate nature.... The usefulness of this spirituality is about to end."[82]

Ruether hoped that her socialist and antiracist feminism could bridge a gap between what was positive in prophetic socialist approaches, on one side, and countercultural critiques that were "elitist, privatistic, aesthetic, and devoid of a profound covenant with the poor and oppressed of the earth," on the other: "Combining the values of world-transcending Yahweh with those of the world renewing Ba'al in a post-technological religion of reconciliation with the body, the woman, and the world, its salvation myth will not be one of divinization and flight from the body but of humanization and reconciliation with the earth.... [This is not] the will to power of a monolithic empire, obliterating all other identities before the one identity of the master race, but a poly-linguistic appreciativeness that can redeem local space, time and identity."[83]

Almost all the elements of C&C's discourse on liberation theology met in this article: feminism, empire, the master race and its Others, ecological critique, and the theme of realism divided against itself. Like C&C at large, it maintained modest hopes for creative dialogue among all these concerns. Its goal was to strengthen particular communities and transform larger power hierarchies.

10

Ongoing Debates about Race, Postmodernity, and the Reagan Era

C&C's most important changes were complete by the late 1970s, and the main value of telling its story is to analyze how its liberation paradigm emerged. Still, many subsequent developments were interesting, and it is worthwhile to follow *C&C*'s story from its founding in 1941 to its death in 1993. This chapter provides a highly selective account of major issues from *C&C*'s last fifteen years. This is not the proper place for a blow-by-blow account of these years. We stand so close in time to the final decade that it remains difficult to gain perspective. Also, *C&C* addressed so many issues, overlapping so much with earlier themes, that a thorough overview would risk becoming diluted and/or redundant.

My rationale for brevity is different from the lament, commonly voiced by neoconservatives and liberal centrists, that *C&C* became predictable. True, *C&C* was predictable in steering left of neoconservatism, as well as in writing so much about Reinhold Niebuhr not being a neoconservative as to bore upcoming generations. Also, perhaps one might argue that *C&C* had *always* been predictable and remained so. Beyond this it is hard to discover any trend toward greater predictability. *C&C*'s political line was not set in stone, and it is simply incorrect to claim that *C&C*'s interests were narrower after the mid-1970s than in earlier years.

Consider eight issues that fell in my sample during the mid-1980s. Some of their topics were unsurprising: whole issues on Niebuhr, South Africa, and the Catholic bishops' pastoral letter on the economy, plus articles on the arms race, feminism, and Central America. However, there was also a report on Lakota efforts to regain control of the Black Hills; a poem by black poet June Jordan; an article on farming families; a defense of some hostages in an airline hijacking who were vilified for attempting to mediate between their captors and the press; and an analysis of how new communications technologies would affect conditions of work, as opposed to more typical concerns about their impact on consumers.[1]

Perhaps this all falls within a predictable spectrum of interest. But read on. There was also a "seamless garment" argument against abortion (the type that applies "Thou shall not kill" equally to the arms race and to pregnant women) by a *C&C* editor. There was a discussion of Renaissance art that portrayed Jesus with explicit genitalia, including a painting of the resurrected Christ with a prominent erection. (*C&C*'s reviewer was skeptical about a book that treated such art as an exemplary celebration of Christ's incarnation.) In the midst of Reagan's presidency, one writer called for a Constitutional amendment to allow presidents to serve more than two terms.[2] Columnist Will Campbell even offered a qualified defense of the Ku Klux Klan after it opened fire on five members of the Communist Workers Party (CWP) who were protesting one of its rallies. Campbell reported that the spouse of a Klansman asked him: "Preacher, tell me how come it's just fine for us to send our boys all the way across the ocean to kill some people who never bothers us, people we never even saw who the government tell us might be Communists, but when some people are right here in our country wearing signs saying they're Communists and that they're going to kill us [a slogan of the CWP demonstration was 'Death to the Klan'], and well, if our boys kills them, they get put in jail?" When Campbell said he was opposed to all killing, she replied, "Well, you must not love the Lord and your country like we do around here." Campbell concluded that the violence "was not a reflection of hayseed bigots but a reflection of the national mood, cultivated and manipulated for half a century."[3]

Whatever we might say about this set of articles, *predictable* is hardly the word that springs to mind. It bears repeating that I have not gone fishing for the greatest diversity I could discover: all these examples appeared in just eight randomly chosen issues published over two and a half years, four each under the leadership of *C&C* editors Bob Hoyt and Leon Howell.

Another variation on the charge of predictability was that *C&C* became intellectually flatter, even anti-intellectual at times. There is somewhat more truth to this perception. *C&C* did "dumb down" to some degree, turning after the early 1980s toward shorter articles and less engagement with emergent intellectual debates. However, it makes no sense to compare Niebuhr's best writing from the 1940s with *C&C*'s less persuasive articles from the 1980s, such as one that called for a national protest against Denny's restaurants, based on a possible racist subtext of Christmas mugs that changed from frowning dark figures (such as green reindeers) to white smiling ones.[4] This is like comparing *C&C*'s early apologetics for South African bantustans with the strongest articles by Ruether in the 1970s.

To gauge the contribution of the later *C&C* to wider intellectual debates, consider the book reviews in the ten issues from my sample that appeared around 1990. They treated twenty books—four times more than in similar periods around 1960 and 1970—including such novels as Toni Morrison's *Beloved* and Salmon Rushdie's *Satanic Verses,* as well as a wide range of social and historical writing.[5] Subjects ranged from Kitty Kelly's "unauthorized biography" of Nancy Reagan to Eric Voegelin's five-volume synthesis of intellectual history. *C&C* joined discussions of well-known books such as Susan Sontag's *AIDS and Its Metaphors,* and promoted neglected books such as Ward Churchill's exposé of FBI repression of the American Indian Movement.[6] Of course, *C&C* also followed Protestant social thought, since the overlapping territory between this and wider intellectual debates was *C&C*'s distinctive niche. This particular sample reviewed John Cobb and Herman Daly's *For the Common Good* (a contribution to debates about ecology), Douglas Meeks's *God the Economist* (a theological case for democratic socialism), and Mary Hunt's *Fierce Tenderness: A Feminist Theology of Friendship.*[7]

Although these reviews suffered from the compressed presentation that *C&C* demanded from its writers in these years, many were important critical contributions in their own right. For example, Mike Miller's comments about *Minds Stayed on Freedom,* an oral history of the civil rights movement, cautioned against *C&C*'s tendency to romanticize the role of ministers in the civil rights movement and avoid thinking critically about the period.[8] At least in the book review section, *C&C* was more consistently interesting in its final decade than in earlier years.

New Priorities on a Range of Issues

Let us consider some new explorations that were especially important. To be sure, the underlying standpoints they reflected did not change a great deal after *C&C*'s radical turn, except in a few cases such as the debate about abortion. *C&C* maintained a sort of limping Great Society approach, somewhere between the left fringe of liberalism and the "responsible" wing of radicalism. Rather than exploring how to push out liberalism's leftward boundaries from within a dominant coalition, *C&C* now adopted a standpoint of responsible opposition. Still, various emergent concerns became important, alongside issues that I have already flagged such as Central America solidarity and the sex war in feminist theory.

First, *C&C*'s long-standing interest in the arms race kicked into high gear during the early 1980s, after idling in the background since the Cuban missile crisis. During Ronald Reagan's first term, military issues were *C&C*'s number one concern, rivaled only by its passion for Latin American radicalism.[9] *C&C*'s underlying motives were captured by a high-ranking Mormon, Edwin Brown Firmage, who called the arms race idolatry and asked, "Can the state itself demand our allegiance, our affirmation, in a decision to destroy hundreds of millions of people?" Firmage stated, "Only a people who possessed no love for, identification with, or responsibility toward those who have lived before and those who will live after us could continue on the path we are now upon. If we see ourselves as part of a continuing chain of being extending into the past and the future, we must abide the consequences of our stewardship toward our fathers and mothers, our daughters and sons. . . . Our hearts must go out in both directions, past and future."[10]

Addressing conservatives who dismissed such exhortations as bleeding heart utopianism, *C&C* joined "sober" debates about policy proposals and two major religious statements of the mid-1980s by Catholic and Methodist bishops. *C&C* consistently called for cuts in military spending, with the savings shifted toward social programs.[11] It extended long-standing debates about whether nuclear deterrence was defensible as a lesser evil, whether visions of peace were realistic, and how just war criteria could justify the risk of a war that might destroy all life on earth.

C&C also promoted activism to slow down the military machine. It was most comfortable with moderate approaches such as the nuclear freeze movement (which called for a halt to nuclear testing and production by both the United States and the Soviets) and legal demonstrations against the arms race.[12] Yet *C&C* was also open to more radical actions that were less concerned about pragmatic results in mainstream politics. The Plowshares Eight, a group that included Daniel Berrigan, entered a nuclear weapons plant and destroyed the nose cone of a missile with a sledgehammer, thus symbolically beating swords into plowshares. They saw their act as analogous to sabotaging a Nazi extermination camp, and they hoped to turn their trial into a forum to declare the arms race illegal under international law.[13] For the government prosecutors and the presiding judge, on the other hand, this was an open-and-shut case of destroying private property. The *C&C* reporter who covered the trial sympathized with the activists and attempted to open a dialogue about their positions with the judge, Samuel Salus. Unfortunately, the days of harmony between *C&C* and high-ranking judges were over. Salus wrote: "I was well aware that you were consorting with, and sympathizing with, the fringe press during the entire trail. . . . It was obvious you weren't there to view the facts objectively. . . . Your confusing thought process and logic appalls me since it has been represented to me that you were a professor of journalism."[14]

Second, *C&C* increasingly focused on the class structure of the United States. It attacked the myth of middle-class success, which justifies the status quo through the idea that any individual has a more or less equal chance to succeed through hard work. In the mid-1970s John Raines reported that if one counted not only income (the usual measure in mainstream analyses) but also control of capital, 10 percent of the population owned over half the wealth, and the richest 0.5 percent owned a quarter. These figures nearly provoked nostalgia as a lesser evil when *C&C* updated the numbers in 1990. After two terms of Reaganomics, the share of the top 10 percent had risen to more than two-thirds of the common wealth, and just four hundred people owned 40 percent of the fixed capital. However, recall how the early *C&C* had defended U.S. capitalism on the grounds that it provided a tolerable dispersion of power. Either set of figures called this into question. Raines showed that class mobility was rare and that low-income people were set up to fail in prevailing institutions, including the educational system, which liberals had seen as a level playing field. The United States was "a country of wage earners and wealth owners, with little mobility between."[15]

C&C's thirty-fifth anniversary symposium in 1976 focused on economic class. Its panel ranged across *C&C*'s liberal-radical continuum, with democratic socialist Michael Harrington near its center of gravity. Harrington distanced himself from more radical panelists, cautioning that confrontation politics would backfire. He promoted national health insurance, tax reform, and a full employment bill, despite the limitations of these measures, because he hoped they could move the nation from point A to B along a path ultimately leading to Z. Since this required knowing where Z is, Harrington presented a structural analysis of the economy. He argued, for example, that the *Wall Street Journal* had threatened a capital strike if President Carter followed through on campaign promises about guaranteed income policies. According to Harrington, mainstream debates about the free market versus economic planning were misleading. "We already have national planning"—and its goal was to maximize corporate profits. Government subsidies of freeways, suburbs, and mechanized agriculture had led directly to urban decay through white flight and unemployment. These decisions were "utterly rational in terms of the corporate structure of the society, so long precisely as you did not count the social costs as costs; so long as you socialize the costs and privatize the benefits. . . . If we are to get out of the pickle we find ourselves in, we have to change this systemic structure of corporate domination."[16]

C&C was never tempted by the fashionable idea that the collapse of centralized command economies in Eastern Europe called this basic analysis into question. If anything was in question, it was whether democratic movements could mobilize enough power to shift more of the ongoing government intervention away from corporate welfare and toward greater public goods, within a system that used the market to allocate resources. When Michael Novak stated that "the natural logic of capitalism leads to democracy," *C&C* was incredulous:

> It is clear that capitalism does not require, nor necessarily encourage, democracy. Elements of the German bourgeoisie helped Hitler come to power. . . . Nor have capitalist societies and their ruling classes shown any notable reluctance to have democracy destroyed in Italy, Japan, Argentina, Brazil, or other countries. . . . In countries with more ambitious and comprehensive welfare states than we have in America—Sweden, Holland, Denmark, England, Israel—there has been no concurrent erosion of political freedoms. . . . [However,] the freedom to hire labor at semi-starvation wages or the freedom of old people to starve to death for lack of pensions has been curtailed.[17]

In 1991 the *Century* published a "Post-Communist Manifesto" by two leading ethicists, Max Stackhouse and Dennis McCann. Taking aim at positions like *C&C*'s, they claimed that "everyone who holds to a 'preferential option for the poor' must now embrace capitalism." *C&C* editor Tom Kelly responded, "There is no great point in picking away at all the old bones of 1950s corporate liberalism." He asked how an intellectual could seriously propose that the collapse of the Soviet Union discredited every form of "political control of the marketplace." Stackhouse and McCann spoke of a reformed capitalism that "uses law, politics, education, and especially theology to constrain the temptations to exploitation," but they gave evasive responses to such critics as John Cobb, who asked exactly how such constraints would operate in practice. Similarly *C&C* asked what sense it made, within the framework of the *Century*'s realist logic, to say that "all politics and economics must be conducted under the context-transcending principles of truth, justice, and love." As Kelly pointed out, "The question unasked is whether a capitalist system is capable of such conduct. The historical record is certainly not encouraging."[18]

Third, *C&C* began to address ecology and the global agricultural system. In part, this simply reflected concern about what was called "world hunger"—large-scale poverty and starvation in Africa, Asia, and Latin

America—while adding little to earlier treatments of development and dependency. Some writers advanced proposals for increasing food yields through agricultural versions of development, while others stressed empowering the hungry by combating dependency.[19] However, another part of *C&C*'s coverage was new. Just as Harrington showed how maximizing corporate profits was irrational if social costs such as deteriorating cities were factored into the analysis, economists including E. F. Schumacher insisted that unlimited growth was irrational because of its ecological costs. The world economy was like a huge factory that could churn out more profits every year, but only because it was guided by an accounting system blind to a major fact: it was generating current income by depleting its *capital*. This capital included nonrenewable energy sources and the capacity of the ecosystem to absorb pollution before breaking down.[20] Thus the earth was like a spaceship using up its limited supply of air and water at an alarming rate. This was a problem no matter what kind of astronaut was at the controls, whether capitalist or socialist. John Cobb and Herman Daly extended this argument, showing how economic costs that did not fit orthodox models of short-term supply and demand were dismissed by mainstream economists as "externalities." This was true "even though the 'externality' may be a rather significant one—like the capacity of the earth to sustain life!"[21]

During its last decade, *C&C* increasingly integrated concerns such as the carrying capacity of the planet, the impossibility of unlimited growth, and the need for technologies to produce food and other needs in a decentralized way, with a stress on long-term ecological sustainability. Not all of *C&C*'s third world voices embraced ecology as a priority, and some of its first world voices agreed with Langdon Gilkey that technology was a "historical fate, something irreversible and unstoppable."[22] However, *C&C* began to call for appropriate technologies and write about technocrats and scientists as purveyors of one ideology among others. Ecological arguments became a standard part of *C&C*'s countercultural discourse; they also blended with other issues, as when a writer suggested that a poor family might not care about old-growth forests, but "ask that same family to protest a paper mill that is spewing particulates into the air in its neighborhood, soiling its clothes, homes, and endangering its health . . . well, you get the picture."[23]

Fourth, *C&C* increasingly shifted attention away from top-down policy debates toward local community organization. We have seen that this trend began in the 1960s, but it increasingly moved toward the center of *C&C*'s vision. *C&C* followed Cesar Chavez's United Farm Workers for many years, promoting its grape and lettuce boycotts and discussing related issues such as the risks of pesticides, efforts by the growers and the Teamsters Union to break the UFW, and the role of Mexican popular spirituality in the movement.[24] As the New Deal coalition slowly crumbled, *C&C*'s hopes for such movements bore increasing weight. An early example of the shift occurred during the 1972 election, when *C&C* reported from the border town of Crystal City, Texas, with members of José Angel Gutiérrez's Raza Unida Party. Their candidate for governor was defeated by an elite pro-business candidate, much as Richard Nixon crushed George McGovern in the national election. Still, at the local level people mobilized against electoral fraud, using mass protest strategies similar to those later used by Corazón Aquino supporters in the Philippines. They won the key local post of sheriff for Raza Unida. The moral of this story was that, despite McGovern's debacle, there was still hope for organizing locally through "people power."[25] *C&C* frequently returned to this moral, seeking to sustain hope for local church-based activism in the face of retreats by national ecumenical organizations. Even as *C&C*'s staff burned out and threw in the towel in the early 1990s, they were developing a major series on the church in the city.[26]

The spirit of such coverage shined through *C&C*'s interview with Leon Sullivan, the pastor of Philadelphia's Zion Baptist Church and founder of Opportunities Industrialization Centers (OIC), which promoted job training initiatives and strategies for black economic self-help. Sullivan, a politically moderate African American, had given up on social action by white churches. He said that anything that these churches ought to do, such as buy inexpensive housing and integrate it directly, was blocked by conservative parishioners. Meanwhile, leaders of black denominations were "concerned about how many angels can dance on the end of a needle. . . . They better be worrying about who's going to eat." Yet Sullivan said, "OIC is the church. I founded it from the basement of my church. OIC is as much the church as a prayer meeting. It's the church in another form. We have a thousand ministers involved in OIC in a hundred cities. . . . That is the church in action!"[27]

Fifth, *C&C* moved toward somewhat greater engagement with the popular media. Some of its high-brow attitudes lingered on, especially in its tendency to ignore television or argue that, as one writer put it, "Christian worldviews are fundamentally at odds with those of Western television culture."[28] Editor Leon Howell made a revealing comment in his report on a *C&C*-organized seminar at a Presbyterian retreat center. Writing in this center's newsletter to a readership somewhat like *C&C*'s, Howell reported that one presenter had "introduced the most unusual of all subjects in these seminars: a two-hour session on MTV to a group almost totally ignorant of its content. Her primary point: How can the church speak to a generation weaned on a technology so alien to most of us?"[29] At the time that Howell wrote these words, MTV had been in existence for ten years and had been gaining influence steadily, especially among youth but with a large ripple effect in many other areas. Few people fluent in popular music would have described themselves as ignorant of its content, and it comes as no surprise that there was little discussion of music in a journal produced by people who could call MTV "alien to most of us."

Nevertheless, *C&C*'s tastes were beginning to change, as the MTV seminar itself suggests. Occasional articles about popular music did appear.[30] Somewhat more consistently, *C&C* discussed Hollywood films. For example, its review of Martin Scorsese's controversial *Last Temptation of Christ* pegged it as "a movie so faithful to the book that it is equally long and boring," and an essay on the book and film versions of Margaret Atwood's *The Handmaid's Tale* made brilliant comments about the strengths and weaknesses of film, as well as the challenge of representing fundamentalism in the media."[31] Also, *C&C* began to relate its standard repertoire of concerns to emergent discussions of popular culture. For example, one thriving subgroup of liberation theologians worked with the concept of popular religion; often they promoted the "inculturation" of Christianity into diverse cultures as an alternative to more arrogant and imperialistic approaches. In this context, Cox described how he traveled to Costa Rica for a conference but found few of the virtuous base communities that *C&C* valorized as authentic refuges set apart from the modern world. Instead, his hosts drove him to a bar in a Toyota, where he proceeded to drink Pepsi, dance to reggae music, and watch a World Cup soccer match on a Sony television. "Into which culture are we supposed to inculturate Christianity?" Cox asked. Perhaps some people were breaking away from older cultures for good reasons. Perhaps it was even appropriate for liberationists to embrace certain aspects of the emerging postmodern culture "that young people everywhere seem to be shaping so adroitly out of the countless global inputs that now reach the most remote hamlet."[32]

Sixth, *C&C* began regular coverage of Native American issues. It got off to a rough start when the issue that launched its coverage began, "Tobacco is a noxious weed; from the devil it doth proceed."[33] Although these words were not intended to insult the role of tobacco in native religion (they introduced an editorial against the tobacco lobby), they unfortunately appeared alongside a graphic of a ceremonial pipe. Then the first article on native issues, an overview of struggles to enforce treaty rights, appeared under a title ("This Land Was Their Land") that worked at cross-purposes with its major argument, which was the need to stress ongoing present-day struggles. The second article was an interview with Principal Chief Wilma Mankiller of the Cherokee nation, and it also stressed the contemporary activities of Indian peoples. Mankiller highlighted her efforts to address economic problems of the people and her no-nonsense pragmatism; she even mentioned that the previous chief, who shared her goals for the tribe, was a Republican bank president. Unfortunately, *C&C* billed this interview as a "report/reflection" by Steve Lawler, "an Episcopal priest from Oklahoma [who] has taken a high school group to the Cherokee Nation on a work group." Mankiller's name did not appear on the title page or in the annual index.[34]

After thus threatening to destroy its credibility in Indian country, *C&C* recovered nicely. We have seen how Vine Deloria and Robert Allen Warrior were respected voices in *C&C*'s debates about liberation theology. *C&C* attracted other excellent Native American writers (notably Anna Lee Walters and Jace Weaver) and addressed a range of relevant issues, as when it mobilized readers against a hydroelectric project in James Bay that threatened both the native people and the region's ecosystem, or when it published a minicontroversy about Kevin Costner's politically correct Western film, *Dances with Wolves*.[35] Warrior emerged as *C&C*'s most assured voice. In an award-winning article he suggested that "any of you who are prompted by *Dances with Wolves* to make a trip out to Indian country to get in touch with the earth should go soon, before your destination of choice is contaminated by a tribally-owned toxic waste dump."[36] By 1993 *C&C* had earned the right to say, in Warrior's words, that it "has been the only [white] alternative press journal that regularly carries news from Indian country. *C&C* readers who have followed this coverage now know more than most informed people about the struggle for American Indian religious freedom, federal Indian policy, economic development, identity politics, and other topics."[37]

Evolving Debates about Theology, Racial Difference, and Postmodernism

Let us consider an address by Chung Hyun-Kyung to the 1991 WCC assembly as a marker of how far *C&C*'s discourse on liberation theologies had moved during the previous two decades. Speaking as an Asian-American feminist, Chung said that it was "time to reread the Bible from the perspective of birds, water, air, trees, and mountains, the most wretched of the earth in our time." She addressed the conference theme, "Come Holy Spirit," with a preamble that began: "Come Spirit of Hagar, Egyptian, black slave woman exploited and abandoned by Abraham and Sarah, the ancestors of our faith. . . . Come. The spirit of indigenous people of the earth, victims of genocide during the time of colonialism and the period of great Christian mission to the world. . . . Come. . . . The spirit of Earth, Air, and Water, raped, tortured, and exploited by human greed and money. Come. The Spirit of soldiers, civilians, and sea creatures now dying in the bloody war in the Gulf. Come. The spirit of our Liberator, our brother Jesus, tortured and killed on the cross."[38] Chung went on to suggest Kwan In, a goddess of Korean popular religion, as an image for the Christian Holy Spirit. Chung's explorations provoked intense criticism from less adventurous theologians, who pressed for clarity about how she distinguished between the Holy Spirit and other spirits and among various kinds of Christians and oppressed beings.[39]

There are no easy answers to these questions, and Chung's words—more a poetic lament than a systematic academic statement—introduce a set of issues that were central to *C&C*'s evolving debates about liberation theologies. How should one articulate a perspective that blends local differences (even down to specific sea creatures) with a global consciousness? How should one respond to the proliferation and radicalization of approaches based on cultural differences (even the differences between humans, birds, and air)? How should one judge the value of classic prophetic Christianity (that of Abraham and Sarah) in the light of evolving intellectual trends?

Recall *C&C*'s symposium on "Whatever Happened to Theology?" in which Frederick Herzog linked Friedrich Schleiermacher's ideas about progress to Nat Turner's rebellion and concluded, "Whoever has ears, let them hear." By the 1980s this critique reflected *C&C*'s common wisdom, and in general the results were positive for *C&C*'s critical consciousness. Unfortunately, some people developed a condition different from the deafness Herzog complained about. They came to hear with such sensitive ears that the result was paralysis. They became so zealous in learning from Others, so solicitous of the feelings of the oppressed, and so ashamed of their own privilege, that they often argued themselves into corners where they had little to contribute as allies. The results were not necessarily more edifying than when conservatives ignored liberation theology as a nonevent, although the explanation ("Since I'm not oppressed, I have nothing to say") was more flattering. Speaking to males who responded to feminism in this way, Beverly Harrison said: "Often the feminist analysis is heard by men as a call to deny your own personal power, to abrogate all leadership, or to renounce all personal strength, to embrace passivity. This, of course, is not what is required. More often, what is called for is a more direct and self-aware owning of the power that is already yours, making it more directly accountable to those affected by it. . . . Feminism is a call to genuine strength in both women and men, a strength born of the power of relationship."[40]

At times this advice was also relevant for *C&C's* white women. Consider an article by Susan Thistlethwaite in which she attacked the false universals of liberalism and called whites to pay more attention to racial differences. Thistlethwaite dismissed the neoorthodox claim that liberal theological arguments were based too heavily on experience. On the contrary, she argued, liberals should pay *greater* attention to experience, because their concept of experience was so abstract and universalistic that Audre Lorde's critique was apt: the master's tools could not dismantle the master's house. "What is the theory behind racist feminism?" asked Thistlethwaite. "Liberalism."[41] She approached the specifics of black female experience through black women's literature.

Thus far, Thistlethwaite identified a promising way to explore overlaps and differences between black and white women without assuming terms of debate that were biased toward whites. Unfortunately, from this point forward her assumption of incommensurable differences between (more or less unified) black and white communities became a runaway train that threatened to derail. She argued that, because of these differences, Carol Christ was being a racist when she drew on the famous lines of black playwright Ntozake Shange, "I found god in myself / & I loved her / I loved her fiercely." No doubt it is important to clarify the difference between Christ's style of goddess spirituality and the stronger sense of grounded collective struggle in much literature by black women. But Thistlethwaite's judgment was extremely sweeping. She took it for granted that Christ could not cite Shange while still understanding racial differences, and she dismissed with contempt a male reviewer's claim (from Shange's book jacket) that Shange "writes with such exquisite care and beauty that anyone can relate to it."[42] But if whites could not relate to black experience, one wanted to know how Thistlethwaite herself could say anything about it. She was honest enough to raise this question, but could only respond that she must "guard against facile universalizing." She said, "I began to wonder whether it is possible" to "encounter this difference wholly and completely, and not move to universals"—that is, to a position she had identified as "racist feminism."[43]

Thistlethwaite was a hair's breadth from claiming that any overlapping experiences which could be discovered between Shange and herself were "false universals" and that trying to speak about them was racist. But why should whites care about black women's literature, if by definition they could not understand it? And how many black writers really agreed that they could not communicate with whites or that their books were about incommensurable racial differences? (For starters, Alice Walker's *Meridian,* one of the texts Thistlethwaite discussed, undermined this idea.)[44] Of course, communicating "wholly and completely" is impossible, even between two straight white males who are best friends, and miscommunication across large cultural divides and power imbalances carries dangers that should not be underestimated (as *Meridian* also powerfully argues). Thus, in the end, Thistlethwaite's cautions stood as crucial questions to pose on a case-by-case basis.[45] In her formulation, however, they stood in a posture of hair-trigger suspicion toward whites who said anything about race, with a possible exception for whites who said only that they might be racists if they said anything else. White women could not even seek "points of agreement" with blacks without extending a "racist feminism" in which "white experience will continue to be the universal."[46]

Not all *C&C* writers jumped on this train of thought. After Delores Williams attacked Rosemary Ruether for trying to speak about black women, Ruether snapped back with none of the politeness associated with "politically correct" discourse. She asked how Williams could be so sure that she could dismiss Ruether's stated commitment to a pluralism of feminist approaches. Ruether had lost all patience with arguments "declaring that [white feminists] can't speak for black feminists and then attacking them for not speaking for black feminists."[47]

Also standoffish toward a radical stress on cultural difference was Cornel West, *C&C*'s leading African American voice during the 1980s. Like James Cone, West had roots in the black church. But West ranged more widely than Cone with his center(s) of gravity in African American cultural studies, pragmatist philosophy, and neo-Marxian theory. He was more oriented to multiracial politics in the framework of democratic socialism, and his writing was more oriented toward interdisciplinary cultural studies than toward Protestant seminaries. In the 1980s West stated that liberation theologies had "galvanized new intellectual energies throughout the religious academy" but that unfortunately they "lack[ed] serious philosophical substance." A case in point was Cone, whose "religious claims reek of hermetic fideism."[48]

West's own approach to religion was difficult to summarize. Most striking was his astonishing range of interests, which, as one reviewer put it, can "leap from Kierkegaard to KRS-One in a single bound."[49] West's *C&C* articles (which are collected in his 1988 *Prophetic Fragments*) discussed various aspects of black politics, the music of Prince and Marvin Gaye, black-Jewish relations, Protestant seminary education, and many books such as Michael Harrington on socialist strategy and Jackson Lears and Richard Fox on *The Culture of Consumption*.[50] This breadth was both West's strength and his Achilles' heel, since it showcased his brilliant analyses but also spread his work rather thin. The price of entering debates on so many fronts was to leave some intellectual strings hanging. West was content to make bold connections and to leave it for his rapidly growing readership to explore them in more detail.

Three themes came up repeatedly: historicism, pragmatism, and radical democracy. West was a historicist because he denied that objective foundations of knowledge were possible, and he insisted that all thought and action were done from specific perspectives, situated within complex social totalities that have multiple layers of meaning. This meant that all theological claims had to be understood contextually and that all "objective" academic claims were laden with moral implications. Steering between appeals to objective transcendental truths and subjectivist relativism, he sought to build persuasive rational arguments for his positions using moderate forms of pragmatism. That is, he assessed positions by asking whether they would have productive consequences within specified contexts. Questions about Truth and philosophical grounding of truth claims were out; questions about the power of language to shape experience were in, along with explorations of how people *used* language in specific situations. West kept his distance from forms of pragmatism that were preoccupied with science, that embraced an anti-intellectual practicalism, or that had slid too far down the slippery slope that sometimes leads from principled pragmatism to relativistic nihilism. Above all, he pressed apolitical neopragmatists (and, indeed, intellectuals of all stripes) to pay more attention to social and political theorists such as W. E. B. Du Bois and Stuart Hall.[51]

By clarifying what kind of pragmatism West defended, we also describe what kind of historicist he was: his history was framed in terms of neo-Gramscian socialism, that is, a version influenced by Antonio Gramsci that stresses cultural hegemony, as I discuss in my introduction. Compared with other scholars with overlapping interests, West was, and remains, notable for a flexible conception of hegemony (giving serious attention to both race and religion along with class), his attention to the tragic dimensions of life (relating historicist readings of theologians such as Niebuhr and Kierkegaard to downbeat postmodernists), and his calls for coalitions rather than internecine warfare between liberals and various stripes of radicalism. West's core norms, when it is time to judge whether a given pragmatic praxis is appropriate, are its adequacy to the full complexity of human life and its ability to "enable oppositional activity" (defined in terms of his rainbow socialism).[52] West is not interested in seeking additional foundations to undergird these commitments, believing it a futile quest that critics should "evade" in favor of pragmatic praxis.

West's role during his *C&C* years is easy to misread from the vantage point of the late 1990s. In the early 1980s, he was making groundbreaking contributions to the broad discourse of liberation theology, showing how race, class, and religion could be theorized together within a broad neo-Marxian approach to U.S. cultural history and how cultural studies approaches could be a bridge between liberation discourses and establishment theologies. A decade later, this role was sometimes forgotten as he drifted away from theology and was attacked from the left for moderating his earlier positions and speaking as a liberal pundit.[53] West was also increasingly tempted by jeremiads that appealed to a purer age located in the 1960s and / or outside capitalist commodity culture; for example, in his 1993 best-seller *Race Matters,* he correlated morality and democracy with families and churches (especially during the civil rights era) while he correlated hedonism and despair with the market (especially during the Reagan era).[54] At his best West has maintained the more defensible thesis that families, churches, and popular culture have *all* been places of cultural contestation throughout the postwar period. Still it remains unclear whether the popular reception of his work will amplify the aspects of his vision that overlap most with conservatism, as opposed to the radical dimensions that he clearly intends. His whirlwind of television appearances, linked to the pragmatic sail-trimming in his critiques, is in some ways reminiscent of Niebuhr's shifting alliances in the 1940s, raising equally complex questions about the trade-offs it implies.

Although these questions intensified in the 1990s, they are not entirely new. In my *C&C* review of West's 1989 book, *The American Evasion of Philosophy,* I commented:

> The key critical question is whether West can, in practice, evade past weaknesses of pragmatism through his use of radical social theory and his professions of faith. Can his appeals to pragmatic contextualization keep enough distance from the existing status quo to maintain a vision of radical alternatives? Can his appeal to future progress toward democracy avoid strengthening entrenched ideologies of nationalism and economic growth? What trade-offs are involved when he . . . boldly invokes a new American jeremiad with a "universal consciousness that promotes an all-embracing democratic and libertarian moral vision"?[55]

By the 1980s, so much of the academic discussion about such issues was channeled through poststructuralist cultural theories that these theories became impossible for *C&C* to ignore. Yet, because *C&C* gave only sporadic attention to these very complicated debates, this book is not the right place to explore them in detail. Suffice it to say that poststructuralists stressed how discourse (that is, language and symbolic communication more generally) shaped the lived experience of everyday life. In the strongest versions of poststructuralism, language even constituted reality: people did not speak languages, but languages "spoke" people, that is, determined how they understood themselves and their world. Poststructuralists in many varieties were incredulous (or, as their critics preferred, cynical) toward claims of objectivity and universality, including general ethical principles. They argued that such claims normalized an unjust status quo and silenced its underdogs. In essence, poststructuralism was an attitude and a set of analytical tools that exposed, deflated, and relativized these rhetorics by calling into question their objectivity—not by appealing to a deeper reality but through a radical pluralism of alternative discursive realities, all of which were unstable. *C&C*'s utopians such as Alves, its neopragmatists such as West, and its champions of textual difference such as Thistlethwaite all drew upon this broad intellectual paradigm to some extent. However, a group of feminist theologians in *C&C*'s wider network pressed poststructuralist arguments the hardest.[56] First among their targets of suspicion were transcendent prophetic rhetorics.

Such theologians were more likely to be reviewed in *C&C* than to write *C&C* articles, and this was true in the case I will discuss, West's review of Sharon Welch's *Communities of Resistance and Solidarity.* In both this book and her subsequent *Feminist Ethic of Risk,* Welch used sweeping poststructuralist arguments to frame a version of liberationist contextualism. As I noted in my introduction, she upheld an ethic of risk as an alternative to an ethic of control that presupposed a standpoint of objectivity and top-down power. This position opposed Niebuhrians such as Dennis McCann who argued that the realists' refusal to correlate historical projects with images of God's kingdom, coupled with their supposed "religious disinterestedness," had better pragmatic results than "solidarity with the oppressed." Welch contended that even when realist metaphors were deployed with liberationist intentions, they presupposed an "erotics of domination" that reinforced hierarchical thinking and short-circuited liberating results. "Doctrines that affirm the absolute power of God . . . reinforce a human desire for absolute power," and allow elites to rationalize their dominance, since elites could "regard themselves as merely the agents of a higher power."[57]

Something like Welch described did frequently happen in the alliance between *C&C* and cold war elites, but this does not yet prove that Welch identified a fatal flaw in *all* prophetic theologies that stress divine transcendence. In his review, West agreed that there had been a postmodern breakdown of trust in transhistorical truths and that therefore no yardstick existed that could evaluate theologies in every context. He saw four possible responses: paralyzing skepticism, the cynical idea that might makes right, "intuitionism" (or a priori appeals to faith), and "critical self-situating contextualism." He placed Welch in his third category of intuitionism; in this sense, he saw her appeal to communities of resistance as a sophisticated postmodern version of Cone's "hermetic fideism." West advocated the fourth approach: a theological method "couched in historical narratives and social analyses" that could "sustain vital communities and possibly persuade others outside" because it provided good reasons that were framed "within the language of a struggling community." In this way, West tried to have his postmodern cake and eat it, too. From within a specific historical tradition and community, analyzed through a historicist method, he held out the possibility of "all-embracing moral visions" that referred to God. In contrast to Welch's claim that universal visions were "intrinsically correlated with oppression," West claimed that, as a matter of empirical fact, oppressed people struggling against domination frequently used universalist discourses to state their "critiques of the present and their visions of the future."[58] As *C&C*'s history drew to a close, this exchange between Welch and West represented *C&C*'s debate about the future of the prophetic tradition at its most sophisticated.

The Battle with Neoconservatives in the Reagan Era

To say the least, Michael Novak's expulsion from *C&C*'s board in 1975 did not mean that *C&C* was able to ignore neoconservatives after this time. Afloat on a river of foundation grants and complacent about their alliance with Republican leaders, Novak and Richard John Neuhaus carried out a wide range of efforts to delegitimate their former colleagues. These included such publications as Novak's *Will It Liberate?* which argued along the lines of the *Century*'s "Post-Communist Manifesto," and Neuhaus's journal *First Things*, a project of his Institute on Religion and Public Life.[59] They also included such organizations as the Ethics and Public Policy Center (founded by Ernest Lefever) and the Institute for Religion and Democracy (IRD), a group run by an unlikely combination of Methodist evangelicals and previously irreligious labor organizers who began as cadres of the sectarian left before converting to neoconservatism.[60]

All these groups participated in a wider neoconservative network, drew on generous funding by conservative foundations, and aggressively promoted their theories of the new class and democratic capitalism.[61] One of the most incisive critiques of the movement comes not from the left but from an even more conservative writer, Paul Gottfried, who complains, "The view of recent American social reform is of a train that became derailed at the time its neoconservative passengers elected to get off. Those on their Right are dismissed as racists and anti-Semites for failing to board the same train; those too far to the Left are viewed with contempt for staying behind too long. Only those who rode the train of Progress for the proper time span and left with the right people are entitled to the redemptive label 'democrat.'"[62] Gottfried writes bitterly about neoconservative successes in taking over institutions and funding sources of an older paleoconservative right. In one famous skirmish of this war, the leaders of the extreme right-wing Rockford Institute, who funded Neuhaus during the 1980s, became so distressed about Neuhaus's views that they "flew from Illinois to New York, where they locked down Neuhaus' Manhattan office, carted away furniture, and left Neuhaus with his personal belongings waiting for a taxi cab on Madison Avenue," forcing him to scramble for a new configuration of foundation backers.[63] In Gottfried's view, neoconservatives were squandering their largess on public relations, rather than doing research that could command the respect of scholars. "The annual budget of any one of the big conservative think tanks exceeds the combined budgets of all left-of-center think tanks," said Gottfried. (For example, the 1985 budget for the American Enterprise Institute was $12 million, and just one conservative "star"—Allan Bloom, author of *The Closing of the American Mind*—received $3 million in grants from the Olin Foundation over three years, which was more than double the entire *C&C* budget for the same period.)[64] With such generous support, continued Gottfried, neoconservatives "should be able to conduct serious research. But according to their critics, not just on the left but among trained social-science researchers of all stripes, they generally do not; most just disseminate opinions."[65]

It is not always easy to judge the balance of opinion and serious argument emanating from the neoconservative world—the results are mixed, as in any large movement—but in any case neoconservatives often targeted *C&C* and its allies for criticism. The IRD fulminated about the "disgrace" that churches would subsidize *C&C*'s "extremist political views," in which "the principle of Reinhold Niebuhr [was] totally abandoned."[66] More often the attacks focused on *C&C*'s wider ecumenical matrix; for example, the IRD's greatest coup was persuading the *Reader's Digest* and *Sixty Minutes* to showcase their attack on the NCC.[67]

Neoconservatives presented themselves as fair-minded and objective, and for a time *C&C* spent considerable energy debating with them. John Bennett and Leon Howell both wrote several articles documenting and dissecting their thinking.[68] In a 1986 symposium called "Reinhold Niebuhr Today" occasioned by Richard Fox's biography of Niebuhr, *C&C*'s reviewers tried to halt what they considered a neoconservative hijacking of Niebuhr's authority (as well as what they considered Fox's insufficient appreciation of Niebuhr as a theologian). True, symposium articles by Herbert Edwards, Beverly Harrison, and M. M. Thomas stressed the limits of Niebuhr's oppositional voice on race, gender, and international issues, much as I have documented in this book.[69] For example, Thomas recalled that after the Suez Crisis he had submitted an article to complain that Niebuhr "was making recognition of sin an apology for it," but that *C&C* had refused to print it.[70] Still, it was a long way from these critiques to granting that Niebuhr was a precursor of full-scale neoconservatism. Bennett said that the "celebration of American capitalism, which [neoconservatives] would free from most governmental intervention, is alien to Niebuhr's acceptance of a mixed economy."[71] Ronald Stone's judgment was compelling: "The American Enterprise people can use Niebuhr's critique of communism, but I do not see how [they] can speak of Niebuhr's 'profound contribution to the theology of democratic capitalism'—unless [they] mean to affirm the gains of the New Deal and the present mixed economy of social-welfare capitalism [in forms advocated by] the left wing of the Democratic party."[72]

In the face of the right's success, *C&C* sometimes backpedaled in search of compromise. One writer judged that the right's "influence can be salutary for the nation as a whole," because even its intolerance might be preferable to "a condition in which morality is not widely demanded."[73] The NCC's Peggy Shriver called on liberals to stress the values they shared with "Uncle Ed from Indiana." She also took the bait of engaging with Neuhaus after he reported that he had asked a cross-section of Protestant leaders for a reaction to the following proposition: "On balance and considering the alternatives, American power is a force for good in the world." Almost unanimously, said Neuhaus, his informants judged that mainline Protestant leaders would deny this proposition or "so equivocate in their answer [that] in effect they too would be saying no." Their posture was "basically one of hostility," and Neuhaus believed that this "clearly excludes them as a candidate for providing cultural leadership." Shriver took it upon herself to prove that church leaders did not really hate America.[74]

Unfortunately, Neuhaus showed limited interest in constructive debates about the strengths and weaknesses of the religious left. He had asked, "Is America a force for good?" Clearly the answer depended on the implied alternatives. Does the United States measure up to the normative vision of the biblical prophets or Catholic social teaching? Is its record on race better than South Africa's? Is its record on economic justice better than Sweden's? Are we comparing it to a vision of how capitalism is supposed to work in some theoretical future, creating harmony through growth that trickles down to everyone, or to the way that capitalism shapes everyday life in Harlem today? Are we comparing the United States to a sophisticated vision of democratic socialism or to life in a Soviet death camp? Moreover, was *C&C* supporting or trashing the U.S. role in the world when it lobbied its own government to support mixed economies, economic redistribution, and democratic freedoms in Latin America? A key *C&C* debating point when discussing Central America was that leftist Nicaragua had a much better record on civil liberties than the quasi-fascist U.S. allies, El Salvador and Guatemala. No one said Nicaragua was perfect. Yet neoconservatives hammered on press censorship in Nicaragua while the United States funded a war against its government—at the same time that opposition journalists in El Salvador were simply tortured and murdered by death squads linked to the United States, who used the argument that freedom of the press was irrelevant during a war.

One suspects that my questions are an example of what Neuhaus had in mind when he accused leftists of "equivocating" in their baptism of the United States, so that they were "clearly excluded" as leaders. For him, ideals of collective justice—whether based on socialism, the New Deal, or Christianity—were rejected if they challenged neoconservative priorities. Neuhaus then interpreted proposals informed by these ideals in light of their actual or forecasted relationship to abstract concepts of totalitarianism. He went on to link them to nightmare images of Stalinist death camps, Nazi aggression, and a supercilious new class. If, at the end of this process, you were presented with the stark alternative of democracy versus totalitarianism, and you preferred to live in Neuhaus's hypothetical capitalist utopia rather than a real Soviet death camp, then congratulations—you "agreed" that left-liberal critiques had been discredited. By a similar logic, one might poll people about whether a vision of classless utopia appeals to them more than the prospect of living in a Haitian slum. Could such a poll prove that an old-style Marxian command economy was "a force for good in the world," or would people "so equivocate" that they remained capable of criticizing the old Soviet Union, as *C&C* had always done? It barely matters, with a premise so flawed.

A revealing exchange ensued when Peter Steinfels wrote a concise, confident, and extremely damning critique of the IRD for defining issues in a narrow and slanted way that fit seamlessly within a well-funded neoconservative campaign against liberalism. (On this point, left-liberals and the far right agreed; Gottfried went so far as to call the IRD a "front organization" for corporate interests.)[75] Neuhaus responded in an aggrieved tone that he was an "upper and lower case Democrat" who "didn't get a penny" from participating in the IRD. He did not intend to function as an apologist for Ronald Reagan, but only to uphold democracy against totalitarianism and keep the gospel aloof from all ideologies. Steinfels replied curtly that whether or not Neuhaus *intended* to baptize Reaganism, he clearly *did* baptize it, and that even if one was willing to grant that Neuhaus sincerely desired to be apolitical, it was "ridiculous to believe that money has nothing to do with the intellectual offensive" of the IRD. If Neuhaus did not like the way Steinfels described his relation to Reaganism—he had used the term *condottieri*, "a metaphor that sat somewhere between the sordid image of 'mercenary' and the altogether elevated one of 'champion'"—then Neuhaus should suggest something better. Would he prefer "proxy"? That was a term which Novak had used to describe his relationship with business executives who wanted independent intellectuals to refute their critics. "The one thing I find truly frustrating" about Neuhaus, said Steinfels, "is his public air of studied innocence"—a posture that Steinfels had by this time revealed as either profoundly hypocritical or remarkably unselfcritical.[76]

Increasingly, *C&C* concluded that Neuhaus and his ilk were not interested in honest debate, and their tone shifted. Consider *C&C*'s review of Neuhaus's book, *The Naked Public Square*. As we have already noted, this was a lament about rising pluralism framed as a treatise on the dangers of secularism and the loss of overarching religious values which, according to Neuhaus, formerly "clothed" the nation in a common moral purpose. *C&C* old-timer Arthur Moore judged that Neuhaus's vision clearly included "the specter of a 'Christian America' with all its ominous historic associations," despite Neuhaus's efforts to evade this problem. Moore observed: "Neuhaus is fond of telling us (and telling us and telling us) that casting out one devil [i.e., drawbacks of the old 'clothed' public square] will bring seven others to take their place. He does not tell us whether bringing the original devil back will drive out the seven replacements or whether we will then simply have eight devils."[77]

When theologian Edward Norman argued along neoconservative lines that Christians should stand aloof from all political ideologies, theologian Dorothee Sölle made no effort to disguise her disgust. She summarized Norman's views as follows: "Christianity is Platonism for the people" and nothing but "an ideological substitute to keep the uneducated masses, who couldn't read the *Politeia* anyway, in their place." Perhaps Norman should ask why people were turning from his understanding of Christianity toward the radical positions he disdained. "Wouldn't it be thinkable that this has to do with some major events in this century—say Auschwitz? How many gas chamber deaths does a theologian need before understanding where we come from? . . . Frankly this soup smells like hot water. A spirituality that is stripped of human need, of any desire, becomes bloodless."[78]

Sölle was not trying to find a meeting of the minds with neoconservatives; she was searching for forms of community that could channel her passion for change, within a structure of power dominated by neoconservatives. She feared that the churches were not up to this task. After one of the many defeats of the left during the 1970s, she said, "I needed a church in which to weep and to pray and to experience solidarity. What I found instead . . . was a small group of friends, enough to retell the story of dying and rising but not enough to discover a new language appropriate to our own situation."[79]

The most popular response to this bleak picture, in *C&C* during its last decade, was to hitch hopes to multicultural alliances and to energies from outside the U.S. middle class, above all from Latin America. Still, in the end, a white professional like Sölle also had to face the issue of hope closer to home. Pressed against the ropes of despair, in some of the most profound essays *C&C* ever published, Sölle struggled to find the language she needed. Was Norman correct? "Is the content of faith the belief in humankind's sinful nature and not in the new creation? Did Jesus come to bring a pessimistic description of human life and the nature of human beings?" Was human history "a closed meaningless circle of eating and being eaten?"[80]

For Sölle, the heart of faith was a struggle against cynicism, against the flattening of human relationships into capitalist commodities, and against all forms of individualism and exploitation that destroy meaningful forms of community. Holding onto religion—at least the types that interested Sölle—was not capitalist brainwashing, as many leftists assumed. On the contrary, to give up on religious meaning was exactly what capitalism *wanted* you to do. In short, for Sölle the question of hope was the question of faith. Sölle was driven back to the sources of her faith, for which she used the images of father, mother, sister, fountainhead, living wind, light, and water of life. Spirituality was not access to a "higher power" but "oneness with the whole, intimate connection." God was the "ground . . . love, depth, sea."[81] Whether this would be enough, it remained to be seen.

11

Producing *C&C* and (Sometimes) Balancing the Budget

If I were writing a history of the Chevrolet Camaro, it would be easy for me to focus on the changing styles and specifications over the years, as opposed to the intentions of particular engineers, the office politics shaping their decisions, and the relative profit margins of alternative designs. Of course, all these factors would be part of the story, and no one could write a book about the Camaro without taking them into account. So, too, with *C&C*. Institutional considerations and the idiosyncrasies of *C&C* personnel are woven inextricably into the story I have just told. Still, my main interest in both *C&C* and the Camaro is in the end result. How did it feel to drive a Camaro? What did one read when *C&C* arrived in the mailbox? I know a little bit about changes in the Camaro and would not mind learning more—but I have almost no interest in the names of specific Chevrolet designers and the detailed financial calculations behind their decisions. Similarly, there are definite limits to my interest in *C&C*'s budget and office politics.

Nevertheless, *C&C* is unlike the Camaro in a major respect. The changes in what *C&C* felt like to read were *constituted* largely by its changes in personnel. General Motors can replace one executive with little change in its overall character, but the same is not true of a tiny operation like *C&C* where the personnel directly shape the product. This point should already be clear from my main narrative; nevertheless, there is more to say about it. While writing this book I have often fretted about the trade-offs before saying that "*C&C*" said thus and so—as opposed to giving a specific name that would strike a specialist as essential and a nonspecialist as distracting. When in doubt, I assumed that specialists could consult my footnotes. Still I must stress that "what *C&C* said" was constituted by a consensus of specific editorial board members (in the early years) or particular exchanges between *C&C*'s editors and writers (in later years). From the beginning, and increasingly after 1970, contributors spoke in their own voices within a forum called *C&C*, more than they embodied "what *C&C* believed." One goal of this chapter is to focus on how specific mixes of people came together at particular times, under institutional arrangements that channeled their voices in distinctive ways.

Another goal is to explore how *C&C* thrived as an institution for a time, and why it failed in the end. This matter cannot be swept under the rug, for a car or a magazine. It simply will not do to say that calculations about profit margins are secondary to the experience of driving a Camaro—if there is no Camaro to drive. Why is there no longer a *C&C* to read? Is there any future for journals of its kind? Let us bear in mind three points to orient this discussion, to keep the details I will discuss from appearing like a mass of trees in a shapeless forest. First, as I have stressed throughout the book, the contours of this forest were shaped by *C&C*'s changing relationships with the larger society. Second, a thumbnail description of a *C&C* budget can be summarized in the formula 2/3: 2/3: 1/3: 1/3. Around two-thirds of the expenses were for printing, mailing, and other nonsalary items. These costs were roughly matched by two-thirds of the income from subscriptions and other standard business sources such as advertising, reprint permissions, and rental of the mailing list. One-third of the budget went for salaries; this was matched by one-third of the income from contributions. As we will see, there were significant variations on this formula; the figures often fluctuated by 10 percentage points or more. Still, for the broad sweep of *C&C*'s history, this formula provides a rough-and-ready benchmark.[1]

Third, journals like *C&C* can rarely survive without some kind of benefactor. This point is worth unpacking with comparative data. The average magazine makes 55 percent of its income from advertising, but journals of opinion are lucky if they make 10 percent.[2] (*C&C* earned 3 percent toward the end.) A 1983 study by the *Los Angeles Times* found that the *New York Review of Books* stood almost alone among leading political journals in making money. Closer to the norm was William F. Buckley's *National Review,* which had lost money for twenty-eight years in a row, including $600,000 in 1981. This journal could only survive because Buckley made an exception for his principle of letting the free market determine which enterprises should live or die. He routinely sent out a year-end fund appeal and covered the shortfall out of his own pocket.[3] The *Nation* had lost money in 115 out of 118 years, despite paying its most famous columnist "in the high two figures."[4] *Mother Jones* performed even worse, losing half a million dollars a year despite a solid 10 percent of its budget from advertising and a tax-exempt foundation to reduce costs. The *New Republic* required almost $3 million in subsidies between 1974 and 1983 from publisher Martin Peretz, whose spouse was an heir of the Singer Sewing Machine fortune. The founders of *Tikkun,* Nan Fink and Michael Lerner, invested $1.5 million of their own money in the venture during its first four years, including a $350,000 annual subsidy.[5] In short, as the *Los Angeles Times* summarizes, "Journals of opinion—'thought-leader' magazines, as they are often called in the Madison Avenue advertising community—have historically lost money in America. Many such magazines have long since gone out of business and virtually all of those still publishing lose money regularly. . . . A moneyed patron seems the only real 'insurance policy' on which any journal of opinion can ultimately depend."[6]

Religious "thought-leaders" face especially acute challenges, largely because their advertising incomes tend to be lower.[7] Moreover, many of the larger religious magazines, such as the *Lutheran* and *Presbyterians Today,* are bankrolled by denominations for in-house communication and feature content shackled to a least common denominator—a model remote from *C&C* and its main competitors. Thus religious magazines with an intellectual or political edge need patrons at least as much as their secular cousins do. *First Things* reports that it generates only two-thirds of its income from subscriptions and other standard sources—roughly in line with *C&C*'s historic percentages—and the remainder comes from fund appeals, grants, and support from Neuhaus's Institute on Religion and Public Life, which has no separate budget for *First Things* within its program. (Foundation grants account for 75 percent of the institute's budget.)[8] The *Witness,* an Episcopalian journal with politics somewhat like *C&C*'s, lives by spending down an inherited multimillion-dollar endowment that provided a $200,000 annual subsidy in 1992.[9] The *Presbyterian Layman,* a newspaper devoted to attacking the liberal wing of the Presbyterian Church, has a circulation of 520,000—with "subscribers" who pay nothing for their subscriptions. (Many treat it as junk mail.) Yet its budget is $1.4 million a year, including $1.1 million from "contributions," plus grants from the Pew Charitable Trust.[10] *Sojourners* survives partly by means of contributions and largely because its staff—much larger than *C&C*'s—works for subsistence wages ($10,500 per year in 1988) and lives in the intentional community that produces the magazine.[11]

One possible solution, for journals written by academics, is to make the publication a project of a university or professional organization. If the journal gains enough respect, it can attract people who write for free as part of their academic careers. It can command high-priced institutional subscriptions from libraries. It also may be able to arrange subsidies, some of which appear on budgets only as absences, that is, as resources that are presupposed: convenient libraries, inexpensive telephones, office space, computer networking, graduate student assistants, and released time from teaching for editors. Not the least important is professional networking through conferences, visiting lecturers, and so on. The interdisciplinary journal *Soundings* provides one example. It began as an arm of an organization now called the Society for Values in Higher Education (SVHE), which was founded in 1924 to carry out a "set of tactics by which Protestant university divinity schools sought to influence American higher education."[12] SVHE had historic connections to Yale and Vanderbilt Universities and solid backing from foundations including Rockefeller, Hazen, Lilly, and Danforth. In addition to the ongoing advantages that *Soundings* enjoys as an arm of the SVHE, the University of Tennessee provides a substantial cash subvention plus office space, help with accounting, and released time for its distinguished editor.[13] By the standards of academic journals, this is not a lucrative deal. On the other hand, many academic journals survive on less.[14]

Both *C&C* and its closest cousin, the *Christian Century*, represent a middle ground between independent magazines like *Sojourners* and university-sponsored journals like *Soundings*. Just as the *New York Review of Books* was an unusual success story in the *Los Angeles Times* study, so the *Century* stands almost alone among independent liberal Protestant journals in the "solvent" category. It covers 75 percent of its budget from subscriptions and 20 percent from advertising, so that minimal contributions can cover the rest. But even in this best case scenario, it is hard to imagine the *Century* attaining or sustaining its present strength without its long-term relationships with associates at the University of Chicago, such as senior editor Martin Marty. The less weight one assigns to this factor, the more unique the *Century*'s success appears.[15]

Against this background, *C&C*'s survival strategy comes into clearer focus. We can summarize it as a five-part recipe: two parts grounding in academia (like *Soundings*), two parts appeals for contributions (like *First Things*), and one part reliance on underpaid writers and staff (like *Sojourners*). Unlike *Soundings*, which has so far enjoyed a secure academic home, *C&C* faced the challenge of first being weaned from Union Seminary subsidies, then adjusting to an erosion of support from its second line of defense at the Interchurch Center, a building across the street from Union which houses many national ecumenical offices. Lacking a benefactor with deep pockets, *C&C* drew on a broad base of small contributors. Its typical pattern—except during the 1960s and the last few years—was to send out a Christmas appeal summarizing the gravity of the latest deficit, then count many checks of $50 and $100, and a handful in the low four figures, as they rolled in from subscribers.[16]

In brief, *C&C* collapsed because of dwindling institutional resources coupled with a rising gap between contributions and expenses. Contributions did not exactly dry up—indeed, they increased—but they did not keep pace with rising costs for printing, postage, and salaries. Eventually staff morale ran out. It remains controversial in *C&C*'s old circles whether, during this process, plausible survival strategies were left unexplored. I will return to this question after discussing how *C&C*'s history unfolded.

From the Institutional Foundations to the Crisis of the Early 1950s

C&C was not a unique departure for Niebuhr, simply because it was a journalistic attempt to convert the Protestant world to his views. Rather, it was the major new journal among many other religious and secular outlets where he was involved. Throughout his career Niebuhr wrote for such influential journals as *Foreign Affairs, Yale Review, Commentary, New Leader, Partisan Review, Atlantic Monthly,* and *Life.*[17] In the late 1930s Niebuhr often wrote for the *Nation,* which followed a path roughly similar to his own from the bandaged but unbowed pacifism of longtime editor Oswald Garrison Villard to the internationalism of new editor Freda Kirchwey.[18] He also wrote for *New Republic,* another left-liberal journal of kindred spirit to *C&C* that embraced World War II and the centralized administrative policies used to pursue it. Many of these journals dwarfed *C&C*. *Partisan Review* roughly matched it at 7,000, but the *Nation* and *New Republic* boasted 45,000 and 41,000, respectively. The *Atlantic* reached 156,000, whereas *Life* worked on a whole different plane with 5.2 million.[19]

Despite Niebuhr's prolific writing for general circulation journals, his major efforts appeared in Christian journals. *C&C* was the place where he redirected most of his energy for religious-political advocacy from former outlets at the *Century,* the pacifist *World Tomorrow,* and his own *Radical Religion.* Recall that he wrote dozens of articles each year for the *Century* during the 1920s and turned down the job of associate editor in 1925. From 1928 to 1934, he was associate editor at *World Tomorrow,* until the same question posed in the debate over *Moral Man and Immoral Society*—is violent class struggle necessary for economic justice?—led to such intense disputes in pacifist circles that *World Tomorrow* folded and merged with the *Century.*[20] In the course of this dispute, Niebuhr resigned as chair of the Fellowship of Reconciliation and shifted many of his organizational commitments to a newly formed Fellowship of Socialist Christians, which provided him "his own personal megaphone" in *Radical Religion.* As we have seen, by 1939 this group was calling itself the Frontier Fellowship, and the journal was renamed *Christianity and Society.*[21] It ran parallel to *C&C* (even sharing the same office) from 1941 until 1956, when *C&C* finally absorbed it.

Although *C&C* shared important things with these precursors and competitors, it was unique—and became uniquely symbolic of splits within Protestant circles—because of the particular coalition that brought it together and its targeted audience. Unlike the *Nation* it was explicitly religious, and it aimed for a broader group of educated Protestant readers than the hard-core Niebuhrian devotees who read *Christianity and Society.* In short, it aimed to make realists out of *Century* readers. Its format of brief lead editorials, feature articles, and a final section called "World Church: News and Notes" was a "conscious clone" of the *Century,* and it rapidly "deprived the *Century* of its longtime monopoly at the apex of the liberal, interdenominational press."[22]

Niebuhr did not act alone in founding *C&C.* If he had not been at Union Seminary, *C&C*'s birth would have been inconceivable, at least in the form it took. Alongside Niebuhr at the center of planning were Henry Sloane Coffin, Henry Pitney Van Dusen, and Francis Pickens Miller, a well-known social gospel writer.[23] Coffin had excellent connections in the New York establishment as a member of the Yale Corporation, longtime pastor of the Madison Avenue Presbyterian Church, and president of Union from 1926 to 1945. Van Dusen took over as Union's president in 1946, raising large funds from corporate sources including the Rockefeller and Luce fortunes, and working harmoniously with Union board members including Luce, John Foster Dulles, and Benjamin Strong, president of U.S. Trust Company.[24] Niebuhr played the main role in organizing *C&C*'s editorial board, which he chaired, and a larger board of sponsors. He drew on his own impressive contacts, as well as those of other founders. Along with Coffin, Van Dusen, and Miller, these included F. Ernest Johnson, a social gospel leader at the Federal Council of Churches; Edward Parsons, Episcopal bishop of California; Henry Smith Lieper of the WCC; and John Bennett, who was then teaching at the Pacific School of Religion but returned to Union in 1943.[25]

The board of sponsors, chaired by Coffin until his death in 1954, was a Who's Who of Protestants committed to internationalism—including ecumenical leader John Mott, Methodist bishop Francis McConnell, and Princeton University president Harold Dodds. By no means were all of them in total agreement with Niebuhr's views. In fact, Martin Marty has selected sponsor Ivan Lee Holt, a Methodist bishop, as a typical representative of the *Century*'s social gospel outlook during the 1930s; Marty also presents F. Ernest Johnson as a moderate, midway between liberalism and Niebuhrian radicalism.[26] *C&C*'s backers represented a coalition of Niebuhrians moving toward moderation, social gospelers moving toward Niebuhr's positions, and others who agreed about the specific issue of the war despite ongoing differences on other issues.

Given such a high-powered set of supporters, the magazine's appearance and operations were modest. As I noted in chapter 2, the match between the urgency of *C&C*'s message and its bare-bones production standards could result in a rough eloquence that was quite compelling. Nevertheless, *C&C* was not visually pleasing, and its writing was not consistently polished, although this varied from writer to writer. *C&C* appeared twenty-five times a year in an eight-page, two-column format completely devoid of graphics other than headlines, occasional notices in boxes, and a header bearing its name and the subheading "A Bi-Weekly Journal of Christian Opinion." The fonts and margins were small and narrow, so that three-page *C&C* articles often fill ten pages when anthologized in books. Near the end of issues, *C&C* printed lower priority articles in even smaller type, with the point of changeover depending on how many words were being packed into the issue. *C&C* often announced that it paid no salaries or honoraria, although in 1942 it hired a secretary for Niebuhr. Subscriptions ($1.50 per year) and contributions paid for the printing and postage. Union provided the office, and the editors volunteered their time, although to some degree many of them worked on Union "company time."

After the war, some of *C&C*'s backers thought it had served its purpose and should end, but there is scant evidence that the inner circle agreed. A 1946 statement of purpose stressed that crises continued: the danger of isolationism, responsibility for the "organization of a world community," and the need to strengthen the resources of churches.[27] By 1948 the editorial board had expanded so much that it split into a core editorial board and a larger group of contributing editors.[28] The core consisted of Niebuhr, Bennett, Van Dusen, Johnson, and Liston Pope, dean of Yale Divinity School. Two more joined in 1950 and 1951: M. Searle Bates, a longtime China missionary hired by Union after Mao's triumph, and Amos Wilder, a biblical scholar from Chicago Theological Seminary and later Harvard. By 1957 several people had died or drifted away, including Pope, Coffin, Parsons, and founders Howard Chandler Robbins and Rhoda McCulloch (the only female board member before the 1970s). Four key people had been added: Union theologian Robert McAfee Brown and Duke University ethicist Waldo Beach, who joined the editorial board in 1954, as well as Northwestern University political scientist Kenneth Thompson and Vanderbilt (later Union) social ethicist Roger Shinn, who became contributing editors in 1955. Other new contributing editors included two academics, William May and William Lee Miller, and the executive secretary of the NCC's department of racial and cultural relations, J. Oscar Lee. Lee was the first African American on *C&C*'s masthead; after McCulloch left in 1951, he was the only one who was not a white male.

The boards were in charge of *C&C*'s writing and decision making. In 1954 Wayne Cowan, a young journalist with experience as a missionary in Japan, was hired as the secretary, with a warning that his job might end in a few months if the journal folded. By the 1970s Cowan would become *C&C*'s most influential person, but he describes his job in the 1950s as a "go-fer"—a "stable boy running across Broadway from our office to the seminary to hitch up the editorial horses." Members of the board would meet in Union's refectory. They discussed their response to current events and divided the tasks of writing. The secretary shuttled between these editors and *C&C*'s cramped office in Union's Reed House, where it moved in 1947 and where it shared space for a time with the *Interpreter's Bible* and *Christianity and Society*. The secretary collected drafts of articles and did some editing. Cowan recalls that Niebuhr's manuscripts typically had "lead sentences half a page in length and heavily Germanic in form" with frequent misspellings. Then the secretary and circulation staff assembled the journal and mailed it.[29]

At the level of sponsor—the outer ring of the three concentric circles making up *C&C*'s leadership—*C&C* added Benjamin Mays of Morehouse College, Eugene Barnett of the YMCA National Council, Harry Emerson Fosdick of Riverside Church, and Benjamin Strong of Union's board.[30] People from all three boards—editors, contributors, and sponsors—constituted the board of sponsors and attended retreats once or twice a year. This was *C&C*'s closest thing to a business meeting, although Cowan recalls the gatherings more as discussion groups. Often the entire board signed editorials that the national press found newsworthy.

One role of the various boards was to promote subscriptions and raise funds. Detailed records are not available between 1945 and the 1960s, but the main outlines are clear. Along with fund appeals in the magazine, *C&C* sent targeted mailings to potential subscribers, especially seminary mailing lists. There was an ambitious initial push for circulation during World War II, centering on letters to mailing lists of all kinds; for example, John Mackay, president of Princeton Seminary, wrote the elders of the synod of Pennsylvania, and the Council on Foreign Relations lent a 1,500-name mailing list.[31] After the war these efforts tapered off, and *C&C* did not revive them on a large scale until the 1960s.[32] However, among *C&C* records (extremely unsystematic for these years) there is some evidence of mailings to potential contributors. For example, one 1953 editorial note refers in passing to "Dr. Coffin's fund appeal" to which five hundred subscribers responded, and there is a folder of thank-you notes from Niebuhr acknowledging gifts in the $50 to $100 range.[33] *C&C* also approached individuals. Internal histories report that in the 1950s "we received small grants (about $2,000) from a family foundation in the Midwest" and Walter Lippmann made a $2,000 donation in 1954.[34] Roger Shinn recalls when Henry Luce stopped funding *C&C*, presumably because he found its politics too left-wing, and when John Mackay offered to seek support from the Pew Foundation, but Niebuhr "replied that he would not accept help from so reactionary an organization."[35]

Before *C&C*'s birth, its projected budget was $15,000—an income of $10,000 in subscriptions and $5,000 in contributions, and expenses of $8,000 for printing and postage and $6,000 for salaries. By 1942, after the opening push to establish the journal, the actual income settled in at $11,000—$7,000 from subscriptions and $4,000 from contributions. This required scaling back the operation, with the largest impact on salaries, which were cut in half to $3,000. Not until 1954 did *C&C*'s finances reach the start-up point envisioned in 1940—a $15,000 budget including $5,000 from contributions. Unfortunately, by then *C&C* had a $1,800 deficit, its subscriptions had doubled in price, and—most ominously—circulation had fallen by 50 percent since the end of World War II. In this context *C&C* seriously considered folding.

Not all of *C&C*'s decline of the early 1950s should be attributed to economics, because *C&C* was palpably demoralized by its battle with McCarthyism and many of its key themes were becoming stale. One issue from 1953—published within a month of Van Dusen's endorsement of bantustans and Niebuhr's call for the execution of the Rosenbergs—led with an editorial packed with such rhetoric as this: "The arc of communist violence from Korea to Malaya and Tibet, and tightening totalitarianism in China, set against the relatively sound performance in the Panmunjom negotiations . . . [plus several other similar things] have brought real changes in the outlook of responsible leaders from Hokkaido to Java to New Delhi—changes in which we can rejoice."[36]

The rest of this issue included a poorly edited piece by Niebuhr in which he rehashed an argument about democracy that he had been making for more than ten years, a somewhat fresher book review called "Corruption in Government: A Perennial Issue," which called for more religious influence on public morality, and a Church News Section that first summarized and then reprinted two lengthy and bland WCC resolutions.[37] There were several typographical errors. On the brighter side, most of this issue avoided the extremely dense font sizes that *C&C* increasingly used at the time.

This sense of cutting corners in production, linked to diminishing passion about *C&C*'s message, was exacerbated in 1952 when Niebuhr suffered a series of strokes that drastically reduced his energy. Although this cut down his whirlwind of travel more than his writing for *C&C*, it still required major adjustments. Bennett was the key person who filled the gap. In 1953 he became co-chair of the board; an editorial note said that this "formally recognizes what has been the actual situation for the past years."[38] By the early 1960s he was *C&C*'s de facto leader.

Despite the relative drop in *C&C*'s organizational energy during the early 1950s, *C&C* still exuded confidence that it had a prophetic word to speak, and even in illness Niebuhr was far more prolific than most of his colleagues. Thus the internal discussion about *C&C*'s future focused on finances. Only a few insiders—notably Coffin—believed that the magazine had outlived its usefulness.[39] In 1954 *C&C* published an increasingly desperate series of appeals for contributions, bulk orders, and cut-rate subscriptions to boost circulation. It culminated in a statement from Niebuhr, which was published in large print in a half-page box. It said, "We do not promise or threaten to go on forever. We merely desire to serve the Church and our generation as long as a sufficient number of friends regard our services as worthwhile."[40] The results were encouraging—Lippmann's gift by itself wiped out the deficit—and *C&C* forged ahead.

An Anomalous Decade of Institutional Growth and Health

In 1956, *C&C* introduced what it called a "new look." By this time a few changes had already evolved. Letters to the editor, rare in the 1940s, had become common, and there was no longer a "World Church: News and Notes" section in every issue. Now *C&C* made further changes. The header graphic—which was virtually its *only* graphic—no longer printed its name horizontally across the top. Instead the title appeared on two lines, with the word "Christianity" directly above "Crisis" and the "C's" aligned in a sort of rudimentary logo. The subtitle, "A Journal of Christian Opinion" became "A Christian Journal of Opinion." (This was supposed to signal that *C&C* did not claim *the* sole legitimate Christian position.)[41] *C&C* moved dates and subscription information to the bottom of the front page, made the masthead smaller, and changed the font to a more streamlined Helvetica style. The result was a breezier and more contemporary feel—insofar as this is possible for a type-heavy journal on plain paper with no graphics—which underlined *C&C*'s newly announced plans to expand coverage of the arts.[42] Niebuhr grumbled to Cowan that he "had a conversation with Mrs. Justice Frankfurter on the phone last night and she doesn't like the new format either."[43]

Despite Niebuhr's reservations, *C&C*'s new look symbolized that it had survived its brush with death and was gaining energy for the future. *C&C*'s confident editorial voice had a counterpart in institutional strength from the mid-1950s to the late 1960s. Most important, *C&C* continued to attract distinguished writers. By 1964 its board grew to seventeen members, still weighted heavily toward white male seminary professors. Key additions since 1957 included Tom Driver and Robert Lynn of Union, Harvey Cox of Harvard Divinity School, and Robert Spike of the NCC Commission on Religion and Race.[44] The thirteen contributing editors included stalwarts in old age (Francis P. Miller), up-and-coming writers (Arthur Moore, Stephen Rose), academics (Charles West), and de facto "foreign correspondents" who reported from Britain (Herbert Butterfield), France (J. B. Duroselle), India (M. M. Thomas), and Latin America (Richard Shaull.)[45] Paul Nitze, Niebuhr's colleague from the State Department policy planning team, was a contributing editor from 1960 to 1961, before resigning when he became assistant secretary of defense. M. M. Thomas was the only non-white on either board between 1962 (when Lee resigned) and 1965.

After 1954 *C&C*'s circulation began an upward trend that continued through 1966. From 4,500 in 1954, circulation steadily grew to 9,000 by 1961 and 16,500 in 1965. *C&C* set a goal of 25,000 by its twenty-fifth anniversary in 1966, but actually peaked at 18,700 in January 1967.[46] Its percentage of income from contributions—33 percent in 1954—shrank to 10 percent by 1961, and reached a low of 4 percent in 1968.[47] *C&C* even began to pay its writers small honoraria in 1963, and it finished 1966 with assets of $50,000—this was the economic muscle it was flexing when it divested from South Africa. Improving finances enabled *C&C* to hire Frances Smith (the only woman on its masthead) as associate editor with responsibilities for promotion from 1962 to 1966. The efforts of Cowan and Smith during these years produced a surge in subscriptions. In 1965, the budget reached $100,000, with almost $20,000 earmarked for promotion.[48] *C&C* churned out direct mail solicitations and advertised in periodicals such as the *Christian Century, United Church Herald, Ramparts, Harper's,* and the *New York Times.*[49] It loved to reprint endorsements, such as one from *Newsweek,* which said that *C&C* had "secured a permanent position of leadership in Protestant journalism."[50] *C&C* also sought out endorsements from pundits and politicians. This could lead into delicate negotiations, as when Senator Eugene McCarthy proposed to say that *C&C* was in the tradition of men like C. S. Lewis and Charles Williams as well as Geoffrey Francis Fisher, archbishop of Canterbury—not *C&C's* preferred role models, to say the least! Cowan suggested that McCarthy's endorsement "might seem a bit confusing" unless he changed the names to Niebuhr, Bennett, and Tillich.[51]

In the late 1950s *C&C* began to increase some of its issues from eight to twelve pages. In 1960 it produced six twelve-pagers and eighteen eight-pagers, for a yearly total of 216 pages. By 1964 every issue had at least twelve pages, and many had sixteen, for an annual output of 292. This trend peaked around 350 in the late 1960s, dropped back into the low 300s during the early 1970s, then rose to more than 400 in the 1980s.

C&C's most striking visual change was the addition of graphics and advertising. At first they only appeared in special issues designed for bulk sales, beginning with a 1961 issue on Africa. *C&C's* first cover graphic was ultra-minimalist—a gray outline of a map of Africa—and Harper's bought two advertisements for books about religion in Africa. Later in the year, *C&C* followed with an unprecedented twenty-page issue on civil rights. This issue not only had a cover graphic—a black and white sketch of a civil rights worker—but even a few drawings illustrating its articles.[52] *C&C* began to churn out special issues regularly. Gradually it recruited advertisers for regular issues and persuaded them to sell books that were not about topics addressed in the issues. By 1968 most issues had three pages of ads, often featuring *C&C's* only graphics, and the advertisers included CALCAV (which often bought full-page ads), the *Saturday Evening Post,* the summer school of Union Seminary, and an enterprising group that offered workshops on changing clergical roles in times of revolution. Publishers became less careful about targeting ads to *C&C* constituents: they probably sold few books with an endorsement from William F. Buckley, and one wonders how many subscribers were actually tempted by *God Is for Real, Man*—"the book that HAPPENS," featuring "street gang teenagers" who "cool it with their elders and cut through adult hypocrisy."[53]

Subscribers surveys from 1967, 1982, and 1990 show that *C&C* readers were highly educated (above 90 percent college graduates, more than half with higher degrees), professional (40–45 percent clergy and 15 percent teachers), members of mainline denominations (60–70 percent from Presbyterian, Methodist, Episcopal and United Church of Christ), and religiously committed (in 1990, 70 percent attended church at least twice a month and 80 percent were active in other church activities). Along with *C&C,* they read *Christian Century* and secular magazines such as the *New Yorker.* Roughly speaking, these patterns are consistent with impressions of earlier years, although the Catholic readership was probably not 10 percent during the 1940s, as it was after 1967.[54]

During this period *C&C* began a long-standing tradition of offering free books with Christmas gift subscriptions, and the selections provide an interesting barometer of its transformation. In 1958 subscribers could choose between Niebuhr's *The World Crisis and Christian Responsibility* (a collection including the essay that became "Ideological Special #256") and Cowan's *What the Christian Hopes For in Society* (a set of *C&C* articles upholding liberal hope against more pessimistic forms of Christian realism). In 1960, *C&C* offered another collection of its own articles on Protestant-Catholic relations, and in 1966 it offered Cowan's *Witness to a Generation,* a "best of *C&C*" retrospective produced for its twenty-fifth anniversary.[55] Other typical selections in the mid-1960s included Harvey Cox's *Secular City,* Charles Silberman's *Crisis in Black and White,* Robert Short's *Gospel according to Peanuts,* and two books by Robert McAfee Brown, *Observer in Rome* (on Vatican II) and *The Collected Writings of St. Hereticus* (from his satirical column). In 1970 *C&C* offered *Seize the Time* by Black Panther leader Bobby Seale and *The Trial of the Catonsville Nine* by Daniel Berrigan. In later years, Richard Barnet's *Roots of War* (1973) and José Míguez Bonino's *Doing Theology in a Revolutionary Situation* (1975) catered to radicals, while Arthur Simon's *Bread for the World* (1975) aimed at moderates. Many choices were idiosyncratic, such as Peter Berger's *Rumor of Angels* (1969), Margaret Mead's *Culture and Commitment* (1970), and Carlos Castaneda's *Journey to Ixtlan* (1973).

Polarization and Reorganization, Late 1960s to Mid-1970s

Along with *C&C*'s radicalization came institutional crisis. In disputes like the one provoked by Cox's "Enough Is Enough" article, the editorial board fell apart. An editorial lamented that *C&C* had "relied on a tangible and active consensus" but "like our public discourse [this] has become fragmented."[56] Cowan became editor in 1968, but Bennett and Niebuhr remained the keys to *C&C*'s prestige, as well as the leaders with the best chance to hold the board together. However, by this time Niebuhr was fading. After 1966 he quit the board, and his health continued to decline until he died in 1971. (As we have seen, his family removed his name from the masthead in 1972.) Bennett became the sole chair of the board and remained active from across the street as president of Union, but conflicts within Union increasingly claimed his attention, and in 1970 he left New York. All this unfolded at the same moment as Nixon's election, the collapse of civil rights organizing, and the inability of the peace movement to end the war. (Bennett's farewell ceremony, at Union's 1970 commencement, was a service of mourning for massacred students at Kent State.)[57]

Into this situation came data impossible to ignore—circulation collapsed from 1969 to 1973, and *C&C* could not balance its books. From a 1967 high of 18,700, circulation fell to 17,000, its first drop since 1954. It briefly rallied after a mailing featuring the (revised) endorsement by Senator McCarthy, but then it went into free fall, declining by 3,000 in 1969 alone. Finally it stabilized between 1973 and 1975 in the 8,500 range (the same level as before Frances Smith's hiring in 1961.) Assets dipped as low as $15,000, and advertising decreased to only one or two pages per issue.[58] Advertising income, which peaked at 9 percent of the budget in 1970, fell to 4 percent in 1976 and stabilized around 3 percent from the late 1970s until the end. In 1969, *C&C* mailed its first eight-page issue since before 1960—although for the year it still averaged 13 pages per issue.

Organizationally, 1969 was *C&C*'s worst year since its near-demise in 1954. The board was in disarray, Bennett was preoccupied with the Black Manifesto controversy, and Cowan was on sabbatical at Stanford. (Robert Lecky was interim editor, assisted by Leon Howell.) Things improved little during the next two years. *C&C* discussed scenarios for survival including merging with *Christian Century* and / or *Commonweal*, cooperating with James McGraw's Methodist-based *Renewal*, which was trying to become "the magazine of the black church," and converting into a newsletter like *I. F. Stone's Weekly*.[59]

Once again, *C&C* considered folding. In fact, the journal *Church and State* even wrote that its closing "had been announced." Cowan recalls, "I thought it was gone. . . . I was so sure of it that I was already experiencing grief."[60] However, a fund-raising effort by Shinn, Arthur Moore, George Younger, and William Ellis boosted assets to a tolerable cushion of $44,000, and *C&C* pressed on. It dissolved the dysfunctional editorial board and reorganized with a new board of directors, chaired by Shinn, which was responsible for business decisions, plus a streamlined board of contributing editors that replaced the editorial board on the masthead.[61] Since this group was more diverse than the old board—and less centered on Union, so that it could not meet from week to week—a major trend after 1971 was for power to flow to the staff. Until the end *C&C*'s basic product, the writing that constituted its Camaro coming off the line, remained dependent on the contributors, but structurally they became more like a roster of writers.[62]

Despite its 1971 reprieve, *C&C* remained unsure whether it could survive until at least 1975, and it was preoccupied with defining the new roles of the staff until at least the end of the decade.[63] It balanced the books in 1972 only by replacing two full-time staff members with one part-time person. However, by 1973 it raised enough money to hire a business manager. In addition, Virginia Sixeas of the Sisters of Notre Dame worked at no cost to *C&C* between 1973 and 1975.[64] With the staff thus expanded, *C&C* pulled out of its organizational spiral. Circulation stabilized after 1973, reached 11,000 in 1976, and shot up to all-time highs in the 17,000–20,000 range between 1977 and 1980. After 1972, *C&C* ran budget surpluses for the rest of the decade and built its assets to $85,000. Unfortunately, this required contributions representing one-third of its budget for the decade. Salaries accounted for around 40 percent of expenses. In short, *C&C* reverted to financial arrangements somewhat like it used before the 1960s boom, with staff leadership and grants from mainline denominations taking up the slack from the reduced role of Union faculty.[65]

C&C's looks greatly improved during this crisis. Until 1969, cover art and inside graphics appeared only on special occasions. But in 1970, assistant editor Robert Harsh began producing far more sophisticated layouts. By 1971, half the issues had eye-catching covers. Thereafter they all did, and *C&C*'s venerable front-page template disappeared forever. At first *C&C*'s artists were influenced by the iconoclastic style of the counterculture—they liked political juxtapositions, muted gestures toward psychedelia, and unpredictable touches such as varying the fonts of headlines. One cover used a photo of an automobile junkyard, cut in pieces and set against a background of newspaper stock price listings.[66] Until it settled down in the mid-1970s, *C&C* was tempted by a week-by-week reinvention of style that produced inconsistent artistic results. Still, on balance the new graphics—combined with a higher grade of paper, an attractive new logo, and articles on the cutting edge of international debates such as Ruether's "Mother Earth and the Megamachine" and Moltmann's "Open Letter to José Míguez Bonino"—made the journal appear newly vital and energetic even as its finances deteriorated.

After the mid-1960s, articles became more important than editorials. This was a boost in overall quality, since by this time the articles were typically stronger, but it broke with tradition. Until 1971 *C&C* limped along with editorials in most issues, but in 1972 it published only four editorials all year, and by the late 1970s it had abandoned them. For a time it compensated with a feature called "Skandalon" (by Shinn, unsigned) that spoke in a voice somewhat like earlier editorial notes and ran on the inside front cover.[67]

Since *C&C*'s reputation hinged on its writers, its most important changes were in personnel. During the second half of the 1960s, younger writers including Cox and Rose had become increasingly central, and it had added two leading black scholars, Vincent Harding to the contributing editors (1965–71) and C. Eric Lincoln to the editorial board (1967–71). This still left its boards 90 percent white and 100 percent male. Subtractions included

Amos Wilder and F. Ernest Johnson, who retired in old age, Robert Spike, who was murdered in 1966, and Tom Driver, who resigned in 1970 because he found *C&C* too conservative. Additions included Howard Moody, a Baptist minister and activist, and Michael Novak, the first Catholic in *C&C*'s inner circle.[68]

After the reorganization in 1972, half the names on *C&C*'s masthead remained familiar: Brown, Cowan, Cox, Moody, Moore (after 1974), Novak, and Shinn, along with Bennett, who remained active from California as "senior contributing editor." This group averaged fifteen years on the masthead.[69] However, in an effort to reduce *C&C*'s domination by white male seminary professors, half the names were new. They featured the foremost black and feminist theologians, James Cone and Rosemary Ruether, plus William Stringfellow, a theologian in the Daniel Berrigan mold, John Fry, an ethicist from the Pacific School of Religion, and James McGraw, editor of *Renewal* and *C&C*'s leading voice for gay pride. On the secular front *C&C* added anthropologist Margaret Mead, socialist economist Robert Lekachman (in 1974), and Frank Baldwin, a specialist in Asian history. Vivian Lindermayer joined the staff as editorial associate in 1971 and began her steady rise through the ranks. To keep this increased diversity from being swallowed up, seventeen names were removed from the masthead, including fourteen white males.[70] Some were people like Thompson from *C&C*'s conservative wing who no longer fit, although others including Shaull and Harding were radicals. Many were inactive contributors under the old format.

This transformation could be painful for old-timers. Of course, it upset budding neoconservatives like Novak. He suggested in 1971 that more direction should come from a senior editor who would generate ideas, and he offered himself as an adviser to the staff in the upcoming months.[71] (Recall that in 1975 Cowan kicked Novak off the board, despite objections from Shinn and Brown, as well as questions about who held the authority to make such decisions.) Moderates, too, were unsettled. Bennett pressed Cowan for additions to the first slate of contributing editors that he proposed internally, to give it more weight at the moderate end of *C&C*'s spectrum of debate.[72]

The readers' surveys of 1982 and 1990 showed relatively few changes since 1967. Subscribers remained highly educated, religiously committed, and weighted toward the mainline denominations (45 percent remained clergy, which contrasts with 80 percent at the *Century* and 30 percent at *First Things* and *Sojourners*). Yet despite an overall impression of continuity, some changes were important. The percentage of women doubled from 20 percent in 1967 to 40 percent in 1990, and the percentage of nonwhites rose from 2 percent to as much as 10 percent, given the generous estimate that *C&C* liked to quote. Thus, even though *C&C* remained a largely white enterprise, its bloc of readers who were not white men increased from 20 percent to nearly 50 percent. *C&C* also worried about its aging constituency; 25 percent of its readers were over 65. (*First Things* readers were 85 percent male, and 29 percent were over 65.)[73]

Readers identified a shifting set of issues as concerns, roughly mirroring changes in *C&C*'s printed text. It is hard to judge whether this reflects a new group of readers or the same people changing in tandem with *C&C*. There was also some tendency for readers to shift from well-heeled liberal journals such as the *New Yorker* to more movement-oriented journals such as the *Nation*. Recall that by 1990 the combined bloc of *Sojourners* and *The Other Side* readers was two-thirds as large as the group of *Century* readers. However, the interest in secular movement journals was surprisingly low, with only 10 percent of *C&C* subscribers reporting that a single choice from among six leading movement journals was one of their favorites.[74] (In contrast, 15 percent of *First Things* readers also subscribe to the *National Review*—by far their most popular choice—compared with 5 percent who read the *Century* and 2 percent who read *Commonweal*.)[75] In 1990, 28 percent called themselves progressive or democratic socialist; 34 percent were unqualified liberals; and a bloc of 25 percent was "somewhat liberal," moderate, or conservative. There was one lonely anarchist.[76]

Some readers of this book may interpret *C&C*'s personnel changes and its 1969–74 collapse of circulation in light of the hypothesis, discussed in my introduction and chapter 7, that left-liberal shifts by mainline Protestants cause institutional decline, as readers "vote with their feet" by defecting to the right. Such a diagnosis of *C&C*'s problems might support the idea that Protestants took a wrong turn in the 1960s, lurching too far to the left, and that the cure is to back up and revitalize center liberalism. Elsewhere I have discussed the strengths and weaknesses of this hypothesis; here I will summarize my conclusions.[77]

First, when I tried to test the simplest version of this hypothesis—that "voters" rejected a takeover of *C&C* by a new group of people—I discovered a fair amount of evidence that tends to minimize this as a factor. I compared the rate of turnover on *C&C*'s staff and central boards in different decades. For whatever these numbers may be worth—and we must approach them with all due caution—I found no increase in the turnover between 1966 and 1976, compared with earlier years. In fact, in key respects there was *less* turnover, depending on how complicated "apples and oranges" comparisons are made.[78] The highest turnover in *C&C*'s core of writers and editors happened between 1956 and 1966, which were years of evolving change set unmistakably within a continuous tradition—and the period of *C&C*'s greatest *growth* and self-confidence. In this regard, a hypothesis about subscribers voting with their feet against leadership discontinuity works at cross purposes. If we link these factors, readers appear to have voted with their feet *in favor of* discontinuities.

Second, if we refine the hypothesis and speculate that readers voted with their feet against *C&C*'s emergent radical *ideas,* whether of continuous boards or discontinuous staffs, we must explain why circulation reached an all-time high in 1978 and subsequently stabilized in the 13,000 range, that is, higher than at any time before 1963. It might be possible to press forward, explaining away these "votes for radicalism" as a result of promotion, since *C&C* offered many loss-leader subscriptions to seminarians in the late 1970s. Unfortunately, this does not work unless the 1969–74 "votes against radicalism" and the "votes for the vital center" in the early 1960s are also explained away because of similar factors. Almost all of the 1967–75 decline came in an atmosphere of crisis when, according to Cowan, "promotional efforts fell by the wayside."[79] What little promotion that *C&C* tried showed results: a 1968 mailing increased circulation, and another in 1972 slowed a downward curve that was steady in previous and later years. Promotion accounted for only 7 percent of the budget during the free fall of 1970 and 1971, compared with 20 percent during the boom years of the early 1960s and the late 1970s. (It later stabilized around 15 percent.)

Undaunted, one might persist. Suppose we bracket these problems by postulating that with enough money one can promote anything, irrespective of content, in this postmodern era. Then one might ask why *C&C* had the self-confidence and vitality to promote aggressively in some periods but not in others. Decreased efforts around 1970 were obviously related to *C&C*'s internal polarization and its relationship to larger political changes, just as the crisis of 1954 was linked to Niebuhr's stroke and demoralization about McCarthyism. Yet this is quite different from simply assuming that a leftward drift in content *caused* a decline. The preferred causal chain in the "radicalization-causes-decline" hypothesis runs from polarization that makes conservative readers leave, to lowered institutional vitality, to reduced promotion, to even more readers defecting on the right. But consider a counter-example that remains interesting, although it is somewhat speculative. We have noted how *C&C* insiders were instrumental in organizing CALCAV. *American Report,* the CALCAV magazine, competed with *C&C* during its short life from 1970 to 1974—it was even edited by past *C&C* editor Robert Lecky and future *C&C* editor Robert Hoyt. It is quite possible that some *C&C* readers switched to *American Report,* not because they saw *C&C* as betraying them on their left but because *American Report* had greater financial resources and was less burdened by sustaining a "responsible" debate on its right. If so, *C&C*'s loss of vitality and lack of promotion would translate into *C&C*'s lower priority compared with an alternative produced by the "excess vitality" of its own leaders. Readers would vote with their feet against *C&C*'s radical turn by abandoning it on the *left*.[80]

All this is speculative, and the rise and fall of *American Report* was certainly not a primary factor shaping *C&C*'s fate. However, my speculations dovetail with unambiguous evidence for a third point. Subscriber defection around 1970 was clearly not only on the right. True, when people like Novak dropped away, like-minded subscribers no doubt followed them. A survey of readers whose subscriptions had lapsed turned up many responses, including "End the War! Yes! Excuse the Anarchists! No!" and "Too polemical, hence unbalanced and superficial."[81] Yet the same survey also turned up respondents such as the seminarian who said, "*C&C* is a dreadful bore—inane liberality, inane commentary—you guys are in no crisis. . . . I'm really quite sorry for you. . . . Maybe my uncle Howard would be interested—he's quiet and gutless. You'd probably get on very well."[82] Others added that *C&C* was "written by men for men," was "cold-blooded and intellectual," and had "become too conservative and oriented toward the establishment."[83] Another large group found *C&C* too negative: some apparently wanted fewer attacks on the establishment, and others wanted more explorations of radical alternatives. Many sensed that the center was collapsing with nothing satisfying to replace it. Robert Harsh described *C&C* as "stale" and "sadly limited." When he joined *C&C*'s staff, his friends "all wished me well *despite* the job [and] said that if I couldn't kick the magazine back to life maybe I could help it die gracefully. . . . Now I could only watch my friends wave good-bye as I faded off (to the right) into the stodgy liberalism we all distrusted so much."[84]

C&C's institutional strategy—and moral commitment—was to build a new constituency on the expanding radical part of its spectrum to compensate for losses on the shrinking conservative part. It sought to maintain the liberals in its core constituency and recover former readers abandoning it on the left. Equally important, it sought allies from a new generation of Protestants who were turning toward secular political movements and popular culture, and from constituencies outside the crumbling coalition of cold war liberalism, notably feminists and racial minorities.

This strategy kept *C&C* alive for two more decades, but it did eventually reach the dead end predicted by the radicalization-causes-decline hypothesis. For the sake of the argument, let us continue to discount the positive and accentuate the negative, interpreting *C&C*'s ultimate collapse in light of its 1967–74 declines, and stressing that its circulation was lower during the 1980s than it was from 1963 to 1968. Was *C&C*'s left turn a success in the cold pragmatic terms of *maximizing* its institutional health? At first glance, the answer might appear to be no, because within *C&C*'s huge pool of prospective new constituents among youth, only a few were seriously prepared to consider alliances with establishment Protestants. *C&C* was seeking allies for its vision of religious-political change, while Protestantism at large was ambivalent about this vision and giving highly mixed signals. *C&C* could not solve this problem by itself. However, I suspect that if it had tried to stay the course of liberal centrism or convert to neoconservatism, it would have lost more of its old readers and gained fewer new ones—although it may well have landed more foundation grants. Against those who see a leftward shift in mainline Protestantism causing institutional decline, I insist that if this is true, then the mainline is between a rock and a hard place. *Not* shifting will also cause institutional decline. *Former* "vital center" strategies do not necessarily translate into credible *current* ones. It is crucial to confront why the former coalition collapsed and to respond to the forces that led to this collapse.

The Later Years

Whatever the pragmatic implications of *C&C*'s left turn in the early 1970s, it continued in roughly the same vein until the end. I have noted a few variations such as a more centrist political line during the early 1980s and a turn toward shorter articles after 1985; if they made a significant difference, they probably alienated the radical wing of *C&C*'s constituency more than its moderates, and its academic readers more than its clergy. In any case, if the issue is *C&C*'s content, the point to accentuate is continuity.

Personnel is a different issue. Turnover continued in the contributing editors. Notable departures included James Cone, Robert Lekachman, and William Stringfellow. Among the key additions were Union faculty members Beverly Harrison, Larry Rasmussen, and Delores Williams, along with ethicists Alan Geyer and Elizabeth Bettenhausen, and several leading liberationists, including Carter Heyward, Susan Thistlethwaite, Gayraud Wilmore, Robert Allen Warrior, and Cornel West.[85] *C&C*'s final masthead listed twenty contributing editors, including seven women, four people of color, and numerous veterans like Bennett, Brown, Cox, Ruether, and Shinn.

Equally important were changes in the staff. Among others who passed through the office, Margaret O'Brien Steinfels rose to executive editor and business manager from 1982 to 1984. Gail Hovey replaced her in this role until 1987, then became managing publisher until 1990. Tom Kelly joined *C&C* in 1982 and rose to associate editor with responsibilities for layouts.

J. Richard Butler became managing publisher from 1991 to the end, after holding key NCC jobs including the directorship of Church World Service. Recall that Lindermayer had been on the scene since 1971; by the end she was a major force, especially after 1990 when she was managing editor.[86]

Above all, the job of editor had become crucial as *C&C* changed from a faculty-run collective to a stand-alone staff operation. Thus the most important staff change occurred in the early 1980s, when Cowan was eased out of the editor's chair. Cowan's loss was Robert Hoyt's gain, as he rose from associate editor in 1977 to executive editor (under Cowan) in 1978, then editor from 1982 to 1985. Cowan remained as "editor-in-chief" between 1982 and 1984 and "editor-at-large" thereafter, but—to make a long story short—there was not enough room at *C&C* for both of them. Cowan, who had nurtured *C&C* for three decades and called it his "bride," faced a situation in which Hoyt could send him a memo stating, "You are not the manager, you are not even the left-fielder; you are in the bull pen, where your skills and experience can be called into play when they are felt to be needed."[87] The ultimate outcome was that both left *C&C*, with Howell taking over the reins in 1985.[88] Thickening the plot was an application from Lindermayer and Hovey for the editorship.

For people aware of *C&C*'s inner workings, controversy still swirls around the interpretation of these changes.[89] Was Cowan victimized at the moment of a health crisis—he suffered from a rare form of brain infection at a crucial stage of the process—or had he simply ceased to be effective? Was Hoyt an aggressive Machiavellian as he moved toward the center of operations, or was he simply a virtuous problem-solver stepping decisively into a power vacuum?[90] Was Hoyt too conservative, or was he himself a victim of unjust charges by Cowan supporters who exploited *C&C*'s lingering anti-Catholicism during the in-fighting? Was Lindermayer stopped from rising to coeditor and hampered in her role as managing editor by the sexism of old-timers, or did she simply depart too far from *C&C*'s historic norm as a first-generation Greek-American, a non-Protestant, and (in her own words) "not a *C&C* 'natural'"? Her final, less-than-glowing comment about *C&C*'s founder was that she "didn't find the Niebuhrian journalistic tradition half-bad."[91]

Luckily, we can sidestep most of these questions as inconsequential for *C&C*'s overall trajectory. However we imagine resolving them, the "Camaro" does not turn out much different in the long run. Only two consequences are worth noting, besides the energy expended in internal strife. First, we have seen that under Hoyt's leadership, when Peggy Steinfels was also a rising force, *C&C* leaned toward a more centrist position on its liberal-radical continuum. Recall how Hoyt even offered neoconservative

James Finn a column—provoking bitter internal controversy—and invited the head of the National Right to Life Committee to join a *C&C* abortion forum.[92] Viewed from a stronger left-feminist point of view this was, as a former chair of *C&C*'s board puts it, "a moment of danger."[93]

To speculate about how this moment might have unfolded, it is interesting to consider *Commonweal,* which recruited Steinfels as editor after she left *C&C* and features Hoyt as senior writer. In her final *C&C* article, Steinfels underlined the difference between *C&C*'s deeply rooted Protestant character and focused commitment to left-feminist politics, as compared with her more Catholic and less politicized sensibility.[94] *Commonweal* clearly reflects this difference, even though it overlapped with *C&C* throughout the two journals' careers. Its spectrum of debate about gender and sexuality was more traditional, and it was far more concerned with Catholic doctrine and liturgy.[95] Given the journals' distinctive histories, *C&C* could not have turned out "just like *Commonweal*" if Hoyt and Steinfels had continued, but it certainly would have been *more* like *Commonweal.* Whatever one thinks about the merits of this path, it probably would not have prolonged *C&C*'s life. In fact, it may well have shortened it. Partly for this reason, Hoyt wrote at *C&C*'s death, "I know with certainty something that others may suspect. . . . Nobody else but Leon Howell could have kept *C&C* going in the difficult years since he took over as editor."[96]

This brings us to the second significant outcome of the leadership change of the mid-1980s, Howell's innovations as editor. Howell was a safe choice for extending Cowan's contacts in the world of ecumenical Protestantism, although someone combining his approach with stronger academic credentials might have been safer.[97] Given his experience in journalism, he was a solid choice from the business point of view, and he beefed up *C&C*'s credibility in investigative journalism. Howell built up a partial surrogate for the old editorial board, which had discussed issues and reported its conclusions in *C&C.* This was the editorial advisory panel, an informal group that met at Union. Some contributing editors participated, such as Union professor Larry Rasmussen, but this group was centered on a larger group of people based near Union, such as Riverside Church minister David Dyson, Methodist bureaucrat Betty Thompson, and Lutheran minister Barbara Lundblad (a board member). Unlike the old board, its only official role was to advise the staff.[98] Howell also revived *C&C*'s tradition of running editorials that commented, pundit-style, on current events. After abandoning editorials in the 1970s, *C&C* had used them sparingly in the early 1980s, but Howell wrote an editorial for most issues. Without the consensus of a strong editorial board behind them, they rarely attracted media attention.

We have noted that Howell shortened and simplified *C&C* articles. In an effort to increase circulation, he also tried to recruit regular columnists who could give *C&C* a more reader-friendly personality.[99] When *C&C* opted to hire Howell rather than promote Hovey and Lindermayer (or search for an established scholar), one of the implications was another road not taken—a road that would have made fewer changes of this kind and paid more attention to emergent debates in the Christian left academy, especially related to feminism. Although Howell and Lindermayer tried to downplay their friction over these matters, the tension was obvious to people close to the journal. Indeed, the friction was clear to anyone who read the masthead and saw that Lindermayer was in charge of book reviews, and then compared her section to the rest of the magazine.

As I noted in my introduction, many approaches pioneered by *C&C* during the 1960s and 1970s became common wisdom in the mainstream Protestant academy. This was not necessarily a bad thing for *C&C,* but it meant that *C&C*'s niche became less distinctive. Some of the debates earlier channeled through its pages moved elsewhere. By around 1980, work in a liberationist paradigm was part of the regular mix of debate in established journals like *Theology Today.* The *Journal of Religious Ethics* (founded in 1973) and the *Journal of Feminist Studies in Religion* (founded in 1985) became major forums in their fields. In this context *C&C* became less central to evolving discussions. Some of its best writers migrated elsewhere just as its financial woes intensified.

C&C did not help this problem with its policy of shorter articles after the mid-1980s. Here it is instructive to return to the comparison with *Sojourners,* which survives not solely through volunteer labor but because it aims for a wider readership than *C&C*—its circulation has often been four or five times higher. This in turn helps explain its less intellectual approach. A more popular approach is neither good nor bad in itself, but it translates into less respect in academia. Howell was experimenting with a shift in a similar direction. Unfortunately, this eroded support among *C&C*'s historic base of professors in Protestant higher education. We have seen that *C&C*'s readers were highly educated, including fully 25 percent in professions or the academy. In 1992, their top suggestion for improvement, from 33 percent of all readers surveyed, was for more in-depth articles.[100] It is easy to multiply anecdotal evidence about how the later *C&C* received reduced respect in the Society of Christian Ethics and the American Academy of Religion. A typical comment from Max Stackhouse appeared in the *New York Times* postmortem on *C&C:* "It was boring, predictable, and filled with empty leftish clichés."[101] Some of this loss of respect overlaps with the syndrome discussed in chapter 9, in which liberation theologies—no matter what their intellectual quality—were not considered serious scholarship. But this only explains half of the problem. *C&C* really did dumb down in some significant ways. Its goal after the mid-1980s was to expand circulation, partly through simplification and popularization, while retaining its core constituency. The actual result was to hold circulation steady while eroding the loyalty of this constituency. One can only speculate whether the alternatives were worse, so that once again (as in the *Commonweal* scenario) the road not taken would also have been a dead-end street.

It bears repeating, however, that the differences in the paths represented by Hoyt, Howell, and Lindermayer (or any realistic alternative that one might imagine) remain variations within a tradition—whether an empty leftish rut or a classic Camaro style—that was not going to change a great deal in the short term. The most decisive issue for *C&C*'s future was the same cycle of rising expenses that caused other journals to seek patrons. During this period several important religious journals did fold.[102] *C&C* survived only under increasing stress. Its circulation held steady after the mid-1970s, but its costs of publishing soared. In 1978 there was a 32 percent jump in the postage bill; in 1990 the bill for postage, rent, and printing added $28,500 in costs, and a 5 percent cost-of-living raise added an additional $10,000.[103] Symbolic of *C&C*'s predicament was the question of where to rent office space. Recall that at first Union provided an office, and in 1947 *C&C* moved across the street into a building that Union purchased for student housing during its postwar boom years. However, Union's financial crisis forced it to sell this building to the Jewish Theological Seminary in 1978. (This was an interesting episode in *C&C*'s engagement with religious diversity, especially since part of this building had housed St. Vladimir's Russian Orthodox Seminary until 1962; in fact, *C&C* moved into a room that had been its chapel.)[104] For a decade, JTS maintained the rent at the below-market rate which *C&C* was by then paying Union. However, during *C&C*'s last four years the rent soared from $3,000 to $20,000.[105]

Around 1980, *C&C*'s costs of publishing, not including salaries, were about 80 percent of its earned income. Not enough was left over for *C&C* to pay its salaries (roughly 40 percent of its budget) with earned income, but *C&C* could survive with contributions that accounted for about 30 percent of the budget, which stood around $300,000 in 1981. A decade later, non-salary publishing costs substantially exceeded earned income; the 1993 budget projected them at 125 percent. Thus contributions had to rise faster than the overall budget, which had ballooned to $500,000 by the 1990s. Typical totals for contributions, not adjusted for inflation, grew from less than $100,000 per year before 1980 to more than $200,000 after 1990. (They even reached $300,000 in the last year, but this was an artificially high figure reflecting emergency contributions at the end.) Even so, toward the end, *C&C* could not balance its budget. With each passing month its reserve fund lost more money.

C&C tried many angles to make ends meet. By 1991 this "biweekly" appeared only seventeen times per year.[106] It switched to pulp paper in 1981, making the magazine's graphics inferior to *Sojourners*, which used glossy paper and more color, as well as *First Things*, which struck a refined pose with expensive paper and an elegant layout.

More importantly, *C&C* spent increasing staff time raising money. Although *C&C* relied on contributions throughout its history, money had rarely been a central preoccupation infusing its day-to-day operations. Its leaders held secure academic jobs, and only the people hired to do promotion spent much time worrying about fund appeals. By the late 1980s, *C&C* was controlled by a non-academic staff who worried all the time about raising money. Lindermayer complained of "moments when *C&C* seems more like a fund-raising machine than a magazine."[107] For all *C&C*'s laments about spiraling postage rates, its salary costs rose just as fast, inching up to 45 percent of the budget in the last few years.[108] This fed a downward spiral. The more money *C&C* had to raise, the more staff time this required, and the more staff time, the more money was needed. Increasingly *C&C* depended on wealthy individual donors and foundation grants.[109] This style and scale of fund-raising was not sustainable. The staff burnout it caused was the immediate occasion for *C&C*'s collapse.

Throughout this process *C&C* leaned more heavily on allies in the Interchurch Center. By this time it was financially independent of Union, although it still drew on the school for work study students, meeting rooms, and the critical matter of recruiting writers. As the academic collective model receded into the past, the board of directors picked up the slack. Both the board and editorial advisory panel were dominated by people from New York ecumenical circles, such as *C&C*'s longtime lawyer William Ellis, publisher Louis Oliver Gropp, Donald Wilson of the Presbyterian Church, and Audrey Miller of the WCC's Friendship Press.[110] By 1988 the twenty-two-member board included only three professors in a sea of ecumenical bureaucrats and business leaders.[111]

C&C's path of least resistance in fund-raising was to seek grants for special projects from sources in the ecumenical network, such as a grant from the Densford Fund of Riverside Church for coverage of Native American issues, and a $10,000 grant from the Episcopal Church Foundation for 1992 to increase readership.[112] Shortly before *C&C* folded, the

Lilly Foundation provided $50,000 for writing on urban ministry, but such large-scale funding was an exception in the magazine's career.[113] Insofar as *C&C* had big-ticket benefactors, most of them came from in and around the Interchurch Center.

C&C thus linked its fortunes to allies who were also embattled and beleaguered. We have seen that Union faced a crisis so acute that transferring *C&C* to a new landlord was the least of its concerns. It lost half of its faculty between 1970 and 1974. This was merely more dramatic, not less severe, than pressures inside the Interchurch Center. In 1968 the NCC had 187 program staff, but by 1989 it had only 61.[114] Several national church offices left New York, with much talk about saving money and reconnecting with the heartland; for example, the United Church of Christ moved to Cleveland and the Presbyterian Church (U.S.A.) moved to Louisville. Offices that maintained part of their operations in New York faced extreme stress. In 1988 one of *C&C*'s strongest allies, the National Division of the United Methodist Board of Global Ministries, was forced to eliminate seventeen positions. In 1996 the WCC faced a 16 percent cut in staff, on top of 20 percent cuts earlier in the decade, because it had racked up a $16.5 million deficit against a $64 million income.[115] These cuts came from budgets that were not large to begin with. In 1978, the NCC's entire budget was only 80 percent of the budget of Billy Graham's organization—and $24 million of its $30 million total was spent by the program unit that included the NCC's relief agency, Church World Service.[116]

Much of this crisis resulted from ideological conflicts similar to those inside *C&C*, expanding the picture I have painted of liberals and radicals divided against themselves while both were under attack from conservatives. Another part resulted from sociopolitical crises in the city of New York. To state the matter bluntly, fewer people wanted to live in Manhattan on the border of Harlem. This compounded Union's crisis and helped provoke the exodus of ecumenical bureaucrats from Morningside Heights. Thus it weakened *C&C*'s resource pool and affected its vitality in ways somewhat tangential to its ideological strife. Yet as long as journals still thrive in the Big Apple, there is only so far one can push the external explanations. The key problems were internal to the Protestant world.

Elizabeth Verdesi diagnosed the NCC's problems (and by extension *C&C*'s) in her response to an analysis by Tracy Early that summarized the NCC's crumbling finances. Early commented that "the NCC has managed to annoy the center and scandalize the right without exciting the left."[117] Verdesi explained why one such "unexcited" group, Church Women United (CWU), had left the NCC: CWU programs were undercut by NCC fees for its core budget; CWU wanted to recruit Roman Catholics and an NCC connection held it back; and CWU had the "passion to be on the cutting edge of social issues, without waiting for the NCC's ponderous machinery to approve." Moreover, Verdesi continued, related problems were undermining an NCC working group to which she currently belonged. Whenever the group met, it spent half its time "trying to understand the NCC's convoluted finances and finding means to raise funds" for its single staff person. Meanwhile, its denominational backers demanded evidence that the group had accomplished anything worth funding. "How can anything worthwhile happen when the Working Group must spend so much energy merely surviving?" asked Verdesi. She then asked (echoing Early) whether her committee had been set up to fail. Did the NCC function "to carry on certain programs, including some too hot to be handled by the denominations, but ones that would never be strong enough to be effective? Isn't this how church bodies . . . all too often operate? Say the right words, pass the resolution, appoint the committee. . . . But then consciously or unconsciously we structure those concerns in such a way that nothing will really happen."[118]

Verdesi's complaints barely need rewriting if we substitute *C&C* for NCC. Too much of *C&C*'s effort was spent merely surviving, and *C&C*, too, had a "ponderousness" that hampered efforts to move in fresher intellectual directions, improve its graphics, and recruit new constituencies. Is there a more vivid example of setting oneself up for failure than trying to produce a journal in the 1990s without a serious use of desktop computers?[119] As one interviewee summarized, "*C&C* walked with a limp for so long that it forgot there was any other way to walk."[120] Who could blame readers if they cut loose?

In the harsh light of pragmatic church politics, it may be too much to expect leaders of ecumenical Protestantism to support a project—whether an NCC agency or a journal—that was committed to significant social critique but was *not* set up to fail. (Consider how much flak the Presbyterians received in 1993 from the *Presbyterian Layman* simply for supporting a gathering of Christian feminists called the Re-Imagining Conference.) And *C&C* was not blameless; its enemies could point to real weaknesses. Still, *C&C*'s historic backers in the mainline churches can find money for enterprises—even admittedly imperfect ones—that they consider priorities. Denominations subsidize seminaries and journals like the *Lutheran;* few suburban churches fail to find enough money for spacious parking lots. If they cannot build support for operations like *C&C*—which have some potential to become less blameworthy if they are not set up to fail—then what will be the long-term consequences? Projects *become* priorities, despite the efforts of well-funded attackers like the IRD, through allies who actively build support for them. For a textbook case in setting up Christian feminism for failure, consider defunding all the journals that provide a counterweight to the *Presbyterian Layman.* At some point, pragmatic retreat shades into complicity. What makes sense as a concession to avoid paralyzing controversy begins to function more like a death wish—a preference to let an institution go to the grave with an older generation, rather than facilitate the changes needed to set it up for success with another generation. Commenting on Union Seminary, James Washington says that "the role of the ecumenical seminary depends on one's perspective of how the ecumenical movement has changed. It is no longer run by white Protestant males . . . but its disposition depends on to what degree those who still long for the old days allow peaceful, healthful change to take place. After all, they do still control the money."[121]

Delores Williams made a related comment about *C&C.* Refusing to strike the suggested celebratory / nostalgic tone in its final issue, she asked, "Where are the well-heeled, financially prosperous Christian liberals who could afford to endow this journal?" For Williams, *C&C*'s death symbolized "the impotence of Christianity" in the face of the "economic aspects of the new world order." Jim Gittings's article in the same issue summed up the question posed by *C&C*'s death with his title, "Ecumenism: Dead in the Water?"[122]

The Bottom Line: Was This Death Inevitable?

Must it be so? Did *C&C* really have to die? I believe that the answer is yes and no: a continuing life was imaginable, although not without major changes. Let us summarize the factors we have considered. Recall my argument about *C&C*'s fate at its macro level, that is, the way its overall trajectory relates to long-term trends in our society. This book as a whole has described the polarization between the neoconservative and liberationist wings that emerged from *C&C*'s classic liberal constituency. *C&C* took the left fork of this divide and tried to sustain a conversation between moderates and radicals within the left-liberal camp. Along with the rise of neoconservative power since 1968, institutional resources and prospects for alliances with elites (things that Niebuhr's *C&C* could presuppose) increasingly followed the neoconservatives toward the right. Meanwhile, the upcoming generation of *C&C*'s core constituency divided. Some remained loyal, others defected toward more radical positions and / or various forms of identity politics—and the largest group never entered *C&C*'s pool of potential subscribers at all because of the problems of mainline Protestantism in holding the interest of youth. Within this dwindling constellation of resources, *C&C*'s choices were defensible in self-interest terms (although for *C&C* the moral content was primary). No doubt *C&C* alienated many readers when it turned toward radical and feminist positions around 1970—but it probably would have lost more readers if it had tried to stay the course of centrist liberalism. Similarly, I doubt that rethinking its basic liberation paradigm would have helped *C&C* in 1993, although there are some ways that it might have become more vital for a new generation, notably by more engagement with emergent academic debates and popular culture.

What about explanations for *C&C*'s failure at the micro level of budgets, personnel, and so on? Although I have noted many significant factors, the major reason why *C&C* folded was dwindling institutional resources compared with expenses. Circulation remained steady and shifts in content were limited, but costs for salaries, postage, and rent escalated markedly. *C&C* always had a precarious financial existence and a symbiotic relationship with the New York ecumenical network. Financial crises at Union in the 1970s led *C&C* to turn toward benefactors in the Interchurch Center, but these allies faced their own crises throughout the 1980s. Like almost all journals of opinion, *C&C* needed some kind of "angel." When it failed to find one, it began to spend excessive time on fund-raising. Eventually its staff burned out from the stress. Viewed in this light, the final outcome appears inevitable: the viability of this model of Camaro was coming to an end. There is no ambiguity about this point if we assume that *C&C* had to retain the institutional configuration it adopted after the mid-1970s. There was no way forward without major change.

At the same time, *C&C*'s final process of closing was extremely abrupt. As one interviewee put it, "After crying wolf all these years, at the end *C&C* hardly cried wolf at all."[123] On March 2, 1993, *C&C* mailed an emergency appeal to subscribers. It said that *C&C* needed a major infusion of money—a quarter million dollars a year above current income for three years—and it was hoping for a miracle. Otherwise, it would fold.[124] One month earlier, Howell had informed the executive committee that he planned to retire. A special task force on *C&C*'s options for the future had been hastily formed; it was asked for a recommendation in less than a month.[125]

The "hope for a miracle" language in the March 2 letter was a compromise. It was vague enough to appease people on the task force, plus their allies in and around the editorial advisory panel, who were trying to imagine a "leaner and meaner" *C&C*.[126] However, it basically assumed that death was a foregone conclusion unless someone offered an endowment large enough to allow the staff to stop scrambling for grants, but otherwise continue with minimal changes. The letter to readers spoke in generalities about money for a transitional process and more promotion.

An internal document that provided a rationale for the $250,000 request was not much more specific: it envisioned using $85,000 a year to hire two new editors (one to replace Howell) and $100,000 for a reserve fund, fund-raising, and promotion.[127]

The deadline for this miracle to appear was immediate. The letter was mailed on March 2, the final vote was taken before the end of the March, and *C&C*'s last issue was dated April 12, 1993 (that is, the issue was in production throughout March). Even though *C&C* quoted Niebuhr's famous words from the 1954 crisis—"We do not promise or threaten to go on forever" but "merely desire to serve the church and our generation as long as a sufficient number of friends regard our services as worthwhile"—*C&C* was leaning strongly toward folding before it mailed the appeal.[128] Once it became clear that no angel would appear with half a million dollars, the issue being tested was not how much support could be mobilized for a new vision of *C&C* but whether *C&C* could pay off its bills, including the severance pay owed to the exiting staff. Despite much talk about dying with dignity and *C&C* going out "at the top of its game," the major impression was of panic. *C&C*'s leaders believed that they had already exhausted every option and that a quick death was the only responsible course of action, like putting a wounded animal out of its misery rather than watching it bleed to death slowly.

Studying internal documents and interviewing *C&C* insiders, I found little evidence that *C&C* fully investigated two survival strategies that seem obvious to me, from my dual vantage point as *C&C*'s historian and an academic. It made little effort to reroot itself in a larger academic institution, as *C&C* rooted itself in Union during its first thirty years, and as umpteen academic journals root themselves all the time. Nor did it seriously consider restructuring and downscaling its staff, shifting some responsibilities to an editorial collective committed to *C&C* as part of ongoing academic commitments. (Again, this was *C&C*'s basic strategy for thirty years, one that many academic journals pursue with success, but one that *C&C* abandoned for a stand-alone professional staff by the 1980s.) *C&C* did make some tentative explorations in both these directions, but they were too little and too late.[129]

Projections from *C&C* budgets allow speculation that the magazine's institutional prospects might have been hopeful if it had pursued these strategies more patiently. The new venture could not have been a financial powerhouse, but its budget might have stabilized in line with its historic pattern. *C&C* never really entered the world of desktop publishing, and it could have easily switched to a monthly format. If it had done so while holding onto 10,000 subscribers—recall that circulation was stable at 13,000—

it should have been able to bring nonsalary costs in line with subscription and advertising income. In fact, it might have covered these costs plus one salary line if it had found an institutional home willing to subsidize some costs for office space, computer networking, accounting, and so on. Such a scenario seems plausible in light of the resources that seminaries pour into in-house journals of various kinds.

At that point the key to solvency would have been cutting salary costs through creating an editorial collective, bringing the payroll into line with reasonable projections of income from contributions and / or endowment income. Such a downsizing scenario also seems plausible in light of the pressures to publish or perish among young academics. If this model had succeeded, significant salary costs for seeking grants and editing could have been eliminated, and the remaining shortfall might have been manageable through a traditional year-end appeal to subscribers, ideally supplemented by a push for an endowment during the transitional period. This, too, seems plausible at least in the short run. *C&C* raised $225,000 a year over its last four years; my projections only assumed ongoing subsidies between $75,000 and $100,000, plus one-time contributions for transition costs. All of this is speculative, but if this scenario is in fact credible, then the cause of *C&C*'s death appears as much a lack of morale and imagination as a lack of resources.[130]

Of course, the factors of morale and resources are mutually reinforcing. In *C&C*'s final days, the problem of imagining a viable future was not leisurely and abstract. It was the decision of a severely overburdened staff and board, facing deficits that were growing with each passing month. If *C&C* failed, it was set up to fail. For years it tried to address problems that it could not solve by itself, and there is plenty of blame to go around.

I began this book talking about bridge-building, and I want to end it the same way. *C&C* attempted to create a discourse that could bridge several divides: between generations within liberal Protestant social thought, among several contentious communities committed to liberation theologies, and between religious communities and public issues. Despite many imperfections, *C&C* sustained this approach from the late 1960s until 1993. Over time, demoralization and inadequate resources created a situation where it could not imagine how to continue.

One of *C&C*'s most insightful obituaries, by editorial advisory panel member Maxine Phillips, appeared in *Dissent* magazine. It built on an analogy between the Democratic Party and mainline Protestant institutions, setting both within a neoconservative dominant culture. Is it possible to imagine the Democratic Party as a vehicle for addressing concerns of African Americans, women, low-income people, and others who seek changes in the U.S. class structure and foreign policy? The question is not whether a politician like Bill Clinton can do this but whether one can imagine elements of the party, perhaps only at a local level, that can enact policy changes from within the system and / or respond constructively to pressures from more radical movements? If we cannot imagine this, does this imply giving up on addressing these concerns at all, at the level of policy? Are Clinton's efforts to distance himself from the left and co-opt Reagan Democrats really the best hope of the left? Is there no imaginable bridge to concretely empowering people further to the left?

Similarly, can we imagine institutions of mainline Protestantism that are vehicles for the energies of young people who value cultural pluralism, presuppose the gains of feminism, and have postmodern cultural sensibilities? Why would the brightest activists, musicians, and artists of this generation ally themselves with existing churches? Again, the question is not whether a neighborhood Presbyterian church in its present form can do this—we know that such churches have been losing this generation's allegiance—but whether there are spaces within the church that can generate this energy. Does the only hope for mainline churches lie in becoming more like fundamentalists—which is roughly the Protestant version of writing off the left and courting Reagan Democrats? Will this have the same results in youth and minority apathy that we see in voter turnout on election day? Should the left-liberals within Protestantism simply give up and leave the church to atrophy, just as radicals write off the Democrats? It is easy to understand why they would do so; still one wonders where they will go. Presupposing such reasoning Phillips wrote as follows:

> C&C could never be a magazine only for people concerned about specific issues or constituencies. It had to be a magazine of the coalition. That coalition no longer holds in the Democratic party, nor does it hold in mainline Protestantism. This does not mean the end of liberalism among Protestants. There are plenty of people out there staffing soup kitchens, involved in urban ministry and peace and justice activities. Still, there is no strong institutionally identifiable movement for the "left" as there appears to be for the right. Did C&C collapse because it was too anchored to dying institutional structures? It tried to bridge the space between what was and what is being born. The bridge couldn't bear the weight, but the space must still be crossed.[131]

Conclusion: Waiting for the Ghost of Tom Joad

As we approach the year 2000 and look back on the history of *C&C,* it is time to set aside the classic liberal complaint about Niebuhr's Christian realism: that his vision was too pessimistic about the prospects for U.S. society and human progress in general. If anything, Niebuhr's postwar ideas appear excessively optimistic in retrospect. Yes, they were grim and chastened compared with more idealistic positions that came before and after. Although this point has become a cliché, it bears repeating, especially when we compare Niebuhr with the most uncritical optimists on the current scene, the apologists for free market capitalism. And yes, Niebuhr's pragmatic rather than purist approach to social activism has important strengths. It deserves greater respect from some groups on the left whose aspirations are more sweeping. Surely pragmatic success belongs somewhere amid a larger list of virtues, even for those of us who find Niebuhr's definitions of "real practical results" overly narrow.

The point I would stress, however, is Niebuhr's basic confidence about the future of liberalism—an optimism that is now very much in question. At *C&C's* inception, Niebuhr imagined the western world as a house about to be destroyed by a tornado of fascism, yet even then he had enough confidence to expound on his vision for the postwar global order, defending this as "imperialistic realism." To be sure, he never tired of stressing the harsh realities of geopolitical conflict and the failures of Enlightenment idealism. Nevertheless, he believed that a democratic capitalism suitably tempered by the checks and balances of the New Deal was the best system that one could hope for. More pointedly, it was worth promoting on a global scale and fighting for, even up to the brink of a nuclear war. In

1959, despite significant injustices that still occupied his attention, Niebuhr's summary judgment in *C&C* was that "in the modern day domestic problems have been tolerably solved."[1]

By the mid-1990s, Bruce Springsteen's vision seemed more compelling, as he sang in a quiet authoritative voice reminiscent of Woody Guthrie, behind the moan of a harmonica like Bob Dylan's:

> Shelter line stretchin' 'round the corner
> Welcome to the new world order
> Families sleepin' in their cars in the southwest
> No home, no job, no peace, no rest.[2]

In Springsteen's North America, the New Deal coalition, which had been part and parcel of *C&C*'s earlier hopes, appeared to be down for the count. True, the president was a Democrat, but in the name of consensus Bill Clinton promoted policies as much like Nixon's as Kennedy's—and still he found himself on the defensive against attacks from the right, as when a leading politician compared him to Joseph Stalin: "Behind our New Deals and New Frontiers and Great Societies you find, with only a difference of power and nerve, the same sort of person who gave the world its Five-Year Plans and Great Leaps Forward."[3] After nearly two decades of rule by people with similar perceptions, the richest 1 percent of the U.S. population owned about 40 percent of the marketable wealth—up 100 percent since Ronald Reagan's first term and rapidly rising—and the real wages of production and nonsupervisory workers had fallen almost 20 percent between 1973 and 1989.[4] Of course, some people were successfully riding the wave of economic growth. For them Springsteen was a whiner, and what the country really needed was less affirmative action and more tax relief for the rich. However, huge numbers had already been swamped by this wave, especially in the inner cities, and many people were anxious about the future: women one divorce away from poverty, families at risk of losing medical insurance with their next layoff or move, possible victims of corporate downsizing (not least in the lower ranks of academia), and parents concerned about their children in a nation where prisons were a leading growth industry and the labor market increasingly pressured workers to sell their labor for less in a race to the bottom with everyone else, anywhere in the world. Springsteen spoke to their fears:

> Highway patrol choppers comin' up over the ridge
> Hot soup on a campfire under the bridge
> . . .
> Waitin' for when the last shall be first and the first shall be last
> In a cardboard box 'neath the underpass.[5]

Whereas Niebuhr watched his tornado from afar, Springsteen surveyed a landscape that had already been leveled by a tornado. He sang of a steelworker in Youngstown, a city with "smokestacks reaching like the arms of God into a beautiful sky of soot and clay." His father had worked in the mill after World War II, but

> Now the yard's just scrap and rubble;
> He said, "Them big boys did what Hitler couldn't do."
> These mills they built the tanks and bombs
> That won this country's wars
> We sent our sons to Korea and Vietnam
> Now we're wondering what they were dyin' for.

For this worker, the promise of democracy was being betrayed. The military-industrial policies that had paid his salary appeared as a deal with the devil, symbolized by Springsteen's image of the steel mill as a scene from hell.

> From the Monongahela valley
> To the Mesabi iron range
> To the coal mines of Appalachia
> The story's always the same
> Seven hundred tons of metal a day
> Now sir you tell me the world's changed.
> Once I made you rich enough
> Rich enough to forget my name.[6]

Conservatives did not ignore such issues entirely, but their proposed solutions called for more of what had caused the problems in the first place: more unbridled growth and downward pressure on wages; more scapegoating of feminists, people of color, and nonmilitary bureaucrats; and more attacks on institutions that seek to minimize the human costs or share the profits, on the grounds that they were unrealistic and uncompetitive. Gary Dorrien successfully challenges their economic logic at the level of theory. For example, he asks how conservatives can attack left-liberal reforms as interfering with the free market at the same time that corporate welfare (subsidies, bailouts, tax breaks, etc.) exceeds $100 billion per year. In other words, the question is not *whether* but *how* the economy will be politicized. Dorrien suggests plausible policies that could build economic democracy within a market economy. What he has not yet shown—and he is not alone in this—is how his suggestions (such as a Swedish plan to democratize control of corporate capital) can become a rallying point for successful U.S. coalition politics.[7]

Dorrien's speculations on the policies he could implement if he held power are an essential contribution, yet they remain far removed from the world that Springsteen evokes. At least for the moment, Springsteen can only narrate credible hopes in small-scale acts of solidarity and resistance. A white Texan who has been incited by the Klan to murder a Vietnamese immigrant puts his knife back in his pocket at the decisive moment, recognizing the common threads of their lives. An impoverished Mexican farmer dreams of a better life and prays for the "saints' blessings and grace to carry me safely to your arms, there across the border." An agent of the border patrol sees a young woman in a holding pen with a child in her arms, and she looks like the wife he is mourning; he abandons his job and helps her cross the line. Sixty years earlier, in *The Grapes of Wrath,* his novel about the Great Depression, John Steinbeck had said all we need to know about people who equate the New Deal with Stalinism. When a migrant worker asks his boss to define the "reds" he so despises, this is the answer: "A red is any son-of-a-bitch that wants thirty cents an hour when we're paying twenty-five!"[8] Springsteen evokes a passage from this novel, Tom Joad's last words to his mother before he becomes a fugitive from the laws made by such bosses.

> Now Tom said "Mom, wherever there's a cop beatin' a guy,
> Wherever a hungry newborn baby cries . . .
> Wherever somebody's strugglin' to be free
> Look in their eyes Mom you'll see me.[9]

Approaching the twenty-first century, Springsteen is searching for the ghost of Tom Joad. In the 1930s, Tom Joad's commitments drew explicitly on the Bible and religious mysticism. "Maybe it's like [Preacher] Casey says," Tom tells his mother. "A fella ain't got a soul of his own, but on'y a piece of a big one."[10] In the new century, what role will Protestant social thought play for upcoming generations who live in this post–New Deal landscape of the super-rich and the unemployed, the technological elite and the prison-industrial complex, the Promise Keepers and battered wives, the militias and the scapegoated migrant workers? Will there be a role for academics like those who gravitated to *C&C,* those engaged with public religion from the standpoint of various underdogs? Neoconservatives content to swim with the corporate sharks can move to such journals as *First Things,* which contradicts most of Niebuhr's cherished ideals of social justice but does emulate him in one respect: he worked from within the "realistic" horizon of New Deal liberalism, and they do the same thing presupposing the horizon of the neoconservative new world order. Liberals from the more staid wing of *C&C*'s old constituency can still opt for the *Christian Century*. Counterculturalists with relatively low demands for academic sophistication can move to *Sojourners*. Those reluctant to embrace these options are adrift. Who can blame them for defecting to religious apathy or turning toward various academic venues less engaged with public religion?

The problem is not lack of prospective interest. *C&C*'s circulation remained fairly steady to the end, at numbers lower than peaks in the mid-1960s and late 1970s but higher than any time before 1963. Polls bear out Maxine Phillips's comment that *C&C*'s death in 1993 "does not mean the end of liberalism among Protestants. There are plenty of people out there staffing soup kitchens, involved in urban ministry and peace and justice activities."[11] It is easy to find people with sharp social critiques, serious moral and spiritual interests, and a wary interest in Christianity. Springsteen is just one among many other popular artists who articulate criticisms of social oppression and alienation, often employing Christian symbolism.

Still the question remains: What is the legacy of *C&C* for people who resonate with these ideas? When I first began to study these issues, as a graduate student at Yale Divinity School in the 1980s, I commonly heard political and theological positions like *C&C*'s denigrated in neoconservative terms. *C&C* was an example of the false consciousness of a new class of cultural elites, a long-discredited replay of an uncritically optimistic social gospel, a nonserious example of the decline of real theology, a betrayal of tradition disguised as a effort at revitalization, and an accommodation to a liberal culture that required transcendent critique. Niebuhr's name came up repeatedly as a warrant for these judgments.

I was convinced that this was bad social thought, since I found pluralist and neo-Marxian approaches more illuminating than neoconservatism on most issues. And since the central religious arguments I found in the best texts of *C&C* bore such a tangential resemblance to the characterizations of "radical theologies" that were being rejected, I increasingly understood that the gap between these perceptions was a matter of paradigm conflict: liberation theologies were written to address one set of problems and judged according to another set. Analyzing how this paradigm conflict unfolded and how it related to larger struggles for hegemony in postwar U.S. history has been the goal of this book.

As I have been at pains to show, however, there was continuity as well as change at *C&C*: its changes took place within a continuous tradition. This is what *C&C* leaders such as John Bennett chose to stress about their history. And at Yale, despite the problem of translating between paradigms, I resisted giving up the search for a common language for conversation with the Niebuhrian tradition, because I believed then—and still believe—that a religious-political language of human sin, the power of God to radically critique shortcomings of human cultures, and the dangers of human pride can be helpful and good. (Indeed, the critical and deconstructive dimensions of this language—although not its theological grounding—are not hard to relate to a postmodern idiom that has been common wisdom in much of the humanities.)[12] The issue was how to deploy this broad tradition of social criticism appropriately in concrete historical situations made up of flesh-and-blood people. Within a Niebuhrian paradigm, which *particular* sins, shortcomings, and prideful acts were under scrutiny? (In the postmodern idiom, which were being targeted for deconstruction?) Which underdogs in what power hierarchies were being supported? Were they the most appropriate ones? I dismissed pretensions to a neutral scrutiny of all the possibilities, whether these were pretensions of speaking objectively, as if from nowhere, or of speaking contextually but trying to be situated everywhere at the same time. Particular options were inescapable.

At its inception, *C&C* had appealed to the transcendent power of God to judge prideful human acts as made concrete in Adolf Hitler and Joseph Stalin. *C&C*'s leaders had launched attacks on the complacent acceptance of liberal capitalism—unambiguously in the 1930s, and as a significant theme (however overshadowed at times) even at the height of the cold war. But at Yale in the Reagan era, the Niebuhrian God primarily attacked human pride made concrete—not in contemporary fascists and corporate oligarchs but in the supposed accommodation of liberation theologians (and other radicals) to U.S. dominant culture. It was as if the German Confessing Church that opposed Nazism came back—but was unable to distinguish between the pride of Hitler and the pride of Jews who resisted the Holocaust. I even heard comparisons between the German liturgy imposed by Hitler and the feminist movement for gender-inclusive language. In both cases, so the argument went, humans were daring to revise religious traditions for historical reasons. Of course, it was quite obvious, at least to me, that traditions continually change and that the different historical circumstances made all the difference in this case.[13]

If the issues were framed in this way, I thought it was clear that some form of radical theology was the most appropriate application of Niebuhrian insights, given the realities of our current situation. Long ago, when I first began the research that led to this book, I hoped that by tracing the concrete application of Niebuhrian rhetorics over time, I could convince my theological colleagues of this point—that they should stop using Niebuhr to resist radical theologies, and start using him to learn from them.

Since then I have become more of an interdisciplinary historian and less of a theologian with each passing year, and I have come to frame the central analytical issue more broadly. The question is not whether liberation theologies are the preferred academic theologies: some are and some are not, depending on the theologian and the issue. The central issue is how Protestant social thought relates to hegemonic power structures and various counterhegemonic movements, no matter what paradigms they use for theology and social analysis. All kinds of people can learn from studying this issue, but it holds special interest for those who would like to see Protestants collaborating less with elite power structures and making larger contributions to movements for social justice. This is a crucial question, not only for religious people who need broader secular allies but also for secular activists and cultural workers who need religious allies. Bridges need to be built from both sides. Despite its limitations, *C&C* was among the better bridges that we had. If it is not replaced, I believe that this represents a significant loss for the left at large, as well as an example of what is, in effect, a sort of death wish on the part of liberal Protestantism.

I decided to mention the comparison between Hitler and inclusive language after I read Adrienne Rich's poem "The Burning of Paper Instead of Children," which takes its title from Daniel Berrigan's words at his trial for napalming draft records at Catonsville ("Apologies, good friends, for this fracture of good order, the burning of paper instead of children"). Rich describes her neighbor's outrage after her children burned a math textbook. "The burning of a book," says the neighbor, "arouses terrible sensations in me, memories of Hitler; there are few things that upset me so much as the idea of burning a book."[14] Similarly, my neoconservative colleagues at Yale were upset when various academic radicals (including myself) turned against established religious-political paradigms. Of course, we did not literally burn books, but we did revise and partly repudiate some inherited approaches based on our sense of the necessary priorities: to focus on great issues of unnecessary suffering and struggles for social justice, and to judge our writing by how well it articulated and responded to these issues.

Rich's poem reflects on the limits of received language for talking about such matters. She says, "People suffer highly in poverty and it takes dignity and intelligence to overcome this suffering," and she calls language "a map of our failures."[15] I suppose that most readers of this book can supply all too many examples of these problems. Indeed, the effort required to set such awareness aside and move on with the everyday business of life—what some might call alienation, or callousness, or the absence of grace, or even realism—can hardly fail to weigh heavily on anyone, whether consciously or measured in denial. Yet to articulate these problems clearly and address them constructively is no easy matter.

In debates in the academy during the past few years, there has been a productive tension between Audre Lorde's use of Rich's work when she said, "The Master's Tools Will Never Dismantle the Master's House," and Hazel Carby, who replied that "the Master appropriated these tools along with the labor of those he exploited, and it is high time that they be reclaimed."[16] This difference in emphasis, more than any other on the current intellectual scene, captures the tension between *C&C*'s best separatist, nationalist, and countercultural voices on one side, and those who want to reclaim aspects of its pragmatic progressivism in an oppositional way, on the other. My reason for citing Rich is not to take sides in this debate—in fact, my sympathies tilt toward Carby—but because Rich helps us reflect, one last time in these pages, on the purposes and limits of writing about human suffering. Dorothee Sölle puts the matter this way:

> Asked to write a poem about peace
> I feel shame for those who ask
> do they live on a different planet
> what are their hopes
> and for whom?
>
> Gases meant for rice farmers
> have been tested
> they can be harmless
> if the humidity and the wind
> are right
>
> So I'd suggest
> We talk about the wind.[17]

Throughout its history, *C&C* addressed issues that cannot easily be reduced to academically respected prose or "responsible" policy proposals: issues of deep suffering and passion, utopian hope, understandings of God. It tried to write about them in a broadly accessible way and to maintain a bridge between its ideal vision and the pragmatic possibilities attainable in a world that it understood as tragic. How can this be done? What are the best trade-offs, since it is hard to imagine how anyone could do this in a satisfying way? In a broad sense, these were *C&C*'s questions throughout its history, and they remained profound problems even when *C&C*'s writing about them was formulaic or moralistic. These became my problems in interpreting *C&C*'s history. They will remain problems as long as people explore how religious traditions might contribute to social justice.

Christian realism sought to build on the concrete realities of experience, but—whether it succeeded or ended with false universals and Munich analogies run amok—it was caught between the limitations of its language and the suffering of the poor. Liberation theologies speak about empowering oppressed people, but they do so in books that compete in publishing markets and academic prestige markets. Books that analyze liberation theologies and try to imagine the standpoints of underdogs are also caught in this tension. The point is not to question whether books about struggles for justice are worth writing. ("Speaking of the wind," continues Sölle, "It can be lenient / Rice plants can be merciful".) Rather, it is to remember that their uses are limited.

I conclude with a poem by W. H. Auden, written after the fall of Poland to the Nazis during *C&C*'s original crisis:

> Defenseless under the night
> Our world in stupor lies:
> Yet, dotted everywhere
> Ironic points of light
> Flash out wherever the just
> Exchange their messages:
> May I, composed like them
> Of Eros and dust,
> Beleagured by the same
> Negation and despair
> Show an affirming flame.

C&C reprinted this poem in a eulogy for Michael Harrington, an activist and scholar whose favorite phrase was "I want to be on the left of the possible." *C&C* called Harrington "a pragmatist in a field of ideologues who was yet grounded in theory and principles."[18] These words make an equally fitting eulogy for *C&C* itself, if we widen their resonance to take in the full breadth of *C&C*'s interests. Sadly, Auden's poem reads almost as well today, as a comment on the victims of the new world order, as it did when it was first written.

Appendix: A Note on Sources and Research Methods

This appendix discusses my system for analyzing *C&C*'s text, my use of *C&C*'s internal records, and the personal interviews I conducted. I examined every page of *C&C*'s published text, at least to the extent of noting the titles of articles and skimming for their general arguments. However, since fifty-two volumes of *C&C* represent a huge number of pages with a great deal of repetition, I identified a random cross section of issues to examine more closely. It represents slightly over 10 percent of *C&C*'s total output. Every four months, I selected the first issue of the month and read it from cover to cover. I coded all its articles' major and secondary themes as part of my standard note-taking; this is the basis for my claims about the proportions of *C&C*'s subjects in various periods. Since *C&C* had yearly rhythms that affected the sample—such as a summer slump and a tradition of publishing sermons at Christmas—I systematically rotated the months I examined.

In addition, as I worked through the text, I studied all the articles that seemed especially significant for *C&C*'s ongoing transformation, whether or not they fell in my random sample. Often these choices were obvious, as when articles introduced new subjects or started major controversies. At other times my selection process was more intuitive. Articles falling into this category represent another 10 percent of *C&C*'s total output. All in all, I took notes on almost eighteen hundred articles; only the most important are cited in my footnotes.

This book began as a dissertation, published in 1992, which focused only on *C&C*'s career from its founding until the mid-1970s. At this stage of research, before *C&C* folded, I did a relatively limited amount of archival work. The main reason was that the "archives" to which I had access consisted of three none-too-large cardboard file boxes with a hodgepodge of contents, most of which I later found scattered through the larger *C&C* archives. These were culled out by Leon Howell, in consultation with other staff, during a 1992 research trip to New York. They contained an interesting mix of correspondence, financial records, and miscellaneous mementos. Some of my footnotes in the current book cite photocopies and notes from these boxes of documents. At the dissertation stage, they gave ample evidence for my purposes, since I conceived my project primarily as a case study of transformations in Protestant social thought, as reflected in *C&C's* published text. Also, I was aware of the in-fighting among *C&C* staff during the 1980s. I was relieved to be able to bracket this subject, to ask *not* to study the documents about it, and to change the subject when people in interviews lobbied me to write their spins on the story into my book.

When *C&C* stopped publishing in 1993, only three months after I finished the dissertation, I reconsidered my decision to end my narrative in the 1970s. I knew that many readers would be aware of *C&C's* failure and curious about why it happened. Also, it became desirable to make the book a complete history of *C&C* from its beginning to its end. I might not have been so eager to expand, if I had known how much extra work these later stages of research would cost through upsetting the structure and proportion of my earlier manuscript, although I would like to believe that the work of rethinking my arguments in light of the changes of the 1980s and 1990s has made this a stronger book. Be that as it may, the expanded project had a significantly larger archival component.

When *C&C* folded, it left behind eighteen large boxes of documents, now housed in Union Seminary's Burke Library, plus another dozen boxes of financial records stored in the Interchurch Center. As far as possible, I made use of these documents, and I am indebted to the librarians at Burke, who went beyond standard library and archives practice in providing me with access to *C&C* records before they could be processed and officially prepared for research purposes; many archives routinely refuse access to all unprocessed materials. Unfortunately, the *C&C* records arrived at Burke in a rather disorganized form during the scramble to close the journal, and they remain largely uncataloged except for a rough inventory of the contents of the boxes, now supplemented by a few notes that I left to orient future researchers. Even such basics as a complete set of minutes and accurate labels of boxes are lacking. I was unable to find minutes from 1945 to 1957, but I did find two sets of 1976–78 minutes that are not the same. Because of these constraints and the large volume of papers, I was unable to work through every box systematically or to devise a satisfying scheme for a scientific cross section. Quite likely some useful aspects of these records remain untapped. However, I believe that I have examined the most relevant material in ample amounts for present purposes.

In addition to analyzing *C&C*'s text and archives, I spoke with many people who have been involved with *C&C*, directly or indirectly. It should come as no surprise that these informants provided some of the more interesting data either off the record or in contexts where this was ambiguous and I have erred on the side of discretion. In some cases these comments have been essential in informing my arguments about *C&C*'s inner workings. Many of these conversations were lengthy prearranged formal interviews with influential *C&C* figures. However, it is difficult to know where to end my list of "expert informants," since I often discovered, upon informally telling a friend or acquaintance about my research, that our small talk turned into an important "interview." For example, Susan Thornton told me at a Halloween party about her experience in the Black Manifesto sit-in when she was a Union seminarian; Mary Shepard shared childhood memories of Henry Sloane Coffin's church and information about the breakup of Union Seminary's board of directors; and I have checked my analysis of *C&C* against the recollections of a whole range of people. The formal interviews and some of the more important conversations are listed below. Once again, I thank each and every one for their insights and cooperation.

John C. Bennett, Claremont, California, 18 November 1989
Arthur Brandenburg, phone interview, 23 June 1994
Robert McAfee Brown, Claremont, California, 17 November 1989
Richard Butler, Minneapolis, 14 October 1991; New York City, 27 June 1994
James Cone, New York City, 30 June 1994
Wayne Cowan and Arthur Moore, New York City, 5 February 1992
Wayne Cowan and Betty Thompson, New York City, 24 June 1994
Tom Driver, New York City, 6 February 1992
Charles Foster, Atlanta, 22 June 1995
Louis Oliver Gropp, New York City, 29 June 1994
Beverly Harrison, New York City, 5 February 1992, 31 May 1995
Casey Hayden and Paul Buckwalter, Tucson, 15 July 1996
Leon Howell, New York City, 4 February 1992, 7 February 1992
Karen Lattea, phone interview, June 1994
Vivian Lindermayer, New York City, 6 February 1992, 29 June 1994
David Little, Knoxville, 6 March 1996
Dick Lundy, Minneapolis, various conversations, 1991–92
Mary Ann Lundy, Louisville, 24 March 1991
Mary McNamara, New York City, 30 June 1994
Gary MacEoin, Claremont, California, 18 November 1989

Audrey Miller, New York City, 24 June 1994
Howard Moody, New York City, 4 February 1992
Joy and B. Davie Napier, Claremont, California, 17 November 1989
Maxine Phillips, New York City, 28 June 1994
Larry Rasmussen, New York City, 9 February 1992, 28 June 1994
Rosemary Radford Ruether, San Francisco, 21 November 1992
Letty Russell, San Francisco, 21 November 1992
Mary Shepard, Minneapolis, 15 October 1991
Roger Shinn, Southbury, Connecticut, 2 June 1995
Frances Smith, New York City, 6 February 1992
Peggy Steinfels and Robert Hoyt, New York City, 1 July 1994
Kathleen Talvacchia, New York City, 29 June 1994, 1 June 1995
James Wall, phone interview, July 1996
Robert Allen Warrior, San Francisco, 22 November 1992
James Washington, New York City, 28 June 1994, 30 May 1995
Don Wilson, New York City, 24 June 1994

Notes

Preface

1. Cornel West, "Martin Luther King Jr.: Prophetic Christian as Organic Intellectual," in *Prophetic Fragments* (Grand Rapids: Eerdmans, 1988), 3–12; see also his "The Paradox of the Afro-American Rebellion," in *The Sixties without Apology*, ed. Sohnya Sayres et al. (Minneapolis: Univ. of Minnesota Press, 1984), 44–58.

Introduction

1. "The Crisis of Commitment," *Rockland Record,* 1 Dec. 1966, photocopy from *C&C* archives, page number illegible. As discussed in the appendix, *C&C*'s records are now generally sorted into boxes with folders, notebooks, and other materials. However, I began my research before the records were in this form. Therefore, if I know the current box and folder for a document, my notes cite these; if not (as in this case), I cite a photocopy in my possession, from records available at an earlier stage of my research, using the formula "photocopy from *C&C* archives."

2. This decision is discussed in Editors, "Toward Disengagement from South Africa," 28 Nov. 1966, 261–63. All citations in these footnotes are from *Christianity and Crisis* unless otherwise noted.

3. "The Crisis of Commitment," *Rockland Record;* "*Crisis* Continues," *Time,* 25 Feb. 1966, photocopy from *C&C* archives, page number illegible. It is easy to multiply citations in this vein; for example, "Christian Realism," *Newsweek,* 28 Feb. 1966, 61, wrote that "*C and C* has now secured a permanent position of leadership in Protestant journalism" and that "many of *C and C*'s views are shared by Protestantism's leading churchmen; indeed, many of the journal's former editors are now solid members of the liberal establishment in church, government, and foundation posts."

4. Walter LaFeber, *America, Russia, and the Cold War,* 2d ed. (New York: Wiley, 1972), 40–41.

5. Martin Marty, *The Religious Press in America* (New York: Holt, Rinehart and Winston, 1963), 57. On *C&C*'s place in the wider world of U.S. religious journalism, see Marty, "The Religious Press," in *Encyclopedia of the American Religious Experience,* ed. Peter Williams and Charles H. Lippy (New York: Scribner, 1988), 1697–1709; and Edward Tabor Linenthal's essay on *C&C* in *Religious Periodicals of the United States: Academic and Scholarly Journals,* ed. Charles Lippy (Westport, Conn.: Greenwood Press, 1986), 131–34.

6. Leon Howell, "Ernest Lefever at the Edge of Power," 2 Mar. 1981, 44. The Senate Foreign Relations Committee rejected Lefever's nomination in June 1981. Instead, he became an adviser to Secretary of State Alexander Haig on international terrorism and continued as the director of the Ethics and Public Policy Center at Georgetown University, a key node in the network of neoconservative foundations and think tanks.

7. Lary May, introduction to *Recasting America: Culture and Politics in the Age of Cold War,* ed. Lary May (Chicago: Univ. of Chicago Press, 1989), 7.

8. Harvey Cox, "*Playboy*'s Doctrine of Male," 17 Apr. 1961, 56–58, 60; Records of *Christianity and Crisis,* box 1, folder labeled "Reprint Requests," Vivian Cadden (of *Redbook*) to Wayne Cowan, 6 Apr. 1964, Archives of the Burke Library, Union Theological Seminary (New York, N.Y.). Hereafter, citations from these records are truncated to "*C&C* records, box number," plus more detailed information if available. Use of these materials is by courtesy of the Burke Library of Union Theological Seminary in the City of New York. The library takes no responsibility for any possible infringement of copyright laws in the publication of its materials.

9. Niebuhr, "Report on Germany," 14 Oct. 1946, 6–7; Richard Wightman Fox, *Reinhold Niebuhr: A Biography* (New York: Pantheon, 1985), 228–29.

10. Niebuhr, "The King's Chapel and the King's Court," 4 Aug. 1969, 211–12. Clippings in *C&C* records, box 10, scrapbook. Similar evidence is scattered throughout *C&C*'s archives.

11. The Crisis of Commitment," *Rockland Record.*

12. "Christian Realism," *Newsweek,* 28 Feb. 1966, 61. FBI surveillance of civil rights and peace organizations in which Bennett played major roles are documented in Mitchell Hall, *Because of Their Faith: CALCAV and Religious Opposition to the Vietnam War* (New York: Columbia Univ. Press, 1990), and James Findlay, *Church People in the Struggle: The National Council of Churches and the Black Freedom Movement, 1950–1970* (New York: Oxford Univ. Press, 1993). By 1971 *Newsweek* was still respectful of Bennett; in its "*C and C* in Crisis," 22 Mar. 1971, 97–98, it called him "for more than 20 years the most sophisticated theological voice in American politics." However, by this time *Newsweek*'s major argument about *C&C* was that a "whirling cycle of theological fads, from secular to revolutionary theology, diminished the magazine's intellectual coherence."

13. Although coverage peaked in the 1960s, it was not trivial in later years. *C&C* records, box 10, scrapbook, collects various citations and reprints from mainstream media; for example, in "An American Tragedy," *Baltimore Sun,* 24 Feb. 1981, A15, Congresswoman Barbara Mikulski states, "I learned more concrete information [about Central America] from a Maryknoll handout and *Christianity and Crisis* magazine than I had from my own government."

14. Marty, "Religious Press," 1704. It is simply not correct that *C&C*'s interests became narrower. Whether it became "less critical" is more complicated; Marty has a point that *C&C* became less critical *of radical causes.* However, it became more critical of centrist and conservative causes and of the dominant culture in general.

15. Richard John Neuhaus, "Desperately Pastoral," *First Things,* Aug./Sept. 1991, 61; Podhoretz to *C&C,* 17 Feb. 1966, in *C&C* records, box 24, folder labeled "Anniversary night."

16. Gayraud Wilmore, "What Seeds, What Flowers?" 12 Apr. 1993, 86–87.

17. For more discussion see chapter 7.

18. Henry Pitney Van Dusen, "A First Glimpse of South Africa," 16 Feb. 1953, 10–13; Ernest Lefever, "Africa: Tribalism versus the State," 27 Dec. 1965, 281, 279–80. These are extreme examples from *C&C*'s conservative wing, but speaking for *C&C*'s mainstream, Niebuhr also stated that the United States had been a "tutor in civilization to [African] primitive cultures" and that unfortunately in the Congo "the Belgians set untutored tribesmen adrift before they could govern themselves." See Niebuhr, "Laos and Cuba: Problems for Review," 23 Jan. 1961, 209–10; Niebuhr, "The Changing United Nations," 3 Oct. 1960, 133–34.

19. See, e.g., 'Bola Ige, "Africa of the Sixties," 20 Mar. 1961, 35–37; Albert Van Den Heuvel, "A Letter to a White South African Friend," 28 Dec. 1970, 284–86; Beyers Naudé, "The Challenge of Political and Social Justice," 20 Jan. 1975, 323–25; Terry Swicegood, "Funeral at Cradock," 16 Sept. 1985, 342–43; Desmond Tutu, "South Africa's Blacks: Aliens in Their Own Land," 26 Nov. 1984; C. Eric Lincoln, "How Now, America?" 1 Apr. 1968, 59.

20. Dorothee Sölle, "Faith, Theology, and Liberation," 7 July 1976, 139.

21. Bennett, "Retrospect and Prospect," 27 Dec. 1976, 312–13.

22. Niebuhr, "Imperialism and Irresponsibility," 24 Feb. 1941, 6; Angus Dun et al., "Christian Conscience and Weapons of Mass Destruction," 11 Dec. 1950, 165; S. Macon Cowles, "Can We Abolish Jim Crow in the Armed Services?" 18 Oct. 1948, 134; Niebuhr, "Sex Standards in America," 24 May 1948, 65–66.

23. Ursula Niebuhr, "Women and the Church, and the Fact of Sex," 6 Aug. 1951, 108, 109; Reinhold Niebuhr, "The Moral and Political Judgments of Christians," 6 July 1959, 99.

24. Wayne Cowan and Vivian Lindermayer, "An Anniversary Statement," 15 Nov. 1976, 258–61; Bennett, "After Thirty Years," 22 Mar. 1971, 38–40. For more on Forman's Black Manifesto, see chapter 6.

25. Linda Barufaldi and Emily Culpepper, "Androgyny and the Myth of Masculine/Feminine," 16 Apr. 1973, 71; Carter Heyward, "Suffering, Redemption, and Christ," 11 Dec. 1989, 384. Barufaldi and Culpepper's WITCH was identified as the Women's Inspirational Theology Conspiracy from Harvard. On the more famous WITCH called Women's International Conspiracy from Hell, see Alice Echols, *Daring to Be Bad: Radical Feminism in America, 1967–1975* (Minneapolis: Univ. of Minnesota Press, 1989), 96–100, 116–19.

26. Robin Lovin, *Reinhold Niebuhr and Christian Realism* (Cambridge: Cambridge Univ. Press, 1995), 240.

27. There was less continuity than meets the eye on the presidential issue, since *C&C* was more bullish about some candidates than others. Also, its debates started out pitting Democrats versus Republicans, but increasingly evolved into a discussion between Democrats and people alienated from the electoral process. *C&C* formally endorsed a presidential candidate only once, in 1964, but its sympathies were usually obvious.

28. To analyze paradigms is to identify basic components of a group's "way of seeing" or "construction of reality" and to explore how they change. Thomas Kuhn, *The Structure of Scientific Revolutions*, 2d ed. (Chicago: Univ. of Chicago Press, 1970), used this approach to analyze scientific theories. Kuhn defines a paradigm as a system of interpretation that can organize and explain a certain body of evidence for a community that accepts it. Over time, anomalies that cannot easily be explained within a given paradigm become so overwhelming that the community breaks toward a new one—one that uses different standards of evidence to construct reality in a different way. Anthony F. C. Wallace, "Revitalization Movements," *American Anthropologist* 58 (1956): 264–81, compares groups to organisms, and individuals to cells. Just as cells have DNA to coordinate their work, paradigms orient people in the world and help them meet their collective needs. If a new situation introduces stress into the system, people will try to revitalize it with new hierarchy of values and behaviors. This entails a shift like an earthquake and results in a new way of seeing "reality." William McLoughlin uses Wallace's theory to frame his *Revivals, Awakenings, and Reform: An Essay on Religion and Social Change in America, 1607–1977* (Chicago: Univ. of Chicago Press, 1978).

29. For more elaboration see my "Evolving Approaches to U.S. Culture in the American Studies Movement: Consensus, Pluralism, and Contestation for Cultural Hegemony," *Canadian Review of American Studies* 23 (1993), no. 2: 1–55. Examples of the approach I have in mind include Michael Bérubé, *Public Access: Literary Theory and American Cultural Politics* (New York: Verso, 1995); Nancy Fraser, *Unruly Practices: Power, Discourse, and Gender in Contemporary Social Theory* (Minneapolis: Univ. of Minnesota Press, 1989); Bruce Grelle, "Hegemony and the 'Universalization' of Moral Ideas: Gramsci's Importance for Religious Ethics," *Soundings* 78 (1995), no. 3–4: 519–40; Stuart Hall, "Gramsci's Relevance for the Study of Race and Ethnicity," *Journal of Communication Inquiry* 10 (1986), no. 2: 5–27, and other articles in this special issue on Hall; Richard Johnson, "What Is Cultural Studies Anyway?" *Social Text* 16 (1986): 38–80; George Lipsitz, *Time Passages: Collective Memory and American Popular Culture* (Minneapolis: Univ. of Minnesota, 1990); and Cornel West, *Keeping Faith: Philosophy and Race in America* (New York: Routledge, 1994).

30. Not all ways of being an underdog are equally significant, and not all kinds of resistance deserve equal weight. The main measure of a helpful analysis of hegemony is its ability

to integrate multiple factors of power at the same time, while still maintaining a focus on factors that deserve priority in particular contexts. (For example, left-handed people may be underdogs, but a left-handed warden is not an underdog in a prison full of right-handed inmates.) I agree that "some differences are playful; some are poles of world historical systems of domination. Epistemology is about knowing the difference," as Donna Haraway says in "Manifesto for Cyborgs: Science, Technology, and Socialist Feminism in the 1980s," in *Feminism/Postmodernism*, ed. Linda Nicholson (New York: Routledge, 1990), 202–3. Even Ernesto Laclau and Chantal Mouffe, *Hegemony and Socialist Strategy: Towards a Radical Democratic Politics* (London: Verso, 1985), who have an unusually wide-open approach to identifying "the hegemonic"—the opposite end of a continuum from some Gramscian approaches that are too rigidly focused on economic structure and insufficiently clear in their commitment to democracy—argue that within any larger hegemonic ensemble of relations there are historically specific "nodal points" that have more weight than others. From this point of view, defining hegemony is not arbitrary, and the concept of oppositionality does not dissolve into a fancy way of talking about any and all forms of cultural turbulence. For example, I argue in chapter 7 that neoconservatives are misleading when they argue that the decisive nodal point in recent U.S. hegemonic systems is something called "the new class" and that the later *C&C* was an example of this class—so that in this sense *C&C* was hegemonic rather than counter-hegemonic. My analysis of neoconservatism follows Gary Dorrien, *The Neoconservative Mind* (Philadelphia: Temple Univ. Press, 1993), and other sources cited in chapter 7.

31. See, e.g., Godfrey Hodgson, *America in Our Time* (New York: Vintage, 1976); Steve Fraser and Gary Gerstle, eds., *The Rise and Fall of the New Deal Order, 1930–1980* (Princeton: Princeton Univ. Press, 1989); Sydney Ahlstrom, *A Religious History of the American People* (New Haven: Yale Univ. Press, 1972); and Tom Engelhardt, *The End of Victory Culture: Cold War America and the Disillusioning of a Generation* (New York: Basic Books, 1995). Two excellent bibliographic articles are William Chafe, "America since 1945," in *The New American History*, ed. Eric Foner (Philadelphia: Temple Univ. Press, 1990), 143–61; and Jon Wiener, "Radical Historians and the Crisis in American History, 1959–1980," *Journal of American History* 76 (1989), no. 2: 399–434. For cautions about overstressing consensus see Marty Jezer, *The Dark Ages: Life in the United States, 1945–1960* (Boston: South End Press, 1982); Winifred Breines, *Young, White, and Miserable: Growing Up Female in the Fifties* (Boston: Beacon Press, 1992); Doug McAdam, *Political Process and the Development of Black Insurgency, 1930–1970* (Chicago: Univ. of Chicago Press, 1982); and George Lipsitz, *A Rainbow at Midnight: Labor and Culture in the 1940s* (Urbana: Univ. of Illinois Press, 1994).

32. David Farber, ed., *The Sixties: From Memory to History* (Chapel Hill: Univ. of North Carolina Press, 1994). My point is not to hold Farber personally responsible; on the contrary, he has opened an important discussion, and the limitations of his collection simply reflect the priorities common among twentieth-century cultural historians, as James Lorence and James Grinsel show in "Amen: The Role of Religion in History Teaching," *AHA Perspectives*, Oct. 1992, 20–23. For more discussion of this issue, which is most severe in twentieth-century studies and among people with leftist politics, see my "Three Challenges for the Field of American Studies: Relating to Cultural Studies, Addressing Wider Publics, and Coming to Terms with Religions," *American Studies* 38 (Summer 1997): 117–46. Although my argument at this point overlaps in part with texts such as Stephen Carter, *The Culture of Disbelief* (New York: Anchor Books, 1993); and George Marsden, *The Soul of the American University: From Protestant Establishment to Established Nonbelief* (New York: Oxford Univ. Press, 1994), my main point is quite different. Where they present moderate-to-conservative Christians as underdogs on the defensive against a secular liberal establishment, I am more inclined (as I argue in chapter 7) to see such Christians as constituting part of the establishment, at least on many key issues, and commanding respect in the mainstream media along the lines suggested by Mark Silk, *Unsecular Media: Making News of Religion in America* (Urbana: Univ. of Illinois Press, 1995). My major point is that secularized academics often fail to appreciate the importance of religions relative to other concerns (as documented by Silk, among others) and are too quick to assume that all Christians are conservatives.

33. Benedict Anderson, *Imagined Communities* (New York: Verso, 1983).

34. José Casanova, *Public Religions in the Modern World* (Chicago: Univ. of Chicago Press, 1994), chap. 1 and passim, surveys the discussion of secularization theory and makes a valuable distinction between three distinct meanings of secularization: (1) secularization as the differentiation of political and religious institutions at least in the west, which he defends as the valid core of the theory; (2) secularization as the decline of religious practice, which is not supported by the evidence; and (3) secularization as privatization of religious practice, which is a common trend but not a necessary one, and which should not be considered normative.

35. Figures cited by Paul Boyer, *When Time Shall Be No More: Prophecy Belief in Modern American Culture* (Cambridge: Harvard Univ. Press, 1992), 2–3, 13–15, from polls in the 1980s; the 85 percent figure includes half who defend literal inerrancy and half who gave scope for symbolic interpretation. See George Gallup and Jim Castelli, The *People's Religion: American Faith in the 90s* (New York: Macmillan, 1989). For a summary of data on religion and U.S. politics, see Robert Booth Fowler and Allen Hertzke, *Religion and Politics in America: Faith, Culture, and Strategic Choices* (Boulder, Colo.: Westview Press, 1995).

36. Pat Robertson, *The New World Order* (Dallas: Word, 1991), 92, 174–76; Janice Peck, *The Gods of Televangelism: The Crisis of Meaning and the Appeal of Religious Television* (Cresskill, N.J.: Hampton Press, 1993), 129–34. See also Michael Lind, "Rev. Robertson's Grand International Conspiracy Theory," *New York Review of Books,* 2 Feb. 1995, 21–25. At one time Robertson controlled the fifth largest television network in the United States, after the three major networks and Fox.

37. George Marsden, *Religion and American Culture* (New York: Harcourt Brace Jovanovich, 1990), 1, citing Gallup polls; Peck, *Gods of Televangelism,* 136, citing Robertson's producer.

38. See, e.g., Winifred Breines, "Whose New Left?" *Journal of American History* 75 (1988), no. 2: 528–45; see also Paul Buhle, *Marxism in the United States: Remapping the History of the American Left* (London: Verso, 1987). I thank Gary Kulik for encouraging me to think about my work in this context.

39. Doug Rossinow, "'The Breakthrough to New Life': Christianity and the Emergence of the New Left in Austin, Texas, 1956–1964," *American Quarterly* 46 (1994), no. 3: 309–40. For a sample of other research showing how religion relates to Farber's themes, see Findlay, *Church People in the Struggle;* Hall, *Because of Their Faith;* James Farrell, *The Spirit of the Sixties: The Making of Postwar Radicalism* (New York: Routledge, 1996); Sara Diamond, *Roads to Dominion: Right-wing Movements and Political Power in the United States* (New York: Guilford Press, 1995); Garry Wills, *Under God: Religion and American Politics* (New York: Simon and Schuster, 1990); Gregory Calvert, *Democracy from the Heart: Spiritual Values, Decentralism, and Democratic Idealism in the Movement of the 1960s* (Eugene, Ore.: Communitas Press, 1991); and Taylor Branch, *Parting the Waters: America in the King Years, 1954–63* (New York: Simon and Schuster, 1988). See also John McGreevy, "Racial Justice and the People of God: The Second Vatican Council, the Civil Rights Movement, and American Catholics," *Religion and American Culture* 4 (1994), no. 2: 221–54, an article that is profitably read in dialogue with George Lipsitz, "The Possessive Investment in Whiteness: Racialized Social Democracy and the 'White' Problem in American Studies," *American Quarterly* 47 (1995), no. 3: 369–87. Of course, I do not argue that *C&C,* or religious ideas and institutions more generally, were solely responsible for the movements of the 1960s. If *C&C* was on the cutting edge of anything, it was the relatively unglamorous task of legitimating a more radical critique for selected middle-class intellectuals with modest political power.

40. Stuart Hall, "On Postmodernism and Articulation: An Interview with Stuart Hall," *Journal of Communication Inquiry* 10 (1986), no. 2: 53–54.

41. Bill Weinberg, "Rumbles of War, Rumors of Peace," *Nation,* 6 Feb. 1995, 166. On Ruiz, see Michael Tangeman, *Mexico at the Crossroads: Politics, the Church, and the Poor* (Maryknoll, N.Y.: Orbis Books, 1995); Gary MacEoin, *The People's Church: Bishop Samuel Ruiz of Mexico and Why He Matters* (New York: Crossroad / Continuum, 1996); and Alma Guillermoprieto, "The Shadow War," *New York Review of Books,* 2 Mar. 1995, 34–43.

42. For a sophisticated treatment of rap and exemplary model of cultural studies, see Tricia Rose, *Black Noise: Rap Music and Black Culture in Contemporary America* (Middletown, Conn.: Wesleyan Univ. Press, 1994). For more on this growing field see Nick De Genova, "Check Your Head: The Cultural Politics of Rap Music," *Transition* 67 (Fall 1995): 22–47; Robin D. G. Kelley, "Kickin' Reality, Kickin' Ballistics: 'Gangsta Rap' and Postindustrial Los Angeles," in *Race Rebels* (New York: Free Press, 1994), 183–227; and Michael Eric Dyson, *Reflecting Black: African American Cultural Criticism* (Minneapolis: Univ. of Minnesota Press, 1993).

43. Here I bracket a huge discussion in religious studies about what, if anything, is *unique* and untranslatable about religion. This is by no means a trivial issue, since the stress on uniqueness by many religion scholars is a major stumbling block for dialogues with secularists. I take up this question in "Three Challenges for the Field of American Studies." My argument here can proceed whether or not there is anything absolutely unique to religion, something which cannot be translated into the language of history or sociology. If not, then learning to use distinctive religious discourses to communicate with religious people is no more esoteric and mysterious than learning to speak Spanish if one moves to Mexico or Los Angeles. If so, that is, if some things simply do not translate, we will bracket them in this book and leave them for another day. For an excellent discussion of this issue see William Scott Green, "The Difference Religion Makes," *Journal of the American Academy Religion* 62 (1994), no. 4: 1191–1207.

44. On trends in American Studies see my "Evolving Approaches to U.S. Culture in the American Studies Movement"; Giles Gunn, *The Culture of Criticism and the Criticism of Culture* (New York: Oxford Univ. Press, 1987); Linda Kerber, "Diversity and the Transformation of American Studies," *American Quarterly* 41 (1989), no. 3: 415–31; Michael Denning, "'The Special American Conditions': Marxism and American Studies," *American Quarterly* 38 (1986), no. 3: 356–80; Gene Wise, "'Paradigm Dramas' in American Studies," *American Quarterly* 31, bibliography issue (1979): 293–337; and George Lipsitz, "Listening to Learn and Learning to Listen: Popular Culture, Cultural Theory, and American Studies," *American Quarterly* 42 (1990), no. 4: 615–36. Niebuhr's major contributions to consensus scholarship are *The Irony of American History* (New York: Scribner, 1952) and *The Children of Light and the Children of Darkness* (New York: Scribner, 1944). To place Niebuhr within U.S. historiography, see David W. Noble, *The End of American History: Democracy, Capitalism, and the Metaphor of Two Worlds in Anglo-American Historical Writing, 1890–1980* (Minneapolis: Univ. of Minnesota Press, 1985), 65–89; and Richard Reinitz, *Irony and Consciousness: American Historiography and Reinhold Niebuhr's Vision* (Cranbury, N.J.: Associated Univ. Press, 1980).

45. Simone Weil, quoted in Elisabeth Schüssler Fiorenza, "Feminist Theology as a Critical Theology of Liberation," *Churches in Struggle: Liberation Theologies and Social Change in North America,* ed. William K. Tabb (New York: Monthly Review Press, 1986), 48.

46. Allan Bloom, *The Closing of the American Mind* (New York, 1987), 314; Arthur Schlesinger Jr., "When Ethnic Studies Are Un-American," *Wall Street Journal,* 23 Apr. 1990. See also E. D. Hirsch, *Cultural Literacy: What Every American Needs to Know* (Boston: Houghton Mifflin, 1987).

47. Robert Bellah et al., *Habits of the Heart: Individualism and Commitment in American Life* (Berkeley: Univ. of California Press, 1985); William Dean, *The Religious Critic in American Culture* (Albany: State Univ. of New York Press, 1994). On *Habits* see Charles Reynolds and Ralph Norman, eds., *Community in America: The Challenge of Habits of the Heart* (Berkeley: Univ. of California Press, 1988). On Dean see my review of *Religious Critic* in *Soundings* 78 (1995), no. 3–4: 661–65. To relate these texts to long-standing debates about civil religion the best places to start are Russell Richey and Donald Jones, eds., *American Civil Religion* (New York: Harper and Row, 1974), which reprints Bellah's 1967 "Civil Religion in America," 21–44; Casanova, *Public Religions in the Modern World;* and Noble, "Robert Bellah, Civil Religion, and the American Jeremiad," *Soundings* 65 (1982): 88–102. See also Mary Douglas and Steven Tipton, ed., *Religion in America: Spirituality in a Secular Age* (Boston: Beacon Press, 1982).

48. Rich quoted in Audre Lorde, "The Master's Tools Will Never Dismantle the Master's House," in *Sister Outsider* (Freedom, Calif.: Crossing Press, 1984), 112; Hazel Carby, "The Politics of Difference," *Ms,* Sept. / Oct. 1990, 85. See also "Interview: Audre Lorde and Adrienne

Rich" and "Age, Race, Class, and Sex: Women Redefining Difference," in *Sister Outsider,* 81–109, 114–23. For a symposium that shows how these issues ramify through a range of concerns on the left, see Stanley Aronowitz et al., "Special Section: Radical Democracy," *Socialist Review* 93 (1994), no. 3: 5–149; my own position is closest to the contribution by Michael Omi and Howard Winant, 127–34.

49. See, e.g., Andrew Parker et al., *Nationalisms and Sexualities* (New York: Routledge, 1991); Amy Kaplan, "Left Alone with America: The Absence of Empire in the Study of the American Culture," in *Cultures of United States Imperialism,* ed. Amy Kaplan and Donald Pease (Durham: Duke Univ. Press, 1993), 3–21. Even without entering the huge territory of multicultural and feminist scholarship, Casanova, *Public Religions in the Modern World,* chap. 2, points to several pairs of publics and corresponding privates: The public state versus private economy; the public economy versus private realm of family; and public intrapersonal exchanges in groups (including families) versus the private realm of individual subjectivity. A call for "more public engagement" might garner widespread agreement, but one person might be agreeing to strengthen the state's regulative power, another might be supporting a feminist movement opposed to state policies, and yet another could be valorizing the "realities" of economics at the expense of feminism.

50. Bruce Robbins, ed., *The Phantom Public Sphere* (Minneapolis: Univ. of Minnesota Press, 1993); x, xxiii. See also Robbins, "Some Versions of U.S. Internationalism," *Social Text* 45 (Winter 1995): 97–124. On Lippmann, see his *The Essential Lippmann: A Political Philosophy for Liberal Democracy* (New York: Random House, 1963); and Arthur Schlesinger Jr., "Walter Lippmann: The Intellectual vs. Politics," in *Walter Lippmann and His Times,* ed. Marquis Childs (New York: Harcourt, Brace, 1959), 189–225.

51. Nancy Fraser, "Rethinking the Public Sphere: A Contribution to the Critique of Actually Existing Democracy," *Social Text* 25/26 (1990): 56–80.

52. West, *Keeping Faith;* Cornel West, *The American Evasion of Philosophy* (Madison: Univ. of Wisconsin Press, 1989). For a *C&C* essay linking West to issues of this section, see my "Cornel West: Can Pragmatism Save?" 16 Dec. 1991, 394–97; see also my discussion in chapter 10. Many essays in West's first collection of essays, *Prophetic Fragments,* were originally published in *C&C.*

53. Orientations to the spectrum of postwar Protestantism subject include Wade Clark Roof and William McKinney, *American Mainline Religion: Its Changing Shape and Future* (New Brunswick, N.J.: Rutgers, 1987); George Marsden, *Understanding Fundamentalism and Evangelicalism* (Grand Rapids: Eerdmans, 1991); Nancy Ammerman, "North American Protestant Fundamentalism," in *Fundamentalisms Observed,* ed. Martin Marty and R. Scott Appleby (Chicago: Univ. of Chicago Press, 1991), 1–66; Wade Clark Roof, *A Generation of Seekers: The Spiritual Journeys of the Baby Boom Generation* (San Francisco: Harper, 1993); and Clyde Wilcox, *Onward Christian Soldiers? The Religious Right in American Politics* (Boulder, Colo.: Westview Press, 1996). Especially valuable for connecting this literature to *C&C* are Robert Michaelsen and Wade Clark Roof, eds., *Liberal Protestantism: Realities and Possibilities* (New York: Pilgrim Press, 1986); and William Hutchison, ed., *Between the Times: The Travail of the Protestant Establishment in America, 1900–1960* (New York: Cambridge Univ. Press, 1989).

54. My article, "Interpreting the 'Popular' in Popular Religion," *American Studies* 36 (Fall 1995): 127–37, addresses related issues through an analysis of Roger Finke and Rodney Stark, *The Churching of America , 1776–1990* (New Brunswick, N.J.: Rutgers Univ. Press, 1992); and R. Laurence Moore, *Selling God: American Religion in the Marketplace of Culture* (New York: Oxford Univ. Press, 1994). For additional discussion of these matters, see chapter 7.

55. Ellen Messer-Davidow, "Manufacturing the Attack on Higher Education," *Social Text* 36 (Fall 1993): 40–80; Leon Howell, "Funding the War of Ideas," *Christian Century,* 19 July 1995, 701–3, and additional citations in chapters 10 and 11.

56. For an overview of these trends see David Lotz, ed., *Altered Landscapes: Christianity in America, 1935–1985* (Grand Rapids: Eerdmans, 1989), esp. 312–41. See also R. Laurence Moore, *Religious Outsiders and the Making of Americans* (New York: Oxford Univ. Press, 1986); and R. Stephen Warner, "Work in Progress toward a New Paradigm for the Sociological Study

of Religion in the United States," *American Journal of Sociology* 98 (1993), no. 5: 1004–93. Two fine samplers of recent work in the multicultural paradigm are David Hackett, ed., *Religion and American Culture: A Reader* (New York: Routledge, 1996); and Thomas Tweed, ed., *Retelling U.S. Religious History* (Berkeley: Univ. of California Press, 1996). Marty, "American Religious History in the 1980s: A Decade of Achievement," *Church History* 62 (1993): 335–77, argues that U.S. religious historians, who were once too centered on the Protestant establishment, are now like a pendulum swinging too far in the opposite direction. For example, "At the end of the ecumenical century, there were [only three] books on ecumenism and not one from the Protestant-Orthodox participant mainstream" (335). It is not completely clear how to interpret Marty's data, since he cites many thematic studies based on mainstream Protestant materials, and he states that civil religion was "relatively slighted" despite the massive literature on Bellah's *Habits of the Heart.* Nevertheless, he documents a strong pluralist trend.

57. Bill Kellerman, "Apologist of Power: The Long Shadow of Reinhold Niebuhr's Christian Realism," *Sojourners,* Mar. 1987, 15.

58. Fox argues along similar lines in "Niebuhr's World and Ours," in *Reinhold Niebuhr Today,* ed. Richard John Neuhaus (Grand Rapids: Eerdmans 1989), 1–18.

59. Cal Thomas, "Peace Movement Doesn't See Flaw in the Human Character," *St. Paul Pioneer Press,* 29 Jan. 1991, 9A.

60. Niebuhr, "John Coleman Bennett: Theologian, Churchman, and Educator," in *Theology and Church in Times of Change: Essays in Honor of John Coleman Bennett,* ed. Edward LeRoy Long and Robert T. Handy (Philadelphia: Westminster Press, 1970), 235. See also Glen Bucher, "Christian Realism after Niebuhr: The Case of John C. Bennett," *Union Seminary Quarterly Review* 41 (1986): 43–58.

61. Bennett's most systematic treatment of Niebuhr's later career is his 1982 afterword to his 1956 essay, "Reinhold Niebuhr's Social Ethics." This appears both in the second edition of *Reinhold Niebuhr: His Religious, Social, and Political Thought,* ed. Charles Kegley (New York: Pilgrim Press, 1984), 132–41; and as Bennett, "Niebuhr's Ethic: The Later Years," 12 Apr. 1982, 91–95.

62. Amid a massive literature, three outstanding texts on the relation of Niebuhrian and liberation theologies are Gary Dorrien, *Soul in Society: The Making and Remaking of Social Christianity* (Minneapolis: Fortress Press, 1995); Craig Nessan, *Orthopraxis or Heresy: The North American Theological Response to Latin American Liberation Theology* (Atlanta: Scholars Press, 1989); and Arthur McGovern, *Liberation Theology and Its Critics* (Maryknoll, N.Y.: Orbis Books, 1989). Two concise orientations to the literature on Niebuhr are the bibliographies in Fox, *Reinhold Niebuhr,* 326–32, and Kegley, *Reinhold Niebuhr,* 531–68. Two outstanding single-volume overviews of Niebuhr scholarship are Kegley, *Reinhold Niebuhr;* and Richard Harries, *Reinhold Niebuhr and the Issues of Our Time* (Grand Rapids: Eerdmans 1988). The leading biography (in a crowded field) is Fox, *Reinhold Niebuhr,* and a fine selection of essays is Robert McAfee Brown, *The Essential Reinhold Niebuhr* (New Haven: Yale Univ. Press, 1986). Two concise introductions to liberation theologies are Dorothee Sölle, *Thinking about God* (Philadelphia: Trinity Press International, 1990); and Rebecca Chopp, *The Praxis of Suffering: An Interpretation of Liberation and Political Theologies* (Maryknoll, N.Y.: Orbis Books, 1986). For a representative range of liberation approaches see Susan Thistlethwaite and Mary Potter Engel, eds., *Lift Every Voice: Constructing Christian Theologies from the Underside* (San Francisco: Harper and Row, 1990); Chopp and Mark Lewis Taylor, eds., *Reconstructing Christian Theology* (Minneapolis: Fortress Press, 1994); Marc Ellis and Otto Maduro, eds., *Expanding the View: Gustavo Gutiérrez and the Future of Liberation Theology* (Maryknoll, N.Y.: Orbis Books, 1990); and Tabb, *Churches in Struggle.*

63. Bennett, "Reinhold Niebuhr's Social Ethics," in Kegley, *Reinhold Niebuhr,* 100–101.

64. Fox, *Reinhold Niebuhr;* Smith, *The Emergence of Liberation Theology: Radical Religion and Social Movement Theory* (Chicago: Univ. of Chicago, 1991); Cone, *Martin and Malcolm and America: A Dream or a Nightmare?* (Maryknoll, N.Y.: Orbis Books, 1991); Robert Wuthnow, *The Restructuring of American Religion: Society and Faith since World War II* (Princeton: Princeton Univ. Press, 1988).

65. Henry Sloane Coffin, "'American Freedom and Catholic Power,'" 2 May 1949, 49–50. Important Catholics at *C&C* included editors Bob Hoyt and Peggy Steinfels and board members Rosemary Ruether and Michael Novak.

66. Carol Christ and Judith Plaskow, eds., *Womanspirit Rising: A Feminist Reader in Religion* (San Francisco: Harper and Row, 1979). Contributors to this groundbreaking volume who wrote for *C&C* or had strong connections included Christ, Sheila Collins, Nelle Morton, Rosemary Ruether, Phyllis Trible, and Penelope Washbourn. More than half of the Christian writers in this collection were *C&C* contributors, and a quarter of its Christian articles either appeared originally in *C&C* or were reprinted there.

67. John C. Bennett and Roger Shinn interviews.

68. Cowan to Schlesinger, 25 Apr. 1963, *C&C* records, box 1, untitled folder.

69. Sharon Welch, *A Feminist Ethic of Risk* (Minneapolis: Fortress Press, 1990), esp. 103–23. See also her *Communities of Resistance and Solidarity* (Maryknoll, N.Y.: Orbis Books, 1985).

70. Ronald Stone, "The Contribution of Reinhold Niebuhr to the Late Twentieth Century," in *Reinhold Niebuhr,* ed. Charles Kegley, 72. For more in this vein see Stone, "Christian Realism and Latin American Liberation Theology," in *The Church's Public Role: Retrospect and Prospect,* ed. Dieter Hessel (Grand Rapids: Eerdmans, 1993), 109–24; Stone, *Reinhold Niebuhr: Prophet to Politicians* (Nashville: Abingdon, 1972); Charles Brown, *Niebuhr and His Age: Reinhold Niebuhr's Prophetic Role in the Twentieth Century* (New York: Trinity Press International, 1992); and Donald Meyer, *The Protestant Search for Political Realism, 1919–41,* 2d ed. (Middletown, Conn.: Wesleyan Univ. Press, 1988). In chapter 10 I discuss Welch's response to a related argument, Dennis McCann's *Christian Realism and Liberation Theology* (Maryknoll, N.Y.: Orbis Books, 1982).

71. My thinking on this issue is indebted to Beverly Harrison, "The Role of Social Theory in Religious Social Ethics: Reconsidering the Case for Marxian Political Economy," in her *Making the Connections: Essays in Feminist Social Ethics* (Boston: Beacon Press, 1985), 54–80, and her review of Fox's biography in "Niebuhr: Locating the Limits," 17 Feb. 1986, 35–39. See also Cornel West's analysis of Niebuhr in *Prophetic Fragments,* 144–54, and *American Evasion of Philosophy,* 150–65.

72. William McGuire King, "The Reform Establishment and the Ambiguities of Influence," in Hutchison, *Between the Times,* 168–92.

73. David Berreby, "Clifford Geertz: Unabsolute Truths," *New York Times Magazine,* 9 Apr. 1995, 44–47, helps explain my vow when he dubs this the OTOH-BOTOH style—an acronym for "on the one hand" (OTOH) "but on the other hand" (BOTOH).

74. Paul Tillich, "Beyond Religious Socialism," *Christian Century,* 16 June 1949, 732–33.

75. Cowan and Lindermayer, "An Anniversary Statement," 15 Nov. 1976, 259. *C&C*'s most famous attack on parasites occurred in its opening editorial, "The Crisis," 10 Feb. 1941, 2. Cowan and Lindermayer quoted a somewhat more tactful Niebuhr comment about World War II parasites from his retrospective article in the twenty-fifth anniversary issue, "A Christian Journal Confronts Mankind's Continuing Crisis," 21 Feb. 1966, 11–13.

76. Shaull, "Liberal and Radical in an Age of Discontinuity," 5 Jan. 1970, 340; Bennett, "After Thirty Years," 22 Mar. 1971, 40.

77. Carby, "Politics of Difference," 85; Rosemary Ruether "A Radical-Liberal in the Streets of Washington," 12 July 1971, 144.

Chapter 1

1. Quotation from Fox, *Reinhold Niebuhr,* 72, referring to the period between the world wars. Since the 1956 founding of *Christianity Today,* the *Century* has had an powerful evangelical competitor—one which currently dwarfs it in circulation.

2. Editorial comment on "How My Mind Has Changed" series, *Christian Century,* 4 Oct. 1939, 1194. The essays were mostly but not exclusively from prominent Protestant church leaders.

3. Niebuhr, "Ten Years That Shook My World," *Christian Century,* 26 Apr. 1939, 542, 543.

4. A great deal has been written about these issues, and I have made no attempt to be comprehensive. My general understanding relies most heavily on Ahlstrom, *Religious History of the American People;* Robert Handy, *A Christian America? Protestant Hopes and Historical Realities,* 2d ed. (New York: Oxford Univ. Press, 1984); Hutchison, *Between the Times;* Marty, *Modern American Religion,* vol. 2: *The Noise of Conflict, 1919–1941* (Chicago: Univ. of Chicago Press, 1991); Meyer, *Protestant Search for Political Realism;* and Ronald White and C. Howard Hopkins, eds., *The Social Gospel* (Philadelphia: Temple Univ. Press, 1976).

5. See, e.g., Engelhardt, *The End of Victory Culture.*

6. Marty, *Righteous Empire* (New York: Dial, 1970); Conrad Cherry, ed., *God's New Israel: Religious Interpretations of American Destiny* (Englewood Cliffs, N.J.: Prentice Hall, 1971); Ernest Tuveson, *Redeemer Nation* (Chicago: Univ. of Chicago Press, 1968); Ahlstrom, "Annuit Coeptis: America as the Elect Nation," in *Continuity and Discontinuity in Church History,* ed. F. Forrester Church and Timothy George (Leiden: Brill, 1979), 315–37. Because of the way U.S. history unfolded, Protestant versions have been the most influential, as well as the most relevant to this book. However, Roman Catholic versions should not be forgotten, given their distinguished pedigree in the Americas reaching from Christopher Columbus through Cardinal Spellman to Michael Novak.

7. Jane Tompkins, *Sensational Designs: The Cultural Work of American Fiction* (New York: Oxford Univ. Press, 1985); Paul Erickson, *Reagan Speaks: The Making of an American Myth* (New York: New York Univ., 1985); Garry Wills, *Reagan's America,* 2d ed. (New York: Penguin, 1988); Michael Rogin, *Ronald Reagan: The Movie and Other Episodes in Political Demonology* (Berkeley: Univ. of California Press, 1987).

8. Catherine Albanese, *Sons of the Fathers: The Civil Religion of the American Revolution* (Philadelphia: Temple Univ. Press, 1976), 201–2; Ahlstrom, "Annuit Coeptis," 320–21; Noble, "The Sacred and the Profane: The Theology of Thorstein Veblen," in *Thorstein Veblen,* ed. Carlton C. Quayley (New York: Columbia Univ. Press, 1968), 72.

9. Sacvan Bercovitch, *The American Jeremiad* (Madison: Univ. of Wisconsin Press, 1978); see also Noble, "Robert Bellah, Civil Religion, and the American Jeremiad."

10. Noble, *End of American History,* 1–14; see also Noble, "Revocation of the Anglo-Protestant Monopoly: Aesthetic Authority and the American Landscape," *Soundings* 79 (1996), no. 1–2. This argument implies that it is better to speak about U.S. and European variations on a modern jeremiad rather than a unique American jeremiad.

11. My analysis follows Noble, *End of American History,* esp. 16–64. See also Noble, *The Paradox of Progressive Thought* (Minneapolis: Univ. of Minnesota Press, 1958).

12. Linda-Marie Delloff, "C. C. Morrison: Shaping a Journal's Identity," in Delloff et al., *A Century of* The Century (Grand Rapids: Eerdmans, 1987), 11.

13. On these issues see the works of William Appleman Williams. His "Frontier Thesis and American Foreign Policy," *Pacific Historical Review* 24 (1955): 379–95, makes an especially clear link between his argument and classic themes of the American jeremiad. *Empire as a Way of Life* (New York: Oxford Univ. Press, 1980) is a good synthetic statement; other works include *The Tragedy of American Diplomacy,* 2d ed. (New York: Delta, 1962), and *The Contours American History* (Chicago: Quadrangle, 1961). On his relation to recent trends in history, see Noble, "Revocation of the Anglo-Protestant Monopoly"; Noble, *End of American History,* 115–40; Bradford Perkins, "*The Tragedy of American Diplomacy:* Twenty-five Years Later," *Reviews in American History* 12 (1984): 1–18; Thomas Paterson et al., "Round Table: Exploring the History of American Foreign Relations," *Journal of American History* 77 (1990), no. 1: 171–244; and Dina M. Copelman and Barbara Clark Smith, eds., "Excerpts from a Conference to Honor William Appleman Williams," *Radical History Review* 50 (1991): 39–70.

14. Fox, *Reinhold Niebuhr,* 78–79.

15. On Beard's career after World War I, see Noble, *End of American History,* 41–64. See also Richard Hofstadter, *The Progressive Historians: Turner, Beard, Parrington* (New York, Knopf, 1968). For a concise example of reasoning similar to Beard's, see Norman Thomas, "The Pacifist's Dilemma" (1937), in *The* Nation, *1965–1990: Selections from the Independent Magazine of Politics and Culture,* ed. Katrina Vanden Heuvel (New York: Thunder's Mouth Press, 1990), 139–44.

16. See, e.g., Noam Chomsky, *Towards a New Cold War* (New York: Pantheon, 1982), and works by Williams cited above.

17. On race and the exceptionalist tradition see Barbara Andolsen, *Daughters of Jefferson, Daughters of Bootblacks: Racism and American Feminism* (Macon, Ga.: Mercer Univ. Press, 1986); Richard Drinnon, *Facing West: The Metaphysics of Indian-Hating and Empire Building* (Minneapolis: Univ. of Minnesota Press, 1980); Reginald Horsman, *Race and Manifest Destiny* (Cambridge: Harvard Univ. Press, 1981); Rogin, *Ronald Reagan;* and Ronald Takaki, *Iron Cages: Race and Culture in Nineteenth-Century America,* 2d ed. (New York: Oxford Univ. Press, 1990). A key theme in Copelman and Smith, "Excerpts from a Conference to Honor William Appleman Williams," is assessing Williams's contribution in light of such work.

18. Often specific people are hard to place on this continuum. For example, William Jennings Bryan, an archetypal Progressive reformer, carried the banner of fundamentalism at the Scopes trail. William Bell Riley, an archetypal fundamentalist, was involved in Progressive reforms early in his career (later he drifted toward extreme anti-Semitism and support for the fascist Silver Shirts). See Lawrence Levine, *Defender of the Faith: William Jennings Bryan, the Last Decade, 1915–1925* (New York: Oxford Univ. Press, 1965) and William Vance Trollinger Jr., *God's Empire: William Bell Riley and Midwestern Fundamentalism* (Madison: Univ. of Wisconsin Press, 1991).

19. Morrison quoted in Linda-Marie Delloff, "C. C. Morrison: Shaping a Journal's Identity," 43. At this time Morrison was not yet the editor, but was a young minister involved with the journal.

20. Jane Addams, *Twenty Years at Hull House* (1910; reprint, New York: New American Library, 1960); DeAne Lagerquist, "Women and the American Religious Pilgrimage: Vida Scudder, Dorothy Day, and Pauli Murray," in *New Dimensions in American Religious History: Essays in Honor of Martin E. Marty,* ed. Jay Dolan and James Wind (Grand Rapids: Eerdmans, 1993), 208–29. On the strengths and limitations of this alliance, see the discussion of Frances Willard and Mother Jones in Robert Craig, *Religion and Radical Politics: An Alternative Christian Tradition in the United States* (Philadelphia: Temple Univ. Press, 1992), 46–82.

21. On the relations among social gospel leaders, industrial workers, and business elites see Liston Pope, *Millhands and Preachers* (1942; New Haven: Yale Univ. Press, 1965); Henry F. May, *Protestant Churches and Industrial America* (New York: 1949); Marty, *Modern American Religion,* 2:384–86 and elsewhere; Meyer, *Protestant Search for Political Realism,* 55–129; Moore, *Selling God,* 172–203; and Herbert Gutman, "Protestantism and the American Labor Movement: The Christian Spirit in the Gilded Age," *American Historical Review* 72 (1966), no. 1: 74–101.

22. Dean Peerman, "Forward on Many Fronts: The *Century,* 1923–1929," in *A Century of* The Century, ed. Delloff et al., 32, discusses the Gary case and cites Robert Moats Miller, *American Protestantism and Social Issues, 1919–39* (Chapel Hill: Univ. of North Carolina Press, 1958). J. Theodore Hefley, "Freedom Upheld: The Civil Liberties Stance of the *Christian Century* between the Wars," *Church History* 37 (1968): 177–94, documents a solid record of support for civil liberties on issues such as the trial of Sacco and Vanzetti and antilynching efforts. However, on the issue of race, Hefley summarizes the *Century's* position as "Anglo-Saxonism," which held that "(1) the white race is superior to the colored races, and (2) the Anglo-Saxon cultural tradition is the most illustrious attainment of any of the world's racial or linguistic stocks" (189).

23. Unsigned editorial, "For President," *Christian Century,* 28 Oct. 1936, 1414–16. Numerous letters of protest were printed on 4 Nov. 1936, 1467–68.

24. On issues intersecting in the temperance movement, see Craig, *Religion and Radical Politics,* 50–62; Linda Gordon, "Family Violence, Feminism, and Social Control," *Feminist Studies* 12 (Fall 1986), no. 3: 453–78; Paul Johnson, "Bottom's Up: Drinking, Temperance, and the Social Historians," in *Reviews in American History* 13 (Mar. 1985): 48–53; and Roy Rosenzweig, *Eight Hours for What We Will: Workers and Leisure in an Industrial City, 1870–1920* (New York: Cambridge Univ. Press, 1983). Immigrant religious leaders were by no means unanimous in fighting Prohibition; Jay Dolan, *The American Catholic Experience: A History from Colonial Times to the Present* (Garden City, N.Y.: Image Books, 1985), 326, says, "Crusading for temperance was as Catholic as going to Sunday Mass."

25. Here I am bracketing several major issues in the interpretation of fundamentalism and premillennialism that are better left for another book. Although these movements were largely predisposed to resist new intellectual and social trends and were often pessimistic about major aspects of U.S. destiny, the issues are complex. By the nineteenth century, evangelical theology had already made major changes in response to the Enlightenment themes of individual human autonomy and reason; fundamentalism continued some of these emphases on human autonomy and adaptation to urbanization and capitalist individualism. Also, premillennialism is compatible with hopes for many kinds of earthly progress—as the examples of William Jennings Bryan and Pat Robertson make clear. On these issues, see (in addition to citations in the introduction) Leonard Sweet, ed., *The Evangelical Tradition in America* (Macon, Ga.: Mercer Univ. Press, 1984); Timothy Weber, *Living in the Shadow of the Second Coming* (Chicago: Univ. of Chicago Press, 1987); and Moore, *Religious Outsiders and the Making of Americans,* 128–49. Further complicating matters, Betty DeBerg, *Ungodly Women: Gender and the First Wave of American Fundamentalism* (Minneapolis: Fortress Press, 1990), argues persuasively that the two issues most commonly mentioned as provoking fundamentalists—the rise of pluralist industrial cities and the growth of scientific and historical critical approaches—should move over and give space to a third, equally important factor—changes in the Victorian gender system.

26. Cited in Delloff, "C. C. Morrison: Shaping a Journal's Identity," 44.

27. A standard history of theological liberalism is William Hutchison, *The Modernist Impulse in American Protestantism* (Cambridge: Harvard Univ. Press, 1976). See also H. Richard Niebuhr, *The Kingdom of God in America* (New York: Harper, 1959).

28. Albert Schenkel, *The Rich Man and the Kingdom: John D. Rockefeller Jr. and the Protestant Establishment* (Minneapolis: Fortress Press, 1995), 176, quoting fundamentalist leader John Roach Stratton. Stratton refers to Park Avenue Baptist Church, the congregation that voted to build Riverside Church across the street from Union Seminary and move into it in 1926. Rockefeller contributed $32 million to this project (178). On Fosdick's place amid a spectrum of social gospel leaders see Dorrien, *Soul in Society,* 60–68.

29. Max Stackhouse, "Rauschenbusch Today: The Legacy of a Loving Prophet," *Christian Century,* 25 Jan. 1989, 76. See also Rauschenbusch, *A Theology for the Social Gospel* (Nashville: Abingdon, 1918); Meyer, *Protestant Search for Political Realism,* esp. 130–44; Dorrien, *Reconstructing the Common Good: Theology and the Social Order* (Maryknoll, N.Y.: Orbis Books, 1990), 16–47.

30. It bears repeating that paradigm change does not mean complete discontinuity; it only implies a new hierarchy of concern that reorients a worldview. This is a crucial issue when using paradigmatic analysis to interpret Niebuhrians, because they typically proposed ideas that were in considerable tension and held them together in one package described as a "dialectic." Therefore, a paradigm could shift simply by reshuffling components of the system, for example, by making the Y hand the X hand.

31. Niebuhr, "The Blindness of Liberalism," *Radical Religion* 1 (1936), cited in Dorrien, *Soul in Society,* 107.

32. Handy, "The Second Disestablishment," in *A Christian America?* 159–84. Three articles in Hutchison, *Between the Times,* explore relationships between the Protestant establishment and key "outsiders": David Wills, "An Enduring Distance: Black Americans and the Establishment," 168–92; Benny Kraut, "A Wary Collaboration: Jews, Catholics, and the Goodwill Movement," 193–229; and Virginia Lieson Brereton, "United and Slighted: Women as Subordinated Insiders," 143–66. Marty, *Modern American Religion,* vol. 2, highlights various aspects of interreligious strife between the wars. See also Moore, *Selling God,* 204–39.

33. Handy, "The American Religious Depression, 1925–35," in *Religion in American History,* ed. John Mulder and John Wilson (Englewood Cliffs, N.J.: Prentice Hall, 1978), 431–44; Paul A. Carter, *Decline and Revival of the Social Gospel: Social and Political Liberalism in American Protestant Churches, 1920–40* (Ithaca: Cornell Univ. Press, 1954).

34. Bruce Barton, *The Man Nobody Knows* (1925; reprint, New York: Charter Books, 1962); Schenkel, *The Rich Man and the Kingdom,* 141–44.

35. Miller, *American Protestantism and Social Issues.*

36. Fox, *Reinhold Niebuhr,* 49–53.

37. Richard Pells, *Radical Visions and American Dreams* (New York: Harper and Row, 1973); Studs Terkel, *Hard Times* (New York: Washington Square, 1970).

38. On the flag episode and Niebuhr's relation to Ward, see Robert Handy, *A History of Union Theological Seminary in New York* (New York: Columbia Univ. Press, 1987), 184–93. For more on Ward see Meyer, *Protestant Search for Political Realism,* 145–49 and passim; Marty, *Modern American Religion,* 2:290–97, and Craig, *Religion and Radical Politics,* 186–99.

39. Niebuhr, *Moral Man and Immoral Society* (New York: Scribner, 1932); *Reflections on the End of an Era* (New York: Scribner, 1935).

40. John Haynes Holmes's review of *Reflections on the End of an Era* in *Herald Tribune Books,* cited in Fox, *Reinhold Niebuhr,* 152–53.

41. The classic example is Meyer's *Protestant Search for Political Realism.* In the 1988 "Introduction to the Wesleyan Edition," pp. ix–xxxv, Meyer remained unmoved by a generation of revisionism, attacking David Noble and William Appleman Williams as throwbacks to the 1930s. Of course, Meyer did not make up the evidence he uses to excoriate the social gospelers. Insofar as my book presents Morrison at his strongest, this should be understood less as an endorsement than as an effort to shift the scholarly discussion so that it does not screen out the good light that is available to throw on the social gospelers. Rauschenbusch is often attacked for holding simple-minded positions that a fair-minded reader of his books does not discover, and Morrison's arguments (flawed though they are) are rarely noted in the literature.

42. For an orientation to the literature on Barth, see George Hunsinger, *Karl Barth and Radical Politics* (Philadelphia: Westminster Press, 1976); Will Herberg, "Introduction: The Social Philosophy of Karl Barth," in Barth, *Community, State, and Church* (Gloucester: Smith, 1968), 1–17.

43. For a fully nuanced version of this claim, presenting Niebuhr in the context of American pragmatism, see Lovin, *Reinhold Niebuhr and Christian Realism.* For cautions not to go overboard with the idea, see (along with Lovin) Langdon Gilkey, "Reinhold Niebuhr as Political Theologian," in *Reinhold Niebuhr and the Issues of Our Time,* ed. Richard Harries (Grand Rapids: Eerdmans, 1988), 157–82.

44. On Niebuhr's relation to Barth, see Niebuhr, "Intellectual Autobiography," in *Reinhold Niebuhr,* ed. Charles Kegley, 15–16; Fox, *Reinhold Niebuhr,* 117 and elsewhere; and Stone, *Reinhold Niebuhr: Prophet to Politicians,* 122–25. Helpful overviews of Bennett's theology include Bucher, "Christian Realism after Niebuhr," and Daniel Day Williams, "The Theology of John Coleman Bennett," in *Theology and Church,* ed. Long and Handy. Later in his career, Bennett embraced Barth as an ally, for example, in his *Radical Imperative* (Philadelphia: Westminster Press, 1975), 15.

45. John Bennett, "A Changed Liberal—But Still a Liberal," *Christian Century,* 8 Feb. 1939, 179.

46. Ibid., 181, 180. As Bennett often acknowledged, his intellectual path largely paralleled Niebuhr's in his early years, although he was far less polemical toward liberal theology. His first major books, *Social Salvation: A Religious Approach to the Problems of Social Change* (New York: Scribner, 1935) and *Christianity—and Our World* (New York: Hazen, 1936), defended hopes for socialist progress in a context of lowered expectations. Bennett was already alarmed about fascism in *Social Salvation,* and by the time he published *Christian Realism* (New York: Scribner, 1941), it was his major concern.

47. Robert Calhoun, "A Liberal Bandaged but Unbowed," *Christian Century,* 31 May 1939, reprinted in *The Christian Century Reader,* ed. Harold Fey and Margaret Frakes (New York: Association Press, 1962), 121. Calhoun's essay was the sole representative of the 1939 "How My Mind Has Changed" series in this "best of the *Century*" retrospective. On the so-called Younger Theologians group (later renamed the Theological Discussion Group) and its relation to politics see Heather Warren, "Intervention and International Organization: American Reformed Leaders and World War II," *American Presbyterians* 74 (1996), no. 1: 42–56.

48. Calhoun, "Liberal Bandaged but Unbowed," 121.

49. Ibid., 118.

50. Cited in Peerman, "Forward on Many Fronts," 42.

51. On the antifascism of 1930s pacifists in the *Century*'s mold, see Lawrence Wittner, *Rebels against War: The American Peace Movement, 1933–1960* (New York: Columbia Univ. Press, 1969), 16–18. See also James Schneider, *Should America Go to War? The Debate over Foreign Policy in Chicago, 1939–1941* (Chapel Hill: Univ. of North Carolina Press, 1989), which documents complex differences among antiwar groups, including two committees led by *Christian Century* editors. Schneider shows that Protestant clergy were overwhelmingly antiwar and pro-neutrality in 1939 (29 and passim), but he does not fully confront the issue of imperialism. He characterizes speeches against British imperialism as mere "Anglophobia" (201) and summarizes one *Chicago Tribune* argument about the drawbacks of imperialism in Asia by commenting that the *Tribune* "did not believe that commercial interests in the Pacific justified risking war with Japan" (153), even though part of the *Tribune*'s argument was that the United States could trade with Japan without attempting to police Asia.

52. In a 1927 series, *Century* managing editor Paul Hutchinson lamented, "America has come to be lumped with those nations whose primary interest in China is the securing of settled markets, whether for the winning of dollars or the winning of souls." Cited by Peerman, "Forward on Many Fronts," 31.

53. Stanley Jones, "Apply the Gandhi Method to Japan!" *Christian Century*, 8 Feb. 1939, 184–85; unsigned editorial, "Infected with Bolshevik Communism?" *Christian Century*, 8 Feb. 1939, 174–75. The charge was made before the Dies committee by a leader of the conservative Lutheran Church–Missouri Synod.

54. Unsigned editorial, "Foreign Policy and Public Opinion," *Christian Century*, 8 Feb. 1939, 175–77.

55. Unsigned editorial, "Invitation to a Holy War," *Christian Century*, 18 Jan. 1939, 78; letters to the editor, *Christian Century*, 8 Feb. 1939, 188–89.

56. Unsigned editorials: "Our Frontier Is on the Potomac," *Christian Century*, 15 Feb. 1939, 206–7; "Well Said, Mr. President," 13 Sept. 1939, 1095–96; "Keep the Arms Embargo!" *Christian Century*, 20 Sept. 1939, 1126–27.

57. Oswald Garrison Villard, "Who Rules America?" *Christian Century*, 23 July 1941, 933–34; editorial, "To Your Battle Stations," *Christian Century*, 5 Nov. 1941, 1360–61.

58. Unsigned editorial, "Is Neutrality Immoral?" *Christian Century*, 12 Nov. 1941, 1399–1400. This was an explicit response to an article in *C&C;* it is extremely bitter about Niebuhr's debating tactics, which had not presented the *Century*'s position at its strongest.

59. Unsigned editorial, "A War for Imperialism," *Christian Century*, 26 Nov. 1941, 1463–65. Luce's essay is widely reprinted, including in William Appleman Williams et al., *America in Vietnam: A Documentary History* (New York: Anchor, 1985), 22–28. On Luce see John K. Jessup, ed., *The Ideas of Henry Luce* (New York: Atheneum, 1969).

60. Unsigned editorial, "Why We Differ," *Christian Century*, 10 Dec. 1941, 1535, 1538.

61. Unsigned editorial, "An Unnecessary Necessity," *Christian Century*, 17 Dec. 1941, 1565, 1566; letters to the editor, 31 Dec. 1941, 1640–42.

Chapter 2

1. Unsigned editorial, "The Crisis," 10 Feb. 1941, 1, 2. According to Fox, *Reinhold Niebuhr*, 196, this article was written by Francis Miller, a founding member of *C&C*'s board. Miller's religious-political views in the mid-1930s are discussed in Marty, *Modern American Religion*, 2:311–15.

2. Unsigned editorial, "The Crisis," 10 Feb. 1941, 3.

3. Niebuhr, "Imperialism and Irresponsibility," 24 Feb. 1941, 6.

4. The quote is Richard Rovere's, and it is cited by Fox, *Reinhold Niebuhr*, 234.

5. On parallel developments at the *Nation* and *New Republic*, see Richard Pells, *The Liberal Mind in a Conservative Age* (New York: Harper and Row, 1985), 10–18; and Margaret Morley, "Freda Kirchwey: Cold War Critic," in *Redefining the Past: Essays in Diplomatic History in Honor of William Appleman Williams*, ed. Lloyd Gardner (Corvallis: Oregon State Univ. Press, 1986), 157–68.

6. The *Century*'s circulation in 1946 was 34,000. According to Pells, *Liberal Mind in a Conservative Age*, 11, *Partisan Review* had 7,000, while the *Nation* boasted 45,000. (The *Atlantic* reached 156,000, and *Life* worked on a whole different plane with 5.2 million.)

7. Fox, *Reinhold Niebuhr*, 168. This judgment raised hackles in Niebuhrian circles, provoking numerous reminiscences about the power of Niebuhr's prayers and sermons. Fox's point stands for Niebuhr's writing in *C&C*, but to round out the view see Ursula Niebuhr, ed., *Remembering Niebuhr: Letters of Reinhold and Ursula Niebuhr* (San Francisco: Harper and Row, 1990).

8. Kellerman, "Apologist of Power," does insinuate such doubts for the postwar period; with HUAC on his trail, Kellerman speculates, Niebuhr "toed the line." For a different view, see Fox, *Reinhold Niebuhr*, 207–8.

9. Paul Merkley, *Reinhold Niebuhr: A Political Account* (Montreal: McGill-Queens Univ. Press, 1975), 151.

10. See, e.g., Henry Sloane Coffin, "The Continuing Pacifist Menace," 16 Nov. 1942, 1–3; Bennett, "A False Christian Nationalism," 23 Mar. 1942, 6–7; John Knox, "Can Evil Always Be Overcome with Good?" 8 Mar. 1943, 2–4; unsigned editorial, "On a Certain Christian Defeatism," 5 May 1941, 2; Robert Fitch, "The New Menace in Isolationism," 9 Feb. 1942, 5–6.

11. For an overview see John Foster Dulles et al., "Six Pillars of Peace," 13 May 1943, 5–6 and 28 June 1943, 6–8. Writers included Dulles, Harold Dodds (president of Princeton University), Sumner Wells (undersecretary of state), Arthur Hays Sulzberger (publisher of the *New York Times*) Francis Sayre (assistant secretary of state); Joseph Ball (senator) and Thomas Dewey (governor of New York). For more on this group, which distributed 500,000 copies of its handbook even before the "Six Pillars" project (which was as an abridgment for even wider dissemination), see Warren, "Intervention and International Organization," 49–51.

12. James Hudnut-Beumler, "The American Churches and U.S. Intervention," in *The Church's Public Role*, ed. Dieter Hessel, 140. On Dulles and his religious connections see Mark Toulouse, *The Transformation of John Foster Dulles: From Prophet of Realism to Priest of Nationalism* (Macon, Ga.: Mercer Univ. Press, 1985); and Joel Kovel, "John Foster Dulles and His Terrible Swift Sword," in *Red Hunting in the Promised Land: Anticommunism and the Making of America* (New York: Basic Books, 1994), 64–86.

13. Unsigned editorial, "Whether We Live or Die," 5 May 1941, 2; Howard Chandler Robbins, "Afterthoughts on the Farewell Address," 8 Mar. 1943, 1–2; Bennett, "An Opportunity Neglected," 7 Aug. 1944, 1–2; Albert Gailord Hart, "Justice in Defense Financing," 22 Sept. 1941, 4–6.

14. See, e.g., Samuel McCrea Cavert, "The Church in World Wars I and II," 15 Oct. 1942, 2–4. This is a common theme in the literature on Niebuhr and in histories of twentieth-century Protestantism. Marty, *Modern American Religion*, 2:390, provides a typical summary when he says that "the concept of holy war always struck [Niebuhr] as idolatrous. . . . He could only see fighting the impending war as a negative task, a burden. In the end Niebuhr's attitude has to be described as one of acquiescence to the necessity of fighting." This provided "a tinge of moderation in the bitter polemics" around the war.

15. Unsigned editorial, "The Crisis," 10 Feb. 1941, 2, 3. At this time *C&C* did not advocate a declaration of war, but it argued that the situation required supporting the lend-lease bill that supplied U.S. arms to Britain, as well as granting "sweeping powers" to President Roosevelt.

16. F. Ernest Johnson, "Shall the Church Pray for Victory?" 15 June 1942, 1–2; Niebuhr, "Does the Church Pray?" 15 June 1942, 3–4; W. Burnett Easton, "Praying for Victory," 10 Aug. 1942, 6–7; Harry Lincoln Boardman, "Correspondence," 5 Oct. 1942, 8.

17. F. Ernest Johnson, "Denominational Pronouncements on the War," 7 Aug. 1944, 7, quoting an official Presbyterian statement. This article as a whole, pp. 6–8, shows that disagreements about peace and imperialism continued among Protestant leaders.

18. I discuss *C&C*'s writing on these issues in later sections.

19. Niebuhr, "Death of the President," 30 Apr. 1945, 4–6; Niebuhr, "Winston Churchill and Great Britain," 2 May 1955, 51–52.

20. Unsigned editorial, "Is the Bombing Necessary?" 3 Apr. 1944, 1–2; Robert Handy cites this article as evidence of wartime criticism in his *C&C* retrospective, "Continuity and Change through Twenty Years," 6 Feb. 1961, 9; Stone, *Reinhold Niebuhr,* 110, asserts that Niebuhr "disagreed with the program of saturation bombing," with no specific citation. Charles Brown, *Niebuhr and His Age,* 188, has the best nuance. He cites this article with the comment that Niebuhr "questioned the change from 'precision' to 'obliteration' bombing," and says that Niebuhr regarded the bombing as a "tragic necessity" despite his questions.

21. *C&C* Board of Sponsors, "The Church and the Chaplains," 1 Nov. 1943, 1; unsigned editorial, "Our Ministry to the Armed Forces," 1 Nov. 1943, 2–3; Chaplain Karl Olsson, "Correspondence," 30 Apr. 1945, 6; Spurrier, "The Church and the Soldier's Sex Problem," 11 Dec. 1944, 4–6; unsigned editorial notes, 7 Aug. 1944, 2; quotation from Major General F. H. Osborn, "The Soldier Gets His Bearings," 7 Aug. 1944, 5.

22. Handy, *History of Union Theological Seminary,* 200–203.

23. These activities are summarized in Merkley, *Reinhold Niebuhr,* 189–90. King, "The Reform Establishment and the Ambiguities of Influence," discusses 1940s ecumenical commissions and their relation to government.

24. In my random sample of wartime articles, ten out of sixty-two had this as their major focus, and many others touched on it, especially beginning in 1943. For more information about my sample, see the appendix. See, e.g., Board of Sponsors, "Statement on Post-War Settlement," 1 Nov. 1943, 3; Justin Wroe Nixon, "Power Politics within World Government," 1 Nov. 1943, 4–6; Charles Taft, "Anglo-American Economic Relations," 11 Dec. 1944, 5–7; Frederick Pollock, "Notes on European Post-War Economic Problems," 3 Apr. 1944, 3–6; Niebuhr, "Common Counsel for the United Nations," 5 Oct. 1942, 1–2; Paul Kwei, "The Treatment of Japan," 30 Apr. 1945, 2–4. In 1942 *C&C* featured a lengthy series on many issues relating to planning a postwar order including "Jewish Problem and Its Solution," "National Sovereignty and International Federation," "Small Nations and European Reconstruction," and many others; for an overview see "Post-War Reconstruction," 9 Feb. 1942, 6.

25. Unsigned editorial, "The Crisis," 10 Feb. 1941, 3.

26. Niebuhr, "Imperialism and Irresponsibility," 24 Feb. 1941, 6.

27. Niebuhr, "Plans for World Reorganization," 19 Oct. 1942, 3–6; Niebuhr, "Anglo-American Destiny and Responsibility," 4 Oct. 1943, reprinted in *God's New Israel: Religious Interpretations of American Destiny,* ed. Conrad Cherry (Englewood Cliffs, N.J.: Prentice Hall, 1971), 303, 304.

28. Paul Boyer, *By the Bomb's Early Light: American Thought and Culture at the Dawn of the Atomic Age* (New York: Pantheon, 1985), 9–10, 211.

29. Rhoda McCulloch, "Japan's Surrender," 17 Sept. 1945, 1–2; Niebuhr, "Our Relations to Japan," 17 Sept. 1945, 5–7. On racist dimensions of the U.S.-Japanese war, see John Dower, *War without Mercy: Race and Power in the Pacific War* (New York: Pantheon, 1986).

30. Boyer, *Bomb's Early Light,* 214.

31. Cited in Fox, *Reinhold Niebuhr,* 224; Fox goes on to show that Niebuhr's own positions "were far more equivocal."

32. Boyer, *Bomb's Early Light,* 202–3, 226–27.

33. Oldham commission of the British Council of Churches, "The Era of Atomic Power," 10 June 1946, 4.

34. Angus Dun et al., "Christian Conscience and Weapons of Mass Destruction: Report of a Commission Appointed by the Federal Council of Churches of Christ in America," 11 Dec. 1950, 165. Boyer discusses the document in *Bomb's Early Light,* 346–47.

35. Georgia Harkness and Robert Calhoun, "The Two Dissenting Opinions," 25 Dec. 1950, 175.

36. See, e.g., E. Lansing Bennett, "Correspondence," 22 Sept. 1941, 8. Outside my random sample, the most notable exception to *C&C*'s rule was Elton Trueblood, "Vocational Christian Pacifism," 3 Nov. 1941, 2–5.

37. Niebuhr, "Japan and the Christian Conscience," *Christian Century,* 10 Nov. 1937, cited in Marty, *Modern American Religion,* 2:389. For an authoritative statement of the position in *C&C* see Dun et al., "Christian Conscience and Weapons of Mass Destruction," 163.

38. *C&C* board member John Mackay joined a Presbyterian support committee for religious objectors, even though some of these objectors had been expelled from Union Seminary after refusing to register for the draft. Handy, *History of Union Theological Seminary,* 199, and two photocopies in author's possession, "Redeeming a Pledge," pamphlet of the Council for Presbyterians in Civilian Public Service," ca. 1942; "Peace Fellowship Honors and Seeks Out World War II Objectors," Newsletter of Presbyterian Peace Fellowship, ca. 1990. George Houser, "Resisting the Draft," *Christian Century,* 16 Aug. 1995, 774–77, is a memoir by one of these pacifists; he was expelled from Union but later became a frequent *C&C* contributor.

39. A. J. Muste, "The H-Bomb as Deterrent," 14 June 1954, 77–79. See also Muste, "Correspondence," 14 Nov. 1949, 150–51.

40. Bennett, "Response to Muste," 14 June 1954, 77.

41. See William McLoughlin, *Billy Graham, Revivalist in a Secular Age* (New York: Ronald Press, 1960), 50–51; Dwight Wilson, *Armageddon Now! The Premillennarian Response to Russia and Israel since 1917* (Grand Rapids: Baker Book House, 1977), 153–54; and Erling Jorstad, *The Politics of Doomsday* (Nashville: Abingdon, 1970), 50 and passim.

42. Examples cited in Boyer, *Bomb's Early Light,* 196, 201, 200. See also Wittner, *Rebels against War,* 180–81. Boyer surveys a variety of religious and peace movement positions, 211–29 and passim, showing that *C&C* was far more nuanced than the evangelical precursor of *Christianity Today, United Evangelical Action,* which said, "If the people [who control the bomb] are saved Christians, it will do the world no harm. If they are pagans, beware" (199). However, the Catholic press tended to oppose the bomb in stronger terms, as did the secular African American press.

43. Boyer, *Bomb's Early Light,* 211, 229.

44. F. Ernest Johnson, "Our Date with Destiny," 14 Apr. 1947, 1–2.

45. Thomas J. McCormick, *America's Half-Century: United States Foreign Policy in the Cold War* (Baltimore: Johns Hopkins Univ. Press, 1989), 78–79; Bruce Cumings, ed., *Child of Conflict: The Korean-American Relationship, 1943–53* (Seattle: Univ. of Washington Press, 1983), 49.

46. Liston Pope, "The Shift in American Policy," 24 July 1950, 98. On Korea, see Cumings, *Child of Conflict,* and Cumings, "Reckoning with the Korean War," *Nation,* 25 Oct. 1986, 393, 406–9. See also Howard Schonberger, "The Cold War and the American Empire in Asia," *Radical History Review* 33 (1985): 139–54.

47. LaFeber's influential *America, Russia, and the Cold War* uses Niebuhr as his representative cold war liberal, presenting him moving (in Paul Merkley's words) in "lock-step conformity with official Cold War policy." Merkley, *Reinhold Niebuhr,* 207–8, provides a concise summary of LaFeber's argument with some mild qualifications.

48. Specifically, in my cross section of 158 articles from 1945 to 1956, the major theme of 47 was the cold war in Europe, and 26 more focused on other foreign policy issues.

49. I rated all the articles in my sample on a scale from 1 to 5, with 1 representing articles that would have been of exclusive interest for religious readers, and 5 representing pieces that could equally well have been published in a purely secular journal. Between 1945 and 1956, fully 48 of 158 articles were rated 1, whereas only 8 were rated 5. The rest—more 2's than 4's—held interest for nonreligious people, but parts of their arguments were especially relevant for the religious. Most of the 1's and 2's had clear sociopolitical dimensions; *C&C* simply expressed these concerns in ways that held limited interest outside religious circles.

50. See, e.g., Tillich, "Theology of Missions," 21 Mar. 1955, 35–38; John Dillenberger, "Tillich's Use of the Concept 'Being,'" 16 Mar. 1953, 30–31; Langdon Gilkey, "Morality and the Cross," 5 Apr. 1954, 35–38.

51. See, e.g., Roger Shinn, "The Problem Beneath the Problems of Christian Living" (review of H. Richard Niebuhr, *Christ and Culture*), 17 Sept. 1951, 117–20; Bennett, "Karl Barth in Translation" (review of *Church Dogmatics*), 1 Oct. 1956, 122–23. Robert Bilheimer, "A Long Step Forward: Second Interpretation" (review of a major World Council of Churches document), 13 Oct. 1952, 133–35.

52. See, e.g., Ursula Niebuhr, "Partakers in His Resurrection," 30 Mar. 1953, 33–34; Paul Scherer, "It's Christmas Again!" 13 Dec. 1954, 164–65; Edward P. Parsons, "Gospel of Resurrection," 29 Mar. 1948, 33. *C&C* always published at least one such article at Christmas and Easter.

53. See, e.g., Fritz Kunkel, "Psychotherapy: A Contribution to Religious Life and Thought," 7 July 1947, 3–5 (correlating sin and neurosis); James Pike, "Religion in Higher Education and the Problem of Pluralism," 8 Jan. 1951, 178–79; Niebuhr, "Weakness of Common Worship in American Protestantism," 28 May 1951, 68–70 (calling for higher liturgical styles); Charles Drake, "Battle on the Revised Standard Version," 6 July 1953, 90–92.

54. See, e.g., Bennett, "'The Responsible Society' at Evanston," 12 July 1954, 90–92; M. Searle Bates, "World Council as Seen at Evanston," 20 Sept. 1954, 115–18; Robert Searle, "Distinctive Features of Protestant Cooperation in New York City," 19 Sept. 1949, 117–19; Umphrey Lee, "Tragedy of Disunion," 14 Oct. 1946, 1–2; Henry Pitney Van Dusen, "The Unity of Christendom: An Historical Footnote," 4 Feb. 1952, 2, 8. Most "World Church: News and Notes" sections had at least one story on ecumenism.

55. Niebuhr, "Democracy, Secularism, and Christianity," 2 Mar. 1953, 24.

56. Will Herberg, "Faith and Politics: Some Reflections on Whittaker Chambers's *Witness*," 29 Sept. 1952, 124; Niebuhr, "False Defense of Christianity," 12 June 1950, 73.

57. Fox, *Reinhold Niebuhr*, 233–34, 201, 229. Fox notes that "The Fight for Germany" also appeared in *Time* and *Reader's Digest*, and that Niebuhr's simultaneous *C&C* reflection covering similar ground, "Report on Germany," 14 Oct. 1946, 6–7, was considerably more nuanced.

58. F. Ernest Johnson, "Our Date with Destiny," 14 Apr. 1947, 1–2.

59. Bennett, "Some Impressions from Geneva," 14 Oct. 1946, 5.

60. See, e.g., Shinn, "War Wounds in Europe," 17 Sept. 1945, 2–5. This was among *C&C*'s rare articles at this time which told concrete stories about the human impact of war, rather than speaking in an abstract voice that focused on the options of elite planners. See also Cynthia Nash, "People Displaced," 3 Mar. 1947, 3–6.

61. Heinz-Horst Schrey, "German Church between Russia and America," 2 Aug. 1948, 108.

62. Merkley, *Reinhold Niebuhr*, 199.

63. Fox, *Reinhold Niebuhr*, 228–29, citing "The Fight for Germany." A typical *C&C* argument along similar lines was Niebuhr, "Two Forms of Tyranny," 2 Feb. 1948, 3–5.

64. See, e.g., Niebuhr, "The Moral and Political Judgments of Christians," 6 July 1959, 99–104, esp. 100–101; Niebuhr, "Report on Germany," 14 Oct. 1946, 6–7.

65. Cited in Fox, *Reinhold Niebuhr*, 235, which gives additional citations on the Barth-Niebuhr debate.

66. Karl Barth, "Karl Barth's Letter on German Remilitarization" (17 Feb. 1951), in *Witness to a Generation: Significant Writings from* Christianity and Crisis, *1941–1966*, ed. Wayne Cowan (New York: Bobbs-Merrill, 1966), 251, 252. Cowan does not mention that *C&C* tended to oppose Barth's position at the time.

67. See, e.g., Charles West, "Challenge for the East: Josef Hromadka," 19 Oct. 1953, 131–34; see also Henry Smith Leiper, "Christian Honesty in Communist Lands," 22 Jan. 1951, 185–86, who argued that Christian writings from Eastern Europe cannot be trusted because they are coerced by the government. Two more useful barometers of this discussion are Bennett, "East and West in Amsterdam," 4 Oct. 1948, 122–23; and W. A. Visser't Hooft, "What Can Churches Do for Peace?" 12 June 1950, 77, which said no to "even considering the possibility of universal mass murder and the self-destruction of mankind."

68. Josef Hromadka, "A Voice from the Other Side," 19 Mar. 1951, 29, 27. Hromadka was commenting on a statement from a 1950 WCC meeting in Toronto, which endorsed the UN policy and said that "the aggressive imperialism of the police state [is] the most virulent form of man's disobedience to God" (cited by Hromadka, 28). Despite Hromadka's stinging attacks, *C&C* did not break with him until 1957, when he refused to denounce the Soviet invasion of Hungary. Bennett then said in "A Matter for Regret," 21 Jan. 1957, 190, "It is hard to see how his many friends in the West . . . can again take seriously what he says." See also Anonymous, "A Hungarian Answers Hromadka," 4 Mar. 1957, 19–24.

69. M. Searle Bates (a board member and a former China missionary) was important in keeping the issue alive. Chinese counterparts of Hromadka sometimes received space. See, e.g., Y. T. Wu, "The Reformation of Christianity," 23 Jan. 1950, 187–88. This anti-imperialist argument was published with a reply from missionary Robbins Strong, 188–89, who said, "It is probably inevitable that any world power will appear to be imperialistic."

70. Niebuhr, "Should We Be Consistent?" 6 Feb. 1950, 1–2.

71. Bennett, "The Problem of Asiatic Communism," 7 Aug. 1950, 109-11. Arguing along similar lines, Henry Pitney Van Dusen, "Positive Policy for Asia," 14 Nov. 1949, 145–46, spoke of a broad-based Asian "revolution" in which "the deep motivation of the masses is . . . nationalist, [with] aspirations parallel[ing] those of our own Republic in the days of its birth."

72. Pope, "The Communist Threat in South Africa," 9 Aug. 1954, 106; Niebuhr, "The New Nations: Seeds, Buds, and Flowers," 30 Mar. 1959, 34–35; anonymous missionary in South America, "Crisis of Democracy in Latin America," 14 May 1951, 59, 60.

73. Niebuhr, "Laos and Cuba: Problems for Review," 23 Jan. 1961, 209–10; Niebuhr, "Our Latin Policy," 2 Apr. 1961, 42–43. Ernest Lefever, "Africa: Tribalism versus the State," 27 Dec. 1965, 279, 280.

74. Niebuhr, "The Moral and Political Judgments of Christians," 6 July 1959, 101. On the Dutch statement see J. G. Mees, "The Dutch Church's Stand on Indonesia," 2 May 1949, 51–53.

75. Niebuhr, "Editorial Notes," 2 May 1955, 51. This was a response to the founding of a nonaligned voting bloc in the UN at the Bandung Conference of 1955. On U.S. relations with the Philippines and Indonesia as imperialist, see Gabriel Kolko, *Confronting the Third World* (New York: Pantheon, 1988). For more on *C&C*, colonialism, and empire see George Shepard, "The Challenge of Colonialism and Racialism," 6 Feb. 1956, 3–6.

76. Board of Sponsors, "Program of *Christianity and Crisis*," 16 Feb. 1948, 11–13.

77. Will Scarlett, "Point Four," 22 Mar. 1954, 25. See also Bennett, "Is It the End of Point Four?" 2 Nov. 1953, 137–38 and WCC Division of Studies, "Common Christian Responsibility toward Areas of Rapid Social Change," 19 Sept. 55, 115–17.

78. Charles Gilkey, "Have We Any Spiritual Capital for Export?" 3 Mar. 1947, 1–2.

79. Robert Good, "The Danger of Disillusionment with Africa," 20 Mar. 1961, 33, 34. See also George Houser, "Our Faltering UN Strategy on Africa," 20 Mar. 1961, 38–41.

80. Roy Blough, "Toward an International Economic Policy," 29 Apr. 1963, 78.

81. Unsigned editorial note, 3 Apr. 1944, 2; Eugene Barnett, "Beirut, Palestine, and the Middle East," 14 May 1951, 114–17; Herman Reissig, "Another Look at the Arab-Israeli Problem," 16 Apr. 1956, 44–46; Alan Geyer, "Christians and 'The Peace of Jerusalem,'" 10 July 1967, 160–64.

82. Van Dusen, "A First Glimpse of South Africa," 16 Feb. 1953, 12. Neither the African National Congress nor the more radical Congress of the People was mentioned in the article, and Van Dusen did not seem to have either in mind when speaking of "moderation"—probably he was thinking of the Liberal Party. However, some *C&C* writers supported the ANC; see Pope, "Communist Threat in South Africa," 9 Aug. 1954, 105–6; and Z. K. Matthews's two-part article, "The Crisis in South America" (corrected to "South Africa" in the second installment), which ran on 10 Nov. 1952, 146–49, and 24 Nov. 1952, 154–59. Aside from Pope, *C&C* insiders simply did not care much about Africa at this time.

83. The "fallen nature" quotation and much of my thinking on this issue is indebted to Noble, *End of American History*, 144.

84. Niebuhr, "The Moral and Political Judgments of Christians," 6 July 1959, 99.

85. From a sample of 158 articles between 1946 to 1956, this figure represents 25 articles from a catchall category of "domestic liberal issues," plus 12 more focused on race relations or religion in the public schools.

86. Bennett, *Christianity and Communism* (New York: Association Press, 1948), 109, 125.

87. Ibid., 116, 112. Bennett, "The Responsible Society' at Evanston," 12 July 1954, 90–92, argued similarly, upholding the anticapitalist rhetoric of WCC documents but assuring *C&C* readers that this was only an attack on laissez-faire capitalism, not the New Deal.

88. Bennett, "Reinhold Niebuhr's Social Ethics," in *Reinhold Niebuhr*, ed. Charles Kegley, 126, 129.

89. Niebuhr, "Democracy, Secularism, and Christianity," 2 Mar. 1953, 20.

90. Niebuhr, "The Theme of Evanston," 9 Aug. 1954, 111.

91. Bennett, "Retrospect and Prospect," 27 Dec. 1976, 312–13.

92. Fox, *Reinhold Niebuhr*, 197. Fox discusses the heyday of *Radical Religion* on 167–69, calling it Niebuhr's "own personal megaphone." He says that "at its peak it had only a thousand subscribers . . . but [in the late 1930s] its influence extended throughout the church" (168).

93. Ibid., 255. Merkley, *Reinhold Niebuhr,* 203, says Niebuhr left the *Nation* in 1951 because he perceived the new editor, Alvarez del Vayo, as pro-Soviet.

94. William Lee Miller, "The Government and the Steel Strike," 30 Nov. 1959, 169. For an article calling for bolder clergy support for labor, see anonymous southern labor leader, "The Minister and Industrial Peace," 29 Mar. 1948, 37–38.

95. Pope, "Vacuum on the Left," 6 Aug. 1951, 105–6; see also Pope, "Social Problems Then and Now," 7 Feb. 1955, 3–4. In the 1930s Pope wrote a classic study, *Millhands and Preachers,* on the relationship of churches from various social classes to a 1929 Communist-led textile strike in Gastonia, North Carolina.

96. Francis P. Miller, "Christian Ethics and Practical Politics," 9 June 1952, 77–80.

97. Brown, "Confessions of a Political Neophyte," 19 Jan. 1953, 186–92. Justice Felix Frankfurter liked this article so well that he bought a few extra copies for academic friends, according to Shinn, "Reinhold Niebuhr in His Letters," 18 Nov. 1991, 375.

98. Robert Fitch, "Heresy Trial in California," 12 June 1950, 77–79.

99. Stephen Whitfield, *The Culture of the Cold War* (Baltimore: Johns Hopkins Univ. Press, 1991), 21, 42. The politician in question was Albert Canwell, Washington State Legislative Fact-Finding Commission on Un-American Activities. On the right in the 1950s, see Diamond, *Roads to Dominion.*

100. F. Ernest Johnson, "The Loyalty Dragnet," 12 Nov. 1951, 146. See also Pope, "The Great Lie," 17 Apr. 1950, 41–42; John Mackay, "The New Idolatry," 6 July 1953, 93; Niebuhr, "Editorial Notes," 6 July 1953, 90.

101. Bennett, "Protestant Clergy and Communism," 3 Aug. 1953, 109.

102. Niebuhr, "Editorial Notes," 16 Mar. 1953, 26. For a later pro-Rosenberg article see Paul Lehmann, "The Rosenbergs, Then and Now: History's New Light," 17 July 1978, 185–87. For recent evidence about the case based on records from the USSR, see Walter Schneir and Miriam Schneir, "Cryptic Answers," *Nation,* 14 Aug. 1995, 152–53. It reveals that Julius was in fact a spy, but provides no direct evidence that he passed atomic secrets. It also shows that the FBI knew at the time of the trial that Ethel was *not* a spy.

103. Fox, *Reinhold Niebuhr,* 255; Merkley, *Reinhold Niebuhr,* 206. The quotation is from Niebuhr, "Why Is Communism So Evil?" in *The World Crisis and Christian Responsibility,* ed. Ernest Lefever (New York: Association Press, 1958), 50. Lefever says this article was reprinted from the *New Leader;* Merkley calls the State Department version a "shamelessly distorted" argument and seems to imply that some of this distortion was introduced by the State Department. *C&C* offered the Lefever book free with new subscriptions in 1958.

104. Bennett, *Radical Imperative,* 8–9.

105. Niebuhr, "Our Fifteenth Birthday," 7 Feb. 1955, 2; Niebuhr, "Ten Fateful Years," 5 Feb. 1951, 2.

106. Board of Sponsors, "Program of *Christianity and Crisis,*" 16 Feb. 1948, 11–13.

107. Charles Malik, "The Crisis of Faith," 2 Oct. 1950, 122, 123, 125. It is possible to imagine Niebuhr's self-critical instincts leading him to hesitate before publishing this piece, but in any case it brought to the surface logic implicit in his thinking and that of other *C&C* writers.

108. Cited in Kovel, *Red Hunting,* 71. Kovel's speculations about religion and the psychological dynamics of the cold war are stimulating. He adds that Dulles was enough of an internationalist and moralist that he "must have known enough about the real story of colonization . . . to be appalled at what he was writing." But "How could Dulles be appalled at what he was writing, when he wrote in order not to be appalled? And he wrote, or thought in this way precisely because he had the kind of conscience that tells a man that he must see himself as the moral light and redeemer of the world." Kovel relates his insights about U.S. foreign policy elites to liberation theologies in his "Liberation Theology / Liberation Spirituality," *Zeta,* Feb. 1990, 101–3.

109. Kovel, *Red Hunting,* 50, citing Mr. X [George Kennan], "The Sources of Soviet Conduct," *Foreign Affairs* 25 (1947): 566–82.

Chapter 3

1. Niebuhr, "School, Church, and the Ordeals of Integration, 1 Oct. 1956, 121–22.

2. Findlay, *Church People in the Struggle,* 20, 87, reports that in the Till case, the NCC "did not want to criticize the verdict of a jury" and that in 1964 the NCC general secretary gave the FBI an internal document of the NCC Commission on Religion and Race that listed all participants in SNCC's Oxford orientation session for Mississippi Freedom Summer.

3. In Findlay, *Church People in the Struggle,* only 28 out of 250 pages treat the period before 1963. In part, Cone's *Martin and Malcolm* can be read as a reflection on how much whites in general, and white churches in particular, can be trusted as allies of blacks. Intensive studies of the 1960s like Findlay's, as well as studies exploring a longer time frame, are both important evidence for answering this question.

4. Edward Parsons, "Reflections on the San Francisco Conference," 30 Apr. 1945, 1–2.

5. Lee was director of the NCC's Department of Racial and Cultural Relations; on his role at the NCC see Findlay, *Church People in the Struggle,* chap. 1, esp. 19. I cannot speak with complete confidence about percentages because *C&C* published some writers whom I cannot identity. Clearly the overwhelming majority were whites, and I have checked the identities of most people who wrote on race relations.

6. Benjamin Mays, "Church Will Be Challenged at Evanston," 9 Aug. 1954, 107. Mays was a member of *C&C*'s board of sponsors, its least active circle of leaders. On Mays and other black leaders who worked with the white religious establishment, see Wills, "An Enduring Distance: Black Americans and the Establishment," in *Between the Times,* 168–92; and Mays, *Born to Rebel: An Autobiography* (Athens: Univ. of Georgia Press, 1987).

7. Frank Graham, "The Need for Wisdom: Two Suggestions for Carrying Out the Supreme Court's Decision against Segregation," 30 Apr. 1955, 66, 67, 66.

8. Azza Salama Layton, manuscript circulated at 1996 NEH seminar on the Roots and Legacies of the 1960s, 145, 147-48. Layton's examples are from a State Department memorandum to the White House that lobbied for a stronger U.S. civil rights policy. This memorandum in turn cited Nkrumah's autobiography.

9. Niebuhr, "Editorial Notes," 2 May 1955, 50–51; Niebuhr, "School, Church, and the Ordeals of Integration," 1 Oct. 1956, 121–22; Herbert Edwards, "Niebuhr, 'Realism,' and Civil Rights in America," 3 May 1986, 12–15, provides a concise retrospective summary of Niebuhr's views on civil rights.

10. Niebuhr, "Bad Days at Little Rock," 14 Oct. 1957, 131. See also Colbert Cartwright, "The Church, Race, and the Arts of Government," 16 Feb. 1959, 12–14.

11. S. Macon Cowles, "Can We Abolish Jim Crow in Armed Services?" 18 Oct. 1948, 134; Edward Parsons, "The Crisis in Negro Rights," 7 June 1948, 73–74.

12. Stiles Lines, "The Race Dilemma in South Carolina," 21 July 1952, 100.

13. See, e.g., Waldo Beach, "Storm Warnings from the South," 19 Mar. 1956, 30.

14. "Church News and Notes: Desegregation," 19 Mar. 1956, 31. A comprehensive article by J. Oscar Lee, "Churches and Race Relations—A Survey," 4 Feb. 1957, 4–7, included two paragraphs about the boycott, stressing its "religious motivation" evidenced in nonviolence. On the role of black churches in Montgomery see Branch, *Parting the Waters.*

15. Ernest Campbell and Thomas Pettigrew, "Vignettes from Little Rock," 29 Oct. 1957, 128–36.

16. Waldo Beach, "The Courage of Self-Restraint," 14 Oct. 1957, 129.

17. Malcolm X with Alex Haley, *The Autobiography of Malcolm X* (New York: Grove, 1964); Malcolm X, *The End of White World Supremacy: Four Speeches by Malcolm X,* ed. Imam Benjamin Karin (New York: Seaver Books, 1971). See also Cone, *Martin and Malcolm and America;* and Michael Eric Dyson, "X Marks the Plots: A Critical Reading of Malcolm's Readers," *Social Text* 35 (1993): 25–55.

18. Quotation from Waldo Beach, "Storm Warnings from the South," 19 Mar. 1956, 28. It is important to note that this was a Y hand qualification in Beach's mind, and that on balance Beach was trying to build support for the NAACP.

19. Liston Pope, "Revolution in Race Relations," 27 Nov. 1950, 154. Pope later published a full-length study with a strong integrationist argument, *The Kingdom beyond Caste* (New York: Friendship Press, 1957).

20. Lines, "The Race Dilemma in South Carolina," 21 July 1952, 102.

21. Of these eight articles, four were either very short "News and Notes" pieces or letters to the editor; only two appeared after 1951. Since my sample includes a few names I cannot identify, these numbers reflect some guesses about the sex of writers based on their first names.

22. Elaine Tyler May, *Homeward Bound: American Families in the Cold War Era* (New York: Basic Books, 1988); Breines, *Young, White, and Miserable.* For concise overviews of U.S. women's history see Linda Gordon, "U.S. Women's History," in Foner, *The New American History,* 185–210; and Sara Evans and Harry Boyte, *Free Spaces: The Sources of Democratic Change in America* (New York: Harper and Row, 1986), 69–108.

23. Elisabeth Schüssler Fiorenza, "Changing the Paradigms," *Christian Century,* 5 Sept. 1990, 796, 797.

24. Parsons, "Reflections on the San Francisco Conference," 30 Apr. 1945, 1. This is the same article cited earlier that posed an alternative between the rule of international law and the "chaos of jungle ethics." Warren Holleman, "Reinhold Niebuhr on the United Nations and Human Rights," *Soundings* 70 (1987): 329–54, analyzes how the Niebuhrians related to the UN during the cold war era.

25. F. Ernest Johnson, "Our Date with Destiny," 14 Apr. 1947, 1–2.

26. Edward Parsons, "A Tract for Any Time," 2 Oct. 1950, 125, 127. Boys' school quote from Whitfield, *The Culture of the Cold War,* 43. On Schlesinger see Pells, *Liberal Mind in a Conservative Age,* passim; on his links with Niebuhr, see the many comments on their relationship in Fox, *Reinhold Niebuhr,* 225–81, as well as Schlesinger, "Reinhold Niebuhr's Role in American Political Thought and Life," in Charles Kegley, *Reinhold Niebuhr,* 189–222. For more examples of links between male cold war ideology and rigid gender/sexual boundaries see Rogin, *Ronald Reagan;* and May, *Homeward Bound.*

27. On this subject see Rosemary Skinner Keller, "Women and Religion," in Lippy and Williams, *Encyclopedia of the American Religious Experience,* 1558–59; and Robert Wuthnow, *Restructuring of American Religion,* 227–29. A useful case study is Sally Purvis, *The Stained-Glass Ceiling: Churches and Their Women Pastors* (Louisville: Westminster Press, 1995). Large increases in female seminary students did not occur until the 1970s; see Conrad Cherry, *Hurrying toward Zion: Universities, Divinity Schools, and American Protestantism* (Bloomington: Indiana Univ. Press, 1995), 250–53.

28. Joan Kelly-Gadol, "The Social Relation of the Sexes: Methodological Implications of Women's History," in *Feminism and Methodology: Social Science Issues,* ed. Sandra Harding (Bloomington: Indiana Univ. Press, 1987), 15–28, focuses on the relationship of gender to the mode of production in a society, and argues that it is possible to predict women's status by placing societies "on a scale, where, at one end, familial and public activities are fairly merged, and, at the other . . . sharply differentiated." On the place of this approach within the complex world of feminist theory, see Alison Jaggar and Paula Rothenberg, *Feminist Frameworks,* 2d ed. (New York: McGraw-Hill, 1984), and additional citations in chapter 8.

29. Niebuhr, "Editorial Note," 31 Oct. 1949, 138; Kenneth Kaby, "Correspondence," 28 Nov. 1949, 158.

30. Ursula Niebuhr, "Women and the Church, and the Fact of Sex," 6 Aug. 1951, 109, 108; Betty Rice, "Report on a Meeting on 'Women and the Church,'" 6 Aug. 1951, 111. Niebuhr's "order of creation" statement should not necessarily be interpreted as a self-conscious polemic against gay/lesbian/bisexual rights, as it would be if written today. Homosexuality appeared to be outside the conscious horizon of her article, and the polemic was against women's rights advocates perceived as "soft" on affirming motherhood and sex-role differentiation. Of course, many gays and lesbians would also be "soft" on related issues, but in this case Niebuhr does not seem to have them in mind.

31. Cyril Richardson, "Women in the Ministry," 10 Dec. 1951, 166, 167 (emphasis in the original); "World Church: News and Notes," 21 July 1952, 102–3.

32. In addition, Elizabeth Morrow, a member of Union Seminary's board, was a *C&C* sponsor in the 1940s and 1950s.

33. At the eve of the explosion of female seminary enrollments in the 1970s, Union had 20 percent compared with an average of 10 percent for the Association of Theological Schools. See Cherry, *Hurrying toward Zion,* 250–53.

34. Handy, *History of Union Theological Seminary,* 192, 296, 179.

35. Ibid., 260, 224–25; Mary Ann Lundy interview. From 1945 to 1963 Union's president was Henry Pitney Van Dusen, a *C&C* board member.

36. Anne McGrew Bennett, *From Woman-Pain to Woman-Vision: Writings in Feminist Theology,* ed. Mary Hunt (Philadelphia: Fortress, 1989).

37. Mildred McAfee Horton and the general situation of female leaders in mainline Protestantism are discussed in Virginia Lieson Brereton, "United and Slighted: Women as Subordinated Insiders," in Hutchison, *Between the Times,* 143–66. On Ursula Niebuhr see Fox, *Reinhold Niebuhr,* passim; and Ursula Niebuhr, *Remembering Niebuhr.* For a discussion of how much Ursula subordinated her career to Reinhold's, see the exchange among several of Niebuhr's colleagues reported in Neuhaus, *Reinhold Niebuhr Today,* 48–51. Fox's contribution to this volume, "Niebuhr's World and Ours," 1–19, stressed Niebuhr's assumption of patriarchal authority and his relatively small contribution to housework and child care. In response to Fox's article, Shinn commended Niebuhr for helping with kitchen chores (when he was not traveling) and said that, despite accepting prevalent cultural patterns, the Niebuhrs "adjusted more than most families of their era to the challenges of a two-career couple" (51).

38. Quoted in Neuhaus, *Reinhold Niebuhr Today,* 51.

39. Cited in Whitfield, *Culture of the Cold War,* 185.

40. Niebuhr, "Sex Standards in America," 24 May 1948, 65–66; Niebuhr, "Sex and Religion in the Kinsey Report," 2 Nov. 1953, 138-40.

41. Niebuhr, "Sex and Religion in the Kinsey Report," 140–41.

42. Seward Hiltner, "Niebuhr on Kinsey," 11 Jan. 1954, 180. A response by Niebuhr, 182–83, concedes some of Hiltner's points and speaks about the "disintegrat[ion] of male dominance"—a disintegration that Niebuhr claimed to support.

43. Whitfield, *Culture of the Cold War,* 186–87.

44. Beverly Harrison, "Keeping Faith in a Sexist Church," in her book *Making the Connections,* 207.

45. *C&C* was also hostile toward evangelical and fundamentalist Protestants, but paid less attention. In 1956 *C&C* engaged in a controversy about Billy Graham, which I discuss in chapter 7. In some ways *C&C*'s attitudes toward Jews paralleled those toward Catholics, but with a smaller element of fear. Aside from a dispute about the Israel-Palestine conflict, which I discuss in chapter 4, *C&C* paid little attention to Jews during this period.

46. Whitfield, *Culture of the Cold War,* 92–99, provides examples of anticommunism by Spellman and the Catholic press, along with cautions about overgeneralizing. Gary MacEoin, *Memoirs and Memories* (Mystic: Twenty-third Publications, 1986), is a fine case study of Catholic conservatism and institutional authoritarianism by an informed observer who later became an important *C&C* writer. To place Catholic conservatives in a larger framework, see Dolan, *American Catholic Experience.*

47. Douglas Horton, "Emperor and Democracy in Japan," 4 Feb. 1946, 3. This article accepts popular stereotypes about the fanatical devotion of Japanese to the emperor, as discussed in Dower, *War without Mercy.* Horton's quoted sentence assumes a similar relationship between Catholic laity and the pope.

48. See, e.g., Charles Kean, "Protestant Reaction to Roman Catholic Pressure," 10 Nov. 1947, 2–5.

49. Karl Barth and Father Jean Daniélou, S.J., "Catholicism, Protestantism, and the One True Church (An Exchange of Letters)," 13 Dec. 1948, 162–64.

50. Most Christians who retreat from exclusive universal truth claims to more qualified and situated truth claims also assume, unless they embrace pure relativism, that within specified contexts there are responses which are better or worse, more appropriate and less appropriate—thus giving rise to possible conflicts in a more delimited framework.

51. Henry Sloane Coffin, "American Freedom and Catholic Power," 2 May 1949, 49–50. Religious liberals were not unique in worrying about this. Liberal philosopher Sidney Hook called Roman Catholicism "the oldest and greatest totalitarian movement in history," according to Whitfield, *Culture of the Cold War,* 91.

52. Fitch, "Catholic Church as a Power Polity," 10 Nov. 1947, 5, 6.

53. Paul Blanshard, *American Freedom and Catholic Power* (Boston: Beacon, 1949).

54. From the beginning, *C&C* often endorsed the teaching of religious values in public schools, and in the early 1960s it devoted much attention to proposals to allow limited public support for Catholic schools, especially through released time arrangements. *C&C* also spoke against the secularization of public education; for example, it endorsed the so-called Regent's Prayer, which was declared unconstitutional in 1962. See Niebuhr, "The Godly and the Godless," 13 Dec. 1948, 161–62; Bennett, "Aid to Parochial Schools: Two Considerations," 1 May 1961, 61–62; Harry Stearns, "Shared Time: Answer to an Impasse?" 18 Sept. 1961, 154–57; Joseph Cunneen, "Parochial Schools and the National Common Good," 18 Sept. 1961, 157–60.

55. M. Searle Bates, "O'Neill versus Blanshard: Review of *Catholicism and American Freedom,*" 9 June 1952, 75–77. Smith cited in James Hennesey, S.J., "Roman Catholics and American Politics, 1900–1960," in *Religion and American Politics,* ed. Mark Noll (New York: Oxford Univ. Press, 1990), 311.

56. Edwin Kennedy, "Preserving Our Protestant Heritage," 26 Nov. 1951, 154; Van Dusen, "An American Embassy at the Vatican—What Is at Stake?" 21 Jan. 1952, 190; Bennett, "The Vatican Appointment," 26 Nov. 1951, 153.

57. Niebuhr, "Catholics and Politics: Some Misconceptions," 23 June 1952, 84.

58. Niebuhr, "The Race Problem in America," 26 Dec. 1955, 169–70; Bennett, "Editorial Notes," 27 Dec. 1954, 170–71.

59. On the history of *Commonweal,* which was *C&C*'s closest cousin in the Catholic world, see Rodger Van Allen, *The Commonweal and American Catholicism: The Magazine, the Movement* (Philadelphia: Fortress Press, 1974). He extends his history in *Being Catholic: Commonweal from the Seventies to the Nineties* (Loyola Univ. Press, 1993).

60. Bennett, "A Protestant View of Roman Catholic Power," 4 Aug. 1958, 114–16, and 15 Sept. 1958, 120–23. This material appeared in Bennett's *Christians and the State* (New York: Scribner, 1958).

61. Archbishop Robert Lucey, "The Catholic Position on Church and State," 26 Apr. 1948, 53–54.

62. Ibid., editor's introduction, 53.

63. John Courtney Murray, *We Hold These Truths: Catholic Reflections on the American Proposition* (New York: Image, 1964). Bennett provided a very positive summary of Murray's views in "A Protestant View of Roman Catholic Power," 15 Sept. 1958, 122–23.

64. Many of these articles are collected in Cowan, ed. *Facing Protestant-Roman Catholic Tensions* (New York: Association Press, 1960).

65. See, e.g., Brown, "Shadow over the Council," 14 Dec. 1964, 246–47, and "The Unfinished Agenda of Vatican II," 20 Sept. 1965, 187–90. See also the issue of 1 Oct. 1962 with articles on Vatican II by Brown, Shinn, Phillip Scharper, and George Lindbeck, as well as continuing coverage in articles such as Brown, "Appraisals of Vatican II, Session Two," 3 Aug. 1964, 164–67; and George Lindbeck, "A Definitive Look at Vatican II," 10 Jan. 1966, 291–95.

66. Brown, "Senator Kennedy's Statement, 16 Mar. 1959, 25–26; Carol George, *God's Salesman: Norman Vincent Peale and the Power of Positive Thinking* (New York: Oxford Univ. Press, 1993), 200–205. The blind prejudice quote is from a press conference by Niebuhr and Bennett under the auspices of the Liberal Party, and was reported in the *New York Times.* For a similar attack in *C&C* see Bennett, "The Roman Catholic 'Issue' Again," 19 Sept. 1960, 125–26.

67. Cowan, "In Twenty-five Years You Pick Up a Lot of Memories," 17 Sept. 1979, 211. Running as a Bennett editorial on 7 Mar. 1960, the statement still received national press coverage.

68. Will Herberg, *Protestant, Catholic, Jew,* rev. ed. (New York: Anchor, 1960), was widely cited in *C&C* circles and among historians of U.S. religion. On Herberg, see James Hudnut-Beumler, *Looking for God in the Suburbs: The Religion of the American Dream and Its Critics, 1945–1965* (New Brunswick: Rutgers Univ. Press, 1994), 110–30.

69. Herberg, "The Sectarian Conflict over Church and State: A Divisive Threat to Our Democracy," 2 Feb. 1953, 7. Herberg quoted Niebuhr, who in turn said in an introduction (2) that Herberg should be harsher toward Catholics.

70. Herberg, "Protestantism in a Post-Protestant America," 5 Feb. 1962, 4, 5.

71. Stephen Rose, "Bishop Myers and the Pope," 10 July 1967, 164–65. This was not typical of *C&C*'s reasoning.

72. This argument supports Wuthnow, *Restructuring of American Religion,* esp. 71–80, which argues similarly about the diminishing importance of denominational boundaries after the 1950s, linked to political realignment within denominations.

Chapter 4

1. Bennett, "An Anniversary and an Arrest," 26 May 1958, 70. On the Catholic Worker movement, see Nancy Roberts, *Dorothy Day and the Catholic Worker* (Albany: SUNY Press, 1984); James Forest et al., eds., *A Penny a Copy: Readings from the Catholic Worker* (Maryknoll, N.Y.: Orbis Books, 1995); June O'Connor, *The Moral Vision of Dorothy Day: A Feminist Perspective* (New York: Crossroad, 1991); and Craig, *Religion and Radical Politics,* 174–228.

2. Charles DeBenedetti, *An American Ordeal: The Antiwar Movement of the Vietnam Era* (Syracuse: Syracuse Univ. Press, 1990), 9–13, discusses a 1955 protest against air raid drills similar to the 1958 protest, and is generally helpful for placing *C&C* within the larger currents of the peace movement, esp. 9–51. See also Maurice Isserman, *If I Had a Hammer: The Death of the Old Left and the Birth of the New Left* (New York: Basic Books, 1987), 173–85.

3. Bennett, "Epilogue: Issues for the Ecumenical Dialogue," in *Christian Social Ethics in a Changing World* (New York: Association Press, 1966), 379–80. Carl-Henric Grenholm, *Christian Ethics in a Revolutionary Age: An Analysis of the Social Ethics of John C. Bennett, Heinz-Dietrich Wendland, and Richard Shaull* (Uppsala: Verbum, 1973), discusses these issues in detail. See also Bennett, "The Geneva Conference 1966," 11 July 1966, 153–54. This conference provoked a famous attack by Paul Ramsey which I take up in chapter 6.

4. Bennett, "It Is Difficult to Be an American," 25 June 1966, 165–66; Eugene Carson Blake, "The Church in the Next Decade," 21 Feb. 1966, 17.

5. Bennett, "Developments in the Middle East," 18 Mar. 1957, 26; Bennett, "The Nuclear Dilemma," 11 Nov. 1961, 200–203.

6. For more on these points, see chapter 11. Briefly, the major issues in *C&C*'s crisis of the early 1950s were that Niebuhr suffered a stroke, which greatly reduced his energies, and this compounded the belief of some backers that *C&C* had served its purpose and should die a natural death after World War II.

7. This symposium took up the entire issue of 3 Mar. 1958 and included articles on Episcopalians, Southern Baptists, Christian Church/Disciples of Christ, Methodists, and Presbyterians; see especially the editorial introduction by Waldo Beach, "Southern Church and the Race Question," 3 Mar. 1958, 17–18. See also Beach, "Changing Mind of the South," 9 Sept. 1962, 119–22. As in earlier years, I cannot speak with complete confidence about percentages because *C&C* published writers whom I cannot identity. However, few articles clearly spoke about "us" and meant African Americans. In my cross section from 1957 to 1965 I can identify only one article by an African American, and it is not focused on race issues.

8. John David Maguire, "When Moderation Demands Taking Sides," 26 May 1961, 114–17; John C. Raines, "My Second Education," 21 Oct. 1991, 324–26. *C&C* also promoted freedom riding in editorials and letters from other seminary professors and freedom riders, e.g., Gaylord Noyce and Brown, "Correspondence," 7 Aug. 1961, 146–48. Maguire became a board member in 1965.

9. See, e.g., Beach, "The Sit-Down Boycott," 21 Mar. 1960, 27; Cowan, "Look-In on the Sit-Ins," 9 Jan. 1961, 203; Stephen Rose, "Why They Go to Mississippi," 3 Aug. 1964, 158–59; Kenneth Underwood and Elden Jacobson, "Probing the Ethics of Realtors," 29 May 1961, 96–99; Phillip Wogaman, "The Fair Housing Controversy in California," 3 Aug. 1964, 161–64; Thomas Pettigrew, "Our Caste-Ridden Protestant Campuses," 29 May 1961, 88–91.

10. The specific numbers were 12 on race, 14 on general domestic issues, 10 on the European cold war, and 8 on third world issues, out of a sample of 79 from 1960 to 1965. For the full period between 1957 and 1965, concentration on civil rights was less pronounced, with race as the major theme of 16 of 127 articles—compared with about 20 each for the European cold war, third world issues, and domestic liberalism. From 1965 to 1970 16 of 98 focused on race.

11. Roger Shinn, "The Burning Issue," 29 May 1961, 83. As if this had been *C&C*'s approach all along, Shinn staked out a middle ground between King, who "may be too ungrudging in attitude, too Christian" to be an effective leader, and the Nation of Islam, which "adopt[ed] the intransigence formerly the exclusive mark of white segregationists."

12. King, "From the Birmingham Jail," 27 May 1963, 89–90. For a full text of King's letter, see James M. Washington, ed., *A Testament of Hope: The Essential Writings of Martin Luther King Jr.* (New York: Harper and Row, 1986), 289–302.

13. Harold Fleming, "Universal Suffrage for Negroes," 29 May 1961, 86; Niebuhr, "Civil Rights and Democracy," 8 July 1957, 89. See also Shinn, "Power of the Franchise," 4 Mar. 1963, 23.

14. Gary Oniki, "Residential Desegregation: Confrontation for the Churches," 29 May 1961, 95.

15. Prentiss Pemberton, "Law Enforcement in Northern Cities," 8 July 1963, 124–25. Stephen Rose, "Epitaph for an Era: A Firsthand Report from Birmingham," 10 June 1963, 103–10, was one of the longest articles *C&C* ever published.

16. James Cone, *Martin and Malcolm and America.* See also William Van Deburg, *New Day in Babylon: The Black Power Movement and American Culture, 1965-1975* (Chicago: Univ. of Chicago Press, 1992); Gayraud Wilmore, *Black Religion and Black Radicalism,* 2d ed. (Maryknoll, N.Y.: Orbis Books, 1984); and Michael Omi and Howard Winant, *Racial Formation in the United States: From the 1960s to the 1980s,* 2d ed. (New York : Routledge and Kegan Paul, 1992). For more citations on black political movements, see chapter 6.

17. Cowan, "Racism in Reverse," 23 June 1958, 87. On Powell see Martin Kilson, "Adam Clayton Powell Jr.: The Militant as Politician," in *Black Leaders of the Twentieth Century,* ed. John Hope Franklin and Aug. Meier (Urbana: Univ. of Illinois Press, 1982), 259-76.

18. Robert Spike, "The Black Muslims," 29 May 1961, 99–100. This was a review of C. Eric Lincoln, *The Black Muslims in America* (Boston: Beacon Press, 1961).

19. Spike, "James Baldwin's Confession," 4 Feb. 1963, 5. Baldwin was not close to the NOI, but he agreed with some of its criticisms of Christianity and said, "I certainly refuse to be put in the position of denying the truth of Malcolm X's statements simply because I disagree with his conclusions or in order to pacify the liberal conscience" (4). See James Baldwin, *The Fire Next Time* (New York: Dell, 1964). *C&C* first wrote about Baldwin's argument when it appeared in the *New Yorker;* later the book was offered to *C&C* subscribers as part of a Christmas promotion.

20. Tom Driver, "Baldwin's *Blues for Mister Charlie,*" 22 June 1964, 125, 126. Frances Smith, "Winds of Change," 24 Dec. 1962, 230–31, raises similar points in relation to *The Fire Next Time.*

21. Bennett, "The Problem of Violence," 22 June 1964, 123.

22. Charles Lawrence and Tom Driver, "Continuing the Conversation: Baldwin's *Blues,*" 201–2. Lawrence taught sociology at Brooklyn College.

23. Spike, "The Black Muslims," 100.

24. Shinn, "Testing of the Church," 8 July 63, 122–23. Findlay, "Religion and Politics in the Sixties: The Churches and the Civil Rights Act of 1964," *Journal of American History* 77 (1990), no. 1: 66–91.

25. Frances Smith, "Churches and the Filibuster," 27 Apr. 1964, 69–70.

26. Shinn, "Civil Rights: Morality and Practical Politics," 11 Nov. 1963, 197–98; Niebuhr, "The Mounting Racial Crisis," 8 July 1963, 122.

27. St. Hereticus (a.k.a. Robert McAfee Brown), "Making the Bible 'Relevant,'" 15 Apr. 1963, 60.

28. Brown, "Correspondence," 13 Oct. 1952, 135–36; Bennett, "The Candidacy of Mr. Nixon," 25 Jan. 1960, 209–10.

29. Kenneth Thompson, "The Decade of the Fifties: A Decade without Greatness," 28 Dec. 1959, 190–91. The quiz show scandal was addressed in several *C&C* editorials and one article.

30. Beverly Harrison interview; Fox, *Reinhold Niebuhr,* 271–72.

31. Niebuhr, "One Year of the New Frontier," 5 Feb. 1962, 1–2; John Brademas, "President Kennedy and the 87th Congress: A Preview," 9 Jan. 1961, 204–7.

32. Adlai Stevenson, "The Survival of a Free Society," 11 Jan. 1960, 204, 207, with introduction by Bennett, 201. It appears in Cowan, *Witness to a Generation.*

33. For example, Bennett, "Needed: Enterprise, Public and Private," 14 Apr. 1958, 46, called for public investment and argued that economic justice was the "test of the 'new capitalism.'" Robert Lekachman, "Dilemmas of Economic Growth," 26 Dec. 1960, 192–95, argued that growth alone could not solve social problems; there was a need to decide what to produce and how to allocate it. He hoped that Kennedy could blend growth with national economic planning.

34. Bennett, "The Labor Reform Act of 1959," 21 Sept. 1959, 124.

35. Niebuhr, "Hoffa and the Teamsters," 28 Oct. 1957, 137, 138; Richard Baker, "New York's Newspaper Strike," 19 Jan. 1959, 198–99.

36. Editorial Board, "An Open Letter to the AMA," 11 June 1962, 97–98; Bennett, "'The Most Exploited Americans,'" 9 Jan. 1961, 203–4; Gordon Bjork, "Crisis in the International Monetary System," 1 Apr. 1968, 59–62; Shinn, "The Moral Meaning of Transportation," 3 Oct. 1966, 209–10.

37. See, e.g., Howard Moody, "The City: Necropolis or New Jerusalem?" 17 Sept. 1962, 152–56; Gibson Winter, "The New Christendom in the Metropolis," 26 Nov. 1962, 206–11; George Younger, "Power Structures of Urban Life," 26 Nov. 1962, 211–15.

38. Stephen Rose, "The Grass Roots Church," 25 June 1966, 168–71. Rose replied to a symposium of critics in "The Grass Roots Church: Response to Critics," 8 Aug. 1966, 186–89. See also Cox, "Reinvesting the Churches' Wealth in Inner Cities," 9 Dec. 1968, 294–95.

39. Bennett, "The Goldwater Nomination," 3 Aug. 1964, 157.

40. Editorial Board, "We Oppose Senator Goldwater!" 5 Oct. 1964, 181–83; Baker, "Pattern on the Right?" 14 Dec. 1964, 247. See also Cowan, "'Total Victory' at the Cow Palace," 3 Aug. 1964, 159–61, and *C&C* records, box 10, scrapbook, collects many press clippings about *C&C*'s endorsement such as a 31 July 1964 *Boston Globe* article entitled "Goldwater Denounced by Protestant Papers" with a large headline and picture, a *New York Post* editorial "Goldwater and Godliness," 30 Oct. 1964, and a retort from the *Arizona Republic,* 3 Aug. 1964, that Bennett "seems to have trouble distinguishing between the word of God and the word of the New York Liberal party which he serves as vice-chairman."

41. To dramatize the contrast I am making, compare Williams's *Empire as a Way of Life* or Rogin's *Ronald Reagan,* with works by Richard Hofstadter such as the *Progressive Historians* or Seymour Martin Lipset, "Religion and Politics in the American Past and Present," in *Religion and Social Conflict,* ed. Robert Lee and Martin Marty (1964; reprint, New York: Oxford Univ. Press, 1984), 55–126. On the relation of Niebuhr to Hofstadter and Williams, see Noble, *End of American History,* 90–140.

42. Niebuhr, "Protestant Individualism and the Goldwater Movement," 14 Dec. 1964, 248–50; Rose, "The Great Cowboy," 3 Aug. 1964, 167–68. It should be noted that Niebuhr presented Goldwater individualism as a residual tradition that was increasingly out of date.

43. Letter from Goldwater to Bennett, 31 May 1966; see also Goldwater to Shinn, 16 June 1966, photocopy from *C&C* archives.

44. Paul Ramsey, "Is God Mute in the Goldwater Candidacy?" with response by Bennett, 21 Sept. 1964, 175–79.

45. Wayne Cowan interview; minutes of the board of directors of *Christianity and Crisis,* 9 Nov. 1967, and internal correspondence on tax exemptions, photocopies from *C&C* archives.

46. Phillip Berrigan, "Letter from a Baltimore Jail," 22 July 1968, 168–70; William Rickenbacker's endorsement of Reagan in "Presidential Forum," 22 July 1968, 165–66. Other articles in the forum included endorsements of Hubert Humphrey (by David Little), Eugene McCarthy (by Howard Moody), and Robert Kennedy (by Cox) on 10 June 1968, 127–33; and of Nelson Rockefeller (by J. Irwin Miller) and Richard Nixon (by Senator Mark Hatfield) on 22 July 1968, 163–68. Hatfield reasoned that Nixon offered the best chance of ending the war.

47. Ivar Berg and Marcia Freeman, "The Job Corps: A Business Bonanza," 31 May 1965, 119; Sargent Shriver, letter, 9 Aug. 1965, 178–80, was an angry response from the head of the bureaucratic umbrella that covered the Job Corps.

48. Paul Younger, "The Revolt of the Welfare Poor," 6 Jan. 1969, 329–32.

49. Dan W. Dodson, "The Dynamic City," 15 Sept. 1969, 229.

50. Niebuhr, "The Changing United Nations," 3 Oct. 1960, 133–34; Lefever, "Africa: Tribalism versus the State," 27 Dec. 1965, 281, 279.

51. Thompson, "The Monroe Doctrine, 1823–1960," 8 Aug. 1960, 118–19.

52. Elisha Greifer, "Needed: A Theory of Revolution," 3 Apr. 1961, 49, 50; Louis Hartz, *The Liberal Tradition in America* (New York: Harcourt Brace, 1955); Stanley Elkins, *Slavery: A Problem in American Institutional and Intellectual Life* (Chicago: Univ. of Chicago Press, 1959). Elkins was not apologizing for slavery; in fact, he compared it to a Nazi concentration camp. His text helped underpin the controversial Moynihan report discussed in chapter 6.

53. Greifer, "Needed: A Theory of Revolution," 51–52. Greifer is citing Walt Whitman Rostow, *The Stages of Economic Growth, a Non-Communist Manifesto* (Cambridge: Cambridge Univ. Press, 1960), and Seymour Martin Lipset, *Political Man* (New York: Doubleday, 1959).

54. Greifer, "Needed: A Theory of Revolution," 51.

55. Fox makes a similar point in *Reinhold Niebuhr,* 275. A distinction between "acceptable 'authoritarian' and unacceptable 'totalitarian' states" was made famous by Jeanne Kirkpatrick during the early years of the Reagan administration.

56. Niebuhr, "Can Democracy Work?" *New Leader* (28 May 1962), 9, cited in Stone, *Reinhold Niebuhr,* 193. On the Roosevelt quotation and Trujillo, see LaFeber, *America, Russia, and the Cold War,* 255. Niebuhr criticized the U.S. invasion of the Dominican Republic in "Caribbean Blunder," 31 May 1965, 113–14, suggesting U.S. policy toward Puerto Rico as a better model.

57. Bennett, "Senator Fulbright Speaks Out," 13 Apr. 1964, 57–58. See also Bennett, "Cuba and the Monroe Doctrine," 15 Oct. 1962, 173–74. In an interesting foreshadowing of *C&C*'s future, Wayne Cowan's articles about Cuba were friendlier to Castro than most other *C&C* treatments. Cowan, "Premier Castro and Cuba," 11 May 1959, 62–63, portrayed Castro as a moderate leader who "represents the ideals and aspirations of his people"; Cowan argued that U.S. policy should be "adapted to the realities" of Cuba. See also Cowan, "Cuban-American Relations, 16 Feb. 1959, 10–11. Both articles appeared early in the revolution, before Castro was driven into an unambiguous alliance with the USSR.

58. In 1955 the WCC refocused its vision of "the responsible society" from Europe to the third world and reoriented its postwar refugee work toward international development. As explained in WCC Division of Studies, "Common Christian Responsibility toward Areas of Rapid Social Change," 19 Sept. 1955, 116, the new initiative sought to teach first world Christians "the economic implications of world community and the role of economic and technical aid from the West." For the third world it sought "responsible emancipation" from tradition, which created danger points similar to Greifer's—the breakdown of rural life and a rising urbanization which caused threats to family and community morals and a threat of left-wing social movements. "Responsible emancipation" meant avoiding these dangerous trends, promoting economic growth, and instituting liberal democracy.

59. McLeod Bryan, "Whither African Nationalism?" 2 May 1960, 59-61.

60. Anonymous "African Christian," "Further Comment on Africa and the Church," 27 June 1960, 95.

61. 'Bola Ige, "Africa of the Sixties," 20 Mar. 1961, 35–37.

62. Cowan, "Church and Society at Geneva," 19 Sept. 1966, 202, 203. Thomas was a *C&C* contributing editor from 1958 to 1972. In his "Asian Security and Development," 3 May 1965, 98–99, Thomas called for a Southeast Asian Marshall plan—but stated that it must be linked to nationalism and "some pattern of socialism" or it will "take a neocolonial form," which would drive nationalists into an alliance with communism.

63. Paul David Devanandan, "Foreign Aid and the Social and Cultural Life of India," 5 Aug. 1957, 108, 111. On Devanandan's relations to Union, see Handy, *History of Union Theological Seminary,* 240–44.

64. Dan Wasserman cartoon, photocopy, publication information unknown, ca. 1980.

65. Bennett interview. See also Stone, *Reinhold Niebuhr,* 180–91.

66. "Editor's introduction to 'Europe's Crisis and America's Dilemma,'" 7 Jan. 1957, 181.

67. Thompson, "Europe's Crisis and America's Dilemma," 7 Jan. 1957, 182, 184–85, 186.

68. Niebuhr, "Situation in the Mid-East," 15 Apr. 1957, 42–43; Niebuhr, "The New International Situation," 12 Nov. 1956, 151; Niebuhr, "Comments on 'Europe's Crisis and America's Dilemma,'" 7 Jan. 1957, 186.

69. V. E. Devadutt, "Correspondence," 10 June 1957, 79–80.

70. Bennett, "Comments on 'Europe's Crisis and America's Dilemma," 7 Jan. 1957, 187, 188. Bates, "Comments on 'Europe's Crisis and America's Dilemma,'" 7 Jan. 1957, 186–87, tended to support Bennett.

71. Bennett, "Developments in the Middle East," 18 Mar. 1957, 26.

72. On this change see Joseph Blau, *Judaism in America* (Chicago: Univ. of Chicago Press, 1976), 73–91.

73. Henry Sloane Coffin, "Perils to America in the New Jewish State," 21 Feb. 1949, 9–10.

74. On 21 Mar. 1949, *C&C* published twelve letters responding to Coffin's article, ten of which were sharply opposed. Two follow-ups on 2 May 1949 and 13 June 1949 defended Coffin's position on the state of Israel (but not on domestic issues).

75. Niebuhr, "The Unresolved Religious Problem in Christian-Jewish Relations," 12 Dec. 1966, 279, 280, 281.

76. Karl Baehr, "The Arabs and Israel," 3 Oct. 1949, 123, 124. Baehr was director of the American Christian Palestine Committee, and Niebuhr was a board member.

77. S. A. Morrison, "Israel and the Middle East," 11 July 1949, 94, 96.

78. Eugene Barnett, "Beirut, Palestine, and the Middle East," 14 May 1951, 116. This was a report from an ecumenical conference in Beirut concerned with refugee relief.

79. See, e.g., Niebuhr, "New Hopes for Peace in the Middle East," 28 May 1956, 65; Herman Reissig, "Another Look at the Arab-Israeli Problem," 16 Apr. 1956, 44–46.

80. Marshall Wingfield, "Arab and Israeli," 29 Oct. 1951, 142, 140–41.

81. Paul Scherer, "The Near East Kaleidoscope," 21 Sept. 1953, 114–19.

82. Niebuhr, "The Situation in the Middle East," 4 Aug. 1958, 109–10; Niebuhr, "Disaster in U.S. Foreign Policy," 15 Sept. 1958, 117; Thompson, "Lebanon: New Elements of Crisis," 4 Aug. 1958, 110.

83. Herbert Butterfield, "Western Policy and Colonialism," 4 Aug. 1958, 112, 113. William Irwin, "Correspondence," 15 Sept. 1957, 124 took exception to the idea that the United States was on the wrong side in India and the Philippines.

84. Butterfield, "Internationalism and the Defense of the Existing Status Quo," 10 June 1957, 76. *C&C* later quoted Butterfield in its most famous statement against the Vietnam war: *C&C* Editorial Board, "We Protest the National Policy in Vietnam," 7 Mar. 1966, 33–34.

85. Bennett, "The Great Conflict of Opinion," 11 May 1959, 61–62.

86. Bennett, "A Condition for Coexistence," 28 Apr. 1958, 53; Bennett, "Official Complacency and Nuclear Tests," 9 June 1958, 77–78; "Sino-American Relations as Viewed at Cleveland," 8 Dec. 1958, 171–72. The NCC document was not pro-communist—it simply argued that recognition was a lesser evil. Still it provoked intense debate at the conference, as well as attacks from *Christianity Today.* This in turn provoked a *C&C* editorial by Brown, "Differ-

ence of Opinion versus Distortion of Fact," 2 Mar. 1959, 18–19, which accused the evangelicals of McCarthyism. Thompson, "The NCC in a Nuclear Age," 8 Dec. 1958, 170, attacked from within *C&C*, lamenting a "return to essentially uncritical pacifist thinking."

87. Niebuhr, "Editorial Notes," 27 Apr. 1953, 51. See also Niebuhr, "Stalin—Deity to Demon," 16 Apr. 1956, 42–43.

88. M. Searle Bates, "Is There a New Russia since Stalin?" 11 Nov. 1957, 148, 150.

89. Thompson, "The Aftermath of Summitry," 13 June 1960, 81–82.

90. Niebuhr, "Limited Warfare" (review of Henry Kissinger, *Nuclear Weapons and Foreign Policy*), 11 Nov. 1957, 146; Niebuhr, "One Year of the New Frontier," 5 Feb. 1962, 1–2.

91. Niebuhr, "Why *Christianity and Crisis*?" 8 Feb. 1960, 1–2; Niebuhr, "The Decade of the Fifties: A Decade of Dizzy and Rapid Change," 28 Dec. 1959, 191–92. Niebuhr's thinking after 1950 on the limits of U.S. power in Asia and the primacy of Europe was roughly allied with Hans Morgenthau's theories about the end of "bi-polarity" in international politics. However, Merkley, *Reinhold Niebuhr*, 191–93, argues that Niebuhr "could not come to terms *intellectually* with what Morgenthau saw as the end of 'bi-polarity.'" Both could make specific analyses about the United States getting bogged down in Asian wars, but Niebuhr continued to see these wars in a basically bipolar framework, whereas Morgenthau didn't expect the USSR to be able to benefit.

92. Bennett, *Christianity and Communism* (New York: Association Press, 1948), 61–62.

93. Bennett, "The Nuclear Dilemma," 11 Nov. 1961, 200–203. For a specific application of this argument to the situation in Germany, see Bennett, "Berlin: Restraint and Discrimination in a Crisis," 18 Sept. 1961, 149–50.

94. These quotations are from a more detailed version of the argument, "Christian Ethics and International Affairs" (5 Aug. 1963), in Cowan, *Witness to a Generation*, 96, 97. Years later, in "The Bishop's Pastoral, A Response," 30 May 1983, 203, Bennett regretted that he had "half-apologized for [making his criticisms] because I did not want to make deterrence less credible."

95. Niebuhr, "Comment on 'The Nuclear Dilemma,'" 11 Nov. 1961, 202; Hans Morgenthau, "The Nuclear Discussion Continued," 11 Dec. 1961, 223; Paul Tillich, "Comment on 'The Nuclear Dilemma,'" 11 Nov. 1961, 204.

96. Paul Ramsey, "Dream and Reality in Deterrence and Defense," 25 Dec. 1961, 232.

97. Thompson, "Comment on 'The Nuclear Dilemma,'" 11 Nov. 1961, 202–3.

98. Carl Mayer, "Moral Issues in the Nuclear Dilemma," 19 Mar. 1962, 36-38. See also Eduard Heimann's contribution to the debate, 16 Apr. 1962, 59.

99. Niebuhr, "Correspondence," 2 May 1962, 48.

100. Bennett, "Ethics and Tactics in a Crisis," 10 Dec. 1962, 223.

101. Bennett, "Christian Realism," 16 Apr. 1962, 51-52. Bennett, "The Nuclear Discussion Continued,'" 11 Dec. 1961, 223. See also DeBenedetti, *An American Ordeal*, 45-46.

102. Shinn, "Changing Tides of History," 13 Apr. 1964, 58; Bennett, "Liberalization versus Liberation," 6 Jan. 1964, 246. See also Bennett, "New Lead in Foreign Policy," 8 July 1963, 123–24.

Chapter 5

1. Joseph Fletcher, *Situation Ethics: The New Morality* (Philadelphia: Westminster Press, 1966), 98, cited in Long and Handy, *Theology and Church*, 141 (for *C&C*'s debate about Fletcher, see below); Robert Spike, "The Beat Bit," 28 Apr. 1958, 56; Tom Driver, "Baldwin's *Blues for Mister Charlie*," 22 June 1964, 123–26.

2. Helpful overviews of these debates include Deane William Ferm, *Contemporary American Theologies: A Critical Survey* (New York: Seabury, 1981), 41–94; David Tracy, *Blessed Rage for Order: The New Pluralism in Theology* (New York: Crossroad, 1975), 3–42; Daniel Callahan, ed., *The Secular City Debate* (New York: Macmillan, 1966); Harvey Cox, ed., *The Situation Ethics Debate* (Philadelphia: Westminster Press, 1968); Long and Handy, *Theology and Church;* Martin Marty and Dean G. Peerman, eds., *New Theology #3* (New York: Macmillan, 1966); and Marty and Peerman, eds., *New Theology #4* (New York: Macmillan, 1967).

3. Among seventy articles in my cross-section in 1946–47 and 1962–63, only one addressed the arts and culture as its primary theme, although several did discuss theology or domestic politics in ways that shaded into cultural analysis. Midway between these two dates, in 1956–57, seven of thirty-eight articles focused unambiguously on the arts.

4. M. Searle Bates (for Editorial Board), "The Extension of the Crisis," 16 Apr. 1956, 43; Amos Wilder, "Christianity, the Arts, and the Mass-Media," 8 Aug. 1955, 105–6.

5. Paul Tillich, "Beyond Religious Socialism," *Christian Century,* 16 June 1949, 732–33.

6. In this connection it is instructive to note that Tillich had close connections to the Frankfurt school (e.g., he was the director of Theodor Adorno's dissertation). On the relation between Tillich's views on culture and various themes of these book, see Kelton Cobb, "Reconsidering the Status of Popular Culture in Tillich's Theology of Culture," *Journal of the American Academy of Religion* 63 (1995), no. 1: 53–84, Richard Nelson, "The Progressive Jeremiad, Critical Theory, and the End of Republican Virtue," *Clio* 16 (1987), no. 4: 359–79, esp. 370–72, and Marsha Hewitt, *Critical Theory of Religion: A Feminist Analysis* (Minneapolis: Fortress Press, 1994).

7. This question about the oppositionality of 1950s literary canons touches on a huge literature in American studies that is better left for a book focusing on a different journal. I discuss these issues in my "Evolving Approaches to U.S. Culture in the American Studies Movement." See also Gunn, *Culture of Criticism;* Denning, "The Special American Conditions"; and Noble, "American Studies and the Burden of Frederick Jackson Turner: The Case of Henry Nash Smith and Richard Hofstadter," *Journal of American Culture* 4 (1981): 34–45. Postwar cultural critiques based on canonical nineteenth-century male literature were significant but circumscribed. Often they shaded into nostalgia for a lost time of fading values opposed to the inexorable triumph of capitalism, and often they functioned to define a national identity (articulated by a "national literature") that could be conscripted for the cold war. For an example of hard-hitting but circumscribed criticism in the postwar analysis of the literary canon, see Leo Marx, *The Machine in the Garden: Technology and the Pastoral Idea in America* (New York: Oxford Univ. Press, 1965). On literary critics' bias toward New England males see Tompkins, *Sensational Designs.*

8. Ralph Ellison, *The Invisible Man* (1952; New York: Vintage, 1982); Arthur Miller, *Death of a Salesman* (1949; New York: Viking, 1958); Jack Kerouac, *The Dharma Bums* (1958; New York: Penguin, 1976). For connections between such literature and larger social history see Breines, *Young, White, and Miserable,* 127–66; Jezer, *The Dark Ages;* and Lipsitz, *Time Passages.* For an illuminating description of a confrontation between James Wechsler, a liberal of the *C&C* type, and Kerouac, see Todd Gitlin, *The Sixties: Years of Hope, Days of Rage* (New York: Bantam, 1987), 54–66.

9. Robert McAfee Brown, "The Kingdom of Camus," 14 Apr. 1958, 46–47; William May, "Albert Camus: Political Moralist" (24 Nov. 1958), cited in Cowan, *Witness to a Generation,* 224. See also Brown, "The Kingdom of Camus," 14 Apr. 1958, 46–47; and Julian Hartt, "Albert Camus: An Appreciation," 8 Feb. 1960, 7–8.

10. Nathan Scott, "Meaning of the Incarnation for Modern Literature," 8 Dec. 1958, 173, 174. On Scott's relation to larger themes in *C&C*'s history, see his "Day by Day," in *Theologians in Transition: The* Christian Century *"How My Mind Has Changed" Series,* ed. James M. Wall (New York: Crossroad, 1981), 134–42.

11. Scott, "Meaning of the Incarnation," 174; Scott, "Beneath the Hammer of Truth," 1 Oct. 1956, 126. Sidney Lanier, "*J.B.*: Togetherness in Uz," 27 Apr. 1959, 59–60. See also Julian Hartt, "William Faulkner: An Appreciation," 8 Aug. 1962, 217–19. Amos Wilder, "Strategies of the Christian Artist," 3 May 1965, 92–95, commended *The Final Beast* by Frederick Buechner, a former Union Seminary student, as an exemplary novel that was unabashed in its positive theology.

12. Niebuhr, "Editorial Notes," 6 Feb. 1956, 2–3; Tillich, "Correspondence," 5 Mar. 1956, 6. This exchange carried extra resonance for *C&C* insiders, because Tillich was a leading force behind not only *C&C*'s turn toward art but also some of its initiatives on sexuality. Insiders suggest that some of *C&C*'s concerns about sexual representation in literature can be understood as veiled reactions to Tillich's promiscuity and habit of sexually harassing female students.

13. Lundy interview; Betty Friedan, *The Feminine Mystique* (New York: Dell, 1963).

14. Robert Spike, "The Beat Bit," 28 Apr. 1958, 56.

15. Kilmer Myers, "The Parish Church and Delinquency," 17 Mar. 1958, 34; George Todd, "Correspondence," 31 Mar. 1958, 43.

16. Paul Elmen, "The Order of Troilus and Cressida," 13 Apr. 1964, 63–66; Lynn Harold Hough, "An Adequate Christian Culture," 7 Feb. 1949, 2–3; Bennett, "Lincoln's Religious Insights," 8 Feb. 1960, 2–3; William Scheide, "Thoughts on Protestant Church Music," 6 Aug. 1956, 107. Hough's article on Spiller was a rare *C&C* treatment of literature during its early period when it usually focused single-mindedly on the cold war. Interestingly, Hough was among *C&C*'s least repentant Progressives.

17. Henry Pitney Van Dusen, "John Foster Dulles: Man of Faith," 20 June 1959, 111.

18. Tom Driver, "The Gospel according to St. Matthew" (16 June 1966), and Sidney Lanier, "Wine of the Country—Sweet and Dry" (15 Mar. 1961), in Cowan, *Witness to a Generation*, 225–32.

19. Barbara Sargent, "Correspondence," 17 Oct. 1955, 130, 134, 136. Eugene Carson Blake, "Correspondence," 28 Nov. 1955, 106, was a reply by the president of the NCC, stating that Sargent's approach would alienate everyone and that she must "criticize from within the body."

20. Fred Myers, "Hollywood and the Military," 17 Feb. 1964, 19–20; Arnold Hearn, "Some Commandments Violated," 26 Nov. 1956, 163–64.

21. Brown, "The Need for Theological Precision," 20 Sept. 1965, 183–84.

22. Frances Smith, "Fairness for the Fair Sex," 17 Sept. 1962, 146–47. Smith worked for *C&C* from 1962 to 1966 and was the only woman listed on the masthead between 1950 and 1972.

23. Harvey Cox, "Playboy's Doctrine of Male," 17 Apr. 1961, 58; Vivian Cadden (of *Redbook*) to Cowan, 4 June 1964, *C&C* records, box 1, folder labeled "Reprint Requests." The article appeared in numerous anthologies and was repeatedly reprinted by *C&C* to sell in bulk orders. For example, *C&C* advertised one reprint on 22 July 1963, but by 14 Oct. 1963 it had sold out again. For more on the general subject see Theodore Peterson, "Playboy and the Preachers," *Columbia Journalism Review* 5 (Spring 1966): 32–35.

24. Harvey Cox, "Miss America and the Cult of The Girl," 7 Aug. 1961, 143, 144, 145. "The Girl," *Time*, 11 Aug. 1961, 40.

25. Robert Fitch , "Christian Criticism of Literature," 29 Apr. 1957, 52, 53.

26. Burnet Easton, "Correspondence," 5 Aug. 1957, 111–12.

27. Tom Driver, "Literary Criticism and the Christian Conscience: A Reply to Mr. Fitch," 8 July 1957, 91–93. See also Driver, "Dramatic Art and Public Morality," 31 Oct. 1960, 157–60.

28. Fitch , "The Obsolescence of Ethics," 16 Nov. 1959, 163; Fitch, "Correspondence," 16 May 1960, 71–72. Big Daddy was a character in *Cat on a Hot Tin Roof.*

29. An influential discussion of this issue is James Gustafson, "Context versus Principles: A Misplaced Debate in Christian Ethics," in Marty and Peerman, *New Theology #3*, 69–103.

30. Fitch, "Obsolescence of Ethics," 164–65.

31. Eugene Carson Blake, "The Church in the Next Decade," 21 Feb. 1966, 17.

32. Roger Shinn, "Theological Ethics: Retrospect and Prospect," 131 (commenting on Fletcher, *Situation Ethics*); Dale Johnson, "Era of the Catchy Title," 13 June 1966, 132–33. In fairness, let us note that for Fletcher, initiating a nuclear war could be a *wrong* application of agapeic calculus. For critiques of Fletcher by several *C&C* figures, see Cox, *The Situation Ethics Debate.*

33. Paul Lehmann, *Ethics in a Christian Context*, 117, cited in Shinn, "Theological Ethics: Retrospect and Prospect," 132.

34. Alexander Miller, "Unprincipled Living: The Ethics of Obligation," 21 Mar. 1960, 28, 29, 30.

35. Paul Ramsey, "Faith Effective through In-Principled Love," 30 May 1960, 76–78. Fitch mentions gull-like swoops in "Obsolescence of Ethics," 165.

36. Miller, "Unprincipled Living," 28, 30; Fitch and Miller, "Correspondence," 16 May 1960, 71–72.

37. Tom Driver, "On Taking Sex Seriously," 14 Oct. 1963, 176, 177. The article appears in Cowan, *Witness to a Generation*, 144–50.

38. I discuss Tom Driver's argument about gay males in chapter 8. It was quite hostile by current standards, but since it did not reject gay and lesbian relationships categorically, it was *C&C*'s least negative stand on the issue before the late 1960s. Documents concerning *C&C*'s internal debate about this article can be found in *C&C*'s archives, box 1. Bennett worried that it "creates an atmosphere of permissiveness" and that some passages were of "dubious taste."

39. Harvey Cox, "Evangelical Ethics and the Ideal of Chastity" (27 Apr. 1964), in Cowan, *Witness to a Generation,* 151, 158.

40. Shinn and Niebuhr memos to Cowan, *C&C* records, box 1, folder labeled "Article correspondence Jan. 1964." Niebuhr, "Christian Attitudes toward Sex and Family," 27 Apr. 1964, 75. See also Bennett, "Toward a Fresh Discussion of Sex Ethics," 14 Oct. 1963, 173, which was a disclaimer introducing Driver's article on sexual ethics. Bennett said that even though "specific absolutes have lost their power," there was still a need to find "landmarks."

41. Cowan, "In Twenty-five Years You Pick Up a Lot of Memories," 17 Sept. 1979, 231; Ramsey, "On Taking Sexual Responsibility Seriously Enough," 6 Jan. 1964, 247–51; Ramsey and Edward Brown, "Correspondence," 11 Nov. 1963, 204–7. The central issue for Ramsey was to endorse sex only within heterosexual marriage; however, within this context he attacked Driver's dualistic approach to sexuality.

42. Shinn, "Theological Ethics: Retrospect and Prospect," 129.

43. St. Hereticus (a.k.a. Brown), "The Gospel according to St. Hereticus—Scripture Lesson for Easter" (16 Mar. 1959), in Cowan, *Witness to a Generation,* 160–62; Lehmann, "Protestantism in a Post-Christian World," 5 Feb. 1962, 8, 10.

44. For example, gender and sexuality were a major focus of only 3 of 127 articles in my random sample from 1957 through 1964, compared with around 40 on international politics.

45. Gilkey, "Secularism's Impact on Contemporary Theology" (5 Apr. 1965), in Cowan, *Witness to a Generation,* 127–28, defined secularity as a modern attitude that "emphasizes the here and now, the tangible, the manipulable, the sensible, the relative, and the this-worldly." It was an all-pervasive "cultural Geist within which all forms of thought, including the theological, must operate if they are to be relevant and creative." It was naturalistic, temporal, relativistic, and emphatic about human autonomy. Not everything that *C&C* published on theology fits neatly into the argument on secularity. As always, *C&C* published a stream of miscellaneous essays on theology and occasional writings (mainly sermons) tending toward the "inspirational." Here are a few examples of theological articles with themes that weave in and out of the discussions described here but that are not necessarily responding primarily to them: Daniel Day Williams, "Jesus Christ, the Beginning," 4 Apr. 1960, 35–39; Williams, "The Vulnerable and the Invulnerable God," 5 Mar. 1962, 27–30; Brown, "The Protestant Spirit," 14 Nov. 1960, 164–67; Tillich, "The Divine Name," 2 May 1960, 55–58 (a straight sermon); and a whole issue on H. Richard Niebuhr, 25 Nov. 1963. Two valuable summaries of theological trends in *C&C* circles are Shinn, "The Shattering of the Theological Spectrum," 30 Sept. 1963, 168–71; and Brown, "Theology and the Gospel: Reflections on Theological Method," in *Theology and Church,* ed. Long and Handy, 15–34.

46. Here, to simplify my presentation, I follow *C&C*'s X hand and correlate the secular move with a linear and Progressive sensibility. However, it is crucial to remember that there is another possible spin on this point—one that I find equally illuminating—that interprets secular theology as *less* linear and Progressive than neoorthodoxy. Sometimes, especially in deconstructionist parts of the death of God camp, contextualists correlated neoorthodox searches for order and coherence with linear logic, and understood the secular move as an acceptance of pluralism and breakdown of overarching teleological meaning.

47. Alan Paton, "Africa, Christianity, and the West" (26 Dec. 1960), in Cowan, *Witness to a Generation,* 123.

48. Henry Pitney Van Dusen, "The Use and Abuse of 'Paradox,'" 20 Feb. 1956, 17–18.

49. Bennett, "The Kingdom of God," 13 June 1960, 85–88; see also Francis P. Miller, "The Silence about the Kingdom of God," 13 June 1960, 83–84.

50. John A. T. Robinson, *Honest to God* (Philadelphia: Westminster Press, 1963); Bennett, "*Honest to God:* A Most Welcome Event," 11 Nov. 1963, 201, 202; Robert Bellah, "*Honest to God:* 'It Doesn't Go Far Enough,'" 11 Nov. 1963, 200–201; Paul Lehmann, "*Honest to God:* A Call to Integrity," 11 Nov. 1963, 198–99.

51. Bennett, "Karl Barth in Translation," 1 Oct. 1956, 123. This was Bennett's initial review of Barth's *Church Dogmatics* when it began to appear in English.

52. Lehmann, "Chalcedon in Technopolis," 12 July 1965, 149–150, citing Cox, *The Secular City,* rev. ed. (New York: Macmillan, 1966), 111–12. Terry Eagleton, *The New Left Church* (Baltimore: Helicon, 1966), was a theological argument, drawing heavily on literary arguments, which overlapped considerably with arguments like Cox's; Eagleton later became a major figure in British New Left literary criticism and cultural studies.

53. Lehmann, "Chalcedon in Technopolis," 149.

54. David Little, "The Social Gospel Revisited," 12 July 1965, 151.

55. Harvey Cox, "Cox on His Critics," in Callahan, *Secular City Debate,* 85–88. See also George Younger, "Does the Secular City Revisit the Social Gospel?" 18 Oct. 1965, 217–19, which attacked Little and defended Cox as "post-Barthian" and "post-Niebuhrian," by which Younger meant that Cox presupposed them. *C&C*'s special issue on Cox included other reviews. Charles West, "What It Means to Be Secular," 12 July 1965, 148, said that Cox's "great weakness" was an inability to speak of God when human powers fail, especially in the face of death. Kilmer Myers, "Where Is the Church?" 12 July 1965, 153, questioned his lack of attention to churches and advanced a rather sweeping theology of "the Church." *C&C*'s entire debate is reprinted with other essays in Callahan, *Secular City Debate,* 59–88.

56. William Hamilton, "Radicalism and the Death of God," 13 Dec. 1965, 272, 273; Gabriel Vahanian cited in Lehmann, "Protestantism in a Post-Christian World," 5 Feb. 1962, 8. Incidentally, Hamilton had broken into *C&C*'s pages eight years earlier with "Moralism and Sex Ethics: A Defense," 28 Oct. 1957, 140–42, which supported traditional teachings on premarital chastity. *C&C* reprinted this article for church youth groups; a 6 Jan. 1958 notice stated that *C&C*'s first run of reprints sold out before Christmas.

57. Examples of *C&C* insiders weighing in on the national stage include Bennett, "In Defense of God," *Look,* 19 Apr. 1966, 69–76; and John Cogley, "Niebuhr Scores Death-of-God Theory," *New York Times,* 12 June 1966, page number illegible, both collected with related materials in *C&C* records, box 18, scrapbook.

58. Langdon Gilkey, "Secularism's Impact on Contemporary Theology" (5 May 1965), in Cowan, *Witness to a Generation,* 128, 129.

59. Sydney Ahlstrom, *Religious History of the American People,* 947.

60. Gilkey, "Secularism's Impact," 130, 129, 132.

61. Niebuhr, "Faith as the Sense of Meaning in Human Existence," 13 June 1966, 128. For a key Bennett statement on related issues, see Bennett, "The Church and the Secular," 26 Dec. 1966, 294–97.

62. Shinn, "Theological Ethics: Retrospect and Prospect," 136, emphasis in the original.

63. Fully 14 of 80 articles in my cross section for 1961 through 1965 focused on Catholic issues; however, this sample may be skewed because it included a special issue on Vatican II. This figure also includes some articles on tax support for Catholic schools. For *C&C*'s coverage of Vatican II see the citations in chapter 3.

64. Bennett and Niebuhr, "*Pacem in Terris:* Two Views," 13 May 1963, 83. *C&C* also broached the issue of Roman Catholic natural law theories in the *Secular City* symposium. Michael Novak wrote that Cox offered grounds for dialogue with Catholics because Cox was advocating natural law in a good sense—not the "non-historical, abstract, immutable" kind but the kind that results when "the dimension of supernature [*sic*] is collapsed to 'coincide' with the dimension of the profane." Given Cox's efforts to persuade Little that he passed muster as a Barthian, Cox was understandably noncommittal about Novak's proposal, calling it "wonderfully provocative." Novak, "Secular Style and Natural Law," 26 July 1965, 165–66; Cox, "Cox on His Critics," 88.

65. Niebuhr, "The Moral and Political Judgments of Christians," 6 July 1959, 102.

66. Richard Rubenstein, "Jews, Christians, and Magic," 30 Apr. 1962, 65–68; William Hamilton, "Radicalism and the Death of God," 273.

67. Arthur Hertzberg, "Correspondence," 11 June 1962, 104; Hertzberg, "Jews and the Death of God," 7 Feb. 1966, 8.

68. Richard John Neuhaus, *The Naked Public Square* (Grand Rapids: Eerdmans 1984). For more citations on public religion see the introduction and my discussion of evangelicals in chapter 7. Reynolds and Norman, *Community in America* and Hutchison, "Past Imperfect: History and the Prospect for Liberalism," in Michaelsen and Roof, *Liberal Protestantism: Realities and Possibilities,* 65–84, are especially valuable contributions.

69. Herberg, "Protestantism in a Post-Protestant America," 5 Feb. 1962, 3–6; Lehmann, "Protestantism in a Post-Christian World," 5 Feb. 1962, 7–10 (with discussion, 11–12); Brown, "Protestantism on the Wane?" 5 Feb. 1962, 2–3. Brown was not ready to give up Niebuhr's Puritan analogy; he also described the post-Protestant mission as a "pilgrim role."

70. The presentations are summarized in John Maguire, "The Morning Session," 30 May 1966, 108–9; and Hannah Arendt et al., "Highlights of the Afternoon Session," 30 May 1966, 112–19. *C&C* records, box 24 contains many documents from the planning of this conference.

71. "Highlights of the Afternoon Session," 30 May 1966, 114, 116; Humphrey, "A Tribute to Reinhold Niebuhr," 30 May 1966, 120–23. Joel Kovel, "Love Hubert, He Was a Liberal?" *Zeta* (Sept. 1991), 88–91, is highly illuminating for understanding the conflict between Humphrey and more radical elements of the New Deal coalition—and by extension for interpreting *C&C*'s polarization.

Chapter 6

1. James Kuhn, "Is Federal Initiative Finished?" 3 Feb. 1969, 1.

2. Harvey Cox, "Enough Is Enough!" 16 Sept. 1968, 194.

3. Will Campbell and James Holloway, "Up to Our Steeple in Politics," 3 Mar. 1969, 38, 39. The "sign of Jonah" alludes to a comment by Jesus about the prophet Jonah, and implies that Christians should work through sacrifice and suffering rather than demonstrations of power.

4. Pete Young, "Saints, Maniacs, and Hypocrites," 3 Mar. 1969, 42.

5. Cox, "Enough Is Enough!" 16 Sept. 1968, 193; Jonathan and June Bingham, "Correspondence," 14 Oct. 1968, 243. For a wider range of comments see Tom Driver et al., "Election '68: A Symposium," 14 Oct. 1968, 232–38. Among the many people who weighed in, Novak and Driver supported Cox. William May, Shinn and three other letter writers besides the Binghams supported Humphrey.

6. Ramsey's point of department was the 1966 WCC conference in Geneva, which I discussed in chapter 4. Dorrien, *Soul in Society,* 173–78, treats the conference and Bennett's role as organizer. To place the debate in a wider context, see Jeffrey Hadden, *The Gathering Storm in the Churches* (New York: Doubleday, 1969).

7. Bennett, "A Critique of Paul Ramsey," 30 Oct. 1967, 247–50; Ramsey, "Paul Ramsey Replies," 27 Nov. 1967, 281. W. G. Onions, "Correspondence," 8 Jan. 1968, 13–14, pointed out that throat-slitting by the Vietcong was not endorsed by Bennett, did not seem to justify napalming civilians, and (unlike the use of napalm) was not an official U.S. government policy. Shinn, "Paul Ramsey's Challenge to Ecumenical Ethics," 30 Oct. 1967, 246, tried to make peace by taking a middle ground; he agreed that churches should try to speak from consensus, and said it was necessary "to distinguish between authentic and false revolution."

8. Ramsey, "Political Repentance Now!" 28 Oct. 1968, 247.

9. Herman Reissig, "Correspondence," 23 Dec. 1968, 320; Lefever, "Correspondence," 25 Nov. 1968, 289. See also Cowan, "On Being Discriminate about Political Reality," 25 Nov. 1968, 283–86.

10. William Van Etten Casey, S.J., "Correspondence," 25 Nov. 1968, 289.

11. Cox, "Correspondence," 23 Dec. 1968, 322.

12. C. Eric Lincoln, "How Now, America?" 1 Apr. 1968, 57. On black political movements of the 1960s, see Clayborne Carson, *In Struggle: SNCC and the Black Awakening of the 1960s* (Cambridge: Harvard Univ. Press, 1981); Manning Marable, *Race, Reform, and Rebellion: The Second Reconstruction in Black America, 1945–1982* (Jackson: Univ. Press of Mississippi, 1984); Stokely Carmichael and Charles Hamilton, *Black Power: The Politics of Liberation in America* (New York: Vintage, 1967); Robert Brisbane, *Black Activism: Racial Revolution in the United States* (Valley Forge, Pa.: Judson Press, 1974); and McAdam, *Political Process and the Development of Black Insurgency.*

13. Lincoln, "How Now, America?" 56, 59.

14. "The Editors" [Blank front page with short italicized note], 29 Apr. 1968, 85. On the Poor People's Campaign see also James McGraw, "An Interview with Andrew J. Young," 22 Jan. 1968, 324–30; and Eric Blanshard, "Accessories after the Facts," 6 Jan. 1969, 332–35, a postmortem that was nearly despairing, despite its subtitle, "The Poor People's Campaign Did Accomplish Something."

15. Niebuhr, "The Mounting Racial Crisis," 8 July 1963, 122.

16. Shinn, "The Assassination of Malcolm X," 22 Mar. 1965, 46. The "chickens" comment alluded to Malcolm's famous comment about John Kennedy's death, discussed in Malcolm X with Alex Haley, *The Autobiography of Malcolm X* (New York: Grove, 1964), 300–302.

17. Shinn, "Upheaval in Los Angeles," 20 Sept. 1965, 181–82.

18. John Pratt, "The White House and the Ghetto," 27 June 1966, 149–51; Malcolm Boyd, "Maintaining Humanness in the Freedom Movement," 4 Oct. 1965, 201–2. Many other articles discussed riots over the following years, e.g., Spike, "Riots as Communication," 19 Sept. 1966, 194–95; and Charles Millar, "Detroit after the Riots," 16 Oct. 1967, 233–36.

19. Robert Spike, "Fissures in the Civil Rights Movement," 21 Feb. 1966, 18–21; Benjamin Payton, "New Trends in Civil Rights," 13 Dec. 1965, 268–71.

20. Pratt, "White House and the Ghetto," 149; John David Maguire, "'To Fulfill These Rights," 11 July 1966, 160; Cowan, "In Twenty-five Years You Pick Up a Lot of Memories," 17 Sept. 1979, 231; Wayne Cowan and Arthur Moore interviews. Moynihan refused the offer of space to respond in *C&C.*

21. This follows the typology in Van Deburg, *New Day in Babylon,* as informed by Omi and Winant, *Racial Formation in the United States.*

22. James Breeden, "Demythologizing Black Power," 8 Aug. 1966, 185. George Younger, "The Defeat of New York's Civilian Review Board," 12 Dec. 1966, 283–86, made Wilkins's fears of backlash concrete and credible, without defending the backlash.

23. Lincoln, "If This Be Black Power . . . ," 11 Dec. 1967, 288. See also Lincoln, "Social Maturity in Mississippi?" 2 Feb. 1970, 1–2, which pointed to signs of growing racial harmony in the South.

24. *Autobiography of Malcolm X,* 278–82; Assata Shakur, *Assata: An Autobiography* (Westport, Conn.: Lawrence Hill, 1987), 181, 132–33.

25. Howard Moody, "White Integrationists and the 'Black Power' Movement," 17 Oct. 1966, 225.

26. Malcolm Boyd, "Maintaining Humanness in the Freedom Movement," 4 Oct. 1965, 200; Moody, "White Integrationists," 226. See also Boyd, "Black Voice, White Voice," 16 Oct. 1967, 236–39.

27. See Saul Alinsky, *Rules for Radicals: A Pragmatic Primer for Realistic Radicals* (New York: Vintage, 1972); for his impact on community organizing since the 1960s see Harry Boyte, *The Backyard Revolution: Understanding the New Citizen Movement* (Philadelphia: Temple Univ. Press, 1980), 50–55.

28. Rose, "Saul Alinsky and His Critics," 20 July 1964, 143–52; Bennett, "The Church and Power Conflicts," 22 Mar. 1965, 47–51. *Christian Century* editor Kyle Haselden wrote to deny *C&C*'s charges and to accent his agreements with Bennett, 19 Apr. 1965, 84. Two passionate letters denounced Alinsky, 28 Dec. 1964, 266–68. As discussed in chapter 9, there were limits to Bennett's support of black power; in this controversy he sided with King against black nationalists and said the church should be all-inclusive. Still it was only a small step from Bennett's 1965 article to the logic of black power as it dominated the movement after 1966.

29. Payton, "New Trends in Civil Rights," 269. Payton was far from a black power militant; here his bottom line suggestions basically proposed an expansion of existing Great Society programs. For more on Payton see Findlay, *Church People in the Struggle,* 177–87.

30. Spike, "Fissures in the Civil Rights Movement." 19. For less dismissive examples of engagement with mainstream policy debates see Bennett, "The Kerner Report," 1 Apr. 1968, 54–55; and James Tillman, "A Dissent from the Kerner Report," 1 Apr. 1968, 62, 66.

31. Leon Howell, "The Delta Ministry," 8 Aug. 1966, 190, 192. Findlay, *Church People in the Struggle,* 111–68, offers a detailed history of the ministry, which had roots in the 1930s and was revitalized by the NCC as an extension of Mississippi Freedom Summer in 1964. It began in 1964 with primary commitments to a Head Start program (linked to civil rights ideologies). Later in the decade it turned toward economic development (linked to black power ideologies).

32. Findlay's *Church People in the Struggle* documents how Spike was killed in 1966, shortly after he broke with his former allies such as Moynihan and was replaced as head of the Commission on Religion and Race. Findlay says that "a small group of national Methodist officials conducted a systematic review in 1980 of the available evidence"; they believe that "probably he was assassinated" and "that government officials, directly or indirectly, played a role in [his] death" (175). Findlay doubts that Spike was important enough to be killed for his views on race, although he had risen high enough to sit in Lyndon Johnson's family box when he spoke before a joint session of Congress in 1965 (169). Complicating matters, and providing Findlay's major hypothesis about the murder, was the fact that Spike was gay and may have been killed in a cruising incident gone awry. Largely because of a desire to cover this up, *C&C* said little about the case, although (as discussed in chapter 8) it published a few articles attacking the police harassment of gays during the following year.

33. John Fry, "So Grow Up!" 22 July 1968, 170–72; Cox, "Preventive War against the Black Panthers," 5 Jan. 1970, 337–38.

34. Gil Scott-Heron, "The Revolution Will Not Be Televised," audio recording in author's possession, recording information unknown, ca. late 1960s. "Tune in, turn on, and *drop* out" was the advice of Timothy Leary, a well-known guru of the campus counterculture.

35. Waldo Beach, "Civil Disobedience and the Churches," 13 June 1966, 126–27. Bennett, "Defending Angela Davis," 13 Dec. 1971, 266–67.

36. Frye Gaillard and Pamela Owens, "Trial in Mecklenberg: Justice or Harassment?" 12 Nov. 1973, 223–27; Robert Maurer, "North Carolina's Buried Treasure: The Ben Chavis Case," 24 May 1976, 125–27. See also Howell, "Bourbons and Blacks in Mexico City," 11 Nov. 1968, 270–71, on black cultural politics at the 1968 Olympics; and Howard Moody, "The Trials of Julius, the Just," 16 Mar. 1970, 41, on the Chicago Seven trial which Moody described as a "kangaroo court."

37. Robert Harsh, "Inside Attica," 29 May 1972, 127–38. See also Tony Fitch and Julian Tepper, "No Time to Talk: Hour by Hour at Attica" and "The Politics of Prisons," 18 Oct. 1971, 211–16. Fitch and Tepper were legal observers inside Attica.

38. John S. Baerst, "Correspondence," 2 Oct. 1972, 217–19; Bernard Barton, "Hogwash about the Black Panthers"; and Herbert Aptheker, "Yes, Virginia, There Is Police Harassment," 16 Mar. 1970, 51.

39. James Forman, "The Black Manifesto," in *Black Theology: A Documentary History,* ed. Gayraud Wilmore and James Cone (Maryknoll, N.Y.: Orbis Books, 1979), 1:84.

40. Handy, *History of Union Theological Seminary,* 280–82. Union eventually raised $750,000 of its million-dollar goal, mostly from one board member. It gave only $25,000 of it, including $5,000 pledged by students, to Forman's group, which was called the National Black Economic Development Conference. NBEDC was related to the Inter-religious Foundation for Community Organizing (IFCO). In the end, IFCO wound up receiving most of the donations earmarked for grassroots social action, with the understanding that they would be divided among various groups. On these issues see Wilmore, *Black Religion and Black Radicalism,* 202–15 and Findlay, *Church People in the Struggle,* 212.

41. Handy, *History of Union Theological Seminary*, 285, 260, 308, and general discussion 280–310. In an interview with Mary Shepard, whose family moved in the social circles of Union board members, she commented that many male board members with high-level corporate connections resigned and were replaced by females who lacked similar power, although they were well connected through their families. (The most notable case was Rosalind Havermayer, a former leader of Union's "women's committee" who became president in the 1970s.) Shepard felt ambivalent because she understood that "the women were doing what needed to be done," but the change represented a substantial withdrawal of corporate support. Of course, Union's problems were not all caused by its internal politics—the larger social crisis of New York City also loomed large.

42. Howell and Robert Lecky, "Reparation Now?" 26 May 1969, 141; Rose, "Colonial Brokerage," 9 June 1969, 159–60; Wilmore, *Black Religion and Black Radicalism*, 205.

43. Donald Robinson, "Reparations and the Colonial Analogy," 4 Aug. 1969, 222, 223. See also Neuhaus, "The Prodigals Return," 23 June 1969, 174–75. For an argument somewhat similar to Robinson's, seeking to delegitimate a movement style of organization on the grounds that it has unelected and therefore unrepresentative leaders—but written in a neo-Marxian vein and directed at black ministers—see Adoph Reed, *The Jesse Jackson Phenomenon* (New Haven: Yale Univ. Press, 1986).

44. Rose, "Can We Get It Together?" 11 Jan. 1971, 292–93; Bennett, "After Thirty Years," 22 Mar. 1971, 40.

45. "Summary Results, *Christianity and Crisis* Readership Survey," ca. Sept. 1967; "Results of Readership Survey," ca. Sept. 1990, *C&C* internal documents, photocopies from *C&C* archives. Howell, "Who Reads *C&C*: Your Portrait in Numbers," 3 Feb. 1992, 4–5, claimed an unambiguous 10 percent nonwhite readership, but the 1990 poll actually showed 90 percent claiming to be "non-Hispanic white," 5 percent claiming to be black, Latino or Asian American, and 2.5 percent each claiming "other" or giving no answer.

46. Bennett, Cowan, and Moore interviews; Hubert Humphrey, "A Tribute to Reinhold Niebuhr," 30 May 1966, 120–23; Cowan, "In Twenty-five Years You Pick Up a Lot of Memories," 17 Sept. 1979, 231; internal *C&C* correspondence about inviting Humphrey in *C&C* records, box 24, numerous folders. See also Fox, *Reinhold Niebuhr*, 284–85. This episode is often mentioned in Niebuhr scholarship and broader U.S. religious histories.

47. On the Vietnam War, see Marilyn Young, *The Vietnam Wars, 1945–1990* (New York: HarperPerennial, 1991); McCormick, *America's Half-Century;* Williams et al., *America in Vietnam;* Eric R. Wolf, *Peasant Wars of the Twentieth Century* (New York: Harper Torchbooks, 1973).

48. D. T. Niles, "Asian Comment on the U.S. in Vietnam," 19 Apr. 1965, 83.

49. The extent, timing, and meaning of North Vietnamese aid to the South is hotly disputed, with doves accenting the Vietcong's strong popular roots in the south and hawks presenting the Vietcong as a front for an external invasion. Secretary of State Dean Acheson set the tone for the dominant U.S. evaluation of this debate when he said "question whether Ho as much nationalist as Commie is irrelevant. All Stalinists in colonial areas are nationalists." Cited in Williams et al., *America in Vietnam*, 95.

50. Bates, "Indochina: The Configuration of Forces," 14 June 1954, 73–74. Niebuhr, "Editorial Notes," 31 May 1954, 66, argued that the French needed (nonmilitary) aid after the fall of Dienbienphu because "armistice will practically turn the three Indo-Chinese states over to communism," but at the same time the United States could not help them unless they "liquidate the colonial past with as much speed and grace as possible." See also Bates, "Queries on U.S. Policy in South and East Asia," 3 Oct. 1955, 121–22.

51. Niebuhr, "The Problem of South Vietnam," 5 Aug. 1963, 142–43. "Bastard" quote from Niebuhr, "Can Democracy Work?" *New Leader*, 28 May 1962, 9, cited in Stone, *Reinhold Niebuhr*, 193.

52. Cumings, "Reckoning with the Korean War," 407, provides the "glut of Chinamen" citation and accents the Korea-Vietnam connection. As early as 1965, Walter Washington, "Correspondence," 14 July 1965, 168, cut to the heart of this issue. He said there was a Chiang analogy and a 38th parallel analogy. The United States was following the Korean analogy, but the Chiang analogy was more likely.

53. "Editorial Comment," 2 Nov. 1964, 209. This question framed three articles in a special issue: a dove, a hawk, and a middle position calling for "responsible involvement": Senator Wayne Morse, "The U.S. Must Withdraw," 2 Nov. 1964, 209–13; Frank Trager, "To Guarantee the Independence of Vietnam," 2 Nov. 1964, 213–15; and Alan Geyer, "Vietnam's Greatest Need: Political Aid," 2 Nov. 1964, 216–19.

54. Kenneth Thompson, "Christian Realism and Foreign Policy," 21 Feb. 1966, 26; Henry Pitney Van Dusen, "U.S. Policy in Asia," 20 Sept. 1965, 193, 192. Such statements continued, although with decreasing frequency, throughout the decade. See, e.g., Thompson, "Democracy, Communism, and Neutralism in Asia," 30 Mar. 1964, 41–42; M. Searle Bates, "China: The Human Scene," 19 Apr. 1965, 80–83, Thompson, "The Arrogance and Agony of Power," 17 Apr. 1967, 75–79; Bates, "China Is Still There," 4 Mar. 1968, 25–26.

55. Niebuhr, "Vietnam: An Insoluble Problem," 8 Feb. 1965, 1–2.

56. Reinhold and Ursula Niebuhr, "The Peace Offensive," 24 Jan. 1966, 301–2, called the war "unfortunate," complained that the United States was "physically ruining an unhappy nation in the process of 'saving' it," and said that the Munich analogy was "fallacious reasoning from inexact analogies." However, the Niebuhrs were more prone than Bennett to qualify their opposition, laying more stress on a Korean analogy for de-escalating the war. Presumably this included keeping South Vietnam, like South Korea, as a pro-western client—precisely the crumbling goal that U.S. policy was already trying to salvage through escalation.

57. Bennett, "Where Are We Headed in Vietnam?" 8 Mar. 1965, 29–30. Other examples include "Editorial," 20 July 1964, 141–42; Bennett, "Senator Fulbright Speaks Out," 13 Apr. 1964, 57–58; Bennett, "Have Negotiations Lost Their High Priority?" 29 Nov. 1965, 249–50; Bennett, New Stage of the War," 20 Sept. 1965, 182–83.

58. Bennett, "From Supporter of War in 1941 to Critic in 1966," 13–14.

59. *C&C* Editorial Board, "We Protest the National Policy in Vietnam," 7 Mar. 1966, 34; Thompson's "Christian Realism and Foreign Policy" also appeared in this issue, which was the Twenty-fifth Anniversary Issue and the occasion for a great deal of press coverage. Thompson took the opportunity to compliment *C&C*'s "senior editor," pointedly excluding Bennett.

60. Bates, Brown, Shinn, and Driver, "Vietnam Addendum," 18 Apr. 1966, 74–80 (Shinn quotation, 78). Ramsey, "To Speak the Whole Political Truth," 13 June 1966, 134, pointed out that this display of dissensus in consensus might "call into question the value of the [statement]."

61. Driver, "Vietnam Addendum"; Vincent Harding, "Vietnam: History, Judgment, and Redemption," 18 Oct. 1965, 215–17.

62. Editorial Board, "We Protest the National Policy in Vietnam," 33, 34.

63. Peter Berger, "A Conservative Reflection about Vietnam," 6 Mar. 1967, 34, 33, 35.

64. Bennett, "It Is Difficult to Be an American," 25 June 1966, 166.

65. See, e.g., "World Churchmen Condemn U.S. Rise in Vietnam Force," *New York Times*, 24 July 1966; Nat Hentoff, "Review of the Press: Summer Madness," *Village Voice*, 11 Aug. 1966, *C&C* records, box 18, scrapbook.

66. "More Crisis than Christianity," *Danville (VA) Register*, 23 July 1966, *C&C* records, box 18, scrapbook.

67. Morley Safer, "Mr. Safer Reports," 27 June 1966, 141, 140. The officer was Arthur Sylvester, assistant secretary of defense for public affairs. Safer also received anonymous death threats. See also Arthur Moore, "The Question of Credibility," 28 June 1965, 133–34.

68. King's speech appears in Washington, *Testament of Hope*, 231-44. See also Andrew Young, "Thirtieth Anniversary Speech," 3 May 1971, 80–82.

69. Other CALCAV leaders with strong *C&C* connections included Michael Novak, William Sloane Coffin (Henry Sloane Coffin's nephew), and Richard Fernandez (later on *C&C*'s board of directors). Robert Lecky and Robert Hoyt edited both *C&C* and CALCAV's *American Report*.

70. For a detailed study of CALCAV, see Hall, *Because of Their Faith;* for a fine summary, see Hall's "CALCAV and Religious Opposition to the Vietnam War," in *Give Peace a Chance: Exploring the Vietnam Antiwar Movement*, ed. Melvin Small and William Hoover (Syracuse: Syracuse Univ. Press, 1992), 35–52. Hall argues, in a similar vein as DeBenedetti, *An American Ordeal,* that there was a decline from moderate and effective antiwar organizing into more radical and irrational styles later in the decade.

71. William MacKaye, "Christians Concerned about Vietnam," 6 Mar. 1967, 38, 42–43; MacKaye, "Clergy in the Capitol," 4 Mar. 1968, 36–37. MacKaye was the religion editor of the *Washington Post.* For a sample of CALCAV outreach, see its widely circulated book, Robert McAfee Brown, Abraham Heschel, and Michael Novak, *Vietnam: Crisis of Conscience* (New York: Association Press, 1967). To place CALCAV within a wider range of opinion on the war, see David Levy, *Debate over Vietnam* (Baltimore: Johns Hopkins Univ. Press, 1991), 91–102; and Daniel Hallin, "The Uncensored War: The Media and Vietnam," in *Major Problems in the History of the Vietnam War,* ed. Robert McMahon (Toronto: Heath, 1990), 546–55. On CALCAV's relations with Roman Catholics, see Patricia McNeal, *Harder than War: Catholic Peacemaking in Twentieth-Century America* (New Brunswick: Rutgers Univ. Press, 1992), 159–63.

72. Two examples of decorous lobbying and "sober" policy analysis were Bennett, "The War and the Local Church, 2 Oct. 1972, 215–16; and John Kenneth Galbraith, "Vietnam: The Moderate Solution," 7 Aug. 1967, 185–90.

73. Bennett, "The Place of Civil Disobedience," 25 Dec. 1967, 299; Driver, "The Frustration of Dissent," 13 Nov. 1967, 266–67; Shinn, "The Trial of Captain Dale E. Noyd," 1 Apr. 1968, 63–66; Howell, "Student Conscience and the Draft," 26 June 1967, 148–50; and the special issue on draft resistance, 22 Dec. 1969.

74. Anne Bennett "A Visit to Vietnam," 7 July 1969, 187–90; Rose, "From Viet Nam to Empire," 3 Mar. 1969, 44; Handy, *History of Union Theological Seminary,* 293.

75. Corita Kent, "Fold-out Poster of Dan Berrigan's Germantown Sermon," 21 Sept. 1970, 186; Philip Berrigan, "Letter from a Baltimore Jail," 22 July 1968, 168–70; Philip Berrigan, "Fact and Fancies from Prison," 11 Dec. 1967, 292–93. On the controversy sparked by the Berrigans, including commentary by several *C&C* insiders, see William Van Etten Casey, ed., *The Berrigans* (New York: Avon, 1971), who cites the poem, 60. *C&C* ran special issues on the Berrigans on 21 Sept. 1970 and 15 May 1972. However, not all *C&C* insiders were unambiguous supporters, especially at the beginning. See Richard Shaull, "Realism and Celebration," 1 Nov. 1968, 272–73; and the editorial introduction to Berrigan, "Letter from a Baltimore Jail," 168.

76. Niebuhr cited in Fox, *Reinhold Niebuhr,* 288, 285; Niebuhr, "A Time for Reassessment," 1 Apr. 1968, 55–56; Stone, "An Interview with Reinhold Niebuhr, 17 Mar. 1969, 48–52.

77. Harsh, "A Proposal for a New Theological Magazine," pp. 3–4 of internal document from 1970, *C&C* records, box 10, scrapbook.

78. George Williamson Jr., "The Pentagon Papers and the Desecration of Pragmatica," 1 May 1972, 99–104. Widely read statements with similar arguments include Kellerman, "Apologist of Power"; and LaFeber, *America, Russia, and the Cold War.*

79. Harrison and Bennett, "Response to 'The Pentagon Papers and the Desecration of Pragmatica,'" 1 May 1972, 104–7.

80. Beverly Harrison, "Feminist Realism," in *Ethics in the Present Tense: Significant Writings from Christianity and Crisis Magazine, 1966–1991,* ed. Leon Howell and Vivian Lindermayer (New York: Association Press, 1991), 191–97; Harrison, *Our Right to Choose: Toward a New Ethic of Abortion* (Boston: Beacon Press, 1983). Harrison's powerful blend of realism and socialist feminism is best showcased in her *Making the Connections.*

81. David Hawk, "Thirtieth Anniversary Speech," 3 May 1971, 82.

82. Chomsky, *Towards a New Cold War.* See also Chomsky, *Turning the Tide: U.S. Intervention in Central America and the Struggle for Peace* (Boston: South End Press, 1985). My *Protestantism and U.S. Foreign Policy: An Essay in Historiography* (master's thesis, Luther Northwestern Seminary, 1987), 84–94, relates Chomsky's arguments to cold war revisionists like William Appleman Williams, as well as works in religious studies such as Walter Capps, *The Unfinished War: Vietnam and the American Conscience* (Boston: Beacon Press, 1982).

83. Tucker, *The Radical Left and American Foreign Policy* (Baltimore: Johns Hopkins Univ. Press, 1971) argued that all variations of radical theory ("revisionism") based reductively on the structural need of U.S. capitalism to expand in the third world were indefensible. But all forms of radical critique that were *less* economistic than this straw version of Leninism turned out, as Tucker set up his argument, to be indistinguishable from establishment real-

ism as practiced after the Tet offensive. After all, it was not difficult for realists to grant that the United States presided over an empire. Niebuhr had long stressed the conflict between democratic and communist empires, and neorealists soon used the idea of national security to portray the United States as *defensive* empire—with the borders to be "defended" in Eastern Europe, the border of China, or (as in the famous NSC-68 document, produced in part by *C&C*'s own Paul Nitze) wherever the "absence of order among nations" becomes intolerable. Furthermore, realists had concluded that it was in their interest to withdraw from Vietnam. Didn't this prove the naiveté of radicals who claimed that U.S. capitalism had no choice but to be imperialist? (Chomsky, *Towards a New Cold War,* 416, comments, "By Tucker's logic, one could prove that corporate managers do not pursue the maximization of profit, since sometimes they shut down an inefficient plant.") Thus dismissing revisionism, Tucker continued searching for what the *really* realistic U.S. self-interest might be. Tucker's "The Purposes of American Power," *Foreign Affairs* (Winter 1980–81), 241–74, judged that domination of Central America was merely a justifiable "want" which might turn out, like Vietnam, to cost more than it was worth. But Tucker portrayed himself as the wise and tough-minded realist (and perhaps also a "Leninist" in terms of his 1971 argument) who understood the structural economic necessity for the United States to have a "right of access to the oil supplies of the Persian gulf" (247), which consequently needed to be militarily defended even at the risk of nuclear war. Chomsky, *Towards a New Cold War,* 216–29, discusses Tucker's argument.

84. Useful orientations to this debate include "Round Table: Exploring the History of American Foreign Relations," *Journal of American History* 77 (1990), no. 1: 171–244; Melvyn Leffler, "The American Conception of National Security and the Beginnings of the Cold War, 1945–48," *American Historical Review* 89 (1984), no. 2: 346–400; John Lewis Gaddis, "The Emerging Post-Revisionist Synthesis on the Origins of the Cold War," *Diplomatic History* 7 (Summer 1983): 171–90; Thomas McCormick, "Drift or Mastery: A Corporatist Synthesis for American Diplomatic History," *Reviews in American History* 10 (1982): 318–30. I discuss these issues in more detail in *Protestantism and U.S. Foreign Policy,* 57–72.

85. Carolyn Eisenberg, "Wise Men, Foolish Choices," *Nation,* 25 May 1992, 700–704, makes a similar point about testing the limits and presupposed goals of elite policy through her dialogue with Melvyn Leffler, who is one of the most judicious scholars who works with the concept of national security.

Chapter 7

1. Of ninety-eight cross-section articles in the late 1960s, twenty-one focused on miscellaneous international issues other than Vietnam, and twenty focused on domestic liberal issues not exclusively tied to race.

2. Niebuhr, "David and Goliath," 26 June 1967, 141–42; Thompson, "The Mideast and the Cold War," 10 July 1967, 159–60; Stone, "Interview with Reinhold Niebuhr," 49.

3. Balfour Brickner, "No Ease in Zion for Us," 18 Sept. 1967, 200–204; Bennett, "A Response to Rabbi Brickner," 18 Sept. 1967, 204–5; Bennett, "Further Thoughts on the Middle East," 26 June 1967, 142.

4. Alan Geyer, "Christians and 'The Peace of Jerusalem,'" 10 July 1967, 161; Shinn, "The Tragic Middle East," 15 Sept. 1969, 235.

5. *C&C* followed Lebanese politics closely throughout the 1970s and 1980s, largely through NCC leader J. Richard Butler, who later became *C&C*'s business manager. See, e.g., Butler, "Religions and Rivalries in Lebanon," 21 Aug. 1978, 190–92; Butler, "The Sources of Lebanon's Agony," 10 May 1982, 131–33. See also Margaret O'Brien Steinfels, "Scandal of the Wholly Innocent," 26 Dec. 1983, 492–93; Dale Bishop, "Lebanon: Infinite Forces in a Small Place," 16 Sept. 1985, 351–54.

6. Geyer, "Christians and 'The Peace of Jerusalem,'" 161.

7. Cowan, "In Twenty-five Years You Pick Up a Lot of Memories," 232; Cowan, "The Palestinian Time Bomb," 5 Oct. 1970, 200; Wayne Cowan and Richard Butler interviews. See also Robert Hoyt, "Israel and 'Palestine': On the Taming of Ogres," 17 July 1978, 179–81.

8. A. Roy Eckardt, "Anti-Israelism, Anti-Semitism, and the Quakers," 20 Sept. 1971, 186.

9. Editors, "About this Issue," 20 Sept. 1971, 128 (which introduces a special issue, *More on the Middle East*); A. Denis Baly, "The Search for Peace: A Modest Defense," 20 Sept. 1971, 186–91; Landrum Bolling, "The Quaker Report, Continuing the Discussion," 29 Nov. 1971, 253–57. Bolling was an Earlham professor and one of the authors of the AFSC report. In an exchange of letters with Baly, 4 Oct. 1971, 206–8, Eckardt became even more outraged.

10. Steven Swartzchild, "The Quaker Report, Continuing the Discussion," 29 Nov. 1971, 259–61; Arthur Hertzberg, "The Quaker Report, Continuing the Discussion," 29 Nov. 1971, 259. Eckardt, "Dr. Eckardt Replies," 10 Jan. 1972, 298, called Swartzchild an "anti-Semitic Jew."

11. Israel Shahak, "More on Jerusalem," 20 Mar. 1972, 63. His organization was the Israel League for Human and Civil Rights.

12. Franklin Littell, "Letter: *C&C, Deutsches Christentum,* and a "Renegade Jew," 1 May 1972, 111; letters from Cowan to Littell, 20 Apr. 1972 and 1 May 1972, and letter from Littell to Cowan, 24 Apr. 1972, photocopies from *C&C* archives. On Littell's and Eckardt's claims that Shahak did not represent Jewish opinion, see Noam Chomsky, *The Fateful Triangle: The United States, Israel, and the Palestinians* (Boston: South End Press, 1983), which argues that Jewish self-interest properly understood implies criticizing Zionist policies since the 1940s and that many Israelis agree. A more representative Jewish statement is Elie Wiesel, *A Jew Today* (New York: Random House, 1978). Eric Black, *Parallel Realities: A Jewish-Arab History of Israel-Palestine* (Minneapolis: Paradigm Press, 1992) incisively summarizes the arguments on both sides.

13. William MacKaye, "Middle East War Issue Fractures Bond Linking Liberal Protestants," *Washington Post,* 6 May 1972, in *C&C* records, box 10, scrapbook.

14. Shahak, "An Open Letter to Franklin M. Littell and 'Christians Concerned for Israel,'" 20 Apr. 1972, photocopy from *C&C* archives. Chomsky, *Fateful Triangle,* documents many such atrocities.

15. MacKaye, "Middle East War Issue Fractures Bond"; letter from Bennett to Ursula Niebuhr, 19 Apr. 1972, photocopy from *C&C* archives; Cowan, "An Announcement," 29 May 1972, 129. For the *New York Times* spin on these developments see its "Journal Drops Niebuhr's Name," 8 May 1972, page illegible, *C&C* records, box 10, scrapbook.

16. Bennett et al., "The General Assembly Vote: Zionism and Racism," 22 Dec. 1975, 319–20.

17. See, e.g., Arthur Moore, "The Middle East War," 26 Nov. 1973, 238–39; John Lindner with Robert Hoyt, "Up from the Summit: A Mid-East Agenda for the President," 13 Nov. 1978, 266–72; Stanley Hoffman, "Peace Needs These Friends," 12 July 1982, 214–15; Rosemary Ruether, "Intifada: New Forms of Resistance," 8 Jan. 1990, 409–10; Elissa Sampson, "Israel, Aid, and American Interests," 21 Oct. 1991, 333–36.

18. Chomsky, "Continuing the Discussion: Intervention in the Middle East?" 15 Sept. 1975, 210, quoting Mattityahu Peled.

19. Ruether suggested that the best role for U.S. Christians in the Israel-Palestinian conflict was to transform U.S. culture so that Jews were not forced to choose between assimilation into a purportedly "universal" culture that actually liquidated Jewish identity, or second-class citizenship (with an underlying threat of violence) that made Zionism necessary. Citing Arthur Waskow, she argued in "Christian Anti-Semitism and the Dilemma of Zionism," 17 Apr. 1972, 93, that "Israel has become a part of the *Galut* (exile)" but that a more positive concept of Jewish identity in the United States could help open the way to "a survival not based on exclusive control of a Jewish state at the expense of Palestinians." See also Ruether, "Anti-Semitism and the State of Israel: Some Principles for Christians," 6 Nov. 1973, 240–43; and Ruether, "Listening to Palestinian Christians," 4 Apr. 1988, 113–15. Ruether's major work on this subject is *Faith and Fratricide: The Theological Roots of Anti-Semitism* (Minneapolis: Seabury, 1974); to place it in a wider Christian theological context see John Pawlikowski, "Christology, Anti-Semitism, and Christian-Jewish Bonding," in Chopp and Taylor, *Reconstructing Christian Theology,* 245–68.

20. Robert Lekachman, "Energy and the American Future: The Case for Nationalization," 4 Mar. 1974, 30–34; Lekachman, "Oil and Power: Intervention in the Middle East?" 23 June 1975, 158; Shinn, "Oil and Power: Intervention in the Middle East?" 23 June 1975, 159.

21. Christopher Rand, "Continuing the Discussion: Intervention in the Middle East?" 15 Sept. 1975, 207–8; Chomsky, "Continuing the Discussion: Intervention in the Middle East?" 211. See also Paul Jacobs, "Middle East Report," 2 Apr. 1973, 45–55.

22. *C&C*'s criticism of the Gulf War was less extensive and confident than one might have expected. The only articles in my cross section that directly addressed the war were Howell, "Defining Moments: Crisis, Meaning, History," 4 Feb. 1991, 3–4; Kari Points, "The Gulf War and Women," 10 June 1991, 193–95; Jim Douglass, "Turned Away from the Holy Land," 21 Oct. 1991, 334–36; James Fine, "Iraq Now: Relief Held Hostage," 21 Oct. 1991, 336–38. For a postmortem on the war that speaks about differences among *C&C* readers, see Editors, "War's End: More Anguish than Joy," 18 Mar. 1991, 77.

23. Harvey Cox, "Gustavo's Grandchildren," 12 June 1989, 194–96 discusses allies in several countries. Typical pieces on the Philippines include Paul Sherry, "Filipino Rewrites," 12 June 1972, 150–51; Gareth Porter, "Philippine Catholics: Hierarchy and Radicals," 16 June 1986, 203–6; and John Dear, "Silencing an Aquino Critic," 10 Sept. 1990, 264–65. Outside Latin America, developments in southern Africa were the most important; major *C&C* foci included economic divestment, Beyers Naudé's Christian Institute, WCC support for the African National Congress and other radical groups; and the *Kairos Document* on South African liberation theology. See, e.g., Cowan, "South Africa and the Banks: A Progress Report," 23 Jan. 1967, 321; Howell, "The Ecumenical Movement on Trial," 6 Mar. 1967, 39–42; Naudé, "The Challenge of Political and Social Justice," 20 Jan. 1975, 323–25; Albert Van Den Heuvel "A Letter to a White South African Friend," 28 Dec. 1970, 284–86; Allan Boesak, "To the Minister of Justice, Pretoria: We Cannot Obey God and You," 26 Nov. 1979, 298; Charles Villa-Vicencio, "The Theology of Apartheid," 13 Mar. 1978, 45–49; Gail Hovey, "Soweto: Keeping Faith with the Children," 16 June 1986, 195–96; Terry Swicegood, "Funeral at Cradock," 16 Sept. 1985, 342–43; Vernon Rose, "Kairos in South Africa," 16 June 1986, 208–9. WCC funding for African radicals is documented in Ernest Lefever, *Amsterdam to Nairobi: The World Council of Churches and the Third World* (Washington: Ethics and Public Policy Center), 91–96.

24. Paul Abrecht, "The Revolution Implicit in Development," 23 June 1969, 178.

25. On these issues see Ronald Chilcote and Joel Edelstein, ed., *Latin America: The Struggle with Dependency and Beyond* (New York: Wiley, 1974), esp. 1–88; Chilcote, ed., *Dependency and Marxism: Toward a Resolution of the Debate* (Boulder, Colo.: Westview Press, 1982); and texts on cold war revisionism such as McCormick, *America's Half-Century*, and Chomsky, *Towards a New Cold War*. See also Richard Barnet and Ronald Müller, *Global Reach: The Power of the Multinational Corporations* (New York: Simon and Schuster, 1974); Harry Magdoff, *Imperialism from the Colonial Age to the Present* (New York: Monthly Review, 1978); and Jack Nelson, *Hunger for Justice: The Politics of Food and Faith* (Maryknoll, N.Y.: Orbis Books, 1980). Many texts in Latin American liberation theology touch on these issues, either overtly or by presupposing dependency analysis. For an application to the politics of international debt during the 1980s see Walden Bello and Claudio Saunt, "International Debt Crisis, Year Five," 23 Nov. 1987, 403–10.

26. Without denying dependency, it remained true that markets had virtues in allocating resources compared with command economies, that supply and demand theory has important analytical uses, and that socialist economies sometimes have good reasons to seek access to international capital and trade. Useful discussions of these issues include Dorrien, *Soul in Society;* Charles Lindblom, *Politics and Markets: The World's Political Economic Systems* (New York: Basic Books, 1977); and Carl Parrini, "Theories of Imperialism," in *Redefining the Past: Essays in Diplomatic History in Honor of William Appleman Williams*, ed. Lloyd Gardner (Corvallis: Oregon State Univ. Press, 1986), 65–84. McGovern, *Liberation Theology and Its Critics*, 156–76, provides a very useful assessment of criticisms of dependency theory by Michael Novak and Paul Sigmund.

27. Shaull, "New Revolutionary Mood in Latin America," 1 Apr. 1963, 46, 47; Cowan to Schlesinger, 25 Apr. 1963, *C&C* records box 1, untitled folder.

28. Bennett, "Latin American Policy Questions," 1 Apr. 1963, 43; Bennett did urge readers to take Shaull's analysis seriously.

29. See, e.g., Emilio Castro, "Christian Response to the Latin American Revolution," 16 Sept. 1963, 160–63; Mauricio Lopez, "Dialogue across the Rio Grande," 9 Jan. 1967, 307–10; Shaull, "The Second Latin American Church and Society Conference," 2 May 1966, 89–91; Gonzalo Castillo-Cardenas, "Bogotá Revisited," 20 Mar. 1967, 54–56; Míguez Bonino, "Missionary Planning and National Integrity," 24 June 1968, 140–43.

30. Shaull, "Next Stage in Latin America," 13 Nov. 1967, 264–66; Shaull, "National Development and Social Revolution: Parts I and II," 20 Jan. 1969, 347–48, and 3 Feb. 1969, 9–12; Paulo Freire, *The Pedagogy of the Oppressed* (New York: Seabury Press, 1970).

31. On CEBs see Thomas Bruneau, *The Political Transformation of the Brazilian Catholic Church* (New York: Cambridge Univ. Press, 1974); Gary MacEoin, *Puebla: A Church Being Born* (New York: Paulist Press, 1980); Smith, *Emergence of Liberation Theology;* Sergio Torres and John Eagleson, eds., *The Challenge of Basic Christian Communities* (Maryknoll, N.Y.: Orbis Books, 1981). See also Michael Candelaria, *Popular Religion and Liberation: The Dilemma of Liberation Theology* (Albany: SUNY Press, 1990). *C&C* produced a special issue on CEBs in 1981, introduced by Phillip Berryman, "Latin America: 'Iglesia que Nace del Pueblo,'" 21 Sept. 1981, 238–42.

32. Cowan, "An Interview with Ivan Illich," 4 Aug. 1969, 218, 214.

33. William Wipfler, "The Price of 'Progress' in Brazil," 16 Mar. 1970, 44–48. It became a staple of *C&C* promotion to claim that this was the first major article on this issue published in the United States. On Brazil see also Thomas Quigley, "Brazil: New Generals versus Renewal Bishops," 1 Apr. 1974, 61–64. On Chile, see Dale Johnson, "Chile: The Counterrevolution," 29 Oct. 1973, 211–16; and Bennett, "Election in Chile," 5 Oct. 1970, 201–2. See also John Stockwell, "Uruguay: Do We Subsidize Repression?" 2 Oct. 1972, 211–13; Sergio Arce Martinez, "Working for the Revolution," 28 June 1971, 132–34; Cowan, "Interview with Marcio Moreira Alves," 20 July 1970, 155–60; and Wipfler, "Latin America: U.S. Colony," 3 Apr. 1972, 68–75. Human rights in Latin America and other countries was the theme of *C&C*'s thirty-fifth anniversary banquet. See Brown et al., "Church, State, and Human Rights," 27 Dec. 1976, 302–13.

34. Dorothee Sölle, "Upon the Murder of Elizabeth Kaseman," 9 Sept. 1980, 171; David Dyson, "The Valley of the Shadow: El Salvador," 8 Jan. 1990, 404–5; Jorge Lara-Braud, "'El Pueblo Unido Jamas Sera Vencido,'" 12 May 1980, 114, 148–50.

35. Dean Kelley, "What to Do When the FBI Knocks: A Primer for Pastors," 2 May 1977, 86–92; "Nicaragua and the World" (interview with Miguel D'Escoto), 12 May 1980, 146.

36. Grant Wacker, "Searching for Norman Rockwell," in *Piety and Politics: Evangelicals and Fundamentalists Confront the World,* ed. Richard John Neuhaus and Michael Cromartie (Lanham, Md.: Ethics and Public Policy Center, 1987), 330–31; Milton Coalter, John Mulder, and Louis Weeks, eds., *The Mainstream Protestant "Decline"* (Louisville: Westminster Press, 1990), 19.

37. Kirk Hadaway, "Denomination Defection: Recent Research on Religious Disaffiliation in America," in Coalter et al., *The Mainstream Protestant "Decline,"* 108

38. See Marty, "Religion in America since Mid-Century," in *Religion in America: Spirituality in a Secular Age,* ed. Mary Douglas and Steven Tipton (Boston: Beacon, 1982) 275; Hutchison, "Past Imperfect: History and the Prospect for Liberalism," in Michaelsen and Roof, *Liberal Protestantism,* 65–84. For a thorough study of the demographic issues, see Hadaway and David Roozen, eds., *Church and Denominational Growth: What Does (and What Does Not) Cause Growth and Decline* (Nashville: Abingdon Press, 1993). For an elegant summary see William McKinney and Wade Clark Roof, "Liberal Protestantism: A Sociodemographic Perspective," in Michaelsen and Roof, *Liberal Protestantism,* 37–50. For general citations on evangelicalism and its relationship to liberal Protestants, see the introduction.

39. See, e.g., Dean Kelley, *Why Conservative Churches Are Growing* (New York: Harper and Row, 1972); and Finke and Stark, *The Churching of America, 1776–1990.* See also Leonard Sweet, "Can a Mainstream Change Its Course?" in Michaelsen and Roof, *Liberal Protestantism,* 235–62; and Peter Berger, "From the Crisis of Religion to the Crisis of Secularity," in Douglas and Tipton, *Religion in America,* 14–24. For more on this issue, see my "Interpreting the 'Popular' in Popular Religion," *American Studies* 36 (Fall 1995): 127–37, which includes an extended analysis of Finke and Stark.

40. Dean Hoge, Benton Johnson, and Donald Luidens, *Vanishing Boundaries: The Religion of Mainline Protestant Baby Boomers* (Louisville: Westminster Press, 1994). The authors argue that mainline has two options: either "recapture authority" or adapt to the desires of lay liberals. They lean toward the first approach because they see the leading cause of defection as eroding boundaries of belief, fed by weak "plausibility structures" in local churches and relativism in the general culture. They fear that adapting to these trends would increase the mainline's problems in the long run. If so, their data suggest that the mainline is between a rock and a hard place. Luidens distances himself from a conservative reading of this analysis in "Fighting 'Decline': Mainline Churches and the Tyranny of Aggregate Data," *Christian Century*, 6 Nov. 1996, 1075–79.

41. David E. Anderson, "Goodbye to Pat Robertson," 4 Apr. 1988, 106–7. For a book-length version of the argument see Steve Bruce, *The Rise and Fall of the New Christian Right: Conservative Protestant Politics in America, 1978–1988* (Oxford: Clarendon Press, 1988).

42. Marty, "Religion in America since Mid-Century," 281.

43. On the spectrum of evangelical political thought see Robert Booth Fowler, *A New Engagement: Evangelical Political Thought, 1966–1976* (Grand Rapids: Eerdmans, 1982); and Carol Flake, *Redemptorama: Culture, Politics, and the New Evangelicalism* (New York: Penguin, 1984).

44. James Davison Hunter, *Evangelicalism—the Coming Generation* (Chicago: Univ. of Chicago Press, 1987); Richard Quebedeaux, *The Young Evangelicals* (New York: Harper and Row, 1974).

45. This episode in *C&C*'s history has been retold more than any other besides its founding and its debate about Vietnam. See, e.g., Fox, *Reinhold Niebuhr*, 265–66; Mark Silk, *Spiritual Politics: Religion and America since World War II* (New York: Simon and Schuster, 1987), 101–3; and Silk, "The Rise of the 'New Evangelicalism,'" in Hutchison, *Between the Times*, 286–89.

46. Niebuhr, "Editorial Notes," 20 Feb. 1956, 18–19; Van Dusen, "Correspondence," 2 Apr. 1956, 40; William Farmer, "Cynicism and the Revival," 2 Apr. 1956, 35–38; Bennett, "An Editor Replies," 2 Apr. 1956, 38. See also Van Dusen, "The Challenge of the 'Sects,'" 21 July 1958, 103–6.

47. Bennett, "The Resourceful Mr. Pew," 11 June 1956, 75; L. Nelson Bell, "Correspondence: Mr. Pew and Mr. Bell," 1 Oct. 1956, 127. Marty, *The Religious Press in America*, 57, estimates that in 1963 *Christianity Today* received a subsidy of $225,000 per year from "wealthy laymen." *C&C*'s entire income in 1965 was around $100,000.

48. Bennett, "The Roman Catholic 'Issue' Again," 19 Sept. 1960, 125–26. A careful reading of Bennett's "underworld" passage reveals that he distinguished the NAE from an older Paul Blanshard type underworld. However, the media reported the story as if he had linked them, and indeed a major point of his argument was that the new Citizens' Committee for Religious Freedom exhibited many of the same old problems in a more genteel form. In any case, Bennett later told Peale (whose son was attending Union Seminary at the time) that he never meant the "underworld" label to apply to him. Meanwhile, Graham claimed that he could not recall initiating the anti-Kennedy lobbying or attacking Kennedy's moral character at the original meeting. See George, *God's Salesman*, 200–211.

49. Rev. Jerry Bryant, "The Biblical Doctrine of Warfare," cited in A. G. Mojtabai, *Blesséd Assurance: At Home with the Bomb in Amarillo, Texas* (London: Secker and Warburg, 1987), 135.

50. Niebuhr, "The King's Chapel and the King's Court," 4 Aug. 1969, 211–12. Pete Young, "Trading Absolution for Support," 9 June 1969, 162–66, was a harsher attack that Bennett criticized internally (Leon Howell interview). See also Elliott Wright, "Raising the Christian Canopy: The Evangelical's Burden," 19 Mar. 1973, 35–40.

51. Nancy Hastings Sehested, "Smiling through a Sunday Morning," 20 July 1992, 244–45; Campbell, "On Silencing Our Finest," 16 Sept. 1985, 340–42. See also Brown, "Listen, Jerry Falwell!" 22 Dec. 1980, 360–64. On the Southern Baptist Convention, see Alan Neely, "Just Stir 'em Up: How the SBC Got That Way," 4 Mar. 1991, 71–72, a review of Nancy Ammerman's *Baptist Battles: Social Change and Religious Conflict in the Southern Baptist Convention* (New Brunswick: Rutgers Univ. Press, 1990).

52. Advertisement, 7 Aug. 1972, 196; John Howard Yoder, "Evangelicals at Chicago: A New Openness to Prophetic Social Critique," 18 Feb. 1973, 23–26; Marlin Van Elderen, "Evangelicals and Liberals: Is There a Common Ground?" 8 July 1974, 151–55; Quebedeaux, "Evangelicals: Ecumenical Allies," 27 Dec. 1971, 286–88; Quebedeaux, "The Evangelicals: New Trends and New Tensions," 20 Sept. 1976, 197–202.

53. Campbell, "The World of the Redneck," 27 May 1974, 118.

54. Cox, *Religion in the Secular City: Toward a Postmodern Theology* (New York: Simon and Schuster, 1984), 267. See also Campbell et al., "*Religion in the Secular City*: A Symposium," 20 Feb. 1984, 35–45, especially the comments by Campbell, Douglas Sturm, and Cornel West. I discuss *Religion in the Secular City* in "Evangelical Popular Religion as a Source for North American Liberation Theology? Insights from Postmodern Popular Culture Theory," *American Studies* 33 (Spring 1992): 63–82. Cox continued in this vein in *Fire from Heaven: The Rise of Pentecostal Spirituality and the Reshaping of Religion in the Twenty-first Century* (Reading, Mass.: Addison-Wesley, 1995).

55. "Results of Readership Survey," *C&C* internal document, ca. Sept. 1990; "Summary Results, *Christianity and Crisis* Readership Survey," *C&C* internal document, ca. Sept. 1967; "About the People Who Read *C&C*," *C&C* promotional brochure, 1982, photocopies from *C&C* archives.

56. Thompson, "Tides and Trauma," 5 Apr. 1971, 62–63. Ramsey did return, in an exception that proves the rule, for a 1980 abortion symposium in which he was paired with the head of the National Right to Life Committee against more liberal panelists. See Dellapenna et al., "Continuing the Discussion: A Middle Ground on Abortion?" 31 Mar. 1980, 70–80.

57. Novak, "Election '68: Let the Republicans Have It," 14 Oct. 1968, 236; Novak, "Hypocrisies Unmasked," 12 May 1969, 125.

58. Berger, "A Conservative Reflection about Vietnam," 6 Mar. 1967, 33–35. Neuhaus, "Cambodia, Salonika, and the Antichrist," 3 Aug. 1970, 169–72 used similar logic, but showed as much passion for attacking contextual ethicists as he did for criticizing the invasion of Cambodia. Useful overviews of Berger's intellectual trajectory are Hudnut-Beumler, *Looking for God in the Suburbs*, 145–66; and Dorrien, *The Neoconservative Mind*, 265–322.

59. Berger, "Reflections on Law and Order," 9 Dec. 1968, 298, 297.

60. Novak, "Healing Class Tensions in a Sick Society," 8 June 1970, 117–18 (citing Tom Wicker). See also Novak, "The Volatile Counter-Culture," 25 May 1970, 107–13, a response to Myron Bloy, "Counter-Culture and Academic Reform, 27 Apr. 1970, 85–90.

61. George Scialabba, "A Calling to Solidarity?" 23 Oct. 1989, 339. On the new class see Barbara Ehrenreich, "The 'New Class': A Bludgeon for the Right," in *Fear of Falling: The Inner Life of the Middle Class* (New York: Pantheon, 1989), 144–95; Dorrien, *Neoconservative Mind;* and B. Bruce-Briggs, ed. *The New Class?* (New Brunswick: Rutgers Univ. Press, 1979). See also the discussion in Robert Wuthnow, *Restructuring of American Religion*, 157–58, and the analysis of Berger by James Davison Hunter in Wuthnow et al., *Cultural Analysis: The Work of Peter L. Berger, Mary Douglas, Michel Foucault, and Jurgen Habermas* (London: Routledge, 1984), 21–77. For a sort of "minority report" on new class analysis, written from a stance friendly to the left, see Richard Flacks and Jack Whalen, *Beyond the Barricades: The Sixties Generation Grows Up* (Philadelphia: Temple Univ. Press, 1989), 277–80; Flacks links this to a more elaborate vision that cites A. J. Muste as a role model in his *Making History: The Radical Tradition in American Life* (New York: Columbia Univ. Press, 1988). See also Elizabeth Walker Mechling and Jay Mechling, "Hot Pacifism and Cold War: The American Friends Service Committee's Witness for Peace in 1950s America," *Quarterly Journal of Speech* 78 (1992): 173–96. Farber, "The Silent Majority and Talk about Revolution," in *The Sixties: From Memory to History*, 291–316, is useful for relating neoconservatives to broader developments in the society.

62. Novak "Unmasking Self-Interests," 4 Oct. 1971, 197–98. Novak, "Programmatic Suggestions for a New Ethnic Politics," 22 Jan. 1973, 309–11.

63. Novak, "Argument: The New Ethnicity," 2 Oct. 1972, 216–17; Novak, "The Politics of Surprise," 9 Aug. 1972, 175–76. It was unclear what to make of his words about Nixon, since they appeared in a new *C&C* feature called "Argument," which was designed to stir up debate, and Novak still claimed he opposed the war.

64. Letters: Cowan to Novak, 9 May 1975; Novak to Cowan, 13 May 1975; Shinn to Cowan, 20 May 1975; Brown to Cowan, 20 May 1975; Cowan to Novak, 5 June 1975; Novak to Cowan, 12 June 1975, photocopies from *C&C* archives. Part of Novak's complaint was about the *process* of *C&C*'s decision making.

65. Depending on how one defines "inner circle," a few internal skirmishes continued. Perhaps the most important concerned James Finn, a former editor of *Commonweal,* who was associated with *Worldview* magazine and the neoconservative Freedom House. Finn became a regular *C&C* columnist for a time under Hoyt's editorship until his suspicion of third world radicals pushed him beyond the boundaries of *C&C*'s tolerance. See, e.g., Finn, "Looking Back on Grenada," 2 Apr. 1984, 102–3 (supporting the U.S. invasion); and Finn, "The Body Snatchers," 12 Dec. 1983, 469–70 (attacking the Philippine left). The most heated conflict occurred in 1981 after Finn signed a *New York Times* advertisement that began: "We—a group of intellectuals and religious leaders—applaud the American policy in El Salvador," as discussed in Eric Hochstein with Ronald O'Rourke, "A Report on the Institute on Religion and Democracy," *IDOC Bulletin* 8–9 (1982): 21. For *C&C*'s response, see Cowan et al., "Dear Jim: Why Did You Sign?" 11 May 1981, 131–33; and Finn, "Why I Signed That Ad," 25 May 1981, 152–54.

66. Andrew Young, "Thirtieth Anniversary Speech," 3 May 1971, 81. King's speech is also a paradigmatic moment for mapping *C&C*'s relation to African American social movements; see Brenda Gayle Plummer, *Rising Wind: Black Americans and U.S. Foreign Affairs, 1935–1960* (Chapel Hill: Univ. of North Carolina Press, 1996), 317–18.

67. Shinn, "Ferment on the Campus," 14 June 1965, 126–27; Mark Juergensmeyer, "The Battle of People's Park," 9 June 1969, 169–71; special issue on *Theological Education,* 14 Apr. 1969, with numerous articles including Bennett's moderate "Priorities in Theological Education," 87–90, and J. Archie Hargreaves's more radical "Blackening Theological Education," 93–98. Cherry, *Hurrying toward Zion,* 213–40, discusses the intersection between seminarians and New Left organizations. He estimates that one hundred Union students were active at Columbia in 1968, including one student (Daniel Pellegrom) who was president of the Columbia University Student Council.

68. Cowan, "On Being Discriminate about Political Reality," 25 Nov. 1968, 283, 284; Malcolm Diamond, "Prophecy and Fanaticism," 8 Jan. 1968, 314.

69. Cited in David Henry, "Recalling the Sixties: The New Left and Social Movement Criticism," *Quarterly Journal of Speech* 75 (1989): 103.

70. Henry F. May, "Meditation on an Unfashionable Book," 27 May 1968, 120–22; Fox, *Reinhold Niebuhr,* 288. See also William May, "Marcuse: Apologist for Intolerance," 22 Mar. 1971, 47–50, Ross Terrill, "Utopians or Revolutionaries," 7 July 1969, 191–95.

71. Kuhn, "The Columbia Revolution," 27 May 1968, 113; Bennett, "The Columbia Revolution: II," 24 June 1968, 138–39; Ramsey, "Political Repentance Now!" 252.

72. Dylan, "Ballad of a Thin Man," from *Highway 61 Revisited,* Columbia Records, 1965.

73. Stephen Rose, "Experiment in Secular Ecumenicity," 13 Nov. 1967, 260–63; Huston Smith, "Psychedelic Theophanies and the Religious Life," 26 June 1967, 144–48.

74. Harsh, "Proposal for a New Theological Magazine," 2, 9.

75. Ibid., 9; David Miller, "More on Play," 6 Mar. 1972, 48.

76. Stringfellow, "Jesus the Criminal," 8 June 1970, 119–22; Scott and Glenda Hope, "In Praise of Intimacy," 28 June 1971, 134–35; Louis Chapin, "Just History," 26 July 1971, 163–64; Myron Bloy Jr., "Superstar and the New Saxons," 28 Dec. 1970, 280–83.

77. Franklin Sherman, "Church and Society at Detroit," 27 Nov. 1967, 276, 278.

78. Gammer Gurton, "Come, Play with Me!" 13 Dec. 1971, 274. Vivian Lindermayer, "More on Play," 6 Mar. 1972, 48, restated Gurton's critique: "To what extent is the play theories' conception of personal liberation dependent on the oppression of another class of people? To what extent is their notion of a 'radical consciousness' just another leisure class phenomenon that can be absorbed quite easily . . . by an oppressive society?"

79. Cox, *The Feast of Fools: A Theological Essay on Festivity and Fantasy* (Cambridge: Harvard Univ. Press, 1969); Cox, *The Seduction of the Spirit: The Use and Misuse of People's Religion* (New York: Simon and Schuster, 1973), quotation 17; Cox, *Turning East: The Promise and Peril of the*

New Orientalism (New York: Simon and Schuster, 1977). In *Just as I Am* (Nashville: Abingdon, 1983), 156, Cox called *Seduction of the Spirit* the book "I am probably least pleased with" and *Turning East* a "detour from my continuing theological interests."

80. Driver, "Review: The Seduction of the Spirit," 7 Jan. 1974, 285, 284; Marty, "Time Now to Think of Turning Baptist," 17 Oct. 1977, 237. Cox, "Light from the East: A Report from Naropa," 24 Jan. 1977, 326–29, covered some of the same ground as *Turning East.*

81. St. Hereticus (a.k.a. Brown), "E. Pluribus Marty," 3 Apr. 1977, 76–77.

82. Campbell and Holloway, "Up to Our Steeple in Politics," 38–39; Young "Saints, Maniacs, and Hypocrites," 43. Young's article was part of a "balanced" symposium, Arthur Moore et al., "The Steeple in Perspective: Four Views," 3 Mar. 1969, 40–44. Ellul's works include *The Technological Society* (New York: Vintage, 1964); *Violence: Reflections from a Christian Perspective* (New York: Seabury, 1969); and *Jesus and Marx: From Ideology to Gospel* (Grand Rapids: Eerdmans, 1988).

83. Cox "The End of an Era," 6 Jan. 1969, 325–26.

84. Kuhn, "Is Federal Initiative Finished," 3 Feb. 1969, 1–2; letter from Arthur Moore to Cowan, 29 Oct. 1973; Brown, "What Can We Do?" 11 Jan. 1971, 295. See also Rose, "Can We Get It Together?" 11 Jan. 1971, 292–93.

85. Shaull, "Liberal and Radical in an Age of Discontinuity," 5 Jan. 1970, 340.

86. Bennett, "After Thirty Years," 22 Mar. 1971, 40; Ruether, "A Radical-Liberal in the Streets of Washington," 12 July 1971, 144.

Chapter 8

1. Cowan, "About this Issue," 2 Oct. 1972, 210, citing an anonymous reader.

2. Tom Driver, "Review: *The Seduction of the Spirit,*" 7 Jan. 1974, 283.

3. Dom Helder Camara, "The Force of Right or the Right of Force?" 5 Aug. 1974, 176. See also his book, *The Desert Is Fertile* (Maryknoll, N.Y.: Orbis Books, 1976).

4. Mary Lou Suhor, "Just What Do Women Want?" 26 June 1978, 162–63.

5. Ibid., 163; Driver, "Review: *The Seduction of the Spirit,*" 284.

6. Alice Echols, *Daring to Be Bad,* 44–45; Sara Evans, *Personal Politics: The Roots of the Women's Liberation in the Civil Rights Movement and the New Left* (New York: Vintage, 1979), 189–92.

7. Cover art, 5 Oct. 1970; Kathy Mulherin and Jennifer Gardner, "Growing Up a Woman," 5 Oct. 1970, 202–9.

8. Arthur Moore, "The Question of Credibility," 28 June 1965, 133–34; Bennett, *Radical Imperative,* 109. Even Howard Moody, one of *C&C*'s first insiders to make serious alliances with feminists, wrote in his "Abortion: Woman's Right and Legal Problem," 8 Mar. 1971, 31, that "I don't believe for one moment that abortion is more important than self-determination for Black communities," the Vietnam war, or even "working with Chavez" [the leader of a Chicano farm workers' union.]

9. Harvey Cox, "The Cultural Captivity of Women," 31 May 1971, 110. Ten years earlier, Cox had also mentioned showgirls and even cited *The Second Sex* by Simone de Beauvoir, but he mainly attacked "The Girl" as an example of degraded consumer society that oppressed everyone regardless of sex. Thus he said that the Rockettes "bear an ominous similarity to the faceless retinues of goose-steppers and the interchangeable mass exercises of explicitly totalitarian societies." Cox, "Miss America and the Cult of The Girl," 7 Aug. 1961, 146.

10. According to Jackson Carroll, Barbara Hargrove, and Adair Lummis, *Women of the Cloth: A New Opportunity for Churches* (San Francisco: Harper and Row, 1981), 7, the percentages of female M.Div. students in mainline denominational seminaries in 1980 ranged from 21 percent for southern Presbyterians to 45 percent for the United Church of Christ. See also Cherry, *Hurrying toward Zion,* 250–53; and the Cornwall Collective, *Your Daughters Shall Prophesy: Feminist Alternatives in Theological Education* (New York: Pilgrim Press, 1980). According to Handy, *History of Union Theological Seminary,* 296–97, 323, in 1972 Union adopted an unusually strong affirmative action goal of making its faculty, staff, and student body half fe-

male and one-third minority. At the time its student body was 20 percent female and 3 percent black; by 1984 it was half female and one-eighth black. On gender (not race) Union was fairly representative of the schools where *C&C* readers clustered.

11. To place *C&C*'s versions of feminism within a broader spectrum, see Evans, *Personal Politics;* Echols, *Daring to Be Bad;* Nicholson, *Feminism/Postmodernism;* Jaggar and Rothenberg, *Feminist Frameworks;* Karen Hansen and Ilene J. Philipson, eds., *Women, Class, and the Feminist Imagination: A Socialist-Feminist Reader* (Philadelphia: Temple Univ. Press, 1989); Judith Plaskow and Carol Christ, eds., *Weaving the Visions: New Patterns in Feminist Spirituality* (San Francisco: Harper and Row, 1989); Gayle Graham Yates, *What Women Want: The Ideas of the Movement* (Cambridge: Harvard Univ. Press, 1975); and Ellen Willis, "Radical Feminism and Feminist Radicalism," in Sayres, *The Sixties without Apology,* 91–118.

12. Kathy Mulherin and Jennifer Gardner, "Growing Up a Woman," 202–9. On the pro-woman line see Echols, *Daring to Be Bad,* 91–92, 143–46.

13. Penelope Washbourn, "The Religious Dimensions of Sexuality," 9 Dec. 1974, 284. See also Washbourn, "Becoming Woman: Menstruation as Spiritual Experience," in Plaskow and Christ, *Womanspirit Rising,* 246–58.

14. Linda Barufaldi and Emily Culpepper, "Androgyny and the Myth of Masculine/Feminine," 16 Apr. 1973, 70, 71. On the better known WITCH see Echols, *Daring to Be Bad,* 96–100, 116–19.

15. Cox, "Eight Theses on Female Liberation," 4 Oct. 1971, 199.

16. Carol Christ, "Letter," 13 Dec. 1971, 276; Anne Bennett, "Letter," 10 Jan. 1972, 298–99.

17. Anne Bennett, *From Woman-Pain to Woman-Vision.* John Bennett coauthored parts of this book; Harrison commented that, because of her influence, he had probably read more feminist theology by the early 1990s than any other man in the country above the age of forty (Harrison interview).

18. Brown, "Joke Telegrams," in 3 May 1971 issue, passim.

19. In an interview, Rosemary Ruether refused to describe herself as a *C&C* insider and insisted that her importance to the journal was based not on active participation in institutional decisions but on her writing moving in harmony with *C&C*'s evolving concerns. Mead was seventy-one years old in 1972, and she was relatively inactive at *C&C.* She died in 1978. For a hostile treatment of Mead's relation to second wave feminism, see Louise Newman, "Coming of Age, but Not in Samoa: Reflections on Margaret Mead's Legacy for Western Liberal Feminism," *American Quarterly* 48 (1996), no. 2: 233–72. For a friendlier analysis of the school of anthropology that she helped pioneer in the 1920s and 1930s, see George Marcus and Michael Fischer, *Anthropology as Cultural Critique* (Chicago: Univ. of Chicago Press, 1986).

20. Rosemary Ruether, "The Search for Soul Power in the White Community," 27 Apr. 1970, 83–85; Ruether, "A Radical-Liberal in the Streets of Washington," 12 July 1971, 144. Since 1976 Ruether has taught at Garrett-Evangelical Seminary.

21. Major texts by Ruether include *Sexism and God-Talk: Toward a Feminist Theology* (Boston: Beacon, 1983), *To Change the World: Christology and Cultural Criticism* (New York: Crossroad, 1981), *Disputed Questions: On Being a Christian,* 2d ed. (Maryknoll, N.Y.: Orbis Books, 1989), and *Gaia and God: An Ecofeminist Theology of Earth Healing* (San Francisco: Harper, 1992).

22. Ruether, "The Persecution of Witches: A Case of Sexism and Ageism?" 23 Dec. 1974, 291–95; Ruether, "Catholic Bishops and 'Women's Concerns,'" 16 May 1988, 175–76; Ruether, "Working Women and the Male Workday," 7 Feb. 1977, 3–8; Ruether, "Why Socialism Needs Feminism and Vice Versa," 28 Apr. 1980, 103–8.

23. For an incisive interpretation of this "sex war" in feminist theory with a good bibliography see Echols, *Daring to Be Bad,* 288–91. For an idea of one extreme in this debate see Mary Daly, *Beyond God the Father* (Boston: Beacon Press, 1973), 123, which compares the 1960s sexual revolution to large-scale gang rape by an invading army. At the other extreme, Barbara Ehrenreich, Elizabeth Hess, and Gloria Jacobs, *Re-Making Love: The Feminization of Sex* (New York: Anchor, 1986), identifies a "women's sexual revolution" in such cultural realms as Beatlemania and (in a highly circumscribed way) Marabel Morgan's *The Total Woman.*

Readers should be aware that I am not a neutral observer of this debate, since I published a *C&C* article leaning toward the pro-eroticism side. I was sufficiently uncomfortable with the end result after several rounds of cuts and *C&C* editing that I prefer not to cite it, but I published a more nuanced version as "Like a Sermon: Popular Religion in Madonna Videos," in *Religion and Popular Culture in America,*" ed. Bruce Forbes and Jeffrey Mahan (Univ. of California Press, forthcoming).

24. Tom Driver, "A Stride toward Sanity," 31 Oct. 1977, 246; Raymond Lawrence, "Toward a More Flexible Monogamy," 18 Mar. 1974, 43.

25. Ruether, "The Personalization of Sexuality," 16 Apr. 1973, 62.

26. Ruether, "The Sexuality of Jesus: What Do the Synoptics Say?" 29 May 1978, 135; Tom Driver, "A Stride toward Sanity," 31 Oct. 1977, 243–46; Phipps, *Was Jesus Married?* (New York: Harper and Row, 1970).

27. Ruether, "Personalization of Sexuality," 62; Harrison interview.

28. Mary Pellauer, "Porn Is Big Business," 13 May 1985, 174–75; Margaret O'Brien Steinfels, "Here She Is! Miss America!" 17 Sept. 1984, 320; Susan Brooks Thistlethwaite, "Battered Women and the Bible: From Subjection to Liberation," 16 Nov. 1981, 308–11.

29. Pamela Cooper-White, "Borders: Sex in the Parish House," 4 Feb. 1991, 22–23; Susan Brooks Thistlethwaite, "Sexual Harassment: To Protect, Empower," 21 Oct. 1991, 329. Marie Fortune, "On *Sex in the Parish,*" 18 Nov. 1991, 367–69. For a book-length approach to this subject see Fortune, *Love Does No Harm: Sexual Ethics for the Rest of Us* (New York: Crossroad / Continuum, 1995).

30. Barry Morris, "Correspondence," 10 June 1991, 207.

31. Gallop cited in Margaret Talbot, "A Most Dangerous Method: The Disturbing Case against Jane Gallop, Feminist Provocateur," *Lingua Franca* (Jan. / Feb. 1994), 39.

32. Kilmer Myers, ". . . But the Bishop's Not Convinced," 13 Dec. 1971, 275–76.

33. Daniel Corrigan et al., "An Open Letter," 16 Sept. 1974, 185, 188; Carter Heyward, "In and Through," 29 July 1974, 188–94.

34. John Thompson, "Women and Religion: Psychic Sources of Misogyny," 2 Apr. 1979, 74.

35. Daly, post-Christian introduction to *The Church and the Second Sex,* 2d ed. (New York: Harper and Row, 1975), 6, cited in Ferm, *Contemporary American Theologies,* 12. For a range of articles on ordination see Betty Gray, "Women Priests Now?" 23 July 1973, 148–51; Heyward and Suzanne Hiatt, "The Trivialization of Women," 26 June 1978, 158–62; Robert Hoyt, "The Vatican on Women Priests," 7 Mar. 1977, 36–37, Jackson Carroll et al., "Women in Ministry: How Are They Doing?" 4 Apr. 1983, 110, 117–20.

36. Franklin Littell, "Abortion in Norway: A Comment," 6 Mar. 1961, 27; Richard Fagley, "Christian Approaches to Responsible Parenthood," 25 Jan. 1960, 215.

37. John Leo, "Rethinking Birth Control," 26 July 1965, 160, 161.

38. Green, "Abortion and Promise-Keeping," 15 May 1967, 109–13.

39. Ramsey, "Abortion and the Law," 7 Aug. 1967, 195–96; Ruth Sprague, "Abortion: The Right to be Wanted," 2 Oct. 1967, 221. Sprague worked for the United Church Board for Homeland Ministries. In fairness we should note that Green had not entirely ignored male promise keeping and responsibility; he pointed out that this was presupposed by child support laws.

40. Bennett, "The Abortion Debate," 20 Mar. 1967, 47. Bennett, "Editorial," 30 Sept. 1968, 214; Bennett, "Avoid Oppressive Laws!" 8 Jan. 1973, 286–87. Edward Fiske, "Toward a Code of Behavior for Ecumenists," *New York Times,* 26 Mar. 1967, in *C&C* records, box 18, scrapbook, reveals readers throughout the country listening in on this *C&C* versus *Commonweal* debate.

41. Daniel Callahan, "Abortion: Thinking and Experiencing," 8 Jan. 1973, 295–98; Michael Novak, "Programmatic Suggestions for a New Ethnic Politics," 22 Jan. 1973, 309–11.

42. Howard Moody, "Church, State, and the Rights of Conscience," 8 Jan. 1973, 294; Moody, "Abortion: Woman's Right and Legal Problem," 8 Mar. 1971, 28. One of the most vehement anti-Christian writers on the left today, Katha Pollitt, paid respect to Moody's commitments in "No God, No Master," *Nation,* 22 Jan. 1996, 9. (This represents a mixed bag for *C&C*'s reputation in the *Nation,* since the main point of Pollitt's article was to attack Cox.)

43. Margaret Mead, "Rights to Life," 8 Jan. 1973, 288–92.

44. Paid advertisement, "A Call to Concern," 3 Oct. 1977, 222.

45. Robert Hoyt, "A Call to Reflection," 31 Oct. 1977, 253-55.

46. Paid advertisement, James Burtchaell, C.S.C., "A Call and a Reply," 14 Nov. 1977, 271, 270.

47. Burtchaell, "Continuing the Discussion: How to Argue about Abortion II," 26 Dec. 1977, 315, 316, emphasis in the original. As a concession to pragmatic politics, Burtchaell supported legalizing—without morally condoning—first-trimester abortions after rape or incest and in case of birth defects.

48. Bennett and Hoyt, "Continuing the Discussion: How to Argue about Abortion," 14 Nov. 1977, 264–66.

49. Harrison, "Continuing the Discussion: How to Argue about Abortion II," 26 Dec. 1977, 311, 313.

50. Vivian and Eric Lindermayer, "Continuing the Discussion: How to Argue about Abortion II," 26 Dec. 1977, 317.

51. Harrison, "Continuing the Discussion: How to Argue about Abortion," 313. For a full statement of Harrison's views, see *Our Right to Choose,* which "aims to make it harder for anyone to speak of abortion as 'a moral dilemma' without giving women's well-being central standing in the discussion" (x). Mary Seger reviewed *Our Right to Choose* in "Abortion: A Feminist Perspective," 31 Oct. 1983, 410–14. My thinking about this impasse over human personhood and its centrality to the debate has been influenced by Carl Cohen, "How Not to Argue about Abortion," *Michigan Quarterly Review* 29 (1990), no. 4: 567–82. Cohen suggests that moderate pro-choice arguments should defend the changing moral status of fetuses, especially based on when the brain (and therefore consciousness) develops.

52. Margaret O'Brien Steinfels, "Consider the Seamless Garment," 14 May 1984, 172–74; Joseph Dellapenna et al., "Continuing the Discussion: A Middle Ground on Abortion?" 31 Mar. 1980, 70–80 (with Ramsey and Carolyn Gerster defending antiabortion positions). This symposium responded to Mary Segers, "Abortion Politics and Policy: Is There a Middle Ground?" 18 Feb. 1980, 21–27.

53. Vivian Lindermayer, "Thinking about Abortion," in Howell and Lindermayer, *Ethics in the Present Tense,* 188; this first appeared as the introduction to Beverly Harrison et al., "Pro-choice Forum: Abortion: How Should Women Decide?" 14 July 1986, 232–47. See also Gail Hovey, "The Abortion Debate Now: Questions of Value," 11 Sept. 1989, 251–52; and Segers, "Abortion Politics 1992: A Guide," 19 Oct. 1992, 353–55.

54. Tom Driver, "On Taking Sex Seriously," 14 Oct. 1963, 178–79.

55. Anonymous letter, "A Very Sick Society," 13 June 1966, 135; Howard Moody, "Homosexuality and Muckraking," 27 Nov. 1967, 270–71. See also Shinn, "Persecution of the Homosexual," 2 May 1966, 84–85.

56. Richard John Neuhaus, "Cambodia, Salonika, and the Antichrist," 3 Aug. 1970, 172.

57. James McGraw, "The Scandal of Peculiarity," 16 Apr. 1973, 67.

58. Norman Pittenger, "Homosexuality and the Christian Tradition," 5 Aug. 1974, 181.

59. James Nelson, "Homosexuality and the Church," 4 Apr. 1977, reprinted in Howell and Lindermayer, *Ethics in the Present Tense,* 168–82. Virginia Ramey Mollenkott, "Human Rights and the Golden Rule: What the Bible Doesn't Say about Sexuality," 9 Nov. 1987, 384. Mollenkott extended Nelson's biblical arguments in her discussion of the words *malakos* and *arsenokoites* in I Cor. 6:9 and I Tim. 1:10, which are often understood to condemn homosexuality. According to Mollenkott, *malakos* was understood until the twentieth century to mean masturbation, not homosexuality. For the first four centuries *arsenokoites* was understood as a male prostitute, and recent studies have also translated *malakos* with this meaning. In other words, just as condemning sex between a female prostitute and a male does not necessarily condemn all straight sex, when the Bible condemns *arsenokoites* it may only be rejecting a specific form of sexual abuse between powerful adult males and the call boys of ancient Rome, not necessarily condemning all sex between consenting same-sex adults.

60. Carter Heyward, "Coming Out: A Journey without Maps," 11 June 1979, reprinted in Howell and Lindermayer, *Ethics in the Present Tense,* 183.

61. Gail Hovey, "In the Matter of Rose Mary Denman," 9 Nov. 1987, 379–80, and other articles in the same issue. See also Tracy Early, "The Struggle in the Denominations: Shall Gays Be Ordained?" 30 May 1977, 118–22; Jeffrey Gros, "A Gay Church in the NCC?" 2 May 1983, 167–71; Jim Gittings, "Clergy and Sexuality: The Pot Still Simmers," 20 July 1992, 250–52. For a collection of documents on these issues, see John J. Carey, ed., *The Sexuality Debate in North American Churches, 1988–1995* (Lewiston, N.Y.: Edward Mellen Press, 1996).

62. John B. Cobb Jr., "Is the Church Ready to Legislate on Sex?" 14 May 1984, 183, 184.

63. Charles Kirkley, "'Fidelity in Marriage . . . Celibacy in Singleness,'" 14 May 1984, 186–88; John W. Espy, "Continuing the Discussion: Homosexuality and the Church," 30 May 1977, 116–17.

64. Myron Madsen et al., "Reader's Responses: Homosexuality and the Church," 18 July 1977, 175. Madsen was president of the Greater New Orleans Federation of Churches.

65. Editors, "The Debate on Homosexuality: We Vote for Change," 30 May 1977, 114, 116.

66. "Calvin Gay," "You Spoke from Ignorance," 30 Oct. 1978, 254. "Calvin Gay" came out of the closet in Merrill Proudfoot, "Coming to Terms with Calvin Gay," in *Called Out: The Voices of Lesbian, Gay, Bisexual and Transgendered Presbyterians,* ed. Jane Adams Spahr (Gaithersburg, Md.: Chi Rho, 1995), 183–90.

67. On AIDS see, e.g., Jan Zita Grover, "Global AIDS: The Epidemic(s)," 12 June 1989, 197–99, and Grover, "Women and AIDS," 8 May 1989, 146–48; Chris Adams, "AIDS and Changing Realities," 11 Sept. 1989, 257–59. For a sample of other issues see Don Martin, "Gay Fathers and the Church," 15 Oct. 1984, 373–74; Paul Siegel, "Homophobia: Types, Origins, Remedies," 12 Nov. 1979, 280–84; Marvin Ellison, "Theology Born in Resistance," 12 June 1989, 185–86; Donna Minkowitz, "The Christian Right's Antigay Campaign," 12 Apr. 1993, 99–104.

68. Louie Crew, "At St. Luke's Parish, the Peace of Christ Is Not for Gays," 30 May 1977, 136–40; John Fortunato, "The Last Committee on Sexuality (Ever)," 18 Feb. 1991, in *Ethics in the Present Tense,* ed. Howell and Lindermayer, 204–5.

69. Louie Crew, "Barry and Me, and the Angels," 2 Mar. 1993, 52–53.

Chapter 9

1. Gustavo Gutiérrez, *A Theology of Liberation,* Trans. Caridad Inda and John Eagleson (Maryknoll, N.Y.: Orbis Books, 1973), 6–12.

2. Bennett, *Radical Imperative,* 135, accents this point. He claims that Luther, Schleiermacher, Rauschenbusch, and Niebuhr all agree with Gutiérrez that theology is "critical reflection on experience," and he says that Niebuhr was deeply influenced by his pastorate in Detroit and his "continuous response to social situations and political choices."

3. Bennett et al., "Symposium: Christian Realism: Retrospect and Prospect," 5 Aug. 1968, 176, 182. The participants included Bennett, Cox, Driver, Shaull, Shinn, Alan Geyer, and Robert Lynn.

4. F. Ernest Johnson, "Denominational Pronouncements on the War," 7 Aug. 1944, 7.

5. Carol Christ, "Whatever Happened to Theology?" 12 May 1975, 113.

6. "Christian Realism: Retrospect and Prospect," quotation by Shinn, 187.

7. Sally Bentley and Claire Randall, "The Spirit Moving: A New Approach to Theologizing," 4 Feb. 1974, 5.

8. Valerie Saiving, "The Human Situation: A Feminine View" (1960), reprinted in Plaskow and Christ, *Womanspirit Rising,* 25–42; Daphne Hampson, "Reinhold Niebuhr on Sin: A Critique," in Richard Harries, *Reinhold Niebuhr and the Issues of Our Time,* 46–60; Judith Plaskow, *Sex, Sin, and Grace: Women's Experience in the Theologies of Reinhold Niebuhr and Paul Tillich* (Lanham, Md.: Univ. Press of America, 1980).

9. We must not *equate* the Christian / post-Christian continuum with the socialist feminist / cultural feminist polarity, if for no other reason than that large numbers of feminists of all stripes rejected Christianity. But even within *C&C* there were many exceptions to the generalization I have proposed. For example, Washbourn was a moderate Christian theologian influenced by cultural feminism, and Heyward first gained fame in *C&C* for the "liberal" Christian issue of female ordination, but was more friendly to radical cultural femi-

nism than most at *C&C.* (Heyward's last published words in *C&C,* in "Nonviolent Ways," 12 Apr. 1993, 82, were "Blessed Be!") A fine orientation to the Christian/postchristian continuum is the introduction to Plaskow and Christ, *Womanspirit Rising,* 1–24. In recent years this bipolar way of thinking about feminist spirituality has been recognized as overly simple. On multicultural issues see Plaskow and Christ, *Weaving the Visions,* and on methodological issues see Serene Jones, "Women's Experience between a Rock and a Hard Place: Feminist, Womanist, and Mujerista Theologies in North America," *Religious Studies Review* 21 (1995), no. 3: 171–79.

10. Representative anthologies include Judith Weidman, ed., *Christian Feminism* (San Francisco: Harper and Row, 1984); Ann Loades, *Feminist Theology: A Reader* (Philadelphia: Westminster Press, 1990); and Rita Nakashima Brock et al., eds., *Setting the Table: Women in Theological Conversation* (St. Louis: Chalice Press, 1995). An excellent book-length introduction is Letty Russell, *Human Liberation in Feminist Perspective* (Philadelphia: Westminster Press, 1974).

11. Cullen Murphy, "Women and the Bible," *Atlantic,* Aug. 1993, 45.

12. Phyllis Trible, "Good Tidings of Great Joy: Biblical Faith without Sexism," 4 Feb. 1974, 16, 12, 14. A version of this argument appears in Plaskow and Christ, *Womanspirit Rising,* 74–84.

13. Elisabeth Schüssler Fiorenza, *In Memory of Her: A Feminist Theological Reconstruction of Christian Origins* (New York: Crossroad, 1983). For a *C&C* review see Marianne Micks, "Jesus and Women: A Feminist View," 17 Oct. 1983, 388–90.

14. Diane Tennis, "The Loss of the Father God: Why Women Rage and Grieve," 8 June 1981, 164–70. For an argument skeptical of hierarchical images, see Dorothee Sölle, "Mysticism, Liberation, and the Names of God," 22 June 1981, 179–85.

15. Anonymous minister cited by Grailville Work Group on Myths and Images, "Myths and Images of Women: A Drama in Three Parts," 4 Feb. 1974, 12.

16. Cynthia Eller, *Living in the Lap of the Goddess* (Boston: Beacon Press, 1995); Margot Adler, *Drawing Down the Moon: Witches, Druids, Goddess-Worshippers, and Other Pagans in America Today* (Boston: Beacon Press, 1979); Starhawk, *Dreaming the Dark,* 2d ed. (Boston: Beacon Press, 1988).

17. Mary Daly, *Gyn/Ecology: The Metaethics of Radical Feminism* (Boston: Beacon Press, 1978), 84. See also Daly, *Beyond God the Father* (Boston: Beacon Press, 1973), which should be read with the "Original Reintroduction" to the second Beacon edition, 1985. A concise orientation to Daly's work is her "Sin Big," *New Yorker,* 26 Nov. 1996, 76–88. On her place in broader feminism, see Echols, *Daring to Be Bad,* 250–53.

18. Carter Heyward, "Ruether and Daly, Theologians: Speaking and Sparking, Building and Burning," 2 Apr. 1979, 66–72. See also Margaret Miles, "Mary Daly: Creation Recrafted," 26 Nov. 1984, 447–50, which found Daly's *Pure Lust: Elemental Feminist Philosophy* (San Francisco: Harper, 1992) attractive in certain ways, but in the last analysis judgmental and esoteric, only convincing for people who already assumed Daly's premises.

19. Carol Christ, *Laughter of Aphrodite: Reflections on a Journey to the Goddess* (San Francisco: Harper and Row, 1987); Christ, "The New Feminist Theology: A Review of the Literature," *Religious Studies Review* 3 (1977), no. 4: 203–12; Christ, "Feminist Thealogy?" 29 Apr. 1985, 161–62.

20. Rosemary , "Continuing the Discussion: A Further Look at Feminist Theology," 24 June 1974, 142; Ruether, "A Religion for Women: Sources and Strategies," 10 Dec. 1979, 307–9; Ruether, "Female Symbols, Values, and Context," 12 Jan. 1987, 460–64. Ruether was criticized for excessive interest in goddess spirituality in Delores Williams, "The Color of Feminism," 29 Apr. 1985, 164–65; and Robert Imbelli, "Ruether's Reconstruction," 29 Apr. 1985, 159–60. She responded in "For Whom, with Whom, Do We Speak Our New Stories?" 13 May 1985, 183–86.

21. Grailville Work Group on Myths and Images, "Myths and Images of Women: A Drama in Three Parts," 4 Feb. 1974, 8, 9. In preparing this play, they drew on Elizabeth Cady Stanton's 1895 book, *The Woman's Bible.* Sheila Collins introduced the play, pp. 7–8.

22. Catherine Keller, "The Step Beyond Metaphor," 9 Nov. 1987, 386–88; Sallie McFague, *Models of God: Theology for an Ecological Nuclear Age* (Minneapolis: Fortress Press, 1987); Nelle Morton, *The Journey Is Home* (Boston: Beacon, 1985).

23. Carter Heyward , "Suffering, Redemption, and Christ," 11 Dec. 1989, 382, 384. Her arguments are developed in greater detail in *The Redemption of God: A Theology of Mutual Relation* (Lanham, Md.: Univ. Press of America, 1982), *Our Passion for Justice* (New York: Pilgrim, 1984), and *Speaking of Christ* (Cleveland: Pilgrim Press, 1989). She restates them in "Lamenting the Loss of Love: A Reply to Colin Grant," *Journal of Religious Ethics* 24 (1996), no. 1: 23–29. For a mixed *C&C* review of *Redemption of God* see Virginia Ramey Mollenkott, "Who's Redeeming Whom?" 4 Apr. 1983, 123–24.

24. Heyward, "Suffering, Redemption, and Christ," 382.

25. Mary Daly, "The Qualitative Leap beyond Patriarchal Religion," *Quest* (1975): 32, cited in Ferm, *Contemporary American Theologies*, 83–84.

26. Rosemary Ruether, "Crisis in Sex and Race: Black Theology versus Feminist Theology," 15 Apr. 1974, 67–73.

27. Carol Anderson et al., "Continuing the Discussion: A Further Look at Feminist Theology (Part One)," 24 June 1974, 140, 141. See also Sheila Collins, "Continuing the Discussion: A Further Look at Feminist Theology (Part Two)," 24 June 1974, 141–42.

28. Ruether, "Continuing the Discussion: A Further Look at Feminist Theology," 24 June 1974, 142.

29. See, e.g., June Jordan, "How Shall We Know His Name," 18 May 1986, 191–94; bell hooks, "On *A Raisin in the Sun*," 6 Feb. 1989, 21–22; Pauli Murray, "Black, Feminist Theologies: Links, Parallels, and Tensions," 14 Apr. 1980, 86–95; Emilie Townes, "The Dream and the Nightmare," 18 Nov. 1991, 362–64; Ada Maria Isasi-Diaz, "A Platform for Original Voices," 12 June 1989, 191–92; Kwok Pui-Lan, "The Gospel and Culture," 15 July 1991, 223–24; Rigoberta Menchú, "The Indigenous Future," 1 Feb. 1993, 19.

30. A sample of *C&C* articles by Williams includes her "Womanist Theology: Black Women's Voices," 2 Mar. 1987, 66–70; "The Color Purple," 14 July 1986, 230–31; "Summing Up the Negatives," 12 June 1989, 183–84; "The Color of Feminism," 29 Apr. 1985, 164–65; "Talking Back," 9 Oct. 1989, 317–19; and "Lethargy in Christendom," 12 Apr. 1993, 90–91.

31. Howell, "The Crises Continue: The Legacy Remains," 3 Feb. 1986, 4, makes the "almost half" claim about articles in volume 44 (Feb. 1985 through Jan. 1986), but I was unable to corroborate his numbers, finding about 30 percent. (My count was based on indexed articles and reviews; it has a small margin of error, since I could not identify every name.) *C&C*'s figure was roughly in line with comparable numbers in secular left journals, which ranged in 1990 between 43 percent female writers in the *Progressive*, through the *Nation* with 20 percent, to the *Monthly Review* in last place with 12 percent. See "Women and the Nation," *Nation Associate* 11 (Fall 1991), no. 2: 4–5.

32. Ruether, "Feminist Theology in the Academy," 4 Mar. 1985, 61. It is interesting to compare Ruether's stages to the more complex typology suggested by Rita Brock (following Peggy MacIntosh): (1) just like a man, (2) add women and stir, (3) women as victims, (4) women centered, and (5) add everyone. See Brock, "What Is a Feminist? Strategies for Change and Transformation of Consciousness," in *Setting the Table*, 3–24. For a symposium on Ruether's article (which included the criticisms I have already cited by Imbelli and Williams), see Elizabeth Bettenhausen et al., "A Feminist Future: Responses and Reflections," 29 Apr. 1985, 158–65. "Sisterhood" quotation from Pauli Murray, "Black, Feminist Theologies," 92, citing a Nelle Morton essay that was later reprinted in *The Journey Is Home*.

33. See, e.g., Andrew Young, "Thirtieth Anniversary Speech," 3 May 1971, 80–82. King's writings are collected with a helpful introduction in James Washington, *A Testament of Hope*. See also Albert Raboteau, "Martin Luther King and the Tradition of Black Religious Protest," in *Religion and the Life of the Nation: American Recoveries*, ed. Rowland Sherrill (Urbana: Univ. of Illinois, 1990), 46–63.

34. E. Franklin Frazier and C. Eric Lincoln, *The Negro Church/The Black Church since Frazier* (New York: Schocken, 1974). Joseph Washington, *Black Religion* (Boston: Beacon Press, 1964), was often discussed by black theologians; for a concise survey of Washington's career (which later turned toward a black power approach) see Ferm, *Contemporary American Theologies*, 41–58. For a more recent interpretation of the black church see C. Eric Lincoln and Lawrence Mamiya, *The Black Church in the African American Experience* (Durham: Duke Univ. Press, 1990).

See also Albert Raboteau, "The Black Church: Continuity and Change," in Lotz, *Altered Landscapes*, 77–91; and James Washington, ed., *Conversations with God: Two Centuries of Prayers by African Americans* (San Francisco: HarperCollins, 1995), especially Washington's superb introduction, xxiii–li.

35. Charles Lawrence, "The Separated Darker Brethren," 22 Feb. 1965, 19.

36. See, e.g., Wilmore, *Black Religion and Black Radicalism*, 135–66.

37. See, e.g., Cone, "Black Consciousness and the Black Church," 2 Nov. 1970, 244–49; and Leon Watts II, "The National Committee of Black Churchmen," 2 Nov. 1970, 237–43, among many other articles in a special double issue on the black church. *C&C*'s interview, Leon Sullivan and James McGraw, "Churchism Is Dead!" 10 Jan. 1972, 290–95, which I discuss in chapter 10, was related to this same trend. Indeed, Sullivan's Zion Baptist was *C&C*'s exemplary kind of black church, despite—or perhaps *because* of—its moderate stance compared with more militant black theologians.

38. Cone, *Black Theology and Black Power* (New York: Seabury, 1969). See also his *God of the Oppressed* (New York: Seabury, 1975) and a number of articles in Cone and Wilmore, *Black Theology: A Documentary History.*

39. Cone, "Who Is Jesus Christ for Us Today?" 14 Apr. 1975, 84.

40. Cone, *Black Theology and Black Power,* 151.

41. J. Deotis Roberts, *Liberation and Reconciliation: A Black Theology* (Philadelphia: Westminster Press, 1971), 9–48; Roberts, *A Black Political Theology* (Philadelphia: Westminster Press, 1974), 178–89, 205–22. *C&C* seldom wrote about Roberts; one exception was Pauli Murray, "Black, Feminist Theologies," 14 Apr. 1980, 86–95.

42. Cone, "Theological Reflections on Reconciliation," 22 Jan. 1973, 308. See also Cone, "Christian Theology and the Afro-American Revolution," 8 June 1970, 123–25. Cone's full response to Roberts is in *God of the Oppressed,* 163–246. By "death" Cone meant that in biblical theology, reconciliation had come through Jesus' death; whites could not insist on reconciliation without following Jesus' model of sacrificial commitment to struggle for justice.

43. Archie LeMone, "When Traditional Theology Meets Black and Liberation Theology," 17 Sept. 1973, 177–78. Cone's relation to the Black Manifesto and the NCBC are discussed in Wilmore, *Black Religion and Black Radicalism* 192–219, and Cone, *My Soul Looks Back* (Maryknoll, N.Y.: Orbis Books, 1986), 41–63.

44. Bennett, "Fitting the Liberation Theme into Our Theological Agenda," 18 July 1977, 165; Bennett, *Radical Imperative,* 127–28.

45. Julius Lester, "Review: *The Black Experience in Religion,*" 31 Mar. 1975, 75; this was a review of C. Eric Lincoln, ed., *Black Experience in Religion* (Garden City, N.Y.: Anchor, 1974). Lester praised many of its essays, but focused his article on attacking Cone.

46. Ruether, "Crisis in Sex and Race," 69. On Garrett-Northwestern, see Cone, *My Soul Looks Back,* 36. For an overview of the range of black religious groups see Hans Baer and Merrill Singer, *African American Religion in the Twentieth Century: Varieties of Protest and Accommodation* (Knoxville: Univ. of Tennessee Press, 1992).

47. Cone, "Theological Reflections on Reconciliation," 22 Jan. 1973, 303–8; Cone, *Spirituals and the Blues: An Interpretation* (New York: Seabury, 1972); Cone, "Who Is Jesus Christ for Us Today?" 14 Apr. 1975, 81–85.

48. Cone, "Report: Black and African Theologies: A Consultation," 3 Mar. 1975, 51.

49. Major statements of Cone's later positions, along with *Martin and Malcolm and America,* include *For My People: Black Theology and the Black Church* (Maryknoll, N.Y.: Orbis Books, 1991) and the second volume of Wilmore and Cone, *Black Theology: A Documentary History* (Maryknoll, N.Y.: Orbis Books, 1993).

50. Gutiérrez, *A Theology of Liberation,* cited in Thomas Sanders, "The Theology of Liberation: Christian Utopianism," 17 Sept. 1973, 168.

51. Jürgen Moltmann, "An Open Letter to José Míguez Bonino," 29 Mar. 1976, 57–63. For Moltmann's more elaborated views see his *Theology of Hope* (New York: Harper and Row, 1967); for Míguez Bonino's see *Doing Theology in a Revolutionary Situation* (Maryknoll, N.Y.: Orbis Books, 1975) and *Toward a Christian Political Ethics* (Philadelphia: Fortress, 1983).

52. Gutiérrez, *A Theology of Liberation*, 232–38. See also Gutiérrez, *The Power of the Poor in History* (Maryknoll, N.Y.: Orbis Books, 1984).

53. Theodore Roszak, *The Making of a Counter Culture* (Garden City, N.Y.: Doubleday, 1969), 124.

54. Rubem Alves, "Magic and Theory," 31 May 1971, 110–11.

55. Cox, "Radical Hope and Empirical Probability," 13 May 1968, 97–98. This article was prompted when Jürgen Moltmann spoke at Duke University on the same day that Martin Luther King Jr. was murdered.

56. Thomas Sanders, "The Theology of Liberation: Christian Utopianism," 170, 172.

57. Alves, "Christian Realism: Ideology of the Establishment," 17 Sept. 1973, 175, 176.

58. These debates are documented in detail by Nessan, *Orthopraxis or Heresy;* McCann, *Christian Realism and Liberation Theology;* and Dorrien, *Soul in Society,* among many others.

59. Bennett, "Continuing the Discussion: Liberation Theology and Christian Realism," 15 Sept. 1973, 197; for a related argument see Carol Christ, "Whatever Happened to Theology?" 12 May 1975, 113.

60. Sanders, "Thomas Sanders Replies," 26 Nov. 1973, 249–51. Jürgen Moltmann, "Open Letter to José Míguez Bonino," 60.

61. Alexander Wilde, "Continuing the Discussion: Liberation Theology and Christian Realism," 15 Sept. 1973, 205, 206.

62. On these political developments see Daniel Levine, ed. *Churches and Politics in Latin America* (Beverly Hills: Sage, 1979); Penny Lernoux, *Cry of the People* (New York: Penguin, 1980); Smith, *The Emergence of Liberation Theology;* and Michael Jiménez, "Citizens of the Kingdom: Toward a Social History of Radical Christianity in Latin America," *International Labor and Working Class History* 34 (Fall 1988): 3–21.

63. Two valuable bridges between this issue and wider debates on the academic left are Tom Moylan, "Denunciation/Annunciation: The Radical Methodology of Liberation Theology," *Cultural Critique* 20 (Winter 1991–92): 33–64; and Denys Turner, "Religion: Illusions and Liberation," in *The Cambridge Companion to Marx* (Cambridge: Cambridge Univ. Press, 1991), 320–37.

64. Brown, endorsement on the cover of Gutiérrez, *Theology of Liberation*. Both Brown and Cox wrote many books popularizing Latin American theology: e.g., Robert McAfee Brown, *Theology in a New Key* (Philadelphia: Westminster Press, 1978) and *Gustavo Gutiérrez* (Louisville: John Knox, 1980); Cox, *The Silencing of Leonardo Boff: The Vatican and the Future of World Christianity* (Oak Park, Ill.: Meyer-Stone, 1988).

65. Frederick Herzog, "On Liberating Liberation Theology," published as the introduction to Hugo Assman, *Theology for a Nomad Church* (Maryknoll, N.Y.: Orbis Books, 1975), 1–23 (Assman's comment was made at the 1975 Theology in the Americas Conference, and is cited by Herzog on p. 16) See also Herzog, *Justice Church: The New Function of the Church in North American Christianity* (Maryknoll, N.Y.: Orbis Books, 1980). In *C&C*, John Fry attacked Herzog's "Liberation Theology Begins at Home," 13 May 1974, 94–98, as uncritical about the weaknesses of the Bible as the "power center" for liberation. See Fry and Herzog, "Liberation Theology: Continuing the Discussion," 14 Oct. 1974, 224–29.

66. Jon Sobrino, *Christology at the Crossroads: A Latin American Approach*, trans. John Drury (Maryknoll, N.Y.: Orbis Books, 1978); Anna Peterson, *Martyrdom and the Politics of Religion: Progressive Catholicism in El Salvador's Civil War* (Albany: State Univ. of New York Press, 1996).

67. Beverly Harrison, "Challenging the Western Paradigm: The 'Theology in the Americas' Conference," 27 Oct. 1975, 254. Harrison discusses the Herzog/Assman confrontation on 253–54.

68. Two excellent works for understanding changes on the Latin American religious-political scene since the early 1980s are Anna Peterson, "Religion in Latin America: New Methods and Approaches," *Religious Studies Review* 21 (1995), no. 1: 3–9; and Rowan Ireland, *Kingdoms Come: Religion and Politics in Brazil* (Pittsburgh: Univ. of Pittsburgh Press, 1991); on the theological scene see also Ellis and Maduro, *Expanding the View*. For *C&C*'s treatment

of evangelicals in Latin America see Laura O'Shaughnessy, "Evangelicals' Latin Future," 18 Mar. 1991, 93–95; and Ken Serbin, "Latin American Catholics: Postliberationism?" 14 Dec. 1992, 403–7. For barometers of *C&C*'s theological discourse in the late 1980s see Larry Rasmussen, "New Dynamics in Theology," 16 May 1988, 178–83; and Ruether et al., "Symposium: Liberation Theology Here and Now," 12 June 1989, 181–96. This symposium included little that *C&C* had not said many times before in a fresher voice, with a few exceptions such as Donna Bivens, "Passion and Compassion, Together," 12 June 1989, 188–89; Michael Zweig, "Gustavo Gutiérrez Is a Revolutionary," 12 June 1989, 184–85; and Brady Tyson, "Brazil: End of an Era?" 12 June 1989, 193–94, which featured straight talk about the collapsing movement in Brazil. See also Gutiérrez, "The 'Preparatory Document' for Puebla: Retreat from Commitment," 18 Sept. 1978, 211–13.

69. A good example is the 12 May 1980 special issue on "Central America: A Season of Martyrs" with articles by Oscar Romero, Jorge Lara-Braud, William Wipfler, and others. See also Andrew Reding, "Central America: Some of the Truth," 12 Nov. 1984, 412–25; Thomas Quigley, "Salvador: Metaphor versus Truth," 2 Feb. 1981, 2, 13–14; Anne Nelson, "El Salvador's Struggle: The Revolution Has a History," 13 June 1983, 231–38; Gary MacEoin, "Latin America: Three Authors, a Single Theme," 13 June 1983, 244–45; Phillip Berryman, "El Salvador's National Debate," 12 Dec. 1988, 440–42.

70. Renny Golden and Michael McConnell, "Sanctuary: Choosing Sides," 21 Feb. 1983, 31–36; Howell, "A New Reformation: Interview with John Fife," 22 Oct. 1986, 313–15; Eric Jorstad, "Time for Faith and Courage?: Interview with Jim Oines," 22 Oct. 1986, 313, 315–18. James Gittings, "Some Notes on the Search for Sanctuary," 13 Jan. 1986, 543–47, reported that one defendant in the conspiracy trial, Sister Darlene Nicgorski, had been ordered to work on sanctuary by the Sisters of Saint Francis, and therefore had sixteen hundred coconspirators. Christian Smith, *Resisting Reagan: The U.S. Central America Peace Movement* (Chicago: Univ. of Chicago Press, 1996) is among the best studies of the movement, with an overview of the church networks in which *C&C* participated (111-15). Smith emphasizes the role of *C&C*'s journalistic counterpart, *Sojourners*, and stresses that it is "no accident that the U.S. Central American peace movement emerged primarily out of the religious community" (167–68).

71. Index to volume 42, 24 Jan. 1983, 462; Frances Smith, "A Brief History of *Christianity and Crisis*," 5.

72. Safer, "Mr. Safer Reports," 27 June 1966, 140. For citations on new class theory, see my discussion in chapter 7.

73. Neuhaus et al., "The Hartford Debate," 21 July 1975, 170, 178.

74. Ibid., 172, 174, 178.

75. Gordon Kaufman, "Whatever Happened to Theology?" 12 May 1975, 111. The larger symposium ran on pp. 106–20, with a wide range of contributors.

76. Van Harvey, "Whatever Happened to Theology?" 12 May 1975, 108; Harvey, "What Is the Task of Theology?" 24 May 1976, 121. Berger, "Different Gospels: The Social Sources of Apostasy," *This World* 17 (1987): 6–17, is a polished statement (reflecting a somewhat later stage in Berger's thinking) on the relation between new class theory and theology.

77. Herzog, "Whatever Happened to Theology?" 12 May 1975, 115, 116, 117. For two mainstream media spins on this symposium, see Kenneth Briggs, "Religious Thinkers Feel Christian Theology Demands Changes," *New York Times*, 6 May 1975, L 27, and John Dart, "Churchmen Fear for Theology," *Los Angeles Times*, 27 May 1975, in *C&C* records, box 10, scrapbook.

78. Jan Milic Lochman with responses by George Houser and Cone, "Violence: The Just Revolution," 10 July 1972, 163–67. Another major theme was the effort to make peace between *C&C*'s socialists and feminists; see, e.g., Ruether, "Consciousness-Raising at Puebla: Women Speak to the Latin Church," 2 Apr. 1979, 77–80. Still another was a debate (rampant in North American religious circles) about whether Christians could be Marxists, although it must be said that by the 1970s *C&C* was bored with this question. According to Harrison, "Challenging the Western Paradigm," 251, delegates at a 1975 liberation theology conference in Detroit did not care about Marxism as the "philosophy of history or the theory of

instant, violent revolution." They "pleaded only for global and class analysis as critical to the theological task" and were "more to be faulted for their superficial, overgeneralized and ill-informed rejection of contemporary Marxist imperialist and class analysis" than for doctrinaire Marxism. On relations between Christianity and Marxism, see especially José Míguez Bonino, *Christians and Marxists: The Mutual Challenge to Revolution* (London: Hodder and Staughton, 1976); Lochman, *Encountering Marx: Bonds and Barriers between Christians and Marxists* (Philadelphia: Fortress Press, 1977); West, *Prophesy Deliverance: An Afro-American Revolutionary Christianity* (Philadelphia: Westminster Press, 1982); and Arthur McGovern, *Marxism: An American Christian Perspective* (Maryknoll, N.Y.: Orbis Books, 1981). See also José Porfirio Miranda, *Marx and the Bible* (Maryknoll, N.Y.: Orbis Books, 1974).

79. Sylvia Marcos, "Mexican Women: An Interview," 2 July 1990, 221–22.

80. Robert Allen Warrior, "Canaanites, Cowboys, and Indians: Deliverance, Conquest, and Liberation Theology Today" (11 Sept. 1989), reprinted in *Ethics in the Present Tense,* ed. Howell and Lindermayer, 45–51. At the level of historical reconstruction (as opposed to the canonical text) Norman Gottwald, *The Tribes of Yahweh: A Sociology of the Religion of Liberated Israel, 1250–1050 B.C.E.* (Maryknoll, N.Y.: Orbis Books, 1979), presents the conquest as an agrarian class war that pitted a peasant coalition against urban overlords, somewhat like in recent Central American revolutions. Gottwald stresses that the Canaanite people of the land (read: Indians) were recruited for the Yahwist coalition before the war, and that their violence targeted the upper class and their collaborators. He valorizes the Yahwists' decentralized (although male-dominated) society during the years between the conquest and the Davidic monarchy.

81. James McGraw and Vine Deloria Jr. "God Is Also Red," 15 Sept. 1975, 198. For a richer version of the argument, see Deloria, *God Is Red* (New York: Dell, 1973).

82. Rosemary Ruether, "Mother Earth and the Megamachine," 13 Dec. 1971, 271. This article was reprinted in Plaskow and Christ, *Womanspirit Rising,* 43–52.

83. Ibid., 272.

Chapter 10

1. Dee Anne Dodd, "Black Hills Not for Sale," 16 June 1986, 198; June Jordan, "Bobo Goetz a Gun," 13 May 1985, 190–91; Max Glenn, "Oklahoma: Faith Community and Family Farm," 3 Nov. 1986, 384–86; Jean Bethke Elshtain, "On the Stockholm Syndrome," 16 Sept. 1985, 354–56; John Wicklein, "Technology Untamed," 17 Sept. 1984, 335.

2. Margaret O'Brien Steinfels, "Consider the Seamless Garment," 14 May 1984, 172–74; Margaret Miles, "The Sexual Christ of the Renaissance," 17 Sept. 1984, 333–34; Isidore Silver, "Restoring Political Restraints: Repeal the 22nd Amendment," 14 May 1984, 178.

3. Will Campbell, "Commie-Killing: Ethics, Law, Geography," 14 May 1984, 175, 176.

4. Kimberly Parsons Chastain and D. Kevin McNeir, "Race and Culture in a Coffee Cup," 2 Mar. 1993, 55–56.

5. Jewell Handy Gresham, "America's Past, America's Ghosts," 4 Apr. 1988, 116–20; Lindermayer, "Satanic Verses: Whose Islam?" 8 May 1989, 131–32.

6. Arthur Moore, "His and Hers Biographies," 10 June 1991, 205–6; Shinn, "Rethinking History," 8 May 1989, 149–50; Jan Zita Grover, "AIDS: Metaphors and Real Life," 11 Sept. 1989, 268–70; Robert Allen Warrior, "Hot Pursuit: FBI versus AIM," 12 Dec. 1988, 447–49.

7. Norman Gottwald, "God, Community, Household, Table," 14 May 1990, 150–54; Larry Rasmussen, "A World out of Scale," 14 May 1990, 154–58; Kathleen Sands, "Friendship as Revelatory," 10 June 1991, 202–4.

8. Miller, "Mississippi Movement Memories," 21 Oct. 1991, 338–40. Another review published during these years but falling outside my sample, George Scialabba's "From Enlightenment to Redemption: Christopher Lasch, Culture, and the Critique of Progress," 18 Nov. 1991, 351–54, won a citation for excellence in reviewing from the National Book Critics Circle. This was not even Scialabba's best *C&C* review; better was "A Calling to Solidarity?" 23 Oct. 1989, 335–39, on Ehrenreich's *Fear of Falling* and Reynolds and Norman's *Community in America.*

9. Of ninety-three articles in my cross section from 1981 to 1984, sixteen focused on nuclear issues. This compared with ten on Central America and twelve on feminism and/or related gender issues.

10. Edwin Brown Firmage, "Allegiance and Stewardship," 1 Mar. 1982, 50, 52. Firmage was identified as the great-great-grandson of Brigham Young, a former Mormon bishop, law professor at the University of Utah, and leader in the opposition to the MX missile.

11. See, e.g., Bishop Roger Mahony, "Becoming a Church of Peace Advocacy," 1 Mar. 1982, 37–44; Alan Geyer, "The Peace Pastoral Reconsidered," 21 Jan. 1985, 524–26; Sidney Lens, "Deep Roots of the Arms Race," 13 May 1985, 177–79; Bennett, "Nuclear Deterrence Is Itself Vulnerable," 13 Aug. 1984, 296–300.

12. A. Lin Neumann, "June 12 in Central Park: A Quiet, Gentle 'No,'" 12 July 1982, 205–8, shows how *C&C* related to conflict behind the scenes at a key national protest, for which Nuclear Freeze organizers claimed the major credit. The organizers closest to *C&C*—the Riverside Church Disarmament Program, Fellowship of Reconciliation, and the Committee for a Sane Nuclear Policy—became embroiled in bitter controversy, both with peace groups that were more vulnerable to red-baiting—the War Resisters League, Women's International League for Peace and Freedom, and the U.S. Peace Council—and with Herbert Daughtry's Black United Front, which demanded a larger leadership role in the march.

13. Daniel Berrigan, "Two Commandments for Lawbreakers," 28 Apr. 1981, 116–20.

14. Liane Ellison Norman and Samuel Salus, "The Trail of the Plowshares Eight: The Judge and a Reporter on the Law and the Facts," 11 May 1981, 138. Salus threatened to sue *C&C* for publishing his letter to Norman; see Cowan, "Dear Judge Salus," 8 June 1981, 175–76.

15. John Raines, "The Middle Class: Unmasking the American Myth," 15 Apr. 1974, 73–77; Ruether, "The Gap Widens," 10 Sept. 1990, 277–78; see also Gar Alperovitz, "Politics . . . and Beyond," 4 Apr. 1988, 108–13. Raines obtained his data from a prestigious study by the University of Michigan; Ruether reviewed (and took her data from) Andrew Winnick, *Toward Two Societies: The Changing Distribution of Income and Wealth in the U.S. since 1960.* For more on the complexities of quantifying class inequalities in the United States see my discussion in the conclusion. See also Raines et al., "Continuing the Discussion: The Crisis of the Middle Class," 29 Sept. 1975, 224–27.

16. Paul Sweezy et al., "The Human and Social Costs of the U.S. Economic System," 29 Nov. 1976, 289. Other typical treatments include Gar Alperovitz, "The Coming Break in Liberal Consciousness," 3 Mar. 1986, 59–65; and Dorrien, "Economic Democracy," 10 Sept. 1990, 271–74. Two fine anthologies with articles on economics by *C&C* contributors are Michael Zweig, ed., *Religion and Economic Justice* (Philadelphia: Temple Univ. Press, 1992); and Tabb, *Churches in Struggle.* See also Mary Hobgood, *Catholic Social Teaching and Economic Theory: Paradigms in Conflict* (Philadelphia: Temple Univ. Press, 1991).

17. Tom Blackburn, "Novak's Capitalism with a Human Face," 24 May 1982, 147.

18. Max Stackhouse and Dennis McCann, "A Postcommunist Manifesto: Public Theology after the Collapse of Socialism," *Christian Century,* 16 Jan. 1991, 44, 45; John Cobb, "Sustainable Community," *Christian Century,* 23 Jan. 1991, 81–82; Tom Kelly "Manifestos, Marx, and the *Christian Century,* 18 Mar. 1991, 76–77. Cobb's comments were part of Barbara Andolsen et al., "Responses to a Postcommunist Manifesto: Ethics, Economics, and the Corporate Life," *Christian Century,* 23 Jan. 1991, 77–85.

19. For example, Shinn's "Population Crisis: Exploring the Issues," 5 Aug. 1974, 170–75, endorsed the "green revolution" to address overpopulation, but Camara, "The Force of Right or the Right of Force?" 177, called first world concerns about overpopulation an "escape valve" to evade core issues of world economic redistribution. Denis Goulet aimed for the middle of *C&C*'s liberal-radical continuum with a parallel rhetoric of "revolutionary change" and "creative incrementalism." See Goulet, "World Hunger: Putting Development Ethics to the Test," 26 May 1975, 125–32. See also Charles Birch, "Ordering the World as a Sustainable Global Economy," 24 Nov. 1975, 282–84, and *C&C*'s special issue on hunger and world food, 3 Feb. 1975. Books on hunger influential in *C&C* circles include Frances Moore Lappé, *Food First: Beyond the Myth of Scarcity,* 2d ed. (New York: Ballantine Books, 1978); Arthur Simon, *Bread for the World* (New York: Paulist Press, 1975); and Nelson, *Hunger for Justice.*

20. E. F. Schumacher, *Small Is Beautiful: Economics as If People Mattered* (New York: Harper and Row, 1973), 12–20. See also Wendell Berry, *The Unsettling of America: Culture and Agriculture* (New York: Avon, 1977); and Jeremy Rifkin with Ted Howard, *The Emerging Order: God in the Age of Scarcity* (New York: Ballantine, 1979).

21. Larry Rasmussen, "A World out of Scale," 14 May 1990, 156.

22. Gilkey cited in Abrecht, "Technology: New Directions in Ecumenical Social Ethics," 28 Apr. 1975, 95. Abrecht mapped a wide spectrum of opinion and tried to promote as much peace as possible. Roger Shinn, Sheila Collins, and Margaret Maxey, "The NCC and Nuclear Power," 10 May 1976, 105–10, was an acrimonious exchange about whether *C&C* should take a "balanced" approach to the pros and cons of nuclear energy. For an excellent overview of Christian debates about the environment see Laurel Kearns, "Saving the Creation: Christian Environmentalism in the United States," *Sociology of Religion* 57 (1996), no. 1: 55–70.

23. Ellie Goodwin, "Nexus of a New Environmentalism," 2 Mar. 1993, 54. See also William Somplatsky-Jarman, "For a More Inclusive Environmental Agenda," 14 May 1990, 144–45; Rasmussen, "Earth Patriotism, Earth Ethics," 20 July 1992, 243; Herman Daly, "Bios, Theos, Logos," 12 July 1982, 216–18; Shinn, "The End of a Liberal Dream," 16 Mar. 1981, 52–56; and *C&C*'s 14 May 1990 special issue about Earth Day.

24. Glen Gersmehl, "The Vision of Cesar Chavez," 11 Jan. 1971, 296–300; John Fry, "No More Table Grapes Again!" 9 July 1973, 137–39; Harry Bernstein, "Cesar Chavez Fights a Two-Front Battle," 20 Aug. 1979, 197–200.

25. John Fry, "Election Night in Crystal City," 27 Nov. 1972, 253–57.

26. Leon Howell, "The City: God's Arena," 16 Nov. 1992, 371, introduces a special issue on the subject, which in turn kicked off a new initiative (cut short by *C&C*'s death) supported by the Lilly Endowment. Other examples in this vein include Wende Marshall, "Organizing Community: Asking Questions," 16 Nov. 1992, 375–76; Howell, "Minority Coalitions: A Place in the Sun," 2 Feb. 1987, 15–18; Harry Boyte, "The Secular Left, Religion, and the American Commonwealth," 16 May 1983, 183–86; George Todd, "Ecumenism Where Church Members Live," 6 Feb. 1989, 15–17; Jim Gittings, "Ecumenism: Dead in the Water?" 12 Apr. 1993, 78–79. A related trend under Howell's leadership was beefed-up coverage of the labor movement, e.g., Laura McClure, "Labor News Notes," 10 June 1991, 192–93.

27. Sullivan and McGraw, "Churchism Is Dead," 295.

28. Laurien Alexandre, "Church and Media: Lots to Learn," 26 Nov. 1990, 378. She cited William Fore, who was an important *C&C*'s writer on the media over the years; see, e.g., his "Public Television," 6 Mar. 1967, 36–38, and "Deprogramming Television: A Manual for the People," 2 May 1977, 93–95. See also Cox, "Religion, Politics, Television," 17 Nov. 1987, 408–9.

29. Howell, "Ghost Ranch and *Christianity and Crisis*," *Ghost Ranch Journal* (Winter 1994): 7–8. These seminars were an annual event, led by a rotating slate of *C&C* board members. They continued in a ghostly way even after *C&C* died.

30. See, e.g., Rose, "Bob Dylan Meets Jesus," 12 Nov. 1979, 274–76; West, "In Memory of Marvin Gaye," 11 May 1984, 220–21; Michael Eric Dyson, "Rap, Race, and Reality," 16 Mar. 1987, 98–100; Mark Hulsether, "Popular Culture, Oppositional Ends," 22 Oct. 1990, 328–30.

31. Tom Driver, "Jesus: God, Man, and Movie," 10 Oct. 1988, 338; Pat Aufderheide, "Feminist Nightmares," 14 May 1990, 158–60. See also Scorcese interviewed by Thomas DePrieto, "Making Jesus Contemporary," 10 Oct. 1988, 342–43. Other typical reviews included Howell, "One Lousy Beanfield," 6 June 1988, 210–11; Kelly, "Defecting from Eternity," 1 Aug. 1988, 278–80.

32. Cox, "Inculturation Reconsidered," 13 May 1991, 140, 142. See also Cox, "Seven Samurai and How They Looked Again," in Ellis and Maduro, *Expanding the View*, 60–72.

33. Howell, "Smoke Gets into More than Your Eyes," 1 Aug. 1988, 259.

34. Steve Lawler, "The Importance of Cultural Diversity: A Talk with the Chief of the Cherokee Nation," 1 Aug. 1988, 270–72, identification of Lawler, 258. *C&C*'s usual policy was to index the people who were interviewed.

35. See, e.g., Anna Lee Walters, "Saints, Storytellers, and Survival," 12 Dec. 1988, 450–51; Walters, "Fractured Vessels of a Holy Life," 8 Jan. 1990, 407–8; John Volkman, "Tribal Sovereignty and Federal Indian Policy," 11 Sept. 1989, 265–68; Warrior, "Native American News," 14 May 1990, 140–42; Jace Weaver, "Native Reformation in Indian Country?" 15 Feb. 1993, 39–41; Andrew L. J. James, "Costnerama," 18 Mar. 1991, 78; Kimberly Parsons Chastain, "Costnerama II: A Modest Dissent," 13 May 1991, 142–43.

36. Warrior, "Dancing with Wastes," 15 July 1991, 216. This piece won an award from the Native American Journalists Association.

37. Warrior, "Indians Are Real People," 12 Apr. 1993, 87.

38. Chung Hyun-Kyung, "Welcome the Spirit; Hear Her Cries," 15 Sept. 1991, 220.

39. Samuel Solivan, "Which Spirit? What Creation?" 15 Sept. 1991, 224–26.

40. Beverly Harrison, "Keeping Faith in a Sexist Church," in her book *Making the Connections,* 233–34. Although this did not appear in *C&C,* it is representative because Harrison was Union's leading feminist and her article addressed a readership similar to *C&C*'s.

41. Susan Thistlethwaite, "Narrative and Connection," 2 Mar. 1987, 72.

42. Ibid., 72, 73, citing Ntozake Shange, *for colored girls who have considered suicide / when the rainbow is enuf* (New York: Bantam, 1980). Christ responded in "Connections to the World of Spirit," 28 Sept. 1987, 320.

43. Thistlethwaite, "Narrative and Connection," 75.

44. Alice Walker, *Meridian* (New York: Washington Square, 1977).

45. Difficulties that arise when whites become interested in the rituals of Native Americans provide paradigm cases, both of the dangers of whites devaluing nonwhite literature through false universals, and of the positive reasons to maintain some texts exclusively for subcultural groups. Two outstanding treatments are Paula Gunn Allen, "Special Problems in Teaching Leslie Marmon Silko's *Ceremony,*" *American Indian Quarterly* 14 (1990), no. 4: 379–86; and Wendy Rose, "The Great Pretenders: Further Reflections on Whiteshamanism," in *The State of Native America,* ed. M. Annette Jaimes (Boston: South End Press, 1992), 403–21. Thistlethwaite, "Great White Fathers," 13 Jan. 1992, 416–18; took a sweepingly hostile position, similar to her attack on Christ, toward whites who sought to learn from (and / or reinvent) Native American ritual.

46. Thistlethwaite, "Narrative and Connection," 72. Since her key sentence was ambiguous, I quote it in full: "What is the theory behind racist feminism? Liberalism. Insofar as 'racial relations' are defined primarily as the search for universals, for points of agreement, white power and white experience will continue to be the universal, and hence the relations between black and white women will continue to be racist." Did Thistlethwaite intend to imply that "searching for universals" was only one (unpromising) way of searching for "points of agreement"? Did her qualifier "defined *primarily*" imply other possible roles for a form of universalism that was "secondary"? Might black / white relations "continue to be racist" because of the history and social structure of the United States—no matter how scholars approach difference—leaving it unclear whether searching for "points of agreement" could be a lesser evil in some cases? All these are possible spins that reduce the problems with Thistlethwaite's article. However, apparently her major point was to blur the distinction—in most if not all cases—between racist suppression of difference and the search for "points of agreement" across difference. For a more nuanced version of her argument, see her *Sex, Race, and God: Christian Feminism in Black and White* (San Francisco: Harper and Row, 1989). See also Thistlethwaite, "On *God's Fierce Whimsey,*" 11 Aug. 1986, 277–79, a review of the Mudflower Collective, *God's Fierce Whimsey: Christian Feminism and Theological Education* (New York: Pilgrim Press, 1985). By 1996 Thistlethwaite was defending the pragmatic value of appeals to universal liberal tolerance, at least for feminists talking to news reporters. See her "All the News That Fits: A Review of Mark Silk's *Unsecular Media,*" *Journal of the American Academy of Religion* 64 (1996), no. 4: 853–62.

47. Rosemary Ruether, "For Whom, with Whom, Do We Speak Our New Stories?" 13 May 1985, 184, responding to Delores Williams, "The Color of Feminism," 29 Apr. 1985, 164–65.

48. Cornel West, "The Historicist Turn in the Philosophy of Religion," in *Keeping Faith,* 129. This article and his "Black Theology of Liberation as Critique of Capitalist Civilization" in Wilmore and Cone, *Black Theology: A Documentary History,* 2:410–25, are two of the best places to approach West's theology. It would be very useful to have a single volume bringing together West's scattered essays on religion; there is no ideal approach to his writings on this subject because his two best scholarly books, *American Evasion of Philosophy* and *Keeping Faith,* touch lightly on the subject, while *Prophetic Fragments* and his first book, *Prophesy Deliverance: An Afro-American Revolutionary Christianity* (Philadelphia: Westminster Press, 1982), do not fully reflect his recent thinking.

49. Michael Bérubé, "Public Academy," *New Yorker* (9 Jan. 1995), 78.

50. The most convenient place to find these citations is *Prophetic Fragments.* Citations in *C&C* include "In Memory of Marvin Gaye," 11 May 1984, 220–21; "Sex and Suicide," 10 June 1985, 155–56; "On Black-Jewish Relations," 30 Apr. 1984, 149–50; "Black Politics Will Never Be the Same," 13 Aug. 1984, 302–4; "Christian Theological Mediocrity," 26 Nov. 1984, 439–40; "Harrington's Socialist Vision," 12 Dec. 1983, 484–86; "On Fox and Lears' *The Culture of Consumption,*" 5 Mar. 1984, 66–68.

51. West also calls for an engagement with feminist theorists, but is less prone to cite kindred female scholars such as philosopher Nancy Fraser, legal theorist Patricia Williams, and theologian Rebecca Chopp, as compared with males like Du Bois. Cornel West and bell hooks, *Breaking Bread: Insurgent Black Intellectual Life* (Boston: South End Press, 1991), is his most sustained published engagement with feminism. An exemplary effort to integrate feminist theology with West's methods is Rebecca Chopp, "A Feminist Perspective: Christianity, Democracy, and Feminist Theology," in *Christianity and Democracy in Global Context,* ed. John Witte Jr. (Boulder, Colo.: Westview Press, 1993), 111–29.

52. West, "Historicist Turn," 132.

53. For constructive critiques see Bérubé, "Public Academy"; Robert Gooding-Williams, "Evading Narrative Myth, Evading Prophetic Pragmatism: Cornel West's *The American Evasion of Philosophy,*" *Massachusetts Review* 32 (1991–92): 517–42; and Hulsether, "The Scholar of Religion as Public Intellectual: Some Recent Works by Cornel West," *Method and Theory in the Study of Religion* 8 (1996), no. 4: 377–84. Unfortunately, West has received some criticism in this vein that is highly misleading and unconstructive, such as Adolph Reed, "What Are the Drums Saying, Booker? The Current Crisis of the Black Intellectual," *Village Voice,* 11 Apr. 1995, 31–37; and Leon Wieseltier, "All and Nothing at All: The Unreal World of Cornel West," *New Republic,* 6 Mar. 1995, 31–36.

54. West, *Race Matters* (Boston: Beacon Press, 1993); see also Henry Louis Gates Jr., "Affirmative Reaction: A Conversation with Cornel West on Talent, Tradition, and the Crisis of the Black Male," *Transition* 5 (1995), no. 4: 173–86.

55. Hulsether, "Cornel West: Can Pragmatism Save?" 16 Dec. 1991, 397, quoting West, *American Evasion,* 232. *C&C*'s review of *Prophesy Deliverance* was James Evans Jr., "The Emergence of Cornel West," 16 May 1983, 194–96.

56. Excellent critical orientations to this complex field are Jones, "Women's Experience between a Rock and a Hard Place"; Janet Jakobsen, "Deconstructing the Paradox of Modernity: Feminism, Enlightenment, and Cross-Cultural Moral Interactions," *Journal of Religious Ethics* 23 (1995), no. 2: 333–63; Elizabeth Bounds, *Coming Together/Coming Apart: Religion, Community, and Modernity* (New York: Routledge, 1997); and Marsha Hewitt, "The Social Implications of Feminist Liberation Theology," *Studies in Religion* 22 (1993), no. 3: 323–25. To relate this generation of feminist theologians to *C&C*'s first generation, see Sheila Greeve Davaney, "Problems with Feminist Theory: Historicity and the Search for Sure Foundations," in *Embodied Love: Sensuality and Relationship as Feminist Values,* ed. Paula Cooey et al. (San Francisco: Harper and Row, 1987), 79–95. In this connection an especially revealing exchange is Ruether, "The Development of My Theology," *Religious Studies Review* 15 (Jan. 1989), no. 1: 1–4, with comments by Kathryn Allen Rabuzzi and Rebecca Chopp, 4–11. To place recent feminist theologies in a larger field see Chopp and Taylor, *Reconstructing Christian Theology;* David Griffin, ed. *Varieties of Postmodern Theology* (Al-

bany: SUNY Press, 1989); and Sheila Greeve Davaney, ed., *Theology at the End of Modernity* (New York: Trinity Press International, 1991).

57. Dennis McCann, *Christian Realism and Liberation Theology*, 4–5; Sharon Welch, *Feminist Ethic of Risk*, 111–12.

58. West, "On Sharon Welch's *Communities of Resistance and Solidarity*" (14 Oct. 1985), in *Prophetic Fragments*, 209, 210. It is important to note that Welch's *Feminist Ethic of Risk*, published in 1990, addresses some of West's questions about her first book.

59. Novak, *Will It Liberate? Questions about Liberation Theology* (New York: Paulist, 1986). For *C&C*'s review see Brown, "Liberation as Bogeyman," 6 Apr. 1987, 124–25. For more on *First Things*, see chapter 11.

60. Howell, "Old Wine, New Bottles: A Short History of the IRD," 21 Mar. 1983, 90–91, reports that the IRD received $533,000 in income from 1980 to 1983, 90 percent of which came from six conservative foundations. Hochstein and O'Rourke, "Report on the Institute on Religion and Democracy," describes the religious commitments and political associations of IRD leaders. For example, David Jessup joined a church for the first time just four months before IRD started and never attended its new member class; during the 1960s he had been a member of the Young People's Socialist League (YPSL), an anti-Stalinist splinter of the Old Left much disliked by the mainstream of the New Left because of its passion for sectarian in-fighting. Isserman, *If I Had a Hammer*, 185–202, discusses YPSL and its place in the New Left.

61. Orientations to the broader network and its funding include Messer-Davidow, "Manufacturing the Attack on Higher Education"; Howell, "Funding the War of Ideas"; Diamond, *Roads to Dominion;* and Paul Gottfried, "Funding an Empire," in *The Conservative Movement*, rev. ed. (New York: Twayne, 1993), 118–41.

62. Gottfried, *Conservative Movement*, 125.

63. Diamond, *Roads to Dominion*, 284.

64. Messer-Davidow, "Manufacturing the Attack on Higher Education," 51; Gottfried, *Conservative Movement*, 128. These sources pay little attention to religious journals, but Messer-Davidow reports that the *National Review* received a subsidy of $342,000 in 1989, and the *New Criterion* received over $600,000 in 1989 and 1990. Jon Wiener, "Dollars for Neo-Con Scholars," *Nation*, 1 Jan. 1990, 12–14, reports that just one of the "four sisters" of conservative philanthropy, the Olin Foundation, paid $3.6 million to Bloom and $163,000 to Michael Novak. David Callahan, "Liberal Policy's Weak Foundations," *Nation*, 13 Nov. 1995, 568–71, shows the gap between funding of scholars on the right and the left, despite the larger absolute wealth controlled by centrist foundations such as Rockefeller and Lilly. For example, the American Enterprise Institute and the Heritage Foundation received $10 million in 1992, while four top think tanks on the left received only $1 million each (570).

65. Gottfried, *Conservative Movement*, 120.

66. Tom Kelly, "'They're Ba-a-ck': The IRD's Spring Offensive," 14 Aug. 1989, 236–40.

67. William Rogers and Robert Chandler, "Revisiting 'the Gospel According to Whom?'" 12 Dec. 1983, 479–83. Incidentally, Morley Safer reported this *Sixty Minutes* story.

68. See, e.g., Bennett, "Reaganethics," 14 Dec. 1981, 339–41; Bennett, "Neoconservative 'Realities' versus Third World Realities," 12 Nov. 1979, 276–79; Howell, "Ernest Lefever at the Edge of Power," 2 Mar. 1981, 36–45.

69. Herbert O. Edwards, "Niebuhr, 'Realism,' and Civil Rights in America," 3 Feb. 1986, 12–15; and Beverly Harrison, "Niebuhr: Locating the Limits," 17 Feb. 1986, 35–39; M. M. Thomas, "A Third World View of Christian Realism," 3 Feb. 1986, 8–10. The overall tone of this symposium was far less critical. See, e.g., Bennett, "Comments on Fox's Life of Niebuhr," 3 Feb. 1986, 5–8; and William Lee Miller, "Some Customer," 3 Feb. 1986, 19–22.

70. M. M. Thomas, "Third World View of Christian Realism," 10. Thomas noted Niebuhr's pragmatism and stress on limits to U.S. power, but said, "I cannot recollect Niebuhr's considering the Asian-African situation as an issue of social justice for their peoples" as opposed to "help[ing] the impoverished world to gain greater technical efficiency." He commented that the latter position was "the universal ideology of modern multinational corporations

and American state policy supporting them in all parts of the Third World. Its continuity with Niebuhr's advocacy of 'imperial realism' is, however, disturbing."

71. Bennett, "Niebuhr's Ethic: The Later Years," 12 Apr. 1982, 95. This was also published as an afterward to Bennett, "Reinhold Niebuhr's Social Ethics," in Charles Kegley, *Reinhold Niebuhr*, 132–41.

72. Ronald Stone, "Correspondence: Niebuhr's Social Thought," 15 Sept. 1980, 247. This was a response to John Cooper, "Exchange on Cuba I: A Challenge for John Bennett," 21 July 1980, 203–6.

73. Dean Kelley, "How Much Freedom of Speech Is Allowed to the Churches?" 5 Oct. 1981, 264.

74. Peggy Shriver, "Conflict in the Christian Family: Can You Listen to Your Relatives?" 5 Oct. 1981, 265; Shriver, "Do Church Leaders Really Hate America?" 19 Sept. 1983, 334–35. For another view see J. Mark Thomas, "The New Religious Right: Worshipping a Place That Isn't God," 15 Feb. 1982, 26–29.

75. Gottfried, *Conservative Movement*, 131.

76. Peter Steinfels, "Christianity and Democracy: Baptizing Reaganism," 29 Mar. 1982, 80–85; Steinfels and Neuhaus, "Continuing the Discussion: 'Christianity and Democracy,'" 10 May 1982, 135, 136.

77. Arthur Moore, "Dressing Up the Public Square," 29 Oct. 1984, 406–7.

78. Edward Norman, "A Politicized Christ," 19 Feb. 1979, 18–25; Dorothee Sölle, "Continuing the Discussion: 'A Politicized Christ,'" 19 Mar. 1979, 50, 51–52. Norman's *Christianity and the World Order* (New York: Oxford Univ. Press, 1979) created a dilemma for neoconservatives because they were gratified by its attack on liberals, but its attacks on politicization were so sweeping that they threatened to undermine neoconservative religious apologetics for capitalism. Berger attempted damage control in "Continuing the Discussion: 'A Politicized Christ,'" 19 Mar. 1979, 52–54.

79. Dorothee Sölle, "Faith, Theology, and Liberation: Remembering Christ," 7 July 1976, 141.

80. Ibid., 138.

81. Sölle, "Mysticism, Liberation, and the Names of God," 22 June 1981, 183. Among Dorothee Sölle's many books, I especially recommend *Christ the Representative* (Philadelphia: Fortress, 1967); *Suffering* (Philadelphia: Fortress, 1973); *Strength of the Weak: Toward a Christian Feminist Identity* (Philadelphia: Westminster Press, 1984); *To Work and to Love: A Theology of Creation* (Philadelphia: Fortress Press, 1984); *Thinking about God* (Philadelphia: Trinity Press International, 1990); and *Theology for Skeptics* (Minneapolis: Fortress Press, 1995).

Chapter 11

1. As I discuss in the appendix, I began my research before *C&C*'s records were in even their current rudimentary form; thus parts of this book are based on notes and photocopied documents from records provided by Leon Howell at an earlier stage of my research. Many of the documents about the budget that I used to draft this chapter fall into this category, especially "Comparative Financial Statement, 1970–1975," "Comparative Financial Statement, 1976–1980," "Comparative Financial Statement, 1981–1985," and Cowan, "Recent History of *Christianity and Crisis*," report to board of directors, 11 June 1973. For more detailed figures, see the *C&C* board minutes, most of which are in *C&C* records, box 4 and 5, in plastic notebooks labeled by year. Unless otherwise noted, all budget data used in this chapter are based on these documents, and all information about circulation and personnel changes is based on mastheads and published notes in *C&C* during the years in question.

2. Judith Duke, *Religious Publishing and Communications* (White Plains, N.Y.: Knowledge Industry, 1981), 172. Duke's chapter, "Magazines," pp. 161–81, is a good overview of the subject. See also Marty, *The Religious Press in America*, 3–63, Marty, "The Religious Press," in Lippy and Williams, *Encyclopedia of the American Religious Experience, 1697–1709;* Dennis Voskuil, "Reaching Out: Mainline Protestantism and the Media," in Hutchison, *Between the Times*, 72–91; and Stephen Board, "Moving the World with Magazines: A Survey of Evan-

gelical Periodicals," in *American Evangelicals and the Mass Media,* ed. Quentin Schultze (Grand Rapids: Academie Books, 1990), 119–42.

3. David Shaw, "Care and Feeding of a Magazine," *Los Angeles Times,* 6 Feb. 1993, 1. Messer-Davidow, "Manufacturing the Attack on Higher Education," 51, reports that the *National Review* received a $342,000 subsidy from conservative foundations in 1989.

4. Shaw, "Care and Feeding of a Magazine," 26; the *Nation* columnist is Calvin Trillin. "Vanden Heuvel Faces the *Nation,*" *New Yorker,* 30 Jan. 1995, 37, discusses a change in the *Nation's* patronage, from Arthur Carter to a group including Paul Newman and E. L. Doctorow.

5. Shaw, "Care and Feeding of a Magazine," 25; Nan Fink, "Publisher's Page," *Tikkun* 4 (1989), no. 5: 6–7.

6. Shaw, "Care and Feeding of a Magazine," 1, 24.

7. Duke, *Religious Publishing and Communications,* 172. The average advertising income of religious journals is only 40 percent, less than the revenue from subscriptions, whereas the 55 percent average advertising income for all magazines is twice their percentage from subscriptions.

8. Personal correspondence from Richard John Neuhaus, 25 July 1996. Neuhaus kindly provided these figures, noting that "we do not have a separate budget for *First Things* since it is included in the over-all program of the institute." He estimated annual foundation grants for *First Things* at "somewhat over $100,000" out of a "best estimate [of the] total cost of producing the journal" of $910,000. (This means that the *First Things* budget, like its circulation, is double that of *C&C* during its last few years.) However, Howell's 1995 article, "Funding the War of Ideas," 702, states that Neuhaus's institute received almost $700,000 from four major neoconservative foundations and $900,000 in total grants out of a $1.2 million budget. Gottfried, *Conservative Movement,* 125, says simply that *First Things* is "lavishly funded by Olin and Scaife" foundations. See also Neuhaus, "The First Five Years," *First Things,* Mar. 1995, 66–68; and Neuhaus, "Who You Are," *First Things,* Aug./Sept. 1992, 61.

9. Jeanie Wylie-Kellermann, "Witnessing and Wealth," *Witness* 75 (1992), no. 5: 28–29 provides details and states that some *Witness* board members considered merging with *C&C* around 1990; Wylie-Kellerman, *Witness* annual fund appeal, 1997 (copy in author's possession), estimates that the money will run out as early as 2003. See the board minutes in *C&C* records, box 5, for sporadic discussion about merger from *C&C's* side. Apparently these discussions did not go very far, although I heard them mentioned occasionally in interviews, for example with Butler and Gropp.

10. "Report on 1995 Activities," document provided by the Presbyterian Lay Committee. Howell, "Funding the War of Ideas," 703, reports that Pew has provided $3.7 million since 1968, including $187,000 annually in recent years.

11. Jim Wallis, "*Sojourners* at a Crossroads," *Sojourners,* 6 Apr. 1988, photocopy from *C&C* archives; Karen Lattea interview; photocopies of independent auditors reports kindly supplied by *Sojourners.* Around 1990, *Sojourners* had three times *C&C's* circulation and four or five times as many staff people. Its 1992 budget was $1.2 million, compared with *C&C's* $500,000.

12. Cherry, *Hurrying toward Zion,* 48. SVHE was first called the National Council of Religion in Higher Education and for a time was the Society for Religion in Higher Education before it assumed its current name in 1976. Cherry discusses its full career (45–51).

13. Memo provided by *Soundings,* "Subscription Rate Increase," 25 Aug. 1997. Cash contributions to *Soundings* have ranged from $10,000 to $35,000 in the past few years, with the trend moving downward.

14. For a valuable comparative analysis, see Patrice McDermott, *Politics and Scholarship: Feminist Academic Journals and the Production of Knowledge* (Urbana: Univ. of Illinois Press, 1994). Unfortunately for present purposes, this fine study of *Signs, Feminist Studies,* and *Frontiers* provides little comparative analyses of journals interested in the interface between feminism and Christianity, even though it is focused on the relation between academic discourse and the everyday life of women's communities.

15. Personal correspondence from James Wall, 26 July 1996; Wall interview. See also Marty,

The Religious Press in America, 3–63, Marty, "The Religious Press," in Lippy and Williams, *Encyclopedia of the American Religious Experience, 1697–1709;* Delloff et al., *A Century of* The Century; Mark Toulouse, "The Christian Century and American Public Life: The Crucial Years, 1956–1968," in *New Dimensions in American Religious History: Essays in Honor of Martin E. Marty,* ed. Jay Dolan and James Wind (Grand Rapids: Eerdmans, 1993), 44–83.

16. Many interviews with *C&C* insiders stressed this point. Howell and Lindermayer, *Ethics in the Present Tense,* xvi, acknowledge Anne Hale Johnson, Harle and Kenneth Montgomery, Luther Tucker, and an anonymous couple as important contributors but stress that twelve hundred people made contributions in 1990. Very rarely did any single donor contribute a significant portion of a *C&C* budget. Evidence about donors is scattered throughout *C&C's* archives and came up in several interviews, but I have not gone into details because some documents are marked confidential. For fairly representative published lists, see Howell, "You Gave and Gave," 1 Mar. 1993, 63–66, and "Manna in a Difficult Time," 16 Mar. 1992, 88–91.

17. "Bibliography of the Writings of Reinhold Niebuhr," in Kegley, *Reinhold Niebuhr,* 529–69.

18. For example, "The Way We Were," *Nation Associate,* 11 (Fall 1991), no. 2: 4, cites a 1941 *Nation* analysis in which I. F. Stone presented the war as a struggle for control of Asia and stated that "it was unavoidable and is better fought now when we still have allies left." See also Vanden Heuvel, *The* Nation, *1965–1990;* and Morley, "Freda Kirchwey: Cold War Critic," in Gardner, *Redefining the Past,* 157–68. On Niebuhr's involvement see Merkley, *Reinhold Niebuhr,* 152–53, and Fox, *Reinhold Niebuhr,* 72–75.

19. Pells, *The Liberal Mind in a Conservative Age,* 10–18.

20. Fox, *Reinhold Niebuhr,* 72–75, 105–15, 154–59. *World Tomorrow* began in 1918, flourished from 1926 to 1934 under the leadership of Kirby Page and Sherwood Eddy, merged with the *Century* in 1934, and then was succeeded by the Fellowship of Reconciliation's *Fellowship* in 1936. See Nancy Roberts, *American Peace Writers, Editors, and Periodicals* (Westport, Conn.: Greenwood Press, 1990), 328.

21. Fox, *Reinhold Niebuhr,* 168.

22. Ibid., 196. Other brief accounts of *C&C's* founding include Stone, *Reinhold Niebuhr,* 108–11; Merkley, *Reinhold Niebuhr,* 150–52; and Brown, *Niebuhr and His Age,* 100–101.

23. Bennett interview; Fox, *Reinhold Niebuhr,* 196–97; Handy, *History of Union Theological Seminary,* 199–202. Miller's views in the mid-1930s are discussed in Marty, *Modern American Religion,* 2:311–15.

24. "Eulogy: William Sloane Coffin," 13 Dec. 1954, 163; Handy, *History of Union Theological Seminary,* 211–58, esp. 218–19. See also Schenkel, *The Rich Man and the Kingdom.*

25. Others included Charles Burlingham, John Mackay, Howard Chandler Robbins, and Rhoda McCulloch. Bennett was not on the first masthead but joined in the third issue, and Johnson, Lieper, and Robbins were all added during the first few months.

26. Marty, *Modern American Religion,* 2:374–84. One test of a sponsor's commitment is whether he was present at a key organizational meeting in 1940. Attending were Niebuhr, Coffin, Van Dusen, William Adams Brown, Samuel McCrea Cavert, Sherwood Eddy, W. P. Ladd, John MacKay, John Mott, and Henry St. George Tucker. But many factors affected attendance. Bennett was not present because he then lived in San Francisco. See "Minutes of Meeting at Parkside Hotel," 1 Oct. 1940, *C&C* records, box 10, black Scrapbook. In addition to names already mentioned, the sponsors at *C&C's* inception included William Cochrane, J. Harry Cotton, Frank Porter Graham, Henry Hobson, Douglas Horton, Lynn Harold Hough, William Allen Neilson, Justin Wroe Nixon, William Scarlett, Henry Sherrill, Robert Speer, Charles Taft, and Charles White. There was one woman joining McCulloch among *C&C* leaders—Elizabeth Morrow, a trustee of Smith College and Union Seminary who was most famous for being Charles Lindbergh's mother-in-law. (When he prominently opposed entry in World War II, she was for it.)

27. Board of Sponsors, "Statement of Purpose," 7 Jan. 1946, photocopy from *C&C* archives. *C&C* records, box 10, black scrapbook, contains several 1946 letters on the subject of "shall we continue?" but scant evidence of hesitation among the key players.

28. A number of people, mainly Protestant academics, served as contributing editors after

the war, including James Baker, a bishop from California; Charles Gilkey, dean at the University of Chicago; Umphrey Lee, president of Southern Methodist University; and Lynn Harold Hough, dean emeritus of the Drew School of Theology. All except Hough were on the editorial board before the 1948 split. Contributing editors after the 1948 reorganization also included Coffin, Henry Smith Leiper, John Mackay, Rhoda McCulloch, Francis Miller, Edward Parsons, and Howard Chandler Robbins. William Scarlett served on the editorial board from 1954 to 1955.

29. Cowan, Bennett, and Howell interviews; Cowan, "In Twenty-five Years You Pick Up a Lot of Memories," 17 Sept. 1979, 234, 233.

30. Some notable sponsors who appear on *C&C* letterhead in the 1950s and/or 1960s, but are not mentioned elsewhere in this chapter, include Franklin Clark Fry, Francis Sayre, H. Shelton Smith, James Pike, Edwin Espy, Angus Dun, and Elton Trueblood. Those who signed board of sponsors editorials varied widely depending on who attended the annual meeting. This gives the impression, confirmed in interviews with Bennett and Cowan, that the role of sponsor was fluid, including room for people deeply committed to *C&C* and for others who merely lent their names.

31. Letters from 1942 in *C&C* records, box 10, black scrapbook. This scrapbook documents a 60,000 piece mailing during the war, including 8,000 to a list from Union Seminary, 6,000 each to lists from the FCC and several other seminaries. *C&C* records, box 18, includes a folder with thirty-eight letters to graduating seniors at seminaries around the country. These are personalized letters testifying to *C&C*'s importance signed by deans, presidents, and luminaries from the schools. In later years such seminary appeals became a standard strategy. *C&C* records, box 19, folder labeled "Old Promotions" documents a similar effort in the 1960s; to the end *C&C* relied on seminarians for new subscribers.

32. *C&C* records, box 4, red binder, board minutes for 1960 state that there had been no appeal to friends of the journal since 1956. *C&C* apparently devoted little energy to institutional survival in the late 1950s. The entire documentation saved in *C&C*'s minutes from 1957 in *C&C* records, box 4, red binder takes up only two pages. It summarizes a 9 Dec. 1957 dinner meeting in Union's refectory, with Van Dusen absent even though he was the secretary at the time, in which the main discussion was about the distinction between the editorial board and contributing editors. This "resulted in a motion by Dr. Niebuhr that the distinction be abolished for all practical purposes" and all contributing editors should be invited to editorial board meetings.

33. Editorial note in 2 Feb. 1953 issue; *C&C* records, box 1, folder labeled "Genl correspondence 30 June 1954–."

34. Cowan, "Recent History of *Christianity and Crisis,*" 1; Frances Smith, "A Brief History of *Christianity and Crisis,*" 6.

35. Personal correspondence from Shinn, 14 Mar. 1997.

36. Bates, "The World and Formosa," 2 Mar. 1953, 17.

37. Niebuhr, "Democracy, Secularism, and Christianity," 2 Mar. 1953, 19–20, 24; Robert Handy, "Corruption in Government: A Perennial Issue," 2 Mar. 1953, 21–22; "World Church: News and Notes," 2 Mar. 1953, 23–24; Niebuhr's article added little to the arguments of his *Children of Light and Children of Darkness* (New York: Scribner, 1944).

38. Editorial note, 27 Apr. 1953, 56.

39. Cowan interview; Cowan, "In Twenty-five Years You Pick Up a Lot of Memories," 210.

40. Niebuhr and Bennett, "To the Readers and Friends of *C&C,*" 18 Oct. 1954, 131.

41. Editorial note, 18 Feb. 1957, 9.

42. An important internal document for *C&C*'s changing orientation is Robert McAfee Brown's "A Reader's Report on *C&C,* 1959–1960," in *C&C* records, box 4, board minutes for 1960.

43. Cowan, "In Twenty-five Years You Pick Up a Lot of Memories," 211.

44. Other new members from the mid-1950s to mid-1960s included theologian Joseph Sittler (1955–59), Richard T. Baker and James Kuhn, professors of journalism and business at Columbia, plus Thompson and Shinn, who were promoted from contributing editors. In 1964 the complete list included the additions I have mentioned plus Niebuhr, Bennett, Van

Dusen, Searle Bates, Waldo Beach, Amos Wilder, Robert McAfee Brown, F. Ernest Johnson, and Kenneth Thompson.

45. In 1964 the complete list also included John Mackay, William May, Gibson Winter, George Younger, and William Lee Miller. Others joined and left the contributors during the decade, including ethicist Alexander Miller, theologian John Baillie, critic Sidney Lanier, and people who were fading out of *C&C*'s picture (such as Henry Smith Leiper) or rising toward its inner circle (such as Cox).

46. Figures from editorial notes, 1 Nov. 1965, 223; and Smith, "Brief History of *Christianity and Crisis*," 7.

47. Editorial notice, 13 Nov. 1961; 1968 figure from Cowan, "Recent History of *Christianity and Crisis*," 1.

48. Cowan, *Witness to a Generation*, xvii; Cowan, "Recent History of *Christianity and Crisis*," 2.

49. *C&C* records, box 19, folder called "Old Promotions," has a representative batch of receipts including these journals plus the *Episcopalian*, the *Reporter*, and the *New Republic*.

50. *Newsweek*, "Christian Realism," 28 Feb. 1966, 61, reprinted in many promotions in *C&C* records, box 19.

51. Letter from McCarthy to Cowan, 15 Sept. 1964; letter from Cowan to McCarthy, 18 Sept. 1964, in *C&C* records, box 19, folder labeled "Old Promotions." A final version of the letter appeared in a four-page flyer, ca. 1968, called "An Invitation from Senator Eugene McCarthy," with inside quotations from Martin Luther King Jr., Walter Lippmann, and many others. It retains the references to Lewis and Fisher but adds a sentence mentioning Niebuhr, Bennett, Brown, and Cox (photocopy from *C&C* archives).

52. These special issues appeared on 20 Mar. 1961 and 29 May 1961.

53. Workshop ad, 15 Apr. 1967, 81; CALCAV ad, 3 Nov. 1968, 259; Buckley ad, 2 Feb. 1970, 11; ad for Carl Burke, *God Is for Real, Man* (New York: Association Press, 1967), 6 Mar. 1967, 43. A typical folder called "Advertising Bills Paid" in *C&C* records, box 19, includes bills to the *Saturday Evening Post*, Union's summer school, five religious presses (Association, Augsburg, John Knox, Westminster, and Sheed and Ward), and four other presses (Lippincott, Macmillan, Oxford, and Doubleday).

54. Photocopies from *C&C* archives: "Summary Results, *Christianity and Crisis* Readership Survey," ca. Sept. 1967; "About the People Who Read *C&C*," *C&C* promotional brochure, 1982; "Results of Readership Survey," ca. Sept. 1990. For a summary see Howell, "Who Reads *C&C*: Your Portrait in Numbers," 3 Feb. 1992, 4.

55. Ernest Lefever, ed., *The World Crisis and Christian Responsibility* (New York: Association Press, 1958); Wayne Cowan, ed., *What the Christian Hopes For in Society: Selections from* Christianity and Crisis (New York: Association Press, 1957); Cowan, ed., *Facing Protestant-Roman Catholic Tensions* (New York: Association Press, 1960); Cowan, ed., *Witness to a Generation: Significant Writings from* Christianity and Crisis, *1941–1966* (New York: Bobbs-Merrill, 1966).

56. Editorial note, 7 Feb. 1972, 2.

57. Handy, *History of Union Theological Seminary*, 289–90; Cowan stresses demoralization in "In Twenty-five Years You Pick Up a Lot of Memories," 232, and "Recent History of *Christianity and Crisis*."

58. "Comparative Financial Statement, 1970–1975"; Cowan, "Recent History of *Christianity and Crisis*." The low circulation of just over 8,000 came in mid-1974, according to "Christianity and Crisis Development Plan," ca. 1975, photocopy from *C&C* archives. But 95 percent of the slide occurred between 1969 and 1973.

59. "Transcript of Conversations between *C&C* and *CC*," 6 Mar. 1969; letter from Lecky to Cowan, 14 Mar. 1969; memo from McGraw to Cowan, 18 Feb. 1971; memo from Shinn to Cowan, 30 Mar. 1971; and "*Christianity and Crisis* and *Commonweal*: Some Suggestions for a Publishing Partnership," 7 Mar. 1968—all photocopies from *C&C* archives. There was an element of takeover in some of these scenarios: *C&C* would be swallowed by *Century*, and *Renewal* by *C&C*. The prospective "swallowees" politely advocated a division of labor and portrayed their role as more virtuous. See also Howell, "Notes on Reflection of Six Months at *C&C*," ca. 1970, photocopy from *C&C* archives.

60. Editorial note, 12 July 1971, 138; Cowan, "In Twenty-five Years You Pick Up a Lot of

Memories," 234. A 1971 memo from Moore, photocopy from *C&C* archives, discusses nuts and bolts of severance pay and inventory of furniture for closing *C&C*.

61. "*Christianity and Crisis* Bylaws," ca. 1971, photocopy from *C&C* archives. A precursor of this board had emerged in the mid-1960s, in the context of updating *C&C*'s bylaws, as a sort of metamorphosed board of sponsors. The 4 Dec. 1968 board minutes in *C&C* records, box 4, red binder, discuss reconstituting the sponsors and speculate that *C&C* might build the board of directors into such a group. At this time fifteen out of twenty-three members of the board of directors were on the editorial board, supplemented by William Ellis, Randolph Dyer, Shelby Rooks, John Brademas, Robert Lynn (who left the editorial board in 1967), Dean Wright, Thomas Stewart, and William Savage. By 1976 only Ellis, Bennett, Moore, and Shinn remained among the board's twenty-two members; twelve listed addresses in the Interchurch Center, and several others were also ecumenical bureaucrats. See "Christianity and Crisis Board Members as of June 10, 1976" and "Members of Board of Directors, 4 Dec. 1968, photocopies from *C&C* archives.

62. Many interviews with people who observed *C&C* directly in the 1960s—especially Bennett, Cowan, Howell, Letty Russell, and Shinn—stressed this point. I asked Cowan whether he tried to counteract the shrinking role of the contributing editors; he replied, "We did not try to counteract the Board's atrophying" (personal correspondence, 2 Aug. 1994).

63. Editorial note, "To Our Readers," 17 Feb. 1975, 18, revealed that *C&C* was still in serious danger of closing. *C&C* records, box 5, board minutes from 1976 and 1977, and *C&C* records, box 4, board minutes from 1978 to 1981, include many documents about the status of contributing editors and the relations between the staff and the board. Shinn, treasurer John Brown, and president Michael McIntyre stressed economic accountability. There was much discussion about appropriate salaries for the staff, who did not fit the old model of Niebuhr or Niebuhr's secretary. Increasingly the staff compared its situation not to any job description in academia but to colleagues at other magazines. *C&C* records, box 4, board minutes from 12 May 1977 record Shinn voting no to staff pay increases. But Cowan's "Salary Recommendations," *C&C* records, box 4, board minutes, 21 Jan. 1981, stated that "*C&C* has never been a "movement" enterprise; even though the compensation it can offer has never matched the rates of comparable commercial publications, it is not accepted that it should be in effect subsidized by its professional staff members."

64. Cowan, "Brief History of *Christianity and Crisis*"; editorial note, 27 Oct. 1975, 249.

65. Howell estimated that grants from mainline denominations accounted for 60 percent of contributions in the late 1970s (Butler interview; Howell interview), but significantly less by the mid-1980s.

66. Cover art by Myra Lee Conway, 7 Feb. 1972. Other *C&C* artists included Emily Vializ in the early 1970s and Mark Larson and Candy Berlin at mid-decade. Conway designed the new logo.

67. Skandalon appeared twelve times in 1972 and less thereafter until it disappeared.

68. Several others came and went, including John Maguire of Wesleyan University who served on the board from 1965 to 1971, Robert Lynn, who left the masthead in 1967 but continued as president of the board of directors; Stephen Rose who left in 1971; and Johannes Hoekendijk, a Dutch theologian and ecumenical leader who served from 1965 to 1969. Strictly speaking, Novak was not the first Catholic on *C&C*'s boards, but he was preceded only by inactive French contributing editor J. B. Duroselle.

69. Several had written for *C&C* even longer. Moody and Novak did not join the board until 1967 and 1968, but both had written for *C&C* since the early 1960s; Brown and Shinn wrote a combined twelve years before joining. Another force for stability was the fact that board members who set the tone were disproportionately old-timers (Bennett, Cox, Cowan, Shinn), while its more peripheral members (Mead, Baldwin, Cone, Novak) were disproportionately newcomers. Ruether was an exception as a trendsetting newcomer.

70. The full seventeen included Searle Bates, Kenneth Thompson, Richard Baker, Waldo Beach, John Maguire, James Kuhn, C. Eric Lincoln, William May, J. B. Duroselle, Charles West, George Younger, Gibson Winter, Albert Van Den Heuvel, Vincent Harding, M. M. Thomas, Richard Shaull, and Arthur Moore (who later returned to the masthead).

71. Memo in *C&C* records, box 4, red binder, board minutes, 30 Mar. 1971. Among the people I interviewed, Cone put the most stress on Novak's efforts to become a major *C&C* leader, and recalls that one meeting was even held at Novak's home. Cone does not believe that there was a plausible scenario of Novak seizing control because Bennett and Shinn would have vetoed it.

72. Letter from Bennett to Cowan, 22 Nov. 1971, photocopy from *C&C* archives.

73. Howell, "Who Reads *C&C:* Your Portrait in Numbers," 4–5; Neuhaus, "Who You Are," 61. As I noted in chapter 6, note 45, half of the 10 percent who were not white actually fell in the categories of "other" and "no answer." See "Results of Readership Survey," ca. Sept. 1990, photocopy from *C&C* archives.

74. It is hard to interpret readers' changing tastes in other magazines, because the data include many apples and oranges comparisons. In 1967, 35 percent listed *Saturday Review, Harper's,* and / or the *New Yorker* as publications they liked, compared with only 8 percent who listed the *Nation, I. F. Stone's Weekly,* and / or *Ramparts.* In addition, 14 percent listed the *New Republic* (which was far more liberal then than in the 1990s). By 1990, 11 percent listed *Atlantic, New Yorker,* or *Harper's* under a more stringent criterion—as one of their two favorite journals—compared with 10 percent who chose *Nation, In These Times, Ms., Progressive, Zeta,* or *Mother Jones.* See "Results of Readership Survey," ca. Sept. 1990, and "Summary Results, *Christianity and Crisis* Readership Survey," ca. Sept. 1967, photocopies from *C&C* archives.

75. Neuhaus, "Who You Are," 61. In second place was the *New York Times Book Review* with 8 percent. Another revealing contrast is with *Christianity Today* which had a 55 percent overlap with the *Reader's Digest* in 1976, according to Duke, *Religious Publishing and Communications,* 174.

76. Howell, "Who Reads *C&C,*" 5. Of the 25 percent who were wavering in their liberalism, 16 percent remained "somewhat liberal."

77. For more detail see "Appendix Two: *Christianity and Crisis* and the Hypothesis That Protestant Radicalization Causes Institutional Decline" in the dissertation version of this book, *Liberals, Radicals, and the Contested Social Thought of Postwar Protestantism: Christianity and Crisis Magazine, 1941–1976* (Ph.D. diss., Univ. of Minnesota, 1992). To contextualize my argument, see my "Interpreting the 'Popular' in Popular Religion."

78. In an effort to quantify turnover around 1970 compared with earlier years, I analyzed board members and key editorial staff at each five-year anniversary since *C&C*'s inception. I expected moderate increases in turnover between 1966 and 1971–72. The actual results were surprising. They vary with different methods of relating *C&C*'s classic format (editorial board with peripheral contributing editors) to its 1972 format (single board called "contributing editors"). If we compare apples and apples—only classic format mastheads until they ended in 1971—the 1966–71 turnover was much *lower* than in any previous period. Only 18 percent of the key names were new compared with the previous low of 37 percent in 1951–56. Comparing apples and oranges—the 1966 editorial board and the new 1972 contributing editors—the 1966–72 turnover triples to 57 percent. However, this was the same rate as in 1956–61, lower than in 1961–66 (64 percent), and not much higher than rates in the 1940s (around 45 percent). The numbers came out slightly different when I factored in the entire masthead, including contributors in the classic format who often remained for years in a kind of "editor emeritus" status. But again, the lowest five-year turnover—15 percent—occurred between 1966 and 1971. Working with ten-year instead of five-year periods, the turnover was again higher from 1956 to 1966 (83 percent) than decades before and after (50 percent). I would not place excessive stock in these numbers, because they count Niebuhr the same before and after his stroke, perceive no difference between core writers like Shinn and Cox and inactive people like J. Oscar Lee and Margaret Mead, and—importantly—are blind to the trend for *C&C* to become more staff-driven after 1970. Still, for whatever they are worth, they do not show any more institutional discontinuity from 1966 to 1976 than in earlier years.

79. Cowan, "Recent History of *Christianity and Crisis,*" 5.

80. On *American Report,* see Hall, *Because of Their Faith,* 107–8, 167. *American Report* reached a circulation of 24,000; its reader profile was similar to *C&C*'s, although it was only 50 per-

cent Protestant. Interestingly, it began to flounder in 1973, which was roughly the same time that *C&C*'s circulation began to stabilize.

81. Cowan, "Circular Letter to Lapsed Subscribers," ca. 1969 and "Reactions of Readers: Selected Quotes," photocopies from *C&C* archives. Unfortunately, we do not have complete records of this survey. We only have a folder of purportedly representative responses in *C&C* records, box 10.

82. Barb Teska, letter to *C&C*, ca. 1969 in *C&C* records, box 10, folder on lapsed-subscribers survey.

83. "Reactions of Readers: Selected Quotes" and letter from Ian George, 23 Nov. 1969, in *C&C* records, box 10, folder on lapsed-subscribers survey.

84. Harsh, "Proposal for a New Theological Magazine," 1.

85. Other departures included John Fry, James McGraw, Margaret Mead, and Frank Baldwin; other additions included Middle East specialist Dale Bishop, past or future staff members Gail Hovey, Leon Howell, and Bob Hoyt, and several others who came and went as columnists.

86. Throughout the 1980s *C&C* tinkered with its job titles. "Long-term Development Committee Report," in *C&C* records, box 5, board minutes, 23 Feb. 1987, proposed renaming Howell president, editor, and publisher (with the board's president becoming its chair) and changing Hovey's title to vice-president. In fact, Howell was not voted president, but he did change from editor to editor and publisher. Hovey changed from executive editor to managing editor, Lindermayer from associate editor to senior associate editor, and Kelly from assistant to associate editor—all without any change at the bottom or top of the pecking order.

87. Cowan interview; Hoyt letter to Cowan, 8 Mar. 1985, photocopy from *C&C* archives.

88. Officially, neither left entirely. Cowan remained on the masthead in the symbolic role of "editor-at-large" starting in 1984, but this meant little for day-to-day operations, especially after his salary line was eliminated in 1986. Hoyt returned to the masthead as a contributing editor in 1987.

89. My analysis is based on interviews with almost all the major protagonists in this story plus several informed observers, as well as documents in *C&C*'s archives. Many of the key documents are in *C&C* records, box 3, folder labeled "Wayne Cowan departure." See also *C&C* records, box 4, board minutes, Jan. 1983 to Nov. 1984. Especially important is a 19 Feb. 1984 document by Hoyt and Lindermayer, "Memorandum on Staff Concerns."

90. Another variation on these questions features Howell rather than Hoyt in the Judas role: Was Cowan double-crossed when he agreed to accept the position of editor-at-large, only to see funding for it disappear in 1986? Documents about this episode, including a resignation letter from Robert Lekachman, are in *C&C* records, box 3, folder labeled "Wayne Cowan departure."

91. Vivian Lindermayer, "Editors on *C&C*," 12 Apr. 1993, 84.

92. *C&C* records, box 4, board minutes, 14 Nov. 1983, document the debate about Finn, which led William Wipfler to resign.

93. Donald Wilson interview. Cone and Harrison made related points; their experiences with Hoyt figured prominently in their perception that *C&C* was not a consistent ally of feminism and black theology.

94. Margaret O'Brien Steinfels, "Among the Protestants," 26 Aug. 1985, 317–18; Peggy Steinfels and Robert Hoyt interview.

95. On *Commonweal* see Rodger Van Allen, *The Commonweal and American Catholicism: The Magazine, the Movement* (Philadelphia: Fortress Press, 1974), and *Being Catholic: Commonweal from the Seventies to the Nineties* (Loyola Univ. Press, 1993). See also Marty, "The Religious Press," in Lippy and Williams, *Encyclopedia of the American Religious Experience;* and John Deedy, "The Catholic Press: The Why and the Wherefore," in Marty et al., *The Religious Press in America,* 65–121.

96. Hoyt, "Editors on *C&C*," 12 Apr. 1993, 81. In an interview, Hoyt underlined this point.

97. According to a 29 Jan. 1985 staff memorandum, the committee—chaired by Eileen Lindner and including Beverly Harrison, Roger Shinn, Lou Gropp, and Arthur Moore—

planned to run the job announcement in magazines like the *Christian Century* and *United Methodist Reporter,* as well as the *Columbia Journalism Review* and *Washington Journalism Review*—but the American Academy of Religion's *Openings* and publications of the Society of Christian Ethics were both conspicuous absences. This memo appears in C&C records, box 16, folder labeled "Search Committee"; my analysis also draws on interviews with Shinn, Vivian Lindermayer, and Gropp.

98. A complete list of editorial advisory panel members in 1991–92 included five contributing editors (Dale Bishop, Howard Moody, Arthur Moore, Larry Rasmussen, Delores Williams), eight board members (Barbara Braver, Barbara Lundblad, Audrey Miller, Irving Williamson, Brenda Stiers, Anne Romasco, Louis Gropp, and Lee Hancock), and thirteen others: Ada Maria Isasi-Diaz, Quinton Dixie, David Dyson, Dwain Epps, Donald Johnston, Wende Marshall, Richard Newman, Maxine Phillips, Michael Rivas, Jean Sindab, Peggy Shriver, Betty Thompson, and George Todd. *C&C* records, box 17, includes a thorough paper trail of editorial advisory panel minutes from the last few years, intermingled with notes for staff meetings dealing with *C&C*'s content. Strictly speaking, the panel was in formation before Howell arrived, but its central role was a feature of his years as editor.

99. The move toward columnists started under Hoyt—the first five were James Finn, Robert Lekachman, Peggy Steinfels, Douglas Sturm, and Cornel West (with Randall Forsberg declining); see the discussion in Hoyt, "Editors Report," in *C&C* records, box 4, board minutes, 30 Sept. 1983. Howell hoped to push further, developing writers with big names who could provide signature voices, somewhat like *C&C* versions of Calvin Trillin or Anthony Lewis. In his 12 June 1987 memo to staff, "Front of the Book" in *C&C* records, box 3, folder labeled "Staff Notes," he mentioned Lewis as a model, called for "expert useful provocative shorter comments," and wrote, "As I think I've made clear, I want more good stuff up front and fewer long pieces." Along with pushing contributing editors such as Heyward and West in this direction, he instituted a new masthead category of columnist. The person who came closest to his model was Will Campbell, although Linda Lancione Moyer, Andrew L. J. James, and Mary Pellauer also took on the role, with Pellauer succeeding the most consistently. (All four appeared on the masthead.) Several other excellent writers—notably Gar Alperovitz, June Jordan, and Manning Marable—were groomed for the role but did not write consistently. In *C&C*'s last year Ellie Goodwin, Laura McClure, and Ellen Teninty were listed as columnists, but by then the model was turning; they were more like regular reporters on the environment, labor, and the economy.

100. Howell, "Who Reads *C&C:* Your Portrait in Numbers," 4–5. Another 10 percent suggested more book reviews, which were the most scholarly pieces *C&C* was publishing at this time.

101. Peter Steinfels, "Influential Christian Journal Prints Last Issue," *New York Times,* 4 Apr. 1993, photocopy from *C&C* archives.

102. Duke, *Religious Publishing and Communications,* 162–66, discusses how *United Methodists Today* and the *Christian Observer* folded in the mid-1970s, while seven of ten representative journals struggled with large subscriber losses between 1970 and 1976, including the *Century* (30 percent loss), the *Christian Herald* (30 percent), *America* (40 percent), and *A.D.* (60 percent). The *Christian Herald* and *American Baptist* both folded at about the same time as *C&C,* as discussed in Doug DeBlanc, "The Decline of Two Historic Magazines," photocopied magazine article from *C&C* archives, publication information unknown, ca. 1992.

103. Shinn et al., fund appeal dated 1 Nov. 1978, photocopy from *C&C* archives; Howell, "Editor and Publishers' Report," in *C&C* records, box 5, board minutes, 28 Sept. 1990. Howell, "Editor's Report," in *C&C* records, box 5, board minutes, 16 Nov. 1992, summarizes increases from 1985 to 1992: $10,000 in rent, $7,500 in insurance, $25,000 in postage, plus more than $25,000 in other categories including salaries. See also Howell, "A Few Matters," a 2 Feb. 1992 document written to brief the Task Force to Discuss *C&C* Options. See *C&C* records, box 5, board minutes for 1993.

104. Howell, "On the Street Where We Live," 20 Apr. 1987, 132.

105. Howell and Miller, "Letter to Readers and Friends," 2 Mar. 1993, photocopy in author's possession.

106. Most of this change dates from the late 1980s. Recall that *C&C* first published twenty-five issues a year; entering 1986 it still produced twenty-two. Thereafter, it cut back steadily, finessing its retreat with double issues.

107. Lindermayer, "Managing Editor's Report," in *C&C* records, box 5, board minutes, 25 Sept. 1992.

108. *C&C* records, box 5, board minutes, 20 Nov. 1989, record a vote for raises of 20 percent per year above the cost of living, although this target was never achieved. The total salary bill for a six-person staff in 1991 was $228,000, including salaries, annuities, and funds to allow Howell to commute between Washington (where his spouse worked) and New York. This number (uncorrected for inflation) compares with an average of about $100,000 between 1974 and 1984.

109. Howell, "Editor's Report," *C&C* records, box 5, board minutes, 2 Mar. 1992, states that it had become difficult to get $20,000 a year directly from denominations by the end, a small percentage of *C&C*'s total contributions.

110. I intend these names as representatives of a larger group, including many who made equally important contributions. A short list of other names that recur in documents from the last two decades (often because they held stints as officers or chaired important committees) includes John Brown, Richard Fernandez, O. Sam Folin, Ardith Hayes, Eileen Lindner, Mary Ann Lundy, Mary McNamara, William McKeown, Michael McIntyre, Valerie Russell, Peggy Shriver, B. J. Stiles, Betty Thompson, George Todd, George Webber, and William Wipfler. Not all worked in ecumenical circles (e.g., Folin was a portfolio manager for an investment firm, and Gropp was editor-in-chief at the Hearst magazine, *House Beautiful*), but the majority did.

111. "The 1988 Board of Directors," photocopy from *C&C* archives.

112. Announcement of Densford grant in *C&C*, 1 Aug. 1988, 261. Report on Episcopal Church Foundation grant in *C&C* records, box 5, board minutes, 25 May 1992.

113. Lilly has funded many intellectual projects related to liberal Protestantism (including grants from the Louisville Institute that supported this book), and one of Lilly's key leaders, Robert Lynn, was a former president of *C&C*'s board. However, Lilly typically supports specific projects rather than operating budgets, whereas *C&C* needed ongoing subsidies.

114. Linda-Marie Delloff, "The NCC in New Times: Structural Changes and the Future of Ecumenism," 9 Jan. 1989, 471.

115. "Glasnost for Religion: Top Story of 1989," *Christian Century*, 21 Dec. 1988, 1179; "WCC Faces Financial Crisis," *Christian Century*, 31 July 1996, 743–44.

116. Tracy Early, "State of the Council," 11 Dec. 1978, 297; "CWS Seeks Independence," *Christian Century*, 21 Dec. 1988, 1176. Church World Service later moved toward autonomy in a dispute about the NCC's fees for overhead, and Dick Butler was the head of CWS during much of its battle with the NCC. Butler resigned in 1988; three years later he became *C&C*'s managing publisher.

117. Early, "State of the Council," 301.

118. Elizabeth Verdesi, "The State of the Council: Continuing the Discussion," 15 Jan. 1979, 337–38.

119. *C&C* talked about buying a computer throughout the 1980s. Board minutes for 4 June 1990 in *C&C* records, box 5, report that *C&C* finally bought a modest personal computer with page-composition software and a fourteen-inch monitor. When *C&C* pulled the plug, it still had not finished integrating the PC into its operations.

120. Letty Russell interview.

121. Quoted in Linda-Marie Delloff, "Union Theological Seminary: A Profile," 9 Apr. 1990, 122. See also William McKinney, "The NCC in New Times (I): Finding a Place in the Culture," 9 Jan. 1989, 465–66, an important statement reprinted in *Ethics in the Present Tense.*

122. Williams, "Lethargy in Christendom," 12 Apr. 1993, 90–91; Gittings, "Ecumenism:

Dead in the Water?" 12 Apr. 1993, 78–79. See also Alan Geyer, "Open Moment, Impoverished Witness," 12 Apr. 1993, 82–83.

123. Harrison phone interview, 23 June 1994.

124. Howell and Miller, "Letter to Readers and Friends."

125. Howell, "Editor's Report: A Narrative," in *C&C* records, box 5, board minutes, 1 Mar. 1993, presents Howell's account of the process. The task force included the executive committee of Howell, Audrey Miller, Bill McKeown, Mary McNamara, and Irving Williamson, plus Barbara Braver, Larry Rasmussen, Maxine Phillips, and Betty Thompson. A key meeting of this group was held on 17 Feb. 1993. Although notes from this meeting suggest divided opinion, a 19 Feb. 1993 letter from Miller in preparation for the board meeting of 1 Mar. 1993 states that at this 17 Feb. 1997 meeting "the decision to go out with dignity became the reluctant consensus, barring a miracle" (documents in *C&C* records, box 5, board minutes).

126. *C&C* records, box 17, includes records from student focus groups formed in 1992 and 1993 to strategize about *C&C*'s future. It was organized by consultant Marilyn Clement and loosely related to the editorial advisory panel. There was little overlap between this group and the task force, but its conversations were in the background.

127. "Rationale for the $250,000 Appeal for Each of the Three Years above the Proposed Budget," internal document in *C&C* records, box 5, with 1993 board minutes. This document appeared to assume a staff of at least seven, although at one point it mentioned the possibility that "an independent editorial board—as in *C&C*'s first twenty-five years—could take major editorial responsibilities and a minimal staff of perhaps two people would receive and edit manuscripts initiated by the editorial board." It does not explore the budgetary implications of such a plan.

128. Howell, "To Celebrate and Say Goodbye," 12 Apr. 1993, 75.

129. I have not gone into detail about the seminary negotiations because some of the documents in the *C&C* archives are marked confidential, and some of the people I interviewed about these matters spoke off the record. The one *C&C* conversation that went the furthest was with a seminary that was prepared to negotiate about subsidies that were not trivial. However, the scenario desired by *C&C*—an infusion of cash to maintain and even expand the staff—was not in the cards, and the key decision makers wanted to close before deficits ate up the reserve fund. The main exploratory meeting with this seminary—done in a conference call on 23 Mar.—happened only a week before *C&C*'s self-imposed deadline to pull the plug. In addition to this overture, board members agreed to contact several other seminaries; for example, Arthur Brandenburg approached Emory University and Scholar's Press; he argued emphatically in an interview that the staff failed to follow up on viable prospects he uncovered. As for exploring the possibility of a "leaner and meaner" staff configuration, this was part of the conversations in the task force on options for *C&C*'s future, as well as the student focus groups. However, no definite plan emerged, in part because of the short time frame. Some of the leaders consoled themselves with the hope of reviving *C&C* later; this was a common theme in the 12 Apr. 1993 farewell issue and the interviews I conducted in 1994. In this regard *C&C* went to its death like a patient going into a coma, hoping that a doctor would show up later with a cure.

130. I presented this analysis to *C&C*'s board (which continued to exist in a rump form) during the fall of 1994, eighteen months after *C&C* folded. Among the scenarios we discussed was whether my own blend of scholarly interests and my knowledge of *C&C*'s network suggested that I could play some role in convening a revived editorial board of younger scholars—the working layer of a two-tiered board anchored by bigger names—under the right set of conditions. We never tested this hypothesis because these conditions never came together, and the moment has long since passed. The issues at stake were confidential then, and they remain so now. I only mention this episode because the news is bound to leak out sooner or later, and I do not want anyone to say that I covered it up.

131. Maxine Phillips, "A Better Choice of Comrades," *Dissent* (Winter 1994): 134–36.

Conclusion

1. Unsigned editorial, "The Crisis," 10 Feb. 1941, 3; Niebuhr, "Plans for World Reorganization," 19 Oct. 1942, 5; Niebuhr, "The Moral and Political Judgments of Christians," 6 July 1959, 99.

2. Bruce Springsteen, "The Ghost of Tom Joad," from *The Ghost of Tom Joad* (Columbia Records, 1995). Copyright © 1995 by Bruce Springsteen. Reprinted by permission. All rights reserved.

3. House majority leader Dick Armey, cited in Jack Beatty, "Wages Matter Most," *Atlantic,* Mar. 1996, read on the World Wide Web.

4. Edward Wolff, "How the Pie Is Sliced: America's Growing Concentration of Wealth," *American Prospect* (Summer 1995): 59; Simon Head, "The New Ruthless Economy," *New York Review of Books,* 29 Feb. 1996, 47. Wolff measures wealth in a way that does not include consumer durables (e.g., furniture) or social security and pension funds. Factoring in consumer durables does not affect overall figures very much, but factoring in pensions and promised future social security benefits lowers the share of the richest 1 percent of the population to 22 percent, without reducing the trend toward increasing polarization (Wolff, 61). Of course, the future of social security appears somewhat precarious, especially for younger people.

5. Springsteen, "Ghost of Tom Joad."

6. Springsteen, "Youngstown," from *The Ghost of Tom Joad.*

7. Gary Dorrien, *Reconstructing the Common Good,* 14 and passim. Dorrien stresses the virtues of the Swedish Meidner Plan, which involved a 20 percent corporate tax paid by transferring stock to labor and other democratic groups via mutual funds controlled by them. He says, "I regard the kind of strategy represented by the Meidner Plan as the essence of modern democratic socialism" (166), although he also promotes a range of alternatives including "worker-owned firms, employee stock-ownership plans, national development banks, community-owned corporations, cooperative banks, private ownership of agriculture and small firms, and decentralized economic planning" (14). For a *C&C* spin-off from this book see Dorrien, "Economic Democracy," 10 Sept. 1990, 271–74. For a review raising questions similar to mine, see Manning Marable, "Democratizing the Living Place," 24 Sept. 1990, 298–99. After *C&C* folded, Dorrien continued in a similar vein in his *Soul in Society.*

8. Springsteen, *The Ghost of Tom Joad;* John Steinbeck, *The Grapes of Wrath* (1939; New York: Viking Press, 1972), 407. Steinbeck's commentary on this definition is a classic: "Well, this young fella he think about her, an' he scratches his head, an' he says, "Well, Jesus, Mr. Hines, I ain't a son-of-a-bitch, but if that's what red is—why, I want thirty cents a hour. Ever'body does. Hell, Mr. Hines, we're all reds."

9. Springsteen, "Ghost of Tom Joad."

10. Steinbeck, *Grapes of Wrath,* 570.

11. Maxine Phillips, "A Better Choice of Comrades," *Dissent* (Winter 1994), 134–36.

12. Two of the best analyses placing Niebuhr in dialogue with recent trends in philosophy and critical thought are Lovin, *Reinhold Niebuhr and Christian Realism;* and West, *American Evasion of Philosophy.*

13. In one of the more vivid examples that I recall, a historical lecture that developed this point at some length, the speaker was well aware of historical differences between *Deutsches Christentum* and Christian feminism—this was the presupposition of the ironic joke he was making. However, he was not joking about his resistance to inclusive language or the theological reasoning about it. A self-professed liberal, A. J. McKelway, used similar logic without irony in "Minneapolis: The Real Issue," *Presbyterian Outlook,* 4 Apr. 1994, 6–7, an attack on a feminist theological conference at which former *C&C* writers played major roles. Arthur Cochrane argued similarly in "Bonhoeffer and Barth versus Norman," 16 Apr. 1979, 86–88, a contribution to *C&C*'s debate about Norman's *A Politicized Christ.*

14. Dan Berrigan, cited in William Van Etten Casey, ed., *The Berrigans* (New York: Avon,

1971), 60. Rich, "The Burning of Paper Instead of Children," in *Poems: Selected and New, 1950–1974* (New York: Norton, 1975), 148.

15. Rich, "The Burning of Paper," 150, 151.

16. Lorde, *Sister Outsider,* 112; Carby, "Politics of Difference," 85.

17. Dorothee Sölle, *Revolutionary Patience* (Maryknoll, N.Y.: Orbis, 1977), 34.

18. W. H. Auden, "September 1, 1939," from *W. H. Auden: Collected Poems,* ed. Edward Mendelson. Copyright © 1940 by W. H. Auden. Reprinted by permission of Random House, Inc. Arthur Moore, "Remembering Mike," 11 Sept. 1989, 253–54.

Select Bibliography

What follows is not a comprehensive bibliography. If it were, given *C&C*'s wide interests, I would have to list most of the texts I have read in religious studies, cultural studies, and twentieth-century U.S. history during the past twenty years. Instead, I offer a selective list centering on secondary works in history, social science, and theological ethics that have been especially important in preparing this book, plus a few of the most important books by a few of the most central *C&C* writers. When in doubt, I have aimed to suggest priorities for further reading rather than to be encyclopedic. I have reduced references to literature and film addressed by *C&C*, primary historical documents from the years of *C&C*'s career, classic scholarly texts from outside *C&C*'s inner circle, and citations in cultural studies to a bare minimum. The footnotes provide some additional citations.

Adler, Les K., and Thomas Paterson. "Red Fascism: The Merger of Nazi Germany and Soviet Russia in the American Image of Totalitarianism." *American Historical Review* 75 (1970): 1046–64.

Adler, Margot. *Drawing Down the Moon: Witches, Druids, Goddess-Worshippers, and Other Pagans in America Today.* Boston: Beacon Press, 1979.

Ahlstrom, Sydney. *A Religious History of the American People.* New Haven: Yale Univ. Press, 1972.

———. "The Radical Turn in Theology and Ethics: Why It Occurred in the 1960s." In *Religion in American History,* ed. John Mulder and John Wilson, 445f. New York: Prentice Hall, 1978.

———. "Annuit Coeptis: America as the Elect Nation." In *Continuity and Discontinuity in Church History,* ed. F. Forrester Church and Timothy George, 315–37. Leiden: Brill, 1979.

Anderson, Benedict. *Imagined Communities.* New York: Verso, 1983.

Angus, Ian, and Sut Jhally. *Cultural Politics in Contemporary America.* New York: Routledge, 1989.

Arac, Jonathan, ed. *Postmodernism and Politics.* Minneapolis: Univ. of Minnesota Press, 1986.

Aronowitz, Stanley. *False Promises: The Shaping of American Working-Class Values.* New York: McGraw-Hill, 1973.

Aronowitz, Stanley, et al. "Special Section: Radical Democracy." *Socialist Review* 93 (1994), no. 3: 5–149.

Baer, Hans, and Merrill Singer. *African American Religion in the Twentieth Century: Varieties of Protest and Accommodation.* Knoxville: Univ. of Tennessee Press, 1992.

Barnet, Richard, and Ronald Müller, *Global Reach: The Power of the Multinational Corporations.* New York: Simon and Schuster, 1974.

Bellah, Robert. *The Broken Covenant: American Civil Religion in Time of Trial.* 2d ed. Chicago: Univ. of Chicago Press, 1992.

Bellah, Robert, et al. *Habits of the Heart: Individualism and Commitment in American Life.* Berkeley: Univ. of California Press, 1985.

Bennett, John C. *Social Salvation: A Religious Approach to the Problems of Social Change.* New York: Scribner, 1935.

———. *Christianity—and Our World.* New York: Hazen, 1936.

———. *Christian Realism.* New York: Scribner, 1941.

———. *Christianity and Communism.* New York: Association Press, 1948.

———. *The Radical Imperative: From Theology to Social Ethics.* Philadelphia: Westminster Press, 1975.

Bercovitch, Sacvan. *The American Jeremiad.* Madison: Univ. of Wisconsin Press, 1978.

Berger, Peter. *The Sacred Canopy.* New York: Doubleday, 1967.

Berry, Wendell. *The Unsettling of America: Culture and Agriculture.* New York: Avon, 1977.

Berryman, Phillip. *Liberation Theology.* Oak Park, Ill.: Meyer Stone, 1987.

———. *Religion in the Megacity: Catholic and Protestant Portraits from Latin America.* Maryknoll, N.Y.: Orbis Books, 1996.

Bérubé, Michael. *Public Access: Literary Theory and American Cultural Politics.* New York: Verso, 1995.

Blumenthal, Sidney. *The Rise of the Counter-Establishment: From Conservative Ideology to Political Power.* New York: Perennial Library, 1988.

Bounds, Elizabeth. *Coming Together/Coming Apart: Religion, Community, and Modernity.* New York: Routledge, 1997.

Boyer, Paul. *By the Bomb's Early Light: American Thought and Culture at the Dawn of the Atomic Age.* New York: Pantheon, 1985.

———. *When Time Shall Be No More: Prophecy Belief in Modern American Culture.* Cambridge: Harvard Univ. Press, 1992.

Boyte, Harry. *The Backyard Revolution: Understanding the New Citizen Movement.* Philadelphia: Temple Univ. Press, 1980.

———, ed. *The New Populism.* Philadelphia: Temple Univ. Press, 1986.

Branch, Taylor. *Parting the Waters: America in the King Years, 1954–63.* New York: Simon and Schuster, 1988.

Breines, Winifred. *Young, White, and Miserable: Growing Up Female in the Fifties.* Boston: Beacon Press, 1992.

Brock, Rita Nakashima, et al., eds. *Setting the Table: Women in Theological Conversation.* St. Louis: Chalice Press, 1995.

Brown, Charles. *Niebuhr and His Age: Reinhold Niebuhr's Prophetic Role in the Twentieth Century.* New York: Trinity Press International, 1992.

Brown, Robert McAfee. *Theology in a New Key.* Philadelphia: Westminster Press, 1978.

———. *The Essential Reinhold Niebuhr.* New Haven: Yale Univ. Press, 1986.

———. *Religion and Violence.* 2d ed. Philadelphia: Westminster Press, 1987.

Brown, Robert McAfee, Abraham Heschel, and Michael Novak. *Vietnam: Crisis of Conscience.* New York: Association Press, 1967.

Bruce, Steve. *The Rise and Fall of the New Christian Right: Conservative Protestant Politics in America, 1978–1988.* Oxford: Clarendon Press, 1988.

Bruce-Briggs, B., ed. *The New Class?* New Brunswick: Rutgers Univ. Press, 1979.

Bruneau, Thomas. *The Political Transformation of the Brazilian Catholic Church.* New York: Cambridge Univ. Press, 1974.

Bucher, Glen. "Christian Realism after Niebuhr: The Case of John C. Bennett." *Union Seminary Quarterly Review* 41 (1986): 43–58.

Buhle, Paul. *Marxism in the United States: Remapping the History of the American Left.* London: Verso, 1987.

Callahan, Daniel, ed. *The Secular City Debate.* New York: Macmillan, 1966.

Calvert, Gregory. *Democracy from the Heart: Spiritual Values, Decentralism, and Democratic Idealism in the Movement of the 1960s.* Eugene, Ore.: Communitas Press, 1991.

Candelaria, Michael R. *Popular Religion and Liberation: The Dilemma of Liberation Theology.* Albany: State Univ. of New York Press, 1990.

Capps, Walter H. *The Unfinished War: Vietnam and the American Conscience.* Boston: Beacon Press, 1982.

Carey, John J., ed. *The Sexuality Debate in North American Churches, 1988–1995.* Lewiston: Edward Mellen Press, 1996.

Carmichael, Stokely, and Charles Hamilton. *Black Power: The Politics of Liberation in America.* New York: Vintage, 1967.

Carroll, Peter. *It Seemed Like Nothing Happened: The Tragedy and Promise of the 1970s.* New York: Holt, Rinehart and Winston, 1982.

Carroll, Peter, and David W. Noble. *The Free and the Unfree: A New History of the United States.* New York: Penguin Books, 1977.

Carson, Clayborne. *In Struggle: SNCC and the Black Awakening of the 1960s.* Cambridge: Harvard Univ. Press, 1981.

Carter, Paul A. *Decline and Revival of the Social Gospel: Social and Political Liberalism in American Protestant Churches, 1920–40.* Ithaca, N.Y.: Cornell Univ. Press, 1954.

Carter, Stephen. *The Culture of Disbelief.* New York: Anchor Books, 1993.

Casanova, José. *Public Religions in the Modern World.* Chicago: Univ. of Chicago Press, 1994.

Casey, William Van Etten, ed. *The Berrigans.* New York: Avon, 1971.

Cherry, Conrad. *Hurrying toward Zion: Universities, Divinity Schools, and American Protestantism.* Bloomington: Indiana Univ. Press, 1995.

———, ed. *God's New Israel: Religious Interpretations of American Destiny.* Englewood Cliffs, N.J.: Prentice Hall, 1971.

Chilcote, Ronald, ed. *Dependency and Marxism: Toward a Resolution of the Debate.* Boulder, Colo.: Westview Press, 1982.

Chilcote, Ronald, and Joel Edelstein, eds. *Latin America: The Struggle with Dependency and Beyond.* New York: Wiley, 1974.

Chomsky, Noam. *Towards a New Cold War.* New York: Pantheon, 1982.

———. *The Fateful Triangle: The United States, Israel, and the Palestinians.* Boston: South End Press, 1983.

———. *Turning the Tide: U.S. Intervention in Central America and the Struggle for Peace.* Boston: South End Press, 1985.

Chomsky, Noam, and Edward Herman. *Manufacturing Consent: The Political Economy of the Mass Media.* New York: Pantheon, 1988.

Chopp, Rebecca. *The Praxis of Suffering: An Interpretation of Liberation and Political Theologies.* Maryknoll, N.Y.: Orbis Books, 1986.

Chopp, Rebecca, and Mark Lewis Taylor, eds. *Reconstructing Christian Theology.* Minneapolis: Fortress Press, 1994.

Chopp, Rebecca, and Sheila Greeve Devaney, eds. *Horizons in Feminist Theology: Identity, Tradition, and Norms.* Minneapolis: Fortress Press, 1997.

Christ, Carol. *The Laughter of Aphrodite: Reflections on a Journey to the Goddess.* San Francisco: Harper and Row, 1987.

Christ, Carol, and Judith Plaskow, eds. *Womanspirit Rising: A Feminist Reader in Religion.* San Francisco: Harper and Row, 1979.

Christianity and Crisis. Records. Archives of the Burke Library, Union Theological Seminary in the City of New York.

Clecak, Peter. *Radical Paradoxes: Dilemmas of the American Left, 1945–70.* New York: Harper and Row, 1973.

Coalter, Milton, John Mulder, and Louis Weeks, eds. *The Mainstream Protestant "Decline."* Louisville: Westminster Press, 1990.

Collins, Patricia Hill. *Black Feminist Thought: Knowledge, Consciousness, and the Politics of Empowerment.* New York: Routledge, 1990.

Cone, James. *Black Theology and Black Power.* New York: Seabury, 1969.
———. *Spirituals and the Blues: An Interpretation.* New York: Seabury, 1972.
———. *God of the Oppressed.* New York: Seabury, 1975.
———. *My Soul Looks Back.* Maryknoll, N.Y.: Orbis Books, 1986.
———. *For My People: Black Theology and the Black Church.* Maryknoll, N.Y.: Orbis Books, 1991.
———. *Martin and Malcolm and America: A Dream or a Nightmare?* Maryknoll, N.Y.: Orbis Books, 1991.
Cone, James, and Gayraud Wilmore, eds. *Black Theology: A Documentary History.* Vol. 2: *1980–1992.* Maryknoll, N.Y.: Orbis Books, 1993.
Cowan, Wayne, ed. *What the Christian Hopes For in Society: Selections from Christianity and Crisis.* New York: Association Press, 1957.
———, ed. *Facing Protestant-Roman Catholic Tensions.* New York: Association Press, 1960.
———, ed. *Witness to a Generation: Significant Writings from Christianity and Crisis, 1941–1966.* New York: Bobbs-Merrill, 1966.
Cox, Harvey. *The Secular City.* Rev. ed. New York: Macmillan, 1966.
———. *The Feast of Fools: A Theological Essay on Festivity and Fantasy.* Cambridge: Harvard Univ. Press, 1969.
———. *The Seduction of the Spirit: The Use and Misuse of People's Religion.* New York: Simon and Schuster, 1973.
———. *Turning East: The Promise and Peril of the New Orientalism.* New York: Simon and Schuster, 1977.
———. *Just as I Am.* Nashville: Abingdon, 1983.
———. *Religion in the Secular City: Toward a Postmodern Theology.* New York: Simon and Schuster, 1984.
———. *The Silencing of Leonardo Boff: The Vatican and the Future of World Christianity.* Bloomington: Meyer-Stone, 1988.
———. *Fire from Heaven: The Rise of Pentecostal Spirituality and the Reshaping of Religion in the Twenty-first Century.* Reading, Mass.: Addison-Wesley, 1995.
———, ed. *The Situation Ethics Debate.* Philadelphia: Westminster, 1968.
Craig, Robert H. *Religion and Radical Politics: An Alternative Christian Tradition in the United States.* Philadelphia: Temple Univ. Press, 1992.
Curtis, Susan. *A Consuming Faith: The Social Gospel and Modern American Culture.* Baltimore: Johns Hopkins Univ. Press, 1991.
Daly, Mary. *Beyond God the Father.* Boston: Beacon Press, 1973.
———. *Gyn/Ecology: The Metaethics of Radical Feminism.* Boston: Beacon Press, 1978.
———. *Pure Lust: Elemental Feminist Philosophy.* San Francisco: Harper, 1992.
Davaney, Sheila Greeve, ed. *Theology at the End of Modernity.* New York: Trinity Press International, 1991.
Davaney, Sheila Greeve, and Dwight Hopkins, eds. *Changing Conversations: Cultural Analysis and Religious Reflection.* New York: Routledge, 1996.
Dean, William. *History Making History.* Albany: State Univ. of New York Press, 1988.
———. *The Religious Critic in American Culture.* Albany: State Univ. of New York Press, 1994.
DeBenedetti, Charles. *An American Ordeal: The Antiwar Movement of the Vietnam Era.* Syracuse: Syracuse Univ. Press, 1990.
DeBerg, Betty. *Ungodly Women: Gender and the First Wave of American Fundamentalism.* Minneapolis: Fortress Press, 1990.
Delloff, Linda-Marie, Martin Marty, Dean Peerman, and James Wall. *A Century of* The Century. Grand Rapids: Eerdmans, 1987.
Deloria, Vine. *God Is Red: A Native View of Religion.* New York: Dell, 1973.
Diamond, Sara. *Roads to Dominion: Right-Wing Movements and Political Power in the United States.* New York: Guilford Press, 1995.
Dolan, Jay. *The American Catholic Experience: A History from Colonial Times to the Present.* Garden City, N.Y.: Image Books, 1985.

Dolan, Jay, and James Wind, eds. *New Dimensions in American Religious History: Essays in Honor of Martin E. Marty.* Grand Rapids: Eerdmans, 1993.

Dorrien, Gary. *Reconstructing the Common Good: Theology and the Social Order.* Maryknoll, N.Y.: Orbis Books, 1990.

———. *The Neoconservative Mind.* Philadelphia: Temple Univ. Press, 1993.

———. *Soul in Society: The Making and Remaking of Social Christianity.* Minneapolis: Fortress Press, 1995.

Douglas, Mary, and Steven Tipton, eds. *Religion in America: Spirituality in a Secular Age.* Boston: Beacon Press, 1982.

Duke, Judith. *Religious Publishing and Communications.* White Plains, N.Y.: Knowledge Industry Publications, 1981.

Dunn, Charles, ed. *American Political Theology: Historical Perspectives and Theoretical Analysis.* New York: Praeger, 1984.

During, Simon, ed. *The Cultural Studies Reader.* New York: Routledge, 1993.

Durkin, Kenneth. *Reinhold Niebuhr.* Harrisburg: Morehouse Press, 1989.

Dyson, Michael Eric. *Reflecting Black: African American Cultural Criticism.* Minneapolis: Univ. of Minnesota Press, 1993.

———. "X Marks the Plots: A Critical Reading of Malcolm's Readers." *Social Text* 35 (1993): 25–55.

Echols, Alice. *Daring to Be Bad: Radical Feminism in America, 1967–1975.* Minneapolis: Univ. of Minnesota Press, 1989.

Ehrenreich, Barbara, Elizabeth Hess, and Gloria Jacobs. *Re-Making Love: The Feminization of Sex.* New York: Anchor Books, 1986.

———. *Fear of Falling: The Inner Life of the Middle Class.* New York: Pantheon, 1989.

Eller, Cynthia. *Living in the Lap of the Goddess.* Boston: Beacon Press, 1995.

Ellis, Marc H., and Otto Maduro, eds. *Expanding the View: Gustavo Gutiérrez and the Future of Liberation Theology.* Maryknoll, N.Y.: Orbis Books, 1990.

Ellul, Jacques. *The Technological Society.* Trans. John Wilkinson. New York: Vintage, 1964.

———. *Violence: Reflections from a Christian Perspective.* New York: Seabury, 1969.

———. *Jesus and Marx: From Ideology to Gospel.* Grand Rapids: Eerdmans, 1988.

Ellwood, Robert. *The Sixties Spiritual Awakening: Religion Moving from Modern to Postmodern.* New Brunswick: Rutgers Univ. Press, 1994.

Engelhardt, Tom. *The End of Victory Culture: Cold War America and the Disillusioning of a Generation.* New York: Basic Books, 1995.

Evans, Sara. *Personal Politics: The Roots of the Women's Liberation in the Civil Rights Movement and the New Left.* New York: Vintage, 1979.

Evans, Sara, and Harry Boyte. *Free Spaces: The Sources of Democratic Change in America.* New York: Harper and Row, 1986.

Farber, David, ed. *The Sixties: From Memory to History.* Chapel Hill: Univ. of North Carolina Press, 1994.

Farrell, James. *The Spirit of the Sixties: The Making of Postwar Radicalism.* New York: Routledge, 1996.

Ferm, Deane William. *Contemporary American Theologies: A Critical Survey.* New York: Seabury, 1981.

Fey, Harold, and Margaret Frakes, eds. *The* Christian Century *Reader.* New York: Association Press, 1962.

Fierro, Alfredo. *The Militant Gospel: A Critical Introduction to Political Theologies.* Maryknoll, N.Y.: Orbis Books, 1977.

Findlay, James. *Church People in the Struggle: The National Council of Churches and the Black Freedom Movement, 1950–1970.* New York: Oxford Univ. Press, 1993.

Fitzgerald, Frances. *Cities on a Hill.* New York: Simon and Schuster, 1986.

Flacks, Richard. *Making History: The Radical Tradition in American Life.* New York: Columbia Univ. Press, 1988.

Flacks, Richard, and Jack Whalen. *Beyond the Barricades: The Sixties Generation Grows Up.* Philadelphia: Temple Univ. Press, 1989.

Flake, Carol. *Redemptorama: Culture, Politics, and the New Evangelicalism.* New York: Penguin Books, 1984.
Foner, Eric, ed. *The New American History.* Philadelphia: Temple Univ. Press, 1990.
Fowler, Robert Booth. *A New Engagement: Evangelical Political Thought, 1966–1976.* Grand Rapids: Eerdmans, 1982.
Fowler, Robert Booth, and Allen Hertzke. *Religion and Politics in America: Faith, Culture, and Strategic Choices.* Boulder, Colo.: Westview Press, 1995.
Fox, Richard Wightman. *Reinhold Niebuhr: A Biography.* New York: Pantheon, 1985.
Franklin, Robert Michael. *Liberating Visions: Human Fulfillment and Social Justice in African American Thought.* Minneapolis: Fortress Press, 1990.
Fraser, Nancy. *Unruly Practices: Power, Discourse, and Gender in Contemporary Social Theory.* Minneapolis: Univ. of Minnesota Press, 1989.
———. "Rethinking the Public Sphere: A Contribution to the Critique of Actually Existing Democracy." *Social Text* 25/26 (1990): 56–80.
———. "From Redistribution to Recognition: Dilemmas of Justice in a 'Post-Socialist' Age." *New Left Review* 212 (1995): 68–93.
Fraser, Steve, and Gary Gerstle, eds. *The Rise and Fall of the New Deal Order, 1930–1980.* Princeton: Princeton Univ. Press, 1989.
Frazier, E. Franklin, and C. Eric Lincoln. *The Negro Church/The Black Church since Frazier.* New York: Schocken, 1974.
Freire, Paulo. *The Pedagogy of the Oppressed.* New York: Seabury Press, 1970.
Gates, Henry Louis, ed. *"Race," Writing, and Difference.* Chicago: Univ. of Chicago Press, 1986.
Gitlin, Todd. *The Sixties: Years of Hope, Days of Rage.* New York: Bantam, 1987.
Gottfried, Paul. *The Conservative Movement.* Rev. ed. New York: Twayne, 1993.
Grant, Jacquelyn. *White Women's Christ and Black Women's Jesus.* Atlanta: Scholars Press, 1989.
Grelle, Bruce. "Hegemony and the Universalization of Moral Ideas: Gramsci's Importance for Religious Ethics." *Soundings* 78 (1995), no. 3–4: 519–40.
Grenholm, Carl-Henric. *Christian Ethics in a Revolutionary Age: An Analysis of the Social Ethics of John C. Bennett, Heinz-Dietrich Wendland, and Richard Shaull.* Uppsala: Verbum, 1973.
Griffin, David. *Varieties of Postmodern Theology.* Albany: State Univ. of New York Press, 1989.
Guillermoprieto, Alma. *The Heart That Bleeds: Latin America Now.* New York: Vintage, 1995.
Gunn, Giles, ed. *The Culture of Criticism and the Criticism of Culture.* New York: Oxford Univ. Press, 1987.
Gutiérrez, Gustavo. *A Theology of Liberation.* Trans. Caridad Inda and John Eagleson. Maryknoll, N.Y.: Orbis Books, 1973.
———. *The Power of the Poor in History.* Trans. Robert Barr. Maryknoll, N.Y.: Orbis Books, 1984.
Hackett, David, ed. *Religion and American Culture: A Reader.* New York: Routledge, 1996.
Hadaway, Kirk, and David Roozen, eds. *Church and Denominational Growth: What Does (and What Does Not) Cause Growth and Decline.* Nashville: Abingdon Press, 1993.
Hadden, Jeffrey. *The Gathering Storm in the Churches.* New York: Doubleday, 1969.
Hall, Mitchell K. *Because of Their Faith: CALCAV and Religious Opposition to the Vietnam War.* New York: Columbia Univ. Press, 1990.
Hall, Stuart. "Gramsci's Relevance for the Study of Race and Ethnicity." In *People's History and Socialist Theory,* ed. Raphael Samuel, 5–27. London: Routledge, 1980.
———. "On Postmodernism and Articulation: An Interview with Stuart Hall." *Journal of Communication Inquiry* 10 (1986), no. 2: 53–54.
Handy, Robert. "Christianity and Socialism in America, 1900–20." *Church History* 22 (1952), no. 1: 39–53.
———. "The Protestant Quest for a Christian America, 1830–1930." *Church History* 22 (1952), no. 1: 8–20.
———. *A Christian America? Protestant Hopes and Historical Realities.* 2d ed. New York: Oxford Univ. Press, 1984.
———. *A History of Union Theological Seminary in New York.* New York: Columbia Univ. Press, 1987.

———. *Undermined Establishment: Church-State Relations in America, 1880–1920.* Princeton: Princeton Univ. Press, 1991.

Hansen, Karen, and Ilene J. Philipson, eds. *Women, Class, and the Feminist Imagination: A Socialist-Feminist Reader.* Philadelphia: Temple Univ. Press, 1989.

Harries, Richard, ed. *Reinhold Niebuhr and the Issues of Our Time.* Grand Rapids: Eerdmans, 1988.

Harrison, Beverly Wildung. *Our Right to Choose: Toward a New Ethic of Abortion.* Boston: Beacon Press, 1983.

———. *Making the Connections: Essays in Feminist Social Ethics.* Boston: Beacon Press, 1985.

Hartz, Louis. *The Liberal Tradition in America.* New York: Harcourt Brace Jovanovich, 1955.

Herberg, Will. *Protestant, Catholic, Jew.* Rev. ed. New York: Anchor Books, 1960.

Hessel, Dieter, ed. *The Church's Public Role: Retrospect and Prospect.* Grand Rapids: Eerdmans, 1993.

Hewitt, Marsha. *Critical Theory of Religion: A Feminist Analysis.* Minneapolis: Fortress Press, 1994.

Heyward, Carter. *The Redemption of God: A Theology of Mutual Relation.* Lanham, Md.: Univ. Press of America, 1982.

———. *Our Passion for Justice.* New York: Pilgrim Press, 1984.

———. *Speaking of Christ.* Cleveland: Pilgrim Press, 1989.

Hobgood, Mary E. *Catholic Social Teaching and Economic Theory: Paradigms in Conflict.* Philadelphia: Temple Univ. Press, 1991.

Hoge, Dean, Benton Johnson, and Donald Luidens. *Vanishing Boundaries: The Religion of Mainline Protestant Baby Boomers.* Louisville: Westminster Press, 1994.

Hodgson, Godfrey. *America in Our Time.* New York: Vintage, 1976.

Horowitz, Daniel. "Rethinking Betty Friedan and *The Feminine Mystique:* Labor Union Radicalism and Feminism in Cold War America." *American Quarterly* 48 (1996), no. 1: 1–42.

Howell, Leon, and Vivian Lindermayer, eds. *Ethics in the Present Tense: Significant Writings from Christianity and Crisis Magazine, 1966–1991.* New York: Association Press, 1991.

Hudnut-Beumler, James. *Looking for God in the Suburbs: The Religion of the American Dream and Its Critics, 1945–1965.* New Brunswick: Rutgers Univ. Press, 1994.

Huggins, Nathan. "The Deforming Mirror of Truth: Slavery and the Master Narrative of American History." *Radical History Review* 49 (1991): 25–48.

Hulsether, Mark. "Evolving Approaches to U.S. Culture in the American Studies Movement: Consensus, Pluralism, and Contestation for Cultural Hegemony." *Canadian Review of American Studies* 23 (1993), no. 2: 1–55.

———. "Interpreting the 'Popular' in Popular Religion." *American Studies* 36 (Fall 1995): 127–37.

———. "It's the End of the World as We Know it." *American Quarterly* 48 (1998), no. 2: 375–84.

———. "The Scholar of Religion as Public Intellectual: Some Recent Works by Cornel West." *Method and Theory in the Study of Religion* 8 (1996), no. 4: 377–84.

———. "Three Challenges for the Field of American Studies: Relating to Cultural Studies, Addressing Wider Publics, and Coming to Terms with Religions." *American Studies* 38 (Summer 1997), no. 2: 117–46.

———. "'The Public' and Some of Its Publics." *Bulletin of the Council of Societies for the Study of Religion* 27 (1998), no. 2.

———. "Like a Sermon: Popular Religion in Madonna Videos." In *Religion and Popular Culture in America,* ed. Bruce Forbes and Jeffrey Mahan. Berkeley: Univ. of California Press, 1998.

———. "Sorting Out the Relationships among Christian Values, U.S. Popular Religion, and Hollywood Films." *Religious Studies Review* 25 (1999), no. 1.

Hunsinger, George. *Karl Barth and Radical Politics.* Philadelphia: Westminster Press, 1976.

Hunter, James Davison. *Evangelicalism—The Coming Generation.* Chicago: Univ. of Chicago Press, 1987.

———. *Culture Wars: The Struggle to Define America.* New York: Basic Books, 1991.

Hutchison, William. *The Modernist Impulse in American Protestantism.* Cambridge: Harvard Univ. Press, 1976.

———, ed. *Between the Times: The Travail of the Protestant Establishment in America, 1900–1960.* New York: Cambridge Univ. Press, 1989.

Ireland, Rowan. *Kingdoms Come: Religion and Politics in Brazil.* Pittsburgh: Univ. of Pittsburgh Press, 1991.

Isserman, Maurice. *If I Had a Hammer: The Death of the Old Left and the Birth of the New Left.* New York: Basic Books, 1987.

Jaggar, Alison, and Paula Rothenberg. *Feminist Frameworks.* 2d ed. New York: McGraw-Hill, 1984.

Jakobsen, Janet. "Deconstructing the Paradox of Modernity: Feminism, Enlightenment, and Cross-Cultural Moral Interactions." *Journal of Religious Ethics* 23 (1995), no. 2: 333–63.

Jeffords, Susan. *The Remasculinization of America: Gender and the Vietnam War.* Bloomington: Indiana Univ. Press, 1989.

Jezer, Marty. *The Dark Ages: Life in the United States, 1945–1960.* Boston: South End Press, 1982.

Jiménez, Michael. "Citizens of the Kingdom: Toward a Social History of Radical Christianity in Latin America." *International Labor and Working-Class History* 34 (Fall 1988): 3–21.

Johnson, Richard. "What Is Cultural Studies Anyway?" *Social Text* 16 (1986): 38–80.

Jones, Serene. "Women's Experience between a Rock and a Hard Place: Feminist, Womanist, and Mujerista Theologies in North America." *Religious Studies Review* 21 (1995), no. 3: 171–79.

Kaplan, Amy, and Donald Pease, eds. *Cultures of United States Imperialism.* Durham: Duke Univ. Press, 1993.

Kazin, Michael. *The Populist Persuasion: An American History.* New York: Basic Books, 1995.

Kearns, Laurel. "Saving the Creation: Christian Environmentalism in the United States." *Sociology of Religion* 57 (1996), no. 1: 55–70.

Kegley, Charles, ed. *Reinhold Niebuhr: His Religious, Social, and Political Thought.* Rev. ed. New York: Pilgrim Press, 1984.

Kellerman, Bill. "Apologist of Power: The Long Shadow of Reinhold Niebuhr's Christian Realism." *Sojourners* (March 1987): 14–21.

Kelley, Dean. *Why Conservative Churches Are Growing.* New York: Harper and Row, 1972.

Kovel, Joel. *Red Hunting in the Promised Land: Anticommunism and the Making of America.* New York: Basic Books, 1994.

Lacey, Michael J., ed. *Religion and Twentieth-Century American Intellectual Life.* New York: Cambridge Univ. Press, 1989.

Laclau, Ernesto, and Chantal Mouffe. *Hegemony and Socialist Strategy: Towards a Radical Democratic Politics.* London: Verso, 1985.

LaFeber, Walter. *America, Russia, and the Cold War.* 2d ed. New York: Wiley, 1972.

———. *Inevitable Revolutions: The U.S. in Central America.* New York: Norton, 1984.

Lears, Jackson. "The Concept of Cultural Hegemony." *American Historical Review* 90 (1985), no. 1: 567–93.

Leffler, Melvyn. "The American Conception of National Security and the Beginnings of the Cold War, 1945–1948." *American Historical Review* 89 (1984), no. 2: 346–400.

Lernoux, Penny. *Cry of the People.* New York: Penguin Books, 1980.

Levine, Daniel, ed. *Churches and Politics in Latin America.* Beverly Hills: Sage, 1979.

Levine, Lawrence. *Defender of the Faith: William Jennings Bryan, the Last Decade, 1915–1925.* New York: Oxford Univ. Press, 1965.

——. *Black Culture and Black Consciousness.* New York: Oxford Univ. Press, 1977.

Lincoln, C. Eric. *The Black Muslims in America.* Boston: Beacon Press, 1961.

Lincoln, C. Eric, and Lawrence Mamiya. *The Black Church in the African American Experience.* Durham: Duke Univ. Press, 1990.

Lindbeck, George. *The Nature of Doctrine: Religion and Theology in a Postliberal Age.* Philadelphia: Westminster Press, 1984.

Lindblom, Charles. *Politics and Markets: The World's Political Economic Systems.* New York: Basic Books, 1977.

Linebaugh, Peter. "Jubilating; or, How the Atlantic Working Class Used the Biblical Jubilee against Capitalism, with Some Success." *Radical History Review* 50 (1991): 143–82.

Lippy, Charles H., ed. *Religious Periodicals of the United States: Academic and Scholarly Journals.* Westport, Conn.: Greenwood Press, 1986.

Lipsitz, George. *A Life in the Struggle: Ivory Perry and the Culture of Opposition.* Philadelphia: Temple Univ. Press, 1988.

———. *Time Passages: Collective Memory and American Popular Culture.* Minneapolis: Univ. of Minnesota Press, 1990.

———. *A Rainbow at Midnight: Labor and Culture in the 1940s.* 2d ed. Urbana: Univ. of Illinois Press, 1994.

———. "Listening to Learn and Learning to Listen: Popular Culture, Cultural Theory, and American Studies." *American Quarterly* 42 (1990), no. 4: 615–36.

———. "The Possessive Investment in Whiteness: Racialized Social Democracy and the 'White' Problem in American Studies." *American Quarterly* 47 (1995), no. 3: 369–87.

Loades, Ann. *Feminist Theology: A Reader.* Philadelphia: Westminster Press, 1990.

Long, Edward LeRoy, and Robert T. Handy, eds. *Theology and Church in Times of Change: Essays in Honor of John Coleman Bennett.* Philadelphia: Westminster Press, 1970.

Lorde, Audre. *Sister Outsider: Essays and Speeches.* Freedom, Calif.: Crossing Press, 1984.

Lotz, David, ed. *Altered Landscapes: Christianity in America, 1935–1985: Essays in Honor of Robert T. Handy.* Grand Rapids: Eerdmans, 1989.

Lovin, Robin. *Reinhold Niebuhr and Christian Realism.* Cambridge: Cambridge Univ. Press, 1995.

McAdam, Doug. *Political Process and the Development of Black Insurgency, 1930–1970.* Chicago: Univ. of Chicago Press, 1982.

McCann, Dennis. *Christian Realism and Liberation Theology: Practical Theologies in Creative Conflict.* Maryknoll, N.Y.: Orbis Books, 1981.

McCormick, Thomas J. *Americas Half-Century: United States Foreign Policy in the Cold War.* Baltimore: Johns Hopkins Univ. Press, 1989, 78–79.

McDermott, Patrice. *Politics and Scholarship: Feminist Academic Journals and the Production of Knowledge.* Urbana: Univ. of Illinois Press, 1994.

MacEoin, Gary. *Memoirs and Memories.* Mystic, Conn.: Twenty-third Publications, 1986.

———. *The People's Church: Bishop Samuel Ruiz of Mexico and Why He Matters.* New York: Crossroad / Continuum, 1996.

McFague, Sallie. *Models of God: Theology for an Ecological Nuclear Age. Minneapolis:* Fortress Press, 1987.

———. *The Body of God: An Ecological Theology.* Minneapolis: Fortress Press, 1993.

McGovern, Arthur. *Marxism: An American Christian Perspective.* Maryknoll, N.Y.: Orbis Books, 1981.

———. *Liberation Theology and Its Critics.* Maryknoll, N.Y.: Orbis Books, 1989.

McGreevy, John. "Racial Justice and the People of God: The Second Vatican Council, the Civil Rights Movement, and American Catholicism." *Religion and American Culture* 4 (1994), no. 2: 221–54.

McLoughlin, William. *Revivals, Awakenings, and Reform: An Essay on Religion and Social Change in America, 1607–1977.* Chicago: Univ. of Chicago Press, 1978.

McNeal, Patricia. *Harder than War: Catholic Peacemaking in Twentieth-Century America.* New Brunswick: Rutgers Univ. Press, 1992.

Manis, Andrew Michael. *Southern Civil Religions in Conflict: Black and White Baptists and Civil Rights, 1947–1957.* Athens: Univ. of Georgia Press, 1987.

Marable, Manning. *Race, Reform, and Rebellion: The Second Reconstruction in Black America, 1945–1982.* Jackson: Univ. Press of Mississippi, 1984.

Marsden, George. *Fundamentalism and American Culture.* New York: Oxford Univ. Press, 1980.

———. *Understanding Fundamentalism and Evangelicalism.* Grand Rapids: Eerdmans, 1991.

———, ed. *Evangelicalism and Modern America.* Grand Rapids: Eerdmans, 1984.

Marty, Martin. *Modern American Religion.* Vol. 1: *The Irony of It All, 1893–1919.* Chicago: Univ. of Chicago Press, 1986.

———. "The Religious Press." In *Encyclopedia of the American Religious Experience,* ed. Charles H. Lippy and Peter Williams, 1697–1709. New York: Scribner, 1988.

———. *Modern American Religion.* Vol. 2: *The Noise of Conflict, 1919–1941.* Chicago: Univ. of Chicago Press, 1991.
———. "American Religious History in the 1980s: A Decade of Achievement." *Church History* 62 (1993): 335–77.
———. *Modern American Religion.* Vol. 3: *Under God, Indivisible, 1941–1960.* Chicago: Univ. of Chicago Press, 1996.
Marty, Martin, et al. *The Religious Press in America.* Westport, Conn.: Greenwood Press, 1972.
May, Elaine Tyler. *Homeward Bound: American Families in the Cold War Era.* New York: Basic Books, 1988.
May, Henry F. *Protestant Churches and Industrial America.* New York: Harper and Row, 1949.
May, Lary, ed. *Recasting America: Culture and Politics in the Age of Cold War.* Chicago: Univ. of Chicago Press, 1989.
Merkley, Paul. *Reinhold Niebuhr: A Political Account.* Montreal: McGill-Queens Univ. Press, 1975.
Messer-Davidow, Ellen. "Manufacturing the Attack on Higher Education." *Social Text* 36 (Fall 1993): 40–80.
Meyer, Donald B. *The Protestant Search for Political Realism, 1919–1941.* Berkeley: Univ. of California Press, 1960.
Michaelsen, Robert, and Wade Clark Roof, eds. *Liberal Protestantism: Realities and Possibilities.* New York: Pilgrim Press, 1986.
Míguez Bonino, José. *Doing Theology in a Revolutionary Situation.* Maryknoll, N.Y.: Orbis Books, 1975.
———. *Christians and Marxists: The Mutual Challenge to Revolution.* London: Hodder and Staughton, 1976.
———. *Toward a Christian Political Ethics.* Philadelphia: Fortress Press, 1983.
Miller, Robert M. *American Protestantism and Social Issues, 1919–1939.* Chapel Hill: Univ. of North Carolina Press, 1958.
Mills, C. Wright. *White Collar: The American Middle Class.* New York: Oxford Univ. Press, 1951.
Miranda, José Porfirio. *Marx and the Bible.* Maryknoll, N.Y.: Orbis Books, 1974.
Moore, R. Laurence. *Religious Outsiders and the Making of Americans.* New York: Oxford Univ. Press, 1986.
———. *Selling God: American Religion in the Marketplace of Culture.* New York: Oxford Univ. Press, 1994.
Morris, Brian. *Anthropological Studies of Religion.* Cambridge: Cambridge Univ. Press, 1987.
Morton, Nelle. *The Journey Is Home.* Boston: Beacon Press, 1985.
Nelson, Cary, and Lawrence Grossberg, eds. *Marxism and the Interpretation of Culture.* Urbana: Univ. of Illinois Press, 1988.
Nelson, Cary, Lawrence Grossberg, and Paula Treichler, eds. *Cultural Studies.* New York: Routledge, 1991.
Nessan, Craig L. *Orthopraxis or Heresy: The North American Theological Response to Liberation Theology.* American Academy of Religion Academy Series, ed. Susan Thistlethwaite, no. 63. Atlanta: Scholars Press, 1989.
Neuhaus, Richard John. *The Naked Public Square: Religion and Democracy in America.* 2d ed. Grand Rapids: Eerdmans, 1984.
———, ed. *Reinhold Niebuhr Today.* Grand Rapids: Eerdmans 1989.
Nicholson, Linda, ed. *Feminism/Postmodernism.* New York: Routledge, 1990.
Niebuhr, Reinhold. *Moral Man and Immoral Society.* New York: Scribner, 1932.
———. *Reflections on the End of an Era.* New York: Scribner, 1935.
———. *The Nature and Destiny of Man.* Vol. 1: *Human Nature.* New York: Scribner, 1941.
———. *The Children of Light and the Children of Darkness.* New York: Scribner, 1944.
———. *The Irony of American History.* New York: Scribner, 1952.
———. *The World Crisis and American Responsibility.* Edited by Ernest W. Lefever. New York: Association Press, 1958.
Niebuhr, H. Richard. *Christ and Culture.* New York: Harper, 1951.
———. *The Kingdom of God in America.* New York: Harper, 1959.

Niebuhr, Ursula, ed. *Remembering Niebuhr: Letters of Reinhold and Ursula Niebuhr.* San Francisco: Harper and Row, 1990.

Noble, David W. *The End of American History: Democracy, Capitalism, and the Metaphor of Two Worlds in Anglo-American Historical Writing, 1890–1980.* Minneapolis: Univ. of Minnesota Press, 1985.

———. "Revocation of the Anglo-Protestant Monopoly: Aesthetic Authority and the American Landscape." *Soundings* 79 (1996), no. 1–2: 149–68.

Noble, David W., and Michael Fores. "The Metaphor for Two Worlds: The American West, Industrial Revolution, and Modernization Theory." *Soundings* 68 (1985), no. 2: 139–59.

Noll, Mark, ed. *Religion and American Politics.* New York: Oxford Univ. Press, 1989.

Novak, Michael. *Will It Liberate? Questions about Liberation Theology.* New York: Paulist, 1986.

Novick, Peter. "Historians, 'Objectivity,' and the Defense of the West." *Radical History Review* 40 (Winter 1988): 6–31.

O'Connor, June. *The Moral Vision of Dorothy Day: A Feminist Perspective.* New York: Crossroad, 1991.

Omi, Michael, and Howard Winant. *Racial Formation in the United States: From the 1960s to the 1980s.* 2d ed. New York: Routledge and Kegan Paul, 1992.

Paterson, Thomas, et al. "Round Table: Exploring the History of American Foreign Relations." *Journal of American History* 77 (1990), no. 1: 171–244.

Pells, Richard. *Radical Visions and American Dreams.* New York: Harper and Row, 1973.

———. *The Liberal Mind in a Conservative Age.* New York: Harper and Row, 1985.

Peterson, Anna. *Martyrdom and the Politics of Religion: Progressive Catholicism in El Salvador's Civil War.* Albany: State Univ. of New York Press, 1996.

Plaskow, Judith. *Sex, Sin, and Grace: Women's Experience in the Theologies of Reinhold Niebuhr and Paul Tillich.* Washington: Univ. Press of America, 1980.

Plaskow, Judith, and Carol Christ, eds. *Weaving the Visions: New Patterns in Feminist Spirituality.* San Francisco: Harper and Row, 1989.

Pope, Liston. *The Kingdom Beyond Caste.* New York: Friendship Press, 1957.

———. *Millhands and Preachers.* 1942. New Haven: Yale Univ. Press, 1965.

Rauschenbusch, Walter. *A Theology for the Social Gospel.* Nashville: Abingdon Press, 1918.

Reed, Adolph L. *The Jesse Jackson Phenomenon.* New Haven: Yale Univ. Press, 1986.

Reinitz, Richard. *Irony and Consciousness: American Historiography and Reinhold Niebuhr's Vision.* Cranbury, N.J.: Associated Univ. Press, 1980.

Reynolds, Charles, and Ralph Norman, eds. *Community in America: The Challenge of Habits of the Heart.* Berkeley: Univ. of California Press, 1988.

Ribuffo, Leo. "Why Is There So Much Conservatism in the United States, and Why Do So Few Historians Know Anything about It?" *American Historical Review* 99 (1994), no. 2: 438–50.

Richey, Russell E., and Donald Jones, eds. *American Civil Religion.* New York: Harper and Row, 1974.

Roberts, J. Deotis. *Liberation and Reconciliation: A Black Theology.* Philadelphia: Westminster Press, 1971.

Roberts, Nancy L. *Dorothy Day and the Catholic Worker.* Albany: State Univ. of New York Press, 1984.

———. *American Peace Writers, Editors, and Periodicals.* Westport, Conn.: Greenwood Press, 1990.

Robbins, Bruce, ed. *The Phantom Public Sphere.* Minneapolis: Univ. of Minnesota Press, 1993.

Rogin, Michael. *Ronald Reagan, The Movie and Other Episodes in Political Demonology.* Berkeley: Univ. of California Press, 1987.

Roof, Wade Clark. *A Generation of Seekers: The Spiritual Journeys of the Baby Boom Generation.* San Francisco: HarperSanFrancisco, 1993.

Roof, Wade Clark, and William McKinney. *American Mainline Religion: Its Changing Shape and Future.* New Brunswick, N.J.: Rutgers Univ. Press, 1987.

Rossinow, Doug. "The Breakthrough to New Life: Christianity and the Emergence of the New Left in Austin, Texas, 1956–1964." *American Quarterly* 46 (1994), no. 3: 309–40.

Ruether, Rosemary Radford. *Faith and Fratricide: The Theological Roots of Anti-Semitism.* Minneapolis: Seabury, 1974.

———. *Sexism and God-Talk: Toward a Feminist Theology.* Boston: Beacon Press, 1983.
———. *To Change the World: Christology and Cultural Criticism.* New York: Crossroad, 1986.
———. *Disputed Questions: On Being a Christian.* 2d ed. Maryknoll, N.Y.: Orbis Books, 1989.
———. *Gaia and God: An Ecofeminist Theology of Earth Healing.* San Francisco: Harper San Francisco, 1992.
Russell, Letty. *Human Liberation in Feminist Perspective.* Philadelphia: Westminster Press, 1974.
———. *The Future of Partnership.* Philadelphia: Westminster Press, 1979.
Sayres, Sohnya, et al. *The Sixties without Apology.* Minneapolis: Univ. of Minnesota Press, 1984.
Schenkel, Albert. *The Rich Man and the Kingdom: John D. Rockefeller Jr. and the Protestant Establishment.* Minneapolis: Fortress Press, 1995.
Schneider, James C. *Should America Go to War? The Debate over Foreign Policy in Chicago, 1939–1941.* Chapel Hill: Univ. of North Carolina Press, 1989.
Schumacher, E. F. *Small Is Beautiful: Economics as If People Mattered.* New York: Harper and Row, 1973.
Schüssler Fiorenza, Elisabeth. *In Memory of Her: A Feminist Theological Reconstruction of Christian Origins.* New York: Crossroad, 1983.
Scott, Nathan Jr., ed. *The Legacy of Reinhold Niebuhr.* Chicago: Univ. of Chicago Press, 1974.
Sherrill, Rowland A., ed. *Religion and the Life of the Nation: American Recoveries.* Urbana: Univ. of Illinois Press, 1990.
Silk, Mark. *Spiritual Politics: Religion and America since World War II.* New York: Simon and Schuster, 1987.
———. *Unsecular Media: Making News of Religion in America.* Urbana: Univ. of Illinois Press, 1995.
Small, Melvin, and William Hoover, eds. *Give Peace a Chance: Exploring the Vietnam Antiwar Movement.* Syracuse: Syracuse Univ. Press, 1992.
Smith, Christian. *The Emergence of Liberation Theology: Radical Religion and Social Movement Theory.* Chicago: Univ. of Chicago Press, 1991.
———. *Resisting Reagan: The U.S. Central America Peace Movement.* Chicago: Univ. of Chicago Press, 1996.
Sobrino, Jon. *Christology at the Crossroads: A Latin American Approach.* Trans. John Drury. Maryknoll, N.Y.: Orbis Books, 1978.
Sölle, Dorothee. *Christ the Representative.* Philadelphia: Fortress Press, 1967.
———. *Suffering.* Philadelphia: Fortress Press, 1973.
———. *Strength of the Weak: Toward a Christian Feminist Identity.* Philadelphia: Westminster Press, 1984.
———. *To Work and to Love: A Theology of Creation.* Philadelphia: Fortress Press, 1984.
———. *Thinking about God.* Philadelphia: Trinity Press International, 1990.
Spencer, John Michael. *Protest and Praise: Sacred Music of Black Religion.* Minneapolis: Fortress Press, 1990.
Stone, Ronald. *Reinhold Niebuhr: Prophet to Politicians.* Nashville: Abingdon Press, 1972.
———. "Christian Realism and Latin American Liberation Theology." In *The Church's Public Role: Retrospect and Prospect,* ed. Dieter Hessel, 109–24. Grand Rapids: Eerdmans, 1993.
Storey, John. *Cultural Studies and the Study of Popular Culture: Theories and Methods.* Athens: Univ. of Georgia Press, 1996.
Susman, Warren. *Culture as History: The Transformation of American Society in the Twentieth Century.* New York: Pantheon, 1984.
Tabb, William K. *Churches in Struggle: Liberation Theologies and Social Change in North America.* New York: Monthly Review Press, 1986.
Takaki, Ronald. *Iron Cages: Race and Culture in Nineteenth-Century America.* 2d ed. New York: Oxford Univ. Press, 1990.
———, ed. *From Different Shores: Perspectives on Race and Ethnicity in America.* New York: Oxford Univ. Press, 1987.
Tangeman, Michael. *Mexico at the Crossroads: Politics, the Church, and the Poor.* Maryknoll, N.Y.: Orbis Books, 1995.

Tanner, Kathryn. *Theories of Culture: A New Agenda for Theology.* Minneapolis, Minn.: Fortress Press, 1997.

Taylor, Mark Kline. *Remembering Esperanza: A Political-Cultural Theology for North American Praxis.* Maryknoll, N.Y.: Orbis Books, 1990.

Thistlethwaite, Susan. *Sex, Race, and God: Christian Feminism in Black and White.* San Francisco: Harper and Row, 1989.

Thistlethwaite, Susan, and Mary Potter Engel, eds. *Lift Every Voice: Constructing Christian Theologies from the Underside.* San Francisco: Harper and Row, 1990.

Tillich, Paul. *The World Situation.* Philadelphia: Fortress Press, 1965.

———. *The Theology of Peace.* Edited by Ronald Stone. Louisville: Westminster Press, 1990.

Toulouse, Mark. *The Transformation of John Foster Dulles: From Prophet of Realism to Priest of Nationalism.* Macon, Ga.: Mercer Univ. Press, 1985.

Tracy, David. *Blessed Rage for Order: The New Pluralism in Theology.* New York: Crossroad, 1975.

Treat, James. *Native and Christian? Indigenous Voices on Religious Identity in the United States and Canada.* New York: Routledge, 1995.

Tucker, Robert W. *The Radical Left and American Foreign Policy.* Baltimore: Johns Hopkins Univ. Press, 1971.

Tuveson, Ernest Lee. *Redeemer Nation: The Idea of America's Millennial Role.* Chicago: Univ. of Chicago Press, 1968.

Tweed, Thomas, ed. *Retelling U.S. Religious History.* Berkeley: Univ. of California Press, 1996.

Van Allen, Rodger. *The Commonweal and American Catholicism: The Magazine, the Movement.* Philadelphia: Fortress Press, 1974.

———. *Being Catholic: Commonweal from the Seventies to the Nineties.* Loyola Univ. Press, 1993.

Van Deburg, William. *New Day in Babylon: The Black Power Movement and American Culture, 1965–1975.* Chicago: Univ. of Chicago Press, 1992.

Vanden Heuvel, Katrina, ed. *The* Nation, *1965–1990: Selections from the Independent Magazine of Politics and Culture.* New York: Thunder Mouth Press, 1990.

Wall, James, and David Hein, eds. *How My Mind Has Changed.* Grand Rapids: Eerdmans, 1991.

Warner, Stephen. "Work in Progress toward a New Paradigm for the Sociological Study of Religion in the United States." *American Journal of Sociology* 98 (1993), no. 5: 1004–93.

Warren, Heather. "Intervention and International Organization: American Reformed Leaders and World War II." *American Presbyterians* 74 (1996), no. 1: 42–56.

Washington, James M., ed. *A Testament of Hope: The Essential Writings of Martin Luther King Jr.* New York: Harper and Row, 1986.

———, ed. *Conversations with God: Two Centuries of Prayers by African Americans.* San Francisco: HarperCollins, 1995.

Weaver, Jace. "Original Simplicities and Present Complexities: Reinhold Niebuhr, Ethnocentrism, and the Myth of American Exceptionalism." *Journal of the American Academy of Religion* 53 (1995), no. 2: 231–48.

Weidman, Judith, ed. *Christian Feminism.* San Francisco: Harper and Row, 1984.

Welch, Sharon. *Communities of Resistance and Solidarity.* Maryknoll, N.Y.: Orbis Books, 1985.

———. *A Feminist Ethic of Risk.* Minneapolis: Fortress Press, 1990.

West, Cornel. *Prophesy Deliverance: An Afro-American Revolutionary Christianity.* Philadelphia: Westminster Press, 1982.

———. *Prophetic Fragments.* Grand Rapids: Eerdmans, 1988.

———. *The American Evasion of Philosophy: A Genealogy of Pragmatism.* Madison: Univ. of Wisconsin Press, 1989.

———. *Keeping Faith: Philosophy and Race in America.* New York: Routledge, 1994.

West, Cornel, and bell hooks. *Breaking Bread: Insurgent Black Intellectual Life.* Boston: South End Press, 1991.

White, Donald C., and C. Howard Hopkins. *The Social Gospel: Religion and Reform in Changing America.* Philadelphia: Temple Univ. Press, 1976.

Whitfield, Stephen. *The Culture of the Cold War.* Baltimore: Johns Hopkins Univ. Press, 1991.

Wiener, Jon. "Radical Historians and the Crisis in American History, 1959–1980." *Journal of American History* 76 (1989), no. 2: 399–434.
Wilcox, Clyde. *Onward Christian Soldiers? The Religious Right in American Politics.* Boulder, Colo.: Westview Press, 1996.
Williams, William Appleman. *The Tragedy of American Diplomacy.* 2d ed. New York: Delta, 1962.
———. *Empire as a Way of Life.* New York: Oxford Univ. Press, 1980.
Wills, Garry. *Reagan's America.* Rev. ed. New York: Penguin Books, 1988.
———. *Under God: Religion and American Politics.* New York: Simon and Schuster, 1990.
Wilmore, Gayraud. *Black Religion and Black Radicalism.* 2d ed. Maryknoll, N.Y.: Orbis Books, 1984.
Wilmore, Gayraud, and James Cone, eds. *Black Theology: A Documentary History.* Vol. 1: *1966–1979.* Maryknoll, N.Y.: Orbis Books, 1979.
Wittner, Lawrence. *Rebels against War: The American Peace Movement, 1933–1983.* Philadelphia: Temple Univ. Press, 1984.
Wolf, Eric R. *Peasant Wars of the Twentieth Century.* New York: Harper Torchbooks, 1973.
Wood, Joe, ed. *Malcolm X in Our Own Image.* New York: St. Martin's Press, 1992.
Wuthnow, Robert. *The Restructuring of American Religion: Society and Faith since World War II.* Princeton: Princeton Univ. Press, 1988.
———. *The Struggle for America's Soul: Evangelicals, Liberals, and Secularism.* Grand Rapids: Eerdmans, 1989.
———. *Producing the Sacred: An Essay on Public Religion.* Urbana: Univ. of Illinois Press, 1994.
Wuthnow, Robert, et al. *Cultural Analysis: The Work of Peter L. Berger, Mary Douglas, Michel Foucault, and Jurgen Habermas.* London: Routledge, 1984.
X, Malcolm. *The End of White World Supremacy: Four Speeches by Malcolm X.* Edited by Imam Benjamin Karin. New York: Seaver Books, 1971.
X, Malcolm with Alex Haley. *The Autobiography of Malcolm X.* New York: Grove, 1964.
Yates, Gayle Graham. *What Women Want: The Ideas of the Movement.* Cambridge: Harvard Univ. Press, 1975.
———. "Spirituality and the American Feminist Experience." *Signs* 9 (1983), no. 11: 59–72.
Young, Marilyn. *The Vietnam Wars, 1945–1990.* New York: HarperPerennial, 1991.
Zweig, Michael, ed. *Religion and Economic Justice.* Philadelphia: Temple Univ. Press, 1992.

Index

Building a Protestant Left was designed and typeset on a Macintosh computer system using PageMaker software. The text is set in Palatino and titles are set in Bookman. This book was designed and composed by Sheila Hart and manufactured by Thomson-Shore, Inc. The recycled paper used in this book is designed for an effective life of at least three hundred years.